CIVIC & CORPORATE HERALDRY

CIVIC & CORPORATE HERALDRY

A DICTIONARY OF IMPERSONAL ARMS OF ENGLAND, WALES & N. IRELAND

COMPILED & EDITED BY
GEOFFREY BRIGGS
F.R.S.A., F.S.A.(SCOT)

HERALDRY TODAY
10 Beauchamp Place
London, S.W.3.

Published in Great Britain by
HERALDRY TODAY
10 Beauchamp Place
London S.W.3.

I.S.B.N. 0 900455 21 7

Printed by
Hollen Street Press Ltd.
Slough, Bucks.

CONTENTS

PUBLISHER'S NOTE

All the Armorial Bearings included within this work belong by right to specific corporate bodies and may be used only by the governing bodies of those corporations in their corporate capacity. Any person wishing to depict any arms included within these pages should first of all make certain that the particular corporate body has no objection.

Square brackets [ ] denote the insertion of words which seem desirable to clarify the blazon. When an = sign also occurs it is intended to denote that the term given in the official blazon is at variance with the drawing painted upon the Patent.

ACKNOWLEDGEMENTS

Illustrations by:

Gerald Cobb
Dan Escott
Wendy Gould
Sandra House
Violetta Keeble
Theodora Winney

The illustration on page 37 first appeared as the frontispiece of the illustrated catalogue of the Heralds' Commemorative Exhibition 1484-1934.

Some of the illustrations of the London Livery Companies were originally published in Richard Wallis's "London's Armory" in 1677.

PREFACE

Tradition demands that an author should commence with a few prefatory remarks addressed to his readers. Yet, for the most part, these remain unread; and, again for the most part, deservedly so. If a preface is to serve any useful purpose it must present facts which may not be easily derived from a study of the work itself, which is not to say that its purpose is an acknowledgement of the author's obligations. In the present work these are largely self-evident with respect to the artists and those officials and representatives of the bodies whose armorial bearings are contained herein. Beyond these, however, a particular debt of gratitude is due to three fellow students of this much-neglected branch of the art and science of Heraldry. To H. Ellis Tomlinson, Esq., M.A., F.H.S., Rowland Bretton, Esq., F.H.S., and T. F. B. Turner, Esq., must largely be attributed any merit which this work may possess, for they have with the greatest possible readiness and courtesy made available the results of their labours in this field; its demerits must be attributed to myself.

Acknowledgements having been made, though wholly inadequately, I must now declare the purpose behind the present volume, which follows closely in the tradition of the late Arthur Charles Fox-Davies' "A Book of Public Arms". Such a scheme as he envisaged, which was no less than a complete and definitive account of all impersonal arms borne throughout the world, must be doomed to failure; any publication at the present time must, necessarily, be an optimum selection. What constitutes this optimum selection is, of course, a matter of editorial policy and in the present instance we have restricted the choice to a particular heraldic jurisdiction; namely that of the English Kings of Arms. Since this in itself would embrace virtually the whole world, we have reduced the area under consideration to England, Wales and Northern Ireland. Within this area we have attempted to set forth every known civic and corporate body which *at the present day* bears Arms by *lawful authority*. To these have been added some few unauthorised coats which are so well known that their omission would cause surprise. By including them we do not pretend to condone the actions of their bearers; we would rather that their inclusion in the present number might inspire their bearers to regularise their armorial position, for in the majority of cases the cause of neglect can scarcely be a financial one. It is much to be regretted that one of the Inns of Court shows a lack of respect for the Laws of Arms.

Although this volume is concerned solely with *current* Arms, we have included as a Supplement a list of those Civic Arms, etc., which are now obsolete. This may serve to stimulate further interest. Should there be sufficient demand for further volumes devoted to this branch of heraldry a complete corpus could be built up in the course of time.

We are fully aware that artists and craftsmen who will, we hope, make use of this book in their work, have little time for extensive reading in the more scientific aspects of the subject and for their benefit, as well as for the benefit of others, we include an explanatory introduction and an illustrated glossary of terms.

Finally, I would beg all readers, whoever they may be, to draw to my attention all such errors as they may discover within these pages. However much care is expended on the preparation of such a work errors are bound to arise. It is in the interest of all that these be corrected, and that publicly.

INTRODUCTION

Heraldry had its birth, if not its conception, on the field of battle. Its origin has long been, and is likely to indefinitely remain, a matter of controversy because it derives from many sources of inspiration. It is clear that its earliest function was as a means of identification in the heat of battle but the admirable manner in which it lent itself to identification commended it for similar purposes in everyday life. In an age when few men could read or write some personalised symbol to indicate the individual was sorely needed and nowhere was this need more apparent than in the authentication of official acts. So it is that the seal has played just as large a part as the military ensign and shield in the development of heraldry.

The adoption of seals with distinctive devices by our ancient boroughs seems to have begun towards the end of the twelfth century and the custom of using borough seals afterwards became general. The devices upon these seals were simple in form and more symbolic than those which appeared upon the seals of the baronial and knightly families of the Middle Ages. They exhibited mainly royal, feudal, and ecclesiastical emblems, castles and ships. In short, they were devices appropriate to the town itself; yet they were not specifically appropriate to a specific town. Heraldic arms were subsequently found to provide this much needed specifically appropriate device and when they came to be adopted the previous seal device provided in many cases the "charges" for the shield.

The earliest civic authority to place its present arms upon a seal appears to have been the City of Chester; the present arms appear on its lesser statute merchant seal which was made at some date between 1312 and 1340. The next earliest may have been the City of London (1380 or 1381), though here the arms form only a small portion of the elaborate seal design. However, what is apparently an earlier coat for the City of London appears on the seal bag attached to Edward II's grant of certain new constitutions to the city in 1319. Clearly Civic Heraldry as such came into being about the beginning of the fourteenth century. In the fifteenth century civic arms became more wide-spread; the arms of the borough appear, in that century, on the seals of Great Yarmouth, Kingston-upon-Thames, Droitwich, York, Colchester, King's Lynn, Kingston-upon-Hull, Norwich, Oxford, Shrewsbury, Boston, Lincoln and Ludlow. Now all these civic coats of arms were locally assumed and none were officially recorded before the sixteenth century and then we find a two-fold method of recording them. In the first place we have regular grants of arms, the earliest of which was made by Sir Christopher Barker, Garter King of Arms, to the City of Gloucester on the 18th October 1538, the second being to the Borough of Morpeth on the 20th May 1552. The second method was by entering them at the Heralds' Visitations. Strangely enough no civic shields of arms seem to have been entered at the first Visitations, and the earliest confirmation appears to have been made to Colchester on 26th August 1558. Numerous confirmations were made at subsequent Visitations though in many cases the record was of an armorial seal design only and the tinctures were omitted. Within recent years certain civic authorities have completed the registration by obtaining a certificate signed by all three Kings of Arms declaring the true nature of their arms. Others still have to take this necessary step.

The earliest civic coats consisted of the shield alone and no town would appear to have adopted either a crest or supporters before such were granted by the Kings of Arms; the earliest case of such a grant is that made to Ipswich by William Hervey, Clarenceux King of Arms, in 1561. The badge and standard only appear officially with the grant to Launceston in 1906.

The remaining classes of corporate Arms may be roughly classified as academic, ecclesiastical, and commercial, although certain varieties would appear to present border-line cases. The earliest academic grants of arms, those to Eton College and King's College, Cambridge, were made under the Great Seal by King Henry VI on 1st January 1449 and it seems doubtful if any were in existence before that time; the advent of the Visitations gave impetus to the recording of academic arms by grant and by formal certification. In this way the lead came from the universities but it must be pointed out that the University of Oxford successfully resisted an attempt at Visitation in the summer of 1634. This is the reason why so many of the Oxford colleges bear arms without formal authority; Oxford claims to be exempt from the surveillance of the heralds. But this has not prevented a number of such colleges receiving grants of arms in recent years.

In the ecclesiastical field we are primarily concerned with Bishoprics; the earliest known case of the appearance of arms which can definitely be attributed to an English bishopric is provided by the seal of William of Louth, who was Bishop of Ely from 1290 to 1298. As peers of the realm the bishops were not, of course, liable to visitation but there are numerous records of these "diocesan" arms in the Visitations in the form of Church Notes. Some few bishops actually entered their own arms (with those of their See) at the Visitations; such cases are Cuthbert Tunstall, Bishop of Durham (1530), Richard Barnes, Bishop of Durham (1584), and Toby Mathew, Archbishop of York (1612). The formal granting of arms for bishoprics began only in the eighteenth century, the first instance being, apparently, to the See of Quebec, 16 July 1793. This was by Royal Warrant, which for a number of years was the normal procedure. The Arms of some few deaneries were, however, recorded at the Visitations, Hereford and Canterbury being cases in point. From these upper levels the use of arms has spread downwards and grants are now made to theological colleges, abbeys, and religious orders.

The study of the heraldry of commerce must begin with the Guilds of the Middle Ages. Among these, those of the City of London were outstanding and, naturally, their practices are the best documented. We cannot say when these Guilds began to use arms but it is apparent that by 1451 the use of arms by livery companies was a recognized custom. The earliest known grant of arms to a livery company is that made to the Drapers of London by Sir William Bruges, Garter King of Arms on 10th March 1439. There may have been earlier ones, but if so they have not survived. In addition to the grant to the Drapers' Company, in the period 1439 to 1500 twenty-five patents to livery companies are known and the whole field was kept under constant review in the subsequent Visitations. From these precedents the field of commercial heraldry has spread to a wide variety of business concerns and also to professional bodies.

It would appear that the whole field of impersonal heraldry derives its beginnings from the classes set out above and there would appear to be few classes of legally constituted bodies which may not be eligible for a grant of arms; of these, however, the Kings of Arms must be the sole judges and arbiters. Certainly the field of heraldic display has been much enlivened by their existence, for they have introduced many innovations in the way of new "charges". These are the very backbone of heraldry and in the following pages we shall have to consider a number of them. Meanwhile let us consider the formal presentation of these armorial "achievements", drawing attention to the most recent developments.

The Shield. This, whatever form it may take, is the *sine qua non* of heraldry for without a shield there can be no Arms. All else is by way of embellishment and incapable of separate existence. The one vital feature of the shield is that it is essentially a vehicle for a two-dimensional display; whether the "charges" upon it are merely painted or carved in high relief, they must be capable of being represented as part of a plane surface. Given this, it is only natural that the shield and its charges must be shown in colour—contrasting colour—for how else is one to discern its contents with any degree of confidence. The fundamental rule of heraldry is that colour must not be put next to colour nor metal next to metal. By "next to" we really mean "upon" for, although the shield is a flat surface, its contents are regarded as being built up layer upon layer. The various colours (or tinctures) known to heraldry are few in number and are divided into two principal divisions, namely *metals* and *colours:* the former comprise gold (*Or*) and silver (*Argent*), while the latter include blue (*Azure*), red (*Gules*), green (*Vert*), black (*Sable*), and purple (*Purpure*). To these have been added a number of others which are much less frequently used; they are *Tenne* (which is variously said to correspond to a brownish-yellow or an orange), *Sanguine* (the colour of blood—perhaps dried), *Murrey* (the colour of mulberry juice), *Bleu-céleste* (a clear bright blue), *Carnation* (the colour of flesh), and *Proper* (which indicates that the object is shown in its natural colours). A third class of tincture consists of the furs which fall into two classes; the first is based upon *Ermine* (the winter coat of the stoat) depicted with black tails upon white. When the tails are white upon black it is called *Ermines,* when black upon gold *Erminois,* and when gold upon black *Pean.* These varieties are not as uncommon as some may believe. The second class is based upon *Vair* (which is said to be a representation of the skins of the European Grey Squirrel) shown as alternate panes of blue and white although other colours may occur—in which case they must be specified, the result being designated e.g. *Vairy* argent and gules. The only other fur in this group which we shall meet is *Potent,* this being drawn rather like the heads of crutches; this again is blue and white but other colours may appear, the result then being either *Potent* or and gules or *Potenty* or and gules.

Although the field (as the actual surface of the shield is called) may consist of one tincture alone, it will very often be found compounded of several. This is done according to a regular system and a clear distinction must be made between a division into an equal number of parts and into an odd number of parts. In the one case (if the parts are equal in size) the whole forms the field, in all other cases the field is charged with something. It is much easier to consider initially those cases where the divisions are unequal, for this determines the terminology of the whole. The very simplest of heraldic charges are geometrical figures and these are known as Ordinaries and Sub-ordinaries, although very few armorists are entirely agreed as to which figures to include in which category. These may be horizontal (Chief, Fesse, Bar, with the diminutives of the last), vertical (the Pale and its diminutives), diagonal (the Bend, Bend sinister, and their diminutives) of a combination of one or more of these (Pall, Saltire, Cross). Additionally there are a number or geometrical charges which are objects rather than bands. These are the Quarter, Canton, Lozenge, Fusil, Mascle, Inescutcheon, Roundel, and Annulet. All these, and their smaller relations will be found in the glossary. These charges assist in naming the divisions of the shield since when it is divided into two equal parts it is generally said to be Per fesse, Per pale, etc., and when divided into a number of such divisions is said to be Barry, Paly, Bendy, etc. In the case of an Ordinary then, it must (with the exception of the Canton, Chief and Bordure) be of metal if the field is a colour or *vice versa;* in the case of compound divisions this is usually the case but not necessarily so. The only other type of field encountered in British armory is that which is strewn with a number of charges, in which case the tincture rule applies.

In the case of personal or family arms the reason behind the choice of a particular object very often is simply that the bearer likes the look of it; in corporate heraldry this is seldom the case and each minute detail has its part to play in telling a story. For this reason it is necessary to know the names by which some of the conventional charges are known. We have already given the names of the geometrical charges but there are two types of charge whose name varies with their colour: these are the roundle and the droplet. The roundle, if of a metal, is regarded as a disk and is called a Plate (silver) or a Bezant (gold). In either case it represents a coin. If it is of a colour then it is regarded as a sphere and goes by a variety of names: Torteau (red), Hurt (blue, this is sometimes a bruise, at others a berry), Pellet (black, often a cannonball), Pomme (green, an apple), Golpe (purple, this is a wound), Orange (orange), Guze (murrey, the Turkish word means an eye—a black eye?). Droplets are called gouttes and take their names from the material of which they are regarded as being formed, thus: gold (gouttes d'Or, drops of gold), silver (gouttes de l'eau, drops of water), red (gouttes de sang, drops of blood), blue (gouttes de larmes, tear-drops), black (gouttes de poix, drops of pitch), green (gouttes d'olive, or gouttes d'huile, drops of olive oil). Modern blazon, however, tends to ignore all these niceties of terminology and often specifies the tincture.

From thc foregoing the reader may get the impression that the language is an unintelligible jargon; this is not so, it is in reality quite easy to understand and we hope that the combination of illustrations and glossary will remove all difficulties. The one feature which *must* be understood is the naming of the tinctures, which in older blazons are named but once. This leads to the use of such expressions as "of the field", "of the first", "of the second", "of the last", etc., and to understand these it may be necessary to list the tinctures as they appear in the blazon. "Proper" is usually (but not always) ignored in the enumeration. This can easily lead to confusion, and confusion certainly does occur—even in patents, so the modern tendency to repeat tinctures is a welcome one. We cannot, in the present work, undertake to set out the whole theory of heraldic practice and the interested reader should consult one of the standard works on the subject but the design of a number of new objects in the shape of heraldic coronets calls for comment: these will best be considered under the heading of the Crest.

The helmet. This is set above the shield in the majority of modern Patents but in the nineteenth century its appearance was something of a rarity. The main function of the helmet is of course to provide a suitable vehicle upon which to bear the crest but its special heraldic function is to indicate the rank of the bearer. The type appropriate to a corporate body is that laid down for a gentleman, which is a closed steel helmet set sideways upon the shield. Artistic convenience very often suggests that it should be placed in a position approximating to a three-quarter view, which is certainly preferable; but there are certain grants and exemplifications in which, inexplicably, a totally different type of helmet is depicted. This helmet is of the type appropriate to a Peer of the realm; although it has been shown on paintings of the arms of certain of the London Livery Companies, the only case where it has been seen on Letters Patent making a grant is in the case of the grant of Crest and Supporters to the City of London. In spite of the fact that numerous grants are known in which the helmet is omitted from the painting there can be no doubt that in a fully marshalled achievement it should be shown. We have omitted it in almost all our illustrations to ease the burden of the artists and also to economise in space. Perhaps the same considerations prevailed in these older Patents.

Although we have not yet exhausted discussion of the varieties of helmet this may more conveniently be dealt with under the heading of the *torse and mantling.* The torse is the conventional wreath of twisted silk which unites the crest to the helmet, the mantling being the cloth covering of the helmet itself. All the old manuals deal solely with what is known as "a wreath of the colours" which comprises six twists alternately of the principal metal and colour of the shield. In order to arrive at these "colours" one must read through the blazon and note the metal and colour which first occurs (minor details and the term "proper" being ignored). In those cases where this does not give a satisfactory result then some degree of ingenuity is required. If for example an ermine field bears a lion gules, the "colours" would be argent (from the ermine) and gules; if, on the other hand, the ermine field bore a lion Or then the "colours" would be Or and sable (again from the ermine). Should there be a deficiency in one of the necessary components, such as would be given by the sole charge being proper, then best practice is to use the heraldic colour to which the charge approximates; this is done in the case of Liverpool which has a wreath argent and sable. Should the case be one in which it is impossible to deduce any colours at all, practice would indicate that it should be argent and gules. A field vair would give a wreath argent and azure, whilst if the charge were vair either silver or blue would be added to whatever was the tincture of the field. Having now said that these are the supposed rules we must say that examination of the actual grants of arm indicate an increasing number of anomalous "colours". Very often the colours are specified. In the sixteenth and seventeenth centuries the mantling, whatever the colours of the torse, is usually gules, doubled argent. This is usually stated in the grant although other colours are often specified. Obviously either there is a rule or there isn't. Let us look at the question more closely.

The earliest civic grant of arms with a crest is that to Ipswich in 1561. Here the shield would give or and gules as the colours, but the torse is argent and sable while the mantling is gules doubled argent: the torse is anomalous. In the case of the City of Chester the arms are an exception to all rules. The shield is dimidiated, the helmet is a frontal one, the torse is of three tinctures (gold, gules and azure—exactly those occurring in the shield) and a mantling which is gules to the dexter and azure to the sinister, both doubled argent. This would appear to be a compromise solution to provide liveries for each of the dimidiated coats. One might suppose that the rule must be that the wreath and mantling must consist of a metal and colour, the two items being in agreement, yet an examination of the grant to the Company of Parish Clerks (1582) gives the lie to this for here we have a torse gules and azure with a mantling gules and azure (i.e. divided on each side into the two colours), the lining being ermine on the dexter and gold on the sinister; the only ermine in the whole achievement is the cuff in the crest. Examples of these anomalous wreaths and mantlings could be multiplied *ad nauseam* but it would serve very little purpose. The simple truth behind the selection of the "colours" is that they are the chosen "livery colours" and anyone wishing to make a painting of armorial bearings would be well advised to enquire as to the tinctures of the torse and mantling for these are not always specified in the blazon. We have attempted to give these particulars in all cases where difficulty is likely to be experienced. There is always a reason for the choice of a particular set of colours but this is not necessarily due to heraldic considerations.

The *crest* is set upon the helmet but never directly upon it, for its junction is always (at least in modern times) masked by either a wreath or a coronet. These latter have provided many opportunities for the heraldic designer to exercise his imagination as also for the Kings of Arms to specify the tinctures of the mantling. This is usually done at the present time when a crest coronet occurs. The coronets which one encounters in old grants are the ducal coronet (four strawberry leaves on a rim), mural coronet (of masonry with battlements), the naval coronet (four sterns of ships alternating with sails), eastern coronet and antique coronet (a plain rim heightened with spikes), the crown vallary (a plain rim heightened by pieces of the form of vair), the crown palisado (a plain rim which "palisadoes" affixed), and the ancient crown (four fleurs-de-lys issuing from a rim). To these have been added a second type of ancient coronet (see the crest of the Heraldry Society), the astral crown (four mullets each enclosed by a pair of wings and set upon a rim), the Saxon crown (a rim with four rays terminating in balls), the mercantile crown (eight masts with sails spread set upon a rim) and a whole host of other special coronets which are specifically and individually described. Some of these have proved to be so attractive and so admirably suited to the purpose of indication of rank that they have passed into common use (see the many examples of the coronet of ears of wheat and acorns among the Rural District Councils). There can be no doubt that crests are appropriate to corporate bodies although one school of thought would deny this since they have no head on which to wear the helmet; it was for this reason that the late Sir John Bernard Burke, Ulster King of Arms, refused to allow a helmet (although he would grant a crest) to corporate bodies. One might equally urge that they have no arm on which to carry a shield. Certainly the mediaeval Kings of Arms appear to have had no scruples in the matter for they granted both helmets and crests; the earliest such grant which has come to our notice is that to the Girdlers by John Smert, Garter King of Arms, in 1454. The earliest civic grant of crest would appear to be that to Ipswich. Although in the past it seems to have been forgotten that the crest must be capable of being rendered in the round and attached to the helmet, at the present times things are much better.

The *supporters*. The origin of these decorative additions to the achievement is not at all clear, but whatever their origin may have been it is clear that in the course of time they became associated with the peerage. The early Kings of Arms, however, never looked upon them as the exclusive prerogative of the peerage, and Roger Machado, Clarenceux King of Arms granted them to the Leathersellers' Company in 1505, the earliest civic case being the much quoted grant to Ipswich. During the sixteenth, seventeenth and eighteenth centuries many such grants were made but it appears that this entitlement seems to have been gradually forgotten because by the early nineteenth century a Royal Warrant had become necessary in order to receive such a grant. Indeed the usual formula in these Royal Warrants reads "although the Privilege of bearing Supporters be limited to Peers of the Realm, the Knights of His Majesty's Orders and the Proxies of the Princes of the Blood Royal at Installations except in such cases wherein under particular Circumstances His Majesty or His Royal Predecessors have been pleased to grant an Especial Licence for the use thereof, yet as a further mark of His Royal Favour, His Majesty has been also pleased to grant and assign to . . . the supporters . . . " The origin of this idea must remain a mystery; Liverpool in 1797 did not require a Royal Warrant, nor did Manchester in 1842. The problem was short-lived and seems to have been swiftly removed. At the present time it would appear that virtually any corporate body may receive a grant of arms, crest and supporters, although supporters may not be granted to Urban, Rural and Parish Councils.

The *badge* was reintroduced to heraldry in the year 1905; the earliest grant to a civic authority was made the following year to the Borough of Launceston. This grant included also a standard as was the case with most of these early grants of badge. In the following years many such grants were made but in 1927 the Home Office requested that no further grants be made to civic bodies and accordingly the grants of badges were, for many years, confined to other classes of corporations and to families. The decision was reversed in 1956 when the London County Council decided that it needed to possess an emblem the use of which might be allowed to societies, clubs and other organizations within its area desiring to show the locality to which they belonged; since the use of the Arms of the County Council by such bodies was not only undesirable but also illegal, the badge was the obvious answer. In the case of other corporations the badge might very well be used for display by its employees, sports clubs and social organizations since it represents the mediaeval identificatory emblem of the servant. Since 1956 many more grants of badges have been made and the number grows with each succeeding year.

We will close this brief survey with a short list of first grants which may prove of interest as establishing precedents.

First grant of Arms to a corporate body	10 March 1438/9	(The Drapers' Company)
First grant of Arms to a civic body	18 Oct. 1538	(City of Gloucester)
First grant of Crest to a corporate body	15 Oct. 1454	(The Girdlers' Company)
First grant of Crest to a civic body	29 Aug. 1561	(Borough of Ipswich)
First grant of Supporters to a corporate body	7 Nov. 1505	(Leathersellers' Company)
First grant of Supporters to a civic body	29 Aug. 1561	(Borough of Ipswich)
First grant of Badge to a civic body	26 March 1906	(Borough of Launceston)
First grant of Badge to a corporate body	30 Aug. 1909	(Port of London Authority)
First grant of Arms to a County Council	18 May 1889	(West Sussex County Council)
First grant of Arms to a Borough	18 Oct. 1538	(City of Gloucester)
First grant of Arms to a Urban District	27 Feb. 1906	(Erith UDC)
First grant of Arms to a Rural District	7 Jan. 1938	(Wetherby RDC)
First grant of Arms to a Parish Council	23 Nov. 1927	(Bocking Parish Council)

A GLOSSARY OF HERALDIC TERMS

This glossary makes no pretence to being complete, even with regard to the terms included in the blazons of this volume. For a more comprehensive collection of terms, with illustrations, the reader should consult one of the standard works. For ease of reference Elvin's "Dictionary of Heraldry" is recommended. We have included such terms as have not yet found their way into such dictionaries.

Abbot's Crosier. The pastoral staff of an abbot; it is sometimes maintained that the termination of the volute lies within the curve.
Accolée. A term used to express the position of two shields placed side by side and touching each other.
Achievement of Arms. The shield with all its external ornaments.
Addorsed. A term used to indicate that two charges are placed back to back.
Aesculapius, Rod of. (1) A rod entwined by a serpent; also called a Staff of Aesculapius.
Affrontée. A term applied to an object, particularly the head of an animal, when shown full-face; it is sometimes wrongly used as a synonym for guardant.
Allerion. (2) A bird resembling the eagle, represented without beak or legs.
Amphibane. A monstrous serpent.
Ancient Crown. (3) A coronet characterised by conventional leaves, often shown as fleurs-de-lys, upon a circlet.
Annulet. A ring.
Antique Crown. (4) A coronet composed of pointed rays upon a circlet; often called an Eastern Crown.
Antelope, Heraldic. This beast resembles the Heraldic Tiger but has serrated horns and deer's legs.
Apaumy. A term applied to a hand or gauntlet open and extended, showing the palm; unless otherwise blazoned every hand is understood to be apaumy.
Arched. Bowed or bent in the form of an arch; not to be confused with Embowed.
Argent. Silver, usually represented as white.
Argosy. A large merchant sailing-ship; a galleon or carrack.
Armed. A term applied to the horns, teeth, claws, and tusks of beasts, and the beaks and talons of birds; when applied to an arrow it refers to the head.
Arrondie. A term used to indicate that an object is rounded or curved.
Astral Crown. A coronet consisting of a circlet on which are mounted four stars (three visible), each star being placed between a pair of elevated wings.
Attires. The antlers of a stag; the beast is said to be Attired.
Attired. See Attires; when applied to a human being it is synonymous with vested.
Augmentations. Additions made to Arms by the Sovereign as a special mark of honour.
Azure. Blue.

Badge. A device used by the following of an armiger to indicate their dependence upon him; also placed upon Standards.
Banded. A term applied to sheaves, etc., to indicate that they are tied with a band.
Bar. (5) A sub-ordinary somewhat narrower than the Fesse which it resembles; unlike the latter it may appear in any part of the shield.
Bar gemel. (6) A single charge consisting of two narrow bars in close juxtaposition.
Barbed. A term applied to a rose to indicate the sepals; applied also to an arrow to indicate the head.
Barrulet. (7) A diminutive of the Bar.
Barruly. Barry of at least ten, the precise number being of no consequence.
Barry. (8) A term used to express a field or charge divided into a certain even number of equal horizontal parts; unless otherwise specified the number is six or eight.
Barwise. A term used to indicate that a charge is borne in the manner of a Bar, i.e. horizontally across the field.
Base. The lower part of the shield; hence in base indicates that a charge is so placed. There is also a charge known as a Base; this is formed by parting the lower part of the field from the upper by means of a line, straight or otherwise.
Beaver. An animal; also the visor of a helmet.
Bend. (9) One of the honourable Ordinaries; likewise a Bend sinister.
In Bend. A term used to indicate that several charges are arranged to follow the line of a Bend; not to be confused with Bendwise, in which the charge occupies the position of a bend.
Bendlet. (10) A diminutive of the Bend; likewise a Bendlet sinister.

Bendy. (11) A term used to express a field or charge divided bendwise into an even number of even parts.
Bezant. A gold roundle.
Bezanty. A term used to express a field or charge strewn with bezants.
Billet. (12) A small oblong figure. The height exceeds the breadth, otherwise it becomes a Billet couche or fessewise.
Billetty. A field used to express a field strewn with billets arranged in rows but not one beneath the other.
Bleu celeste. Blue; but a much lighter shade than Azure.
Bluebottle. The cornflower.
Bordure. (13) A sub-ordinary. The illustration shows a bordure per fesse.
Brock. The Badger.
Bugle Horn. A hunting-horn; usually stringed.

Cabled. A term applied to an anchor with a rope cable.
Caboshed. (14) A term applied to the head of a beast when borne full-faced with no part of the neck visible.
Caduceus. (15) The Rod of Mercury; a rod with two wings attached and entwined by two serpents.
Canton. (16) One of the sub-ordinaries, resembling a first quarter of a shield but somewhat smaller; it may be either dexter or sinister as specified.
Caparisoned. A term used to indicate that a war-horse is fully accoutred.
Carnat. Flesh-coloured; often spelled Carnation, etc.
Cartouche. An ornamental figure, often oval, enclosed by scrollwork and serving as a shield.
Catherine wheel. (17)
Celestial Crown. (18) A coronet similar in form to the Antique Crown and having upon each point a star.
Chaplet. (19) A wreath or garland of flowers and leaves; unless otherwise specified the flowers number four and are equidistantly arranged.
Checky. (20) A term used to express a field or charge divided into a number of small squares of alternating tinctures; in the case of a field it is maintained that there must be at least twenty pieces, in the case of an ordinary there must be at least three rows of squares. If there be but one row it will be Compony and if two rows it will be Counter-compony. The term is more usually spelled Chequy.
Cherub. (21) This is usually drawn as the head of an infant between a pair of wings, but a different form appears as a Supporter.
Chevron. (22) One of the honourable Ordinaries.
Chevronel. (23) A diminutive of the Chevron.
Chief. (24) One of the honourable Ordinaries. In chief is frequently used to indicate that charges are placed in the upper part of the shield.
Cinquefoil. (25) A conventional charge resembling a five-petalled flower.
Civic Crown. (26) A garland of oak and acorns; the term is cometimes wrongly used for a Mural Crown.
Clarion. (27) A charge of uncertain origin, resembling a spear rest.
Close. A term applied to the wings of birds when close to the body.
Cockatrice. (28) A monster with the body and tail of a wyvern and the head, comb, wattles and legs of a cock.
Combatant. A term applied to lions rampant face to face; likewise to other aggressive beasts.
Compony. See Checky.
Confronting. A term synonymous with combatant, applied to other beasts.
Conjoined. Linked together; often said to be distinct from interlaced.
Contourne. A term applied to animals facing towards the sinister.
Cornish Chough. (29) A species of crow with red beak and legs.
Cornucopia. The Horn of Plenty.
Cottised. (30) A term used to indicate, though strictly the usuage is incorrect, that an Ordinary is enclosed by its own diminutives; a Cross cottised is enclosed by lines parallel to its limbs.
Couchant. A term applied to animals to indicate that they are lying down; with beasts of the chase the more usual term is lodged.
Counterchanged. A term used to express the alternation of tinctures occurring when charges are placed upon a field or bearing divided into a metal and a colour, the tincture of the charge upon each being that of the other.
Counter-compony. (31) See Checky.
Couped. Cut off in a straight line.
Courant. Running at full speed.
Crescent. (32) A half-moon with the points uppermost.
Crest. A figure attached to the helmet.
Crined. A term used with respect to the colouring of hair, e.g. of a man's head or the horse's mane.
Cross. (33) One of the honourable Ordinaries, existing in numerous forms with specific names:—
- **Bottony.** (34)
- **Cross Crosslet.** (35)
- **Fillet Cross.** A very narrow cross.
- **Flory.** (36)
- **Formy.** (37)
- **Maltese Cross.** (38)

Moline. (39)
Parted and Fretted. (40)
Patonce. (41)
Patriarchal. (42)
Pattée. (43)
Pointed. (44)
Potent. (45)
Pommelée. (46)
St. Anthony's Cross. (47) A Tau Cross.
St. Cuthbert's Cross. (48) A cross pattée quadrate at the centre.
St. James's Cross. (49)
Sercelée. (50)

Crosier. The pastoral staff of a bishop or abbot; often incorrectly used for a cross-staff.

Crown. Unless otherwise described this is represented as a Ducal Coronet.

Crusilly. A term used to express a field or charge strewn with crosses; unless otherwise described cross crosslets are to be understood.

Cubit Arm. (51) A hand and forearm cut off below the elbow.

Current. See Courant.

Dancetty. (52) A zigzag line of partition, differing from indented in having larger indentations which are fewer in number; an Ordinary when dancetty has an indentation opposite a point.

Dexter. The right-hand side of the shield, being to the left of the observer; a dexter hand is a right hand.

Dimidiated. A term applied to charges of which only half is shown in consequence of division.

Displayed. (53) A term applied to the wings of birds when fully open; unless otherwise described the tips are upwards.

Doubled. A term applied to the mantling, etc., to express the lining.

Dovetailed. (54) A line of partition.

Ducal Coronet. (55) A coronet composed of a circlet on which are four strawberry leaves (three visible); this is not the coronet of a Duke.

Eagle. A bird; unless otherwise described it is represented as displayed with the wing-tips uppermost, other birds in the absence of description are represented close.

Earl's Coronet. (56) A coronet composed of a circlet upon which are eight silver balls, raised upon points (five visible), with gold strawberry leaves between the points (four visible).

Eastern Crown. See Antique Crown.

Embattled. (57) A line of partition formed like the battlements of a castle; unless otherwise described an Ordinary is embattled only on the upper side, if embattled on both sides (the crenelles being opposite each other) the correct term is Bretessed, and if a crenelle is opposite a merlon then it is described as Embattled counter embattled.

Embowed. A term used to express an Ordinary or bearing which is bent; an arm embowed has the elbow to the dexter. The term is often used as the exact opposite of Arched or Enarched.

Embrued. Dripping with blood; sometimes wrongly used in the sense of blood-stained.

Enarched. See Arched.

Endorsed. See Addorsed.

Enflamed. A term used to express a beacon, lamp, torch, etc., when ignited; it is often spelled Inflamed.

Enfield. (58) A monster with the head of a fox, the chest of a greyhound, the foreclaws of an eagle, the body of a lion, and the hind-legs and tail of a wolf.

Enfiled. A term used with reference to one or more charges which are passed through another such as a coronet; the charges here are Enfiled and the coronet Enfiles them.

Engrailed. (59) A line of partition in the form of semicircular indents; in a simple line it is often distinguishable with difficulty from engrailed. The criterion is that it must present the appearance of having the points outwards, hence these usually (except in the case of Per chevron engrailed) point away from the more honourable point of the shield. An Ordinary engrailed has the points outwards. It is the exact opposite of invected.

Enhanced. A term used to express any charge borne higher in the shield than its customary position.

Ensigned. A term used to express any charge (or the shield itself) when another is placed immediately above it as though resting upon its upper edge. This is distinct from Surmounted although this latter term is often wrongly used as an equivalent.

Eradicated. Torn up by the roots, applied to trees and plants.

Erased. (60) Torn off, so as to present a jagged edge, in contrast with couped.

Ermine. One of the furs; represented as black tails upon white.

Ermines. One of the furs; represented as white tails upon black.

Erminois. One of the furs; represented as black tails upon gold.

Escallop. (61) A sea shell; the cockle-shell.

Escarbuncle. (62) A conventional charge, derived from the shield-umbo.

Escutcheon. A shield; sometimes spelled Escocheon.

Estoile. (63) A star of six wavy rays.

Face. (64) The head of a lion or leopard when shown full face without the neck being visible is termed a lion's face or a leopard's face.
Fesse. (65) One of the honourable Ordinaries.
Fetterlock (66) A shackle and padlock.
Field. The surface of the shield.
Fimbriated. (67) Having a narrow edging of contrasting tincture.
Fired. Synonymous with Enflamed.
Fitchy. A term applied to a cross to denote that a limb is sharpened to a point from the centre outwards; if the limb has the point attached to it it becomes Fitched, e.g. "at the foot".
Flambeau. A torch.
Flaunch. (68) One of the Ordinaries; always borne in pairs.
Fleam. (69) An ancient lancet.
Fleur de lys. (70) A conventional charge, perhaps based upon the lily.
Flory. A term used to express a field or charge strewn with fleurs-de-lys; see also Cross Flory.
Fleury. Synonymous with Flory.
Flory-counterflory. (71) A term applied to a charge, the edge of which is modified by fleurs-de-lys, the heads alternately outwards and inwards.
Forcene. (72) A term applied to a horse in the position usually called rampant.
Fountain. (73) A roundle barry wavy of six argent and azure; also the architectural work so called.
Fourchée. (74) A term applied to a tail when forked; not to be confused with double-queued.
Fret. (75) A charge consisting of two long pieces in saltire, extending to the edges of the shield, interlaced with a mascle.
Fretted. Interlaced.
Fretty. (76) A term used to express a field or charge overlaid by a number of pieces crossing bendways and bendways sinister, and interlaced; if the pieces are not interlaced then it is termed Trellised.

Garb. (77) A sheaf; unless otherwise described it is a sheaf of wheat.
Gamb. (78) The whole foreleg of a beast, as opposed to a paw.
Garland. See Chaplet.
Gaze. (79) At. A term applied to animals of the deer-kind when standing and showing the full-face; in other beasts called Guardant.
Gemel. See Bar gemel.
Gobony. Synonymous with Compony.
Gorged. Encircled about the neck.
Gouttes. Conventional droplets; their names are varied according to their tincture, thus: argent—d'eau; or—d'or; azure—de larmes; gules—de sang; sable—de poix; vert—d'huile or d'olive. Very often the tincture is expressed without regard to this convention.
Grenade. (80) A bomb in the form of a hollow ball.
Griffin. (81) A monster having the wings, forefeet and head (with the addition of ears) of an eagle, the body, hind legs and tail of a lion; a Male Griffin has no wings but has a number of rays or spikes issuing from its body. The rampant position for a griffin is called Segreant.
Guardant. (82) A term applied to lions, etc., when showing their full face; not to be confused with Affrontee.
Gules. Red.
Gutty. (83) A term used to express a field or charge strewn with gouttes.
Gyronny. (84) A field is said to be gyronny when it is so divided as to form a number of Gyrons; the number must be specified.

Habited. Clothed, or vested.
Henaege Knot. (85)
Horned. To be distinguished from Armed in that it refers merely to the horns.
Hurt. A blue roundle.
Humet. (86) A bar or fesse couped.
Humetty. Couped as applied to an Ordinary.

Incensed. Term applied to beasts, etc., having fire issuing from their mouths and ears.
Indented. (87) A line of partition.
Indented grady. A line of partition resembling steps.
Inescutcheon. A small escutcheon as a charge.
Inflamed. See Enflamed.
Invected. (88) A line of partition being the exact opposite of Engrailed.
Inverted. Turned the wrong way.
Irradiated. Surrounded by rays.
Issuant. (89) A term used to express that a charge arises out of something, e.g. Issuant from the base; not to be confused with Naissant.

Jessed. A term applied to hawks to express that they are fitted with jesses, i.e. the thongs with which the bird was held. N.B. These are distinct from the thongs by which the bells are attached, although it is to these latter thongs that older blazons refer the term.
Jessant-de-lys. (90) A term applied to, e.g. a leopard's face when a fleur-de-lys issues from its mouth. The term Jessant implies throwing out or shooting forth.

Label. (91) A mark of cadency, consisting of a file and pendants.
Lacy knot. (92)
Langued. A term applied to the tongues of beasts.

Latticed. (93) A figure resembling fretty but set upright and of a closer mesh.
Lined. When a cord is attached to a collar, that collar is said to be lined.
Link. A torch.
Lizard. (94) A reptile; also the wild cat of Norway, resembling a Lynx.
Low of Flames. A tongue of flame.
Lodged. The couchant position with respect to beasts of the chase.
Lozenge.
Lozengy. (95) A term used to express a field or charge divided into a number of lozenge-shaped figures.
Lymphad. (96) An old-fashioned ship, or galley, with one mast and provided with oasr.

Martlet. (97) A swallow-like bird without legs.
Mascle. (98) A voided lozenge.
Masoned. (99) Marked in a manner resembling the cement in stone buildings.
Maunch. (100) A type of sleeve.
Membered. A term used to indicate the legs of birds, or at least such birds as have no talons.
Mercantile Crown. A coronet consisting of a circlet on which are raised eight masts (five visible) each with sail spread.
Millrind. (101) The iron affixed to the centre of a millstone.
Mullet. A five-pointed star with straight pointed rays.
Mural Crown. (102) A coronet in the form of a circlet masoned and with crenellations.
Murrey. A purplish-red colour; the colour of mulberry juice; often regarded as synonymus with Sanguine.

Naiant. (103) Swimming; applied to fish in that position.
Naval Crown. (104) A coronet composed of a circlet on which are mounted the sterns and sails of ships alternately.
Nebuly. (105) A line of partition resembling clouds.
Nowed. (106) Tied in a knot.

Ogress. A black roundle.
Opinicus. (107) A monster with the body and fore-legs of a lion, the head, neck and wings of an eagle, and the tail of a camel.
Or. Gold.
Orle. (108) One of the subordinaries forming an inner border.

Pale. (109) One of the honourable Ordinaries.
Palet. (110) A diminutive of the Pale.
Palisado, crown. Same as vallary, which see.
Paly. (111) A term used to express a field or charge divided into an even number of equal pieces by vertical lines.
Paly Bendy. (112) A term used to express a field or charge when divided by a combination of paly and bendy so as to form a series of non-rectangular parallelograms.
Pall. (113) An archiepiscopal vestment; also a geometrical charge resembling it in shape.
Pantheon. A monster.
Party. Signifies divided; unless otherwise described it represents a division per pale.
Paschal Lamb. (114) A lamb depicted as carrying a flag (often charged with the Cross of St. George, and with a halo about its head).
Passant. (115) A term applied to beasts when shown walking.
Pean. One of the furs; represented as gold tails on black.
Pegasus. (116) A winged horse.
Pendant. Hanging; often, indeed usually, spelled Pendent.
Pellet. A black roundel.
Pellety. A term used to express a field or charge strewn with pellets.
Petasus. (117) The helmet of Mercury; represented as a winged morion.
Pheon. (118) The barbed head of a dart; frequently the inner edge of the barbs are engrailed, otherwise it may be a Broad Arrow.
Phoenix. (119) A bird resembling an eagle, always depicted in flames.
Pierced. Perforated; unless otherwise described the perforation is circular.
Piety, In her. (120) A term applied to the pelican when represented in her nest and piercing her breast in order to feed her young with her blood; occasionally, but wrongly, a pelican vulning itself is so described—there must be the nest and young.
Pile. (121) One of the Ordinaries.
Plate. A silver roundel.
Pomeis. A green roundel.
Popinjay. (122) The parrot.
Port. A gateway.
Potent. (123) One of the furs, similar to vair but in the form of crutch-heads; see also Cross Potent.
Pride. (124) In his. A term applied to the peacock with tail displayed.
Purfled. Embroidered.
Purpure. Purple.

Quadrate. Square.
Quarter. (125) An ordinary; also one of the division in a quarterly shield, irrespective of the number of such divisions.
Quarterly. (126) A term used to express a field divided into quarters; there is no limit to the number of such divisions.
Quarter-pierced. (127) Perforated in a square form; in the case of a cross the whole of the intersection is removed.

Quatrefoil. (128) A conventional charge differing from the cinquefoil and trefoil in having four petals or leaves.
Queucd. Tailed. (129) is double queued.

Radiant. A lion of partition.
Radiated. Term applied to an object from which issue rays.
Radiating. Synonymous with Radiated.
Raguly. (130) A line of partition; like the trunk of a tree when lopped of its branches.
Rampant. (131) The usual position of a lion; rearing and standing on the near hind leg.
Rayed. Synonymous with Radiated.
Rayonée, Crown. A coronet composed of a circlet with points as in the Antique but differing therefrom in that the rays are alternately straight and wavy.
Recursant. A term applied to the eagle in trian-aspect with the back turned towards the observer.
Reguardant. (132) Looking behind.
Respectant. A term applied to tame animals when placed face to face.
Reversed. Contrary to the usual position, e.g. upside down.
Riband. A ribbon; also a diminutive of the Bend.
Rising. A term applied to birds when preparing to fly.
Rose. Borne depicted naturally ((133) garden rose stalked and leaved) and heraldically ((134) rose heraldic).
Roundle. A disc-like or spherical figure.
Rousant. Rising.
Rural Crown. A coronet composed of a circlet on which are set oak leaves and acorns alternately.

Sable. Black.
Salamander. (135) A lizard-like creature; usually shown in flames.
Salient. (136) Leaping with both hind feet on the ground.
Saltire. (137) One of the honourable Ordinaries.
Sanguine. A purplish-red; the colour of blood.
Saxon Crown. A coronet composed of a circlet on which are four uprights (three visible) each surmounted by a ball.
Sea-horse. Etc. All creatures (other than those occurring in nature) whose names contain the word sea, e.g. Sea-bear, Sea-horse; Sea-unicorn, are represented with the head and forequarters of the animals and the tail of a fish.
Seax. (138) A Saxon sword.
Segreant. (139) The rampant position of a griffin.
Semée. (140) Synonymous with strewn with.
Sengreen. (141) The house-leek.
Sinister. The left-hand side of the shield, hence to the right of the spectator.
Slipped. (142) A term applied to the stalk of plants.
Soleil, En. Borne upon the sun.
Springing. (143) The salient position when applied to beasts of the chase.
Square pierced. Perforated in square form.
Stafford Knot. (144).
Statant. (145) Standing on all four feet.
Stooping. With lowered head.

Talbot. (146) A hound with long ears.
Tierced. Divided into three, the parts being equal.
Tenne. A tawny yellow; or orange.
Thunderbolt. (147) The emblem of Jupiter
Torteau. A red roundel.
Trefoil. (148) A conventional charge differing from the cinquefoil and quatrefoil in having three petals or leaves.
Tressure. (149) A narrow Orle. Usually Flory.
Trinity. (150).
Triton. (151) A Sea-god, resembling a merman, usually blowing a conch-shell.
Trivet. (152) A frame of iron with three supports.
Tudor rose, or double rose. (153) Is the red heraldic rose of Lancaster charged with the white rose of York.
Tufted. A term applied to the small bunches of hair on Heraldic Antelopes, Unicorns, etc.

Undy. (154) Wavy.
Unguled. A term applied to the hoofs of cloven hoofed animals.

Vair. (155) One of the furs; represented as shield shaped pieces placed base to apex.
Vairy. Vair of other tinctures than argent and azure.
Vallary. (156) Crown. A coronet composed of a rim on which are placed vair-like pieces.
Vert. Green.
Vested. Clothed.
Virolled. A term applied to the garnishing bands of the bugle horn.
Voided. (157) Having the centre removed parallel to the outline.
Volant. Flying.
Vulned. (158) Wounded.

Wake knot. (159).
Water bouget. (160).
Weir. (161) Fish-weir.
Wyvern. (162) A monster resembling a two-legged dragon, the tail being that of a serpent but often barbed.

1 2 3 4 5 6
7 8 9 10 11 12
13 14 15 16 17 18
19 20 21 22 23 24
25 26 27 28 29 30
31 32 33 34 35 36
37 38 39 40 41 42

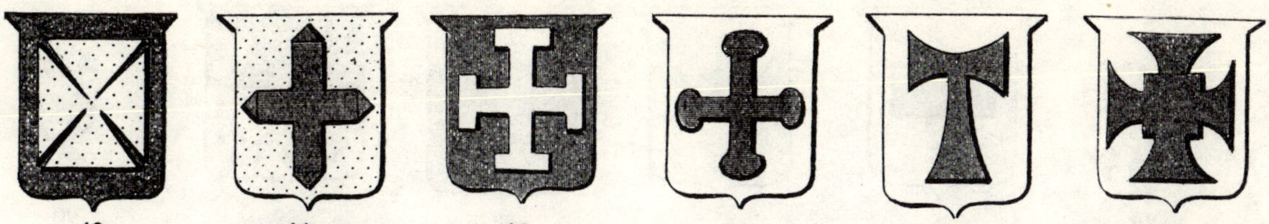

43 44 45 46 47 48

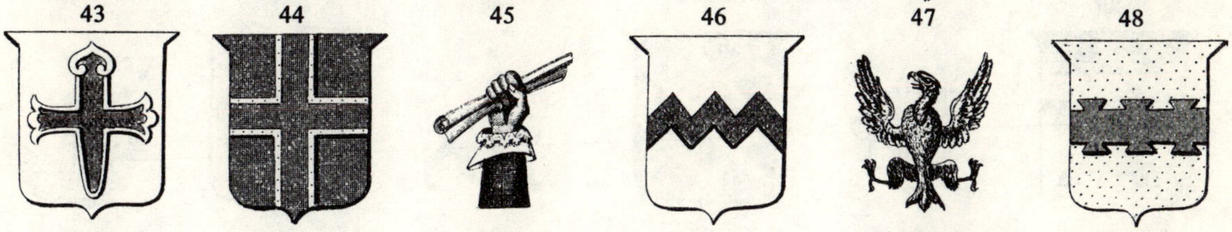

49 50 51 52 53 54

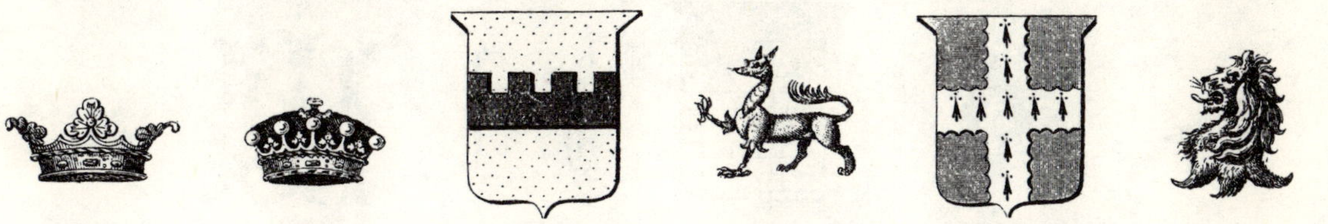

55 56 57 58 59 60

61 62 63 64 65 66

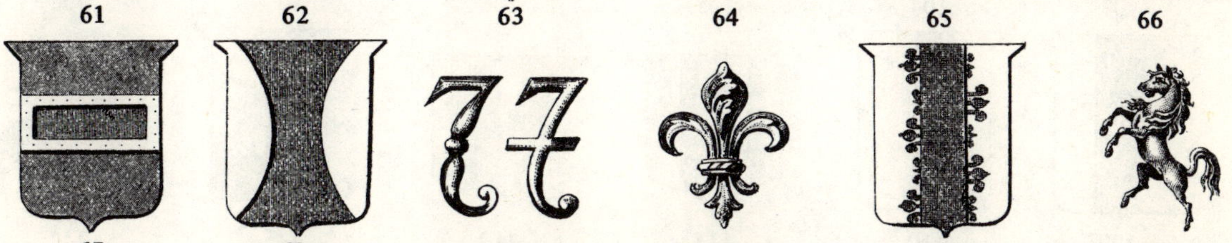

67 68 69 70 71 72

73 74 75 76 77 78

79 80 81 82 83 84

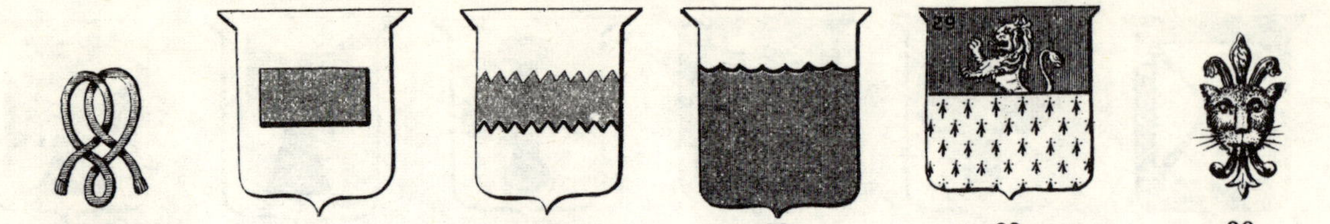

85 86 87 88 89 90

91 92 93 94 95 96

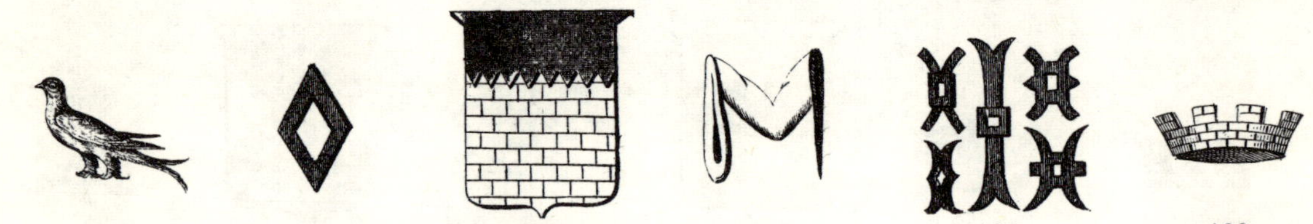

97 98 99 100 101 102

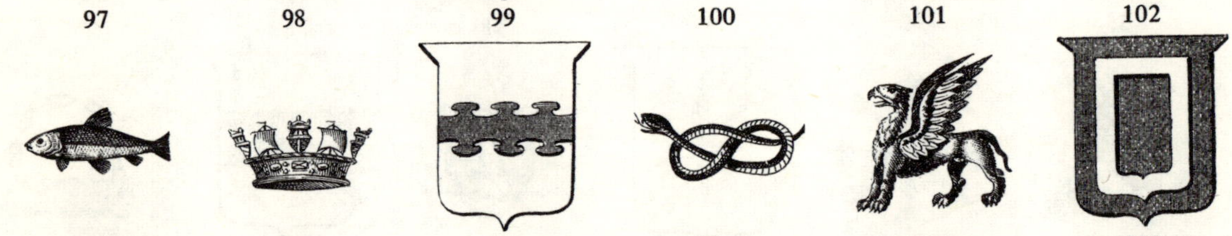

103 104 105 106 107 108

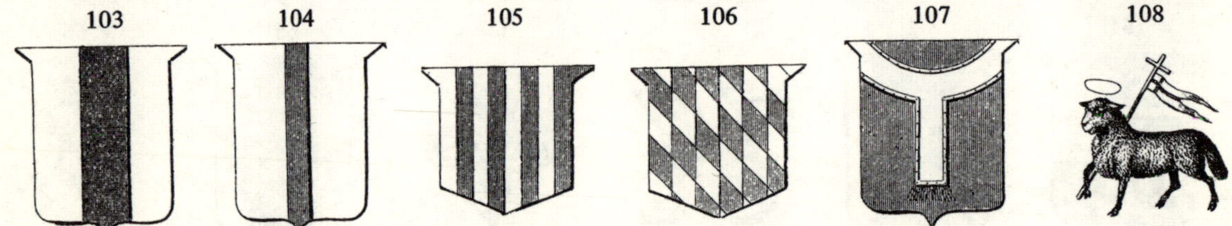

109 110 111 112 113 114

115 116 117 118 119 120

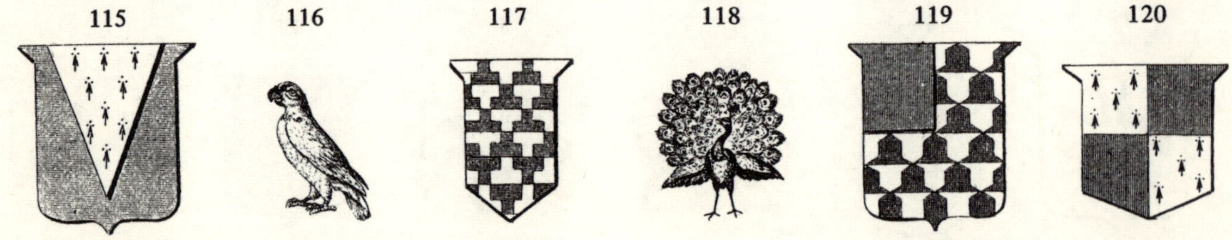

121 122 123 124 125 126

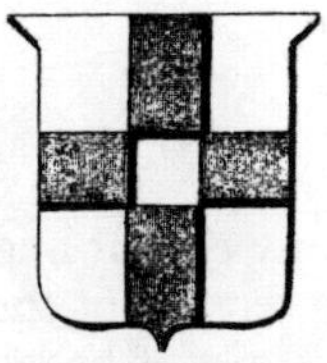
127

128

129

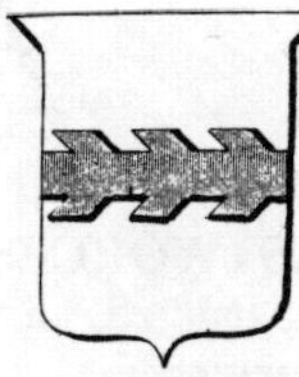
130

131

132

133

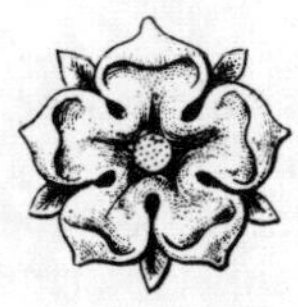
134

135

136

137

138

139

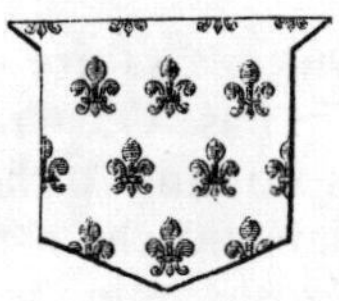
140

141

142

143

144

145

146

147

148

149

150

151

152

153

154

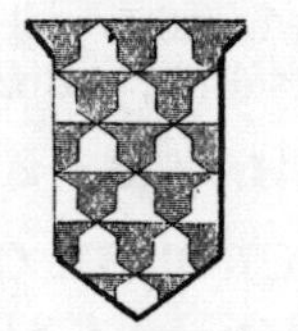
155

156

157

158

159

160

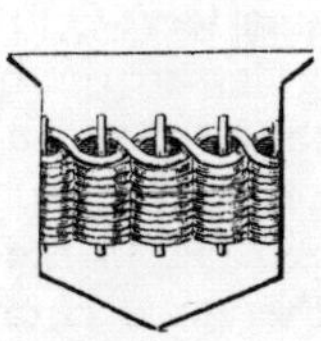
161

162

A

** Denotes Illustration*

THE ABBEY, MALVERN WELLS (WORCESTERSHIRE). Or, a chevron gobony argent and gules between three sprigs of hazel, fructed, slipped and leaved proper. **Crest:** On a wreath of the colours, A unicorn's head argent, armed and crined gules, holding in the mouth a sprig of hazel, fructed, slipped and leaved proper. **Motto:** Ora, labora, lude. **Granted** 8 April 1954 to The Abbey, Malvern Wells, Ltd., for the use of the above girls' school.

THE ABBEY NATIONAL BUILDING SOCIETY. Argent, a cross gules; over all a castle sable. **Crest:** On a wreath of the colours, A lion statant Or gorged with a chain, hanging therefrom a key, wards to the sinister, gules. **Supporters:** On either side a lion Or charged on the shoulder with a billet, that on the dexter sable with a fleur-de-lis Or, that on the sinister ermine with a sword erect gules. **Motto:** Aedificium nostrum bene stat. **Granted** 28 March 1944.

ABBEYS. See Ampleforth; Douai; Ealing.

ABERGAVENNY, BOROUGH OF (MONMOUTHSHIRE).* Gules, a saltire argent between a rose in chief and two fleurs-de-lis in fesse and a portcullis chained in base Or. **Crest:** On a wreath of the colours, Upon the trunk of a tree fessewise, eradicated and sprouting to the dexter, proper, a bull passant argent, pied and unguled sable, gorged with a collar and chain reflexed over the back and charged on the body with two fleurs-de-lis Or. **Motto:** Hostes nunc amici. **Granted** 27 March 1901.

ABERYSTWYTH, BOROUGH OF (CARDIGANSHIRE). Or, in chief two lymphads sable, sails furled argent, flags and pennons flying to the sinister gules, and in base an open book proper, bound also gules and clasped gold, inscribed on the pages with the Arabic numerals 1277 fessewise also sable. **Crest:** On a wreath Or, sable and gules, A representation of the Castle Tower at Aberystwyth proper. Mantled gules, sable and Or. **Supporters:** On the dexter side a dragon reguardant gules supporting a staff Or, flying therefrom a pennon sable charged with a garb gold; and on the sinister side a lion reguardant sable supporting a like staff, flying therefrom a pennon gules charged with a winged wheel Or. **Motto:** Gorau moes gwasanaeth. **Badge:** Within two leeks, the roots crossed in saltire, proper, a lion rampant reguardant sable. **Granted** 15 May 1961.

ABERYSTWYTH. See also Wales, University College of (Aberystwyth).

ABINGDON, BOROUGH OF (BERKSHIRE).* Vert, a cross patonce Or between four crosses pattée argent. **Crest:** On a wreath argent and gules, Out of a mural crown Or masoned azure, set between two wings of the last a stag's head gold, in the mouth two flashes (representing a nuclear flash) argent. **Supporters:** On the dexter side a swan, wings elevated and addorsed, proper standing on a woolpack gules, in the beak a Tudor rose slipped and leaved proper, gorged with a Saxon crown Or, attached thereto a church bell rope of the last reflexed over the back, the dolley of alternate twists of gules, argent and azure; and on the sinister side a like swan standing on a book bound gules edged Or, in the beak three stalks of barley proper, gorged with an ancient crown gold, attached thereto a church bell rope as on the dexter, **Motto:** Faith and Industry. Arms entered at the Visitations of 1566, 1623 and 1666; Crest and Supporters granted 12 March 1962.

ABINGDON

ACCRINGTON

ACKWORTH SCHOOL

ABERGAVENNY

ACCIDENT SURGERY, INSTITUTE OF. Argent, a hurt environed by a snake nowed in chief vert, purfled Or. **Crest:** Out of an ancient crown Or an arm embowed, vested argent, the hand proper grasping a rod of Aesculapius gules, the serpent vert. [Mantled azure, doubled argent.] **Supporters:** On either side a representation of St. Barbara proper. **Motto:** Tend and mend. **Granted** 12 March 1962.

ACCOUNTANTS. See Certified and Corporate Accountants; Chartered Accountants; Cost and Works Accountants; General Accountants; Incorporated Accountants and Auditors.

ACCRINGTON, BOROUGH OF (LANCASHIRE).* Gules, on a fesse argent a shuttle fessewise proper, in base two printing cylinders, issuant therefrom a piece of calico (parsley pattern) also proper; on a chief per pale Or and vert, a lion rampant purpure and a stag current Or. **Crest:** On a wreath of the colours, An oak branch bent from the sinister chevronwise, sprouting and leaved, proper, fructed Or. **Motto:** Industry and Prudence conquer. **Granted** 26 August 1879.

ACKWORTH SCHOOL (ACKWORTH, YORKSHIRE).* Azure, on a chevron argent between three acorns slipped also argent, a chevron sable, thereon as many roses likewise argent, barbed and seeded proper. **Crest:** Issuant from a coronet composed of four roses argent, barbed and seeded proper, set upon a rim Or, a mount vert, thereon a lamb statant, in the mouth a sprig of thyme, leaved and flowered, also proper. **Motto:** Non sibi sed omnibus. **Granted** 15 December 1959.

ACTON TECHNICAL COLLEGE.* Per fesse sable and Or, on a fesse argent between in chief an open book proper and in base a gear-wheel of twenty-five teeth of the first, a barrulet wavy azure [all within a bordure compony Or and sable]. **Crest:** On a wreath of the colours, In front of an oak tree fructed proper, two seaxes in saltire, points upwards, argent, hilted and pommelled Or. **Motto:** Mihi cura futuri. **Granted** 30 August 1951. In the grant the bordure is apparently illustrated but not blazoned.

ACTUARIES, INSTITUTE OF.* Chequy sable and Or, a bend wavy argent; on a chief gold, an open book between two hour glasses proper. **Crest:** On a wreath Or, gules and argent, A woolpack vert charged with a bend wavy argent. **Supporters:** On either side a lion argent charged on the shoulder with a Tudor rose, argent on gules, barbed and seeded proper, and grasping in the interior paw a bezant. **Motto:** Certum ex incertis. Granted 15 March 1956.

AERONAUTICS, COLLEGE OF (CRANFIELD, BERKSHIRE). Per chevron argent and sable, in chief two bars nebuly azure and in base a three-branched torch winged Or, inflamed proper. **Crest:** Issuant from an astral crown, an owl azure. **Motto:** Post nubes lux. **Granted** 1 June 1948.

AGRICULTURAL ENGINEERING, NATIONAL COLLEGE OF. Murrey, a garb of padi proper between two ears of wheat, stalked and leaved; issuant from the base a cog-wheel Or. **Crest:** On a wreath of the colours, In front of an open book proper, edged Or and bound sable, a pair of hands proper grasping a roundel per pale sable and barry wavy of four argent and azure. **Motto:** E natura ingenioque copia. **Granted** 30 May 1967.

AGRICULTURE, ESSEX INSTITUTE OF.* Argent, on a bend gules a bull's head caboshed between two garbs Or; on a chief vert, an Essex plough gold. **Crest:** On a wreath Or and gules, An appletree fructed proper, pendent from a branch thereof by a riband azure an escutcheon gules charged with three seaxes fessewise in pale, blades argent, hilts and pomels Or to the sinister, and cutting edges upwards. **Motto:** Time tries the truth in every thing. **Granted** 24 October 1951.

AIR PILOTS AND NAVIGATORS OF LONDON, GUILD OF. Per pale sable and argent, in chief two wings conjoined and in base a roundel, all counterchanged. **Crest:** On a wreath of the colours, A demi winged lion Or holding in the paws an antique lamp azure, inflamed proper. [Mantled azure, doubled argent.] **Supporters:** On either side a falcon, wings elevated and ad-

ACTUARIES, INSTITUTE OF

ACTON
TECHNICAL COLLEGE

AIR TRAINING, COLLEGE OF

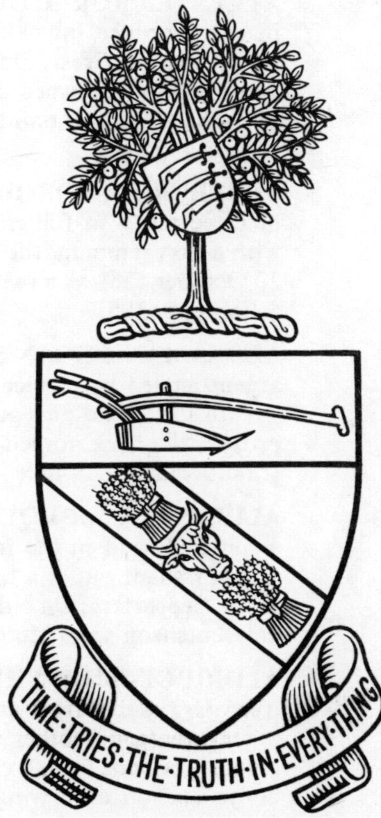

AGRICULTURE,
ESSEX INSTITUTE OF

dorsed, proper, belled Or, the dexter charged on the breast with a sun in splendour gold, the sinister hooded of the last, plumed sable, and charged on the breast with an estoile irradiated argent [the whole upon a compartment of grass, thereon clouds, proper.] **Motto:** Per caelum via nostra. **Granted** 28 September 1956.

AIR TRAINING, COLLEGE OF.* Tierce in pairle reversed bleu celeste, azure and vert, a winged lion rampant, wings elevated and addorsed, Or, grasping in the dexter paw a torch gold, enflamed proper. **Crest:** Issuant from a coronet composed of four mullets set upon a rim azure, a falcon rising Or, beaked and membered gules, the jesses vert. Mantled azure, doubled Or. **Motto:** Look forward. **Badge:** A hurt environed by a wreath of laurel Or; over all, issuant from a coronet composed of four mullets set upon a rim gold, a falcon rising, jessed also gold. **Granted** 30 June 1960.

AIR WARFARE, ROYAL AIR FORCE COLLEGE OF (MANBY, LINCOLNSHIRE).* Azure semée of mullets Or, a cresset, enflamed, proper within a compass-ring gold, lettered sable. **Crest:** Issuant from an astral crown Or, a pelican, wings elevated, azure, gorged with a naval crown gold. [Mantled azure, doubled Or.] **Motto:** Progress. **Granted** 21 June 1951 to The Royal Air Force Flying College (Manby) and regranted 20 July 1962 upon the change in name.

THE ALBERT MIDDLE CLASS COLLEGE IN SUFFOLK, COMMONLY CALLED FRAMLINGHAM COLLEGE. Azure, a chevron between three antique crowns argent, each enfiled with two arrows in saltire Or. **Crest:** On a wreath of the colours, Out of an antique crown, between two branches of olive fructed or, a chestnut horse's head proper. **Motto:** Studio sapientia crescit. **Granted** 5 September 1967.

ALCESTER RURAL DISTRICT COUNCIL (WARWICKSHIRE).* Gules, two Roman swords in saltire proper, hilts and pomels Or, over all a cross engrailed of the last; on a chief azure, three mitres argent. **Crest:** On a wreath of the colours, Out of a wreath of oak proper, fructed Or, a demi bull gules, armed and unguled gold, holding between the legs an escutcheon azure charged with three needles, points downward, in fesse argent. **Motto:** Dirigere non dominari. **Granted** 16 March 1955.

ALDEBURGH, BOROUGH OF (EAST SUFFOLK).* Azure, on water in base an ancient ship of three masts in full sail, a ladder affixed to the side amidships, proper, the mainsail charged with a lion rampant, the fore and aft sails and pennons each charged with a cross, gules. **Granted** 20 October 1561 as a seal (untinctured); Certified (with tinctures) as Arms by the Kings of Arms 5 February 1951.

ALDERMAN COGAN'S SCHOOL (HULL, YORKSHIRE).* Azure, two quill pens in saltire argent enfiled by a ducal coronet Or; on a chief gules, three leaves of the second. **Crest:** On a wreath Or, azure and gules, A pelican's head and neck erased, the beak Or vulning the breast proper, the neck gorged with a chain Or, pendent therefrom a key, wards to the sinister, gold. [Mantled azure, doubled Or.] **Motto:** Constans fidei. **Granted** 20 December 1956.

ALDERSHOT, BOROUGH OF (HAMPSHIRE).* Quarterly gules and vair, in the first quarter a mitre Or and in the fourth two swords in saltire proper, pommelled and hilted of the third. **Crest:** Issuant out of a mural crown, a hind's head proper charged on the neck with a spur-rowel sable. **Supporters:** On either side a lion guardant gules gorged with a collar Or, pendent therefrom an escutcheon vair. **Motto:** Pugna pro patria. **Granted** 7 May 1923.

ALDRIDGE-BROWNHILLS URBAN DISTRICT COUNCIL (STAFFORDSHIRE).* Vert fretty Or, issuant from a base composed of three mounds of earth proper charged with a bar wavy argent, thereon another wavy azure, a beacon sable, enflamed proper. **Crest:** On a wreath of the colours, Issuant from a circlet of bricks azure, a demi eagle Or, charged on the breast with a fleur-de-lys and on each wing with an escallop azure. Mantled gules, doubled Or, **Motto:** Unite to

AIR WARFARE, COLLEGE OF

ALDERSHOT

ALCESTER

ALDEBURGH

ALDERMAN COGAN'S SCHOOL

flourish. **Badge:** An eagle displayed, standing on [and within?] a wreath, Or, beaked, armed and charged on the body with a fleur-de-lys and on each wing an escallop azure. **Granted** 20 December 1968.

ALFORD URBAN DISTRICT COUNCIL (LINCOLNSHIRE—PARTS OF LINDSEY). Barry wavy argent and azure, a lion rampant, queue fourchee, and on a chief sable, a windmill sail of five arms Or between two Lincoln Red Shorthorn bulls' heads caboshed proper, ringed argent. **Crest:** On a wreath of the colours, In front of a demi lion ermine holding between the paws a book Or, charged with a rose gules charged with another argent barbed and seeded proper, seven mascles conjoined gules. **Motto:** Foursquare to all winds. **Granted** 1 October 1965.

ALFRETON URBAN DISTRICT COUNCIL (DERBYSHIRE).* Azure, two chevrons; a chief Or, thereon two crosiers in saltire azure between two cressets sable, fired proper. **Crest:** Out of a mural crown sable charged with three trefoils slipped argent, a mount vert, thereon, between two lozenges issuant sable, an oak tree proper, fructed of five acorns Or. [Mantled azure, doubled or.] **Motto:** Ex terra vires. **Granted** 10 January 1963.

ALLEYN'S COLLEGE OF GOD'S GIFT, COMMONLY CALLED DULWICH COLLEGE.* Argent, a chevron between three cinquefoils gules; a chief ermine, thereon a cinquefoil of the second. **Crest:** On a wreath of the colours, Issuant from flames of fire, a cubit arm, the hand grasping a heart, all proper. **Motto:** Detur gloria soli Deo. **Granted** 1935.

ALL HALLOWS ROMAN CATHOLIC SECONDARY SCHOOL (FARNHAM, SURREY). Argent, a cross throughout gules; surmounting the fesse point in saltire two fronds of palm vert, enfiled by a celestial crown Or. **Crest:** On a wreath of the colours, In front of two keys in saltire, wards upward and outward, Or, a Paschal Lamb passant reguardant proper. **Motto:** Testimonium perhibere veritati. **Granted** 20 June 1962.

ALLHALLOWS SCHOOL (ROUSDON, DEVON).* Tierce in pairle reversed gules, azure and Or, in chief a celestial crown of the third and three lilies slipped vert issuant crosswise from one stalk, the outer lilies depressed by two leaves arrondie growing from the base of the stalk also vert, and in base an otter couchant of the first. **Motto:** Famam extendere factis. **Granted** 22 June 1950.

ALLIANCE ASSURANCE COMPANY LIMITED. Argent, upon a rock issuant from the base proper, inscribed 1824 in gold numerals, a quadrangular castle also proper, pennons flying to the sinister from each tower gules. **Crest:** In front of flames proper issuant from a coronet of four roses argent, barbed and seeded proper, set upon a rim Or, two keys in saltire, wards upwards, sable. **Supporters:** On the dexter side a lion guardant Or, resting the sinister hind leg on an escutcheon argent charged with a rod of Aesculapius gules; and on the sinister side a like lion resting the dexter hind leg on an escutcheon argent charged with an anchor sable. **Motto:** Multi societate tutiores. **Granted** 14 September 1933.

ALLIANCE BUILDING SOCIETY (BRIGHTON, SUSSEX). Gules, within two chevronels Or, three bezants, the whole between three bees gold. **Crest:** On a wreath of the colours, In front of a domed tower sable, masoned argent, perched thereon a martlet Or, two dolphins, heads downwards, in saltire also argent, fins and tails gold. **Motto:** Domus arx certissima. **Granted** 8 June 1954.

ALLIANCE PERPETUAL BUILDING SOCIETY. Gules, on a bend ermine between two castles, three keys, wards downwards, Or. **Crest:** On a wreath argent and gules, Issuant from the battlements of a tower gules, masoned Or, a demi owl, wings expanded, gold. **Supporters:** On either side a winged lion Or supporting a staff proper, flying therefrom a banner gules, masoned gold. **Motto:** Alliance is wisdom. **Granted** 3 September 1939.

ALLEYN'S COLLEGE

ALFRETON

ALDRIDGE-BROWNHILLS

ALLHALLOWS SCHOOL

ALL SOULS' COLLEGE

ALL SOULS' COLLEGE (OXFORD UNIVERSITY).* Or, a chevron between three cinquefoils gules. Entered at the Visitation of 1574 for The College of the Souls of Faithful People deceased.

ALTON RURAL DISTRICT COUNCIL (HAMPSHIRE). Argent, issuant from a base barry wavy of four of the first and vert, a mount also vert, thereon a yew tree proper; on a chief sable, three lions' faces, jessant-de-lys, Or. **Crest:** On a wreath argent and vert, A greyhound sejant sable charged on the shoulder with a cinquefoil argent and resting the dexter forepaw on an open book proper, edged and bound gold. **Motto:** Alto nomine. **Granted** 1 August 1957.

ALTRINCHAM, BOROUGH OF (CHESHIRE). Azure, in chief two garbs and in base a cogwheel Or. **Crest:** On a wreath of the colours, A lion passant guardant Or supporting with the dexter forepaw a staff gules, the truck gold, flying therefrom a banner azure charged with a cornucopia fessewise of the first, the fruit proper. **Supporters:** On the dexter side a unicorn ermine, armed, maned and unguled Or, gorged with a collar gules, pendent thereform by a chain of the last an escutcheon barry of six argent and azure; and on the sinister side a lion Or, gorged with a collar gules, pendent therefrom by a like chain an escutcheon quarterly gules and or, in the first quarter a lion passant argent. **Motto:** Altrincham en avant. **Granted** 30 August 1937.

AMERSHAM RURAL DISTRICT COUNCIL (BUCKINGHAMSHIRE).* Argent, on a mount in base vert a wyvern, wings expanded, gules; on a chief per pale of the last and sable, three plates. **Crest:** Issuant from a Saxon crown Or, a demi lion gules holding in the paws a sprig of beech proper. Mantled gules, doubled argent. **Motto:** Freely we serve. **Granted** 1 May 1953.

THE AMICABLE SOCIETY. See Norwich Union Life Assurance Society.

AMMANFORD URBAN DISTRICT COUNCIL (CARMARTHENSHIRE).* Per fesse dancetté Or and sable, in chief a cross couped of the last. **Crest:** On a wreath of the colours, Issuant from a wreath of oak leaves sable, a demi boar gules, armed Or. **Motto:** Hanfod tref trefn. **Granted** 9 April 1952.

AMPLEFORTH ABBEY AND COLLEGE (YORKSHIRE).* Per fesse dancetté Or and azure, a chief per pale gules and of the second charged on the dexter side with two keys in saltire Or and argent and on the sinister with a cross flory between five martlets of the first. **Motto:** Dieu le ward. Granted 17 May 1921.

AMPTHILL RURAL DISTRICT COUNCIL (BEDFORDSHIRE).* Or, a stag's head [caboshed] gules, between the attires an escutcheon azure charged with three bars wavy of the first encircled by a chaplet of oak fructed proper; on a chief sable, a lion passant guardant gold. **Crest:** On a wreath of the colours, Out of a mural crown, a demi lion gules, gorged with a collar argent charged with three escallops sable, holding between the paws a garb Or. **Motto:** Courage and Skill. **Granted** 11 February 1957.

ANAESTHETISTS OF GREAT BRITAIN AND IRELAND, ASSOCIATION OF. Gules, a rod of Aesculapius proper, in chief two poppy heads Or. **Crest:** On a wreath of the colours, Two mandrakes in pile Or. **Supporters:** On the dexter side a representation of Somnus, holding in the exterior hand a torch downwards, and on the sinister side a representation of Morpheus, both proper. **Motto:** In somno securitas. **Granted** 12 February 1945.

ANDOVER, BOROUGH OF (HAMPSHIRE).* Argent, on a mount vert, in front of an oak tree fructed proper a lion statant guardant gules. **Crest:** On a wreath of the colours, A stag Or resting the dexter forehoof on a lozenge argent charged with a fleur-de-lis azure. **Supporters:** On the dexter side a lion guardant gules; and on the sinister side an eagle, wings elevated and addorsed, azure. **Motto:** Constantia basis virtutum. **Granted** 4 April 1949.

AMERSHAM

AMPLEFORTH
ABBEY AND COLLEGE

AMMANFORD

ANDOVER

ANDREW WEIR INSURANCE COMPANY LIMITED. Argent, on water barry wavy in base proper, a lymphad, sail furled, sable, flags flying to the dexter gules, in chief two phoenixes also sable, their pyres proper; all within a bordure azure charged with three mullets Or. **Crest:** On a wreath Or and azure, A dexter cubit arm, vested azure semée of mullets Or, the hand grasping a beacon inflamed proper. Mantled azure, doubled argent. **Granted** 1 August 1963.

ANGLESEY COUNTY COUNCIL.* Gules, a chevron between three lions rampant Or; a bordure barry wavy of eight azure and argent. **Crest:** Out of an antique crown Or, a demi dragon gules supporting a garb gold. **Supporters:** On the dexter side a bull argent gorged with a wreath of seaweed proper; and on the sinister side a heraldic tiger sable gorged with a wreath of oak also proper fructed Or. **Motto:** Mon Mam Cymru. **Granted** 9 April 1954.

ANGLIA BUILDING SOCIETY (NORTHAMPTON). Per fesse gules and argent, in chief a tower triple towered of the second, the portcullis raised Or, and in base a double rose of the first barbed and seeded proper; all between two keys, wards downwards and outwards, counter-changed. **Crest:** On a wreath of the colours, Upon a mount vert a griffin segreant Or resting the dexter claw upon a builder's trowel, point downward, proper. **Supporters:** On either side a lion guardant Or gorged with a wreath argent and gules, pendant therefrom by a leather guige an escutcheon also gules, that on the dexter charged with a rose argent, barbed and seeded proper, and that on the sinister with a fetterlock gold. **Motto:** Stability. **Granted** 10 September 1956 to the Northampton Town and County Building Society; regranted 1 October 1968 upon the change in name.

ANTIQUE DEALERS. See British Antique Dealers' Association Limited.

ANTRIM COUNTY COUNCIL.* Or, a lion rampant gules holding in the dexter paw a cross crosslet fitchée azure; on a chief vert, between two towers a pale argent, thereon a dexter hand appaumée also gules. **Crest:** On a wreath of the colours, A demi figure representing St. Patrick in a habit vert trimmed with gold, the nimbus Or, holding in the dexter hand a slip of shamrock and supporting over the sinister shoulder a shepherd's crook, proper. **Supporters:** On either side a wolf gules, that on the dexter holding in the mouth a slip of flax flowered, that on the sinister a wheat ear, both stalked and leaved, proper [the whole upon a compartment of basaltic rock proper, representing the Giant's Causeway.] **Motto:** Per angusta ad augusta. **Granted** 28 March 1952.

APOTHECARIES OF THE CITY OF LONDON, WORSHIPFUL COMPANY OF. Azure, Apollo, the inventor of Physic, proper, his head radiant, holding in his left hand a bow and in his right hand an arrow Or, supplanting a serpent argent. **Crest:** On a wreath Or and azure, A rhinoceros statant proper. Mantled gules, doubled argent. **Supporters:** On either side a unicorn Or, armed and unguled argent. **Motto:** Opiferque per orbem dicor. **Granted** 12 December 1617 by William Camden, Clarenceux King of Arms.

APPLEBY, BOROUGH OF (WESTMORLAND). Azure semee of apple leaves proper, three lions passant [in pale] Or, each resting the dexter forepaw on an apple of the same. **Crest:** Issuant from an ancient crown Or, a salamander proper holding in its mouth a sprig of apple-blossom leaved also proper. Mantled azure, doubled Or. **Supporters:** On each side a dragon proper resting the interior hind paw on an apple slipped and leaved Or. **Motto:** Nec ferro nec igni. **Granted** 1 June 1959.

ARCHBISHOP HOLGATE'S GRAMMAR SCHOOL (YORK).* Or, a bend between two bulls' heads couped sable; on a chief per pale azure and barry of four argent and gules, a mitre of the first and a rectorial staff in bend of the third. **Motto:** Vincet amor patriae. **Granted** 20 March 1950.

AMPTHILL

ANGLESEY

ARCHBISHOP HOLGATE'S GRAMMAR SCHOOL

ANTRIM

ARCHITECTS AND SURVEYORS, INCORPORATED ASSOCIATION OF. Quarterly gules and azure, a fesse embattled between three lions' faces Or. **Crest:** On a wreath Or, gules and azure, A representation of the Parthenon proper. [Mantled gules, doubled Or.] **Supporters:** On the dexter side a figure representing an architect of the seventeenth century holding in the exterior hand a plan of St. Paul's Cathedral; and on the sinister side a surveyor of the same period holding in the exterior hand a surveyor's pole, and over the shoulder a surveyor's chain, all proper. **Motto:** Probitate et arte. **Granted** 24 January 1955.

ARDINGLEY COLLEGE (HAYWARDS HEATH, SUSSEX). Azure, on a triple mount in base a Passion cross between six martlets Or; on a chief of the last, between two crosses botonnée sable, a pale engrailed gules charged with an ostrich feather erect argent. **Crest:** On a wreath of the colours, A pelican in her piety proper, beaked and legged Or, gorged with a collar gemel gules, the nest gold charged with a cross botonnee also gules. **Motto:** Beati mundo corde. **Granted** 1942.

ARMAGH, CITY OF [URBAN DISTRICT COUNCIL]. Azure, on a bend embattled between in chief a primatial cross and in base a harp Or, a bendlet gules. **Crest:** On a wreath of the colours, An ancient Irish crown gold. **Motto:** In concilio consilium. **Granted** 10 December 1958.

ARMOURERS AND BRAZIERS OF THE CITY OF LONDON, WORSHIPFUL COMPANY OF.* Argent, on a chevron sable a tournament gauntlet between two pairs of swords in saltire of the first, garnished, pomelled and hilted Or; on a chief of the second, on a plate between two helmets also argent, garnished gold, a cross couped gules. **Crest:** On a wreath of the colours, A demi man in armour argent, garnished Or, open faced, holding in his dexter hand a mace of war proper. Mantled gules, doubled argent. **Granted** 15 October 1556 to The Fraternitye or Guylde of St. George of the men of the mystery of Armerors. To the above the Company customarily adds a second shield (accollé with the first), supporters and motto. A second crest is sometimes seen. These are of no authority. **Arms:** Azure, on a chevron Or between two ewers in chief and a two-handled three-legged pot in base of the second, three roses gules, barbed and seeded proper. **Crest:** On a wreath of the colours, A demi man in armour, couped at the middle of the thighs, all proper, garnished Or, the beaver up, on his head a plume of three feathers, two argent and one gules, round his waist a sash of the last, fringed of the second, holding in his dexter hand a sword erect of the first, hilt and pomel gold. Mantled gules, doubled argent. **Supporters:** On either side a man in complete armour, the dexter proper garnished Or, the sinister all of the last, on their heads plumes of feathers, round their waists a sash, and each holding in the exterior hand a sword, all as in the Crest. **Motto:** We are one. (*Illustration on page* 47, *without supporters*).

ARMS, COLLEGE OF.* Argent, a cross gules between four doves, the dexter wing of each expanded and inverted, azure. **Crest:** On a ducal coronet Or, a dove rising azure. Mantled gules, doubled argent. **Supporters:** On either side a lion guardant argent, ducally gorged Or. **Motto:** Diligent and secret.

ARMS, OFFICERS OF.* Garter King of Arms: Argent, a cross gules; on a chief azure a ducal coronet encircled by a Garter between on the dexter a lion passant guardant and on the sinister a fleur-de-lis, all Or. Clarenceux King of Arms: Argent, a cross gules; on a chief of the second a lion passant guardant ducally crowned Or. Norroy King of Arms: Argent, a cross gules; on a chief per pale azure and of the second a lion passant guardant ducally crowned between on the dexter a fleur-de-lis and on the sinister a key, ward upwards and inwards, all Or. Ulster King of Arms: Or, a cross gules; on a chief of the second a lion passant guardant between on the dexter a harp and on the sinister a portcullis, all of the first. The two latter Arms of Office are borne impaled by Norroy and Ulster King of Arms. Chester Herald: A garb Or ensigned by the Royal Crown proper. Lancaster Herald: A rose gules, barbed and seeded and ensigned by the Royal Crown proper. Richmond Herald: A rose gules, barbed and seeded proper, dimidiating a like rose

ROUGE DRAGON — ROUGE CROIX — BLUEMANTLE

SOMERSET — CHESTER — PORTCULLIS — RICHMOND — WINDSOR

LANCASTER — CLARENCEUX — GARTER — NORROY — YORK

COLLEGE OF ARMS

argent, barbed and seeded and en soleil; the whole ensigned by the Royal Crown likewise proper. Somerset Herald: A portcullis Or ensigned by the Royal Crown proper. Windsor Herald: Issuant from clouds proper upwards seven rays of the sun Or. York Herald: A rose argent, barbed and seeded proper, en soleil Or, ensigned by the Royal Crown proper. Bluemantle Pursuivant: A mantle of estate azure, doubled ermine, corded and tasselled Or. Portcullis Pursuivant: A portcullis chained Or. Rouge Croix Pursuivant: A plain cross gules. Rouge Dragon Pursuivant: A dragon passant gules. Arundel Herald Extraordinary: A horse argent holding in the mouth a sprig of oak proper. Norfolk Herald Extraordinary: Two ostrich feathers in saltire argent, each having a chain Or laid along the quill. Fitzalan Pursuivant Extraordinary: A sprig of oak vert fructed Or.

ARNOLD URBAN DISTRICT COUNCIL (NOTTINGHAMSHIRE).* Per chevron, barry wavy of six argent and azure, and gules, in chief two arrows erect proper, flighted of the third, and in base an oak tree fructed and eradicated Or. **Crest:** On a wreath Or. and gules, Issuant from a circlet composed of eight fleurs-de-lis Or, an eagle rising gules. **Motto:** Alta sententia. **Granted** 26 February 1948.

ARTILLERY COMPANY, "THE HONOURABLE". Argent, a cross gules (being that of St. George) charged with a lion passant guardant Or (being part of the Royal Arms of England); on a chief azure a portcullis of the third between two ostrich feathers erect of the field. **Crest:** On a wreath of the colours, A dexter arm embowed in armour, the gauntlet grasping a pike in bend sinister Or, between two dragons' wings argent each charged with a cross gules. **Supporters:** On the dexter side a pikeman, armed and accoutred, supporting with the exterior hand a pike erect proper; and on the sinister side a musketeer with his matchlock, bandoleers and rest, all proper. **Motto:** Arms pacis fulcra. **Granted** and confirmed by Royal Warrant; exemplified 30 April 1821.

ARUNDEL, BOROUGH OF (WEST SUSSEX).* Or, three martlets sable; on a chief embattled gules, a lion rampant of the first between two cross crosslets fitchée argent. **Crest:** On a wreath of the colours, Upon a fleur-de-lys Or, a swallow rising to the sinister proper. **Motto:** Antiqua constans virtute. **Granted** 14 January 1939.

ARUNDEL HERALD EXTRAORDINARY. See Arms, Officers of.

ASHBY DE LA ZOUCHE RURAL DISTRICT COUNCIL (LEICESTERSHIRE). Argent, on a mount in base, an ash tree proper, within a bordure gules charged with five bezants; on a chief sable, a cinquefoil ermine between two garbs Or. **Crest:** Out of a coronet composed of fleurs-de-lis set upon a rim gules, a demi-lion Or, supporting a staff proper, flying therefrom a banner paly of six gold and azure a quarter ermine. Mantled gules, doubled argent. **Motto:** Deeds, not words. **Granted** 9 February 1956.

ASHBY DE LA ZOUCHE URBAN DISTRICT COUNCIL (LEICESTERSHIRE).* Sable, on a mount in base, a castle triple towered argent; on a chief of the last, a pale gules between two maunches sable, on the pale a demi lion issuant also argent. **Crest:** Out of a mural crown Or, charged with three fleurs-de-lys gules, a bull's head sable, armed also Or, gorged with a collar also sable edged gold and charged with three bezants. Mantled gules, doubled argent. **Motto:** Sans Dieu rien. **Granted** 9 November 1960.

ASHFORD SCHOOL, KENT.* Argent, six torches, three, two and one, sable, inflamed proper; on a chief gules, three cross crosslets fitchee of the field. **Crest:** On a wreath of the colours, A demi unicorn argent, armed, crined and unguled Or, resting the dexter hoof on a terrestrial globe proper. **Motto:** Esse quam videri. **Granted** 20 May 1946 to Ashford School for Girls.

ASHTON-UNDER-LYNE, BOROUGH OF (LANCASHIRE).* Argent, a mullet sable, pierced of the field; in dexter chief a crescent gules. **Crest:** On a wreath of the colours, Upon the battle-

ARNOLD

ARUNDEL

ASHBY DE LA ZOUCHE U. D. C.

ASHFORD SCHOOL

ments of a tower proper, a griffin's head erased gules, charged on the neck with a crescent Or. **Motto:** Labor omnia vincit. **Granted** 7 July 1926.

ASHVILLE COLLEGE AND NEW COLLEGE (HARROGATE, YORKSHIRE). Per chevron gules and argent, a chevron ermine between in chief a dragon's head erased Or between two roses of the second, barbed and seeded proper, and in base issuant from a mount an ash tree also proper. **Motto:** Esse quam videri. **Granted** 14 June 1933.

ASSAY OFFICE, THE. See Birmingham, The Standard of Wrought Plate in.

ASSOCIATED ELECTRICAL INDUSTRIES LIMITED (LONDON). Argent, three escutcheons azure, each charged with a thunderbolt Or fired proper. **Crest:** On a wreath of the colours, A dexter hand proper grasping a thunderbolt Or fired also proper. **Supporters:** On the dexter side an heraldic.antelope argent, attired and collared, pendent from the collar by a chain an escutcheon Or charged with a rose gules barbed and seeded proper; and on the sinister a lion argent, collared, pendent from the collar by a chain Or an escutcheon azure charged with eight arrows in saltire banded argent. **Granted** 1 December 1944.

ASSOCIATION FOR THE PROTECTION OF COMMERCIAL INTERESTS AS RESPECTS WRECKED AND DAMAGED PROPERTY [KNOWN AS THE SALVAGE ASSOCIATION].* Argent, an anchor in bend azure; over all a cross gules. **Crest:** On a wreath of the colours, A terrestrial globe proper encircled with a chain Or. **Supporters:** On the dexter side a cormorant; and on the sinister an albatross, supporting the shield with the interior wings expanded and inverted, proper. **Motto:** Quaerite vera. **Granted** 10 June 1955.

ASSOCIATIONS. See also under the operative term, e.g. for Association of Anaesthetists of Great Britain and Ireland see Anaesthetists of Great Britain and Ireland, Association of.

ASTON CHARITIES TRUST LIMITED (LONDON).* Ermine, a cross raguly gules; in dexter chief a pair of compasses Or. **Crest:** On a wreath argent and gules, Issuant from a circlet of eight bezants, a dove proper holding in the beak a sprig of olive Or. **Supporters:** On the dexter side a dragon; and on the sinister side an emu holding in the beak a horseshoe, all Or. **Motto:** Nihil caritate clarus. **Granted** 26 June 1953.

ASTON IN BIRMINGHAM, UNIVERSITY OF. Azure, five lozenges conjoined in bend Or; on a chief argent, an open book proper, bound gules edged Or, between two hammers erect sable. **Crest:** On a wreath argent, gules and sable, Out of a mural crown sable a cubit arm, vested argent, the hand proper holding a torch gules enflamed also proper, between two branches of laurel Or. **Granted** to the Corporation of the City of Birmingham for the use of the Birmingham College of Technology 18 March 1955; regranted 1 August 1966.

ATHERTON URBAN DISTRICT COUNCIL (LANCASHIRE).* Or, on a bend gules between two lozenges sable, a lion's gamb erased of the field. **Crest:** On a wreath of the colours, A sparrowhawk, wings elevated and addorsed, proper perched on a shuttle Or and resting the dexter claw on a millrind sable. **Motto:** Consilio et prudentia. **Granted** 29 May 1951.

AUCTIONEERS AND LANDED PROPERTY AGENTS, INCORPORATED SOCIETY OF. Tierce in pairle azure, argent and Or, in chief a garb of the third, in base to the dexter a gavel erect sable and to the sinister a T square erect interlaced with an open foot-rule proper. **Crest:** On a wreath of the colours, Issuant from the battlements of a tower argent, a dexter hand holding a flambeau erect fired, both proper. **Supporters:** On the dexter side an ancient Briton holding in the exterior hand a club resting on the shoulder proper; and on the sinister side a Roman citizen holding in the exterior hand a scroll proper. **Motto:** Fortiter, fideliter, feliciter. **Granted** 30 January 1931.

ASHTON-UNDER-LYNE

ASTON CHARITIES TRUST

SALVAGE ASSOCIATION

ATHERTON

AUDENSHAW URBAN DISTRICT COUNCIL (LANCASHIRE).* Per pale argent and gules, a pickaxe and a pierced mullet in pale counterchanged, in dexter chief a rose of the second and in sinister chief a rose of the first, both barbed and seeded proper. **Crest:** On a wreath of the colours, A mill-wheel proper between a rose argent and a rose gules, both barbed and seeded proper. **Motto:** Festina lente. **Granted** 17 November 1950.

AXMINSTER PARISH COUNCIL (DEVON).* Per saltire gules and azure, an orb between in fess two battleaxes erect, the blades inwards, and in base a shuttle, all Or. **Crest:** On a wreath of the colours, Upon a mount vert a minster proper. **Motto:** Steadfast and faithful. **Granted** 10 November 1945 to the former Axminster Urban District Council.

AYCLIFFE DEVELOPMENT CORPORATION (CO. DURHAM). Gules, on a chevron argent between three garbs Or, banded vert, a grenade sable, fired proper; all within a bordure Or. **Crest:** On a wreath of the colours, On a limestone cliff an oak tree fructed with a broken branch and another growing therefrom, all proper. **Supporters:** On either side a lion argent holding in the interior paw in a steel gauntlet a cross patonce gold. **Motto:** Non minima sed maxima petimus. **Granted** 20 September 1956.

AYLESBURY, BOROUGH OF (BUCKINGHAMSHIRE).* Gyronny of six gules and sable, a mute swan rousant proper; on a chief Or, a Saxon crown gules. **Crest:** On a wreath argent and gules, Issuant from a wreath of plaited straw a mount, thereon an Aylesbury duck, all proper. Mantled gules, doubled argent. **Supporters:** On the dexter side a buck proper gorged with a chain Or, pendent therefrom a hexagon argent charged with a garb gules banded Or; and on the sinister side a stag also proper gorged with a chain, pendent therefrom a like hexagon charged with a crescent sable. **Motto:** Semper prorsum. **Badge:** An oval gyronny of six gules and sable, charged with a Saxon crown Or issuant therefrom a mount, thereon an Aylesbury duck proper; the whole environed by a garland of beech leaves vert. **Granted** 5 April 1964.

AYLESBURY

AUDENSHAW

AXMINSTER

B

* *Denotes Illustration*

BACUP, BOROUGH OF (LANCASHIRE).* Azure, on a fesse between two bales of cotton in chief Or and a block of stone with lewis attached in base proper, a fleece sable between two bees volant of the third; in the centre chief point a squirrel sejant of the second. **Crest:** On a wreath of the colours, In front of a bale of cotton Or, a stag [proper] gorged with a collar vair and resting the dexter forefoot on a trefoil slipped gold. **Motto:** Honor et industria. **Granted** 13 March 1883.

BAGSHOT RURAL DISTRICT COUNCIL (SURREY).* Per pale Or and argent, a stag's head caboshed gules, between the attires a ball sable fired in cross proper, on a chief vert charged with two barrulets wavy also argent, a lion passant gold over all. **Crest:** Out of a coronet composed of eight fir cones set upon a rim Or, a mount vert, thereon a falcon close proper, jessed and belled gold. **Motto:** Festina prudenter. **Granted** 20 July 1960.

BAILDON URBAN DISTRICT COUNCIL (YORKSHIRE—WEST RIDING).* Vert, three chevrons and in chief a fleece Or. **Crest:** On a wreath of the colours, A skylark holding in the beak a sprig of gorse slipped and flowered proper. **Motto:** Surgamus ergo strenue. **Granted** 30 September 1952. (*Illustration on page* 49).

BAKERS OF THE CITY OF LONDON, WORSHIPFUL COMPANY OF.* Gules, three garbs Or, on a chief barry wavy of six argent and azure two anchors of the second cabled gules; over all issuant from a cloud proper radiated in chief also Or a cubit arm descending therefrom vested of the third cuffed sable, the hand proper holding a balance gold. **Crest:** On a wreath Or and gules, Two arms embowed issuing out of a cloud proper, holding in their hands a chaplet of wheat Or. Mantled gules, doubled argent. **Supporters:** On either side a buck proper, attired Or, gorged with a chaplet of wheat also Or. **Motto:** Praise God for all. **Granted** 1536 (probably; patent not extant); Crest and Supporters granted 8 November 1590 by Robert Cooke, Clarenceux King of Arms; the whole recorded at the Visitation of 1634. (*Illustration on page* 47).

BALDOCK URBAN DISTRICT COUNCIL (HERTFORDSHIRE).* Or, on a cross between in the first and fourth quarters three chevronels gules, a garb of the first; on a chief sable, a stag's head erased gold between two Madonna lilies proper. **Crest:** On a wreath of the colours, A representation of the head of a Roman centurion's standard of SPQR with thunderbolt, laurel wreath and eagle displayed gold. **Motto:** Sic vos non vobis. **Granted** 10 May 1951.

BALLIOL COLLEGE (OXFORD UNIVERSITY).* Gules, a false escutcheon argent, impaling Azure, a lion rampant argent ducally crowned Or. Recorded at the Visitation of 1574. In practice the relative positions of the two coats are reversed.

BALLYMENA, BOROUGH OF (CO. ANTRIM).* Azure, seven towers, three in pale with two in chief and as many in base Or. **Motto:** Post praelia praemia. **Granted** 26 August 1953.

BALLYMENA ACADEMY. Argent, a humet azure between in chief two dexter hands and in base an ant gules. **Crest:** On a wreath argent, azure and gules, In front of a demi badger proper, an ancient lamp Or enflamed also proper. **Motto:** Tenax propositi. **Granted** 3 December 1958.

BALTIC MERCANTILE SHIPPING EXCHANGE (LONDON). Azure, three bars wavy argent, over all a lighthouse between two lymphads, sails set and pennons flying Or, in chief a pair of wings conjoined gold. **Crest:** On a wreath argent and gules, Two mermen respectant proper supporting a garb Or banded argent and azure. **Supporters:** On the dexter side a sea-lion, and on the

BAGSHOT

BALLYMENA, BOROUGH OF

BACUP

BALLIOL COLLEGE

BANBURY

BALDOCK

sinister side a sea-bear, both Or and charged on the shoulder with a petasus azure. **Motto:** Our word our bond. **Badge:** A garb Or enfiled with a mercantile crown azure, the sails argent. **Granted** 10 December 1957.

BANBRIDGE URBAN DISTRICT COUNCIL (CO. DOWN). Per fess vert and barry wavy azure and argent, a representation of the bridge over the River Bann, in chief a spindle and a shuttle in saltire Or between two mussels argent. **Crest:** On a wreath argent and azure, Issuant from a mural crown gules charged with an escallop argent, a garb Or between two branches of oak leaved and fructed proper. **Motto:** Per Deum et industriam. **Granted** 5 May 1964.

BANBURY, BOROUGH OF (OXFORDSHIRE).* Azure, a sun in his splendour Or; on a chief ermine, a castle of two towers between two pairs of swords, points upwards, in saltire gules. **Crest:** On a wreath of the colours, Mounted upon a horse passant argent, caparisoned Or and gules, a lady in Tudor costume proper. **Supporters:** On either side an ox gules, armed and unguled Or, gorged with a collar argent charged with a bar wavy azure. **Motto:** Dominus nobis sol et scutum. Granted 28 August 1951.

BANGOR, BISHOPRIC OF. Gules, a bend Or guttée-de-poix between two pierced mullets argent. Recorded in the College of Arms. Gules, a bend argent guttée-de-larmes between two pierced mullets of the second. Recorded in the Parliament Roll of 1512.

BANGOR, BOROUGH OF (CO. DOWN). Gules, two lymphads in pale Or, each with a sail argent charged with a dexter hand couped of the field; all between as many flaunches barry wavy argent and azure. **Crest:** On a wreath of the colours, A demi figure representing St. Comgall vested as an abbot of the sixth century reading an open book held in his dexter hand and supporting with his sinister hand a pastoral staff, the crook resting on his shoulder, all proper. **Supporters:** On either side a dolphin vert, finned Or, the dexter charged with a bezant thereon a trefoil slipped also vert and the sinister with a bezant thereon a bull's head caboshed proper. **Motto:** Beannchor. **Granted** 5 April 1951.

BANGOR ENDOWED SCHOOL (BANGOR, CO. DOWN). Azure, within two bendlets, as many bendlets dancettée, all between two mullets Or; a bordure of the last. **Crest:** On a wreath of the colours, A griffin couchant, wings elevated and addorsed, Or. **Granted** 8 July 1954.

BANK LINE LIMITED (LONDON). Or, in front of two anchors in saltire proper an oval cartouche, scrolled Tenné, and charged per bend sinister gules and azure a bendlet argent. **Crest:** Issuant from a mercantile crown Or, two arms proper the hands grasping a lymphad, the sail furled, sable, pennons flying to the dexter gules. **Supporters:** On the dexter side a Triton azure blowing a conch Or; and on the sinister side a seadog gules finned and armed also Or. **Motto:** Per laborem ad honorem. **Badge:** Within a wreath of oak on the dexter and laurel on the sinister proper tied in base with a riband azure, in front of two anchors crossed in saltire also proper a flag flying to the sinister per bend sinister gules and azure a bendlet argent. **Granted** 9 January 1958.

BANKERS, INSTITUTE OF. Pean, a circular chain Or; on a chief gules, an open book gold between two bezants. **Supporters:** On the dexter side a figure representing Themis proper holding in the exterior hand a pair of scales Or; and on the sinister side a figure representing Hermes proper holding in the exterior hand his caduceus Or. **Motto:** Probus et fidelis. **Granted** 30 July 1954.

BANK OF LONDON AND MONTREAL LIMITED. Quarterly gules and argent, a cross quarterly counterchanged between in the first quarter a maple leaf slipped in autumnal tints proper, in the second quarter a sword erect also gules, in the third quarter an ancient ship sails set also proper pennon and flags flying argent each charged with a cross of St. George, and in the fourth quarter a plate charged with a saltire likewise gules. **Crest:** On a wreath of the colours, A morion Or. **Granted** 22 March 1960.

THE ARMORERS

THE BARBER CHIRVRGIONS

THE BAKERS

THE SMITHS

BANK OF LONDON AND SOUTH AMERICA LIMITED. Quarterly argent and gules, in the first and fourth quarters a sword point upwards of the second and in the second and third quarters a Spanish galleon in full sail flags flying of the first; in the fesse point a Spanish morion helmet of the sixteenth century Or. **Crest:** On a wreath of the colours, A condor rising Or. **Granted** 4 September 1960.

BARBERS OF THE CITY OF LONDON, WORSHIPFUL COMPANY OF.* Quarterly, first and fourth, Sable, a chevron between three fleams argent, second and third, Per pale of the second and vert, on a spatter also argent a Tudor rose proper crowned Or; on a cross dividing the quarters gules a lion passant guardant gold. **Crest:** On a wreath argent and sable, An opinicus statant Or. Mantled gules, doubled argent. **Supporters:** On either side a lynx proper [semée of hurts, torteaux, pomeis, bezants and plates] ducally gorged and chained argent. **Motto:** De praescientia Dei. **Granted** 2 June 1569 by Sir Gilbert Dethick, Garter King of Arms, Robert Cooke, Clarenceux King of Arms, and William Flower, Norroy King of Arms to replace earlier grants of 29 September 1451 (Roger Legh, Clarenceux King of Arms) and 10 July 1561 (William Hervey, Clarenceux King of Arms).

BARCLAYS BANK LIMITED.* Argent, an eagle displayed [wings inverted] sable charged on the body and on each wing with a ducal coronet of the field. **Granted** 22 October 1937.

BARKING, LONDON BOROUGH OF.* Per saltire gules and barry wavy argent and azure, in chief between two keys in saltire a sword palewise point downwards, in base two croziers with sudarium in saltire surmounting a lily slipped and leaved, and in the flanks a representation of a Barking well smack in full sail to the sinister and a cogwheel all Or. **Crest:** On a wreath argent and azure, In front of a demi sun in splendour Or, a representation of the curfew tower of Barking proper. **Supporters:** On either side a lion Or, gorged with a collar per pale sable and gules, holding a torch inflamed gold. **Motto:** Dei gratia probemur rebus. **Badge:** A roundel per pale sable and gules, charged with two croziers and a lily as in the Arms. **Granted** 1 September 1965.

BARKING ABBEY SCHOOL (ESSEX). Azure, in chief three lilies in fesse argent, stalked leaved and slipped vert, and in base as many roses Or, barbed and seeded proper; on a bordure gules, eight plates. **Crest:** On a wreath Or and azure, In front of a representation of Barking Abbey Curfew Tower an open book proper, edged Or and bound gules. **Granted** 10 June 1955.

BARNARD CASTLE URBAN DISTRICT COUNCIL (CO. DURHAM).* Gules, in chief a castle and in base a cross formy, the uppermost limb between a crescent and an estoile of seven rays, all within an orle argent. **Crest:** Out of a coronet composed of six cross-crosslets set upon a rim Or, a rock proper, thereon a boar passant argent holding with the dexter forehoof a bow in bend gules. Mantled gules, doubled argent. **Motto:** Nec temere nec timide. **Granted** 4 September 1959.

BARNET, LONDON BOROUGH OF.* Azure, on a mount in base vert, a Paschal Lamb proper; a chief per pale argent and gules, thereon a Saxon crown Or between two roses counterchanged, barbed and seeded proper. **Crest:** On a wreath of the colours [argent and azure], In front of a two-bladed air-screw in pale winged and issuant Or, two swords in saltire points upward proper. Mantled azure, doubled argent. **Supporters:** On the dexter side a lion, and on the sinister side a stag argent; each charged on the shoulder with a cross potent quadrate gules [the whole upon a compartment of fern]. **Motto:** Unitas efficit ministerium. **Granted** 1 January 1965.

BARNSLEY, COUNTY BOROUGH OF (YORKSHIRE—WEST RIDING).* Argent, on a chevron gules between two shuttles fessewise in chief and in base as many pickaxes in saltire proper, a falcon wings elevated and holding in the dexter claw a padlock Or between two boar's heads couped of the last each holding in the mouth a cross patée fitchée in pale of the first; a chief sable, thereon a cross patée between two covered cups also Or. **Crest:** On a wreath of the colours,

BARNARD CASTLE

BARKING

BARCLAYS BANK

BAILDON

BARNET

A gryphon argent, wings elevated sable, resting the dexter claw on an escucheon argent charged with a shuttle palewise sable. **Supporters:** On the dexter side a miner, his pit lamp suspended from his neck, supporting in his exterior hand a pick-axe proper; and on the sinister side a glass-blower, supporting in his exterior hand a blow-pipe, issuant therefrom in base a glass bottle, all proper. **Motto:** Spectemur agendo. Arms and Crest granted 19 October 1869; Supporters granted 13 August 1913.

BARNSLEY HOSPITAL MANAGEMENT COMMITTEE. Per chevron sable and argent, in chief two covered cups of the second and in base a cross formy of the first. **Crest:** On a wreath of the colours, Issuant from a cup sable a rose argent barbed and seeded stalked and leaved proper. **Motto:** Salus infirmorum. **Granted** 27 February 1950.

BARNSTAPLE, BOROUGH OF (DEVON).* Gules, a castle of three towers conjoined argent, the centre tower larger than the others. Recorded at the Visitation of Devon 8 September 1620.

BARROW-IN-FURNESS, COUNTY BOROUGH OF (LANCASHIRE).* Gules, on a bend between a serpent nowed in chief and a stag trippant in base Or, an arrow pointing upwards to a bee volent proper; upon a chief argent, on waves of the sea a paddle-wheel steamship under steam and canvas also proper. **Crest:** On a wreath of the colours. Out of the battlements of a tower a ram's head proper, armed and collared Or. **Motto:** Semper sursum. **Granted** 13 December 1867.

BARRY, BOROUGH OF (GLAMORGANSHIRE).* Or, three bars gemel gules between in chief two fleurs-de-lys azure and in base a dragon passant of the second. **Crest:** On a wreath of the colours, Upon water barry wavy proper, a lymphad sable, sail set argent lozengy also sable, pennons flying gules. **Supporters:** On either side a unicorn argent, armed, crined and unguled Or, gorged with a chain of the last pendent thereform by a like chain an escutcheon, that on the dexter Argent three bars gemel gules and that on the sinister as the Arms. **Motto:** Cadernid, cyfiawnder, cynnydd. **Granted** 31 October 1939.

BASILDON DEVELOPMENT CORPORATION (ESSEX).* Per chevron embattled gules and Or, in chief a fountain between two mullets argent and in base an oak tree proper. **Crest:** On a wreath of the colours, A wyvern sejant sable, transfixed through the breast by a sword in bend Or. **Motto:** Art, industry, contentment. **Granted** 1 February 1950.

BASKETMAKERS OF THE CITY OF LONDON, WORSHIPFUL COMPANY OF.* Azure, three cross baskets in pale argent between a prime and an iron on the dexter and a culling knife and an outsticker on the sinister of the second. **Crest:** On a wreath of the colours, A cradle, therein a child, rocked at the head by a girl and at the feet by a boy vested proper. **Motto:** Let us love one another. **Granted** 12 October 1931.

BATH, CITY AND COUNTY BOROUGH OF (SOMERSET).* Waves of the sea proper, a chief embattled gules; over all a sword erect argent, pomel and hilt Or, the blade charged with a key, ward in chief and to the sinister gold. Recorded at the Visitation of 1623. Certified 4 August 1888. In practice the corporation use a different coat which is here illustrated and may be blazoned per fesse embattled azure and gules, the base masoned sable, in chief two bars wavy, over all a sword erect argent, pomel and hilt Or, between in base two crosses bottonée of the third. These Arms appear in the Collections of the College of Arms.

BATH UNIVERSITY OF TECHNOLOGY. Azure, a sword in pale argent, hilt and pommel and quillons Or, the point ensigned by a Watt governor proper, between in fess two heads of Sul Or. **Crest:** On a wreath Or, argent and azure, Out of a mural crown argent, an eagle, wings expanded and inverted, Or, supporting with the dexter claw a key, wards upward and outward, silver. **Supporters:** On the dexter side a wyvern erect vert charged on the body with mullets, each of six points, Or; and on the sinister side a unicorn sejant erect Or, armed, unguled, crined and

BARROW-IN-FURNESS

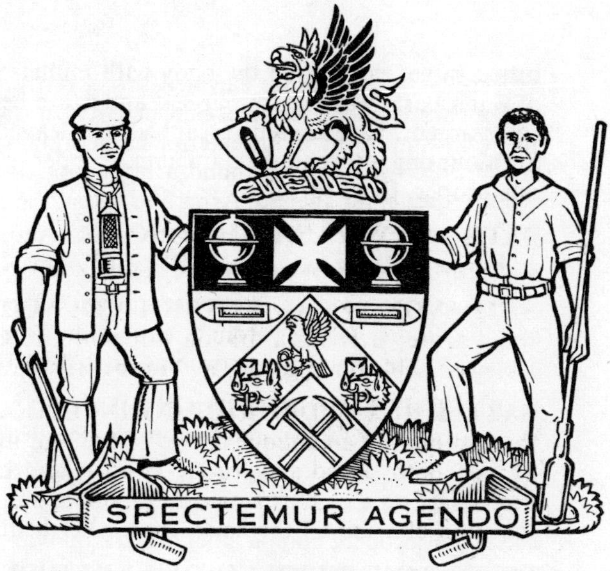

BARNSLEY

BARNSTAPLE

BARRY

BASILDON

tufted sable, charged on the body with mullets of six points vert; the whole upon a compartment of water barry wavy of four argent and azure between two river banks proper, sprouting therefrom roses argent, barbed seeded, slipped and leaved proper. **Motto:** Generatim discite cultus. **Badge:** Surmounting a torch azure, inflamed proper, a lion's face Or, grasping in the jaws a Watt governor proper. **Granted** 15 November 1966.

BATH AND WELLS, BISHOPRIC OF. Azure, a saltire per saltire quarterly counterchanged Or and argent. Recorded in the College of Arms.

BATHAVON RURAL DISTRICT COUNCIL (SOMERSET).* Vert, on a fesse argent a bar wavy azure; over all a dragon rampant Or. **Crest:** On a wreath of the colours, Upon a billet fessewise sable three garbs Or. **Motto:** Rus Gratiis Musisque dignum. **Granted** 19 June 1951.

BATTLE RURAL DISTRICT COUNCIL (EAST SUSSEX).* Argent, a cross gules between in the first quarter an antique crown of the last, in the second a sprig of hop, and in the third a sprig of oak, both leaved and fructed proper, and in the fourth a sword erect of the second, hilt and pomel Or; on a chief per pale gules and azure, a demi lion passant guardant gold conjoined with the stern of a ship of the field. **Motto:** Per bellum patria. **Granted** 20 April 1953.

BEBINGTON, BOROUGH OF (CHESHIRE).* Per chevron azure and Or, in chief a saltire couped argent between two garbs of the second, and in base a lymphad, sail furled, sable, flags flying to the dexter gules. **Crest:** On a wreath of the colours, In front of a rising sun Or, a representation of the Bromborough Market Cross proper. **Motto:** Civitatis fortuna cives. **Granted** 3 January 1934 to the Bebington Urban District Council.

BECCLES, BOROUGH OF (EAST SUFFOLK).* Azure, a bend wavy between two ancient crowns each enfiling two arrows in saltire points downward all Or. **Crest:** On a wreath of the colours, In front of a clump of rushes proper, issuant therefrom a demi lion azure, a dolphin argent. **Supporters:** On the dexter side a dragon, wings inverted and addorsed, gules gorged with a mural crown and supporting a staff Or, flying therefrom a banner argent charged with a cross pommée gules; and on the sinister side a like dragon Or, gorged with a mural crown gules and supporting a staff Or, flying therefrom a banner also gules charged with two keys in saltire Or. **Motto:** Prosperity through fidelity. **Granted** 23 February 1951.

BEDE, COLLEGE OF THE VENERABLE (DURHAM UNIVERSITY). Argent, an ancient Northumbrian cross gules; a chief azure, thereon, between two lions rampant Or, a pale gold charged with a cross patonce also azure. **Crest:** Out of an ancient crown Or, two lions' gambs argent, armed gules, the paws grasping an escallop sable. **Motto:** Ut et alios instruam. **Granted** 31 May 1957.

BEDFORD, BOROUGH OF.* Per pale argent and gules, a fesse azure. **Seal:** Argent, an eagle displayed, wings inverted and head turned toward the sinister, sable, ducally crowned Or, surmounted by a castle of three tiers gold. Recorded at Visitations on 7 June 1566 and in 1634. This seal is usually shown on a shield and is thus illustrated here.

BEDFORD COLLEGE (LONDON UNIVERSITY). Argent, between two flaunches paly bendy Or and sable a cross patée throughout gules voided of the field surmounted by an open book of the second; on a chief of the third, an antique lamp gold enflamed proper. **Granted** 13 August 1913.

BEDFORDSHIRE COUNTY COUNCIL.* Quarterly Or and gules, a fess wavy barry wavy of four argent and azure surmounted by a pale sable charged with three escallops of the third. **Crest:** On a wreath of the colours, Issuant from a wreath of oak Or, a swan's head and neck proper. **Supporters:** On the dexter side a lion gules; and on the sinister side a bull Or. **Motto:** Constant be. **Granted** 12 April 1951.

BATTLE

BECCLES

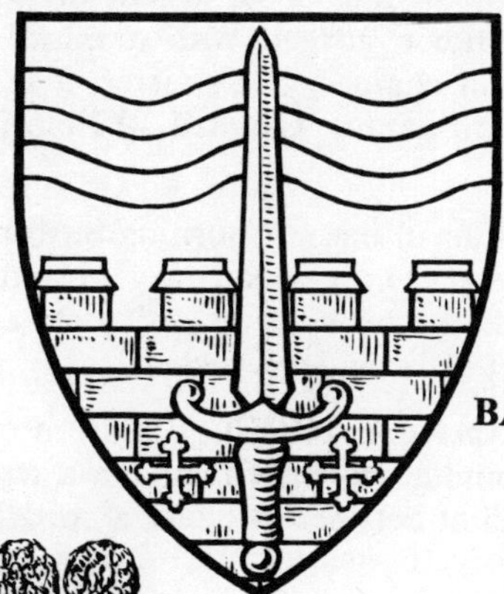

BATH CITY

BATHAVON

BASKETMAKERS COMPANY

BEBINGTON

BEDLINGTONSHIRE URBAN DISTRICT COUNCIL (NORTHUMBERLAND). Argent, a cross formy quadrate between four lozenges sable; on a chief azure, a long-ship, bows on, proper, the sail set also argent charged with a like cross, pennon flying gules, between two lions rampant respectant also proper, each holding in the interior paw as many lightning flashes in saltire Or. **Crest:** On a wreath of the colours, A Bedlington terrier proper, the forepaws on a coal tub loaded sable. **Motto:** De profundis. **Granted** 1 June 1962.

BEESTON AND STAPLEFORD URBAN DISTRICT COUNCIL (NOTTINGHAMSHIRE).* Argent, three barrulets wavy argent, in chief a Tudor rose between two posies each of two purple crocuses and bent grass, and in base three bees, two and one, each bee volant in bend, all proper. **Crest:** On a wreath of the colours, A demi winged bull affrontée argent, armed Or, resting the hooves gules on a serpent proper. **Motto:** Faith, unity and industry. **Granted** 20 August 1959.

BELFAST, CITY AND COUNTY BOROUGH OF.* Party per fesse argent and azure, in chief a pile vair and on a canton gules a bell argent, in base a ship with sails set argent on waves of the sea proper. **Crest:** On a wreath of the colours, A sea-horse gorged with a mural crown proper. **Supporters:** Dexter, a wolf proper, ducally gorged and chained Or; sinister, a sea-horse gorged with a mural crown proper. **Motto:** Pro tanto quid retribuamus. **Granted** 30 June 1890 by Sir John Bernard Burke, C.B.E., Ulster King of Arms.

BELFAST PRESBYTERIAN COLLEGE. Argent, on a mount in base, a burning bush proper; on a chief azure, two inkhorns also argent garnished Or. **Crest:** On a wreath argent and azure, Out of clouds proper, two cubit arms, vested Or, the hands also proper holding aloft a closed book bound gules edged and clasped gold. **Motto:** Veritatem eme et noli vende. **Granted** 1 May 1958.

BELGRAVE MILLS COMPANY LIMITED (OLDHAM, LANCASHIRE). Gules, a chevron ermine between in chief two mascles argent and in base a spindle proper. **Crest:** On a wreath of the colours, A demi ram sable, armed and unguled Or, holding between the feet a spindle as in the Arms. **Granted** 24 March 1923.

BELPER RURAL DISTRICT COUNCIL (DERBYSHIRE).* Per pale vert and sable, a pale wavy argent surmounted of another wavy azure; on a chief dancettée Or, a Tudor rose barbed and seeded between two oak trees couped proper fructed gold. **Crest:** On a wreath of the colours, Issuant from the battlements of a tower gules, a mount vert, thereon a popinjay Or gorged with a collar gules, pendant therefrom a horseshoe sable, resting the dexter claw on an ancient lamp gold enflamed proper. **Motto:** Beau repeyr. **Granted** 31 August 1953.

BENFLEET URBAN DISTRICT COUNCIL (ESSEX).* Tierced in pairle reversed gules, vert and argent, in chief two ancient crowns Or and in base two bars wavy azure. **Crest:** On a wreath Or, gules and vert, Between two horns Or, a Viking ship sable, shields, oars and sail gold, the sail charged with a castle also sable. **Motto:** Societas florebit. **Badge:** A Viking ship as in the Crest on waves barry wavy azure and argent, all within a wreath Or, gules and vert. **Granted** 28 February 1962.

BENNETT MEMORIAL CHURCH OF ENGLAND SECONDARY SCHOOL FOR GIRLS. Vert, a brock passant proper; on a chief argent, three gilly-flowers stalked and leaved also proper. **Motto:** Semper tenax. **Granted** 19 December 1952.

BENTALL'S LIMITED (KINGSTON-UPON-THAMES). Or, a lion rampant queue fourchée azure, [ducally] crowned Or, and on a chief azure, a salmon naiant argent finned gules. **Crest:** On a wreath Or and vert, A leopard statant argent pellety, flying from a crown about the neck Or a scarf parted Or and vert. **Motto:** To strive, to seek, to serve. **Badge:** A leopard statant argent pellety, flying from a crown about the neck Or a scarf parted Or and vert. **Granted** 10 May 1967.

BEDFORDSHIRE C. C.

BEESTON AND STAPLEFORD

BELFAST

BELPER

BEDFORD

BEWDLEY

BENFLEET

BERKSHIRE, COUNTY COUNCIL OF THE ROYAL COUNTY OF.* Azure, two lions passant guardant in pale Or; a bordure embattled ermine. **Crest:** On a wreath of the colours, Upon a mount vert, a stag at gaze Or in front of an oak tree fructed proper. **Supporters:** On the dexter side a lion gules gorged with an ancient crown Or and charged on the shoulder with a Tudor rose proper; and on the sinister side a horse argent gorged with a like crown, pendent therefrom a bezant charged with a pile sable. Arms and Crest [the stag argent] granted 18 July 1947. Crest changed and supporters granted 7 April 1961.

BERWICK-UPON-TWEED, BOROUGH OF.* Per pale azure and gules, upon a mount vert a wych-elm proper and in front of the same a bear passant proper muzzled and chained to the base of the tree with a chain Or. Below the shield, which is ensigned of a coronet proper to a Royal Burgh, upon a compartment suitable to a Burgh Royal, along with this motto, Victoria, gloria, merces, are set for Supporters two bears proper muzzled and chained with chains reflexed over their backs Or. Matriculated in the Public Register of All Arms and Bearings in Scotland 14 November 1958.

BETHLEM ROYAL HOSPITAL AND THE MAUDSLEY HOSPITAL. Argent, two bars sable surmounted of a pickaxe erect azure, in chief a label of five points throughout gules; on a chief azure, a plate radiated Or charged with a cross gules between a chalice Or therein a representation of the Host argent and a basket Or containing loaves of bread of the first. **Supporters:** On either side a dragon guardant azure, armed, langued and the underpart of the wings Or, resting the interior hind claw on a sphere of the last. **Granted** 1 August 1951.

BEVERLEY, BOROUGH OF (YORKSHIRE—EAST RIDING). (i) . . . three bars wavy . . . in chief a castor beaver, its head turned biting at the fur . . . ; (ii) . . . three bars wavy . . . on a chief . . . a castor beaver, its head turned biting at the fur . . . ; (iii) Quarterly, first and fourth, . . . an eagle displayed . . . ducally crowned . . . ; second and third, . . . three bars wavy . . . and in chief a castor beaver, its head turned biting at the fur . . . Recorded as seal devices on shields (untinctured) at the Visitation of 1584-5.

BEWDLEY, BOROUGH OF (WORCESTERSHIRE). Argent, an anchor in pale azure surmounted by a fetterlock Or, within the fetterlock on the dexter side a sword erect of the second, hilt and pommel gold, and on the sinister side a rose gules. Recorded at the Visitation of 1634.

BEXHILL-ON-SEA, BOROUGH OF (EAST SUSSEX).* Ermine, a cross double parted and fretted gules, between in the first quarter a mitre, and in the second a demi lion passant guardant conjoined to the demi hulk of a ship, both Or, in the third an estoile sable, and in the fourth a mallard proper; on a chief argent, above waves of the sea a demi sun in splendour issuing from the upper part of the centre of the chief also proper; all within a bordure azure charged with eight martlets of the third. **Crest:** On a wreath of the colours, On a mound of sand, a Martello tower proper. **Motto:** Sol et salubritas. **Granted** 21 January 1907.

BEXLEY, LONDON BOROUGH OF.* Per saltire Or and barry wavy argent and azure, a saltire gules between in chief an oak tree eradicated proper, fructed Or, and in base a cog wheel gules. **Crest:** On a wreath Or and gules, On the battlements of a port between two towers argent, masoned sable, a horse forcene argent. **Supporters:** On either side a stag gules, attired and unguled Or, gorged with a collar wavy argent thereon a bar wavy azure. **Motto:** Boldly and rightly. **Badge:** A Carrick bend azure surmounting a fess and within and tied about a mascle Or. **Granted** 20 May 1965.

BICESTER URBAN DISTRICT COUNCIL (OXFORDSHIRE).* Barry nebuly Or and gules, a hurt charged with a fleur-de-lys gold. **Crest:** On a wreath of the colours, In front of a fox's mask, two stalks of wheat in saltire, leaved proper. Mantled gules, doubled argent. **Motto:** Ut tibi sic aliis. **Granted** 30 October 1959.

BERWICK-UPON-TWEED

BERKSHIRE

BEXHILL-ON-SEA

BEXLEY

BIDEFORD, BOROUGH OF (DEVON).* Argent, over water barry wavy in base, a stone bridge of three arches proper, masoned Or, issuant from the centre arch an ancient ship, the mast appearing behind the bridge, also proper; on a chief gules three clarions gold. **Crest:** On a wreath argent and azure, An Elizabethan ship in full sail proper, the centre sail charged with a clarion Or. **Motto:** Pro Rege ac Fide audax. **Granted** 12 September 1936.

BINGLEY URBAN DISTRICT COUNCIL (YORKSHIRE—WEST RIDING).* Per chevron argent and vert, in chief two trefoils slipped sable and in base a fleece Or; on a chief gules a millrind gold between two roses also argent, barbed and seeded proper. **Crest:** Issuant from a Saxon crown Or, a bear's head argent, muzzled gules. Mantled vert, doubled Or. **Motto:** Opes industria parit. **Granted** 10 September 1956.

BIRKBECK COLLEGE (LONDON UNIVERSITY).* Chequy Or and sable, on a pale argent a sword gules; a chief of the second, thereon an owl of the third between two antique lamps of the first inflamed proper. **Crest:** On a wreath of the colours, A demi lion reguardant Or resting the sinister paw on an anchor sable enfiled with an eastern crown gold. **Motto:** In nocte consilium. **Granted** 31 December 1948.

BIRKENHEAD, COUNTY BOROUGH OF (CHESHIRE).* Quarterly Or and argent, on a cross gules, between a lion passant of the last in the first quarter, an oak tree issuant from a mount proper in the second, an estoile azure in the third, and two lions passant of the third in the fourth, a crosier in pale of the first and two crescents in fesse of the second. **Crest:** On a wreath of the colours, Upon a rock proper in front of a crosier erect Or a lion [statant] azure resting the dexter paw on an anchor also Or. **Motto:** Ubi Fides ibi lux et robur. **Granted** 28 August 1878.

BIRKENHEAD SCHOOL LIMITED. Quarterly gules and Or, in the first quarter a lion passant argent, over all a crosier erect, crook to the sinister, surmounted by an open book also argent, the pages inscribed with the words BEATI MVNDO CORDE in letters sable. **Crest:** On a wreath of the colours, A coronet composed of eight silver-birch leaves set upon a rim vert. **Motto:** Beati mundo corde. **Granted** 4 March 1959.

BIRMINGHAM, BISHOPRIC OF. Per pale indented Or and gules, five roundels, two, two and one, and in chief two crosses patée, all counterchanged. **Granted** 8 March 1906.

BIRMINGHAM, PROVOST AND CHAPTER OF ST. PHILIP'S CATHEDRAL. Argent, a key in pale wards downwards between in chief two crosses formy and in base two roundels all gules. **Granted** 20 February 1937.

BIRMINGHAM, CITY OF (WARWICKSHIRE).* Quarterly, first and fourth azure a bend of five lozenges Or, second and third per pale indented of the last and gules; over all a fesse ermine, thereon a mural crown of the second. **Crest:** On a wreath of the colours, A mural crown, issuant therefrom a dexter arm embowed, the hand holding a hammer, all proper. **Supporters:** On the dexter side a man habited as a smith (representing Industry) holding in the dexter hand a hammer resting on an anvil proper; and on the sinister side a female figure (representing Art) proper, vested argent, wreathed round the temples with laurel vert, tied by a riband gules, holding in the dexter hand resting on the shield a book bound also gules and in the sinister a painter's palette Or with two brushes proper. **Motto:** Forward. Arms and Crest granted 3 April 1889; Supporters granted 4 April 1889; the whole re-exemplified 31 August 1936.

BIRMINGHAM, THE STANDARD OF WROUGHT PLATE IN. [THE ASSAY OFFICE]. Argent, a cupel proper between in chief two anchors erect sable and in base flames of fire issuant also proper. **Supporters:** On either side a lion guardant Or each charged with a cupel proper. **Granted** 22 January 1925.

BIRKBECK COLLEGE

BINGLEY

BIDEFORD

BIRKENHEAD

BICESTER

BIRMINGHAM, UNIVERSITY OF.* Per chevron, the chief per pale gules and azure, in dexter a lion rampant with two heads, in sinister a mermaid holding in the dexter hand a mirror and in the sinister a comb Or, the base sable charged with an open book proper, with two buckles and straps and edges of the third, inscribed "Per ardua ad alta". Granted 27 August 1900.

BIRMINGHAM CHAMBER OF COMMERCE AND INDUSTRY. Sable, four rods of Mercury conjoined in cross Or; over all in fesse point a mural crown gold within an annulet ermine. **Supporters:** On the dexter side a bear argent winged Or; and on the sinister side a sea horse also argent winged and finned gold; each gorged with a collar of the last, pendent therefrom a purse gules tasselled gold, and each supporting a staff also gules, that on the dexter side flying a banner of the last charged with a Stafford knot likewise gold and that on the sinister side a banner of the last charged with a pear sable slipped and leaved proper [the whole upon a compartment of grass to the dexter and barry wavy argent and azure to the sinister]. **Motto:** Venture and prosper. **Granted** 28 September 1959.

BIRMINGHAM, CITY OF, COLLEGE OF COMMERCE. Azure, a bend of lozenges conjoined between two torches bendwise Or enflamed proper. **Crest:** Within a circlet of eight bezants, an heraldic tiger statant gules, crined and tufted Or. **Motto:** Age quod agis. **Granted** 5 June 1963.

BIRMINGHAM COLLEGE OF FOOD AND DOMESTIC ARTS. Per chevron gules and Or, a chevronel sable between in chief two plates, the dexter charged with a garb of wheat and the sinister with a boar's head couped proper, and in base between two sprigs of bay also proper tied with a riband a flame of fire gules. **Crest:** On a wreath Or and azure, Out of a mural crown Or, a dexter arm embowed, vested argent, the hand grasping a cornucopia inverted also proper. **Granted** 20 September 1962.

BIRMINGHAM COLLEGE OF TECHNOLOGY. See Aston in Birmingham, University of.

BIRMINGHAM GENERAL HOSPITAL. Argent, two chevronels sable; on a pale ermines a rose gules barbed and seeded proper between two trefoils also gules. **Crest:** On a wreath of the colours. Between two mullets Or a cockatrice gules holding in the dexter claw a trefoil gold. **Motto:** Flecta non resiliet. **Granted** 20 June 1933.

BIRMINGHAM UNITED HOSPITALS. Per pale indented Or and azure, to the dexter a cockatrice gules grasping in the dexter claw a trefoil of the second and to the sinister a garb of the first; on a chief ermine a dolphin naiant between two lions rampant also of the second each holding in the sinister paw a bow erect of the third stringed gold. **Crest:** On a wreath of the colours, A demi lion rampant azure holding in the sinister paw a bow erect gules stringed Or. **Granted** 29 April 1939.

BISHOP GROSSETESTE COLLEGE, LINCOLN. Azure, a bend ermine; over all on a cross moline Or a leopard's face gules jessant-de-lys vert. **Crest:** On a wreath Or, azure and vert, A demi-lion pean, the head gules, gorged with a collar gemel and supporting a crosier the head enclosing a cross moline square-pierced Or. **Motto:** No omnia sibi habeat. **Granted** 25 June 1969.

BISHOPS' COLLEGE, CHESHUNT. Azure, on a saltire between in chief a celestial crown and in base a mitre Or, a crozier and a sword, point upwards, in saltire proper. **Crest:** On a wreath of the colours, In front of a mount vert, thereon a Paschal Lamb proper, a fleur-de-lys argent. **Motto:** Qualis fides talis vita. **Granted** 26 February 1952.

BISHOP'S STORTFORD URBAN DISTRICT COUNCIL (HERTFORDSHIRE).* Vert, on a pale argent surmounted by a fess wavy of the last charged with a bar wavy azure counterchanged on the pale, a mitre and a garb proper. **Crest:** On a wreath of the colours, On a mount vert the battlements of a tower proper, issuant therefrom a cross pommelled gules. **Motto:** Pro Deo et populo. **Granted** 20 August 1952.

BIRMINGHAM CITY

BIRMINGHAM UNIVERSITY

BISHOP'S STORTFORD

BLACKBURN R. D. C.

BLABY RURAL DISTRICT COUNCIL (LEICESTERSHIRE). Per fesse indented vert and sable, a saltire Or charged with a saltire purpure; on a chief ermine a maunch of the second between two legs embowed, each hosed and shod with a soft leather shoe of the fifteenth century, couped also purpure. **Crest:** On a wreath of the colours, Set upon a representation of the entrance to the railway tunnel at Glenfield in the Parish of Blaby proper, a saltire, perched thereon an eagle displayed, wings extended fessewise Or. **Motto:** In terra divitiae. **Granted** 20 December 1954.

BLACKBURN, BISHOPRIC OF. Per fesse gules and Or, two keys in saltire wards downwards argent in chief and a rose barbed and seeded proper in base. **Granted** 19 February 1927.

BLACKBURN, COUNTY BOROUGH OF (LANCASHIRE).* Argent, a fesse wavy sable between three bees volant proper; on a chief vert a bugle stringed argent between two fusils Or. **Crest:** On a wreath of the colours, A shuttle Or, thereon a dove wings elevated argent and holding in the beak the thread of the shuttle reflexed over the back and an olive branch proper. **Motto:** Arte et labore. **Granted** 14 February 1852.

BLACKBURN RURAL DISTRICT COUNCIL (LANCASHIRE).* Or, a lion rampant purpure, armed and langued vert; on a chief wavy of the last a bee volant between two fusils gold. **Crest:** On a wreath of the colours, Out of a mural crown Or, charged with three roses gules barbed and seeded proper, a mount vert, thereon a cow statant guardant argent. **Motto:** Serva fidem. **Granted** 23 February 1955.

BLACKPOOL, COUNTY BOROUGH OF (LANCASHIRE).* Barry wavy of eight sable and Or, a seagull volant proper; on a chief argent a thunderbolt also proper between a fleur-de-lis and a lion rampant both gules. **Crest:** On a wreath of the colours, On the battlements of a tower Or, the sails of a windmill saltirewise proper surmounted in the centre by a rose gules barbed and seeded also proper. **Motto:** Progress. **Granted** 10 June 1899.

BLACKPOOL BOYS' GRAMMAR SCHOOL. Azure, three martlets Or; on a chief of the last a passion cross gules between two open books proper bound also gules. **Crest:** On a wreath of the colours, The sails of a windmill proper, thereon in the centre a rose gules barbed and seeded also proper. **Motto:** Meliora sequamur. **Granted** 20 December 1957.

BLACKSMITHS OF THE CITY OF LONDON, WORSHIPFUL COMPANY OF.* Sable, a chevron Or between three hammers argent handled and crowned with open crowns of the second. **Crest:** On a wreath of the colours, A phoenix in flames rising proper. **Motto:** By hammer and hand all arts do stand. [The ancient motto: As God will, so be it]. **Granted** 24 June 1610 by Sir William Segar, Garter King of Arms. (*Illustration on page* 47).

BLACKWELL RURAL DISTRICT COUNCIL (DERBYSHIRE).* Argent, a pickaxe surmounted by a spade, the hafts upwards, in saltire proper within an orle of pellets; on a chief sable three stag's heads caboshed of the field. **Crest:** On a wreath of the colours, A sinister arm embowed holding a Davy safety lamp proper. **Motto:** Lux et humanitas. **Granted** 22 September 1942.

BLAENAVON URBAN DISTRICT COUNCIL (MONMOUTHSHIRE).* Quarterly wavy sable and Or, in the first and fourth quarters a key wards upwards and to the dexter, and in the second and third quarters a lozenge, all counterchanged. **Crest:** On a wreath of the colours, Issuant from a circlet of lozenges conjoined stable, a dexter cubit arm in armour proper charged on the wrist with a buckle fessewise Or, the hand grasping a sword in bend sinister with blade bent downwards also proper, hilt and pomel gold. **Motto:** At spes non fracta. **Granted** 12 May 1952

BLETCHLEY URBAN DISTRICT COUNCIL (BUCKINGHAMSHIRE).* Barry argent and azure, an eagle displayed, wings inverted, Or; on a chief per pale gules and sable a Saxon crown between two bulls' heads caboshed gold. **Crest:** Out of a mural crown Or a demi horse sable

BLACKBURN
CO. BOROUGH

BLETCHLEY

BLACKPOOL

BLAENAVON

BLACKWELL

gorged with a collar gemel and maned argent breathing flames proper and supporting a spear erect gules. **Motto:** Progrediens confirmatur animus. **Granted** 12 April 1955.

BLYTH, BOROUGH OF (NORTHUMBERLAND).* Per fesse gules and azure, on a fesse argent between in chief an ancient crown Or and in base a lymphad proper, flags flying to the dexter gules, three ermine spots sable. **Crest:** Issuant out of a mural crown sable charged with three miner's picks, shafts upwards Or, a demi lion gold holding in the dexter paw a miner's lamp proper. **Motto:** We grow by industry. **Granted** 24 January 1923

BLYTH HARBOUR COMMISSION. Per chevron azure and barry wavy of six argent and of the first, in chief a cross fleury between two lions rampant of the second and in base an ancient two-masted ship in full sail proper. **Motto:** Post salum salus. **Granted** 4 March 1925.

BOGNOR REGIS URBAN DISTRICT COUNCIL (WEST SUSSEX).* Azure, on a pile Or a Saxon crown gules; a chief invected of the second thereon three martlets of the first. **Crest:** On a wreath of the colours, Between two gull's wings azure, a Saxon crown gules. **Motto:** Action. **Granted** 10 April 1935.

BOLDON URBAN DISTRICT COUNCIL (CO. DURHAM).* Azure, within two chevronels three purses Or; in chief two escallops and in base three lilies issuing from one stalk argent. **Crest:** Issuant from a mural crown sable charged with three ears of wheat Or, a demi lion argent holding between the paws an open book of the last bound and clasped gold. **Motto:** Audaces prorsum. **Granted** 20 March 1953.

BOLTON, COUNTY BOROUGH OF (LANCASHIRE).* Gules, two bendlets Or, a shuttle with weft pendent between an arrow, point upwards, and a mule spindle in chief palewise, all of the last and an escutcheon in base of the second thereon a rose of the first barbed and seeded proper. **Crest:** On a wreath of the colours, Upon a rocky moor an elephant statant proper, on its back a castle Or, and thereon a rose as in the Arms, the trappings per pale gules and vert and charged with mitre also Or. **Supporters:** On either side a lion sable, gorged with a wreath argent and sable, each supporting a staff Or, flying therefrom a banner, that on the dexter vair Or and gules, that on the sinister argent on a bend azure three stags' heads caboshed Or. **Motto:** Supera moras. **Badge:** Upon an oval gules encompassed by a garland of six roses gules, barbed, seeded and leaved proper, an arrow, point upwards, enfiled by a crown palisado Or. Arms and Crest granted 5 June 1890; Supporters and Badge granted 25 September 1958.

BOLTON SCHOOL (BOLTON, LANCASHIRE).* Argent, two bends sable, the upper engrailed; on a chief of the second between a rose and a chaplet Or an open book proper. **Crest:** On a wreath of the colours, Between two sprigs of laurel a cock statant proper, combed and wattled gules, facing the dexter on a trumper Or facing the sinister. **Motto:** Mutare vel timere sperno. **Granted** 6 September 1923. The Arms are borne upon a lozenge, without Crest or Motto, for the Girls' Division of the School.

BOOKKEEPERS AND RELATED DATA PROCESSING, INSTITUTE OF, LIMITED. Per fess checky sable and argent and sable, on a pile gules between two quill pens palewise Or two mullets argent, irradiated Or, issuing from those in chief a lightning flash argent, in base a mullet of six points also argent, irradiated Or. **Crest:** On a wreath argent, sable and gules, A demi figure garbed as a Franciscan representing Fra Luca Paciol resting the sinister hand on a book bound gules, edged, clasped and garnished Or, and pointing thereto with a wand proper held in the dexter hand. Mantled sable and gules, doubled Or. **Motto:** Vincit omnia perseverantia. Badge: A male griffin sejant checky sable and argent, the head, neck and foreparts gules, beaked, legged, rayed and tufted, holding in each claw a quill pen Or. **Granted** 20 February 1969.

BOOTHAM SCHOOL (YORK). Argent, on a cross azure a rose of the field barbed and seeded proper between four crosses patée concave also argent. **Motto:** Membra sumus corporis magni. **Granted** 29 June 1931.

BOLDON

BLYTH

BOGNOR REGIS

BOLTON CO. BOROUGH

BOLTON SCHOOL

BOOTLE, COUNTY BOROUGH OF (LANCASHIRE).* Argent, on a chevron between three fleurs-de-lis azure as many stags' heads caboshed Or; on a chief sable three mural crowns of the field. **Crest:** On a wreath of the colours, Upon a rock a lighthouse proper. **Motto:** Respice, aspice, prospice. **Granted** 4 November 1869.

BOROUGH ROAD COLLEGE. Azure, on a chevron argent between in chief two bees volant and in base a cross botony Or, a Saxon crown between two roses gules, barbed and seeded proper. **Motto:** Una mente. **Granted** 15 June 1964 to The British and Foreign Bible Society for the use of the College.

BOSTON, BOROUGH OF (LINCOLNSHIRE—PARTS OF HOLLAND).* Sable, three coronets, each composed of crosses patee and fleurs-de-lys, in pale Or. **Crest:** On a wreath of the colours, A woolpack proper charged with a ram couchant Or, horned sable. Mantled gules, doubled argent. **Supporters:** On either side a mermaid proper, crined and tail-fin Or, ducally crowned azure. **Motto:** Per mare et per terram. Recorded at the Visitation 1 December 1568.

BOSTON RURAL DISTRICT COUNCIL (LINCOLNSHIRE—PARTS OF HOLLAND).* Bendy wavy of six Or and azure, on a chief sable a garb between two pairs of windmill sails gold. **Crest:** On a wreath of the colours, A demi lion guardant Or, ducally crowned azure, supporting a crosier argent. **Motto:** Serve with amity. **Granted** 1 December 1953.

BOURNE URBAN DISTRICT COUNCIL (LINCOLNSHIRE—PARTS OF KESTEVEN).* Or, on a fesse azure between in chief three torteux and in base a Wake knot gules, a bar wavy argent. **Crest:** On a wreath of the colours, Issuant from the battlements of a tower gules, a demi lion ermine holding between the paws an escutcheon azure charged with a fleur-de-lis argent. **Motto:** Vigila et ora. **Granted** 23 July 1953.

BOURNEMOUTH, COUNTY BOROUGH OF (HAMPSHIRE).* Quarterly Or and azure, a cross flory between a lion rampant holding between the paws a rose in the first and fourth quarters, six martlets, two, two, and two, in the second, and four salmons naiant and in pale in the third, all counterchanged. **Crest:** On a wreath of the colours, Upon a mount vert a pine tree proper, in front four roses fessewise Or. **Motto:** Pulchritudo et salubritas. **Granted** 24 March 1891.

BOWDON URBAN DISTRICT COUNCIL (CHESHIRE).* Per chevron arched Or and vert, in chief two yew trees eradicated proper and in base a garb of the first; on a chief gules a lion passant argent. **Crest:** On a wreath of the colours, A demi unicorn ermine, armed, unguled and tufted Or, holding between the hooves a bow proper. **Motto:** Beau don. **Granted** 11 August 1945.

BOWLAND RURAL DISTRICT COUNCIL (YORKSHIRE—WEST RIDING).* Vert, on a pale Or between two roses argent, barbed and seeded proper, a pale sable, thereon a crozier gold. **Crest:** On a wreath of the colours, A stag's head couped Or, gorged with a collar, affixed thereto a chain reflexed round the neck sable, the collar charged with three mullets gold. **Motto:** I will lift up mine eyes. **Granted** 9 April 1954.

BOWYERS OF THE CITY OF LONDON, WORSHIPFUL COMPANY OF.* Sable, on a chevron Or between three floats argent as many pierced mullets of the field. **Crest:** On a wreath Or and azure, Three bows bent gules stringed Or. Mantled sable, doubled ermine. **Motto:** Crecy, Poitiers, Agincourt. **Granted** 10 November 1488 by Sir Thomas Holme, Clarenceux King of Arms.

BRACKNELL DEVELOPMENT CORPORATION (BERKSHIRE).* Vert, three annulets interlaced in pale Or within an orle of eight bezants. **Crest:** On a wreath of the colours, A stag's head erased proper charged on the neck with three annulets interlaced, one and two, Or. **Motto:** Home, Industry, Leisure. **Granted** 18 July 1951.

BOWDON

BOSTON BOROUGH

BOURNE

BOSTON R. D. C.

BOURNEMOUTH

BOOTLE

BRADFIELD COLLEGE (BERKSHIRE). Per chevron vert and azure, in chief two falcons jessed and belled Or and in base a saltire argent. **Motto:** Benedictus es O Domine, doce me statuta tua. **Granted** 16 November 1923.

BRADFORD, BISHOPRIC OF.* Azure, two keys in saltire Or, in chief a woolpack proper corded of the second. **Granted** 4 June 1920.

BRADFORD, CITY AND COUNTY BOROUGH OF (YORKSHIRE—WEST RIDING).* Per pale gules and azure, on a chevron engrailed between three bugle horns stringed Or, a well sable. **Crest:** On a wreath of the colours, A boar's head [sans tongue] erased Or in front of the trunk of a tree sprouting proper. **Supporters:** On the dexter side a ram sable, horned Or and gorged with a wreath of white roses proper; and on the sinister side an Angola [Angora] goat argent, horned Or and gorged with a collar gules, thereon three roses also argent. **Motto:** Labor omnia vincit. **Badge:** A ram's head caboshed argent, horned and crowned with a civic [= mural] crown Or. Standard: Per fesse gules and azure, the bands and lettering Or, fringed of the colours. Arms and Crest granted 18 October 1847; Supporters granted 31 December 1907; Badge and Standard granted 31 January 1908.

BRADFORD, UNIVERSITY OF.* Gules, an open book proper, edged, bound and having seven clasps, between in chief two bugle horns stringed Or and in base a rose argent barbed and seeded proper. **Crest:** On a wreath of the colours, Issuant from the stock of an oak tree sprouting leaves, a cubit arm proper grasping a torch sable, issuant therefrom seven rays of the sun Or. **Supporters:** On either side a falcon, wings addorsed, argent, issuant from the head seven rays of the sun as in the Crest. **Motto:** Give invention light. **Badge:** A torch as in the Crest, pendent therefrom by the string a bugle horn Or. **Granted** 20 February 1967.

BRADFORD AND BINGLEY BUILDING SOCIETY. Per chevron gules and azure, on a chevron engrailed between in chief two roses argent, barbed and seeded proper, and in base a bugle horn stringed Or, three trefoils slipped sable, **Crest:** On a wreath of the colours, Out of a Saxon crown Or a mount vert, thereon a boar's head erased Or sans tongue and armed gules. **Supporters:** On the dexter side a ram argent, armed and unguled Or; and on the sinister side a bear argent; each gorged with a riband azure, pendent therefrom a billet gules charged with a bee volant Or. **Motto:** Labor parit opes. **Granted** 5 August 1964.

BRADFORD PERMANENT BUILDING SOCIETY. Gules, between two bugle horns in fesse stringed, a key in pale, the bow in chief in the form of three thrift flowers conjoined upon one stem, the double wards in the form of two towers, all Or. **Crest:** On a wreath of the colours, Out of a garland of roses argent, barbed, seeded and leaved proper, a tower sable irradiated with rays of the sun and pendent from the battlements thereof a bugle horn stringed Or. **Supporters:** On either side a ram guardant argent, armed, unguled, murally crowned, and holding in the mouth by the string a tasselled purse Or. **Motto:** Protection. **Granted** 1 August 1966.

BRADFORD TEXTILE SOCIETY LIMITED. Ermine, five pallets and as many barrulets fretted Or; on a chief per pale gules and azure an open book argent, edged and bound also Or, between two bugle horns stringed gold. **Crest:** Out of a circlet gules charged with three roses argent, barbed and seeded proper, a demi figure representing St. Blaize in episcopal robes mitred and nimbed, in the dexter hand a crosier and in the sinister hand and resting on the shoulder a woolcomb, all Or. Mantled gules, doubled Or. **Supporters:** On either side a ram sable, armed and unguled Or, gorged with a riband azure, pendent therefrom a pair of scales gold. **Motto:** Consilium contexamus arti. **Granted** 20 August 1959.

BRAINTREE AND BOCKING URBAN DISTRICT COUNCIL (ESSEX).* Gules, on a cross quarter-pierced Or two lions rampant in pale azure and two fleurs-de-lis in fess vert. **Crest:** On a wreath of the colours, In front of two swords saltirewise, hilts in base, argent, enfiled by a mural crown Or, three pirced mullets gules. **Motto:** Hold to the truth. **Granted** 21 March 1927.

BOWLAND

BRADFORD, UNIVERSITY

BRADFORD, BISHOPRIC

BRADFORD

BRACKNELL

BRAINTREE RURAL DISTRICT COUNCIL (ESSEX). Gules, an eagle displayed, wings inverted, Or, in the claws a seax argent, hilt, pommel and quillons Or, in chief a bar wavy argent charged with another sable. **Crest:** Out of a coronet composed of four ears of wheat and as many acorns leaved, set alternately upon a rim Or, a mount vert, thereon a cock statant gold, combed, wattled and legged gules, charged on the breast with a representation of the device or mark of Thomas Paycock of Great Coggeshall sable. Mantled gules doubled argent. **Motto:** Fide et fortitudine. **Granted** 20 December 1962.

BRASENOSE COLLEGE (OXFORD UNIVERSITY).* Tierced per pale, the centre argent thereon an escutcheon of the Arms of the See of Lincoln ensigned by a mitre proper, the dexter side argent a chevron sable between three roses gules barbed and seeded proper, the sinister side quarterly, first and fourth argent a chevron between three bugle horns stringed sable, second and third argent a chevron between three crosses crosslet sable. Recorded at the Visitation of 1575.

BRECKNOCK, BOROUGH OF (BRECKNOCKSHIRE). Vert, a pall wavy argent, thereon another azure; over all a mantle of estate gules doubled ermine. **Crest:** Out of a mural crown Or a longbow and a pitchfork interlaced in saltire proper. **Supporters:** On the dexter side an eagle, wings elevated and addorsed, Or, the under wing charged with a roundel per pale vert and argent thereon an open book proper, bound gules, edged gold; and on the sinister side a dragon gules, wings elevated and addorsed, the underwing charged with a bezant thereon the Roman numerals XXIV sable; each standing on a representation of a walled town in front of the Brecon Beacons. **Motto:** Canmol dy fro athrig yno. **Badge:** A roundel vert charged with a mantle of estate gules doubled ermine encircled by a civic wreath proper and ensigned by a mural crown Or. **Granted** 20 July 1962.

BRECKNOCK RURAL DISTRICT COUNCIL (BRECKNOCKSHIRE).* Quarterly azure and Or, on a fesse wavy between in the first quarter a leaping salmon argent, in the second a beacon enflamed, in the third an oak tree couped proper, and in the fourth a garb gold, a bar wavy of the third. **Crest:** On a wreath of the colours, In front of a Celtic cross of stone proper a dragon passant gules supporting with the dexter claw a quill pen, point downwards argent. **Motto:** Llifa'r dwr, Llewyrcha'r bobl. **Granted** 20 December 1954.

BRECKNOCKSHIRE AGRICULTURAL SOCIETY. Vert, in chief two rams' heads and in base a Hereford Bull's head, all caboshed proper within a bordure barry of ten argent and gules charged with eight martlets sable. **Crest:** On a wreath of the colours, A wyvern's head couped, in the mouth three stalks of wheat, all proper. **Mottoes:** (above crest) Brycheiniog; (below shield) Ei bri ein brant. **Granted** 17 May 1955.

BRENT, LONDON BOROUGH OF.* Per chevron gules and vert, a chevron wavy argent between in dexter chief an orb and in sinister chief two swords in saltire [proper], hilts and pomels Or, points upward, and in base two seaxes in saltire proper, hilts and pomels Or, enfiled through a Saxon crown Or. **Crest:** Issuant from a Saxon crown Or, a mount vert, thereon a lion statant guardant gold, charged on the shoulder with a cinquefoil gules. **Supporters:** On the dexter side a lion guardant Or supporting a staff gules, flying therefrom a banner vert charged with a pair of scales Or; and on the sinister side a dragon azure supporting a staff vert, flying therefrom a banner gules charged with three lilies slipped argent, the stamens Or; the whole upon a compartment of grass divided by a stream of water argent, a pale wavy azure. **Motto:** Forward together. **Granted** 1 September 1965.

BRENTWOOD URBAN DISTRICT COUNCIL (ESSEX).* Per fess rayonée argent and gules, in chief a Cornish chough proper between two pilgrim's staves sable, and in base three Saxon crowns Or. **Crest:** On a wreath of the colours, Issuant from the battlements of a tower azure a demi stag Or. **Motto:** Ardens fide. **Granted** 1 August 1951.

BRENT

BRENTWOOD

BRAINTREE AND BOCKING

BRECKNOCK R. D. C.

BRASENOSE COLLEGE

BRENTWOOD SCHOOL. See Sir Anthony Browne's School.

BREWERS OF THE CITY OF LONDON, WORSHIPFUL COMPANY OF.* Gules, on a chevron engrailed argent between three pairs of barley sheaves saltirewise Or three kilderkins sable hooped gold. **Crest:** On a wreath argent and azure, A demi maiden proper, vested azure fretty argent, crined Or, holding in either hand three ears of barley of the last. Mantled sable, doubled argent. **Motto:** In God is all our trust. **Granted** 29 February 1544 by Thomas Hawley, Clarenceux King of Arms, in place of an earlier grant (23 July 1468) by William Hawkeslowe, Clarenceux King of Arms. (*Illustration on page* 79).

BREWING, INSTITUTE OF.* Gules, two garbs of barley in saltire between three tuns fessewise Or. **Crest:** Issuant out of a coronet composed of four hop cones and as many hop leaves alternately set upon a rim Or, a demi griffin sable supporting a malt shovel gold. **Motto:** Rerum cognoscere causas. **Granted** 5 January 1928.

BRIDEWELL ROYAL HOSPITAL. See Christ's Hospital.

BRIDGEND URBAN DISTRICT COUNCIL (GLAMORGAN).* Vert, a salmon leaping to the dexter proper, on a chief sable a bridge of two arches masoned Or. **Crest:** On a wreath of the colours, A raven proper between two garbs Or. **Motto:** A vo penn bit pont. **Granted** 18 June 1951.

BRIDGNORTH, BOROUGH OF (SHROPSHIRE). Argent, on a rock in base a castle of three towers with spires proper, from the dexter spire a banner of St. George, and from the sinister spire a banner quarterly, gules a lion passant Or and azure a fleur de lys also Or; on a chief vert a lion passant guardant gold. **Motto:** Fidelitas urbis salus regis. **Granted** 14 September 1958. Bridgnorth is now a Rural Borough.

BRIDGWATER, BOROUGH OF (SOMERSET).* Gules, rising from water barry wavy in base proper, the piers of a bridge Or, thereon a castle argent, portcullis raised, thereunder a leopard's face, in chief an estoile of eight points and a fleur-de-lys gold. **Crest:** On a wreath argent and gules, An ancient ship Or in full sail, rigging sable, flags and pennant argent, each charged with a cross gules, the sail also argent charged with a chevron between three garbs of the second. **Supporters:** On either side a lion guardant Or, each gorged with a rope proper, pendent therefrom on the dexter an escutcheon gules charged with two bendlets wavy gold, and on the sinister an escutcheon argent charged with a trivet sable. **Motto:** Opes consilium parit. **Granted** 19 September 1952.

BRIDGWATER BUILDING SOCIETY. Gules, a pallet wavy argent, over all a castle of three degrees and two towers domed Or, the port sable therein a key erect ward upwards to the dexter also Or, and in chief two sprigs of thrift each of three flowers gold. **Crest:** Out of a coronet composed of two fleurs de lys and as many estoiles set upon a circlet Or, a demi dragon gold holding between the paws an escutcheon argent charged with a trivet sable. **Motto:** Consilium parit opes. **Granted** 25 April 1961.

BRIDLINGTON, BOROUGH OF (YORKSHIRE—EAST RIDING).* Per pale sable and argent, three Gothic capital letters B counterchanged, on a chief embattled of the second two barrulets wavy azure. **Crest:** Issuant from a coronet composed of eight roses set upon a rim Or, a sun rising gules. **Motto:** Signum salutis semper. **Granted** 26 September 1934.

BRIDPORT, BOROUGH OF (DORSET).* Gules, upon a base barry wavy of eight argent and azure, a gateway between two towers of the second, in the open port also gules three ropemakers' spinning hooks palewise in fesse Or, in chief a lion passant guardant ducally crowned between two fleurs-de-lys of the last. Recorded (without spinning hooks) at the Visitation 3 October 1565; recorded as above at the Visitation 9 September 1623.

INSTITUTE OF BREWING

BRIDGWATER

BRIDGEND

BRIDPORT

BRIDLINGTON

BRIGHOUSE, BOROUGH OF (YORKSHIRE—WEST RIDING).* Or, on a pale sable between in chief two roses gules, barbed and seeded proper, and in base two crescents of the second, a lion rampant of the field. **Crest:** On a wreath of the colours, Upon the battlements of a tower argent charged with two crescents fessewise sable, a leopard's face of the first between two roses gules, barbed, slipped and seeded proper. **Motto:** Labore et prudentia. **Granted** 28 March 1894.

BRIGHTON, COUNTY BOROUGH OF (EAST SUSSEX).* Argent, two dolphins naiant sable, a bordure azure charged with six martlets Or. **Crest:** On a wreath of the colours, Two dolphins in saltire, heads downwards, sable between as many branches of coral gules. **Motto:** In Deo fidemus. **Granted** 14 April 1897.

BRIGHTON COLLEGE.* Azure, two keys in saltire Or between in fesse two pelicans vulning themselves respectant argent and in chief a closed book of the third, edged and clasped of the second. **Motto:** TO Δ 'EY NIKAT Ω. **Granted** 18 June 1920.

BRIGHTON GRAMMAR SCHOOL.* Per pale gules and azure, a cross crosslet fitchée throughout between two escallops in base Or. **Crest:** On a wreath of the colours, Between a pair of wings a dexter hand couped at the wrist, the index finger pointing to a mullet, all Or. **Motto:** Meliora sequimur. **Granted** 25 July 1960.

BRISTOL, BISHOPRIC OF. Sable, three ducal coronets in pale Or. Recorded in the College of Arms.

BRISTOL, DEAN AND CHAPTER OF THE CATHEDRAL OF THE HOLY AND UNDIVIDED TRINITY OF. Gules, a lymphad, sail set, and in chief three ducal coronets in fesse Or. **Granted** 6 September 1960.

BRISTOL, CITY AND COUNTY BOROUGH OF.* Gules, on the sinister side a castle with two towers domed all argent, on each dome a banner charged with the cross of St. George, the castle on a mount vert, the dexter base water proper, thereon a ship of three masts Or, the rigging sable, sailing from a port in the dexter tower, her fore and main masts being visible and on each a round top of the fifth, on the foremast a sail set and on the mainmast a sail furled of the second. **Crest:** On a wreath Or and gules, Issuant from clouds, two arms embowed and interlaced in saltire proper, the dexter hand holding a serpent vert, and the sinister holding a pair of scales Or. **Supporters:** On either side a unicorn sejant Or, armed, maned and unguled sable. **Motto:** Virtute en Industria. Recorded and confirmed 24 August 1569.

BRISTOL, UNIVERSITY OF. Argent, on a cross quadrate gules, a representation of the Arms of the City of Bristol (with the consent of the Lord Mayor, Aldermen and Citizens), between in pale a sun in splendour and an open book proper, leaved and clasped Or, and inscribed with the words "Nisi quia Dominus", and in the fesse to the dexter a dolphin embowed and to the sinister a horse courant, both of the third. **Motto:** Vim promovet insitam. **Granted** 4 December 1909.

BRISTOL AND WEST BUILDING SOCIETY. Per chevron sable and gules, in chief a balance Or and in base a castle triple towered argent. **Crest:** On a wreath of the colours, In front of two arms embowed in saltire, the hand to the dexter holding a round shield and that to the sinister three sprigs of thrift, a rock, all proper. **Motto:** Security through thrift. **Granted** 25 February 1939.

BRISTOL, CLIFTON AND WEST OF ENGLAND ZOOLOGICAL SOCIETY.* Vert, in chief two elephants' heads affrontée argent and in base a cross bottony Or. **Crest:** On a wreath of the colours, On a mount vert semée of wild flowers, a sapling between a chimpanzee and a gorilla, both sejant, proper and each holding the sapling with the interior forepaw and supporting in front thereof with the exterior forepaw an escutcheon gules charged with a unicorn's head erased Or armed and crined sable. **Motto:** Ask of the beasts & they shall teach thee. **Granted** 20 May 1954 to the Treasurer for the use of the Society.

BRIGHTON

BRIGHTON COLLEGE

BRIGHOUSE

BRISTOL

BRISTOL ROYAL HOSPITAL

BRIGHTON GRAMMAR SCHOOL

BRISTOL COLLEGE OF TECHNOLOGY. Per pale, to the dexter barry undy of eight argent and azure, on a bend Or a dragon volant vert (being part of the Arms of the Company and Fellowship of the Merchant Adventurers of the City of Bristol) and to the sinister the Arms of the said City of Bristol, on a chief sable an open book proper between two cogwheels also argent. **Crest:** On a wreath Or and gules, An owl proper perched on a ship's top rigged Or. **Motto:** Per sapientiam provenite. **Granted** 3 March 1958.

BRISTOL ROYAL HOSPITAL.* Azure, on a pale between two unicorns combatant Or, an antique lamp of the field, inflamed proper, between two hearts gules also inflamed proper. **Crest:** On a wreath of the colours, A demi bull sable, winged, horned, and supporting a rod of Aesculapius Or. **Motto:** Charity universal. **Granted** 15 May 1967.

BRITISH AIRPORTS AUTHORITY.* Azure, a pale argent, over all a port between two towers Or, the portcullis raised sable, the whole ensigned with an astral crown Or. **Crest:** On a wreath of the colours, Out of an astral crown Or, between to the dexter a sprig of two roses gules, barbed, seeded and leaved, and to the sinister two thistles conjoined on one stem proper, a dexter cubit arm vested azure, perched on the glove a falcon wings addorsed proper, belled Or. **Supporters:** On either side a lynx proper, winged Or, the whole upon a compartment of grass, thereon clouds, proper. **Motto:** Salvete portum invecti. **Badge:** A hurt charged with a port between two towers Or, the portcullis raised sable, the whole ensigned with an astral crown Or, all within a bordure of clouds proper. **Granted** 10 October 1967.

BRITISH AND COMMONWEALTH SHIPPING COMPANY LIMITED. Azure, a mercantile crown Or, sails argent; on a bordure gold four towers per fesse sable and gules alternately with as many lions rampant of the last. **Crest:** On a wreath of the colours, A sea lion guardant Or, supporting a ship's rudder erect, tiller to the dexter azure, garnished gold. **Supporters:** On either side a sea-lion guardant Or, supporting a flagstaff proper, flying therefrom a flag azure charged with a saltire argent thereon another gules, and over all a lozenge argent charged with a lion rampant also gules. **Motto:** Tendimus. **Badge:** Within a wreath of oak leaves vert tied with a riband Or, a hurt, thereon a sea-lion guardant gold gorged with a mercantile crown as in the Arms. **Granted** 20 February 1957.

BRITISH ANTIQUE DEALERS' ASSOCIATION LIMITED. Sable, an antique crown Or. **Crest:** On a wreath of the colours, A golden bust of Benvenuto Cellini proper. **Supporters:** On either side a jackdaw, wings elevated, proper, the underside of the wing semée of antique crowns Or. **Motto:** Ars non habet inimicum nisi ignorantium. **Granted** 20 January 1958.

BRITISH ASSOCIATION FOR THE ADVANCEMENT OF SCIENCE.* Azure, ten stars, two of six, four of five, and four of four points, argent (representing the constellation of Libra (The Scales)); over all a balance Or. **Motto:** Sed omnia disposuisti. **Granted** 9 March 1937.

BRITISH BANK OF THE MIDDLE EAST. Or, on water barry wavy in base proper, an Arab dhow also proper; on a chief azure, in Kufic Arabic the words "British Bank of the Middle East" enarched gold. **Supporters:** On either side a date palm proper, fructed Or. **Motto:** Fiducia et Fides. **Granted** 20 June 1957.

BRITISH BROADCASTING CORPORATION.* Azure, a terrestrial globe proper encircled by an annulet Or and seven estoiles in orle argent. **Crest:** On a wreath of the colours, A lion passant Or grasping in the dexter forepaw a thunderbolt proper. **Supporters:** On either side an eagle, wings addorsed, proper collared azure, pendent therefrom a bugle horn stringed Or. **Motto:** Nation shall speak peace unto nation [originally: Quaecunque] **Badge:** A thunderbolt proper, thereon a pellet inscribed with the letters BBC Or. **Granted** 8 March 1927.

BRITISH AIRPORTS AUTHORITY

BRISTOL ZOOLOGICAL SOCIETY

BRITISH BROADCASTING CORPORATION

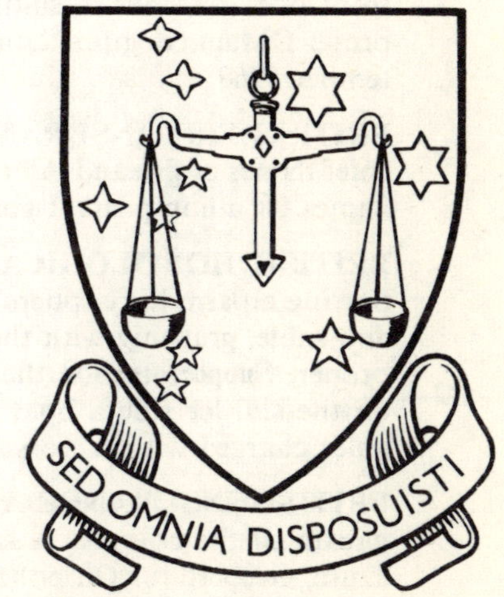

BRITISH ASSOCIATION

BRITISH COMMONWEALTH INSURANCE COMPANY LIMITED. Argent, on water barry wavy proper in base, a lymphad, sail furled, sable, flags flying to the dexter gules, in chief two phoenixes also proper. **Crest:** On a wreath argent and azure, A hand grasping a beacon inflamed proper. **Granted** 7 June 1950.

BRITISH COUNCIL. Or, on a pale gules a lion's face of the first; a chief sable, thereon an open book proper, edged gold. **Crest:** Issuant from an antique crown Or, a cubit arm, vested azure cuffed argent, the hand proper grasping a torch gold inflamed also proper. **Supporters:** On either side a lion reguardant Or gorged with an antique crown azure. **Motto:** Truth will triumph. **Granted** 9 July 1941.

BRITISH DENTAL ASSOCIATION. Sable, issuant from the dexter and sinister base two lions combatant supporting a rod of Aesculapius Or. **Supporters:** On the dexter side a representation of St. Damian holding in the exterior hand a scalpel and a branch of palm all proper; and on the sinister side a representation of the figure of St. Apollonia holding in the exterior hand a pair of forceps gripping a tooth and a branch of palm all proper. **Motto:** Ars, scientia, mores. **Granted** 11 April 1930.

BRITISH DIETETIC ASSOCIATION. Azure, an ibex proper, armed and unguled Or, perched upon the point of a cornucopia gold. **Crest:** On a wreath of the colours, An ibex's head erased proper, gorged with a chain Or, pendent therefrom an escutcheon azure charged with a cornucopia Or. **Granted** 10 June 1958.

BRITISH ENGINEERS, INSTITUTION OF. Or, two barrulets sable; on a chief azure a bridge of three arches throughout proper. **Crest:** On a wreath of the colours, In front of a sun in splendour rising Or, a volcano acting proper. **Motto:** Quod petis hic est. **Granted** 4 May 1950 to The Engineering Delegacy, Limited.

BRITISH EUROPEAN AIRWAYS CORPORATION. Argent, a fesse gules between three astral crowns azure. **Crest:** On a wreath of the colours, In front of a sun in splendour rising Or, a swift volant sable. **Motto:** Clavis Europae. **Badge:** A winged key fessewise, wards downwards and to the dexter, gules. **Granted** 19 November 1946.

BRITISH FEDERATION OF UNIVERSITY WOMEN, LIMITED. Azure, a lozenge ermine surmounted of an open book proper, edged and bound Or, in chief two rams passant argent, armed and unguled gold. **Crest:** On a wreath argent, alternated with azure, gules, and vert, In front of two scrolls in saltire argent each tied with a riband gules an ancient lamp Or inflamed proper. Mantled gules, doubled argent. **Motto:** Amicitiae perficiamus artem. **Granted** 20 September 1960.

BRITISH FIRE INSURANCE COMPANY LIMITED. Per fess embattled gules and sable, in chief flames of fire and in base three crosses botonnée Or. **Crest:** On a wreath of the colours, Upon flames Or a lion passant guardant gules. **Granted** 27 February 1920.

BRITISH HOROLOGICAL INSTITUTE LIMITED. Sable, two lions counter-rampant supporting an armillary sphere Or. **Crest:** On a wreath of the colours, An eagle rising chequy argent and sable, grasping with the talons an hour glass Or, and in the beak a sprig of thyme flowered proper. **Supporters:** On the dexter side a unicorn argent, armed, crined and unguled sable; and on the sinister side a boar erminois gorged with a collar and pendent therefrom an escutcheon gules charged with a cross formy fitchy Or. **Motto:** Vigilantia. **Granted** 20 May 1965.

BRITISH INSURANCE ASSOCIATION. Quarterly azure and gules, a rose Or. **Crest:** On a wreath of the colours, A salamander couchant reguardant inflamed proper, banded and ringed azure. **Supporters:** On either side a lion reguardant Or, armed and langued azure, supporting a staff gules, the truck also Or, flying therefrom a pennon quarterly of the second and of the third, a rose of the last [gold]. **Motto:** Safe guard. **Granted** 8 March 1949.

THE BOWYERS

THE BREWERS

THE EMBRVIDERERS

THE BVTCHERS

BRITISH INTERNAL COMBUSTION ENGINE MANUFACTURERS' ASSOCIATION. Gules, within an annulet argent, inflamed inwards Or, a terrestrial globe proper; on a chief of the second two cog wheels sable. **Crest:** On a wreath of the colours, A cubit arm proper grasping a bezant charged with the symbol of Jupiter sable. **Supporters:** On the dexter side a representation of Vulcan, in his exterior hand a pair of pincers; and on the sinister side a representation of Neptune, in his exterior hand a trident erect, all proper. **Motto:** Toti conterminus orbi. **Granted** 14 February 1946.

BRITISH LIMBLESS EX-SERVICEMEN'S ASSOCIATION.* Azure, in front of a sun in splendour Or, a cross potent per saltire of the first and gules. **Crest:** On a wreath of the colours, In front of a pair of wings conjoined in base argent, an anchor Or between two sheathed swords pilewise, points downwards, the dexter sheathed gules and the sinister azure, both garnished gold, the hilts and pommels also gold. **Supporters:** On the dexter side a lion sejant Or, collared argent, on the collar a daffodil slipped and leaved proper between two roses gules barbed and seeded also proper; and on the sinister side a lion sejant gules, collared argent on the collar a shamrock between two thistles stalked and leaved proper. **Motto:** Service and fortitude. **Granted** 9 May 1958.

BRITISH MEDICAL ASSOCIATION. Per pale Or and azure, a maunch counterchanged; on a chief of the first a lion passant also azure. **Crest:** On a wreath of the colours, In front of two torches in saltire azure enflamed proper, a rod of Aesculapius Or. **Supporters:** On the dexter side a figure representing Hippocrates holding in his exterior hand a pomegranate proper; and on the sinister side a figure representing William Harvey, physician, also proper, holding in his exterior hand an annulet per fesse gules and azure. **Motto:** With head and heart and hand. **Granted** 25 May 1955.

BRITISH OAK INSURANCE COMPANY LIMITED.* Or, on a mount in base vert an oak tree proper; a chief indented gules, thereon a key, wards downwards, of the field. **Supporters:** On either side a talbot sable charged on the shoulder with a dagger, point upwards, argent, pommel and hilt Or. **Motto:** Festina lente. **Granted** 10 May 1937.

BRITISH ORTHOPAEDIC ASSOCIATION. Azure, a scamnum between two cords nowed Or; on a chief paly of four gules and gold a lion passant guardant counterchanged. **Crest:** On a wreath of the colours, On a mount vert a young plane tree in leaf with a crooked stem bound with cords to a straight post on the dexter all proper. **Supporters:** On the dexter side a representation of Hippocrates, habited azure, supporting with his exterior hand a ladder from which a rung has been removed; and on the sinister side a representation of Aesculapius, habited argent, supporting with his exterior hand his staff, all proper. **Granted** 16 July 1952.

BRITISH OVERSEAS AIRWAYS CORPORATION.* Azure, a lion's face winged, the wings enfiled with an astral crown Or. **Crest:** On a wreath of the colours, Upon a mount vert a winged lion passant Or collared of the first, the tips of the wings enveloped in clouds proper. **Supporters:** On the dexter side a winged lion and on the sinister a winged sea lion, both Or, and each gorged with a collar vert. **Badge:** A lion's face winged Or. **Granted** 24 January 1941.

BRITISH OXYGEN COMPANY LIMITED. Gules, two bars nebuly and a bordure nebuly argent. **Crest:** Issuant from a crown of rays gules, a demi lion Or holding in the paws a vine branch slipped, leaved and fructed, proper. **Supporters:** On either side a lion Or, the head rayonée gules, holding aloft in the interior paw a staff of Aesculapius sable, the serpent vert purfled gold. **Motto:** Auris vitalibus vesci. **Badge:** Within an annulet Or encircled with a wreath of green leaves proper, a torteau charged with a lion rampant gold. **Granted** 5 April 1961.

BRITISH PHOTOGRAPHERS, INSTITUTE OF. Sable, a rainbow proper within a bordure argent. **Crest:** On a wreath of the colours, A bezant charged with a demi lion couped holding a torch enflamed proper. **Supporters:** On the dexter side a lion; and on the sinister side a lynx, both

BROMSGROVE

BRITISH OVERSEAS AIRWAYS CORPORATION

BRITISH OAK INSURANCE

BRITISH LIMBLESS EX-SERVICEMEN'S ASSOCIATION

proper. **Motto:** By light to knowledge. **Badge:** A pellet, thereon a bezant charged as in the Crest. **Granted** 23 March 1956.

BRITISH POSTGRADUATE MEDICAL FEDERATION. Paly of eight argent and azure, a rod of Aesculapius Or; on a chief gules a Tudor rose radiated between two open books argent, edged and bound gold. **Granted** 28 August 1950.

BRITISH RAILWAYS BOARD. Vert, on a fess double-cottised argent between in chief three railway wheels of the last and in base a portcullis also argent, two barrulets wavy azure. **Crest:** On a wreath of the colours, A demi lion gules holding between the paws a railway wheel argent. **Supporters:** On either side a lion guardant gules charged on the shoulder with a railway wheel argent. **Motto:** Velociter et securiter. **Badges:** (1) Within an annulet a greyhound courant between two barrulets, all argent. (2) A railway wheel argent charged with a lion's head erased gules. (3) Issuant from coronet composed of two oak leaves, as many roses, barbed and seeded, stalked and leaved, and as many thistles, stalked and leaved, and as many leeks, set upon a rim Or, a demi lion gules holding between the paws a railway wheel argent. **Granted** 17 May 1956 to The British Transport Commission; transferred to the British Railways Board by Royal Warrant 20 February 1963; exemplified 30 April 1963.

BRITISH STANDARDS INSTITUTION. Argent, on a bend gules between a retort proper, the bowl half-filled with liquid azure, and a hank of cotton palewise of the last, a girder couped of the first. **Crest:** On a wreath of the colours, Two hands couped at the wrist holding an open book proper, bound gules edged Or. **Supporters:** On either side a lion guardant gules, that to the dexter holding with the interior forepaw a plumbline Or, and that to the sinister holding in the interior forepaw a plumbline Or, and that to the sinister holding in the interior forepaw a pair of scales gold. **Motto:** Esse quam videri. **Granted** 3 January 1951.

BRITISH TRAVEL ASSOCIATION. Per saltire, the chief azure, the flanks vert, and the base barry wavy argent and azure; in chief a representation of the Royal Crown and in base a dove volant proper. **Crest:** On a wreath of the colours, A caduceus Or supported by two swallows close proper. **Supporters:** Upon a mount vert, issuing therefrom a rose gules and a rose argent, both barbed, seeded, slipped, and leaved, between thistles, shamrocks and leeks all proper, on either side a pegasus, wings addorsed, argent, charged on the shoulder with a sun in splendour proper. **Motto:** Peace through travel. **Badge:** An antique compass rose of sixteen points upon a field argent within a rim Or, four points gules, four points azure, the remainer and the centre all Or, encircled by a wreath of laurel vert. **Granted** (pursuant to Royal Licence) 1 September 1965.

BRITISH TUGOWNERS' ASSOCIATION. Azure, on water in base barry wavy argent and azure, a ship full-rigged with sail furled proper; on a chief Or an orange tree eradicated and fructed, a thistle slipped and leaved, a rose gules barbed and seeded, and a leek, all proper. **Crest:** On a wreath of the colours, In front of an escallop a sea horse between two coils of rope, all proper. **Motto:** In parvis potestas. **Badge:** A bezant charged with a seahorse naiant gules, collared with a rope sable, on water in base barry wavy argent and azure, in chief a bar nebuly sable. **Granted** 5 June 1963.

BRITISH UNITED AID TO CHINA. See Sino-British Fellowship Trust.

BROCKENHURST GRAMMAR SCHOOL (HAMPSHIRE). Per chevron sable and gules, in chief two slips of oak fructed silver and in base a rose argent, barbed and seeded proper. **Crest:** On a wreath of the colours, In front of a hurst of trees a badger resting the dexter forepaw upon an open book proper, edged and bound gules. **Motto:** Inter silvas quaerere verum. **Granted** 20 August 1962.

BRODERERS OF THE CITY OF LONDON, WORSHIPFUL COMPANY OF.* Paly of six argent and azure, on a fesse gules between three lions passant guardant Or, armed and langued

BUDE-STRATTON

BOROUGH OF BUCKINGHAM

BROMLEY

BUCKINGHAMSHIRE COUNTY COUNCIL

BRYANSTON SCHOOL

gules, two broaches in saltire between as many quills of the third. **Crest:** On a wreath argent and gules, A hurt radiated Or and charged with a St. Esprit displayed argent, beaked and membered gules. Mantled gules, doubled argent. **Supporters:** On either side a lion rampant Or gutty de sang. **Motto:** Omnia desuper. **Granted** by William Hawley, Clarenceux King of Arms, 17 August 1558.

BROMLEY, LONDON BOROUGH OF.* Vert, a pierced cinquefoil argent within an orle of [nine] acorns Or. **Crest:** On a wreath of the colours, Two swords in saltire gules, ensigned by an escallop Or. **Supporters:** On the dexter side a dragon, and on the sinister side a horse, both argent. **Motto:** Servire populo. **Badge:** A sword argent, hilt and pomel Or, and a branch of oak fructed proper, in saltire. **Granted** 20 April 1965.

BROMSGROVE RURAL DISTRICT COUNCIL (WORCESTERSHIRE).* Vert, the head of a crosier Or and a sickle proper in saltire. **Crest:** On a wreath argent and vert, Within a representation of the four stones at Clent Hills, a beech tree proper. **Motto:** Dirigere ministrando. **Granted** 25 November 1952.

BROOKLANDS COUNTY TECHNICAL COLLEGE (WEYBRIDGE, SURREY). Per bend sable and vert, on a bend wavy argent between in chief a cogwheel winged Or and in base an open book proper, bound Or, two bendlets wavy azure; over all a fess enarched masoned and embattled proper. **Crest:** On a wreath Or and sable, Between two sprigs of oak fructed, a cubit arm proper grasping a flash of lightning argent. **Motto:** Progress with Industry. **Granted** 9 May 1969.

BRUNEL UNIVERSITY. Azure, a pair of dividers chevronwise proper, in base on a pile reversed Or a lozenge ermine; a chief enarched in the form of a bridge of masonry proper. **Crest:** On a wreath of the colours, A swan, wings addorsed, proper, about the neck a mural crown Or, resting the dexter foot on a cogwheel proper. **Granted** 12 June 1970.

BRUTON SCHOOL FOR GIRLS. See Sunny Hill School.

BRYANSTON SCHOOL (BLANDFORD, DORSET).* Azure, issuant from the base a sun Or. **Motto:** Et nova et vetera. **Granted** 28 January 1928 to the Governors of Bryanston School Incorporated.

B.S.P. [BRITISH STEEL PILING] INDUSTRIES LIMITED. Chequy Or and sable, two flaunches embattled gules, each charged with a lion's face Or. **Crest:** On a wreath Or and gules, Issuant from a castle wall embattled, portcullis raised, Or, the port gules, a mount vert, thereon a stag lodged supporting with the dexter forefoot a pair of dividers proper. **Motto:** We serve Industry. **Badge:** Within an annulet embattled, a male griffin segreant Or, tufted gules. **Granted** 10 November 1967.

BUCKINGHAM, BOROUGH OF.* Per pale sable and gules, a swan rousant, wings inverted and expanded, argent, ducally gorged Or. Recorded at the Visitation of 1566.

BUCKINGHAMSHIRE COUNTY COUNCIL.* Per pale gules and sable, a swan rousant proper, ducally gorged with chain reflexed over the back Or; on a chief of the last a roundel per chevron a cross at the point vert and argent. **Crest:** On a wreath of the colours, On a mount a beech tree eradicated proper, enfiled with a Saxon crown Or. **Supporters:** On the dexter side a stag; and on the sinister side a swan rousant, both proper. **Motto:** Vestigia nulla retrorsum. **Granted** 23 March 1948.

BUDE-STRATTON URBAN DISTRICT COUNCIL (CORNWALL).* Argent, two bars wavy azure within a bordure sable bezantée; on a chief gules a cross formy of the field between two clarions Or. **Crest:** On a wreath of the colours, In front of a sun in splendour Or and upon a sinister hand couped at the wrist and gauntletted, a falcon belled proper, collared compony argent and sable. **Granted** 11 September 1947.

BURNLEY CO. BOROUGH

BUILDING SOCIETIES' ASSOCIATION

BUNGAY

BURGESS HILL

BURNHAM ON SEA

BUDLEIGH SALTERTON URBAN DISTRICT COUNCIL (DEVON). Gules, upon water in base barry wavy argent and azure, an ancient one-masted ship with two sails furled Or, flying from the mast a pennon and from the stern a flag of St. George; on a chief also Or three billets also azure, the centre one charged with two keys in saltire, wards upwards, gold, and the other two each charged with a lion rampant also gold. **Crest:** On a wreath of the colours, In front of a beacon sable enflamed proper, a griffin segreant Or resting the dexter claw upon an escutcheon gules charged with five lozenges conjoined in bend argent and in fesse point a martlet sable. **Motto:** Beau sejour. **Granted** 15 December 1959.

BUILDERS, INSTITUTE OF. Quarterly indented gules and azure, in the first quarter a triple towered castle, in the second quarter a pair of compasses extended points downwards, in the third quarter a plummet, and in the fourth quarter a hammer-head palewise, all Or; on a chief pean a brush, the handle upwards, also Or between two trowels, points upwards, argent, the handles gold. **Crest:** On a wreath of the colours, A lion passant guardant Or resting the dexter fore paw on a terrestrial globe proper. **Motto:** Diligently and faithfully. **Granted** 28 November 1934.

BUILDING SOCIETIES' ASSOCIATION.* Per chevron gules and azure, a chevronel argent between in chief two sprigs of thrift Or and in base a castle of three towers, the portcullis raised, gold. **Crest:** On a wreath of the colours, Issuant from a wreath of thrift proper a demi griffin Or, grasping in the dexter claw a key erect, wards upwards and outwards gules. **Supporters:** On either side a talbot pean charged on the shoulder with a sword erect gules surmounted of a portcullis pendant from the neck by the chains Or. **Motto:** Unitate fortior. **Granted** 30 August 1956.

BUILDING SURVEYORS' INSTITUTE. Per pale azure and argent, on a fesse counterchanged between in dexter chief and base an open book proper, garnished Or, and in sinister chief and base a pair of compasses of the first, a like pair of compasses and book. **Crest:** On a wreath of the colours, A surveyor's level and tripod Or. **Motto:** Via media exempli gratia. **Granted** 3 December 1954, to the Society of Building Surveyors Limited.

BUILDING TRADES EMPLOYERS, see National Federation of.

BUNGAY URBAN DISTRICT COUNCIL (EAST SUFFOLK).* Barry wavy of six vert and argent, a Norfolk wherry in full sail proper, pennon flying gules; a chief Or, thereon a port between two towers sable, the port ensigned by an escutcheon gold charged with a cross also gules. **Crest:** On a wreath of the colours, A representation of the Black Dog of Bungay courant proper upon a ray of lightning fessewise gules. **Motto:** Moribus antiquis pareamus. **Granted** 6 July 1953.

BURGESS HILL URBAN DISTRICT COUNCIL (EAST SUSSEX).* Per fesse azure and gules masoned argent, in chief a two-handled vase Or. **Crest:** On a wreath argent and gules, Upon a hillock vert charged with the wheel of a potter's wheel, a martlet Or. **Motto:** Consilio et prudentia. **Granted** 14 August 1953.

BURNHAM ON SEA URBAN DISTRICT COUNCIL (SOMERSET).* Per chevron Or and argent, on a chevron enarched gules three bulls' heads caboshed also argent, in base as many bars wavy azure; a canton per fesse gules and sable, in chief a demi sun issuant gold. **Crest:** On a wreath of the colours, A representation of the old Burnham lighthouse proper. Mantled gules, doubled Or. **Motto:** Lumen monstro pro salute. **Granted** 1 February 1961.

BURNLEY, COUNTY BOROUGH OF (LANCASHIRE).* Or, a chevron engrailed gules between in chief two fusils and in base a lion rampant sable; a chief wavy of the last, thereon a dexter hand erect couped at the wrist argent between two bees volant of the first. **Crest:** On a wreath of the colours, On a mount vert a stork argent, beaked and membered gules, holding in the dexter foot a stone and in the beak a cotton-flower slipped, both proper. **Motto:** Pretiumque et causa laboris. **Granted** 17 May 1862.

BURNLEY R. D. C.

BURTON UPON TRENT

BURY ST. EDMUNDS

BURY

BUXTON

BURNLEY BUILDING SOCIETY. Argent, a chevron gules between three bees volant proper; on a chief azure a dexter hand appaumé couped Or between two thrift plants, leaved and flowered, also proper. **Crest:** On a wreath of the colours, In front of a perch, thereon a hawk proper, beaked, membered and belled Or, five roses gules, barbed and seeded also proper. **Motto:** By service we progress. **Granted** 15 June 1948.

BURNLEY RURAL DISTRICT COUNCIL (LANCASHIRE).* Per chevron Or and vert, in chief two roses gules, barbed and seeded proper, and in base a bugle horn stringed gold; on a chief wavy sable a sprig of cotton also proper between two pairs of wheat-ears each in saltire and stalked, leaved and slipped of the first. **Crest:** On a wreath of the colours, Issuant from reeds proper, a demi lion purpure, armed and langued vert, gorged with a collar argent charged with three mullets sable and holding in the dexter paw a shuttle palewise also sable, tipped and threaded gold. **Motto:** Bono ruris consulere. **Granted** 8 February 1955.

BURTON UPON TRENT, COUNTY BOROUGH OF (STAFFORDSHIRE).* Barry wavy of six argent and azure; on a chief gules an eagle displayed of the first between two fleurs-de-lis Or. **Crest:** Out of a mural crown Or, a dexter hand proper grasping a lozenge azure charged with a saltire argent. **Motto:** Honor alit artes. **Granted** 26 April 1928.

BURTON UPON TRENT GRAMMAR SCHOOL. Or, on a cross engrailed azure five mullets argent, in the first quarter a mitre of the second. **Motto:** Deus nobiscum. **Granted** 7 October 1955.

BURY, COUNTY BOROUGH OF (LANCASHIRE).* Quarterly argent and azure, a cross party and fretty counterchanged between an anvil sable in the first quarter, a fleece Or in the second, two shuttles in saltire threads pendent proper in the third, and three culms of the papyrus plant issuing from a mount also proper in the fourth. **Crest:** On a wreath of the colours, Upon a mount a bee volant between two flowers of the cotton-tree slipped, all proper. **Motto:** Vincit omnia industria. **Granted** 28 February 1877.

BURY ST. EDMUNDS, BOROUGH OF (WEST SUFFOLK).* Azure, three open crowns Or, each transfixed with two arrows in saltire [points downward] argent. **Crest:** On a wreath of the colours A wolf sejant proper holding a king's head couped at the neck of the last, crowned Or. Mantled gules, doubled argent. **Motto:** Sacrarium regis, cunabula legis. **Granted** 29 November 1606 by William Camden, Clarenceux King of Arms.

BUSINESS AGENTS, INSTITUTE OF, LIMITED. Azure, a caduceus in pale between in fess two purses and surmounted in base by a castle of three towers, all Or. **Crest:** On a wreath of the colours, A demi lynx supporting between the paws a rolled title deed bound with a riband proper, pendent therefrom a key, wards downward and outward, Or. **Motto:** In beneficium amborum. **Granted** 30 July 1968.

BUTCHERS OF THE CITY OF LONDON, WORSHIPFUL COMPANY OF.* Azure, two poleaxes in saltire Or, blades inwards, between two bulls' heads couped in fesse argent; on a chief of the last a boar's head couped gules, tusked of the second, langued of the first, between two bunches of knee-holly vert banded gold. **Crest:** On a wreath of the colours, A bull statant, wings addorsed, Or, the wings lined argent, the head, forequarters, hoofs and tuft of the tail of the first, the hindquarters of the second, armed gules, about the head a nimbus gold. Mantled gules, doubled argent. **Supporters:** On either side a bull with wings addorsed, the head, forequarters, wings, hoofs and tuft of the tail Or, the hindquarters argent, armed gules, about the head a nimbus of the first. **Motto:** Omnia subiecisti sub pedibus, oves et boves. Arms and Crest granted 7 February 1541 by Thomas Hawley, Clarenceux King of Arms; Supporters granted 28 June 1922.(*Illn. on p.* 79).

BUXTON, BOROUGH OF (DERBYSHIRE).* Vert, the rod of Aesculapius Or within an orle of eight fountains. **Crest:** On a wreath of the colours, Upon a rock a buck at gaze proper. **Motto:** Benedicite fontes Domino. **Granted** 31 January 1917.

CAERNARVON

CAERNARVONSHIRE

C

** Denotes Illustration*

CAERNARVON, ROYAL BOROUGH OF.* Gules, a lion passant guardant Or between three plumes, each of three ostrich feathers, argent. **Crest:** On a wreath of the colours, An eagle displayed Or charged on the breast with a plume as in the Arms. **Supporters:** On the dexter side a dragon gules; and on the sinister side an eagle, wings addorsed, Or; each supporting an ostrich feather argent. **Motto:** Brenhinol Brig Gwynedd. **Badge:** In front of a representation of the Eagle Tower of Caernarvon Castle proper, a plume as in the Arms, and on the battlements of the turrets a lion passant guardant gules. **Granted** 1 January 1965.

CAERNARVONSHIRE COUNTY COUNCIL.* Quarterly Or and gules, four lions passant guardant counterchanged; a fesse vert charged with three eagles displayed of the first. **Crest:** On a wreath Or and vert, On a mount vert a port between two towers Or, issuant therefrom a plume of three ostrich feathers argent. **Supporters:** On either side a sea dragon per fesse gules and proper. **Motto:** Cadernid Gwynedd. **Granted** 21 July 1949.

CAERWYS PARISH COUNCIL (FLINTSHIRE). Or, a dragon rampant and on a chief gules a representation of the ash tree called Caerwys Cross proper. **Crest:** On a wreath of the colours, Out of an ancient crown Or, a representation of the Caerwys Eisteddfod harp proper. **Motto:** Tannau arian geiriau arian. **Granted** 5 September 1967.

CAISTOR RURAL DISTRICT COUNCIL (LINCOLNSHIRE—PARTS OF LINDSEY). Vert, a gadwhip and shepherd's crook in saltire between four garbs Or. **Crest:** On a wreath of the colours, Issuant from the battlements of a tower proper, the head of a Roman legionary standard Or. **Motto:** Castrum ruri dat consilium. **Granted** 15 December 1959.

CALNE, BOROUGH OF (WILTSHIRE).* Sable, a tower towered and domed argent between two ostrich feathers of the last, a like feather in the portway, each feather piercing an escrol Or. **Crest:** A mural crown ensigned by a mitre Or, jewelled proper, in front of two archiepiscopal staves in saltire also proper. **Supporters:** On either side a boar gules, armed and crined Or, gorged with a garland of teazels argent. **Motto:** Faith, Work, Service. Arms recorded at the Visitation of 1565. Crest and Supporters granted 10 November 1950.

CALNE AND CHIPPENHAM RURAL DISTRICT COUNCIL (WILTSHIRE). Per fess wavy gules and barry wavy of four argent and vert, issuant in base from a block of Bath stone proper ensigned by a Saxon crown Or, a tree of three branches proper; over all a mitre in fess point issuant therefrom two crosiers in pile Or. **Crest:** Issuant from a rural crown Or, between two sickles, the blades points inward, argent, the hafts gules banded Or, a double headed eagle displayed sable charged on the breast with a magnetic needle erect ensigned by an estoile Or. **Motto:** Virtute in factis. **Granted** 26 November 1968.

CAMBRIDGE, CITY OF.* Gules, a bridge of one arch surmounted by three towers Or, in chief a fleur-de-lys gold between two roses argent, the base barry wavy of the last and azure, thereon three ships each with one mast and yardarm, the sail furled also sable. **Crest:** On a wreath Or and gules, Upon a mount vert a bridge in the form of a castle with two ports and three domed towers,

CALNE

CAMBRIDGE CITY

and between the towers two turrets also domed, argent. **Supporters:** On either side a sea horse, the upper part gules, the nether part proper, finned Or. **Granted** 7 June 1575 by Robert Cooke, Clarenceux King of Arms, and recorded in the Visitation of 1684.

CAMBRIDGE, UNIVERSITY OF.* Gules, on a cross ermine between four lions passant guardant Or, a Bible lying fesseways of the field, clasped and garnished of the third, the clasps in base. **Motto:** Hinc lucem et pocula sacra. **Granted** 9 June 1573 by Robert Cooke, Clarenceux King of Arms, and recorded at the Visitation of 1575.

CAMBRIDGE, READERS IN THE UNIVERSITY OF. Reader of "Devinity": Gules, on a cross ermine between four doves argent, a book of the first, the leaves Or charged in the midst with the Greek letter Theta sable. **Crest:** On a wreath silver and gules, a dove volant argent with an olive branch vert in his beak. Mantled gules, doubled argent. Reader of "Greke": Per chevron argent and sable, in chief the two Greek letters Alpha and Omega of the second and in base a cicado or grasshopper of the first; on a chief gules a lion passant guardant Or charged on the side with the letter G sable. **Crest:** On a wreath of the colours, An owl argent, legs, beak and ears Or. Mantled gules, doubled argent. Reader of Hebrew: Argent, the Hebrew letter Tau sable; on a chief gules a lion passant guardant Or charged on the side with the letter H sable. **Crest:** On a wreath of the colours a turtle dove azure. Mantled gules, doubled argent. Reader of "Lawe": Purpure, a cross moline Or; on a chief gules a lion passant guardant of the second charged on the side with the letter L sable. **Crest:** On a wreath of the colours, a bee volant Or. Mantled gules, doubled argent. Reader of "Phisicke": Azure, a fesse ermines between three lozenges Or; on a chief gules a lion passant guardant of the third charged on the side with the letter M sable. **Crest:** On a wreath Or and azure, A quinquangle silver called "Simbolum sanitatis". Mantled gules, doubled argent. All granted by Robert Cooke, Clarenceux King of Arms, 13 November 1590.

CAMBRIDGESHIRE AND ISLE OF ELY COUNTY COUNCIL.* Or, a double tressure flory counterflory gules, over all on a bend wavy azure three [open] crowns Or; the shield ensigned with a mural crown Or. **Supporters:** On either side a Great Bustard proper, the exterior leg resting on a closed book gules, garnished Or. **Motto:** Sapientes simus. **Badge:** Within an annulet, issuant therefrom four fleurs-de-lys in cross, an open crown Or. **Granted** 1 September 1965.

CAMDEN, LONDON BOROUGH OF.* Argent, on a cross gules a mitre Or; a chief sable, thereon three escallops argent. **Crest:** On a wreath of the colours, Issuant from a mural crown argent, a demi elephant sable, armed Or, about the neck a wreath of holly fructed proper. **Supporters:** On the dexter side a lion and on the sinister side a griffin Or, each gorged with a collar, the dexter argent charged with three mullets sable, the sinister gules charged with three mullets Or, and pendent from the collar of each a fountain. **Motto:** Non sibi sed toti. **Badge:** On a roundel tierced in pairle reversed, gules, azure and sable, fimbriated Or, an elephant's head erased argent, armed Or. **Granted** 10 September 1965.

CAMPBELL COLLEGE (BELFAST).* Gyronny of eight Or and sable, an open book proper, bound gules, edged and clasped gold; on a chief also gules a lion passant guardant of the first supporting with the dexter forepaw an ancient Irish bell argent. **Crest:** On a wreath argent and sable, In front of an Irish bell tower Or, a boar passant sable, armed and langued gold, charged on the body with a trefoil slipped argent. **Motto:** Ne obliviscaris. **Badge:** A plate charged with a boar's head erased sable, armed Or. **Granted** 30 September 1955.

CAMPION HALL, TRUSTEES FOR ROMAN CATHOLIC PURPOSES FOR (OXFORD UNIVERSITY)*. Argent, on a cross sable a plate charged with a wolf's head erased of the second, between in pale two billets of the field, that in chief charged with a cinquefoil and that in base with a saltire gules, and in fess as many plates each charged with a campion flower leaved and slipped proper; on a chief also of the second two branches of palm in saltire enfiled with a celestial crown Or. **Granted** 4 November 1935.

CAMPBELL COLLEGE

CAMBRIDGESHIRE AND ISLE OF ELY

CAMPION HALL

CAMDEN

CAMBRIDGE UNIVERSITY

THE CAMPION SCHOOL (HORNCHURCH, ESSEX). Sanguine, a campion flower and in chief the letters IHS ensigned by a cross with three passion nails in pile below the letters, being the device of the Society of Jesus, between a dexter and a sinister canton Or, each charged with a torch enflamed proper. **Crrst:** On a wreath of the colours, A dove displayed argent, beaked and legged Or, on each wing a campion flower sanguine, the head ensigned by a tongue of flame proper. **Motto:** Auctore Deo. **Granted** 1 June 1967.

CANFORD SCHOOL (WIMBORNE, DORSET).* Barry wavy of six azure and argent, an oak tree eradicated and fructed proper; on a chief of the second an open book of the third. **Motto:** Nisi Dominus frustra. **Granted** 8 September 1924.

CANNOCK RURAL DISTRICT COUNCIL (STAFFORDSHIRE).* Vert, on a pile argent enfiled in base through a Stafford knot Or a stag's head caboshed, between the antlers a bugle horn sable garnished and stringed, the burrs environed of a wreath of laurel leaves Or. **Crest:** Out of a coronet composed of four ears of wheat and as many acorns leaved set alternately upon a rim Or and in front of the head of an oak tree proper fructed Or, a demi archer bearded, in armour, proper, vested from his waist paly argent and gules, slung from the shoulder and at the waist a quiver of arrows Or, and in the hands a bow and arrow drawn to the head Or. Mantled vert, doubled argent. **Motto:** Nec temere nec timide. **Granted** 5 March 1964.

CANNOCK URBAN DISTRICT COUNCIL (STAFFORDSHIRE). Barry of eight vert and sable, a stag's head caboshed between in chief an ancient crown of fleurs-de-lis Or and in base a cross potent quadrate argent. **Crest:** Out of a circlet vert, issuant from flames an oak tree fructed proper, the trunk enfiled with a Stafford knot Or. **Motto:** Labor in venatu. **Granted** 20 February 1951.

CANTERBURY, ARCHBISHOPRIC OF.* Azure, an archiepiscopal staff in pale Or surmounted of a pall argent fringed of the second and charged with four crosses patée fitchée sable. Recorded in the College of Arms.

CANTERBURY, DEAN AND CHAPTER OF THE CATHEDRAL CHURCH OF CHRIST.* Azure, on a cross argent the letters I/X sable. Recorded at the Visitation of 1619.

CANTERBURY, CITY OF (KENT).* Argent, three Cornish choughs proper; on a chief gules a lion passant guardant Or. **Motto:** Ave mater Angliae. Recorded at the Visitation of 1619.

CARDIFF, CITY AND COUNTY BOROUGH OF (GLAMORGAN).* Argent, on a mount vert a dragon rampant gules supporting in front of a leek issuing from the mount a flag staff erect proper, flying therefrom to the sinister a banner of the third charged with three chevronels of the first. **Crest:** A Tudor rose on three ostrich feathers argent issuing out of a mural crown proper. [Mantled gules, doubled argent.] **Supporters:** On the dexter side a goat and on the sinister side a sea horse, both proper; as an Honourable Augmentation, Her Majesty's Royal Badge for Wales, videlicet, within a circular riband argent fimbriated Or bearing the motto Y DDRAIG GOCH DDYRY CYCHWYN in letters vert and ensigned with a representation of the Crown proper an escutcheon per fess argent and vert and thereon a Red dragon passant, pendent by a golden chain from the neck of each supporter. **Mottoes:** (above the crest) Deffro mae'n ddydd; (below the shield) Y ddraig goch ddyry cychwyn. Arms granted 26 August 1906; Crest granted by Royal Warrant 6 October 1906; exemplified 15 February 1907; Supporters granted 25 February 1907; Supporters augmented by Royal Warrant 19 October 1956; exemplified 23 October 1956.

CARDIFF, UNIVERSITY COLLEGE. See South Wales and Monmouthshire, University College of.

CARDIGANSHIRE COUNTY COUNCIL.* Quarterly per pale indented, first sable a lion rampant reguardant Or, second barry wavy of six argent and azure a herring haurient proper,

CANFORD SCHOOL

CANTERBURY

CANNOCK R. D. C.

CANTERBURY, DEAN AND CHAPTER

CANTERBURY ARCHBISHOPRIC

third azure a garb Or banded gules, and fourth sable a chevron between three roses argent barbed and seeded proper; the shield ensigned with a mural crown gold. **Motto:** Golud Gwlad Rhyddid. **Granted** 21 October 1957.

THE CARDINAL WISEMAN SCHOOL (COVENTRY). Azure, issuing from the base the head of an archiepiscopal staff Or, set therein a cartouche scrolled and garnished gold charged with the Arms Sable a chevron ermine between three cronels argent. **Crest:** On a wreath argent and sable, Two dexter cubit arms erect, vested gules, the hands proper supporting a cardinal's hat, tasselled also proper. **Motto:** Omnia pro Christo. **Granted** 20 March 1959.

CARLISLE, BISHOPRIC OF.* Argent, on a cross sable a mitre Or. Recorded in the College of Arms.

CARLISLE, CITY AND COUNTY BOROUGH OF (CUMBERLAND).* Or, on a cross patée between four roses gules, a rose of the field barbed and seeded proper; the shield ensigned by a mural crown having three towers Or and lined gules, the centre tower pierced by a gateway gules. **Supporters:** Upon a mount vert on either side a wyvern gules, armed and langued azure, the wings semée of roses Or barbed vert. **Motto:** Be just and fear not. Shield allowed and mural crown [described as a Crest] and supporters granted 7 July 1924.

CARMARTHEN, BOROUGH OF.* Gules, a castle triple-towered between two ostrich feathers erect in fesse argent, on each of the outer towers a Cornish chough proper respecting the centre tower, and in base a lion passant reguardant Or. **Crest:** On a wreath of the colours A fisherman carrying a coracle proper. **Motto:** Rhyddid hedd a llwyddiant. **Granted** 9 April 1936.

CARMARTHEN RURAL DISTRICT COUNCIL.* Vert, on a pale argent between two garbs Or, a mullet of five points between four mullets of six points gules between two pallets sable; a chief per pale embattled Or and gules, thereon two lions passant guardant counterchanged. **Motto:** Oni heuir ni fedr. **Granted** 21 June 1951.

CARMARTHENSHIRE COUNTY COUNCIL.* Quarterly indented Or and gules, in the first and fourth quarters a dragon rampant and in the second and third quarters a lion rampant, all counterchanged. **Crest:** On a wreath of the colours, A dragon passant gules gorged with a collar flory counterflory and resting the dexter claw on a harp Or. **Motto:** Rhyddid gwerin ffyniant gwlad. **Granted** 28 August 1935.

CARMEL COLLEGE, LIMITED (WALLINGFORD).* Per fesse azure and argent, in chief a seven-branched candlestick between, dexter, a stone tablet and, sinister, an open book, all Or and in base seven scrolls of the Law gules. **Motto:** בכל דרכיך דרעהו . Granted 10 June 1963.

CARMEN OF THE CITY OF LONDON, WORSHIPFUL COMPANY OF.* Or, a sword erect, point upwards, in pale proper, pommel and hilt gules, between two cart wheels in fesse of the last. **Crest:** On a wreath of the colours, A demi cart horse argent, collared sable, resting the sinister hoof on a wheel as in the Arms. **Supporters:** On either side a dray horse argent, harnessed and bridled proper, gorged with a wreath of roses gules, barbed, seeded and leaved also proper. **Motto:** Scite, cito, certe. Arms and Crest granted 28 February 1929; **Supporters** granted 7 April 1938.

CARPENTERS OF THE CITY OF LONDON, WORSHIPFUL COMPANY OF.* Argent, a chevron engrailed between three pairs of compasses sable. **Motto:** Honour God. **Granted:** 24 November 1466 by William Hawkeslowe, Clarenceux King of Arms. (*Illustration on page* 118).

CARRICKFERGUS, BOROUGH OF (CO. ANTRIM). Gules, on water in base barry wavy a castle with three towers proper, in chief two doves respectant argent. **Crest:** On a wreath of the colours, A lymphad flagged azure, the sail Or charged with a billet also azure thereon a lion ram-

CARDIFF

CARDIGANSHIRE

CARLISLE, BISHOPRIC

CARLISLE

pant gold. **Supporters:** On the dexter side an Irish Kerne (warrior) of the sixteenth century vested in a saffron tunic lined azure, with trews and brogues of the last, supporting with the exterior hand a halbert proper, and on the sinister side a knight in chain mail, his head enclosed in a war-helm proper, vested in a surcoat azure. **Motto:** Gloria prisca novatur. **Granted** 12 March 1953.

CASTERTON SCHOOL (KIRKBY LONSDALE).* Barry wavy argent and azure, a cross gules; on a chief argent between two falcons rising sable, beaked, legged and collared Or, the dexter contournée, a pale azure charged with a crescent Or, issuant therefrom flames proper. **Motto:** Cor unum, via una. **Granted** 1 August 1963.

CASTLE DONNINGTON RURAL DISTRICT COUNCIL (LEICESTERSHIRE).* Azure, on a base barry wavy of four azure and argent, a granite rock proper, thereon a castle of three towers silver, that in the centre charged with a maunch sable, in chief two mitres Or. **Crest:** Issuant from a coronet composed of four ears of wheat and as many acorns leaved set alternately upon a rim Or, a demi lion guardant winged Or charged on the shoulder with a cinquefoil pierced ermine and holding in the paws a wagon-wheel proper. Mantled gules, doubled argent. **Motto:** Vires contexamus arti. **Granted** 20 November 1962.

CASTLE WARD RURAL DISTRICT COUNCIL (NORTHUMBERLAND).* Sable, a pale Or, in dexter chief a castle triple-towered, the portcullis raised, argent. **Crest:** On a wreath of the colours, A lion passant guardant Or, charged on the shoulder with an estoile, the dexter forepaw gauntletted gules and grasping a sword in bend sinister argent, hilt and pommel gold. **Motto:** Onward. **Granted** 1 November 1962.

CASTLEFORD, BOROUGH OF (YORKSHIRE—WEST RIDING).* Gules, on water barry wavy in base proper a triple-towered castle Or, in chief two roses argent barbed and seeded proper. **Crest:** On a wreath of the colours, A demi eagle Or gorged with a collar gules, pendent therefrom a miner's lamp proper, and charged on each wing with a Lacy knot sable. **Motto:** Audacter et sincere. **Granted** 3 March 1952 to the Castleford Urban District Council.

CASTLEREAGH RURAL DISTRICT COUNCIL (CO. DOWN).* Quarterly argent and Or, in the first quarter a dexter hand appaumy gules, in the second and third a cogwheel azure, and in the fourth an eagle displayed gules; on a chief vert a rural crown Or. **Crest:** On a wreath of the colours Issuant from the battlements of a tower argent, masoned sable, a demi Irish Elk proper supporting between the legs a ceremonial mace Or. **Motto:** The same to all men. **Granted** 5 October 1966.

CENTRAL ELECTRICITY GENERATING BOARD.* Paly gules and Or two bars dancetty, the upper per pale sable and argent, the lower per pale argent and sable. **Crest:** On a wreath Or, gules and sable A male griffin segreant gules, armed, langued and rayed Or, behind the head a sun in splendour gold. **Supporters:** On the dexter side a lion guardant Or, winged gules, and on the sinister side a dragon gules, winged Or. **Motto:** Power in trust. **Badge:** A male griffin segreant gules, armed, langued and rayed Or, behind the head a sun in splendour gold. **Granted** 6 November 1958.

CENTRAL FLYING SCHOOL, ROYAL AIR FORCE. Sable, on a fesse wavy argent between in chief two wings conjoined and inverted Or and in base an anchor of the third and a sword proper, pommel and hilt gold, in saltire, two bars wavy azure. **Crest:** On a wreath of the colours, Upon the battlements of a tower proper, a pelican gules rising from her nest, gorged with a Naval crown. **Granted** 9 December 1931.

CERTIFIED AND CORPORATE ACCOUNTANTS, ASSOCIATION OF. Gules bezantée, on a pile ermine a cadaceus Or. **Crest:** On a wreath of the colours, An open book proper with leaves bezantée. **Motto:** Meritum, opportunitas, officium. **Granted** 23 January 1934 to the London Association of Certified Accountants Limited.

WORSHIPFUL COMPANY OF CARMEN

CARMARTHEN R. D. C.

CARMEL COLLEGE

CARMARTHEN C. C.

CARMARTHEN BOROUGH

CHADDERTON URBAN DISTRICT COUNCIL (LANCASHIRE).* Argent, between two bendlets engrailed a mullet sable, pierced of the field, between two roses gules, barbed and seeded proper, all between as many griffins segreant also gules, armed and langued azure. **Crest:** On a wreath argent and gules, Upon an anvil proper an eagle, wings elevated and addorsed, azure resting the dexter claw on a shuttle Or. **Motto:** Labor omnia vincit. **Granted** 9 September 1955.

CHAMBER OF SHIPPING OF THE UNITED KINGDOM. Per fess wavy gules and barry wavy of eight argent and azure, an ancient ship of three masts in full sail Or. **Crest:** Out of a Naval crown Or, a dexter arm, the hand grasping a trident proper. **Supporters:** On either side a sea lion reguardant vert gorged with a Naval crown. **Motto:** Salus patriae salis dominatio. **Badge:** A stockless anchor attached to and encircled by its chain cable argent. **Granted** 31 January 1921.

CHAPEL EN LE FRITH RURAL DISTRICT COUNCIL (DERBYSHIRE). Vert, a stag's head caboshed, between the attires a cross formy Or; a chief dancettée of the last, over all in chief a lion passant guardant gules. **Crest:** Out of a circlet vert charged with four gouttes d'eau, the battlements of a tower, issuant therefrom a demi lion argent, collared vairy Or and gules and holding in the paws an escutcheon per pale argent and azure charged with a rose gules barbed and seeded proper. **Motto:** Cave et spera. **Granted** 8 April 1954.

CHAPEL ROYAL OF ST. PETER AD VINCULA IN HER MAJESTY'S TOWER OF LONDON, CHORAL FOUNDATION OF THE. Argent, in front of two keys in saltire, the bows conjoined by a chain and manacles gules, a clarion azure; on a chief embattled per pale gules and azure a lion passant guardant Or. **Crest:** On a wreath of the colours, In front of a representation of the White Tower of London between two trees, a house martin, wings closing, proper. **Motto:** Jubilate. **Badge:** A clarion Or ensigned by a representation of the White Tower of London proper. **Granted** 25 March 1969.

CHARING CROSS HOSPITAL MEDICAL SCHOOL.* Ermine, a Maltese cross gules, thereon on a plate fimbriated Or between four fleurs de lys in cross of the last a rod of Aesculapius sable; on a chief gules between two bezants an open book argent, edged and clasps gold, inscribed with the words IN HOC SIGNO VINCES sable. **Granted** 4 September 1934.

CHARTERED ACCOUNTANTS OF ENGLAND AND WALES, INSTITUTE OF. Argent, on a mount in base, in front of a rudder in bend sinister a female figure proper representing "Economy" habited gules, mantled azure, about the temples a wreath of olive, in the dexter hand a pair of compasses, all proper; a chief of the second, thereon a balance suspended Or. **Motto:** Recte numerare. **Granted** 22 January 1881.

CHARTERED BANK OF INDIA, AUSTRALASIA AND CHINA. Quarterly indented gules and vert, in the first quarter a representation of Britannia, in the second in front of a palm tree an elephant statant, in the third a fleece, and in the fourth a Chinese junk in full sail Or. **Crest:** On a wreath of the colours, Upon a Doric column couped proper a terrestrial globe Or. **Supporters:** On the dexter a lion and on the sinister a griffin proper, each charged on the shoulder with and resting the hind paw upon a bezant. **Motto:** Partes per eoas (original motto: Per mundum orientalem). **Badge:** In front of a bezant a key in bend proper. **Granted** 29 December 1950.

CHARTERED INSURANCE INSTITUTE. Azure, between two chains fessewise three anchors argent, in chief a salamander in flames and in base a garb Or. **Crest:** Out of a Saxon crown Or, an arm embowed in armour proper, the hand also proper grasping by the blade a sword in bend sinister, point downwards, gules. **Supporters:** On the dexter side a sea unicorn argent, the foreparts gules, armed, bearded and finned Or, and on the sinister side a sea lion also argent, the foreparts also gules, finned gold; each holding by the exterior leg a book, the spine turned outwards from the

CASTERTON SCHOOL

CASTLEFORD

CASTLE DONNINGTON

CASTLEREAGH

CASTLE WARD

breast, azure, edged, garnished and with pendent marker also gold. **Motto:** Consilium scientia. Arms granted 25 September 1933; Crest and Supporters granted 3 June 1957.

CHARTERED SHIPBROKERS, INSTITUTE OF. Azure, three ancient ships under sail fessewise in bend Or between four bendlets wavy argent. **Crest:** On a wreath of the colours, In front of two anchors in saltire Or surmounted by a ship's wheel, a mast head with a mast head light, all proper. **Motto:** Our word our bond. **Granted** 10 March 1931.

CHARTERED SURVEYORS, ROYAL INSTITUTION OF.* Azure, within a surveyor's chain in orle and issuant from the chief the capital of an Ionic column argent; on a chief of the last a lion passant guardant of the field. **Crest:** On a wreath of the colours, In front of a Terrestrial Globe proper a pair of dividers Or. **Supporters:** On either side a lion Or supporting a surveyor's ranging rod and resting the interior hind paw upon a log of wood proper. **Motto:** Est modus in rebus. **Badge:** A lion rampant contournée crowned with an ancient crown argent and supporting between the fore paws a ranging rod azure and argent. Arms, Crest and Supporters granted 21 November 1947; Badge granted 1 December 1967.

CHATHAM, BOROUGH OF (KENT).* Argent, a fesse chequy gules and Or between in chief two ancient ships with three masts and sails proper, colours flying of the second, and in base a sword of the fourth, pommel and hilt of the third, surmounted by a trident in saltire and entwined with a wreath of laurel proper. **Crest:** Out of a Naval crown Or, a trident erect enfiled with a wreath of laurel proper. **Motto:** Loyal and true. **Granted** 1 August 1891.

CHEADLE AND GATLEY URBAN DISTRICT COUNCIL (CHESHIRE). Sable, on a fesse dancetty of two points argent another gules between in chief two bulls' heads caboshed also argent and in base an eagle displayed ermine; on a chief azure a garb between two lozenges Or. **Crest:** Out of a mural crown gules, an oak tree proper fructed of five acorns Or, pendent from the upper branches by a riband gules an escutcheon argent charged with a fleur de lys azure. **Granted** 20 December 1955.

CHELMSFORD, BISHOPRIC OF.* Or, on a saltire gules a pastoral staff of the first and a sword argent, pomel and hilt also of the first. **Granted** 12 August 1949. [Illustrated in the Patent as shown].

CHELMSFORD, BOROUGH OF (ESSEX).* Argent, a bridge of three arches proper, in chief two croziers in saltire between as many lions rampant azure, in base two bars wavy of the last. **Crest:** On a wreath argent and azure, Upon a rock proper a crozier in pale Or surmounted by two swords in saltire, points upwards, proper, pommels and hilts Or, interlaced by a wreath of oak vert. **Motto:** Many minds, one heart. **Granted** 6 February 1889.

CHELMSFORD RURAL DISTRICT COUNCIL (ESSEX).* Argent, three bars azure; on a chief indented gules two seaxes in saltire, points upwards, between as many mullets of the field. **Crest:** On a wreath argent and gules, Set upon a garb Or a mullet gules. **Granted** 20 December 1954.

CHELSEA COLLEGE OF PHYSICAL EDUCATION (EASTBOURNE). Azure, a winged bull statant argent, horned and unguled and resting its dexter forefoot on a sphere Or; on a chief also Or between two sea horses vert, the dexter legs raised, a pale ermine, thereon a cross throughout gules surmounted of an open book proper, edged gold. **Motto:** Mens sana in corpore sano. **Granted** 5 June 1958 to Eastbourne Corporation for the use of the College.

CHELSEA POLYTECHNIC.* Azure, a pale between two anchors Or, in the centre chief point an antique crown of the field. **Crest:** On a wreath of the colours, In front of an open book proper, garnished Or, an ancient lamp inflamed gold. **Granted** 4 November 1948.

CHATHAM

CHARTERED SURVEYORS

CENTRAL ELECTRICITY GENERATING BOARD

CHADDERTON

CHELTENHAM, BOROUGH OF (GLOUCESTERSHIRE).* Or, a chevron engrailed gules between two pigeons in chief and an oak tree eradicated in base proper; on a chief azure a cross flory argent between two open books also proper, binding and clasps of the first. **Crest:** On a wreath of the colours, Upon a mount between two branches of oak a fountain, thereon a pigeon, all proper. **Motto:** Salubritas et eruditio. **Granted** 26 February 1877.

CHELTENHAM COLLEGE. Per bend gules and sable, on a bend Or between in chief two swords in saltire proper, pommels and hilts of the second, and in base a fasces palewise of the last, a mullet of the first between two fleurs de lys of the second. **Crest:** On a wreath Or and sable, A boar's head erased sable transfixed by a cross flory fitchy argent. **Supporters:** On either side a wolf argent supporting between the forelegs a staff Or, flying therefrom a banner azure charged with two keys in saltire Or. **Motto:** Labor omnia vincit. Arms granted 7 August 1896; Crest and Supporters granted 7 May 1965.

CHELTENHAM LADIES' COLLEGE.* Sable, on a chevron argent between in chief two martlets of the second and in base a daisy slipped and leaved proper, three mullets of the field. **Motto:** Coelesti luce crescat. **Granted** 30 January 1931.

CHEMICAL ENGINEERS, INSTITUTION OF. Argent, a bend per bend indented azure and gules between in chief a millrind sable and in base a salamander sable in flames proper. **Crest:** On a wreath of the colours, Issuant from waves of the sea proper a dolphin erect vert, finned and bearded gules, between two long S's, being the mathematical signs of an integral, the dexter sign contournée Or. **Supporters:** On the dexter side a figure representing Pallas Athene proper, and on the sinister side a figure representing Hephaestus proper. **Motto:** Firidendo fingere disco. **Granted** 15 October 1963.

CHEMISTRY, ROYAL INSTITUTE OF. Per pale gules and azure, within a voided hexagon Or charged with the alchemical symbols for silver, copper, tin, lead, iron and mercury, sable a sun in splendour gold. **Crest:** On the dexter side a sea-horse (Hippocampus) azure, guttee d'Or finned gold, and on the sinister side a salamander gules in flames Or. **Motto:** Ratio atque usus. **Granted** 12 September 1958.

CHERTSEY URBAN DISTRICT COUNCIL (SURREY).* Vert, a key Or and a sword proper, hilt and pomel Or, wards and point upward, in saltire enfiled through a mural crown argent; a chief wavy barry wavy argent and azure. **Crest:** On a wreath of the colours, In front of a representation of a church proper a pike fessewise Or. **Motto:** Servire contendimus. **Granted** 20 December 1962.

CHESHAM URBAN DISTRICT COUNCIL (BUCKINGHAMSHIRE).* Per fesse Or and gules, a fesse counter company argent and sable between in chief two beech trees couped and in base a swan rousant proper, ducally gorged, chained and reflexed gold. **Crest:** Out of a coronet composed of four lilies and as many chessrooks alternately set upon a rim argent, a buck's head proper. **Motto:** Serve one another. **Granted** 20 February 1961.

CHESHIRE COUNTY COUNCIL.* Azure, a sword erect between three garbs Or. **Crest:** Upon a mural crown gules a lion statant guardant Or between two ostrich feathers argent. **Supporters:** On either side a lion Or supporting between the forelegs an ostrich feather argent. **Motto:** Jure et dignitate gladii. **Badge:** In front of an oval wreath of oak leaves a sword erect, the blade surmounted of a garb, all Or. Arms, Crest and Supporters granted 3 May 1938; Badge granted 23 December 1958.

CHESHIRE COUNTY TRAINING COLLEGE (CREWE). Vert, a sword erect between two garbs Or; on a chief sable an open book proper, bound gold. **Crest:** On a wreath of the colours, On an oak stock, between two branches springing therefrom leaved proper, fructed gold, a squirrel [sejant erect] gules. **Motto:** Doce ut discas. **Granted** 19 July 1957.

CHELMSFORD BOROUGH

CHELMSFORD R. D. C.

CHELTENHAM BOROUGH

CHARING CROSS HOSPITAL

CHELMSFORD BISHOPRIC

CHELTENHAM LADIES' COLLEGE

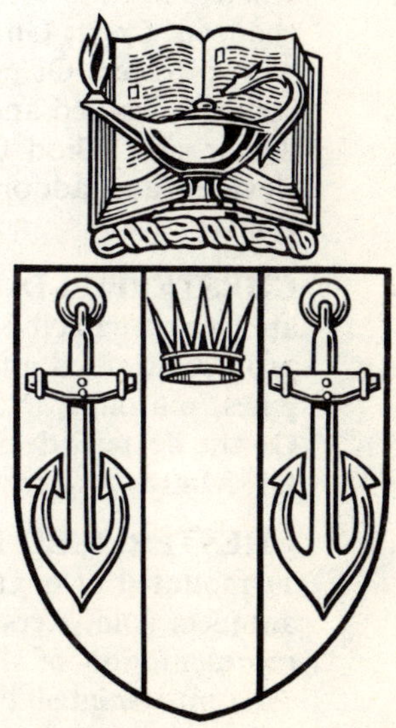

CHELSEA POLYTECHNIC

CHESHIRE POLICE AUTHORITY. Azure, between two garbs in fesse a sword erect supported in chief by two lions passant guardant issuant from the flanks, all Or. **Crest:** On a wreath of the colours, Within two sprays of oak a crown palisado Or, issuant therefrom a wolf's head argent. **Motto:** Tutior quo paratior. **Badge:** Within an oval garland of oak leaves a sword erect Or surmounted by a plume of three ostrich feathers argent bound to the blade with a sword belt Or. **Granted** 10 December 1965.

CHESHUNT URBAN DISTRICT COUNCIL (HERTFORDSHIRE).* Argent, a fess wavy azure surmounted by a pale ermine; on a chief of the second a castle triple-towered Or between a rose gules and a thistle dimidiated, both slipped and leaved, and an oak tree, eradicated and fructed, proper. **Crest:** On a wreath of the colours, A falcon proper, belled and resting the dexter claw on a cross patée Or. On a scroll below the shield the word CESTREHUNT. **Granted** 6 November 1945.

CHESTER, BISHOPRIC OF.* Gules, three mitres, two and one, Or. Recorded in the College of Arms.

CHESTER, CITY AND COUNTY BOROUGH OF (CHESHIRE).* Gules, three lions passant guardant in pale Or dimidiating Azure, three garbs Or. **Crest:** On a wreath Or, gules and azure, A sword erect, hilt and pommel Or, within a sheath sable encircled by a sword belt of the last, both garnished gold. Mantled on the dexter side gules, on the sinister side azure, both doubled argent. **Supporters:** On the dexter side a lion Or gorged with an open crown argent, and on the sinister side a wolf argent gorged with a like crown Or. **Motto:** Antiqui colant antiquum Dierum. **Badge:** On a roundel per pale gules and azure environed by a wreath of laurel Or, a wolf's head argent, langued also azure, issuant from an ancient crown of gold. Arms confirmed, Crest and Supporters granted 3 September 1580 by William Flower, Norroy King of Arms; Badge granted 17 September 1959.

CHESTER DIOCESAN TRAINING COLLEGE (CHESTER). Argent, on a cross gules a garb Or, in the first quarter in front of two swords in saltire proper, hilts and pomels gold, an open book also proper, clasped also gold. **Crest:** On a wreath of the colours, In front of two swords in saltire proper, hilts and pomels Or, a mitre of the last charged with a garb gules. **Motto:** Qui docet in doctrina. **Granted** 5 July 1954.

CHESTER, WREXHAM AND NORTH WALES SAVINGS BANK.* Azure, in front of two croziers in saltire a garb Or; on a chief per pale gules and gold a lion passant guardant counterchanged. **Crest:** On a wreath of the colours, Issuant from a wreath of oak fructed proper a castle of two towers Or ensigned with a trumpet fesswise gold, perched thereon a cock sable, beaked, combed, wattled and membered gules, charged upon the breast with a bezant. **Supporters:** On the dexter side a lion Or and on the sinister side a wolf argent, each winged with dragon's wings elevated and addorsed gules. **Motto:** Vos collocastis, nos custodiemus. **Granted** 15 November 1960.

CHESTERFIELD, BOROUGH OF (DERBYSHIRE).* Gules, a device representing a pomegranate tree as depicted on the ancient Common Seal of the Borough, the tree leaved and eradicated proper, flowered and fructed Or. **Crest:** On a wreath of the colours, Issuant from a mural crown gules, masoned Or, a mount vert, thereon a Derby ram passant guardant proper. **Supporters:** On the dexter side a cock and on the sinister side a pynot, or magpie, proper, each ducally gorged Or. **Motto:** Aspire. **Granted** 10 November 1955.

CHESTERFIELD RURAL DISTRICT COUNCIL (DERBYSHIRE).* Or, a miner's pick sable surmounted of a Tudor rose barbed and seeded proper; on a bordure engrailed also sable eight annulets gold. **Crest:** On a wreath Or and vert, Out of a mural crown argent, masoned sable, a representation of the crooked spire of Chesterfield Parish Church proper. **Motto:** Regnant qui serviunt. **Granted** 20 September 1954.

CHESHAM

CHESTER

CHESHIRE C. C.

CHERTSEY

CHESTERTON RURAL DISTRICT COUNCIL (CAMBRIDGESHIRE). Gules, on a saltire ermine between in chief a cornucopia, the horn Or, replenished proper, in fess two pairs of windmill sails, and in base an eagle, wings displayed and inverted, Or, a closed book gules, garnished and clasped Or. **Crest:** On a wreath argent and gules, In front of a mount vert, thereon a Great Bustard close proper, three fleurs-de-lys sable. **Motto:** Niet zonder arbyt. **Granted** 1 September 1965.

CHICHESTER, BISHOPRIC OF.* Azure, Our Blessed Lord in judgement seated in His throne, His dexter hand upraised Or, His sinister hand holding an open book proper, and out of His mouth a two-edged sword, the point to the dexter, gules. Recorded in the College of Arms.

CHICHESTER, BOROUGH OF (WEST SUSSEX).* Argent guttée-de-sang, on a chief gules a lion passant guardant Or. **Granted** 14 August 1570. The chief is shown indented in an earlier Visitation record.

CHICHESTER COLLEGE OF FURTHER EDUCATION. Argent, on a pale vert between a distaff and a flash of lightning azure, a wheel argent between two bezants; on a chief embattled per bend azure and gules a lion passant guardant between two martlets Or. **Crest:** On a wreath of the colours, In front of a tower gules a sun rising Or. **Motto:** Honour alit artes. **Granted** 1 August 1966.

CHICHESTER RURAL DISTRICT COUNCIL (WEST SUSSEX).* Azure, a fesse wavy argent between six martlets Or; a bordure argent guttée-de-sang. **Crest:** On a wreath of the colours, A seal proper resting the dexter front flipper upon a mitre Or. **Motto:** Adhuc hic hesterna. **Granted** 22 October 1948.

CHIGWELL URBAN DISTRICT COUNCIL (ESSEX).* Or, a stag lodged proper; on a chief gules three axe-heads each in bend sinister, blades downwards, argent. **Crest:** On a wreath of the colours, Issuant from a wreath of oak, a dexter cubit arm, habited vert, the hand proper grasping a riband gules, pendent therefrom a bugle horn Or [contourné]. **Motto:** Non progredi est regredi. **Granted** 9 May 1951.

CHIROPODISTS, SOCIETY OF, LIMITED. Tierced in pairle argent, gules and azure, in chief an escallop per pale of the third and second, to the dexter a rod of Aesculapius, and to the sinister a torch enflamed, both erect Or. **Motto:** Post curam otium. **Granted** 5 November 1946.

CHORLEY, BOROUGH OF (LANCASHIRE).* Or, on a chevron gules three escutcheons argent, each charged with a bluebottle [or cornflower], slipped and leaved, proper; on a chief of the second a crown vallary of the first. **Motto:** Beware. **Granted** 3 July 1882.

CHORLEY RURAL DISTRICT COUNCIL (LANCASHIRE).* Argent, on a pale sable between two cornflowers, stalked, leaved and flowered, proper a standish between two cross crosslets of the field. **Crest:** Out of a coronet composed of eight roses gules, barbed and seeded proper, set upon a rim Or, a mount vert, thereon a bull argent supporting a beacon sable fired proper. **Motto:** Spectemur agendo. **Granted** 28 April 1952.

CHRIST'S COLLEGE (CAMBRIDGE UNIVERSITY).* Quarterly, first and fourth, Azure three fleurs-de-lys, two and one, Or, second and third, Gules three lions passant guardant in pale Or; all within a bordure company argent and azure. Recorded at the Visitation of 1575.

CHRIST'S HOSPITAL AND BRIDEWELL ROYAL HOSPITAL. Argent, a cross gules, in the first quarter a sword erect of the last; on a chief azure a rose of the field, barbed and seeded proper, between two fleurs-de-lys Or. **Granted** 4 May 1955.

CHESTER, WREXHAM AND NORTH WALES SAVINGS BANK.

CHESTERFIELD R. D. C.

CHESTER BISHOPRIC

CHESTERFIELD BOROUGH

CHESHUNT U. D. C.

CHRIST CHURCH COLLEGE (OXFORD UNIVERSITY).* Sable, on a cross engrailed argent a lion passant gules between four leopards' faces azure; on a chief Or a rose of the third barbed and seeded between two Cornish choughs proper. Recorded at the Visitation of 1574-5.

CHURCH IN WALES, REPRESENTATIVE BODY OF THE. Argent, on a cross azure a Celtic cross Or. **Granted** 9 December 1954.

CHURCHILL COLLEGE TRUST, TRUSTEES OF THE (OXFORD UNIVERSITY).* Quarterly, first and fourth, Sable a lion rampant argent on a canton of the last a cross gules, second and third, quarterly argent and gules in the second and third quarters a fret Or on a bend sable three escallops also argent; over all in the fesse point an open book likewise argent. **Crest:** On a wreath of the colours. A lion couchant guardant argent supporting with the dexter forepaw a staff Or, flying therefrom a banner gules charged with ah open book also argent. **Motto:** Forward. **Granted** 17 September 1959.

CIBA FOUNDATION FOR THE PROMOTION OF INTERNATIONAL COOPERATION IN MEDICAL AND CHEMICAL RESEARCH. Sanguine, three regular hexagons Or; on a chief dovetailed gold five annulets interlaced fessewise sable. **Crest:** On a wreath of the colours, A cock sable, combed, wattled and membered gules, supporting with the dexter claw a rod of Aesculapius gold, the serpent proper. **Supporters:** On the dexter side a wyvern Or charged on the shoulder with a sword erect gules, and on the sinister side a lion gold charged on the shoulder with a representation of the Basle staff sable. **Motto:** Consocient gentes. **Granted** 20 December 1957.

CINQUE PORTS, CORPORATION OF THE. Per pale gules and azure, three lions passant guardant dimidiated and conjoined to the hulks of as many ancient ships, all in pale Or. Recorded in the College of Arms.

CIRENCESTER GRAMMAR SCHOOL (GLOUCESTERSHIRE).* Per chevron azure and Or, a chevron between three wolves' heads erased, all counterchanged. **Crest:** A mural crown argent, therein in front of a mitre argent, garnished Or, a slip of two Tudor roses, barbed, seeded and leaved, proper. **Motto:** Dona praesente rape laetus horae. **Granted** 31 March 1958.

THE CITY UNIVERSITY. Murrey, upon a mount a beacon fired Or; a chief of the Arms of the City of London. **Crest:** On a wreath of the colours, In front of a chaplet of laurel Or a dexter hand couped below the wrist proper, vested murrey, holding a torch enflamed Or. **Motto:** To serve mankind. **Granted** 1 August 1966.

CITY AND GUILDS OF LONDON INSTITUTE.* Argent, a cross gules surmounted of a sun Or; a chief of the second, thereon a lion passant gold gorged with a naval crown azure. **Crest:** On a wreath of the colours, A dexter cubit arm, vested bendy sinister argent and gules, the hand proper grasping a sword also gules, the blade enfiled with a mural crown also argent. **Supporters:** On the dexter side a unicorn Or, armed, crined, tufted and unguled argent, and on the sinister side a griffin gold pellettée. **Motto:** Coram Deo laboramus. **Granted** 9 September 1955.

CIVIL ENGINEERS, INSTITUTION OF. Or, on a pale azure between two annulets in fesse sable, a thunderbolt between in chief a sun in splendour of the first and in base a fountain proper. **Crest:** On a wreath of the colours. Upon a billet fessewise azure charged with a fesse wavy argent a representation of the Eddystone lighthouse upon rocks proper. **Supporters:** On the dexter side a beaver and on the sinister a crane, both proper. **Motto:** Scientia et ingenio. Arms granted 17 March 1913; Crest and Supporters granted 31 December 1948.

CLACTON URBAN DISTRICT COUNCIL (ESSEX).* Per chevron azure crusilly argent and gules, in chief two cinquefoils of the second and in base as many swords in saltire Or. **Crest:** On a wreath of the colours, A lymphad gules, sail set proper charged with an escallop Or, anchor of the last, pennant azure and flags flying from the stem and stern of the last each charged with an escallop gold. **Motto:** Lux, salubritas, felicitas. **Granted** 14 April 1938.

CHICHESTER R. D. C.

CHICHESTER BISHOPRIC

CHORLEY R. D. C.

CHIGWELL

CHICHESTER BOROUGH

CHORLEY BOROUGH

CLARE COLLEGE (CAMBRIDGE UNIVERSITY).* Or, three chevronels gules, impaling Or, a cross gules; all within a bordure sable guttée d'Or. Recorded at the Visitation of 1684.

CLEETHORPES, BOROUGH OF (LINCOLNSHIRE—PARTS OF LINDSEY).* Argent, on a bend engrailed between two escallops azure three owls Or. **Crest:** On a wreath of the colours, Upon a rock a pelican argent, vulning herself gules, gorged with a strap also argent, buckle Or. **Supporters:** On the dexter side a Norseman, holding in the exterior hand a shield, and on the sinister side a Cleethorpes fisherman, holding in the exterior hand a net, all proper. **Motto:** Vigilantes. **Granted** 8 September 1936.

CLERGY, CORPORATION OF THE SONS OF THE. Lozengy argent and sable, on a chief purpure a cross patée Or between two books of the first, garnished and clasped of the fourth. **Crest:** On a wreath of the colours, A female figure, the emblem of Charity, vested in a loose garment sable, head, breast, hands, and feet proper, her hair dishevelled Or, accompanied with three naked boys, one on the dexter side and one on each arm of the second, crined of the third. **Motto:** Quod eorum minimis mihi. **Granted** 29 November 1685, by Dugdale, Garter, and St. George, Clarenceux King of Arms, to The Society for the Relief of Clergymen's Widows and Orphans.

CLERKS OF THE PEACE OF COUNTIES AND OF CLERKS OF COUNTY COUNCILS, SOCIETY OF. Quarterly azure and argent, in the first and fourth quarters a lion passant guardant Or, and in the second and third quarters a dragon rampant gules; on a chief sable two quill pens in saltire, points downward, also argent. **Crest:** On a wreath of the colours, An ancient crown Or jewelled proper. **Motto:** Tien le droict. **Granted** 1 November 1960.

CLERKS OF WORKS OF GREAT BRITAIN, INSTITUTE OF, INCORPORATED. Per fesse azure and gules, masoned argent, in chief two towers argent, masoned sable, and in base a spirit level fessewise; over all a plumb line in pale Or. **Crest:** On a wreath Or and azure, Out of the battlements of a tower argent, masoned sable, between two branches of laurel vert, fructed Or, an owl holding in the dexter claw a torch erect Or, enflamed proper. **Supporters:** On either side a lion paly [of four] Or and gules gorged with a collar argent, masoned sable, pendent therefrom by a chain a six-pointed star argent charged with a dexter hand appaume couped at the wrist gules, and resting the interior hind paw upon a block of stone proper. **Motto:** Potestate, probitate et vigilantia. **Badge:** On a roundel per pale argent and gules masoned argent, environed of a chaplet of laurel vert fructed Or, a Tee square and a trowel in saltire proper. **Granted** 2 September 1964.

CLEVEDON URBAN DISTRICT COUNCIL (SOMERSET).* Or, on a pile reversed flory at the point sable between in chief two roses gules, barbed and seeded proper, a lion rampant reguardant of the field. **Crest:** On a wreath of the colours, Issuant from a mount vert a hill cleft at the summit proper. **Motto:** Vigilate et orate. **Granted** 14 August 1933.

CLIFTON COLLEGE.* Argent, a chevron between two trefoils slipped in chief and a garb in base azure; a chief gules, thereon a ducal coronet Or between two books argent, clasped and garnished gold. **Motto:** Spiritus intus alit. **Granted** 8 April 1895.

CLITHEROE, BOROUGH OF (LANCASHIRE).* Azure, on a mount in base vert a castle of three domed towers, each flying a pennon, Or. **Crest:** Issuant from a coronet composed of two crescents Or and as many pierced mullets sable set alternately upon a rim gold, a lion's head erased argent. **Supporters:** On either side a lion purpure gorged with a chain, pendent therefrom an escutcheon Or charged with a rose gules barbed and seeded proper. **Motto:** Stabit saxum, fluet amnis. **Granted** 20 February 1952.

CLITHEROE RURAL DISTRICT COUNCIL (LANCASHIRE).* Barry wavy of eight argent and vert, three whales in fesse haurient, in the mouth of each a crozier Or, and each charged with a rose gules barbed and seeded proper. **Crest:** On a wreath of the colours, Issuant from the battlements of a tower purpure a demi lion vert gorged with a ducal coronet Or, pendent therefrom an

CHRIST CHURCH COLLEGE

CIRENCESTER GRAMMAR SCHOOL

CHRIST'S COLLEGE

CHURCHILL COLLEGE

CITY AND GUILDS

escutcheon argent charged with a pierced mullet sable, holding between the paws a crescent ermine. **Motto:** Nostrum est rura tueri. **Granted** 9 April 1959.

CLOCKMAKERS OF THE CITY OF LONDON, WORSHIPFUL COMPANY OF. Sable, a clock, each of the four pillars of the case based on a lion couchant and capped with a globe surmounted by a cross, and on the dome of the case an Imperial Crown, all Or. **Crest:** On a wreath of the colours, A sphere Or. Mantled gules, doubled argent. **Supporters:** On the dexter side a naked old man, representing Time, holding a scythe and an hour glass, and on the sinister side the figure of an emperor, robed and crowned, holding a sphere, all proper. **Motto:** Tempus rerum imperator. **Granted** 31 January 1672, by Sir Edward Walker, Garter King of Arms.

CLOTHWORKERS OF THE CITY OF LONDON, WORSHIPFUL COMPANY OF.* Sable, a chevron ermine between in chief two havettes argent and in base a teazel cob Or. **Crest:** On a wreath argent and sable, A mount vert thereon a ram statant Or, **Supporters:** On either side a griffin Or pellettee. **Motto:** My trust is in God alone. Arms granted 22 November 1530, by Thomas Benolt, Clarenceux King of Arms; Crest and Supporters granted 25 March 1587, by Robert Cooke, Clarenceux King of Arms. [In the 1587 emblazonment the teazel is gold, stalked and leaved vert.]

COACH- AND COACH-HARNESS-MAKERS OF THE CITY OF LONDON, WORSHIPFUL COMPANY OF. Azure, a chevron between three coaches Or. **Crest:** On a wreath of the colours, Phoebus in his glory sitting in a chariot Or drawn through a cloud proper by four horses argent, reined and bridled Or. **Supporters:** On either side a horse argent, bridled and harnessed sable, the harness studded Or garnished gules, and housed azure with fringe and purfling Or, adorned with plumes of feathers Or, azure, argent and gules. **Motto:** Surgit post nubila Phoebus. **Granted** 17 July 1677, by Sir William Dugdale, Garter King of Arms and Sir Henry St. George, Clarenceux King of Arms.

COAL FACTORS' SOCIETY. Per pale Or and sable, on a bend wavy cotised wavy four lozenges argent conjoined, counterchanged. **Crest:** On a wreath of the colours, On water barry wavy proper a collier brig sable, pennons flying Or, the whole environed by lozenges conjoined sable. **Motto:** Per mare per industriam. **Granted** 20 December 1963.

COALVILLE URBAN DISTRICT COUNCIL (LEICESTERSHIRE). Or, two pallets between six lozenges sable; on a chief azure a maunch between two garbs of the field. **Crest:** Out of a coronet composed of six lozenges gules set upon a rim Or, an oak tree rooted upon a rock proper. **Motto:** Ex terra opes. **Granted** 23 March 1956.

COLCHESTER, BOROUGH OF (ESSEX).* Gules, two staves raguly and couped argent, one in pale surmounted by another in fesse, between two ducal coronets in chief Or, the lower part of the vertical stave enfiled with a like coronet. Confirmed 26 August 1558 and recorded at the Visitation of 1634.

COLERAINE, BOROUGH (CO. LONDONDERRY).* Argent, a chevron azure, in chief two garbs and in base a salmon naiant proper; a chief harry wavy of the first and second, thereon a pale of the first charged with a saltire gules. **Crest:** On a wreath of the colours, Upon a mount vert a castle with two towers proper charged with a dexter hand couped gules. **Supporters:** On either side a dragon per fesse argent and gules charged on the wing with a sword erect of the last. **Motto:** Cuil rathain. **Granted** 24 October 1951.

COLWYN BAY, BOROUGH OF (DENBIGHSHIRE).* Argent, on a mount vert an oak tree proper, fructed Or; on a chief per pale of the last and gules a lion passant guardant counterchanged. **Crest:** On a wreath of the colours, A demi dragon gules holding between the claws a man's head in profile couped at the neck argent. **Motto:** Iechyd, harddwch, heddwch. **Granted** 11 September 1934 to the Colwyn Bay Urban District Council.

CLACTON

CLEETHORPES

CLARE COLLEGE

CLIFTON COLLEGE

CLEVEDON

COLYTON PARISH COUNCIL (DEVON).* Per chevron Or and azure, in chief two torteaux and in base a saltire argent; on a chief of the second semée-de-lys of the first a lion rampant also argent. **Crest:** On a wreath of the colours, In front of two ostrich feathers inclining outwards a sword, point downwards, proper, hilt and pommel Or, and a civic mace gold in saltire. **Motto:** More majorum. **Granted** 15 April 1954.

COMMERCIAL UNION ASSURANCE COMPANY LIMITED.* Sable, a fire beacon and on a chief Or three anchors azure. **Supporters:** On either side a winged lion guardant collared Or. **Motto:** Anchora salutis. **Granted** 14 November 1928.

COMMONWEALTH DEVELOPMENT CORPORATION. Per fesse vert and gules, on a fesse wavy argent between in chief a sun in splendour and in base two stalks of millet leaved in saltire Or, a fesse wavy azure. **Crest:** On a wreath argent and gules, A felling axe, the blade outwards, and a sheaf of paddy Or connected by two lark's heads [= strands of rope] and a true lovers' knot azure. **Supporters:** On either side a sea lion proper, the dexter holding a torch Or inflamed also proper, and the sinister holding a cornucopia, the horn gold and the fruit also proper. **Motto:** Veni Creator. **Granted** 30 October 1948 to The Colonial Development Corporation.

COMMONWEALTH TELECOMMUNICATIONS BOARD. Azure, a bendlet dancetté argent between two cables Or. **Crest:** On a wreath of the colours, Between two wings argent, tipped Or, a dexter cubit arm grasping a thunderbolt and ensigned with a representation of the Royal Crown proper. **Supporters:** On the dexter side a sea horse and on the sinister an eagle close, both proper. **Motto:** Per mare, per aera. **Granted** pursuant to Royal Warrant, 24 August 1950.

COMMONWEALTH UNIVERSITIES, ASSOCIATION OF. Azure, two wings conjoined in base Or surmounted of an open book proper bound gules edged gold, in chief a rose also gules, irradiated Or, and charged with a rose argent, both roses barbed and seeded proper. **Crest:** On a wreath of the colours, A demi terrestrial globe proper ensigned with an ancient lamp argent, garnished Or, enflamed also proper. **Motto:** Scientia commune bonum. **Granted** 20 June 1958 to The Association of Universities of the British Commonwealth; Regranted by Royal Licence to The Association of Commonwealth Universities and exemplified 9 September 1966.

THE CONCRETE SOCIETY. Quarterly per fess wavy Or and argent, an annulet between four lions rampant gules; over all a fesse wavy sable surmounted by a pale sable. **Crest:** On a wreath argent and gules, Out of a mural crown and in front of an annulet Or, a lion rampant gules holding between the forepaws a snowflake azure. **Motto:** Concreti corroboramur. **Granted** 5 September 1967.

CONGLETON, BOROUGH OF (CHESHIRE). Sable, on water in base barry wavy azure and argent a tun between two conger eels argent, a lion statant guardant Or on the tun. **Crest:** On a wreath of the colours, A demi bear muzzled proper, with chain reflexed over the back, and supporting a garb Or. **Supporters:** On the dexter side a wolf argent and on the sinister side a lion purpure, armed and langued Or, about the neck of each a chain, pendent therefrom two keys in saltire Or. **Motto:** Sit tibi sancta cohors comitum. **Granted** 5 September 1967.

CONGLETON RURAL DISTRICT COUNCIL (CHESHIRE).* Azure, on a chevron argent seven gouttés de larmes between in chief two garbs Or and in base a crystal of rock salt proper. **Crest:** On a wreath of the colours, A wolf's head couped argent gorged with a collar azure, pendent therefrom by a ring Or an escutcheon argent three bendlets wavy azure a canton ermine. **Motto:** Rura mihi placent. **Granted** 15 January 1951.

CONNAH'S QUAY URBAN DISTRICT COUNCIL (FLINTSHIRE).* Vert, on water in base charged with three salmon naiant proper a lymphad Or, the sail quarterly gold and gules a bendlet sable. **Crest:** Out of a circlet of steel, flames proper, therein a demi dragon gules holding between the paws a cross fleuretty engrailed sable. Mantled vert, doubled argent. **Motto:** Llwyddiant o Ddiwydiant. **Granted** 30 January 1961.

CLITHEROE BOROUGH

CLITHEROE R. D. C.

COLERAINE

COLCHESTER

THE CARPENTERS

THE CLOCKMAKERS

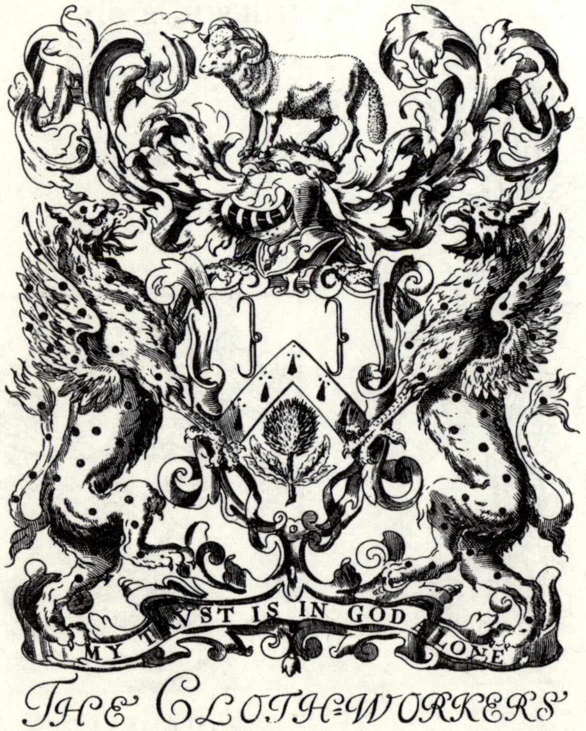

THE CLOTH-WORKERS

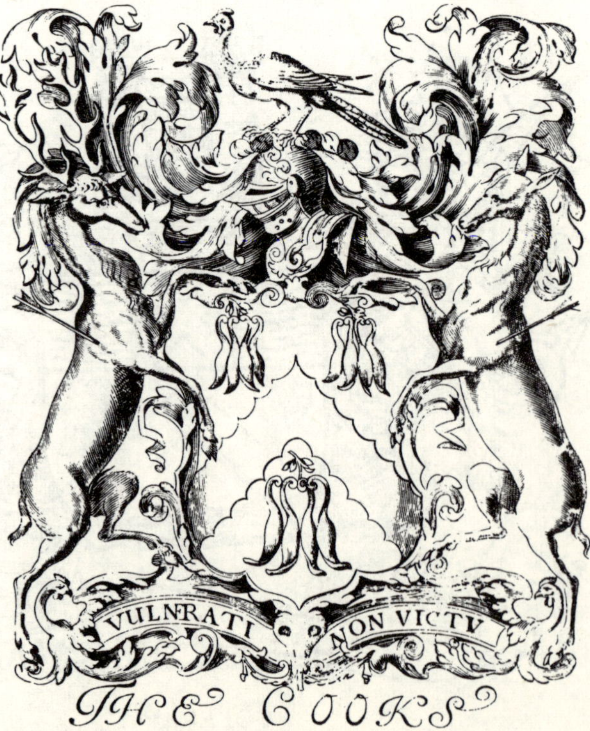

THE COOKS

The Coopers

The Cordwainors

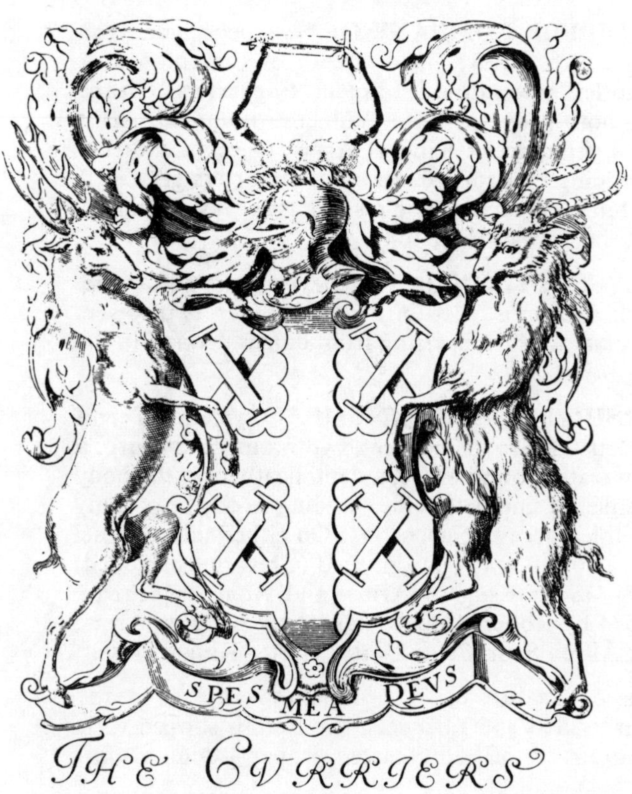

The Curriers

The Cutlers

CONNOR, BISHOPRIC OF. Azure, a lamb passant supporting with the dexter foreleg a staff proper, flying therefrom a pennon argent charged with a saltire gules, between three crosses crosslet Or; on a chief of the last two crosiers in saltire of the field. **Granted** 24 May 1945.

CONSETT URBAN DISTRICT COUNCIL (CO. DURHAM). Argent, a representation of St. Ebba proper supporting with the sinister hand a pastoral staff Or between in chief two swords in saltire also proper, hilts and pomels gold, and in base a miner's lamp likewise proper; two flaunches sable, each charged with a furnace fired also proper. **Crest:** Issuant from a mural crown flames enveloping a sword proper, hilt and pomel Or. **Granted** 17 September 1955.

CONSTANTINE TECHNICAL COLLEGE, MIDDLESBROUGH. Or, on a pale between two lions combatant azure, an open book of the field between in chief a rose argent, barbed and seeded proper, and in base a lymphad also Or. **Crest:** On a wreath of the colours, A lion rampant guardant azure supporting an anchor erect sable, the shank piercing a rose as in the Arms. **Motto:** Facta non verba. **Granted** 30 November 1922.

CONSULTING ENGINEERS, ASSOCIATION OF.* Vert, on a fess wavy argent two barrulets wavy azure; over all a pale Or, thereon four cogwheels throughout and engaged sable. **Crest:** On a wreath Or and gules, Two eagles' heads erased and per fess, the dexter gules and azure, the sinister azure and gules, both beaked and collared, the collars linked by a chain Or. **Motto:** Acer et exactus. **Badge:** Two eagles' heads erased and per fess, the dexter gules and azure, the sinister azure and gules, both beaked and collared, the collars linked by a chain Or. Arms and Crest granted 19 June 1967; Badge granted 16 April 1968.

CONTINGENCY INSURANCE COMPANY LIMITED. Or, a torch fired and a broken spear in saltire proper, between in chief a rose and in the flanks two wheels gules. **Motto:** Ad alios adjuvandos potens. **Granted** 2 February 1931.

COOKS OF THE CITY OF LONDON, WORSHIPFUL COMPANY OF.* Argent, a chevron engrailed sable between three columbine flowers azure. **Crest:** On a wreath of the colours, A mount vert, thereon a cock pheasant proper. Mantled gules, doubled argent. **Supporters:** On the dexter side a buck and on the sinister side a doe, both proper. **Motto:** Vulnerati non victi. Arms granted 13 October 1467 by William Hawkeslowe, Clarenceux King of Arms, to replace earlier one (31 May 1461) by John Wrexworth, Guyenne King of Arms; Crest and Supporters granted 1 August 1614 by William Camden, Clarenceux King of Arms. Each supporter was originally transfixed by an arrow but these were removed at the Visitation of 1687.

COOKSTOWN URBAN DISTRICT COUNCIL (CO. TYRONE). Per chevron vert and azure, in chief two garbs proper and in base a cogwheel, and on a chief Or a port between two towers proper between two dexter hands couped gules. **Crest:** A phoenix rising from flames proper, in the beak a cogwheel gules. **Granted** 6 August 1969.

COOPERS OF THE CITY OF LONDON, WORSHIPFUL COMPANY OF.* Gyronny of eight gules and sable, on a chevron between three annulets Or a royne between two broad axes azure; a chief vert, thereon three lilies argent. **Crest:** On a wreath Or and azure, a demi heathcock, the body azure semee of annulets gold, the wings argent semée of annulets sable, holding in the beak a lily silver slipped and leaved vert. Mantled azure, doubled argent. **Supporters:** On either side a camel gules semée of annulets, bridled Or. **Motto:** Love as brethren. Arms granted (Crest not blazoned) 27 September 1509 by Sir Thomas Wriothesley, Garter King of Arms, and Roger Machado, Clarenceux King of Arms; Supporters granted 1574 by Robert Cooke Clarenceux King of Arms; the whole re-exemplified 20 February 1909 by Sir Alfred Scott Scott-Gatty, Garter King of Arms.

W. T. COPELAND & SONS LIMITED. Gules, on a saltire between in pale two horses' heads and in fess two boars' heads all erased argent, four mullets sable between five trefoils slipped vert. **Crest:** On a wreath of the colours, Between two branches of holly fructed proper a demi griffin,

CONGLETON R. D. C.

COLWYN BAY

CONNAH'S QUAY
U. D. C.

COMMERCIAL UNION

COLYTON

wings addorsed, gules holding a rose argent. **Motto:** Ex igni pulchritudo. **Badge:** A bottle oven proper. **Granted** 10 October 1967.

CORBY URBAN DISTRICT COUNCIL (NORTHAMPTONSHIRE).* Gules, a cross patonce cantoning four oak leaves, each enfiled by a ducal coronet Or. **Crest:** On a wreath of the colours, A corbie, wings elevated, sable, beaked, membered, gorged with a ducal coronet and chained Or, its dexter claw resting on a gad of steel proper. **Motto:** Deeds, not words. **Granted** 3 March 1958.

CORDWAINERS OF THE CITY OF LONDON, WORSHIPFUL COMPANY OF.* Azure a chevron Or between three goats' heads erased argent, horned and bearded of the second. **Crest:** On a wreath of the colours, A goat's head erased argent, the erasures gules, horns wreathed Or and azure. Mantled gules, doubled argent. **Motto:** Corio et arte. **Granted** 25 June 1579 by Robert Cooke, Clarenceux King of Arms.

CORINTHIAN CASUALS FOOTBALL CLUB. Vert, a lion passant guardant in bend Or between two cotises argent; on a canton of the last a cross of St. George surmounted of a football proper. **Crest:** On a wreath argent and vert, a two-headed lion sejant affrontée, the heads turned to the dexter and the sinister Or, supporting with the dexter forepaw a staff, flying therefrom a banner per fesse of white and blue silk, and with the sinister forepaw a like staff, flying therefrom a banner per fesse of pink and dark brown silk, all proper. **Motto:** E duobus unum. **Granted** 10 December 1958.

CORNHILL INSURANCE COMPANY LIMITED.* Azure, a pile reversed issuant from the base and in chief two garbs Or. **Granted** 30 March 1937.

CORNWALL COUNTY COUNCIL.* Sable, fifteen bezants in pile within a bordure barry wavy of eight argent and azure. **Crest:** On a wreath argent and azure, A chough proper resting the dexter claw upon a ducal coronet Or. **Supporters:** On the dexter side a fisherman holding over the exterior shoulder a net, and on the sinister side a miner, resting the exterior hand on a sledge hammer, all proper. **Motto:** One and all. **Granted** 5 April 1939.

CORNWALL, DUCHY OF.* Sable, fifteen bezants. The shield ensigned by the coronet of the Heir Apparent. **Supporters:** On either side a Cornish chough proper, supporting an ostrich feather argent, penned Or. **Motto:** Houmont. Supporters granted by Royal Warrant 21 June 1968.

CORPUS CHRISTI COLLEGE (CAMBRIDGE UNIVERSITY).* Quarterly gules and azure, in the first and fourth quarters a pelican in its piety, and in the second and third three lily flowers slipped and leaved all argent. **Granted** 23 December 1570 by Robert Cooke, Clarenceux King of Arms.

CORPUS CHRISTI COLLEGE (OXFORD UNIVERSITY).* Tierced per pale, the centre argent thereon an escutcheon of the Arms of the See of Winchester ensigned with a mitre all proper, the dexter side azure a pelican Or vulning her breast gules, the sinister side sable a chevron Or between three owls argent on a chief gold as many roses gules barbed and seeded proper. Recorded at the Visitation of 1574-5.

COST AND WORKS ACCOUNTANTS, INSTITUTE OF. Azure, a sun issuant in chief Or, two bezants each charged with a bee volant proper in fesse, and a garb of the second in base; on a chief ermine a pair of scales gold. **Crest:** On a wreath of the colours, In front of a pair of compasses extended Or an open book proper, edged gold. **Supporters:** On either side a lion Or gorged with a collar vairy gules and argent, pendent therefrom an escutcheon also gules, that on the dexter charged with two tally sticks in saltire gold and that on the sinister with an hour glass proper garnished also gold, each resting the interior hind paw on a cog-wheel argent. **Motto:** Profitas accuratio justitia. Arms and Crest granted 5 October 1932; Supporters granted 16 January 1952.

CONSULTING ENGINEERS

CORNWALL, DUCHY OF

CORBY

CORNWALL C. C.

COTTON COLLEGE (OAKAMOOR, STAFFORDSHIRE). Azure, a chevron argent between three estoiles Or, the chevron surmounted by an open book also argent, binding and clasps gold, edged gules. **Motto:** Religioni ac bonis artis. **Granted** 20 October 1929.

COUNCIL FOR NATIONAL ACADEMIC AWARDS. Sable, four steepled towers conjoined by curtain walls argent, between three chaplets of laurel each fructed proper and tied with a riband Or. **Crest:** On a wreath Or and gules, In front of two torches in saltire sable, enflamed proper, a lion's face Or. **Supporters:** On either side a lion Or supporting between the forelegs an apple tree fructed proper, the trunk enfiled through an ancient crown Or. **Motto:** Lauream qui meruit ferat. **Granted** 20 May 1966.

COUNTRY LANDOWNERS' ASSOCIATION. Vert, a chevronel between in chief two garbs and in base a portcullis, a linked chain in orle all Or. **Crest:** On a wreath of the colours, On a mount vert, in front of an oak tree fructed a pile of faggots all proper. **Supporters:** On the dexter side a lion supporting a staff Or, and on the sinister side a dragon gules supporting a spade Or. **Motto:** We serve the land. **Granted** 20 March 1957.

COUNTY COLLEGE (LANCASTER UNIVERSITY). Gules, on three piles, two from the chief and one from the base, Or three roses gules, barbed and seeded proper; over all a chevron azure, and on a chief azure a lion passant Or. **Crest:** On a wreath Or and gules, Issuant from an ancient crown azure a bezant between two oak leaves proper. **Motto:** Sine consilio nihil. **Granted** 30 September 1969 to the University of Lancaster for the use of the County College.

COVENTRY, BISHOPRIC OF.* Gules, a cross potent, quadrate in the centre, argent within a bordure of the last charged with eight torteaux. **Granted** 24 January 1919.

COVENTRY, CITY AND COUNTY BOROUGH OF (WARWICKSHIRE).* Per pale gules and vert, an elephant statant and on his back a castle triple-towered and domed Or. **Crest:** On a wreath of the colours, A cat statant guardant proper. **Supporters:** On the dexter side an eagle, wings elevated and addorsed, sable, langued and legged gules, and on the sinister side a phoenix, wings elevated and addorsed, Or, langued gules, the flames proper. **Motto:** Camera principis. Arms and crest recorded at the Visitations of 1619 and 1682 (on the latter occasion a banner charged with three ostrich feathers was allowed on the centre tower of the castle); Arms and crest confirmed in above form and supporters granted 10 February 1959.

COWBRIDGE, BOROUGH OF (GLAMORGAN).* Party per chevron gules and argent, in chief semée of cross crosslets and two lions rampant of the last, and in base over water a bridge of three arches, thereon a cow passant, all proper. **Crest:** On a wreath of the colours, A cow proper, holding in the mouth an ear of wheat leaved and slipped gold, and supporting with the dexter forehoof an escutcheon Or charged with three chevronels invected gules. **Motto:** Awn rhagom. **Granted** 7 April 1888.

COWBRIDGE RURAL DISTRICT COUNCIL (GLAMORGAN).* Sable, the head of a Celtic cross within an orle composed of eight garbs and at the base a cow's head caboshed Or. **Crest:** On a wreath Or and vert, In front of two wings conjoined in base Or a miner's lamp proper. **Motto:** A fynno Duw a fydd. **Granted** 30 January 1956.

CRAWLEY DEVELOPMENT CORPORATION (SUSSEX).* Or, on a fesse gules between three crows sable, as many chevronels interlaced argent; a bordure azure charged with sixteen martlets gold. **Crest:** On a wreath of the colours, Issuant from a circlet of palisades Or a dexter hand grasping a trowel erect proper. **Supporters:** On the dexter side a stage coachman and on the sinister side a woodman, both proper. **Motto:** By design and endeavour. **Granted** 2 April 1951.

CRAWLEY URBAN DISTRICT COUNCIL (SUSSEX).* Argent, on a cross azure between four acorns leaved and slipped proper, nine martlets volant Or. **Crest:** Out of a crown palisado a demi lion guardant Or brandishing in the dexter forepaw a hammer proper. **Motto:** I grow and I rejoice. **Granted** 9 February 1957.

CORPUS CHRISTI COLLEGE (OXFORD UNIVERSITY)

COVENTRY BISHOPRIC

CORPUS CHRISTI COLLEGE (CAMBRIDGE UNIVERSITY)

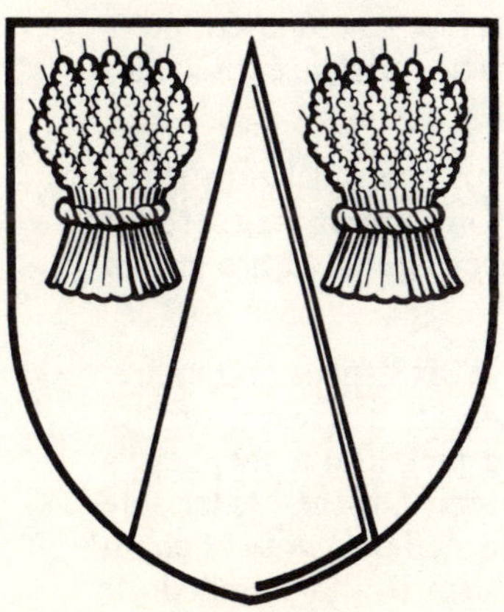

CORNHILL INSURANCE

COVENTRY

CREWE, BOROUGH OF (CHESHIRE).* Ermine, a wheel Or; on a chief wavy azure a maunch between two garbs gold. **Crest:** On a wreath Or and azure, A demi lion argent holding between the claws a cog-wheel Or. **Motto:** Semper contendo. **Granted** 18 March 1955.

CREWKERNE URBAN DISTRICT COUNCIL (SOMERSET).* Or, a lion rampant azure between three torteaux; on a chief ermine a pale sable, thereon three swords in pile, points downwards, proper, pommels and hilts of the first. **Crest:** On a wreath of the colours, Issuant from a wreath of flax flowered proper, the mast of a ship also proper, at the masthead a pennon of St. George, the sail hoisted gules charged with a cross moline Or within a bordure argent guttée de sang. **Motto:** Keep faith. **Granted** 1 June 1949.

CRICKHOWELL RURAL DISTRICT COUNCIL (BRECKNOCKSHIRE).* Per fess wavy Or and gules, a fess enhanced wavy barry wavy azure and argent, in chief between a salmon leaping in bend sinister and a ram's head caboshed all proper a pale sable, thereon a garb gold, in base three towers triple-towered also argent. **Crest:** On a wreath argent and azure, A dragon passant gules supporting with the dexter claw a longbow stringed Or. Mantled azure, doubled argent. **Motto:** Oportet nos progredi. **Granted** 10 February 1960.

CRICKLADE PARISH COUNCIL (WILTSHIRE).* Ermine, a bend wavy azure; on a chief vert a horse courant to the sinister argent. **Motto:** In loco delicioso. **Granted** 2 April 1948.

CROHAM HURST SCHOOL. Per chevron azure and vert, in chief an ancient hand lamp Or, enflamed proper, between a slip of lime and a slip of vine, both leaved and fructed, also proper, in base a sperver gold lined purpure. **Crest:** On a wreath of the colours, A demi lion argent supporting with the paws a key Or, the ward upwards and outwards, all between two posies of dandelion leaved, flowered and seeded proper. **Motto:** Finis coronat opus. **Granted** 1 May 1958.

CROSBY, BOROUGH OF (LANCASHIRE).* Azure, a cross pattée azure, within an orle of ten billets sable. **Crest:** On a wreath of the colours, Issuant from a wreath of holly fructed proper a demi griffin holding in the claws a staff erect proper, flying therefrom to the sinister a banner Azure on a pale argent between two stags' heads caboshed Or a representation of the Waterloo Medal and riband proper. **Supporters:** On either side a sea horse azure, maned, finned and charged on the shoulder with an anchor Or. **Motto:** Vis unita fortior. **Granted** 7 August 1937.

CROYDON, LONDON BOROUGH OF.* Argent, on a cross flory at the ends sable five bezants, between in chief to the dexter two swords azure and gules in saltire and [to the sinister] two keys azure and gules in saltire. **Crest:** Out of a mural crown Or a fountain between a branch of oak leaved and fructed and one of beech slipped proper. **Supporters:** On the dexter side a lion sable and on the sinister side a horse argent, each with a cross formy fitchy pendent from a collar counterchanged. **Motto:** Ad summa nitamur. **Badge:** A fountain charged with a cross flory at the ends sable, thereon five bezants. **Granted** 10 December 1965.

CULFORD SCHOOL (BURY ST EDMUNDS, SUFFOLK). Argent, on a cross azure three crowns Or in fess and two escallops of the first in pale, in the first quarter a lion rampant reguardant of the second. **Crest:** On a wreath of the colours, A book argent edged Or ensigned with a crown proper. **Motto:** Viriliter agite, estote fortes. **Granted** 10 May 1937.

CUMBERLAND COUNTY COUNCIL.* Per fesse vert and barry wavy of six argent and azure, in chief three Parnassus flowers proper. **Crest:** Issuant from a mural crown Or a wreath, on the dexter side of oak fructed and on the sinister side of ash, in front thereof a pick and a shepherd's crook in saltire, and perched upon the crown a curlew, all proper. **Supporters:** On the dexter side a representation of the Dacre Bull at Naworth gules, armed, unguled and collared with a chain reflexed over the back Or, and on the sinister side a roebuck also gules, armed and unguled Or [the whole upon a compartment in the form of a masoned embattled wall Or.] **Motto:** Perfero. **Granted** 19 September 1951.

COWBRIDGE BOROUGH

COWBRIDGE R. D. C.

CRICKHOWELL

CRAWLEY U. D. C.

CREWKERNE

CREWE

CURRIERS OF THE CITY OF LONDON, WORSHIPFUL COMPANY OF.* Azure, a cross engrailed Or between eight shaving knives in saltire argent, handled of the second. **Crest:** On a wreath Or and azure, Out of clouds proper two arms also proper vested in shirt sleeves folded beneath the elbow argent, the hands holding a shaving knife of the last handled Or. **Supporters:** On the dexter side an Elk proper, horned and hooved Or, and on the sinister side a goat argent flashed sable. **Motto:** Spes nostra Deus. **Granted** 8 August 1583 by Robert Cook, Clarenceux King of Arms. (*Illustration on page* 119).

CUTLERS IN HALLAMSHIRE, INCORPORATED COMPANY OF. Argent, on a fess indented vert between three pairs of swords in saltire proper, pommels and hilts sable, eight arrows interlaced saltirewise banded of the field between two garbs Or. **Crest:** On a wreath of the colours, In front of an elephant's head couped Or two swords in saltire as in the Arms. **Motto:** Pour y parvenir a bon foi. **Granted** 13 August 1875.

CUTLERS OF THE CITY OF LONDON, WORSHIPFUL COMPANY OF.* Gules, three pairs of swords in saltire argent, hilts and pomels Or. **Crest:** On a wreath of the colours, An elephant argent, armed and harnessed Or, bearing on its back a castle Or thereon two pennons displayed, the dexter argent a cross gules, the sinister a pennon of the Arms of the Cutlers' Company. **Supporters:** On either side an elephant argent, armed Or. **Motto:** Pour parvenir a bonne foy. **Granted** 10 May 1622 by Sir William Segar, Garter King of Arms, to replace an earlier grant (7 May 1476) by Thomas Holme, Clarenceux King of Arms, which was confirmed (12 October 1530) by Thomas Benolt, Clarenceux King of Arms, and (22 October 1590) by Robert Cooke, Clarenceux King of Arms. (*Illustration on page* 119).

CYMMORODORION, HONOURABLE SOCIETY OF. Quarterly Or and gules, four lions passant guardant counterchanged, those on the dexter contourny. **Crest:** On a wreath of the colours, A dragon passant gules supporting with the dexter paw a lance Or, flying therefrom a pennon per fesse argent and vert. **Supporters:** On the dexter side a figure representing St. David vested in ecclesiastical robes and supporting with the exterior hand a cross staff proper and on the sinister side a figure representing an Arch Druid vested also proper holding in the exterior hand a sceptre Or. **Motto:** Cared doeth yr encilion. **Granted** 11 November 1953.

CRAWLEY
DEVELOPMENT CORPORATION

CROYDON

CRICKLADE

CROSBY

CUMBERLAND

D

** Denotes Illustration*

DANCING, ROYAL ACADEMY OF.* Per pale wavy gules and Or, a fess dancetty counterchanged, in the dexter chief a pentacle of the second. **Crest:** On a wreath of the colours, A figure representing Terpsichore proper. **Supporters:** On either side a doe guardant proper winged Or. **Motto:** Salus et felicitas. **Granted** 20 April 1937. The shield is shown here with a diaper pattern on it.

DARLINGTON, COUNTY BOROUGH OF (CO. DURHAM). Per pale azure and argent, to the dexter a representation of St. Cuthbert's cross proper and to the sinister two pallets vert; on a chief also argent a representation of the steam engine "Locomotion" and tender also proper. **Crest:** On a wreath of the colours, Two lions combatant argent supporting between them with the forlegs a civic mace Or. **Supporters:** On the dexter side a wyvern sejant, severing the neck a falchion proper [hilt and pomel Or], and on the sinister side a lion [ducally] crowned Or. **Motto:** Floreat industria. Arms and Crest granted 20 May 1960; Supporters granted 10 October 1967.

DARLINGTON RURAL DISTRICT COUNCIL (CO. DURHAM). Gules, on a fesse argent between in chief two garbs Or, each enfiled by a circlet of steel proper the circlets conjoined by a steel chain also proper, and in base a Shorthorn bull's head caboshed gold, a bar azure charged with a barrulet wavy also argent. **Crest:** On a wreath of the colours, A demi lion argent, the body and tail passing through a false escutcheon Or, holding with the forepaws by the blade a representation of the Conyers falchion, point downwards, proper. **Motto:** Optima petamus. **Granted** 19 June 1959.

DARTFORD, BOROUGH OF (KENT).* Gules, on a fess argent between in chief a jester's head habited in a fool's cap couped at the neck Or between two bezants, each charged with an ear of wheat proper, and in base an anvil of the third, a barrulet wavy azure. **Supporters:** On the dexter side a hermit holding in the exterior hand a staff and on the sinister side a prioress holding in the exterior hand a pastoral staff proper. **Motto:** Tenax et fidelis. **Granted** 4 September 1933.

DARTFORD GRAMMAR SCHOOL FOR GIRLS. Vert, in front of a fesse wavy argent charged with two barrulets wavy azure a horse rampant [forcene] also argent; on a chief of the last between two open books proper [edged Or, bound gules] a pale murrey charged with a torch Or. **Crest:** On a wreath of the colours, A pomme, thereon a fesse wavy argent charged with a bar wavy azure; over all a horse as in the Arms. **Granted** 20 June 1956.

DARTFORD RURAL DISTRICT COUNCIL (KENT).* Per fesse vert and gules, on a fesse argent between in chief a garb between two millrinds Or and in base on water barry wavy of the third and azure an ancient galley in full sail oars in action proper, a bar wavy of the fifth. **Crest:** On a wreath of the colours, A pomeis charged with a horse rampant argent. **Motto:** We serve. **Granted** 15 December 1950.

DARTMOUTH, BOROUGH OF (DEVON).* Gules, on water barry wavy in base proper an ancient ship, issuant from the centre thereof the figure of a king, robed, crowned, and holding in his sinister hand a sceptre; on the bow and on the stern of the ship a lion sejant guardant, that to

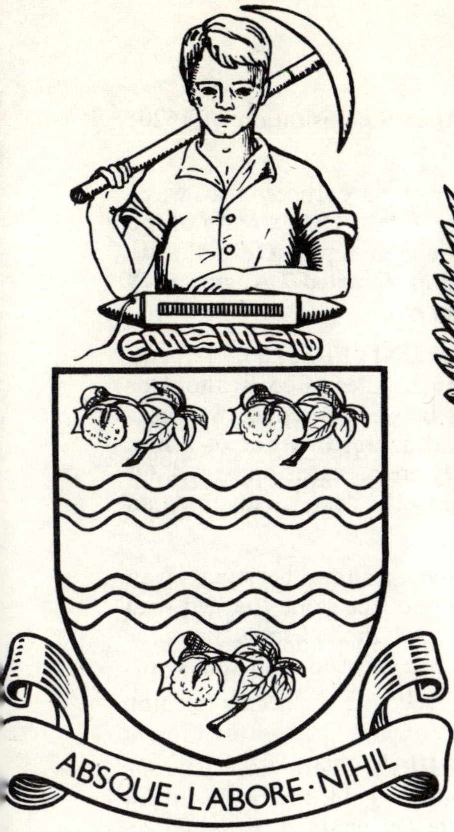

DARWEN

ROYAL ACADEMY OF DANCING

DARTFORD BOROUGH

DARTFORD R. D. C.

the dexter contourné, all Or. Recorded as a seal device (untinctured) at the Visitation of 1620; confirmed by Kings' of Arms Certificate 31 January 1951.

DARWEN, BOROUGH OF (LANCASHIRE).* Or, a fesse wavy with cottices also wavy azure between three sprigs of the cotton tree slipped and fructed proper. **Crest:** On a wreath of the colours, In front of a demi miner habited proper, holding over his shoulder a pick Or, a shuttle fessewise of the last, thread pendent proper. **Motto:** Absque labore nihil. **Granted** 7 August 1878 to The Mayor, Aldermen and Burgesses of the Borough of Over Darwen.

DARWIN COLLEGE TRUST, TRUSTEES OF THE (CAMBRIDGE UNIVERSITY). Argent, on a bend gules cottised vert between two mullets each within an annulet gules three escallops or (for Darwin) impaling Per fess dancetty azure and gules, a caduceus between in chief two roses Or (for Rayne); all within a bordure Or. **Crest:** On a wreath Or and azure, In front of a lion passant Or, murally crowned azure, holding in the dexter forepaw a key erect, wards outwards, Or three escallops argent. **Badge:** A leading rein interlaced azure, the clip to the dexter, entwining an escallop Or. **Granted** 5 January 1966.

DAVENANT FOUNDATION GRAMMAR SCHOOL. Gules, three escallops between seven cross crosslets fitchée, three, one, two, and one, argent, within a bordure of the same charged with eight lows of flame proper. **Crest:** On a wreath argent, gules and sable, A lymphad sable, pennons and flags flying gules, at the masthead a beacon enflamed proper, the sail charged with the Arms. **Badge:** A lymphad as in the Crest, upon a base wavy azure charged with a bar wavy argent, all within an annulet Or. **Granted** 9 November 1961.

DAVENTRY RURAL DISTRICT COUNCIL (NORTHAMPTONSHIRE). Vert, on a pale Or another gules charged with a Roman sword erect proper, hilt and pommel gold, the blade enfiled with a mural crown also gold; on a chief argent three pellets, the centre one charged with a fetterlock of the second, the others with a rose also argent, barbed and seeded proper. **Crest:** On a wreath of the colours, A buck's head argent, attired and gorged with a ducal coronet Or, pendent therefrom a torteau charged with an escarbuncle gold. **Motto:** Power in trust. **Granted** 20 June 1955.

DAWLEY URBAN DISTRICT COUNCIL (SHROPSHIRE).* Gules, three escutcheons argent, the first charged with a cross of the field, the second with a cross erminois, and the third with a cross vert. **Crest:** On a wreath of the colours, A demi triton winding a conch horn and crowned with an antique crown all Or. **Motto:** Trinis catenis vinctus. **Granted** 10 September 1956.

DEAL, BOROUGH OF (KENT) * Per pale gules and azure, three demi lions passant guardant in pale dimidiated with three demi hulks of ships Or; on a chief azure a representation of the Silver Oar of the Cinque Ports. **Crest:** On a wreath of the colours, Two towers proper. **Supporters:** On the dexter side a Roman centurion and on the sinister side a Royal Marine in full dress uniform; the whole upon a rocky mount, all proper. **Motto:** Adjuvate advenas. **Granted** 4 March 1968.

DEBEN RURAL DISTRICT COUNCIL (EAST SUFFOLK).* Barry wavy of six argent and azure, a lymphad Or, flying flags and pennon of St. George; on a chief sable a Saxon crown between two garbs Or. **Crest:** On a wreath of the colours, Issuant from the battlements of a tower Or a demi stag argent, attired proper unguled Or, gorged with a collar gules charged with three escallops Or, pendent therefrom a cross engrailed Or and supporting with the legs an anchor sable. **Motto:** Debentur omnia Deo. **Granted** 30 August 1963.

DEMOLITION CONTRACTORS, NATIONAL FEDERATION OF. Argent, a pinch bar fessewise, point to the dexter, surmounted by a mattock, head upwards, and a shovel, blade downwards, in saltire, all proper. **Granted** 27 November 1948.

DEBEN

DEAL

DENBIGHSHIRE

DARTMOUTH

DAWLEY

DENBIGHSHIRE COUNTY COUNCIL.* Argent, a lion rampant sable; a chief barry wavy Or and azure. **Crest:** On a wreath argent, gules, Or, purpure, argent, and azure, A demi dragon gules, gorged with a mural crown Or, supporting with the dexter fore claw an escutcheon quarterly sable, argent, gules and azure, thereon a ram's head caboshed proper. Mantled gules, doubled Or. **Motto:** Duw a digon. **Granted** 12 March 1962.

DENTON URBAN DISTRICT COUNCIL (LANCASHIRE).* Per pale argent and sable, two bars per pale gules and of the first, in chief three pierced cinquefoils ermine. **Crest:** On a wreath argent and gules, A beaver proper charged with two mullets in pale Or. **Motto:** Persevere. **Granted** 23 March 1936.

DERBY, BISHOPRIC OF. Purpure, a cross potent quadrate argent, in chief three fountains. **Granted** 29 October 1927.

DERBY, COUNTY BOROUGH OF.* Argent, on a mount vert within park palings a buck lodged between two oak trees fructed proper. **Crest:** On a wreath of the colours, A ram passant proper, collared Or, between two sprigs of broom also proper. **Supporters:** On either side a buck charged on the shoulder with a sprig of broom proper. **Motto:** Industria, virtus et fortitudo. **Granted** 12 May 1939.

DERBY COUNTY AND BOROUGH POLICE AUTHORITY. Sable, on a fess between in chief two stags' heads cabossed and in base a ram passant argent, a Tudor rose proper. **Motto:** Vis unita fortior. **Granted** 20 September 1968.

DERBY DIOCESAN TRAINING COLLEGE. Argent, on a pale purpure a cross potent quadrate of the field between a mitre Or and a fountain; a chief sable, thereon an open book proper edged and clasped of the third. **Crest:** On a wreath of the colours, A cross potent quadrate argent charged with a fountain. **Motto:** Dominus frustra. **Granted** 20 December 1950.

DERBY SCHOOL (BURY, LANCASHIRE). Quarterly argent and azure, on a bend of the last between in the second quarter an open book also argent edged and bound Or and in the third quarter a cogwheel also Or, three stags' heads caboshed gold. **Crest:** Out of a coronet composed of four roses gules barbed and seeded proper set upon a rim Or, a demi stag gold gorged with a torse argent and azure and supporting a torch erect also gold enflamed proper. **Motto:** Industria, Constantia, Sapientia. **Granted** 7 September 1959.

DERBY SCHOOL (DERBY). Per pale argent and sable, an open book proper, edged and clasped Or, bound gules, the pages inscribed 1554 in Arabic numerals, the whole ensigned by an ancient crown gold; on a chief gules between two crosses potent quadrate a stag lodged in a park also Or. **Motto:** Vita sine litteris mors. **Granted** 20 November 1962.

DERBYSHIRE BUILDING SOCIETY.* Or, a Tudor Rose proper; on a chief vert between two sprigs of thrift, each of three flowers, a castle of three towers, the portcullis raised, all gold. **Crest:** On a wreath Or and gules, Upon a mount vert a ram passant proper resting the dexter forehoof upon an escutcheon purpure charged with a mitre Or. **Supporters:** On either side a stag proper gorged with a collar of park palings Or and holding in the mouth a sprig of broom also proper. **Motto:** Bene serviendo. **Granted** 20 March 1959.

DERBYSHIRE COUNTY COUNCIL.* Or, a rose gules surmounted by another argent, both barbed and seeded proper; on a chief sable three stags' heads caboshed of the third. **Motto:** Bene consulendo. **Granted** 17 September 1937.

DEVIZES, BOROUGH OF (WILTSHIRE).* Per pale gules and azure, a castle in perspective, the whole forming a hexagon, the front triple-towered, the two outer towers domed, all Or, each dome ensigned by an estoile sable. Recorded at the Visitation of 1565.

DENTON

DERBYSHIRE BUILDING SOCIETY

DERBY CO. BOROUGH

DERBYSHIRE C. C.

DEVON COUNTY COUNCIL.* Argent, a lion rampant gules [ducally] crowned Or; on a chief wavy per fesse azure and barry wavy of the first and fourth an ancient ship argent. **Crest:** On a wreath of the colours, Out of a naval coronet Or a Dartmoor pony's head, in the mouth a sprig of heather, proper. **Supporters:** On the dexter side a Devon bull and on the sinister side a sea lion, both proper. **Motto:** Auxilio divino. Arms granted 11 October 1926; Crest and Supporters granted 6 March 1962.

DEWSBURY, COUNTY BOROUGH OF (YORKSHIRE—WEST RIDING).* Chequey Or and azure, on a chief engrailed sable a cross patonce of the first between two owls argent. **Crest:** On a wreath of the colours, In front of a cross patonce fitchée azure an owl as in the Arms. **Motto:** Deus noster refugium et virtus. **Granted** 24 February 1893.

DIDCOT PARISH COUNCIL (BERKSHIRE).* Vert, two costs in bend sinister surmounted of two costs in bend argent between in chief a gun barrel, in fess two garbs Or, and in base a ram's head erased of the second, armed gold; on a chief sable a mitre also of the second. **Crest:** On a wreath of the colours, Issuant from a wreath of hawthorn, leaved and flowered, a roebuck's head proper. **Motto:** Faith in service. **Granted** 21 July 1952.

DIDSBURY COLLEGE (WESTBURY ON TRYMM, BRISTOL).* Azure, a three-masted ship in full sail, flags flying to the dexter, argent; on a chief wavy of the last a cross couped between two escallops sable. **Motto:** Quo vadis sequimur. **Granted** 12 November 1946.

DIRECTORS, INSTITUTE OF. Argent, on a pale ermine between a castle of three towers and an argosy in full sail sable, a cross and in the first quarter a sword erect Or; on a chief gules a compass card gold. **Crest:** Issuant from a circlet Or with eight thrift flowers leaved proper on the rim, a pair of scales gules, behind the pivot a compass card as in the Arms. **Supporters:** On the dexter side a lion Or gorged with a collar gules charged with [three] bezants, and on the sinister side a dragon gold, winged argent, the underside of the wing charged with a cross gules. **Motto:** Integrity and enterprise. **Granted** 10 March 1952.

DISTILLERS OF THE CITY OF LONDON, WORSHIPFUL COMPANY OF.* Azure, a fesse wavy of water argent between in chief a sun Or drawing up a cloud argent distilling drops of water proper and in base a distillatory double-armed Or with two worms and bolt receivers argent. **Crest:** On a wreath argent and azure, A garb of barley Or wreathed about with a vine branch vert bearing grapes proper. Mantled gules, doubled argent. **Supporters:** On the dexter side a Russian and on the sinister side an Indian savage, each in his proper habit. **Motto:** Drop as rain, distil as dew. **Granted** 18 March 1639 by Sir John Borough, Garter King of Arms (*Illustration on page* 145).

THE DOCK AND HARBOUR AUTHORITIES' ASSOCIATION. Azure, on water in base barry wavy proper an ancient ship, mainsail set, pennons flying, Or; a canton ermine and in sinister chief a mullet gold. **Crest:** On a wreath Or and azure, Standing on a rock a cormorant, in the beak a sprig of laver proper, the dexter claw resting on an escutcheon argent charged with an anchor sable. **Granted** 21 March 1960.

DOCTOR WILLIAMS' SCHOOL, DOLGELLAU. Or, a pile reversed sable ensigned on the top with a fire-beacon proper; on a chief of the second three mullets of six points of the first. **Motto:** Ardua semper. **Granted** 27 October 1932.

DONCASTER, COUNTY BOROUGH OF (YORKSHIRE—WEST RIDING).* Gules, a port between two towers with flags argent, the portcullis raised sable, in chief a Saxon crown Or. **Crest:** On a wreath of the colours, Upon a cushion ermine a lion sejant Or grasping between his paws a staff proper, flying therefrom a banner azure, fringed and tasselled gold, thereon upon waves argent and azure a port between two towers as in the Arms charged with the word DON in letters sable. **Supporters:** On either side a lion sejant Or holding in the mouth a rose argent, barbed, seeded, leaved and slipped proper. **Motto:** Comfort et liesse. **Granted** 28 March 1927.

DEVON

DIDCOT

DEWSBURY

DEVIZES

DIDSBURY COLLEGE

DONCASTER AND DISTRICT JOINT WATER BOARD. Gules, issuant from water barry wavy of six azure and argent in base a port between two conically capped towers argent, the portcullis raised sable, issuant between the towers a rose argent, barbed, seeded, slipped and leaved proper; on a bordure Or nine fountains. **Crest:** On a wreath of the colours, Upon a mount vert a lion sejant Or supporting with the forelegs a valve key proper. **Motto:** Aquam eduxisti eis. **Granted** 5 March 1964.

DONCASTER RURAL DISTRICT COUNCIL (YORKSHIRE—WEST RIDING). Per pale sable and vert, a fesse wavy argent charged with another wavy azure and surmounted by a port between two towers, the portcullis raised, proper, in chief and in base a rose of the third, barbed and seeded also proper. **Granted** 30 October 1947.

DORKING AND HORLEY RURAL DISTRICT COUNCIL (SURREY). Vert semée of [twelve] acorns Or, two bendlets wavy argent. **Crest:** Out of a coronet composed of eight pine cones set upon a rim Or a mount vert, thereon a griffin passant gold, the beak and forelegs azure, and ducally gorged of the last, holding in the dexter claw a hammer erect proper. Mantled vert, doubled argent. **Motto:** E glande quercus. **Granted** 20 March 1959.

DORKING URBAN DISTRICT COUNCIL (SURREY).* Chequy Or and azure, a pale gules, thereon a lion rampant per fesse of the first and argent between in chief a ducal coronet gold and in base a sprig of oak fructed also argent. **Crest:** On a wreath of the colours, Within a mural crown argent a mount vert, standing thereon a Dorking cock proper. **Motto:** Virtute et vigilantia. **Granted** 24 August 1954.

DORSET COUNTY COUNCIL. *Argent, three lions passant guardant in pale and in base a fleur-de-lys gules; the shield ensigned with a mural crown towered Or. **Supporters:** On either side a dragon, wings elevated and addorsed, Or gorged with a Saxon crown gules. **Motto:** Who's afear'd. **Granted** 21 February 1950.

DOUAI ABBEY AND SCHOOL. Azure, three representations of the crown of St. Edmund, King and Martyr, Or; on a chief engrailed of the last an abbot's mitre between two fleurs-de-lys of the field. **Motto:** Dominus mihi adiutor. **Granted** 25 September 1929.

DOVER COLLEGE. Sable, a cross argent between four leopards' faces Or; on a chief of the last the castle with two towers of the field between two open books argent, edged gold bound gules. **Crest:** On a wreath of the colours, A demi man (representing St. Martin) habited as a Roman soldier, holding in his dexter hand a sword with which he divides his cloak, flowing from his shoulders and supported by his sinister hand, all proper. **Motto:** Non recuso laborem. **Granted** 30 January 1931.

DOWN COUNTY COUNCIL.* Vert, on a fess Or fretty gules a fish naiant argent, in chief three garbs Or and in base on water barry wavy of four argent and azure a lymphad, sail furled, pennon and flags flying, Or between two flax flowers slipped and leaved proper. **Crest:** On a wreath of the colours, Out of an ancient crown a dexter cubit arm, vested and cuffed argent, the hand proper grasping a Celtic crozier Or, looped about the shaft a snake, head downwards and to the sinister, vert. **Supporters:** On either side an Irish elk guardant proper. **Motto:** Absque labore nihil. **Granted** 15 December 1967.

DOWNHAM RURAL DISTRICT COUNCIL (NORFOLK).* Or, on a pale wavy double plain cotised azure a pallet wavy argent; a chief azure, thereon three pierced cinquefoils Or. **Crest:** Out of a coronet composed of four ears of wheat and four acorns leaved set alternately upon a rim Or, a winged demi lion argent, the wings Or semée of annulets gules, ducally gorged Or. **Motto:** Rident florentia prata. **Granted** 20 May 1964.

DOWNING COLLEGE (CAMBRIDGE UNIVERSITY).* Barry of eight argent and vert, a griffin segreant Or within a bordure azure charged with eight roses of the first, barbed and seeded proper. **Motto:** Quaerere verum. **Granted** 13 April 1801.

DORKING

DONCASTER CO. BOROUGH

DORSET

DOWNHAM

DRAPERS OF THE CITY OF LONDON, WORSHIPFUL COMPANY OF.* Azure, three clouds with sunbeams issuing proper crowned with Imperial Crowns tripled Or. **Crest:** On a wreath of the colours A mount vert, thereon a ram couchant Or, armed and unguled sable. Mantled gules, doubled argent. **Supporters:** On either side a lion Or pelletty. **Motto:** Unto God only be honor and glory. **Granted** June 1613 by Sir William Segar, Garter King of Arms, to replace earlier grants (10 March 1439) by Sir William Bruges, Garter King of Arms, and (10 July 1561) by William Hervey, Clarenceux King of Arms. (*Illustration on page* 145).

DRIFFIELD URBAN DISTRICT COUNCIL (YORKSHIRE—EAST RIDING). Barry of ten argent and azure, a pale vert charged with a ram's head caboshed proper between in chief and in base an ear of barley leaved Or. **Crest:** Issuing from a circlet sable charged with three roses argent, barbed and seeded proper, a hart's head also proper charged on the neck with two keys in saltire Or. Mantled azure, doubled argent. **Granted** 10 September 1956.

DROITWICH, BOROUGH OF (WORCESTERSHIRE).* Gules a sword of state, point downwards, argent surmounted of two lions passant Or, impaling quarterly, first and fourth, chequy argent and sable, second and third, gules two barrows erect in fesse argent. Recorded at the Visitation of 1634. Certified by John Dunamace Heaton-Armstrong, Chester Herald, in 1952.

DROYLSDEN URBAN DISTRICT COUNCIL (LANCASHIRE).* Or, three bendlets enhanced vert, in base a lamb passant proper supporting a crossstaff flying a banner argent charged wth a cross patée gules. **Motto:** By concord and industry. **Granted** 16 October 1950.

DUDLEY, COUNTY BOROUGH OF (WORCESTERSHIRE). Gules, on a fesse engrailed argent between in chief on a mount vert a representation of the keep of Dudley Castle proper, the sinister tower ensigned with a long cross Or, and in base a salamander in flames also proper, a trilobite between an anchor cabled and a Davy lamp, all of the first. **Crest:** Out of a mural crown Or, a lion's head azure, maned gold, collared ermine. **Supporters:** On either side an angel proper, winged argent, habited gules, girdled Or, and holding in the exterior hand a mural crown gold. **Motto:** Sapiens qui prospicit. **Granted** 20 March 1957.

DUKINFIELD, BOROUGH OF (CHESHIRE).* Quarterly azure and argent, a cross pointed and voided quarterly of the last and sable between in the first quarter a raven close and in the fourth a garb, both Or. **Crest:** Out of a crown palisado Or, a cubit arm, vested azure, cuff argent, hand proper holding an escutcheon of the second charged with a sun in splendour of the first, between two ostrich feathers of the third. **Motto:** Integrity. **Granted** 24 March 1900.

DULWICH COLLEGE. See Alleyn's College of God's Gift.

DUNGANNON URBAN DISTRICT COUNCIL (CO. TYRONE).* Or, a castle proper, in chief a dexter hand gules; on a chief sable a shuttle fessewise of the field. **Crest:** On a wreath Or and sable, A dexter hand grasping a stalk of flax flowered and leaved proper. **Motto:** Dungannon. **Granted** 6 August 1951.

DUNSTABLE COLLEGE. Quarterly Or and gules, a chevron ermine between in chief a hind's head erased and a bugle horn stringed and in base an escallop all counterchanged; a bordure engrained sable. **Crest:** On a wreath of the colours, A buzzard rising gules charged on the breast with an escallop Or. **Motto:** To learn, to do, to serve. **Granted** 1 September 1965.

DURHAM, BISHOPRIC OF. Azure, a cross Or between four lions rampant argent. Recorded in the Parliament Roll of 1512. Azure, a cross patonce Or between four lions rampant argent. Recorded at the Visitation of 1530. The mitre of the Bishop of Durham is encircled by a ducal coronet.

DURHAM, CITY OF.* Sable, a cross argent surmounted by another cross gules. Recorded at the Visitation of 1615.

DOWNING COLLEGE

DOWN

DROYLSDEN

DROITWICH

DURHAM CITY

DUKINFIELD

DURHAM, PRINCIPAL AND GOVERNING BODY OF THE GRADUATE SOCIETY OF THE UNIVERSITY OF. Ermine, a cross formy quadrate gules; on a chief indented sable between three lions rampant argent two lozenges Or. **Crest:** On a wreath argent and gules, Two lions rampant argent supporting a cross formy quadrate gules. Mantled sable, doubled argent. **Granted** 10 February 1966.

DURHAM, UNIVERSITY OF.* Argent, a cross pattée quadrate gules; a canton azure charged with a chevron Or between three lions rampant of the first. **Motto:** Fundamenta ejus super montibus sanctis. **Granted** 18 May 1843.

DURHAM, UNIVERSITY COLLEGE, Azure, a cross patonce Or between four lions rampant argent; on a chief of the last a cross of St. Cuthbert sable between two Durham mitres gules. **Motto:** Non nobis solum. **Granted** 29 May 1912.

DURHAM COUNTY COUNCIL.* Azure, on a cross Or between four lions rampant argent, each ducally crowned gold and grasping in the dexter claw a sword in bend sinister proper pomel and hilt gold, five lozenges sable; the shield ensigned with a mural crown gold. **Badge:** Within a garland of wheat Or three bars wavy azure; over all a lion as in the Arms. **Granted** 30 May 1961.

DURHAM RURAL DISTRICT COUNCIL.* Lozengy argent and sable, in chief two miner's lamps proper and in base a garb Or. **Crest:** Out of a coronet composed of four ears of wheat and as many acorns slipped and leaved set alternately on a rim Or, a lion rampant argent holding in the forepaws a miner's pick erect Or. **Motto:** By faith, foresight and industry. **Granted** 1 February 1962.

DURSLEY RURAL DISTRICT COUNCIL (GLOUCESTERSHIRE). Gules, a Paschal Lamb proper within an orle of [ten] crosses formy argent; on a chief vert between two cartwheels of eight spokes Or an open book also proper, garnished gold, thereon the words HOLY BIBLE in letter sable. **Crest:** Out of a crown vallary Or, a mount of sand, standing thereon a White-fronted Goose close proper. Mantled gules, doubled argent. **Motto:** God with us. **Granted** 12 May 1952.

DYERS OF THE CITY OF LONDON, WORSHIPFUL COMPANY OF.* Sable, a chevron engrailed argent between three bags of madder of the second, corded Or. **Crest:** On a wreath of the colours, A grain tree proper. **Supporters:** On either side a panther proper, incensed gules, crowned Or and semée of roundels gules, azure, vert, purpure and sable. **Motto:** Da gloriam Deo. The Arms are anterior to 1530, no patent for them being extant. At the Visitations of 1530 and 1590, the chevron was recorded as plain but that of 1634 makes it engrailed. The Crest and Supporters were granted 14 November 1577 by Robert Cooke, Clarenceux King of Arms.

DYERS AND COLOURISTS, SOCIETY OF.* Tierce in pairle reversed purpure, Or, and azure, in chief a madder plant eradicated gold and a slip of indigo leaved and fructed also azure and in base between two slips of the grain tree leaved also gold a hexagon argent voided of the field. **Crest:** On a wreath Or and purpure, A Purple Iris flower proper. **Supporters:** On the dexter side a female figure representing the goddess Iris, habited argent with wings Or and holding in the exterior hand a caduceus proper, and on the sinister side a male figure representing a craftsman of the dyer's trade in seventeenth century habit proper, holding in the exterior hand a hank of silk also Or. **Motto:** Scientia coloris ministra. **Badge:** Within a voided hexagon Or a Purple Iris flower proper. **Granted** 20 December 1956.

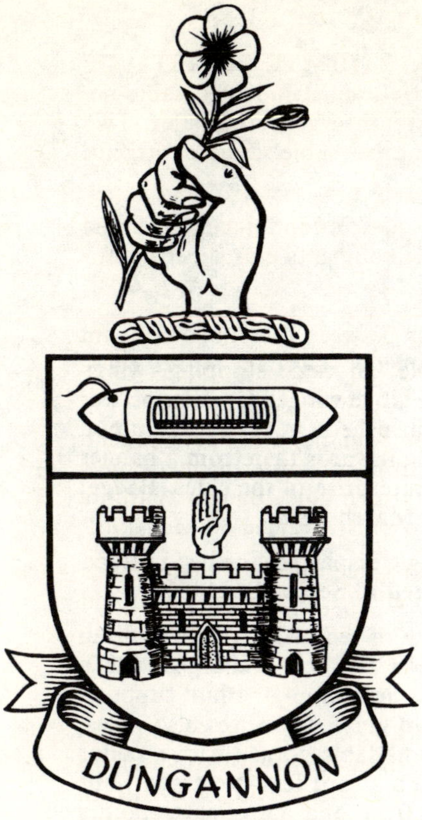

DUNGANNON

DURHAM UNIVERSITY

DURHAM R. D. C.

DURHAM C. C.

DYERS AND COLOURISTS

E

* *Denotes Illustration*

EAGLE AVIATION LIMITED. Per pale nebuly azure and sable, an eagle stooping, wings elevated, Or. **Crest:** On a wreath argent and gules, A demi terrestrial glove winged Or. **Supporters:** On either side the figure of a knight proper, armed cap-a-pie sable garnished Or, vested in a jupon of the Arms and supporting with the exterior hand a staff gold, flying inwards therefrom a banner argent charged with four fusils conjoined in saltire gules. **Motto:** Enterprise in the skies. **Badge:** Within an annulet an eagle stooping, wings elevated, Or. **Granted** 20 March 1958.

EAGLE OIL AND SHIPPING COMPANY, LIMITED. Or, an eagle displayed, the head turned to the sinister; a chief and base sable. **Motto:** Semper vigilans. **Granted** 10 September 1956.

EAGLE STAR INSURANCE COMPANY LIMITED. Barry wavy of ten azure and argent, an eagle displayed Or, pendent from the neck by a guige an escutcheon also azure charged with a mullet of the second. **Crest:** On a wreath of the colours, In front of a demi-lion guardant supporting a trident erect Or and charged on the shoulder with an escallop gules, five roses also gules, barbed and seeded proper. **Supporters:** On either side a lion guardant sable gorged with a collar argent charged with three escallops gules and holding in the mouth a sword fesswise argent, hilt and pommel inwards Or. **Motto:** In aquila stella securitas. **Badge:** In front of a star of seven points Or an eagle recursant volant to the sinister azure. **Granted** 20 February 1957.

EALING, ABBEY OF ST. BENEDICT AT. Sable, a cross potent gules fimbriated Or; on a chief of the last between two ravens also sable a pierced cinquefoil also gules, each foil charged with an ermine spot gold. **Granted** 28 March 1956.

EALING, LONDON BOROUGH OF.* Argent, issuant from a grassy mount in base an oak tree proper fructed Or; on a chief gules three Saxon crowns Or. **Motto:** Progress with unity. **Granted** 1 September 1965.

EAST ANGLIA, UNIVERSITY OF.* Azure, three ancient crowns Or, in chief a castle of three domes argent, flying from each the banner of St. George, the port sable, portcullis raised Or. **Crest:** On a wreath argent, Or, and azure, Issuing from clouds proper an angel vested argent, mantled azure, winged, crined and crowned Or, holding in the dexter hand a sword erect proper, hilt and pomel Or, and in the sinister hand an open book also proper, edged, bound and leathered Or. **Supporters:** On either side a lion guardant Or, pendent from the neck by cords tasselled a purse azure, and holding with the interior paw an ancient crown gold. **Motto:** Do different. **Granted** 5 March 1964.

EASTBOURNE, COUNTY BOROUGH OF (EAST SUSSEX).* Argent, on a fesse double cottised gules a rose Or between two stags' heads caboshed of the field. **Crest:** On a wreath of the colours, A sea horse raising the dexter foot vert. **Motto:** Meliora sequimur. **Granted** 11 January 1928.

EASTBOURNE COLLEGE. Azure, on a cross argent a rose gules; in the first quarter a stag's head caboshed of the second. **Crest:** On a wreath of the colours, In front of an open book proper a stag's head as in the Arms. **Motto:** Ex Oriente salus. **Granted** 21 January 1933.

THE DIERS

THE DRAPERS

THE DISSTILLERS

EASTBOURNE MUTUAL BUILDING SOCIETY. Argent, on a fesse double cotised gules two martlets Or; over all issuant from the base a representation of the Beachey Head Lighthouse proper. **Motto:** Salus per prudentiam. **Granted** 1 March 1960.

EASTBOURNE TRAINING COLLEGE. Per chevron indented grady argent and gules, in chief two Yellow-horned poppies (Glancium flavum) slipped and leaved proper and in base a seahorse supporting between the fins an open book argent. **Motto:** Courage mounteth with occasion. **Granted** 20 November 1963 to The County Borough of Eastbourne for the use of the College.

EAST DEAN RURAL DISTRICT COUNCIL (GLOUCESTERSHIRE).* Barry wavy of six argent and vert, on a pile erminois in chief an oak tree couped proper fructed with eleven acorns Or and in base a stag's head caboshed also proper. **Crest:** Issuant from a coronet composed of four fleurs-de-lys set on a rim Or, a demi figure representing an ancient Forest of Dean miner capped and habited sable, in his mouth a stick transfixing a candle enflamed proper, holding in the dexter hand a pick erect and carrying over the sinister shoulder a hod of coal also proper. **Motto:** Velut silva floreat. **Granted** 9 April 1954.

EAST DOWN RURAL DISTRICT COUNCIL (CO. DOWN). Per chevron vert and Or, on a chevron wavy per chevron wavy argent and azure in chief a salmon naiant proper, between three stalks of barley conjoined Or and two shuttles in saltire Or, and in base a demi figure representing St. Patrick, habited and nimbed Or, supporting over the sinister shoulder a shepherd's crook. **Crest:** On a wreath of the colours, Between six stalks of barley proper a dexter arm embowed, vested and cuffed Or, the hand holding a stalk of three flax flowers proper. **Motto:** Ever looking forward. **Granted** 3 February 1966.

EAST ELLOE RURAL DISTRICT COUNCIL (LINCOLNSHIRE—PARTS OF LINDSEY). Gules, issuant from the base a representation of the Elloe stone proper between two mitres in fesse Or; a chief arched barry wavy of six argent and azure. **Crest:** Out of a circlet vert charged with five wheat ears, an eagle's head Or, in the beak a tulip gules stalked and leaved proper. Mantled gules, doubled Or. **Motto:** Alacres illo coluerunt. **Granted** 16 March 1955.

EAST GRINSTEAD URBAN DISTRICT COUNCIL (EAST SUSSEX).* Vert, a pallet argent surmounted of a sun rising issuant from the base Or; on a chief of the last an ash tree couped proper, enfiled by an ancient crown gules, between a hammer sable and a sword in its scabbard also gules, garnished also argent. **Crest:** Issuant from a circlet Or charged with three roses gules, barbed and seeded proper, a plume of five ostrich feathers azure, the quills gold. Mantled vert, doubled Or. **Motto:** Pratis praesto virentibus. **Granted** 9 September 1955.

EAST KESTEVEN RURAL DISTRICT COUNCIL (LINCOLNSHIRE—PARTS OF KESTEVEN).* Per fesse azure and sable, on a bar cotised argent between in chief three crosses bottony and in base an oak tree eradicated and fructed Or, a barrulet wavy also azure. **Crest:** On a wreath Or and azure, A crane, wings expanded and inverted, proper perched on an anchor fessewise gold. **Motto:** Rus diligenter curate. **Granted** 20 January 1960.

EASTLEIGH, BOROUGH OF (HAMPSHIRE).* Or, on a bend chequy sable and argent between in chief a mitre of the second and in base a lily leaved and slipped proper, three roses gules, barbed and seeded also proper. **Crest:** On a wreath of the colours, In front of a rising sun a winged wheel Or. **Motto:** Salus populi suprema lex. **Granted** 16 January 1934 to the Eastleigh Urban District Council.

EAST MIDLANDS ELECTRICITY BOARD. Azure, a cross raguly couped between in the first quarter an antique crown, in the fourth quarter a fetterlock Or, in the second and third

EAST GRINSTEAD

EAST ANGLIA UNIVERSITY

EASTBOURNE

EALING

EAST DEAN

quarters a rose argent, barbed and seeded proper; on a chief of the second a bear supporting a ragged staff sable between two cinquefoils ermine. **Crest:** On a wreath of the colours, A Viking's ship, oars in action, Or, the sail argent charged with a horseshoe sable, pennant flying gules. **Supporters:** On either side a stag proper, that to the dexter charged on the shoulder with a plate, thereon a Stafford knot sable, and that to the sinister charged on the shoulder with a roundel per chevron a cross at the point vert and argent. **Motto:** Feliciter servimus. **Granted** 10 March 1950.

EAST MIDLANDS GAS BOARD. Or, on a cross raguly vert a fleur-de-lys of the field; a chief gules, thereon a three-tiered castle between two rams' heads caboshed argent. **Crest:** On a wreath of the colours, In front of flames a demi figure of Vulcan holding in the dexter hand four arrows and over the sinister shoulder a hammer, all proper. **Supporters:** On either side a panther [guardant] gules, incensed, charged on the shoulder with a pierced cinquefoil ermine. **Motto:** E mulcibere garae. **Granted** 19 March 1953.

EAST RETFORD, BOROUGH OF (NOTTINGHAMSHIRE).* Or, two choughs, wings elevated and addorsed, respecting one another, their interior legs elevated and the claws conjoined proper. **Crest:** On a wreath Or and sable, A lion passant, queue fourchée, gules resting the dexter paw on an escutcheon Or charged with a representation of a deed proper, the seal pendent also gules. **Supporters:** On either side a unicorn ermine, armed, maned, tufted and unguled Or, gorged with a collar sable charged with three escallops gold. **Motto:** Vetustas dignitatem generat. **Granted** 4 November 1940.

EAST RETFORD RURAL DISTRICT COUNCIL (NOTTINGHAMSHIRE).* Paly wavy of four vert and argent, a stag trippant gules; on a chief sable a sun issuant Or. **Crest:** Out of a circlet composed of four ears of wheat and as many acorns leaved set alternately on a rim Or, a demi greyhound argent gorged with a collar gules, pendent therefrom an escutcheon ermine charged with two piles in pile sable, and holding between the paws an escallop also argent. **Motto:** Famam extendere factis. **Granted** 9 June 1961.

EAST RIDING OF YORKSHIRE COUNTY COUNCIL. See Yorkshire.

EAST SUSSEX COUNTY COUNCIL. See Sussex.

EASTWOOD URBAN DISTRICT COUNCIL (NOTTINGHAMSHIRE).* Lozengy argent and sable; on a chief Or an annulet of the second between two torteaux. **Granted** 17 May 1951.

EBBW VALE URBAN DISTRICT COUNCIL (MONMOUTHSHIRE). Per fesse sable and gules masoned argent, a cross fillet Or, in the first quarter a pair of mill rolls palewise proper, the necks gold, in the second quarter an open scroll of parchment also proper. **Crest:** On a wreath Or and sable, A dragon passant gules, breathing fire proper, gorged with a collar of steel also proper with a chain of the same attached thereto passing between the forlegs and reflexed over the back, and resting the dexter foreclaw on an ingot of steel likewise proper. **Motto:** Iechyd ac addysg. **Granted** 10 March 1958.

ECCLES, BOROUGH OF (LANCASHIRE). Or, on a mount vert the front elevation of an ecclesiastical building masoned proper; a chief azure, thereon between two sprigs of the cotton tree slipped and fructed of the third a pale argent charged with a representation of a Nasmyth Steam Hammer sable. **Crest:** On a wreath of the colours, In front of a rock surmounted by a lighthouse a ship under sail to the sinister, all proper. **Supporters:** On either side a griffin gules supporting between the forelegs a staff Or, flying therefrom a forked pennon argent charged with three boars' heads erased and erect in fess sable langued gules [the whole upon a compartment of grass divided by a stream of water barry wavy argent and azure]. **Motto:** Labore omnia florent. **Badge:** A cog-wheel azure charged with a bezant, thereon and issuant from a mount vert the front

EASTLEIGH

EAST RETFORD BOROUGH

EASTWOOD

EAST KESTEVEN

EAST RETFORD R.D.C.

EGHAM

elevation of an ecclesiastical building masoned proper; all encircled by a wreath of eight roses gules, barbed, seeded and leaved proper. Arms and Crest granted 7 November 1893; Supporters and Badge granted 5 January 1966.

ECCLESIASTICAL INSURANCE OFFICE LIMITED. Azure, a fret Or; over all a portcullis between four passion crosses argent. **Crest:** On a wreath of the colours, In front of a church tower proper a cock Or. **Motto:** Pro ecclesia, **Granted** 1 June 1965.

ECONOMIC INSURANCE COMPANY LIMITED. Per pale Or and sable, three bars couped counterchanged. **Crest:** On a wreath of the colours, A lion rampant guardant supporting with the forepaws and dexter hind paw a key, ward upward and outward, Or. **Supporters:** On the dexter side a Wallaby and on the sinister side a Springbok, both proper. **Motto:** Providentia salus. **Granted** 3 August 1950.

EDGBASTON HIGH SCHOOL FOR GIRLS (BIRMINGHAM). Argent, a pale per pale indented throughout azure and Or between two laurel branches proper. **Crest:** On a wreath argent and vert, A distaff erect between two martins, the dexter contourné proper. **Motto:** Fideliter, fortiter feliciter. **Granted** 25 July 1961.

EGHAM URBAN DISTRICT COUNCIL (SURREY).* Vert, a representation of Magna Carta ensigned by a representation of the crown of King John proper. **Crest:** On a wreath Or and vert, In front of a weeping willow tree and on water barry wavy, a swan proper. **Motto:** Ut homines liberi sint. **Granted** 19 March 1951.

ELECTRICAL ENGINEERS, INSTITUTION OF. Azure, within an annulet flory counterflory at the cardinal points a winged thunderbolt Or; on a chief of the last two bars wavy of the first surmounted with an open book proper garnished gules, on the leaves the words DISCE DOCE in letters sable. **Crest:** On a wreath of the colours, A lion statant guardant Or, armed and langued azure, supporting with the dexter forepaw a caduceus gold. **Supporters:** On either side a pegasus argent, winged, crined and unguled Or, charged on the shoulder with a cross pommelly gules. **Granted** 6 January 1949.

ELECTRICITY COUNCIL. Argent, a male griffin gules, armed, langued and tufted, the beak surmounting a sun in splendour Or; on a bordure azure twelve estoiles argent. **Crest:** On a wreath argent and azure, In front of a demi sun in splendour Or an eagle, wings expanded, sable, beaked and membered Or, the dexter wing charged with a daffodil flower affronté Or and the sinister with a rose gules, barbed and seeded proper. **Supporters:** On either side a lion per fess wavy ermine and ermines, that on the dexter gorged with a collar Or charged with three roses gules, barbed and seeded proper, in the mouth a like rose, slipped and leaved vert, and that on the sinister gorged with a collar azure charged with three daffodil flowers affronté, in the mouth a daffodil slipped and leaved proper. **Motto:** The past is but the prologue. **Granted** 7 March 1966.

ELECTRONIC AND RADIO TECHNICIANS, SOCIETY OF, LIMITED. Azure, a fess wavy, in chief a lightning flash between the signs for vector forces within two cogwheels, and in base a conventional representation of an atom, all within a bordure, all Or. **Crest:** On a wreath of the colours, In front of a conventional representation of an atom Or the head of Mercury proper, crined and wearing a petasus Or. **Motto:** In servitio industriae. **Granted** 15 December 1967.

ELLESMERE COLLEGE (SHROPSHIRE).* Per chevron purpure and Or, two celestial crowns fesswise of the last, in chief a cross flory also gold, in base a raven proper holding in the beak a golden annulet. **Crest:** On a wreath of the colours, Standing on a mount vert a raven as in the Arms. **Motto:** Pro patria dimicans. **Granted** 12 April 1954.

ELLESMERE PORT, BOROUGH OF (CHESHIRE).* Gules, on a bar argent a barrulet sable surmounted of a pale also argent thereon a pallet azure, in the first quarter a beaver, in the second

ELSTREE

ELLESMERE PORT

ENFIELD

ELLESMERE COLLEGE

a cornucopia inverted, in the third a garb and in the fourth a sickle, all Or. **Crest:** On a wreath of the colours, On water barry wavy a lymphad, sail set proper and charged with a cogwheel sable, flags and pennon flying gules. **Supporters:** On the dexter side a sea horse and on the sinister side a tabby cat guardant, both proper. **Motto:** Progrediamur. **Badge:** On a plate encircled by a cable Or, water barry wavy in base, thereon a lymphad proper, the sail argent charged with a cogwheel sable, and flags and pennon flying gules. Arms, Crest and Supporters granted 6 October 1955; Badge granted 20 December 1963.

ELSTREE RURAL DISTRICT COUNCIL (HERTFORDSHIRE).* Ermine, issuant from a base barry wavy of four argent and azure a mount vert, thereon an oak tree proper, fructed and charged on the branches with a Saxon crown Or; on a chief of the last on a pale between two escallops of the third a saltire gold. **Crest:** On a wreath argent and azure, A demi hart proper gorged with a mural crown Or and supporting with the sinister forehoof a cinematograph spool loaded with film, all proper. **Motto:** Do well and fear not. **Granted** 20 March 1957.

ELTHAM COLLEGE. Azure, two pilgrims' staves in saltire argent surmounted by a cross flory Or. **Crest:** On a wreath of the colours, In front of two torches in saltire Or enflamed proper an open book also proper. **Motto:** Gloria filiorum patres. **Granted** 10 May 1935.

ELY, BISHOPRIC OF. Gules, three ducal coronets, two and one, Or. Recorded in the College of Arms.

EMMANUEL COLLEGE (CAMBRIDGE UNIVERSITY).* Argent, a lion rampant azure, armed and langued gules, holding in the dexter forepaw a laurel wreath proper, in the mouth a scroll [of the second] inscribed EMMANUEL in letters Or. Granted 1 January 1589 by Robert Cooke, Clarenceux King of Arms.

EMPIRE TEST PILOTS' SCHOOL (BOSCOMBE DOWN, SALISBURY). Azure semée of mullets Or, on a pale argent a torch enflamed proper. **Crest:** Issuant from an astral crown Or an eagle, wings elevated and addorsed, azure. **Motto:** Learn to test, test to learn. [Original motto: Looking forward]. **Granted** 7 September 1949.

ENFIELD, LONDON BOROUGH OF.* Or, on a fesse wavy vert a bar wavy argent charged with a barrulet wavy azure; over all an enfield rampant gules. **Crest:** On a wreath Or and azure, A stag's head proper, wreathed about the neck a garland of roses gules, barbed, seeded, slipped and leaved proper. **Supporters:** On the dexter side a lion gules gorged with a collar engrailed with chain reflexed over the back and charged with a saltire couped Or, and on the sinister side an enfield gules. **Motto:** By industry ever stronger. **Badge:** On a pentagon wavy Or fimbriated concentrically vert, argent, and azure, argent and vert, an enfield rampant gules. **Granted** 15 August 1966.

ENGLISH AND AMERICAN INSURANCE COMPANY LIMITED.* Quarterly argent and gules, a cross counterchanged within a bordure azure charged with thirteen mullets of the first. **Crest:** Within a coronet composed of four roses gules barbed and seeded proper and as many mullets argent set upon a rim Or, upon waves of the sea a representation of the whaler "Terra Nova" in full sail proper. **Supporters:** On either side a lion Or gorged with a chain gold, pendent therefrom an anchor argent, and supporting a staff proper, flying therefrom a banner also argent charged with a saltire gules. **Motto:** Nunquam non paratus. **Granted** 1 March 1957.

ENNISKILLEN, BOROUGH OF (CO. FERMANAGH). Quarterly gules and azure, a cross argent charged with another cross of the first between in the first and fourth quarters a castle with portcullis raised of the third, flying therefrom a banner of St. George, in the second quarter an open book proper, garnished Or, and in the third quarter three bridges of as many arches in pale of the last. **Crest:** On a wreath of the colours, Perched upon an anchor fessewise sable an eagle, wings displayed, Or. **Supporters:** On the dexter side a Private of the 27th (or Inniskilling) Regiment

ENGLISH AND AMERICAN INSURANCE

EPSOM AND EWELL

ESHER

EMMANUEL COLLEGE

EPSOM COLLEGE

of Foot and on the sinister side an Officer of the 6th (or Inniskilling) Regiment of Dragoons, each in the uniform of the period 1815. **Motto:** Ut proavi in Deo confidemus. **Granted** 12 May 1950.

ENNISKILLEN RURAL DISTRICT COUNCIL (CO. FERMANAGH). Vert, on a fess argent between in chief a wood pigeon and in base a mallard drake, the heads of a Hereford and a Friesian cow couped and respectant, all proper. **Crest:** On a wreath of the colours, A representation of the round tower of Devenish proper. **Granted** 15 November 1966.

EPSOM AND EWELL, BOROUGH OF (SURREY).* Per chevron vert and argent, in chief two horses' heads erased Or and in base as many bars wavy azure. **Motto:** None such. **Granted** 4 September 1937.

EPSOM COLLEGE.* Per pale azure and sable, three fleurs-de-lis Or; on a chief of the last an open book proper inscribed with the words "Olim meminisse juvabit" between in the dexter a lamp and in the sinister a rod of Aesculapius gules. **Crest:** On a wreath of the colours, In front of an eagle's head between two wings azure, three fleurs-de-lis gold. **Motto:** Deo non fortuna. **Granted** 7 June 1910.

EQUITABLE LIFE ASSURANCE SOCIETY.* Gules, a heart Or between six writing pens quilled gold feathered argent. **Crest:** On a wreath of the colours, Issuant from a mural crown argent a pelican in her piety proper. **Supporters:** On either side a griffin sable, winged Or, charged on the wing with a fesse undy gules and gorged with a collar gold, that of the dexter charged with thistles proper and that of the sinister with roses azure barbed and seeded also proper. **Motto:** Sic nos non nobis. **Granted** 6 December 1960.

ESHER URBAN DISTRICT COUNCIL (SURREY).* Azure, a chevron Or between in dexter chief a griffin passant, in sinister chief an eagle displayed argent, and in base on a mount vert a representation of Wayneflete's Tower at Esher Place proper; a chief argent charged with two barrulets wavy of the first. **Crest:** On a wreath of the colours, On a mount vert in front of three silver birch trees proper a lion passant guardant Or. **Granted** 1 June 1957.

ESHTON HALL SCHOOL EDUCATIONAL TRUST, LIMITED (GARGRAVE, YORKSHIRE). Sable, a demi wolf couped Or, gorged with a collar gemel gules, between three open books proper, edged gules, bound and clasped Or. **Crest:** On a wreath of the colours, A demi-wolf Or charged on the neck [shown on the shoulder] with a mullet of six points gules supporting a torch Or enflamed proper. **Motto:** Mens sibi conscia recti. **Granted** 5 March 1964.

ESSEX, UNIVERSITY OF. Gules, three seaxes in pale, cutting edges upwards, argent, pomels and hilts to the dexter Or, in chief an open book proper edged and bound with seven clasps Or. **Crest:** On a wreath of the colours, A wyvern statant argent upon two branches of oak raguly leaved fructed in saltire proper enfiled through an annulet argent. **Motto:** Thought the harder, heart the keener. **Granted** 10 December 1963.

ESSEX COUNTY COUNCIL.* Gules, three seaxes fessewise in pale argent, pomels and hilts Or, points to the sinister and cutting edges upwards. **Granted** 15 July 1932.

ESSEX INSTITUTE OF AGRICULTURE. See Agriculture, Essex Institute of.

ESTATE MANAGEMENT, COLLEGE OF (READING UNIVERSITY). Or, two pallets azure; over all on a fesse engrailed sable a garb of the field between two open books argent edged gold. **Crest:** On a wreath of the colours, An owl perched upon the battlements of a tower proper between two sprigs of oak also proper fructed Or. **Granted** 24 June 1929.

ETON COLLEGE.* Sable, three lilies argent; on a chief per pale azure and gules on the dexter a fleur-de-lis and on the sinister a lion passant guardant Or. **Motto:** Floreat Etona. **Granted** 1 January 1449 by King Henry VI.

EQUITABLE LIFE ASSURANCE

ETON R. D. C.

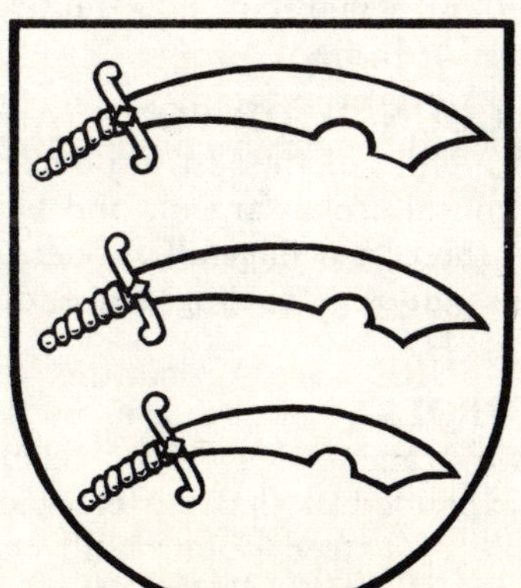

ESSEX C. C.

ETON COLLEGE

ETON RURAL DISTRICT COUNCIL (BUCKINGHAMSHIRE).* Per pale gules and sable, issuant from a plain base barry wavy of four argent and vert a mount of the last, thereon in front of a beech tree Or a swan, wings displayed and inverted, proper; all within a bordure ermine. **Crest:** Out of a coronet composed of four fleurs-de-lys gules set upon a rim Or a demi panther guardant argent semée of hurts, collared gules and holding between the paws an escutcheon also argent charged with a fesse sable thereon three plates. Mantled gules and sable, doubled argent. **Motto:** Consilio et animis. **Granted** 18 November 1960.

EVESHAM, BOROUGH OF (WORCESTERSHIRE).* Azure, a prince's coronet Or between two ostrich feathers in chief argent, the quills bezantée, and a garb in base of the second; all within a bordure sable bezantée. Recorded at the Visitations of 1604, 1634 and 1682.

EVESHAM RURAL DISTRICT COUNCIL (WORCESTERSHIRE).* Azure, on a chevron Or between in chief two cornucopiae proper, the horns Or, and in base a pear tree issuant Or, fructed sable, a chain in chevron padlocked to the dexter and ringed to the sinister azure. **Crest:** On a wreath of the colours, Upon a mount vert in front of a representation of Broadway Tower a lion passant queue-fourchée holding in the dexter forepaw a cross-crosslet fitchée gules. **Motto:** Fervet opus. **Granted** 20 December 1962.

EXETER, BISHOPRIC OF. Gules, a sword erect in pale argent, hilted Or, surmounted of two keys addorsed in saltire, wards in chief, of the last. Recorded in the College of Arms.

EXETER, CITY AND COUNTY BOROUGH OF.* Per pale gules and sable, a castle triangular and triple-towered Or. **Crest:** On a wreath Or and sable, A demi lion gules, ducally crowned and holding between the paws a bale [Or banded azure] surmounted of a cross botonnée gold. [= orb] Mantled azure, doubled argent. **Supporters:** On either side a pegasus argent, crined and unguled Or, the wings [elevated] barry wavy of six of the first and azure. **Motto:** Semper fidelis. **Badge:** In front of two swords in saltire, points upwards Or, a Tudor hat gules, embroidered gold. Arms confirmed and Crest and Supporters granted 6 August 1564 by William Hervey, Clarenceux King of Arms; Badge granted 16 October 1907.

EXETER, UNIVERSITY OF. Argent, a saltire vert surmounted in chief of an open book proper inscribed with the words LUCEM SEQUIMUR; on a chief gules a triple-towered fortress gold; all within a bordure sable bezantée. **Granted** 24 May 1923 to the University College of the South West of England, Exeter; transferred to the University upon its creation.

EXETER COLLEGE (OXFORD UNIVERSITY).* Argent, two bends nebuly sable; a bordure of the last charged with eight pairs of keys endorsed and interlaced in the bows Or, the wards upwards. Recorded at the Visitation of 1574.

EXMOUTH URBAN DISTRICT COUNCIL (DEVON). Argent, two anchors in saltire gules between four fish naiant azure; on a chief of the last ten ancient ships in full sail, five and five, of the field. **Crest:** Issuant from a mural crown argent, and between two *Magnoliae grandiflorae Exmouthiensis* proper, a tower Or, thereon a flagstaff proper, flying therefrom to the sinister a flag also argent charged with a cross gules. Mantling azure, doubled argent. **Motto:** Mare ditat flores decorat. **Granted** 12 February 1947.

EYE, BOROUGH OF (EAST SUFFOLK). Azure, a cross flory between four martlets Or, in chief and issuing from the cross two branches leaved vert, each having three roses argent, upon the branches an eagle with wings expanded of the last, crowned gold. **Crest:** Upon an Imperial Crown Or, the cap gules, an estoile of sixteen points gold charged with a human eye proper. Mantled azure, doubled argent. **Motto** (above the Crest): Oculus in coelum. **Granted** 20 April 1592.

EXETER

EVESHAM BOROUGH

EVESHAM R.D.C.

EXETER COLLEGE

F

** Denotes Illustration*

FAILSWORTH URBAN DISTRICT COUNCIL (LANCASHIRE).* Per pale gules and argent, three bendlets enhanced per pale Or and of the first; on a chief ermine a chapeau of the first, turned up ermine, between two roses also of the first, barbed, seeded, stalked and leaved proper. **Crest:** On a wreath of the colours, Upon a mount vert a griffin segreant gules with three shafts of lightning issuant from the beak Or and supporting a representation of the Failsworth Pole proper. **Motto:** True worth never fails. **Granted** 20 January 1948.

FALMOUTH, BOROUGH OF. Argent, a double-headed eagle displayed sable, each wing charged with a tower Or, in base issuant from water barry wavy proper a rock also sable, thereon surmounting the tail of the eagle a staff also proper, flying therefrom a pennon gules. **Crest:** On a wreath of the colours, Out of a chaplet of oak proper, fructed Or, a representation of the ancient Falmouth Packet Boat in full sail proper. **Supporters:** On either side a lion guardant Or crowned with a Royal Crown of the seventeenth century proper, the dexter holding in the interior forepaw an adze and the sinister in the like paw a pin maul also proper. **Motto:** Remember. **Granted** by Royal Licence 7 March 1961; exemplified 20 June 1961.

FALMOUTH DOCKS AND ENGINEERING COMPANY. Quarterly sable and argent, a cross quarterly of the last and Or between in the first quarter six bezants, three, two and one, in the second quarter a double-headed eagle displayed of the first, in the third quarter on water barry wavy azure and argent a three-masted sailing ship, the mainsail set proper, flags flying gules, and in the fourth quarter the head and shoulders of a man couped affrontée, vested about the dexter shoulder argent and wreathed about the temples with leaves vert, tied at the back with ribands also argent. **Crest:** On a wreath of the colours, Out of a ship's crow's nest two ostrich feathers in saltire, all proper. **Supporters:** On the dexter side a sailor of the Royal Navy of the mid-nineteenth century and on the sinister side a sailor of modern times, both proper. **Motto:** Servimus. **Granted** 22 March 1960.

FAN MAKERS OF THE CITY OF LONDON, WORSHIPFUL COMPANY OF. Or, a fan displayed with a mount of various devices and colours, the sticks gules; on a chief per pale gules and azure, on the dexter side a shaving iron over a bundle of sticks tied together of the first, on the sinister a framed saw in pale gold. **Crest:** On a wreath Or and gules, A hand couped proper holding a fan displayed Or. **Motto:** Arts and trade united. These Arms and Crest are of no authority.

FAR BLETCHLEY TRAINING COLLEGE.* Quarterly vert and azure, on a cross pomelly Or a roundel gules, thereon a horn in bend Or. **Crest:** On a wreath Or and azure, Issuant from a mount vert, between three stalks of wheat Or two poppies slipped and leaved proper, all enfiled through a crown azure. **Motto:** In my end is my beginning. **Granted** 5 March 1966 to The Bletchley Park Training College to be known as Far Bletchley Training College.

FAREHAM URBAN DISTRICT COUNCIL (HAMPSHIRE).* Sable, on water barry wavy in base proper a lymphad Or, the flags argent charged with a cross gules; on a chief of the third a pale between two roses of the fourth, barbed and seeded also proper, charged with as many keys

FAREHAM

FARMERS COMPANY

FAR BLETCHLEY TRAINING COLLEGE

FARNBOROUGH

FAILSWORTH

in bend, wards outwards, the upper of the third, the lower of the second, and interlaced with a sword in bend sinister also of the third, pomel and hilt also of the second. **Motto:** Prest à faire. **Granted** 15 July 1947.

FARMERS, COMPANY OF.* Azure, three ears of wheat in fesse slipped and leaved Or; a chief of the last. **Crest:** On a wreath of the colours, A bull passant gules semée of mullets Or, armed and unguled gold. **Supporters:** On either side a farm labourer proper holding in the exterior hand a sickle also proper [the whole upon a compartment of ploughed land, the furrows receding from the foreground, proper]. **Motto:** Give us our Daily Bread. **Badge:** Two sickles interlaced Or. **Granted** 6 May 1948.

FARNBOROUGH URBAN DISTRICT COUNCIL (HAMPSHIRE).* Per fess dancettée azure and gules, in chief two wings conjoined and expanded fesswise and in base a fir tree couped Or. **Crest:** On a wreath of the colours, In front of two fern leaves in saltire vert a cross couped between two roses Or. **Motto:** Fides et justitia. **Granted** 23 January 1934.

FARNHAM URBAN DISTRICT COUNCIL (SURREY).* Vert, a castle with three towers Or; on a chief argent a mitre of the first, garnished of the second, between a sprig of oak and a sprig of hop, both fructed of the field. **Crest:** On a wreath of the colours, In front of a stag's head affrontée proper issuant from six ears of wheat fessewise, three to the dexter and three to the sinister Or, a stone headed axe also proper and a pastoral staff gold in saltire. **Motto:** By worth. **Granted** 11 October 1950.

FARNWORTH, BOROUGH OF (LANCASHIRE).* Azure, on a chevron between three bees volant Or two cotton cops of the field. **Crest:** Issuant from a coronet composed of six roses gules set upon a rim Or, a stag's head affrontée of the last between two branches of fern proper. **Supporters:** On the dexter side a stag and on the sinister side a lion azure, each gorged with a collar Or charged with three roses gules. **Motto:** Juste nec timide. **Granted** 31 October 1939.

FARRIERS OF THE CITY OF LONDON, WORSHIPFUL COMPANY OF.* Argent, three horseshoes; on a bordure sable three nails pallwise argent. **Crest:** On a wreath of the colours, An arm embowed issuing from clouds from the sinister side all proper, holding in the hand a farrier's hammer azure, hafted and crowned Or. **Supporters:** On either side a horse argent gorged with a collar, pendent therfrom a sword gules. **Motto:** Vi et virtute. **Granted** 11 September 1968.

FARRINGTON'S GIRLS SCHOOL (CHISLEHURST, KENT).* Vert, three roses Or between two barrulets argent, in chief a wyvern between two keys erect, wards to the dexter, of the second and in base an ancient lamp also of the second, inflamed proper. A canton ermine, thereon (with the permission of Her Majesty) the Cypher of Her Majesty Queen Mary also gold. **Motto:** Posside sapientiam. **Granted** 10 March 1928 to The Governing Body and Members of Farrington's Girls' School.

FEATHERSTONE URBAN DISTRICT COUNCIL (YORKSHIRE—WEST RIDING). Quarterly Or and azure, a cross quarterly gules and argent, in the first quarter a lion rampant purpure, in the second three roses argent, in the third a garb also argent, and in the fourth a miner's safety lamp also proper. **Crest:** On a wreath of the colours, Upon a rock an ostrich feather erect between two battleaxes in saltire, all proper. **Motto:** Concilio et animis. **Granted** 23 February 1955.

FELIXSTOWE [COLLEGE] SCHOOL, LIMITED.* Gules, a cross patonce argent between in the first quarter a pelican proper, in the second a garb Or, in the third a cinquefoil gold, and in the fourth a falcon also proper. **Crest:** On a wreath of the colours, In front of an open book proper, bound sable, a lion rampant Or. **Motto:** Fide constantia. **Granted** 19 November 1954.

FELSTED SCHOOL. See Free School of Richard, Lord Riche.

FARNHAM U. D. C.

FARNWORTH

FARRINGTON'S GIRLS SCHOOL

WORSHIPFUL COMPANY OF FARRIERS

FELTMAKERS OF THE CITY OF LONDON, WORSHIPFUL COMPANY OF.* Argent, a dexter hand appaumé couped at the wrist gules between two hat-bands nowed azure, in chief a hat sable, banded azure. **Crest:** On a wreath of the colours, A dexter arm embowed proper, holding in the hand a hat sable banded azure. **Motto:** Decus et tutamen. **Granted** 31 May 1946.

FERMANAGH COUNTY COUNCIL. Barry wavy argent and azure, two flaunches vert; over all a representation of the Watergate at Enniskillen Or, flying from the battlements to the dexter a banner of St. Patrick. **Crest:** Out of a coronet of four shamrocks set upon a rim Or a mount vert, thereon a horse passant argent, caparisoned gules, thereon a knight in full armour, in the dexter hand a sword erect proper [hilt and pomel Or.] **Supporters:** On either side a brock proper charged on the shoulder with a bezant, thereon a dexter hand couped gules. **Motto:** Feor magh eanagh. **Granted** 20 August 1954.

FILEY URBAN DISTRICT COUNCIL (YORKSHIRE—EAST RIDING).* Per fess, in chief azure a representation of Filey Brig proper with the sun shining thereon Or, the base per pale wavy gold and also azure three pallets wavy argent on the last. **Crest:** Within a crown of rays of ancient Rome Or, a seagull proper rising from a rock vert, holding in the beak a fish also proper. Mantled azure, doubled Or. **Motto:** Filey et felicitas. **Granted** 17 July 1952.

FIRE OFFICES' COMMITTEE FIRE PROTECTION ASSOCIATION.* Per fesse wavy gules and barry wavy of four argent and azure, in chief a fire ball Or. **Crest:** On a wreath of the colours, Three torches, one in pale and two in saltire, vert enflamed proper, tied with a cord Or. **Motto:** Protection. **Granted** 8 June 1949.

FISHMONGERS OF THE CITY OF LONDON, WORSHIPFUL COMPANY OF.* Azure, three dolphins naiant embowed in pale argent, finned, toothed, and crowned Or, between two pairs of stockfish in saltire argent, over the mouth of each fish a crown Or; on a chief gules three pairs of keys of St. Peter in saltire Or. **Crest:** On a wreath argent and sable, Two cubit arms, the dexter vested Or cuffed azure, the sinister azure cuffed Or, the hands argent holding an Imperial Crown proper. Mantled on the dexter side gules, doubled Or, on the sinister side azure, doubled argent. **Supporters:** On the dexter side a merman, armed, holding in his right hand a falchion and with his left sustaining the helm and timbre; and on the sinister side a mermaid holding in her left hand a mirror and supporting the Arms with her right hand, all proper. **Motto:** Al worship be to God only. Arms and Crest granted 19 October 1512 by Sir Thomas Wriothesley, Garter King of Arms, and Thomas Benolt, Clarenceux King of Arms. The helmet is usually shown as that of an English Peer. Supporters granted 17 December 1575 by Robert Cooke, Clarenceux King of Arms. (*Illustration on page* 169).

FITZALAN PURSUIVANT EXTRAORDINARY. See Arms, Officers of.

FITZWILLIAM HALL (CAMBRIDGE UNIVERSITY). Lozengy argent and gules; a chief of the Arms of the University of Cambridge. These arms are of no authority.

FLAXTON RURAL DISTRICT COUNCIL (YORKSHIRE—NORTH RIDING).* Argent, three stalks of flax interlaced proper, tied with a riband azure, in chief a Saxon crown gules; all within a bordure vert, thereon eight roses of the first, barbed and seeded also proper. **Crest:** On a wreath argent and gules, Out of a circlet of oak fructed proper a winged lion rampant gules, langued azure, holding in the forepaws a fetterlock Or. **Motto:** Progress with honour and dignity. **Granted** 20 March 1953.

FLEETWOOD, BOROUGH OF (LANCASHIRE).* Per saltire nebuly Or and azure, in chief a rose gules, barbed and seeded proper, in base an ancient galley of the third, and in fesse two martlets of the first. **Motto:** Onward. **Granted** 25 August 1933.

FLETCHERS OF THE CITY OF LONDON, WORSHIPFUL COMPANY OF.* Sable, a chevron between three broad arrows Or, headed and flighted argent. **Crest:** On a wreath of the

FELIXSTOWE [COLLEGE] SCHOOL

FILEY U. D. C.

WORSHIPFUL COMPANY OF FELTMAKERS

'IRE OFFICES' COMMITTEE

FLEETWOOD BOROUGH OF

FLAXTON R. D. C.

colours, An angel proper vested and with wings endorsed Or feathered of many colours, holding in both hands a bundle of arrows also Or, headed and flighted argent encircled with a band sable. Mantled sable, doubled Or. **Motto:** True and sure. Arms granted 12 October 1467 by William Hawkeslowe, Clarenceux King of Arms; Crest granted 1486 by Sir Thomas Holme, Clarenceux King of Arms; the whole confirmed 12 October 1530 by Thomas Benolt, Clarenceux King of Arms and recorded at the Visitation of 1568. (*Illustration on page* 169).

FLINT, BOROUGH OF.* Per fess wavy azure and barry wavy of eight argent and of the first, in chief upon a rock issuant proper a castle of two towers Or, and in base an ancient three-masted ship, sail furled, pennons flying, gold. **Crest:** Out of a coronet composed of four fleurs-de-lis argent and as many mullets Or set alternately upon a rim silver, in front of flames proper a demi eagle displayed gold. **Supporters:** On either side a dragon gules charged on the shoulder with a rose Or, barbed and seeded proper, supporting between the forelegs an ostrich feather erect argent; the whole upon a compartment of rocks proper. **Motto:** Castellum supra fluvium. **Badge:** Upon a pellet environed by a chaplet of roses Or, barbed, seeded and leaved proper, in front of an ostrich feather erect argent a castle as in the Arms. **Granted** 10 October 1962.

FLINTSHIRE COUNTY COUNCIL.* Argent, on a cross engrailed fleury sable between four Cornish choughs proper, a mascle of the field between four plates. **Crest:** On a wreath of the colours, A demi dragon gules supporting with the claws an ostrich feather argent. **Motto:** Gorau Tarian Cyflawnder. **Granted** 12 May 1938.

FOLKESTONE, BOROUGH OF (KENT).* Or, on water barry wavy in base proper an ancient ship with four men's heads therein apparent as represented on the ancient Seal of the Borough of Folkestone also proper; on a chief per pale gules and azure a demi lion passant guardant dimidiated with the hull of a ship gold. **Crest:** On a wreath Or and azure, A demi double-headed eagle displayed sable, beaked Or, charged on the breast with a rose argent, barbed and seeded proper, dimidiated with a fleur-de-lys gold, and on each wing with a ducal coronet also gold. **Supporters:** On the dexter side a figure representing St. Eanswyth proper crowned with an ancient crown and holding in the exterior hand a pastoral staff Or, and on the sinister side a figure representing William Harvey, the physician, also proper holding in the exterior hand a heart gules. **Motto:** Salubritas et amoenitas. **Granted** 25 July 1958.

FOOD TECHNOLOGY, NATIONAL COLLEGE OF. Gules, a beehive proper between three gauntlets argent garnished Or. **Crest:** On a wreath of the colours, A lion sejant gules holding in the dexter paw a torch Or, enflamed proper, and supporting with the sinister a cornucopia also proper. **Motto:** Processus per scientiam. **Granted** 1 November 1956.

THE FOOTBALL ASSOCIATION, LIMITED.* Argent, semée of [ten] Tudor roses proper, three lions passant guardant in pale azure. **Granted** 30 March 1949.

THE FOOTBALL ASSOCIATION OF WALES, LTD.* Ermine, a dragon [rampant] gules; a bordure vert charged with eleven leeks Or. **Motto:** Gorau chwarae cyd-chwarae. **Granted** 30 August 1951.

FOUNDERS OF THE CITY OF LONDON, WORSHIPFUL COMPANY OF.* Azure, a laver-pot between two taper candlesticks Or. **Crest:** On a wreath Or and azure, A fiery furnace proper, two arms of the last issuing from clouds on the sinister side also proper, the sleeves azure, the hands holding a pair of closing tongs sable taking hold of the melting pot in the furnace likewise proper. Mantled gules, doubled argent. **Motto:** God the only Founder. **Granted** 13 October 1590 by Robert Cooke, Clarenceux King of Arms. (*Illustration on page* 169).

FOUNDLING HOSPITAL. Per fesse azure and vert, a young child lying naked and exposed, extending its right hand proper, in chief a crescent argent between two mullets of six points Or. **Crest:** On a wreath of the colours, A lamb argent holding in its mouth a sprig of thyme proper. **Supporters:** On the dexter side a terminal figure of a woman full of nipples proper with a mantle

FOLKESTONE

FLINTSHIRE C. C.

FLINT

vert, the term argent, being the Emblem of Nature, and on the sinister side the Emblem of Liberty, represented by Britannia holding in her right hand upon a staff proper a cap argent, and habited in a vest azure girt with a belt Or, the under garment gules. **Motto:** Help. **Granted** 1747 to The Hospital for the Maintenance of Exposed and Deserted Young Children. Its current title is The Coram Foundation.

FOURTH POST OFFICE BUILDING SOCIETY. Quarterly per pale and per fesse indented azure, gules, gules and Or, in the first and fourth quarters a castle counterchanged, in the second a sprig of thrift flowered gold, and in the third two keys in saltire, wards upward, also gold. **Crest:** On a wreath Or and azure, A demi lion azure, armed and langued gules, ducally gorged and holding in the sinister paw a pair of scales Or. **Supporters:** On the dexter side a lion Or, armed and langued gules, ducally crowned and charged on the shoulder with a portcullis azure, and on the sinister side a like lion counterchanged. **Motto:** Rei custos tuae. **Granted** 15 September 1961.

FOYLE COLLEGE (LONDONDERRY).* Quarterly argent, sable, azure and of the first, a cross quarterly gules and of the first between, in the first quarter a sword erect of the fourth, in the second quarter a tower of the first, in the third quarter a harp Or stringed of the first, and in the fourth quarter a hand appaumée couped at the wrist of the fourth. **Crest:** On a wreath Or and gules, A demi lion argent charged with a trefoil slipped vert and holding between the paws an open book proper, edged Or, thereon the figures 1617 gules. **Motto:** Ne unquam cesseris. **Granted** 31 March 1949.

FRAMEWORKKNITTERS OF THE CITY OF LONDON, WORSHIPFUL COMPANY OF. Argent, a knitting frame sable, garnished Or. **Crest:** On a wreath argent and gules, A lamb passant proper resting the dexter forehoof on a hank of silk fesswise Or. **Supporters:** On the dexter side a student of the University of Cambridge in academical costume of the seventeenth century proper, and on the sinister side a female figure also in seventeenth century costume habited azure, cuffs, cap, neckerchief and apron argent, holding in the dexter hand a knitting needle proper and in the sinister hand a piece of worsted knit gules. **Motto:** Speed, strength and truth united. **Granted** and confirmed 3 February 1933.

FRAMLINGHAM COLLEGE (SUFFOLK). See Albert Middle Class College in Suffolk.

FREEBRIDGE LYNN RURAL DISTRICT COUNCIL (NORFOLK).* Or, on a cross quadrate azure a castle of three domed towers, each flying a pennon to the dexter, between four cross-crosslets fitchy of the first; on a chief sable a lion passant gold. **Motto:** Non sibi sed patriae. **Granted** 21 April 1955.

FREEMASONS:

UNITED GRAND LODGE OF FREE AND ACCEPTED MASONS OF ENGLAND.* Per pale gules and quarterly azure and Or, dexter on a chevron between three castles argent a pair of compasses extended of the third, sinister a cross quarterly of the fourth and vert between in the first quarter a lion rampant of the third, in the second an ox passant sable, in the third a man with hands elevated proper vested of the fifth the robe crimson lined with ermine, and in the fourth an eagle displayed also of the third; the whole within a bordure of the first charged with eight lions passant guardant of the third. **Crest:** On a wreath of the colours, A representation of an Ark supported on either side by a cherub proper, with the motto over in Hebrew characters "Holiness to the Lord". **Supporters:** On either side a cherub proper. **Motto:** Audi, vide, tace. **Granted** by Royal Warrant 19 July 1919; exemplified 29 July 1919.

PROVINCIAL GRAND LODGE OF BUCKINGHAMSHIRE. Per pale gules and quarterly azure and Or, dexter on a chevron between three castles argent a pair of compasses extended of the third, sinister a cross quarterly of the fourth and vert between, in the first quarter a lion rampant of the third, in the second an ox passant sable, in the third a man with hands elevated proper vested of the fifth the robe crimson lined with ermine, and in the fourth an eagle displayed also

THE FOOTBALL ASSOCIATION
OF WALES

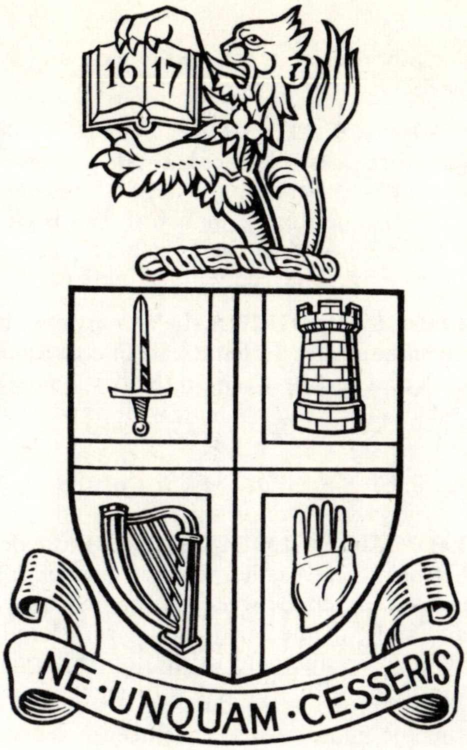

FOYLE COLLEGE

FREEMEN OF THE CITY
OF LONDON

THE FOOTBALL ASSOCIATION

FREEBRIDGE LYNN

FREEMASONS

of the third; the whole within a bordure per pale of the sixth and first charged with six royal swans of the third. **Granted** 3 June 1929.

PROVINCIAL GRAND LODGE OF CHESHIRE. Per pale gules and quarterly azure and Or; dexter on a chevron between three castles argent a pair of compasses extended gold; sinister a cross quarterly of the fourth and vert between, in the first quarter a lion rampant of the third, in the second an ox passant sable, in the third a man with hands elevated proper vested of the fifth the robe crimson lined with ermine, and in the fourth an eagle displayed also of the third; the whole within a bordure of the second charged with six garbs also gold. **Granted** 9 May 1957.

PROVINCIAL GRAND LODGE OF DURHAM. Per pale gules and quarterly azure and Or; dexter on a chevron between three castles argent a pair of compasses extended of the third; sinister a cross quarterly of the fourth and vert between, in the first quarter a lion rampant of the third, in the second an ox passant sable, in the third a man with hands elevated proper vested of the fifth the robe crimson lined with ermine, and in the fourth an eagle displayed also of the third; the whole within a bordure of the second charged with a cross between eight lions rampant of the third. **Granted** 24 July 1922.

PROVINCIAL GRAND LODGE OF GLOUCESTER. Per pale gules and quarterly azure and Or; dexter on a chevron between three castles argent a pair of compasses extended gold; sinister a cross quarterly of the fourth and vert between, in the first quarter a lion rampant of the third, in the second an ox passant sable, in the third a man with hands elevated proper vested of the fifth the robe crimson lined with ermine, and in the fourth an eagle displayed also of the third; the whole within a bordure of the fifth charged with eight horseshoes of the fourth. **Granted** 5 March 1963.

PROVINCIAL GRAND LODGE OF LANCASHIRE (EASTERN DIVISION). Per pale gules and quarterly azure and Or; dexter on a chevron between three castles argent a pair of compasses extended of the third; sinister a cross quarterly of the fourth and vert between, in the first quarter a lion rampant of the third, in the second an ox passant sable, in the third a man with hands elevated proper vested of the fifth the robe crimson lined with ermine, and in the fourth an eagle displayed also of the third; the whole within a bordure vair charged with two stags' heads caboshed of the third and two roses of the first. **Granted** 20 July 1932.

PROVINCIAL GRAND LODGE OF LANCASHIRE (WESTERN DIVISION). Per pale gules and quarterly azure and Or; dexter on a chevron between three castles argent a pair of compasses extended of the third; sinister a cross quarterly of the fourth and vert between, in the first quarter a lion rampant of the third, in the second an ox passant sable, in the third a man with hands elevated proper vested of the fifth the robe crimson lined with ermine, and in the fourth an eagle displayed also of the third; the whole within a bordure per pale of the second and third semé of fleurs-de-lys gold and roses of the first. **Granted** 28 October 1920.

PROVINCIAL GRAND LODGE OF MIDDLESEX. Per pale gules and quarterly azure and Or; dexter on a chevron between three castles argent a pair of compasses extended of the third; sinister a cross quarterly of the fourth and vert between, in the first quarter a lion rampant of the third, in the second an ox passant sable, in the third a man with hand elevated proper vested of the fifth the robe crimson lined with ermine, and in the fourth an eagle displayed also of the third; the whole within a bordure of the first charged with a Saxon crown in chief likewise of the third and three seaxes two erect in fesse and one fessewise in base also proper pomels and hilts gold. **Granted** 27 September 1943.

PROVINCIAL GRAND LODGE OF STAFFORDSHIRE. Per pale gules and quarterly azure and Or; dexter on a chevron between three castles argent a pair of compasses extended of the third; sinister a cross quarterly of the fourth and vert between, in the first quarter a lion rampant

THE FISHMONGERS

THE FLETCHERS

THE FOVNDERS

THE FRVITERERS

of the third, in the second an ox passant sable, in the third a man with hands elevated proper vested of the fifth the robe crimson lined with ermine, and in the fourth an eagle displayed also of the third; the whole within a bordure of the second charged with eight Stafford knots gold. **Granted** 15 December 1944.

PROVINCIAL GRAND LODGE OF SURREY. Per pale gules and quarterly azure and Or; dexter on a chevron between three castles argent a pair of compasses extended of the third; sinister a cross quarterly of the fourth and vert between, in the first quarter a lion rampant of the third, in the second an ox passant sable, in the third a man with hands elevated proper vested of the fifth the robe crimson lined with ermine, and in the fourth an eagle displayed also of the third; the whole within a bordure quarterly of the second and sixth charged with a representation of King Edgar's crown in chief gold, two ostrich feathers erect in fesse argent and an oak sprig in base of the last. **Granted** 24 October 1935.

FREEMEN OF THE CITY OF LONDON, GUILD OF.* Argent on a cross gules enfiled in chief and base by two mural crowns Or a rose of the last, slipped and leaved proper. **Crest:** A mural crown Or, therefrom a dove, wings expanded, proper. **Motto:** Londini defendi tuos Deus optime cives. **Granted** 31 May 1912.

THE FREE SCHOOL OF RICHARD LORD RICHE, COMMONLY CALLED FELSTED SCHOOL (ESSEX).* Gules, a chevron between three crosses botonny Or. **Motto:** Garde ta foy. **Granted** by Royal Warrant 12 April 1963; exemplified 10 September 1963.

FRIMLEY AND CAMBERLEY URBAN DISTRICT COUNCIL (SURREY).* Azure, three owls argent membered Or, each perched on a branch of oak, leaved also argent fructed gold; on a chief of the last a tower also azure between on the dexter a sword in bend proper, hilt and pomel gules, and two keys in bend sinister, addorsed and the bows interlaced, the upper gules the lower azure, and on the sinister two swords in saltire also proper, hilts and pomels also gules. **Crest:** On a wreath of the colours, A demi lion queue fourchée Or, ducally crowned gules, holding with the paws a grenade fired proper. **Motto:** A Deo et Regina. **Granted** 27 February 1956.

FROME URBAN DISTRICT COUNCIL (SOMERSET).* Sable, on a chevron between in chief two sallow trees and in base a teazel slipped Or, a chevron ermine. **Crest:** Out of a Saxon crown Or, a demi dragon, wings elevated and addorsed, gules supporting a crozier gold. **Motto:** Time trieth truth. **Granted** 14 August 1953.

FRUIT AND POTATO TRADES, NATIONAL FEDERATION OF, LIMITED.* Per saltire Or and vert, in fesse two lions combatant of the first; over all in the fesse point a plate charged with a cornucopia gules, the fruit proper. **Crest:** On a wreath of the colours, A sun in splendour Or charged with a cornucopia gules, issuant therefrom a shamrock, a thistle, a garden rose, and a leek, all proper. **Motto:** Unity is strength. **Badge:** A sun in splendour Or charged with a cornucopia as in the Crest. **Granted** 18 March 1955.

FRUITERERS OF THE CITY OF LONDON, WORSHIPFUL COMPANY OF.* Azure, on a mount in base vert the tree of Paradise environed with the serpent between Adam and Eve, all proper. **Motto:** Arbor vitae Christus, fructus per fidem gustamus. There arms are of no authority.

FUEL, INSTITUTE OF. Per fess gules and sable, a sun in splendour Or, emerging therefrom six chains, three in chief Or and three in base argent. **Crest:** On a wreath of the colours, Issuant from a chain embowed sable, six flames proper. **Supporters:** On the dexter side a representation of Vulcan resting the interior foot on an anvil, and on the sinister side a representation of Prometheus resting the interior foot on a rock, all proper. **Motto:** Vires acquirit eundo. **Granted** 10 March 1967.

FULWOOD URBAN DISTRICT COUNCIL (LANCASHIRE).* Per chevron vert and ermine, in chief two stags' heads caboshed Or, in base an oak tree eradicated proper fructed gold; all

FULWOOD

FRIMLEY AND CAMBERLEY

FROME

FYLDE

THE FREE SCHOOL

FRUIT AND POTATO TRADES

within a bordure engrailed of the last. **Crest:** Out of a mural crown Or charged with three roses gules, barbed and seeded proper, a mount vert, thereon a lion passant guardant also proper gorged with a torse argent and azure and resting the dexter forepaw on a fleur-de-lis also argent. Mantled vert, doubled argent. **Motto:** Fortiter et fideliter. **Granted** 2 June 1958.

FURNESS, WITHY & COMPANY LIMITED. Azure, three bars wavy argent, in chief as many capstans of the last, cabled Or. **Crest:** Issuing out of a coronet composed of four trident heads set upon a rim Or, a sea dog proper guttée d'eau. Mantled azure, doubled argent. **Supporters:** On either side a sea hart proper, attires and hooves, dorsal fin and tail Or [the whole upon a compartment vert thereon a launching slipway proper.] **Motto:** Quod mare non novit. **Badge:** A spear erect, hafted gules headed argent, surmounted of two ships' rudders in saltire sable, strapped and hinged Or, the tillers outwards gold. **Granted** 30 September 1957.

THE FURNITURE MAKERS' GUILD. Argent, a chevron dovetailed counterdovetailed gules between three braces and bits each palewise with the bits downwards sable. **Crest:** On a wreath of the colours, A cubit arm grasping a handplane proper. **Motto:** Straight and strong. **Granted** 1 October 1954.

FYLDE RURAL DISTRICT COUNCIL (LANCASHIRE).* Vert, the sails of a windmill saltirewise Or; on a chief indented of the last a rose gules barbed and seeded proper, between two fountains. **Crest:** Out of a coronet of four cinquefoils set on a rim argent, a dexter arm in armour embowed proper, the hand gauntleted also proper and pendent therefrom a buglehorn sable, stringed and garnished Or. **Motto:** Gaudeat ager. **Granted** 20 July 1954.

THE GARDINERS

THE GLASIERS

THE GLOVERS

THE GROCERS

G

** Denotes Illustration*

GAINSBOROUGH RURAL DISTRICT COUNCIL (LINCOLNSHIRE—PARTS OF LINDSEY).* Per pale, barry wavy of six azure and argent, and ermine, on a pale Or a chevron vert between in chief a mitre afrontée gules charged with a fleur-de-lys gold and in base an eagle displayed [wings inverted] also gules. **Crest:** On a wreath Or and gules, A Danish dragon-ship sable, pennon flying azure, the sail Or charged with a boar's head erased of the first armed and langued gules. **Motto:** Trust and triumph. **Granted** 8 October 1952.

GAINSBOROUGH URBAN DISTRICT COUNCIL (LINCOLNSHIRE—PARTS OF LINDSEY).* Vert, on a fesse wavy argent between in chief a cog-wheel between two garbs and in base an ancient crown Or, a fesse wavy azure. **Crest:** On a wreath of the colours, Out of a mural coronet two anchors in saltire Or. **Motto:** Strive for the gain of all. **Granted** 15 March 1950.

GARDENERS OF THE CITY OF LONDON, WORSHIPFUL COMPANY OF.* On a shield representing a landscape the figure of a man habited about the body with a skin delving the ground with a spade all proper. **Crest:** On a wreath argent and vert, A basket of flowers and fruit proper. **Supporters:** On either side a female figure vested argent, wreathed about the temples with flowers and supporting on the exterior arm a cornucopia proper. **Motto:** In the sweat of thy brows shalt thow eate thy bread. Arms and Crest granted by Royal Warrant 9 June 1905; exemplified 8 September 1905; Supporters granted 8 September 1905.

GARSTANG RURAL DISTRICT COUNCIL (LANCASHIRE).* Per fesse gules and argent, a fesse wavy barry wavy of four of the second and azure, in chief two crosiers in saltire Or between as many pierced cinquefoils ermine, and in base a rose of the first barbed and seeded proper. **Crest:** On a wreath of the colours, Upon the battlements of a square tower proper a lion couchant resting the dexter forepaw on a garb Or. **Motto:** Curandum omnium bonum. **Granted** 9 September 1949.

GARTER KING OF ARMS. See Arms, Officers of.

GAS COUNCIL.* Sable, three flames of fire proper; on a bordure Or twelve annulets gules. **Crest:** On a wreath of the colours, A dragon rampant gules holding in the dexter fore claw a torch erect Or enflamed proper. **Supporters:** On either side an owl proper charged on the shoulder with an ogress, thereon a flame of fire also proper. **Motto:** In libertate consilium. **Granted** 3 February 1950.

GAS ENGINEERS, INSTITUTION OF. Per fesse sable and gules, a fess rayonée argent, in base a mount issuant Or; over all a bend also Or charged with a retort between two open books proper, edged and bound and clasped gules. **Crest:** Issuant from a circlet rayonée, two torches in saltire Or inflamed proper. **Supporters:** On the dexter side a lion Or gorged with a circlet rayonnée gules and charged on the shoulder with a torteau, and on the sinister side a bull sable, armed, unguled and gorged with a circlet rayonée Or and charged on the shoulder with a bezant. **Motto:** Assidue exquirendo servire. **Granted** 14 May 1930.

GARSTANG

GAINSBOROUGH U. D. C.

GAINSBOROUGH R. D. C.

GAS COUNCIL

GATESHEAD, COUNTY BOROUGH OF (CO. DURHAM).* Argent, issuant from water in base proper a tower sable between two crosses of St. Cuthbert azure. **Crest:** On a wreath argent and azure, A goat's head erased argent, armed Or, gorged with a riband, suspended therefrom a portcullis sable. **Motto:** Caput inter nubila condit. **Granted** 27 September 1932.

GEMMOLOGICAL ASSOCIATION OF GREAT BRITAIN. Argent, on a cross formy-quadrate throughout quarterly gules and azure a closed book, bound and clasped, Or, jewelled proper, between in chief within an annulet Or a representation of the top plan of a rose-cut diamond proper, in fesse two lozenges argent each charged with a fillet cross sable and in base an annulet Or gemmed argent. **Crest:** On a wreath argent, gules and azure, A demi lynx proper holding between the paws an escarbuncle of eight rays gules each floretty and pommety of a jewel respectively from the base of pearl, ruby, jacinth, topaz, emerald, turquoise, sapphire and amethyst. **Motto:** Omnemque pretiosum lapidem. **Granted** 20 February 1967.

THE GENERAL ACCOUNTANTS' ASSOCIATION. Argent, a balance and on a chief gules an hourglass Or between two open books proper, bound and clasped Or. **Crest:** On a wreath of the colours, Within an arch a sword erect inflamed proper, pomel and hilt Or. **Motto:** Justitia, meritum, fidelitas. **Granted** 5 March 1963.

GENERAL DENTAL COUNCIL. Per fess indented gules and argent, a lion rampant counterchanged holding between the paws a great pearl proper. **Crest:** On a wreath of the colours, A Blackheaded Plover (Pluvianus Aegyptius), wings expanded and inverted, proper. **Supporters:** On the dexter side a representation of Hygeia argent holding in the exterior hand a great pearl, the arm entwined by a serpent also argent, and on the sinister side a representation of Aesculapius argent, holding in the exterior hand a like pearl, the rod argent, resting against the sinister shoulder. **Motto:** Esse quam videri. **Granted** 12 June 1957.

GENERAL PRACTITIONERS, ROYAL COLLEGE OF. Per pale sable and argent, a chevron counterchanged between in chief an opium poppy flower and a gentian flower, both slipped, proper, and in base a Roman lamp Or, inflamed also proper. **Crest:** On a wreath of the colours, An owl proper supporting with the dexter claw a gavel upright Or entwined with a serpent also proper. **Supporters:** On the dexter side a unicorn Or, armed, crined and unguled argent, and on the sinister side a lynx proper, spotted azure, gules, vert, Or and argent, and ducally gorged and chained of the last. **Motto:** Cum scientia caritas. **Granted** 20 June 1961.

GERARD AND REID LIMITED. Quarterly gules and ermine, a lion rampant Or gorged with a ducal coronet, a chain affixed thereto passing between the forelegs and reflexed over the back Or, grasping with the dexter paw a sword in bend sinister proper, pomel and hilt gold. **Motto:** Verbum nostrum satis. **Badge:** Within an annulet Or a lion as in the Arms. **Granted** 20 February 1961.

GILLETT BROTHERS DISCOUNT COMPANY LIMITED.* Azure, a sun in splendour Or between four billets, each per bend argent and Or. **Crest:** On a wreath argent and azure, On a mount vert a ram passant proper, resting the dexter hoof upon a bezant, between two gillyflowers stalked and leaved proper. **Motto:** Deus est nobis sol et scutum. **Granted** 20 May 1964.

GILLINGHAM, BOROUGH OF (KENT).* Argent, a cross gules, in the first quarter an ancient harp, in the second on waves of the sea an ancient ship, in the third issuing out of waves of the sea a rock thereon a fort, and in the fourth quarter a sprig of broom, all proper. **Crest:** On a wreath of the colours, In front of a foul anchor erect two swords in saltire, points upwards, that pointing to the dexter sheathed, all proper. **Motto:** With fort and fleet for home and England. **Granted** 2 April 1904.

GIPPING RURAL DISTRICT COUNCIL (EAST SUFFOLK).* Azure semée of fleurs-de-lys, a bend wavy argent between two ears of wheat, slipped and leaved, Or. **Crest:** On a wreath of the

GILLETT BROTHERS

GATESHEAD

GILLINGHAM

GIPPING

colours, On a mount vert an ash tree proper, in the centre and pendent from the branches by a riband azure an escutcheon sable charged with a leopard's face Or. **Motto:** Domini est dirigere. **Granted** 25 May 1951.

GIRDLERS OF THE CITY OF LONDON, WORSHIPFUL COMPANY OF.* Per fesse azure and Or, a pale counterchanged, three gridirons of the second. **Crest:** On a wreath of the colours, Issuing out of clouds proper irradiated Or a demi-figure of St. Lawrence vested azure, holding in his dexter hand a gridiron and in his sinister hand a book gold. Mantled azure semé of clouds irradiated, doubled ermine. **Motto:** Give thanks to God. **Granted** 15 October 1454 by John Smert, Garter King of Arms.

GIRTON COLLEGE (CAMBRIDGE UNIVERSITY).* Quarterly vert and argent, a cross flory counterchanged between in the first and fourth quarters a roundel ermine and in the second and third quarters a crescent gules. **Granted** 14 February 1928.

GLAMORGANSHIRE COUNTY COUNCIL.* Or, three chevronels gules between as many Tudor roses, barbed and seeded proper. **Crest:** On a wreath of the colours, Issuant from flames proper a demi dragon, wings elevated and addorsed, gules supporting a staff Or, flying therefrom a banner also gules charged with a clarion gold. **Supporters:** On the dexter side a miner supporting with his dexter hand a pick, and on the sinister side a steelworker, both proper. **Motto:** A Ddioddefws a Orfu. **Granted** 15 December 1950.

GLANFORD BRIGG RURAL DISTRICT COUNCIL (LINCOLNSHIRE—PARTS OF LINDSEY).* Ermine, between three pallets wavy azure two croziers addorsed Or; on a chief sable a representation of the Brigg bridge proper. **Crest:** On a wreath argent and azure, Issuant from flames a Lincolnshire Red Shorthorn bull's head proper charged on the neck with three links of chain in fesse argent. **Motto:** Always ready. **Granted** 27 March 1950.

GLASS-SELLERS OF THE CITY OF LONDON, THE WORSHIPFUL COMPANY OF. Azure a Venetian glass cup between a laverpot of white ware on the dexter and a looking-glass on the sinister all proper. **Motto:** Discordia frangimur. These are of no authority.

GLAZIERS OF THE CITY OF LONDON, WORSHIPFUL COMPANY OF.* Argent, two glazing irons in saltire between four closing nails sable; on a chief gules a demi lion passant guardant Or. **Crest:** On a wreath of the colours, A lion's head couped Or between two wings azure. **Supporters:** On either side a boy proper holding in the exterior hand a torch Or, inflamed also proper. **Motto:** Lucem Tuam da nobis Deus. Recorded at the Visitation of 1634; the entry refers to a certificate by Robert Cooke, Clarenceux King of Arms, in 1588. Certified 5 March 1926 by Sir Henry Farnham Burke, Garter King of Arms. (*Illustration on page* 173).

GLENLOLA COLLEGIATE SCHOOL (BANGOR, CO. DOWN). Azure, in base two bars wavy argent, issuant therefrom a cygnet rousant proper. **Motto:** Nisi Dominus frustra. **Granted** 20 September 1961.

GLOSSOP, BOROUGH OF (DERBYSHIRE).* Argent, a rose gules, barbed and seeded proper, between three cross crosslets fitchée and in chief a mural crown of the second. **Motto:** Virtus, veritas, libertas. **Granted** 7 July 1919.

GLOUCESTER, BISHOPRIC OF.* Azure, two keys endorsed in saltire, wards upwards, Or. Recorded in the College of Arms.

GLOUCESTER CATHEDRAL CHURCH, THE DEAN AND PREBENDS OF. Azure, on a fesse Or three crosses formy fitchy of the field; on a canton of the second a demi rose en soleil issuant from the chief line gules between two demi fleurs-de-lys issuant from the flanks also of the field. **Granted** 28 March 1542 by Sir Christopher Barker, Garter King of Arms.

GLOUCESTER, CITY AND COUNTY BOROUGH OF.* Or, three chevronels gules between ten torteaux, three, three, three, and one. **Crest:** Issuant from a mural crown Or a demi lion

GLOUCESTER BISHOPRIC

GIRTON COLLEGE

GLAMORGANSHIRE

GIRDLERS

GLOSSOP

GLANFORD BRIGG

guardant gules holding in his dexter paw a broadsword and in his sinister paw a trowel proper. **Supporters:** On either side a lion gules holding in the dexter forepaw a broadsword proper. **Motto:** Fides invicta triumphat. Arms recorded at the Visitation of 1623. Arms confirmed and Crest and Supporters granted 14 August 1652; regranted 16 April 1945. This achievement replaces an earlier grant of arms (18 October 1538) by Sir Christopher Barker, Garter King of Arms, which was also recorded at the above Visitation.

GLOUCESTERSHIRE COUNTY COUNCIL.* Per chevron gules and Or, in chief two fleeces and in base three chevronels counterchanged; on a chief of the second a billet azure between two billets vert, each charged with a horseshoe gold. **Crest:** On a wreath of the colours, A demi lion reguardant gules gorged with a mural crown and resting the sinister paw upon a horseshoe Or. **Motto:** Prorsum semper. **Granted** 10 December 1935.

GLOUCESTERSHIRE TRAINING COLLEGE. Per pale Or and gules, three chevronels counterchanged; on a chief azure an open book proper, edged, bound and clasped, between two ears of wheat Or. **Crest:** On a wreath of the colours, Out of the battlements of a tower proper a demi lion reguardant azure grasping in the dexter paw a sword erect Or and resting the sinister on a book gules, garnished Or. **Motto:** Labore est orare. **Granted** 2 September 1964.

GLOVERS OF THE CITY OF LONDON, WORSHIPFUL COMPANY OF.* Per fesse sable and argent, a pale counterchanged and three rams salient of the second, armed and unguled Or. **Crest:** On a wreath of the colours, A ram's head argent, armed and issuant from a basket Or, filled with wool argent, between two wings erect gules. Mantled gules, doubled ermine. **Motto:** True hearts and warm hands. **Granted** 20 October 1464 by John Smert, Garter King of Arms.

GODALMING, BOROUGH OF (SURREY).* Party per pale gules and sable, a woolpack argent; on a chief of the last a rose of the first, barbed and seeded proper, between two escocheons also gules, that on the dexter charged with a fesse dancettée between two crosses patée in pale of the third, and that on the sinister charged with three pears in bend leaved and slipped proper. **Crest:** On a wreath of the colours, A mound, thereon a ram statant holding in the mouth a pear leaved and slipped all proper, suspended from the neck by a riband gules an escocheon Or charged with a pair of shears erect points upwards also proper. **Motto:** Libera deinde fidelis. **Granted** 12 June 1893.

GOLBORNE URBAN DISTRICT COUNCIL (LANCASHIRE). Argent, on a cross engrailed between in chief two roses gules, barbed and seeded proper, and in base as many lozenges sable, two spindles fessewise, points upwards, Or. **Crest:** On a wreath of the colours, In front of a garb Or two triangular harrows conjoined by a ring fessewise sable. **Motto:** Fide et fiducia. **Granted** 10 May 1954.

GOLD AND SILVER WYREDRAWERS OF THE CITY OF LONDON, WORSHIPFUL COMPANY OF. Azure, on a chevron Or between two coppers in chief of the second and in base as many points in saltire argent, a drawing iron between two rings sable. **Crest:** On a wreath of the colours, Two arms embowed, vested gules cuffed argent, the hand proper holding an engrossing block Or. **Supporters:** On the dexter side an Indian proper crowned with an Eastern crown Or, vested round the middle with feathers pendent, alternately argent and gules, holding over his shoulder a bar of silver, and on the sinister side a man vested proper, in his sinister hand a hank of silk argent. **Motto:** Amicitiam trahit amor. These are of no authority.

GOLDSMITHS OF THE CITY OF LONDON, WORSHIPFUL COMPANY OF.* Quarterly gules and azure, in the first and fourth quarters a leopard's head affrontée Or, in the second and third a covered cup between in chief two buckles fessewise, all of the last. **Crest:** On a wreath Or and gules, A demi virgin issuing from a cloud proper, in a gown gules and kirtle Or, arms extended, holding in the dexter hand proper a balance gold and in the sinister hand a touchstone proper.

GODALMING

GLOUCESTER CO.

GOLDSMITHS

GLOUCESTERSHIRE C. C.

Mantled gules, doubled argent. **Supporters:** On either side a unicorn Or, the mane, hoofs and tail argent. **Motto:** Justitia virtutum regina. **Granted** 8 November 1571 (with gown of crest, mane, hooves and tail of the supporters purpure) by Robert Cooke, Clarenceux King of Arms; entered at Visitation of 1634 as above on the authority of Henry St. George, Richmond Herald. Certified painting from Garter King of Arms dated 31 March 1891 shows a Peer's helmet.

GOLDSMITHS, NATIONAL ASSOCIATION OF. Quarterly Or and argent, on a cross quarterly gules and azure a lion's face gold; on a chief per pale of the fourth and third a pair of scales of the first. **Crest:** On a wreath Or, gules, azure, argent, gules, azure, A demi figure representing St. Dunstan, nimbed, habited and mitred as a bishop, his dexter hand raised in benediction and his sinister hand resting upon a covered cup all Or. Mantled parted gules and azure, doubled Or and argent. **Supporters:** On either side a unicorn reguardant Or, armed, crined, unguled, and gorged with a chain, aıgent, pendant therefrom an escutcheon quarterly gules and azure, that on the dexter charged with an annulet gold gemmed also argent and that on the sinister with an hourglass also Or. **Motto:** Concordia, Integritas, Industria. **Granted** 15 December 1960.

GOLDSMITHS' COLLEGE (LONDON UNIVERSITY). Argent, a cross gules, on an inescutcheon azure a leopard's face Or; on a chief of the third an open book of the field edged and clasped gold. **Granted** 24th August 1921.

GONVILLE AND CAIUS COLLEGE (CAMBRIDGE UNIVERSITY).* Argent, on a chevron between two chevronels indented sable three escallops Or, impaling Or, semée of flowers gentil, in chief a sengreen above two serpents erect and respecting one other all proper, the serpents' tails bound together and resting on a square stone of green marble in base, and between the serpents a closed book sable, edged gules clasped and garnished gold; all within a bordure company argent and sable. **Crest:** On a wreath of the colours, A dove argent, beaked and membered gules, holding in the beak by the stalk a flower gentil stalked vert. **Granted** 1575 by Robert Cooke, Clarenceux King of Arms.

GOODE, DURRANT AND MURRAY (CONSOLIDATED) LIMITED. Azure, two sea horses respectant Or. **Crest:** On a wreath of the colours, A demi lion guardant gules, winged Or, holding aloft in the dexter paw a trident Or and resting the sinister paw on a bezant. **Motto:** Totis viribus. **Badge:** Two sea horses respectant Or, each supporting a trident gules, the hafts in saltire and enfiled through the tails. **Granted** 10 December 1965.

GOOLE, BOROUGH OF (YORKSHIRE—WEST RIDING).* Or, a lymphad, sail set, oars in action, sable, flags flying to the dexter gules; on a chief of the second three swans argent. **Supporters:** On either side a Viking supporting in the exterior hand a spear proper. **Motto:** Advance. **Granted** 7 October 1933.

GOUDHURST COLLEGE LIMITED. Per chevron azure and Or, on a chevron gules between a sun rising and issuant in chief and on a mount in base a hurst of oak trees proper fructed Or, an open book proper, edged and bound Or. **Crest:** On a wreath argent and gules, On a mount vert a horse forcene argent, about the neck a wreath of hops fructed proper, supporting a garb Or tied with a Stafford knot vert. **Motto:** Ad lucem. **Granted** 7 March.

GOWER RURAL DISTRICT COUNCIL (GLAMORGAN).* Barry wavy of eight argent and azure, on a pile azure a lion between three cross-crosslets Or. **Crest:** Out of a coronet composed of four ears of wheat and as many acorns leaved set upon a rim Or, a mount of heath proper, thereon in front of a lion holding between the forepaws a Maltese cross argent a portcullis chained gold nailed azure. Mantled gules, doubled Or. **Motto:** Gloria ruris divina. **Granted** 20 January 1964.

GOWER

GOOLE

GRAVESEND

GRANTHAM

GONVILLE AND CAIUS COLLEGE

GRANTHAM, BOROUGH OF (LINCOLNSHIRE—PARTS OF KESTEVEN).* Chequy Or and azure, a bordure sable verdoy of trefoils slipped argent. Recorded at the Visitation of 1634.

GRANTHAM AND KESTEVEN GENERAL HOSPITAL. Vert, a stag courant argent; on a chief counter company Or and azure, an apple proper. **Crest:** On a wreath of the colours, Two hands proper supporting a rod of Aesculapius Or. Granted 14 January 1948.

GRAVESEND, BOROUGH OF (KENT).* Argent, a tower gules charged with a bull's head issuing from a ducal coronet, both Or; and vomiting flames of fire proper; all within a bordure azure charged with five fleurs-de-lys and as many buckles Or. **Motto:** Decus et tutamen. **Granted** December 1635 to replace an earlier coat recorded at the Visitation of 1619.

GRAY'S INN. Sable, a griffin segreant Or. These Arms are of no authority.

GREAT DUNMOW PARISH COUNCIL (ESSEX).* Gules, on a chevron between in chief two fleurs-de-lis and in base a lion rampant Or, grasping in the dexter forepaw a civic mace argent, a pomegranate slipped, leaved and seeded, proper, between two mascles chevronwise of the first. **Crest:** On a wreath of the colours, On a woolpack proper a boar passant azure, armed, unguled and charged on the flank with three crescents, two and one, Or, holding in the mouth three stalks of barley and a spray of hops also proper. **Motto:** May Dunmow prosper. **Granted** 20 April 1956.

GREATER LONDON, OFFICE OF THE SHERIFF OF.* Gules, two seaxes in saltire argent, pommels and hilts Or, between in chief a Saxon crown Or and in base a horse courant argent. **Granted** 5 December 1966.

GREATER LONDON COUNCIL.* Barry wavy argent and azure, on a chief gules a Saxon crown Or. **Badge:** On a roundel argent fimbriated gules charged with three bars wavy azure, a torteau thereon a Saxon crown Or. Arms granted 1 September 1965; Badge granted 5 October 1966.

GREAT TORRINGTON, BOROUGH OF (DEVON).* Argent, in base two bars wavy azure, over all a fleur-de-lys sable; all within a bordure engrailed of the last. **Granted** 14 April 1948 in place of the Arms confirmed 6 September 1564 and recorded at the Visitation of 1620 which differed from the above in that all the charges were sable.

GREAT YARMOUTH, COUNTY BOROUGH OF (NORFOLK).* (i) Per pale gules and azure, three lions passant guardant in pale Or dimidiated with as many herrings naiant in pale argent; (ii) Per fesse gules and azure, in chief three lions passant guardant in pale Or and in base as many herrings naiant, two and one, argent; (iii) Azure, three herrings naiant in pale argent. These three coats were all recorded at the Visitation of 1563 and all three were certified by the Registrar of the College of Arms 16 December 1908. The first is that in general use with the Motto: Rex et nostra jura.

GREENWICH, LONDON BOROUGH OF.* Per chevron argent and gules, in chief an hour glass proper between two estoiles azure, and in base three cannon barrels erect palewise proper each surmounted on the breach by a lion's face Or. **Motto:** We govern by serving. **Granted** 1 October 1965.

GRESHAM LIFE ASSURANCE SOCIETY LIMITED.* Argent, a chevron engrailed ermines between two pierced mullets in chief and a pierced cinquefoil in base sable. **Crest:** On a wreath argent and gules, Upon a rock with flames issuant from either side proper a grasshopper Or. **Granted** 21 March 1936.

GRESHAM'S SCHOOL (HOLT, NORFOLK).* Argent, a chevron ermines between three pierced mullets sable; on a chief gules a dolphin naiant also argent, ducally crowned Or, between on the dexter and sinister two keys in saltire, wards upwards and outwards, gold. **Crest:** On a

GREATER LONDON COUNCIL

OFFICE OF THE SHERIFF OF GREATER LONDON

GREAT DUNMOW

GREAT YARMOUTH

GREENWICH

wreath argent and sable, A grasshopper proper supporting a key erect Or, wards to the sinister. **Motto:** Al worship be to God only. **Granted** 16 December 1955.

GREY COLLEGE (DURHAM UNIVERSITY). Gules, a scaling ladder in bend argent between two St. Cuthbert crosses proper [the pectoral cross of St. Cuthbert gold, with a ruby in the middle]. **Granted** 20 May 1960.

GREYFRIARS (OXFORD UNIVERSITY). Argent, in front of the lower limb of a long cross pointed at the foot proper, two arms in saltire, the dexter charnois, the sinister habited in the sleeve of a Franciscan Friar, the hands upwards and appaumée displaying stigmata proper, on a chief azure a Paschal Lamb also proper; over all in dexter flank a crosier erect sable, garnished and headed Or, the head containing a square pierced cross moline, and in the sinister flank an archiepiscopal staff also erect sable, garnished and headed Or, each limb of the cross terminating in a cross formy. **Motto:** Deus meus et omnia. **Granted** 20 June 1958.

GRIMSBY, COUNTY BOROUGH OF (LINCOLNSHIRE—PARTS OF LINDSEY).* Argent, a chevron between three boars' heads couped sable, armed Or, langued gules. Confirmed 1592 and recorded at the Visitation of 1634.

GRIMSBY, CLEETHORPES AND DISTRICT WATER BOARD.* Argent, on a bend engrailed between two fountains, a boar's head erased Or. **Crest:** On a wreath of the colours, Between two escallops Or an owl affrontée argent, beaked and legged gold. **Motto:** E rupe erumpet aqua. **Granted** 8 November 1937.

GRIMSBY RURAL DISTRICT COUNCIL (LINCOLNSHIRE—PARTS OF LINDSEY).* Vert, an ancient ship of three masts Or, each flying a forked pennon of St. George, the mainsail charged with a beehive and the fore and mizzen sails charged with an escallop sable; on a chief wavy also argent two dolphins embowed also vert finned gules. **Crest:** Out of a coronet composed of four ears of wheat and as many acorns leaved set upon a rim Or, a mount vert, thereon an Aberdeen Angus Bull statant proper. Mantled vert, doubled argent. **Motto:** By faith and industry. **Granted** 20 June 1961.

GROCERS OF THE CITY OF LONDON, WORSHIPFUL COMPANY OF.* Argent, a chevron gules between nine cloves sable. **Crest:** On a wreath of the colours, A camel statant Or, bridled sable, on his back two bags of pepper argent powdered with cloves and corded sable. Mantled azure, doubled argent. **Supporters:** On either side a griffin per fesse gules and Or, the underwing azure, beaked and clawed Or. **Motto:** God grant grace. Arms granted with supporters 1532 by Thomas Benolt, Clarenceux King of Arms; Crest granted (the mantling gules, doubled argent) 14 October 1562 by William Hervey Clarenceux King of Arms. Mantling changed at Visitation of 1634. The whole exemplified 8 June 1927 by Norroy King of Arms. (*Illustration on page* 173).

GROVELY MANOR SCHOOL LIMITED. Erminois, three lozenges argent, on the first a saltire gules, on the second a sword in bend sinister, point upwards, enfiled with two keys addorsed in bend, wards upwards, azure, on the third a sprig of laurel vert. **Motto:** Fortiter, fideliter, feliciter. **Badge:** A saltire gules, issuant from each angle a fleur de lys argent. **Granted** 2 November 1931.

GUILDFORD, BISHOPRIC OF.* Gules, two keys conjoined, wards outwards, in bend, the uppermost Or, the other argent, a sword of the third, pommelled and hilted of the second, interposed between them in bend sinister, all within a bordure azure charged with ten woolpacks also argent. **Granted** 30 September 1927.

GUILDFORD, BOROUGH OF (SURREY).* Sable, on a mount vert a castle with two towers enbattled on each tower a spire, from the battlements of the castle rising a tower triple-towered all Or; the whole between two woolpacks in fesse argent; the base barry wavy of the last and azure

GREAT TORRINGTON

GRESHAM'S SCHOOL

GRESHAM LIFE ASSURANCE

RIMSBY, CLEETHORPES WATER BOARD

GRIMSBY R. D. C.

and over all in base a lion couchant guardant also Or. Recorded at the Visitations of 1623 and 1662. Sable, on a mount vert a castle with two towers, on each tower a spire capped with a ball, in front of a tower triple-towered issuant from the battlements argent an escutcheon of France Modern and England quarterly, in the portway a portcullis raised and a key ward downwards and to the dexter Or, over the port two roses also Or, on the mount a lion couchant guardant, his tail extended, gold, on either side of the castle a woolpack argent; the base barry wavy of the last and azure. Painting issued by York Herald 1950.

GUILDFORD RURAL DISTRICT COUNCIL (SURREY).* Per pale azure and sable, issuant from water barry wavy in base proper a mount vert, thereon in front of an oak tree fructed a lion couchant guardant Or; over all on a fesse argent three Cornish choughs also proper. **Crest:** Out of a coronet composed of four ears of wheat and as many acorns slipped and leaved set alternately upon a rim Or, a demi lion argent, around the neck a rope proper, entwisted therewith an anchor fessewise also Or, and between the forelegs a flax-breaker gold. Mantled sable and azure, doubled argent. **Motto:** Fortiter et fideliter. **Granted** 10 May 1960.

GUILDHALL INSURANCE COMPANY LIMITED. Sable, a terrestrial globe Or; on a chief of the second a lion passant guardant of the first. **Supporters:** On the dexter side a representation of the giant Gog and on the sinister side a representation of the giant Magog, both proper. **Motto:** Per terras ubique. **Granted** 10 July 1929.

GUINNESS MAHON HOLDING LIMITED. Per chevron gules and azure, a lion rampant Or, on a chief argent, on waves of the sea in base a barque in full sail proper; and on a bordure Or four trefoils slipped vert and four roses gules, barbed and seeded proper. **Crest:** On a wreath of the colours, A bear couchant ermine, on the shoulder a bezant. **Supporters:** On the dexter side a stag and on the sinister side a bull, both proper and bezanty. **Motto:** Pro bono omnium. **Badge:** Within an annulet Or, on a rocky mount a gannet, wings addorsed, proper. **Granted** 5 September 1969.

GUNMAKERS OF THE CITY OF LONDON, WORSHIPFUL COMPANY OF. Argent, two guns in saltire proper, in chief the letter G, in base the letter Y sable, each crowned with a regal crown, on the dexter side in fesse a gun barrel and on the sinister side three balls, all of the second. These Arms are of no authority.

GUY'S HOSPITAL (LONDON). Sable, on a chevron Or between three leopards' heads argent, each crowned with an Eastern crown of the second, as many fleurs-de-lis azure. **Crest:** On a wreath of the colours, A woman sitting accompanied with three children proper, habited azure, being the emblem of Charity. **Supporters:** On either side an angel proper, habited argent, the hair and wings Or, each holding a book proper, the clasps gold. **Motto:** Dare quam accipere. **Granted** 24 May 1725 to The Corporation for the Management and Disposition of the Charities of Thomas Guy of London.

GWYNEDD POLICE AUTHORITY. Argent, an Edwardian Castle of five towers, three and two, in perspective gules; on a chief wavy vert three eagles displayed Or. **Crest:** On a wreath argent and vert, Issuant from a plume of five ostrich feathers argent a demi dragon gules holding in the dexter claw a key with pentagonal bow and double bit in the form of two letters G addorsed downwards Or. **Motto:** Goreu camp cadw. **Granted** 10 November 1967.

GWYNEDD RIVER AUTHORITY.* Bendy wavy of six argent and vert, a salmon leaping to the sinister proper; on a chief Or two lions passant guardant gules. **Crest:** On a wreath of the colours, Perched upon two tridents in saltire an eagle displayed Or. **Granted** 1 September 1965.

GRIMSBY CO. BOROUGH

GUILDFORD BOROUGH

GUILDFORD BISHOPRIC

GUILDFORD R. D. C.

GWYNEDD RIVER AUTHORITY

* *Denotes Illustration*

H

HABERDASHERS OF THE CITY OF LONDON, WORSHIPFUL COMPANY OF. Barry wavy of six argent and azure, on a bend gules a lion passant [guardant] Or. **Crest:** On a wreath of the colours, Issuing from clouds two naked arms embowed holding a laurel wreath, all proper. **Supporters:** On either side a goat of India argent, flecked gules, membered Or. **Motto:** Serve and obey. Arms granted 13 December 1503 by Roger Machado, Clarenceux King of Arms to replace an earlier grant (16 July 1446) by Roger Legh, Clarenceux King of Arms; Arms confirmed and Crest and Supporters granted 8 November 1570 by Robert Cooke, Clarenceux King of Arms.

HACKNEY, LONDON BOROUGH OF. Per fess sable and argent, a Maltese cross per fess argent and gules between two oak trees eradicated Or fructed gules, and in the [= on a] base gules three bells Or; the whole within a bordure barruly wavy argent and azure. **Crest:** On a wreath argent and gules, On a mount vert a representation of the tower of the parish church of St. Augustine, Hackney, proper. **Badge:** On an ellipse barruly wavy argent and azure, a delf per fess sable and argent, fimbriated Or, charged with a Maltese cross per fess argent and gules, ensigned by a representation of the tower of the ancient parish church of St. Augustine, Hackney. **Granted** 25 July 1969.

HAILEYBURY AND IMPERIAL SERVICE COLLEGE.* Azure, an open book argent bound gules edged and garnished with seven clasps gold and inscribed with the words "Sursum Corda" sable, the initial letters of the third, between three hearts Or, winged of the second; on a chief also Or an anchor cabled and a sword, the point upwards, in saltire of the field. **Crest:** On a wreath Or and azure, A lion sejant guardant erect, crowned with an Eastern crown Or, and holding between the forepaws a scroll with the seal pendent therefrom proper. **Motto:** Fear God, Honour the King. Arms granted 18 August 1943; Crest granted 10 June 1963.

HAILSHAM RURAL DISTRICT COUNCIL (EAST SUSSEX).* Vert, two castles proper, in base an ancient plough Or; on a chief wavy barry wavy of six azure and gold an ancient ship, all argent. **Crest:** On a wreath azure and vert, A hurt semée of mullets of six points argent charged with a martlet Or. **Motto:** Habitare ruri delectationes colere. **Granted** 20 June 1956.

HALESOWEN, BOROUGH OF (WORCESTERSHIRE).* Per pale argent and Or, a lion rampant double queued per pale gules and vert; a chief per pile reversed of the first and azure, thereon in chief two escallops sable and in base a fleur-de-lys of the second. **Crest:** Out of a mural crown Or, an anvil sable, the beak encircled by a chain reflexed over the face gold. **Supporters:** On the dexter side a Canon of the Premonstratensian Order holding in the exterior hand a [closed] book and on the sinister side a gentleman habited in costume of the fifteenth century, all proper. **Motto:** Respice, aspice, prospice. **Granted** 16 September 1937.

HALIFAX, COUNTY BOROUGH OF (YORKSHIRE—WEST RIDING).* Chequy Or and azure, a man's face affrontée [eyes closed] bearded and surrounded by a halo proper. **Crest:** Issuant from a Saxon crown Or a mount vert, thereon a Paschal Lamb proper holding a cross

HAILEYBURY

HALIFAX

HALESOWEN

HAILSHAM

staff gold, flying therefrom a forked pennon argent charged with a cross gules. Mantled azure, doubled Or. **Supporters:** On either side a lion Or holding with the interior paw a rose argent, barbed, seeded, stalked and leaved proper. **Motto:** Except the Lord keep the city. **Granted** 12 April 1948.

HALSTEAD URBAN DISTRICT COUNCIL (ESSEX).* Per chevron vert and azure, in chief two weavers' shuttles erect proper and in base a thunderbolt Or. **Crest:** On a wreath of the colours, In front of a saltire azure, on a mount vert a garb proper. **Motto:** Consilio et prudentia. **Granted** 20 November 1964.

HALTEMPRICE URBAN DISTRICT COUNCIL (YORKSHIRE—EAST RIDING).* Sable, a cross patonce argent, in the first quarter a rose of the second barbed and seeded proper. **Crest:** On a wreath of the colours, Upon a mount vert a stag at gaze proper gorged with a mural crown Or. **Motto:** Haulte emprise. **Granted** 5 February 1952.

HAMMERSMITH, LONDON BOROUGH OF.* Barry wavy argent and azure, two hammers in saltire interlaced with a horseshoe Or; on a chief gules two swords in saltire proper, hilts and pomels Or, a mitre of the last. **Crest:** On a wreath argent and sanguine, Out of a mural crown of six turrets Or an ancient ship, oars in action, sable, sail set, flags and pennon flying sanguine, the sail charged with two hammers in saltire interlaced with a horseshoe Or. Mantled azure, doubled argent. **Supporters:** On each side a male griffin gules, beaked and irradiated Or, armed and langued azure, each gorged with a cord Or, pendent from that of the dexter an escallop, and from that of the sinister a cross crosslet argent. **Motto:** Judge by our labour. **Badge:** Two hammers in saltire interlaced with a horseshoe Or. **Granted** 1 March 1965.

HARDWARE, NATIONAL INSTITUTE OF. Or, a key, wards upwards, between in chief a pair of scales and in base an anvil sable. **Crest:** On a wreath of the colours, A lantern radiant proper suspended from an arch of iron rod sable. **Granted** 12 March 1951.

HARINGEY, LONDON BOROUGH OF.* Sable, eight rays [of lightning] issuing from the fess point throughout Or. **Crest:** On a wreath of the colours, In front of a demi sun in splendour Or a demi cog wheel sable. **Motto:** Progress with humanity. **Badge:** Eight rays [as in the Arms]. **Granted** 10 May 1965.

HARLOW DEVELOPMENT CORPORATION (ESSEX).* Argent, on a cross engrailed sable a fleur de lis Or; on a chief azure three ancient crowns of the third each enfiling two arrows in saltire, points downwards, of the second. **Crest:** On a wreath of the colours, A demi griffin sable holding in the dexter claw by the blade a seax proper, pomel and hilt Or, and charged on the shoulder with a pierced mullet argent. Mantled gules, doubled argent. **Motto:** Members of one another. **Granted** 9 January 1948.

HARLOW URBAN DISTRICT COUNCIL (ESSEX).* Vert, between three lozenges argent a pair of dividers Or enfiled by a mural crown also argent; two flaunches of the last each charged with a mascle gules. **Crest:** On a wreath of the colours, In front of a dexter cubit arm vested in a white shirt-sleeve, the cuff rolled back, the hand grasping an axe, a demi cogwheel proper. **Motto:** In common endeavour. **Granted** 27 September 1957.

HARPENDEN URBAN DISTRICT COUNCIL (HERTFORDSHIRE).* Bendy of six gules and argent, three garbs Or; a chief azure, thereon on a pale between two saltires throughout of the third, a fess dancetté sable. **Crest:** On a wreath of the colours, Within wattled palings proper a mount vert, thereon a hart lodged also proper. **Motto:** Fide et labore. **Granted** 4 February 1949.

HARROGATE, BOROUGH OF (YORKSHIRE—WEST RIDING).* Quarterly argent and gules, a cross counterchanged between in the first and fourth quarters a fountain proper and in the second and third a bugle horn stringed Or; on a chief per pale of the second and azure a lion

HALSTEAD

HAMMERSMITH

HALTEMPRICE

HARLOW

HARINGEY

passant guardant of the first. **Crest:** On a wreath of the colours, Out of the battlements of a tower a trunk of a tree erect entwined by two serpents respecting each other proper, surmounted by a cock sable, combed and wattled gules. **Motto:** Arx celebris fontibus. **Granted** 8 November 1884.

HARROW, LONDON BOROUGH OF.* Or, a fesse arched vert, in chief on a pile gules between a torch sable, enflamed proper, and a quill pen of the fourth, a clarion of the first, and in base upon a mount issuant a hurst of trees of the second. **Crest:** Issuant from a mural crown proper a demi lion holding between the paws an arrow fessewise argent enfiled with a wreath of oak also proper. **Supporters:** On the dexter side a representation of Hygeia supporting with her exterior hand a staff entwined with a snake, and on the sinister side a Benedictine monk supporting with his exterior hand a staff, all proper. **Motto:** Salus populi suprema lex. Arms and Crest granted 3 May 1938 to the former Harrow Urban District Council; Supporters granted 10 September 1954 to the former Borough of Harrow; the whole allowed to the London Borough of Harrow 4 August 1965.

HARROW SCHOOL.* Azure, a lion rampant, in dexter chief two arrows in saltire, points downward, tied in the centre with a bow and enfiled with a wreath of laurel, all argent. **Motto:** (Below shield) Donorum Dei dispensatio fidelis; (above shield and badge) Stet fortuna domus. **Badge:** Two arrows in saltire, points downward, tied in the centre with a bow and enfiled with a wreath of laurel, all argent. **Granted** 3 October 1929 to The Keepers and Governors of the possessions, revenues and goods of the Free Grammar School of John Lyon within the Town of Harrow on the Hill in the County of Middlesex.

HARTLEY UNIVERSITY COLLEGE, SOUTHAMPTON. See Southampton, University of.

HARTLEY VICTORIA METHODIST COLLEGE (MANCHESTER).* Azure, a hart courant between three fleurs-de-lys argent. **Crest:** On a wreath of the colours, A hurt charged with an antique lamp Or, enflamed proper. **Motto:** Ubi spiritus ibi libertas. **Granted** 19 July 1937.

HARWICH, BOROUGH OF (ESSEX).* Gules, a portcullis chained Or, studded and spiked azure. **Crest:** On a wreath of the colours, Upon waves of the sea proper an ancient ship with one mast Or, at the bow and stern turrets and affixed below the top of the mast a tower argent, the sail furled of the last, and flying to the dexter a pennon gules. **Motto:** Omnia bona bonis. **Granted** 15 December 1943.

HASLEMERE URBAN DISTRICT COUNCIL (SURREY).* Per chevron purpure and sable, on a chevron Or between in chief two hinds' heads erased and in base an acorn slipped and leaved argent, a fountain between two hazel leaves proper. **Crest:** Out of a mural crown Or a demi heraldic antelope argent, collared azure, supporting a beacon sable, fired proper. **Motto:** Vita Musis gratior. **Granted** 9 December 1959.

HASLINGDEN, BOROUGH OF (LANCASHIRE). Quarterly Or and argent, on a fesse wavy azure between a lion rampant purpure holding between the paws a cinquefoil ermine in the first quarter, six eagles displayed three, two and one gules in the centre chief point a rose of the last barbed and seeded proper in the second, a cogwheel sable in the third, a pickaxe in bend surmounting a spade in bend sinister entwined by a chain in arch all proper in the fourth, a shuttle fessewise of the first tipped and furnished with the thread pendent of the second. **Crest:** On a wreath of the colours, Upon a mount a rock, thereon a moorcock, holding in the beak a sprig of hazel, between two branches of hazel fructed, all proper. **Motto:** Nothing without labour. **Granted** 25 March 1892.

HASTINGS, COUNTY BOROUGH OF (EAST SUSSEX). Per pale gules and azure, a lion passant guardant Or between in chief and in base a lion passant guardant gold dimidiated with the hulk of a ship argent. Recorded at the Visitation of 1634.

HARLOW U. D. C.

HARPENDEN

HARROGATE

HARROW

HATFIELD COLLEGE (DURHAM UNIVERSITY). Azure, a chevron Or between three lions rampant argent, a bordure ermine. **Crest:** Out of an ancient crown Or a panache of five ostrich feathers ermine charged with a chevron sable. **Motto:** Primus vel in primis. **Granted** 31 May 1957.

HATFIELD RURAL DISTRICT COUNCIL (HERTFORDSHIRE).* Barry of ten argent and azure, a lion rampant ermine, on a chief gules three ducal coronets Or; all within a bordure of the last charged with eight Tudor roses proper. **Crest:** On a wreath of the colours, An oak tree charged with a Tudor rose, all proper. **Motto:** Semper serio. **Granted** 14 May 1945.

HAVERFORDWEST, BOROUGH OF (PEMBROKESHIRE). Barry wavy argent and azure, a lymphad, sails set, proper and flags flying gules; on a chief vert a castle triple-towered between two plumes, each of [three] ostrich feathers argent. **Crest:** On a wreath argent and vert, Out of the battlements of an hexagonal tower a demi man winding a horn proper, habited per pale vert and argent, on his head a steel cap proper. **Supporters:** On the dexter side a dragon gules, the undersides of the wings charged with a cross Or thereon five cinquefoils sable, and on the sinister side a lion sable, about the neck an ancient crown [=Eastern, or antique, crown] with a chain reflexed over the back Or. **Motto:** O lector salve, coeli pateant tibi valve. **Granted** 5 October 1966 to The Borough and County of the Town of Haverford alias Haverfordwest.

HAVERING, LONDON BOROUGH OF.* Per saltire argent and azure, a gem ring Or set with a ruby proper. **Crest:** On a wreath Or and azure, A castellated gateway with three towers Or, masoned sable, the windows and the middle tower domed azure, ensigned by a cross gules, and the outer towers each with a steeple azure, issuant above the port a bull's head and neck affronty proper. **Motto:** Liberty. **Badge:** A bull's head caboshed proper within a gem ring Or set with a ruby proper. **Granted** 1 March 1965.

HAWARDEN RURAL DISTRICT COUNCIL (FLINTSHIRE). Azure, on a bar wavy argent a barrulet wavy of the first and over all a palet sable, in chief a hammer and a pick in saltire argent between two ears of wheat Or and in base a lion rampant also argent; a bordure of the last charged with nine martlets sable. **Crest:** On a wreath of the colours, On three towers conjoined argent a dragon passant gules holding in the dexter claw a feather also argent. **Motto:** Gorau nawdd, nawdd Duw. **Granted** 23 December 1954.

HAYLING ISLAND COUNTY SECONDARY SCHOOL (HAMPSHIRE). Gules, a cross Or between four keys erect, wards to the sinister, argent, on a chief argent three roses gules, barbed and seeded proper; a bordure barry wavy argent and azure. **Crest:** On a wreath of the colours, In front of a rock Or, perched thereon a heron proper, four bezants. **Motto:** With these keys. **Granted** 20 December 1968.

HEALTH, ROYAL SOCIETY OF.* Azure, a fountain radiating Or. **Crest:** On a wreath of the colours, An apple tree leaved and fructed with seven apples proper. **Supporters:** On the dexter side a representation of a figure of Hygeia and on the sinister side a stork, both proper. **Motto:** Salus generis humani. **Granted** 16 September 1949 to the Royal Sanitary Institute.

HELBERT, WAGG AND COMPANY LIMITED. Gules, a lion rampant Or holding between the forepaws a battleaxe erect proper; on a chief argent a pair of scales sable. **Crest:** Issuant from a coronet composed of roses argent, barbed and seeded proper, and bezants set alternately upon a rim company Or and sable, three battleaxes, one erect and two in saltire, also proper. **Motto:** Tiens la foi. **Granted** 13 March 1960.

HEMEL HEMPSTEAD DEVELOPMENT CORPORATION (HERTFORDSHIRE).* Vert, a Tudor rose, gules upon argent, barbed and seeded proper, within a surveyor's chain of the third. **Crest:** On a wreath of the colours, Issuant from a mural coronet gules a mount vert, thereon a stag lodged proper. **Supporters:** On the dexter side a greyhound proper and on the sinister side a stag proper, each gorged with a mural coronet gules. **Motto:** Majora, uberiora, pulchriora. **Granted** 27 January 1948.

HEMSWORTH RURAL DISTRICT COUNCIL (YORKSHIRE—WEST RIDING).* Sable, on a mount in base an oak tree proper, fructed Or; on a chief gules a cross couped gold between

HARWICH

HASLEMERE

HARROW SCHOOL

HATFIELD

HARTLEY VICTORIA
METHODIST COLLEGE

two roses argent, barbed and seeded also proper. **Crest:** Out of a circlet azure charged with a crescent argent between two mullets of six points Or, a bull's head sable, armed gold. **Motto:** Constanter et recte. **Granted** 12 October 1954.

THE HERALDRY SOCIETY.* Quarterly azure and gules, a lion's face crowned with an ancient crown Or within a tressure flory on the outer edge of the same. **Crest:** On a wreath Or, azure and gules, A demi figure of a knight in armour, habited in a tabard of the Arms, his hands gauntleted proper, the dexter holding the hilt and the sinister resting on the quillons of a sword, point downward, also proper, hilt and pomel Or, on his head a chapeau gules turned up ermine encircled by an ancient crown gold. Mantled azure and gules, doubled Or. **Supporters:** On either side an unicorn sable, armed, unguled, crined and tufted Or, wreathed about the neck with a torse argent and gules. **Motto:** Entalenté a parler d'armes. **Badge:** A lion's face crowned with an ancient crown Or within an annulet flory on the outer edge of the same. **Granted** 10 August 1957.

HEREFORD, BISHOPRIC OF.* Gules, three leopards' faces reversed, jessant-de-lis, two and one, Or. Recorded in the College of Arms.

HEREFORD, DEAN AND CHAPTER OF. Or, five chevronels gules. Recorded at the Visitation of 1634.

HEREFORD, CITY OF.* Gules, three lions passant guardant in pale argent; on a bordure azure ten saltires of the second. **Crest:** On a wreath of the colours, A lion passant guardant argent holding in the dexter paw a sword erect proper, hilt and pomel Or. **Supporters:** On either side a lion rampant guardant argent gorged with a collar azure charged with three buckles Or. **Motto:** Invictae fidelitatis praemium. Arms recorded (without bordure) at the Visitations of 1569 and 1634; Arms augmented and Crest and Supporters granted 14 September 1645 by Sir Edward Walker, Garter King of Arms.

HEREFORDSHIRE COUNTY COUNCIL.* Gules, on a fesse wavy between in chief a lion passant guardant argent and in base a Herefordshire bull's head caboshed proper, a bar wavy azure. **Crest:** On a wreath of the colours, A demi lion rampant gules holding in the sinister claw a fleece Or. **Supporters:** On the dexter side a lion guardant Or gorged with a wreath of hops fructed proper and on the sinister side a talbot argent gorged with a collar Or charged with three apples proper. **Motto:** Pulchra terra Dei donum. **Granted** 28 February 1946.

HERNE BAY URBAN DISTRICT COUNCIL (KENT).* Barry wavy of six argent and azure, on a chief of the last a heron Or between two crosses formée fitchee of the first. **Crest:** On a wreath of the colours, A lymphad gules with pennant per fess argent and azure and the sail also argent charged with a bull statant sable, armed and unguled also gules. **Motto:** Ne cede malis. **Granted** 8 June 1948.

HERTFORD, BOROUGH OF.* Argent, on water barry wavy a hart lodged proper. **Supporters:** On either side a lion ermine gorged with a collar, pendent therefrom by a chain gules an escutcheon Or charged with three chevrons also gules. **Motto:** Pride in our past, faith in our future. **Badge:** Within a chaplet of roses gules a hart's head caboshed proper, between the attires an escutcheon Or charged with three chevronels gules. **Standard:** Argent, the bands azure fimbriated and inscribed Pro Hertfordae honore gold, fringed argent and azure. Arms recorded at the Visitation of 1634; Supporters granted 20 October 1937; Badge granted 23 September 1925.

HERTFORD, OFFICE OF THE SHERIFF OF THE COUNTY OF.* Azure, a castle triple towered Or; on a chief argent a hart lodged proper. **Granted** 20 August 1963.

HERTFORD COLLEGE (OXFORD UNIVERSITY). Gules, a stag's head caboshed argent, attired or, between the attires a cross pattée fitched at the foot of the last. These Arms are of no authority.

HAVERING

ROYAL SOCIETY OF HEALTH

HEMSWORTH

HEMEL HEMPSTEAD

HERTFORD RURAL DISTRICT COUNCIL. Azure, on a saltire Or a stag's head caboshed gules; a bordure barry wavy of eight argent and of the first. **Crest:** On a wreath argent and azure, In front of an oak tree proper, fructed Or, a stag salient gold. **Motto:** Pro rure, pro patria. **Granted** 16 April 1951.

HERTFORDSHIRE COUNTY COUNCIL.* Barry wavy of eight azure and argent, an inescutcheon Or charged with a hart lodged proper. **Supporters:** On either side a hart proper gorged with a chain Or and pendent therefrom an escutcheon azure charged with a saltire gold. **Motto:** Trust and fear not. **Granted** 3 June 1925.

HEXHAM URBAN DISTRICT COUNCIL (NORTHUMBERLAND).* Vert, a saltire argent between in chief an ancient crown, in base a mitre, and in fess two garbs Or; a chief wavy barry wavy of six azure and of the second. **Crest:** On a wreath of the colours, A fleshing knife and a beam knife in saltire proper, the upper handles joined by a chain Or, pendent therefrom a fleece gold banded vert. **Granted** 31 August 1953.

HEYWOOD, BOROUGH OF (LANCASHIRE). Or, five pellets between two bendlets engrailed, the whole between as many mascles sable. **Crest:** On a wreath of the colours, In front of the trunk of a tree eradicated fessewise and sprouting to the dexter a falcon rising proper, each wing charged with a pellet, and holding in the beak a sprig of oak also proper, three mascles interlaced Or. **Motto:** Alte volo. **Granted** 14 May 1881.

HIGHWORTH RURAL DISTRICT COUNCIL (WILTSHIRE). Per saltire vert and gules, a saltire argent between in chief a mute swan rousant proper, in base a tower argent, and in fess two hammers erect Or. **Crest:** On a wreath of the colours, On a mount vert, issuant from a crown vallary Or, a garb of wheat proper girt with a circlet per fess embattled sable and argent. **Motto:** Magni consilium pretii. **Granted** 12 March 1968.

HIGH WYCOMBE, BOROUGH OF (BUCKINGHAMSHIRE).* Sable, on a mount vert a swan argent, ducally gorged and chained Or. **Motto:** Industria Ditat. Recorded at the Visitations of 1566 and 1634; Certified circa 1953.

HILLINGDON, LONDON BOROUGH OF.* Per pale gules and vert, an eagle displayed per pale Or and argent, in the dexter claw a fleur-de-lys Or and in the sinister a cog wheel argent; on a chief Or four civic crowns vert. **Crest:** On a wreath of the colours, Issuant from a circlet of brushwood sable a demi lion gules, with wings argent, the underside of each wing charged with a cross gules, and holding between the paws a bezant, thereon a mullet azure. **Supporters:** On the dexter side an heraldic tiger Or, gorged with an astral crown and charged on the shoulder with a rose gules charged with another argent, barbed and seeded proper, and on the sinister side a stag proper, attired and gorged with a circlet of brushwood and charged on the shoulder with two ears of rye slipped in saltire Or. **Motto:** Forward. **Badge:** A roundel vert surmounted of a mullet of seven points argent charged with a mural crown gules. **Granted** 22 March 1965.

HILLSBOROUGH RURAL DISTRICT COUNCIL (CO. DOWN).* Tierced in pairle reversed wavy gules, vert and azure, divided argent, in chief a shuttle erect and an ear of wheat erect, and in base issuant from a mount a representation of the Round Tower of Drumbo Or charged with a sinister hand appaumé couped gules. **Crest:** On a wreath argent and azure, A demi figure representing one of the Old Guard of Hillsborough Castle proper. **Motto:** Ex fide fortis. **Granted** 20 April 1964.

HINCKLEY AND COUNTRY BUILDING SOCIETY. Per pale indented argent and gules, a bordure vert charged with four garbs Or and as many pierced cinquefoils ermine alternately. **Crest:** On a wreath of the colours, Out of a chaplet of thrift flowers proper a mount vert, thereon a castle of three towers, the portcullis raised, Or. **Motto:** Tuta velut cor Angliae. **Granted** 20 February 1959.

THE HERALDRY SOCIETY

HEREFORD BISHOPRIC

HEREFORDSHIRE C. C.

HERNE BAY

HINCKLEY URBAN DISTRICT COUNCIL (LEICESTERSHIRE).* Per pale dancettée argent and gules, on a chief erminois a maunch of the second between two flames of fire proper. **Crest:** On a wreath of the colours, In front of five ostrich feathers argent a ram's head erased sable armed Or. **Motto:** Angliae cor. **Granted** 16 August 1946.

HINDLEY URBAN DISTRICT COUNCIL (LANCASHIRE). Or, between two barrulets wavy azure a hind lodged proper between as many roses gules, barbed and seeded also proper, in base a like rose; a chief wavy sable charged with three mascles of the field. **Crest:** On a wreath argent, azure and sable, Two dragons' heads couped and addorsed sable, in the mouth of each three stalks of wheat, about their necks a chaplet of oak, all proper. **Motto:** Prodesse. **Granted** 10 February 1958.

HITCHIN URBAN DISTRICT COUNCIL (HERTFORDSHIRE).* Gules, on a fesse arched and embattled argent between in chief a lion passant guardant and in base a sheaf of barley Or, a fleshing knife fessewise proper. **Crest:** On a wreath of the colours, Two shepherds' crooks in saltire, pendent therefrom at the point of intersection by a ring a fleece, all proper. **Motto:** Et patribus et posteritati. **Granted** 25 November 1936.

HOLBORN LAW SOCIETY. Ermine, on a cross gules between in chief a pavilion purpure, lined argent, and a lion rampant, and in base a griffin segreant and an open book all proper, the latter edged and bound Or, in front of a sword sheathed, point upwards, a hind lodged, pierced by an arrow, Or. **Crest:** On a wreath argent and gules, In front of a saltire argent a female figure representing Justice blindfolded proper, habited azure, scarf gules, in the dexter hand a pair of scales Or and in the sinister a sword erect proper, hilt and pomel Or. **Motto:** Salus populi suprema lex. **Granted** 10 December 1965.

HOLDERNESS RURAL DISTRICT COUNCIL (YORKSHIRE—EAST RIDING). Argent, a Viking ship in full sail proper; on a chief per pale vert and sable, between two roses argent, each charged with another gules, all barbed and seeded also proper, two stalks of wheat in saltire Or. **Crest:** On a wreath of the colours, A representation of the parish church of Patrington proper. **Motto:** Think right, do right. **Granted** 19 July 1957.

HOLLAND, PARTS OF. See Lincolnshire.

JOHN HOLT AND COMPANY (LIVERPOOL) LIMITED. Argent, a representation of the schooner "Maria" in full sail proper; on a chief azure a mullet between two African manilla coins argent. **Crest:** On a wreath of the colours, A dexter hand in a steel gauntlet grasping an African manilla coin proper. **Supporters:** On the dexter side an African lion and on the sinister side a cormorant, both proper. **Motto:** Quaerere verum. **Badge:** Within an African manilla coin, the opening upward, proper a mullet vert. **Granted** 1 June 1960.

HOLY ISLAND PARISH COUNCIL (NORTHUMBERLAND). Barry wavy argent and azure, a pomeis ensigned with an ancient crown and charged throughout with a Celtic cross Or; on a chief also azure in a landscape a representation of the ruined Priory of Lindisfarne proper. **Crest:** On a wreath Or and azure, A monk seated affrontée and habited in a saffron-coloured robe proper, behind the head a nimbus Or, and holding in the hands an open book gules, garnished gold. **Motto:** Ecce ego, mitte me. **Granted** 10 June 1959.

HOLYWOOD URBAN DISTRICT COUNCIL (CO. DOWN). Vert, a representation of the Priory Church at St. Laiseran at Holywood Or; on a chief sable a cross fourchy between two lozenges gold, that on the dexter charged with an estoile of eight points, and that on the sinister with a dexter hand couped, both gules. **Crest:** On a wreath Or and gules, On a mount vert, in front of a sun rising Or, three oak trees fructed proper. **Motto:** Sanctus boscus. **Granted** 1962.

HEXHAM

HEREFORD

HERTFORDSHIRE C. C.

OFFICE OF THE SHERIFF OF HERTFORD

HOMERTON COLLEGE (CAMBRIDGE). Argent, a leopard's face jessant-de-lys sable between three griffins' heads erased gules; on a bordure azure eight open books proper. **Crest:** On a wreath of the colours, A demi griffin holding between the claws a lozenge argent charged with a leopard's face jessant-de-lys as in the Arms. **Motto:** Respice finem. **Granted** 22 December 1954.

HONOURABLE ARTILLERY COMPANY. See Artillery Company, The Honourable.

HONOURABLE COMPANY OF MASTER MARINERS. See Master Mariners, Honourable Company of.

HONOURABLE SOCIETY OF CYMMORODORION. See Cymmorodorion, Honourable Society of.

HORNCASTLE RURAL DISTRICT COUNCIL (LINCOLNSHIRE—PARTS OF LINDSEY). Or, a castle of two towers gules; on a chief wavy vert a mitre gold between two Lincolnshire Shorthorn bulls' heads caboshed proper. **Crest:** On a wreath of the colours, Out of a wreath of laurel vert a dexter arm embowed in armour, the hand grasping a dexter gauntlet, all proper, the upper arm charged with a sun Or. **Motto:** Defend the right. **Granted** 30 January 1956.

HORNERS OF THE CITY OF LONDON, WORSHIPFUL COMPANY OF. Argent on a chevron between three leather bottles sable as many hunting-horns stringed of the first. These are of no authority.

HORNSEA URBAN DISTRICT COUNCIL (YORKSHIRE—EAST RIDING).* Or, three bars wavy azure, issuant from the base a sun in splendour gules; a chief wavy sable, thereon a fountain between two roses argent, barbed and seeded proper. **Crest:** Issuant from a mural crown Or a sun in splendour gules surmounted of a rose argent, barbed and seeded proper. Mantled gules, doubled Or. **Motto:** Health and happiness. **Granted** 24 June 1955.

HORSHAM URBAN DISTRICT COUNCIL (WEST SUSSEX).* Azure, a lion rampant argent resting the dexter hind foot on a representation of the letter H Or. **Crest:** Issuant from a mural crown Or a demi lion between two lilies in bend sinister, slipped and leaved, proper. **Motto:** Proudly we serve. **Granted** 17 October 1944.

HOSPITAL ADMINISTRATORS, INSTITUTE OF. Or, a cross couped gules; on a chief sable an ancient lamp Or, inflamed proper, between two Ankhs Or. **Crest:** Issuant from a celestial crown Or a cubit arm proper grasping a serpent nowed vert. **Supporters:** On the dexter side a representation of the Egyptian God of Medicine Imhotep and on the sinister side a representation of the Greek Goddess Hygeia, both proper. **Motto:** Fide et constanter. Arms (with the field argent), Crest and Supporters granted 17 June 1948; Arms regranted with the field as above 20 April 1966.

HOSPITAL ENGINEERING, INSTITUTE OF.* Or, on a bend between two cocks sable, three cog wheels Or. **Crest:** On a wreath of the colours, A torch erect, enflamed and entwined by a serpent, all proper. **Motto:** Life in our hands. **Granted** 30 September 1969.

HOSPITAL OF QUEEN ELIZABETH IN DONNINGTON (BERKSHIRE). Per fesse azure and gules, on a fesse Or between three cross crosslets fitchy argent, a bar embattled sable charged with three white roses barbed and seeded proper. **Crest:** On a wreath of the colours, Issuant from a Tudor rose proper a pelican's head and neck Or, vulning herself gules and murally gorged sable. **Motto:** Deo et pauperibus. **Granted** 20 December 1963.

HOUNSLOW, LONDON BOROUGH OF.* Per fesse azure and gules, on a fesse wavy between in chief two wings conjoined in base argent surmounted of a sword erect Or, and in base a lion rampant guardant per fesse Or and argent, a barrulet wavy azure. **Crest:** On a wreath of the colours, Upon ferns proper a talbot passant sable supporting over the dexter shoulder a post horn Or. **Supporters:** On either side a griffin Or gorged with a collar gemel wavy azure and charged on the wings with a seax, the cutting edge inwards proper, pomel and hilt gules. **Motto:** Juncti pro-

HERTFORD BOROUGH

HILLSBOROUGH

HIGH WYCOMBE

HORNSEA

HILLINGDON

grediamur. **Badge:** In front of two wings argent, each charged with two barrulets wavy azure, a seax erect proper, pomel and hilt gules, the blade surmounted of a lion's face Or. **Granted** 3 September 1964. The patent shows two barrulets on the fesse.

HOVE, BOROUGH OF (EAST SUSSEX).* Per chevron, the chief per pale Or and gules, on the dexter a saltire azure surmounted by another argent, and on the sinister two pairs of leg-irons, one chevronwise, the other reversed and interlaced, of the first, the base chequy azure and Or, three martlets, one and two, of the last; all within a bordure ermine charged with six martlets also Or. **Crest:** On a wreath of the colours, Upon a mount of shingle an ancient ship proper with the sail displayed azure semée of cross crosslets Or and on a banner gules flying from the masthead to the dexter a martlet as in the Arms. **Motto:** Floreat Hova. **Granted** 16 December 1899.

HOYLAKE URBAN DISTRICT COUNCIL (CHESHIRE). Vert, two golf clubs in saltire, heads downwards, enfiled with an ancient crown Or, between in chief a fountain charged with an anchor fouled sable and in base a garb gold; two flaunches barry wavy argent and azure. **Crest:** On a wreath of the colours, Upon a sandstone rock an oyster catcher (Haematopus Ostralegus) rising proper. **Motto:** Prespice et prospice. **Granted** 1 November 1960.

HUDDERSFIELD, COUNTY BOROUGH OF (YORKSHIRE—WEST RIDING).* Or, on a chevron between three rams passant sable, as many towers argent. **Crest:** On a wreath of the colours, A ram's head couped argent, armed Or, gorged with a collar sable, holding in the mouth a sprig of the cotton-tree, slipped and fructed, proper. **Motto:** Juvat impigros Deus. **Granted** 12 October 1868.

HUDDERSFIELD BUILDING SOCIETY. Erminois, on a chevron sable between three roses argent, barbed and seeded proper, as many towers argent. **Crest:** On a wreath Or and gules, Out of a garland of thrift flowers proper a demi ram argent, armed and unguled Or, supporting with the legs a key erect, wards outward and upward in the form of the letter H gold. **Motto:** Juvat impigros Deus. **Granted** 5 March 1964.

HUDSON'S BAY COMPANY. Argent, a cross gules between four beavers sable. **Crest:** Upon a cap of maintenance gules turned up ermine, a fox sejant proper. **Supporters:** On either side an elk proper. **Motto:** Pro Pelle Cutem. **Granted** 6th September 1921.

HULL, UNIVERSITY OF.* Azure, a torch fired and enfiled with a ducal coronet Or between on the dexter a rose argent, barbed and seeded proper, and on the sinister a fleur-de-lys of the second; on a chief wavy of the third a dove of the first. **Motto:** Lampada ferens. **Granted** 22 November 1927 to the University College of Hull; recertified on change of status.

HUNSTANTON URBAN DISTRICT COUNCIL (NORFOLK).* Barry wavy argent and azure, on a pile reversed gules two arrows in saltire, points downwards, enfiled with a coronet of four fleurs de lys set upon a rim Or; on a chief also gules a lion passant of the first. **Crest:** On a wreath of the colours, A sea lion Or supporting an ostrich feather erect argent. **Motto:** Alios delectare juvat. **Granted** 9 September 1955.

HUNTING-CLAN AIR TRANSPORT LIMITED. Quarterly, first and fourth gules, six barrulets argent a mullet of seven points azure, second and third gules, on a lozenge argent a lion rampant of the field; all within a bordure of clouds proper. **Crest:** On a wreath of the colours, An owl gold, under the sinister wing an arrow, point to the dexter, azure. **Supporters:** On the dexter side an eagle, wings elevated and addorsed, sable, beaked and membered Or, langued and armed gules, supporting with the sinister claw a staff gold, flying therefrom a banner of the first quarter of the Arms; and on the sinister side a winged lion gules supporting a like staff, flying therefrom a banner of the second quarter of the Arms. **Motto:** Cautus in consilio, alacer in acto. **Badge:** A banner of the first quarter of the Arms to the dexter and a banner of the second quarter of the Arms to the sinister, the staves in saltire Or and enfiled with a circlet of clouds proper. **Granted** 3 December 1954.

HINCKLEY

HITCHIN

HOSPITAL ENGINEERING

HOUNSLOW

HORSHAM

HUNTINGDON AND GODMANCHESTER, BOROUGH OF.* Per fess dovetailed Or and vert, in chief two huntinghorns sable, stringed gules, and in base a fleur-de-lys argent. **Crest:** Out of an ancient crown Or, upon a mount vert, in front of a port between two towers proper, pennons flying gules, a stag's head and neck couped proper. **Supporters:** On the dexter side a man habited as a mediaeval huntsman proper, his bow and quiver Or, the arrows gules flighted Or, and on the sinister side a man habited as a mediaeval oxherd, the goad in his exterior hand proper, tipped Or, both standing upon a representation of the old bridge at Huntingdon also proper. **Motto:** United we advance. **Granted** 5 June 1963.

HUNTINGDON AND PETERBOROUGH COUNTY COUNCIL. Barry argent and azure, on a fess embattled vert a cornucopia between two garbs Or. **Crest:** Issuant from a mural crown Or a demi lion rampant gules gorged with a collar flory counterflory and supporting a staff Or, flying therefrom a banner vert charged with two keys in saltire Or. Mantled azure, doubled argent. **Supporters:** On the dexter side a pikeman of the New Model Army supporting with the exterior hand a pike, and on the sinister side a mited abbot in processional vestments for St. Peter's Day supporting with the exterior hand a crosier and sudarium, all proper. **Motto:** Cor unum. **Badge:** Two keys in saltire surmounted by a buglehorn Or, the strings azure interlaced with the keys. **Granted** 3 April 1965.

HUYTON-WITH-ROBY URBAN DISTRICT COUNCIL (LANCASHIRE). Azure, an eagle, wings addorsed and inverted, Or perched upon a cradle proper, therein an infant also proper swaddled gules; on a chief dancetty of the second three roses also gules, barbed and seeded proper. **Crest:** Issuant from a mural crown Or a demi wolf sable, charged on the shoulder with a fret argent, gorged with a strap gold buckled gules and supporting a staff of the first, flying therefrom a banner azure charged with a cross moline also gold. **Motto:** Cum aquila alte volemus. **Granted** 10 May 1954.

HYDE, BOROUGH OF (CHESHIRE). Argent, a chevron nebuly argent between three lozenges Or; on a chief of the second a flake erect surmounted by a hatter's bow in bend sinister between a cog-wheel and two miners' picks in saltire, therefrom suspended a Davy lamp, all proper. **Crest:** On a wreath of the colours, Upon a pack of cotton prints azure, banded and semée of mascles Or, a sprig of the cotton-tree, slipped and fructed, in bend sinister surmounted of a shuttle furnished in bend proper. **Motto:** Onward. **Granted** 18 July 1882.

HUNSTANTON

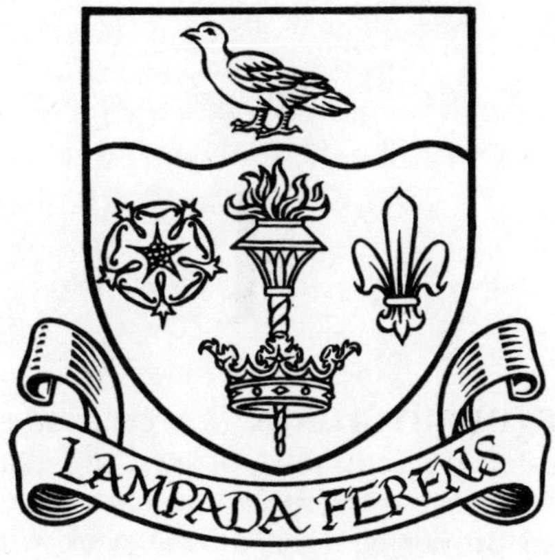

HULL UNIVERSITY

HUDDERSFIELD

HOVE

HUNTINGDON AND GODMANCHESTER

I

ILKESTON, BOROUGH OF (DERBYSHIRE).* Argent, on a saltire sable between two cotton hanks in pale and as many sinister gloves in fesse proper, the astronomical sign for Mars Or; on a chief azure a representation of a piece of Maltese lace fessewise argent. **Crest:** On a wreath of the colours, A bear's head couped proper charged on the neck with the astronomical sign of Mars sable, suspended from the mouth a safety-lamp proper. **Motto:** Labor omnia vincit. **Granted** 24 August 1887.

ILKLEY URBAN DISTRICT COUNCIL (YORKSHIRE—WEST RIDING).* Gules, a stone Celtic cross proper between two fountains; on a chief argent a lion passant guardant sable, armed and langued of the first. **Crest:** On a wreath argent and gules, A mount of rocky moorland proper, thereon issuant from a crown palisado Or a bull salient gules, the horns gold. **Motto:** Per salubritatem opes. **Granted** 4 December 1956.

IMPERIAL COLLEGE OF SCIENCE AND TECHNOLOGY. Per fesse, in chief the Royal Arms of the United Kingdom of Great Britain and Ireland, in base Or, an open book proper inscribed with the word "Scientia". **Motto:** Scientia imperii decus et tutamen. **Granted** by Royal Warrant 1909.

IMPERIAL WAR MUSEUM, TRUSTEES OF THE. Gules, a trophy composed of a spade and hammer with two swords, all in saltire, and conjoined wings in fess surmounted by an anchor, in chief a chain enarched, all Or. **Crest:** Out of an ancient crown Or, in front of an embattled gate gules, the portcullis raised sable, a lion passant guardant crowned Or. **Motto:** That the past may serve. **Badge:** Out of an ancient crown Or, in front of an embattled gate gules, the portcullis raised sable, a lion passant guardant crowned Or. **Granted** 10 February 1969.

INCORPORATED ACCOUNTANTS AND AUDITORS, SOCIETY OF. Argent, an open book, issuant from the dexter chief a sunburst proper; all within a bordure sable charged with six bezants and six plates alternately. **Crest:** On a wreath of the colours, A demi figure of a scribe proper habited sable, holding in the dexter hand a pen and in the sinister an inkhorn also proper. **Motto:** Fides atque integritas. **Granted** 24 January 1929.

THE INDEPENDENT SCHOOLS ASSOCIATION, INCORPORATED.* Argent, two torches in saltire sable, enflamed proper, surmounted by a cross couped gules, thereon a sinister gauntlet also proper. **Crest:** On a wreath of the colours, An eagle supporting with the dexter claw a quadrant proper. **Motto:** Pro liberis. **Granted** 19 December 1952.

INDUSTRIAL SUPERVISORS, INSTITUTE OF. Azure, a fess ermine between in chief an open book proper, bound Or, between two lozenges gold, and in base a pale per pale indented of the last and gules. **Crest:** On a wreath of the colours, Out of a mural crown Or a dexter hand grasping a torch enflamed, all proper. **Motto:** Meritus qui laborat. **Granted** 20 September 1962.

INNER TEMPLE, THE HONOURABLE SOCIETY OF THE.* Azure, a pegasus salient argent. **Motto:** Volat ad aethera virtus. Certified by the three Kings of Arms 10 May 1967.

ILKESTON

ILKLEY

INDEPENDENT SCHOOLS ASSOCIATION

IRLAM

INNHOLDERS OF THE CITY OF LONDON, WORSHIPFUL COMPANY OF. Azure, a chevron argent between three oatsheaves Or; on a chief argent a St. Julian's cross sable. **Crest:** On a wreath of the colours, A star Or appearing out of a cloud proper. Mantled gules, doubled argent. **Supporters:** On either side a horse reguardant argent. **Motto:** Hinc spes affulget. **Granted** 2 December 1634 by Sir Richard St. George, Clarenceux King of Arms.

INNS OF COURT. See Gray's Inn; Inner Temple; Lincoln's Inn; Middle Temple.

INSTITUTES. See under the operative term, e.g., for Institute of Accident Surgery, see Accident Surgery, Institute of.

IPSWICH, COUNTY BOROUGH OF (EAST SUFFOLK).* Per pale gules and azure, in the first a lion rampant gold, armed and langued azure, in the second three demi boats of the third. **Crest:** On a wreath argent and sable, A demi lion Or supporting a ship sable. **Supporters:** Two horses of the sea argent commonly called Neptune's horses, maned and finned gold. Arms confirmed and Crest and Supporters granted 29 August 1561.

IRLAM URBAN DISTRICT COUNCIL (LANCASHIRE).* Argent, a lion rampant gules crowned with an ancient crown Or, holding in the forepaws a flail proper; on a chief indented of three points azure a mitre also Or between two plates each charged with a boar's head couped sable armed Or. **Crest:** Out of a coronet composed of six roses gules, barbed and seeded proper, set upon a rim argent, flames proper, issuant therefrom a demi eagle Or, wings displayed gules, charged on the breast with a fountain and holding in the beak a cross crosslet fitchy erect also argent. **Motto:** Ingenio et consilio. **Granted** 12 April 1955.

IRON AND STEEL INSTITUTE. Sable, a buck's head caboshed and in chief two hawks' bells argent; on a chief rayonné Or the astronomical symbol of Mars of the first. **Crest:** On a wreath of the colours, A miner's pick and gad in saltire sable. **Motto:** Faber fabrum adjuvet. **Granted** 23 March 1908.

IRONMONGERS OF THE CITY OF LONDON, WORSHIPFUL COMPANY OF. Argent, on a chevron gules between three gads of steel azure, three swivels Or. **Crest:** On a wreath azure, gules and argent, Two lizards erect face to face proper coupled with a chain gules. Mantled gules, doubled ermine. **Supporters:** On either side a lizard erect proper. **Motto:** God is our strength; Assher dure. Arms granted 1 September 1455 by William Tyndale, Lancaster King of Arms; ratified and confirmed 28 May 1560 by William Hervey, Clarenceux King of Arms; entered at Visitation of 1568; Supporters granted 10 July 1923.

ISLE OF WIGHT COUNTY COUNCIL.* Azure, a castle triple towered argent between three anchors Or. **Crest:** On a wreath of the colours, A mural crown Or charged with three anchors azure. **Supporters:** On the dexter side a horse and on the sinister side a sea horse, both argent. **Motto:** All this beauty is of God. **Granted** 17 October 1938.

ISLINGTON, LONDON BOROUGH OF. Barry wavy argent and azure, a Maltese cross argent surmounted by an open book proper edged; and on a chief gules, in front of a water bouget sable, an arrow erect proper, barbed and flighted argent. **Badge:** A fountain charged with a crescent and an annulet interlaced Or. **Granted** 3 February 1966.

IPSWICH

INNER TEMPLE

ISLE OF WIGHT

J

JARROW, BOROUGH OF (CO. DURHAM).* Per saltire azure and barry wavy of six argent and of the first, in chief a cross flory of the second, in fess two lymphads sails furled Or, and in base an open book also of the second edged and clasped gold and inscribed with the words "Beda Historia Ecclesiastica" sable. **Crest:** Issuant from an antique crown Or a demi dragon azure, winged vert, holding between the claws a crescent gold. **Motto:** Labore et scientia. **Granted** 3 March 1930.

JESUS COLLEGE (CAMBRIDGE UNIVERSITY).* Argent, a fesse sable between three cocks' heads erased sable, crested and jelloped gules; all within a bordure of the last charged with eight ducal coronets Or. **Crest:** Out of a ducal coronet Or a cock sable, crested and jellopped gules. **Granted** 1575 by Robert Cooke, Clarenceux King of Arms.

JESUS COLLEGE (OXFORD UNIVERSITY). *Either* Vert, three stags trippant argent, attired Or; *or* Azure, three stags trippant argent. Both Arms are of no authority.

JOINERS OF THE CITY OF LONDON, WORSHIPFUL COMPANY OF. Gules, a chevron argent between in chief two pairs of compasses extended at the points and in base a sphere Or; on a chief of the second a pale azure between two roses of the field, barbed and seeded proper, the pale charged with an escallop also of the second. **Crest:** On a wreath Or and azure, A demi savage proper, wreathed about the head and waist with leaves vert, holding in the dexter hand over the shoulder a tilting spear Or, headed argent. Mantled gules, doubled argent. **Motto:** Join loyalty with liberty. **Granted** 10 April 1571. The arms were entered at the Visitation of 1568.

JARROW

JESUS COLLEGE
(CAMBRIDGE UNIVERSITY)

KENSINGTON AND CHELSEA

K

KEBLE COLLEGE (OXFORD UNIVERSITY). Argent, a chevron engrailed gules; on a chief azure three pierced mullets Or. These Arms are of no authority.

KEELE, UNIVERSITY OF. Or, on a chevron gules an open book argent, in base a scythe proper; on a chief wavy of the second a Stafford knot between a fleur-de-lys and a fret of the second. **Crest:** On a wreath of the colours, In front of a laurel vert a representation of Rodin's statue "Le Penseur" Or. **Motto:** Thanke God for all. **Granted** 20 June 1950 to The University College of North Staffordshire.

KEIGHLEY, BOROUGH OF (YORKSHIRE—WEST RIDING).* Argent, on a fess sable between three stag's heads caboshed, a fountain proper; all within a bordure embattled azure. **Crest:** On a wreath of the colours, In front of a dragon's head erased gules, entwined by a serpent Or, a fountain proper. **Motto:** By worth. **Granted** 7 February 1883.

KENILWORTH URBAN DISTRICT COUNCIL (WARWICKSHIRE).* Argent, on a mount in base a castle of three towers gules; on a chief azure two mullets Or pierced gules. **Crest:** On a wreath of the colours, An ostrich feather ermine supported by two lions queue fourchée, the dexter argent, the sinister vert, each gorged with a crown, pendent therefrom an escallop Or. **Motto:** Cives oppidi fundamenta. **Granted** 5 January 1966.

KENSINGTON AND CHELSEA, ROYAL BOROUGH OF.* Gules, a mitre Or; on a chief ermine three crowns Or. **Crest:** On a wreath of the colours, Issuant from a mount vert a broom bush flowered proper. **Supporters:** On the dexter side a boar azure and on the sinister side a winged bull argent, armed and unguled Or. **Motto:** Quam bonum in unum habitare. **Granted** 10 December 1965.

KENT AT CANTERBURY, UNIVERSITY OF.* Per chevron argent and gules, in chief three Cornish choughs proper, and in base a horse rampant argent. **Crest:** On a wreath of the colours In front of a representation of the West Gate of the City of Canterbury proper issuant from water barry wavy of four argent and azure, two crosiers in saltire Or. **Supporters:** On either side a lion passant guardant dimidiated with the hull of an ancient ship Or. **Motto:** Cui servire regnare est. **Granted** 1 June 1967.

KENT COUNTY COUNCIL.* Gules, a horse forcene argent. **Crest:** Issuant from a mural crown proper three masts rigged with courses set and topsails furled proper, flying from each mast-head a pennon argent charged with a cross gules. **Supporters:** On either side a sea lion Or gorged with a collar gules, pendent therefrom an escutcheon, the dexter of the Arms of the See of Canterbury and the sinister of the Arms of the Cinque Ports. **Motto:** Invicta. **Granted** 17 October 1933.

KESTEVEN, PARTS OF. See Lincolnshire.

KETTERING, BOROUGH OF (NORTHAMPTONSHIRE).* Sable, a pelt Or, in chief a cross crosslet fitchy of the last between two fountains each charged with a martlet of the first. **Crest:**

KEIGHLEY

KENT

UNIVERSITY OF KENT

KENILWORTH

On a wreath of the colours, Issuant from a circlet of chain, flames proper. **Supporters:** On the dexter side a griffin reguardant Or, beaked and membered and gorged with a chain reflexed over the back azure, and on the sinister side a Negro proper, habited about the waist with a cloth, and his sinister wrist encircled with a handcuff, pendent therefrom a broken chain azure. **Motto:** Progressio et concordia. **Granted** 26 September 1938.

THE KEW GUILD. Azure, on a fesse argent between two ancient crowns Or, a vine branch proper; two flaunches silver each charged with a flame of fire also proper. **Crest:** On a wreath Or and vert, A dexter hand couped at the wrist holding two sprigs, one of oak and the other of Chinchona, leaved and fructed, all proper. **Motto:** Floreat Kew. **Badge:** On a hurt ensigned by a vine-branch proper and surmounted by an ancient crown Or, a flame of fire also proper. **Granted** 10 December 1962.

KEYNSHAM URBAN DISTRICT COUNCIL (SOMERSET).* Gules, six clarions, three, two and one, Or; a chief wavy barry wavy azure and argent. **Crest:** Out of a Roman corona radiata Or a demi dragon also Or gorged with a brass wire enfiled with a cogwheel proper and holding between the claws an escutcheon argent, thereon a cross sable charged with a leopard's face gold. **Motto:** Maintien le droit. **Granted** 15 June 1962.

KIDDERMINSTER, BOROUGH OF (WORCESTERSHIRE).* Azure, two chevronels Or, each charged with five pellets, between in chief two shuttles chevronwise Or, threaded gules, and in base a bee volant Or. **Crest:** On a wreath of the colours, On a mount vert a kid passant Or holding over the dexter shoulder a long cross gules. **Supporters:** On the dexter side a ram Or, armed and unguled gules, and on the sinister side a stag Or, attired and unguled gules. **Motto:** Deo juvante arte et industria floret. **Badge:** Within a circlet of bezants conjoined a kid Or holding over the dexter shoulder a long cross gules. **Granted** 10 June 1963.

KING EDWARD VII HOSPITAL, WINDSOR.* Argent, on water barry wavy in base a swan proper; on a chief azure a Tudor rose also proper between two fleurs-de-lys Or. **Crest:** On a wreath of the colours, A griffin segreant holding between the forepaws a rod of Aesculapius Or. **Supporters:** On the dexter side a stag argent and on the sinister side a swan rousant proper, each charged with a cross couped gules. **Granted** 12 January 1945.

KING JAMES'S GRAMMAR SCHOOL (KNARESBOROUGH, YORKSHIRE). Azure, on a mount in base vert a castle of two domed towers Or, pennons flying to the sinister argent; a chief Or, thereon two [open] crowns gules. **Crest:** On a wreath of the colours, A demi lion gules, crowned and pendent from a chain about the neck a book Or, grasping in the dexter paw a sprig of oak vert, fructed Or. **Motto:** Quid retribuam Domino. **Granted** 20 December 1966.

KING'S COLLEGE (CAMBRIDGE UNIVERSITY).* Sable, three roses argent; a chief per pale azure and gules charged on the dexter side with a fleur de lis and on the sinister with a lion passant guardant, both Or. **Granted** 1 January 1449 by King Henry VI.

KING'S LYNN, BOROUGH OF (NORFOLK). Azure, three dragons' heads erased and erect Or, in the mouth of each a cross-crosslet fitchy of the last. Recorded at the Visitation of 1563.

KING'S SCHOOL (BRUTON, SOMERSET). Azure, in chief an open crown Or and in base a dolphin naiant argent. **Motto:** Deo juvante. **Granted** 2 November 1921.

KING'S SCHOOL IN MACCLESFIELD. Argent, a lion rampant guardant holding between the forepaws a fleur-de-lys azure, banded Or; on a chief gules three greyhounds' heads couped argent, collared Or. **Granted** 4 March 1968.

KING'S SCHOOL (WARWICK). Gules, a cross flory, in the first quarter a fleur-de-lys Or; on a chief of the second three martlets azure. **Crest:** On a wreath of the colours, Upon a portcullis chained Or a bear argent, muzzled gules, supporting a ragged staff also argent. **Motto:** Altiora

KINGSTON-UPON-HULL

KETTERING

KING'S COLLEGE

KIDDERMINSTER

KEYNSHAM

peto. **Granted** 7 September 1931.

KINGSTON-UPON-HULL, CITY, COUNTY OF THE CITY AND COUNTY BOROUGH OF (YORKSHIRE—EAST RIDING).* Azure, three ducal coronets in pale Or. Recorded without tinctures at the Visitations of 1612 and 1665-6. Tinctures certified by Windsor Herald 1879.

KINGSTON-UPON-THAMES, ROYAL BOROUGH OF.* Azure, three salmon naiant [in pale] argent, finned and tailed gules. **Crest:** On a wreath of the colours, Issuing from a wreath of bay banded Or a demi stag proper gorged with a [ducal coronet] crown Or, pendent therefrom an escutcheon Ermine on a chevron vert between two chevronels the upper one per pale azure and gules and the lower one per pale gules and azure a cross patée or, holding between the forelegs a fountain. **Supporters:** On either side a stag proper gorged with a riband argent, pendent therefrom an escutcheon Azure from the base an elm tree proper in front of a sun rising Or, and resting the interior hind hoof on a charred woodstock; the whole upon a grassy mound proper supported by a fillet wavy per fess wavy argent and azure. **Badge:** A roundel of the Arms encircled by a wreath of elm and bay vert tied with a riband and ensigned by a Saxon crown Or. **Granted** 3 March 1966.

KINGSTON COLLEGE OF TECHNOLOGY (KINGSTON-UPON-THAMES). Per fesse wavy Or and azure, in chief an open book proper, bound azure edged gold, the dexter page charged with a voided hexagon and the sinister with a cogwheel gules, and in base three salmon in pale naiant proper. **Crest:** On a wreath of the colours, Between two sprigs of oak fructed a torch enflamed proper enfiled through a Saxon crown Or. **Motto:** Per scientiam progrediamur. **Granted** 20 November 1963.

KINGSWOOD URBAN DISTRICT COUNCIL (GLOUCESTERSHIRE).* Per chevron vert and Or, in chief two stags' heads caboshed proper crowned with a coronet composed of four fleurs-de-lis set upon a rim of the second, and in base a boar's head erased sable; all within a bordure ermine. **Crest:** On a wreath of the colours, A demi lion gules gorged with a chain Or and holding in the paws a torch erect sable inflamed proper. **Motto:** Face the dawn. **Granted** 21 July 1945.

KIRKBY URBAN DISTRICT COUNCIL (LANCASHIRE).* Azure, a pair of scales Or between in chief two bees volant proper and in base a cross moline gold. **Crest:** Out of a coronet composed of four roses gules, barbed and seeded proper, set upon a rim Or, a mount vert, thereon a cormorant, wings elevated and addorsed, holding in the beak a slip of oak, leaved and fructed, also proper. Mantled azure, doubled argent. **Motto:** Fide et industria. **Granted** 25 November 1958.

KIRKHAM GRAMMAR SCHOOL. Per chevron engrailed Or and azure, in chief two doves, wings elevated and endorsed, of the second, beaked and legged gules, each holding in the beak an olive branch proper, and in base upon a cloud, the sunbeams issuing, an ancient imperial crown tripled also proper. **Crest:** On a wreath of the colours, Upon a book proper a windmill Or. **Badge:** A dove volant Or holding in the beak an olive branch proper. **Granted** 27 June 1929.

KIRKHAM URBAN DISTRICT COUNCIL (LANCASHIRE).* Azure, a dove volant, the dexter wing inverted, holding in the beak a branch of olive Or; on a chief of the last a rose gules, barbed and seeded proper, between two choughs also proper. **Crest:** Issuant from a circlet, thereon mullets gules, a demi lion Or supporting a pastoral staff gules headed sable. **Motto:** Firma et stabilis. **Granted** 4 September 1950.

KIVETON PARK RURAL DISTRICT COUNCIL (YORKSHIRE—WEST RIDING).* Quarterly ermine and azure, on a cross Or between in the first quarter a cock and a magpie combatant proper, in the second quarter a hart trippant, in the third quarter a garb of the third, and in the fourth quarter an oak tree eradicated also proper fructed gold, a torteau charged with a rose argent, barbed and seeded also proper. **Crest:** On a wreath of the colours, A castle of four towers Or. **Motto:** Consilio et animis. **Granted** 11 March 1949.

KING EDWARD VII HOSPITAL

KINGSTON-UPON-THAMES

KLEINWORT, BENSON LIMITED. Per chevron Or and sable, in chief two oak trees eradicated proper, fructed gold, in base a lion rampant also gold; a chief of the second bezantée. **Crest: On a** wreath of the colours, Upon a mount vert three trefoils slipped, the centre one Or the outer ones proper. **Supporters:** On either side a lion Or, gorged with a collar sable charged with a trefoil slipped gold between two bezants, in the paws a sprig of oak leaved and stalked proper, fructed also gold. **Motto:** Nil sine studio. **Granted** 30 July 1959 to Kleinwort Sons and Company Limited; Arms transferred upon change of name 15 June 1962.

KNOTTINGLEY URBAN DISTRICT COUNCIL (YORKSHIRE—WEST RIDING).* Azure, issuant from water barry wavy in base a bridge of two arches proper, in chief a Lacy knot Or between two roses argent, barbed and seeded also proper. **Crest:** On a wreath argent and azure, A cubit arm holding an ancient glass bottle proper. **Motto:** Industria ditat. **Granted** 15 December 1942.

KNUTSFORD URBAN DISTRICT COUNCIL (CHESHIRE). Azure, a saltire between in chief and in base two garbs, and in fesse as many fleurs de lys Or; on a chief barry wavy of four of the first and argent an antique crown gules. **Crest:** Out of a mural crown gules charged with four fusils conjoined Or, a demi lion also gules gorged with a wreath of may and holding in the fore-paws an open book proper, edged and bound gold. **Motto:** Respice, aspice, prospice. **Granted** 22 November 1955.

KIRKBY

KIRKHAM

KINGSWOOD

KIVETON PARK

KNOTTINGLEY

L

LADY MARGARET HALL (OXFORD UNIVERSITY). Or, on a chevron between in chief two talbots passant and in base a bell azure, a portcullis of the field. These are of no authority.

LAKES URBAN DISTRICT COUNCIL (WESTMORLAND).* Vert, five fountains in orle; on a chief dancetty Or the head of a wheelhead cross of stone proper. **Crest:** On a wreath of the colours, On a rock issuant from a wreath of laurel fructed, a Herdwick ram statant guardant proper armed Or. **Motto:** Inter montes et lacus. **Granted** 5 August 1964.

LAMBETH, LONDON BOROUGH OF.* Quarterly per fess wavy, first argent a cross gules, second and third ermine a mullet Or, and fourth chequy Or and azure, over all a pale sable thereon a crosier [= archiepiscopal cross-staff] surmounted by a mitre also Or; all within a bordure sable charged with fifteen bezants. **Crest:** On a wreath of the colours, Upon water proper a Paschal Lamb argent ducally gorged, supporting over the dexter shoulder a crozier [as before, and Or] flowing therefrom a pennon also argent charged with a cross gules. **Motto:** Spectemur agendo. Arms of the former Metropolitan Borough of Lambeth granted by Royal Licence, exemplified 8 March 1966; regranted as above 15 March 1966.

LANCASHIRE COUNTY COUNCIL.* Gules, three piles, two issuant from the chief and one in base, Or, each charged with a rose of the field barbed and seeded proper. **Crest:** On a wreath of the colours, A lion passant guardant proper charged on the body with a mascle gules and resting the dexter forepaw on an escocheon of the above said Arms. **Supporters:** On either side a lion proper gorged with a collar vair, pendent therefrom an escocheon of the following Arms, viz. Gules, three piles, two issuant from the chief and one in base, Or, each charged with a rose gules barbed and seeded proper. **Motto:** In concilio consilium. Arms and Crest granted 31 August 1903, Supporters granted 26 October 1903.

LANCASTER, CITY OF.* Per fesse azure and gules, in chief a fleur-de-lis and in base a lion passant guardant Or. **Crest:** On a wreath of the colours, A lion passant guardant azure semé-de-lis Or. **Supporters:** On either side a lion rampant guardant azure, semé-de-lis and gorged with a collar Or, pendent therefrom an escocheon argent charged with a rose gules barbed and seeded proper. **Motto:** Luck to Loyne. Arms confirmed and Crest granted 19 July 1907; Supporters granted 20 July 1907.

LANCASTER, DUCHY OF. Gules, three lions passant guardant in pale Or, a label of three points azure, on each point three fleur-de-lys Or. **Crest:** On a cheapeau gules turned up ermine a lion statant guardant crowned with a coronet composed of crosses patée and fleurs-de-lys Or, gorged with a label as in the arms [Peer's Helmet, mantled gules doubled ermine] **Motto:** Souveraigne. Exemplified May 1962 [no blazon].

LANCASTER, UNIVERSITY OF.* Or, a fesse wavy argent charged with two barrulets wavy azure between in chief two roses gules barbed and seeded and in base an open book proper bound and clasped; on a chief gules a lion passant Or. **Crest:** On a wreath of the colours, In front of two

LAKES

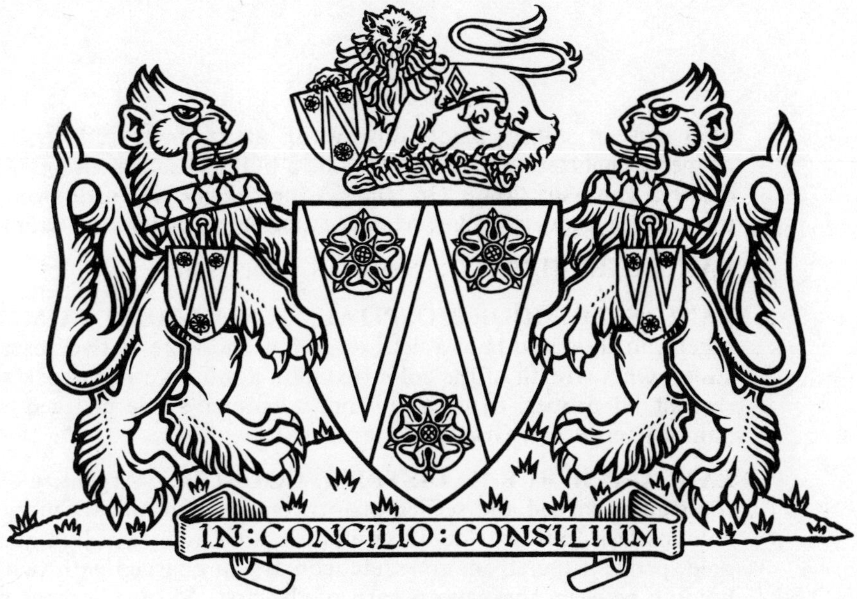

LANCASHIRE

LANCASTER

LAMBETH

quill pens in saltire, points downward, azure, feathered Or, a Herdwick ram's head caboshed proper. **Supporters:** On the dexter side a bull gules, armed, unguled, collared and pendent from the collar a Panassus flower Or; and on the sinister side a dragon gules, collared and pendent from the collar a fleur-de-lys Or. **Motto:** Patet omnibus veritas. **Granted** 20 May 1966.

LANCASTER HERALD. See Arms, Officers of.

LANCASTER MOOR HOSPITAL MANAGEMENT COMMITTEE.* Per saltire azure and argent, in chief and base a fleur-de-lys Or and in fesse two roses gules barbed and seeded proper. **Crest:** On a wreath of the colours, Upon a mount a moorcock supporting a staff entwined with a serpent all proper, flying therefrom a banner azure charged with a full moon argent. **Motto:** Sanitati perducere. **Granted** 28 April 1952.

LANCASTER RURAL DISTRICT COUNCIL. Argent, a fesse wavy azure between sixteen roses gules barbed and seeded proper, ten in chief and six in base. **Crest:** Issuant from a coronet composed of four fleur-de-lys set upon a rim Or, a demi lion guardant azure gorged with a riband gold, pendent therefrom an escutcheon argent charged with two croziers in saltire also azure, and holding between the paws a garb of the first. **Motto:** Semper procedens. **Granted** 30 November 1953.

LANCING COLLEGE.* Argent, on a bend cotised sable a cross couped between two martlets of the first; all within a bordure engrailed azure; the whole surmounted of a chief ermine thereon between two purses Or a pale of the third charged with a lily also Or. **Motto:** Beati mundo corde. **Granted** 1923.

LARNE, BOROUGH OF (CO. ANTRIM). Sable, on water barry wavy in base a four-masted ship in full sail proper; on a chief Or a castle between two shuttles palewise also proper. **Crest:** On a wreath argent and sable, An arm embowed grasping a corran [=ancient Irish sickle] proper. **Supporters:** On either side a swan charged on the breast with a flax flower proper. **Motto:** Falce marique potens. **Granted** 29 August 1952.

LAUNCESTON, ALIAS DUNHEVED, BOROUGH OF (CORNWALL).* Gules, a circular castle of three tiers Or; a bordure azure charged with eight domed towers of the second. **Crest:** Issuant from a ducal coronet Or, a lion's head gules between two ostrich feathers argent. Mantled gules, doubled argent. **Motto:** Royale et loyale. **Badge:** A Keep or castle gold, as in the Arms. **Standard:** Barry of four gules and sable, the latter bezanty, the bands gold inscribed in letters sable; the fringe Or and azure. Arms and crest granted 24 July 1572 by Robert Cooke, Clarenceux King of Arms; Badge granted 26 March 1906.

LAUNDERERS OF THE CITY OF LONDON, COMPANY OF. Per pale Or and argent, a representation of the washing machine invented by Henry Sidgier in the year 1782 between three antique flat irons fired proper. **Crest:** On a wreath argent and azure, A white domestic cat cleaning itself within a circlet of lily flowers and sunflowers alternately proper. **Supporters:** On the dexter side a figure representing the Princess Navsicaa robed purpure, draped over the dexter forearm a piece of white sarcenet, upon the head a diadem, and the interior foot resting upon a washing stone; and on the sinister side a figure representing a laundrymaid of the eighteenth century resting the exterior hand upon a dolly, all proper. **Motto:** Cleanliness is next to Godliness. **Granted** 1 August 1963.

LAW, THE COLLEGE OF. Ermine, on a cross gules a sword sheathed, point upwards, surmounted by an open book proper bound clasped and edged Or; on a chief gules, on a pale ermine between a pair of scales and a portcullis chained, a Saxon crown Or. **Crest:** On a wreath argent and gules, An owl, wings expanded, supporting with the dexter claw a posy of mignonette, stock and lavender, proper. **Motto:** Leges juraque cognoscamus. **Granted** 5 September 1967.

LANCASTER MOOR HOSPITAL

LANCING COLLEGE

LAUNCESTON

LANCASTER UNIVERSITY

LAW SOCIETY, THE INCORPORATED. Ermine, on a cross gules a sword sheathed in pale, point upwards, Or; a chief of the last, thereon a pale of the second charged with a lion passant guardant of the third, between a lion rampant also of the second upon the dexter side and upon the sinister a harp azure. **Crest:** On a wreath of the colours, The figure of Justice represented by a female figure blindfolded, habited azure, mantled gules, in the right hand a balance suspended Or, and in the left a sword erect proper. **Supporters:** On the dexter side a pegasus Or, around the neck a double chain gold and pendant therefrom an escocheon ermine charged with a rose gules; and on the sinister side a lion purpure, around the neck a double chain and pendent therefrom an escocheon Or charged with a trefoil slipped vert. **Motto:** Leges juraque servamus. Arms and Crest granted 4 June 1845; Supporters granted 5 June 1845.

LEAMINGTON SPA. See Royal Leamington Spa.

LEATHERHEAD URBAN DISTRICT COUNCIL (SURREY).* Per saltire vert and barry wavy of six argent and azure, in chief flames proper encircled by a chain of square links, in base a stag's head caboshed Or, between the attires an open book proper bound and clasped also Or. **Crest:** On a wreath of the colours, Issuant from a wreath of oak leaves fructed proper, a swan rousant argent, the sinister wing charged with a sword, point upward, gules. **Motto:** Service links all. **Granted** 6 May 1946.

LEATHERSELLERS OF THE CITY OF LONDON, WORSHIPFUL COMPANY OF. Argent, three roebucks passant reguardant gules attired and unguled sable. **Crest:** On a wreath of the colours, A demi roebuck gules attired and unguled sable. Mantled gules, doubled ermine. **Supporters:** On the dexter side a roebuck Or attired and unguled sable; and on the sinister side a ram argent armed and unguled Or. **Motto:** Soli Deo honor et gloria. Arms and crest granted 20 May 1479 by John More, Norroy King of Arms; Supporters granted (with change in arms) 7 November 1505 by Roger Machado, Clarenceux King of Arms; this new version was confirmed 11 October 1530 by Thomas Benolt, Clarenceux; the original arms and crest and the supporters were certified 3 April 1905 by Sir Alfred Scott Scott-Gatty, Garter King of Arms as confirmed 29 January 1687 by Sir Henry St. George, Clarenceux King of Arms.

LEE CONSERVANCY BOARD. Argent, on water in base barry wavy proper a galley sable, the sail of the first; on a chief wavy of the second semée-de-lis Or three swans also proper. **Crest:** On a wreath of the colours, A hart lodged gules gorged with a Saxon crown and charged on the body with two seaxes in saltire Or. **Supporters:** On either side a dolphin proper charged with a Saxon crown Or. **Motto:** Bene ambulet res nostra. **Granted** 9 May 1935.

LEE CONSERVANCY CATCHMENT BOARD.* Vert gutteé d'eau, a fountain proper. **Crest:** On a wreath of the colours, A pike naiant holding in the mouth a roach, all proper. **Supporters:** On either side a heron proper gorged with an antique crown Or. **Motto:** Je lie au Lee. **Granted** 20 April 1937.

LEEDS, CITY AND COUNTY BOROUGH OF (YORKSHIRE—WEST RIDING)*. Azure, a fleece Or; on a chief sable three mullets argent. **Crest:** On a wreath of the colours, An owl proper. **Supporters:** On either side an owl proper ducally crowned Or. **Motto:** Pro Rege et Lege. Arms recorded at the Visitation of 1666; Crest and Supporters granted 7 November 1921.

LEEDS, UNIVERSITY OF. Vert, an open book proper, edged and clasped gold, inscribed with the words "Et augebitur scientia", between in chief three mullets argent and in base a rose of the last barbed and seeded proper. **Crest:** On a wreath of the colours, A Greek sphinx gules. **Granted** 10 August 1905.

LEEDS AND HOLBECK BUILDING SOCIETY.* Azure, a fesse wavy argent surmounted of a tower Or; on a chief sable three mullets also argent. **Crest:** On a wreath of the colours, An

LEATHERHEAD

LEEDS

LEE CONSERVANCY CATCHMENT BOARD

owl between two sprigs of thrift flowered and leaved proper. **Supporters:** On either side a griffin argent gorged with a collar gules charged with three bezants, pendent from the collar a key also gules, and resting the interior hind paw on a rose also argent barbed and seeded proper. **Motto:** Servate et servite. **Granted** 25 July 1960.

LEEDS INCORPORATED CHAMBER OF COMMERCE. Azure, a fleece Or; on a chief sable a pair of cloth shears extended, points upwards, between a printing press and a cogwheel argent. **Crest:** On a wreath of the colours, An owl argent grasping with the dexter claw a sword, point upwards, of the last hilt and pommel Or. **Granted** 20 February 1951.

LEEDS PERMANENT BUILDING SOCIETY. Per chevron sable and azure, in chief two mullets and in base a triple-towered castle argent. **Crest:** On a wreath argent and azure, Upon the battlements of a tower an owl proper holding with the dexter claw a key Or. **Supporters:** On either side an owl proper gorged with a collar, pendent therefrom by a chain an escutcheon gules charged with a rose argent barbed and seeded proper. **Motto:** Safe and sound. **Granted** 12 January 1949.

LEEK AND WESTBOURNE BUILDING SOCIETY. Or masoned sable, two flaunches of the last each charged with a curlew facing to the centre proper. **Crest:** On a wreath of the colours, Three sprigs of thrift flowered and leaved proper, the stems enfiled with a Stafford knot Or. **Supporters:** On either side a lion gules holding between the forepaws a brick axe proper. **Motto:** Per frugalitatem domus. **Granted** 20 May 1954 to the Leek and Moorlands Building Society.

LEEK URBAN DISTRICT COUNCIL (STAFFORDSHIRE). Azure, a saltire patonce between in chief a Stafford knot, in fess two suns and in base a garb, all Or. **Crest:** Out of a mural crown Or charged with three mulberry leaves proper, a mount of heather, thereon a moorcock also proper resting the dexter claw on a Leek small-weave shuttle gold threaded gules. **Motto:** Arte favente nil desperandum. **Granted** 7 May 1956.

LEGAL AND GENERAL ASSURANCE SOCIETY LIMITED. Azure, a representation of Temple Bar proper, on a point in base Or a rose gules barbed and seeded also proper. **Crest:** On a wreath of the colours, A dragon rampant vert, the wings argent edged and ribbed of the first charged with a cross gules, supporting a fasces in bend proper. **Motto:** Pro salute. **Granted** 19 February 1937.

LEICESTER, BISHOPRIC OF.* Gules, a pierced cinquefoil ermine, in chief a lion passant guardant grasping in the dexter forepaw a cross crosslet fitchée Or. **Granted** 12 August 1949.

LEICESTER, CITY AND COUNTY BOROUGH OF.* Gules, a cinquefoil pierced ermine. **Crest:** On a wreath of the colours, A wyvern sans legs argent strewed with wounds gules, wings expanded ermine. **Supporters:** On either side a lion reguardant gules gorged with a ducal coronet, suspended therefrom by a chain Or a cinquefoil ermine pierced gules. **Motto:** Semper eadem. Arms and Crest recorded at the Visitation of 1619; Supporters granted 2 December 1926.

LEICESTER, UNIVERSITY OF. Gules, an open book strapped proper and buckled and inscribed with the words "Ut Vitam Habeant" in letters Or, between in chief two cinquefoils pierced ermine and in base a horse shoe also Or. **Crest:** On a wreath of the colours, A demi-gryphon segreant Or holding between the claws an open book as in the Arms. **Granted** 3 April 1922 to the Leicester, Leicestershire and Rutland College.

LEICESTER AND RUTLAND POLICE AUTHORITY. Per fess azure and vert, on a fess argent between in chief two pierced cinquefoils ermine and in base a horseshoe Or, a fox courant proper. **Granted** 20 September 1968.

LEICESTERSHIRE COUNTY COUNCIL.* Quarterly per fesse indented argent and gules, in the first quarter a torteau charged with a cinquefoil ermine, in the second quarter a lion rampant

LEEDS AND HOLBECK BUILDING SOCIETY

LEIGH

LEICESTER

LEICESTER BISHOPRIC

double queued also argent, in the third quarter an ostrich feather ermine, and in the fourth quarter a maunch sable. **Crest:** On a wreath of the colours, A fox courant over stubble proper. **Supporters:** On the dexter side a bull sable ducally gorged Or; and on the sinister side a Leicestershire ram proper. **Motto:** For'ard, for'ard. **Granted** 25 January 1930.

LEIGH, BOROUGH OF (LANCASHIRE).* Quarterly gules and argent, a cross quarterly counter-changed between a spear head of the last in the first quarter, a mullet sable in the second, a shuttle fessewise the thread pendant of the last in the third, and a sparrow-hawk close proper in the fourth. **Crest:** On a wreath of the colours, The battlements of a tower proper, issuant therefrom a bear's paw gules holding a javelin erect Or. **Motto:** Aequo pede propera. **Granted** 23 December 1899.

LEIGHTON LINSLADE URBAN DISTRICT COUNCIL (BEDFORDSHIRE). Quarterly Or and gules, a single-arched bridge throughout argent, masoned sable, the keystone charged with an ear of wheat proper, the whole between in chief two celestial crowns and in base a lily plant of three flowers counterchanged. **Crest:** On a wreath of the colours, A water-ouzel displayed proper perched upon two cog-wheels Or, each issuant from a mural crown argent. **Motto:** By truth and diligence. **Granted** 5 January 1966.

LEIGHTON PARK SCHOOL (READING). Sable, six oak leaves, three two and one, Or. **Granted** 1926.

LEOMINSTER, BOROUGH OF (HEREFORDSHIRE). Vert, a lion rampant Or grasping in the sinister paw a lamb argent. **Crest:** On a wreath of the colours, Within a wreath of hop leaves a Herefordshire bull statant guardant proper. **Supporters:** On the dexter side a representation of St. Peter proper holding in the exterior hand two keys, wards downwards and outwards, Or; and on the sinister side a pilgrim supporting his staff with his exterior hand also proper, on his hat an escallop gold. **Motto:** Where Justice rules, there Virtue flows. **Granted** 30 June 1955.

LETCHWORTH URBAN DISTRICT COUNCIL (HERTFORDSHIRE).* Argent, three chevronels gules, over all on a chief embattled azure two roses of the first barbed and seeded proper. **Crest:** On a wreath of the colours, An owl affrontée argent between two sprigs of oak vert fructed Or. **Motto:** Prudens futuri. **Granted** 11 December 1944.

LEWES, BOROUGH OF (EAST SUSSEX).* Checky Or and azure, a sinister quarter gules semée of cross-crosslets argent, thereon a lion rampant Or. Recorded without tinctures at the Visitation of 1634; Certified as above by Kings' of Arms Certificate 10 June 1963; N.B. Certified with the lion also argent by Alfred Scott Scott-Gatty, York Herald, 19 Nov. 1894.

LEWISHAM, LONDON BOROUGH OF.* Tierced in pairle reversed purpure, vert and sable, on a pall reversed argent five bars wavy azure, between in chief two lions' faces each crowned with a Saxon crown and in base a lymphad, sail set, pennon and flags flying, Or. **Crest:** On a wreath Or and purpure, Between two dolphins haurient and addorsed vert a mullet Or, all between two wings displayed argent. **Supporters:** On the dexter side a horse argent, crined and unguled Or; and on the sinister side a stag argent, attired and unguled Or; each gorged with a mural crown gules. **Motto:** Salus populi suprema lex. **Badge:** Within an annulet a Saxon crown Or. **Granted** 7 March 1966.

LEYLAND URBAN DISTRICT COUNCIL (LANCASHIRE).* Argent on a saltire azure between in pale a water-bouget and a rose gules barbed and seeded proper, and in fesse two leopards' faces sable, a martlet Or. **Crest:** Issuant from a rim Or gouttée vert, between two branches of the cotton plant leaved slipped and flowered proper a dexter hand grasping a motor-wheel also proper winged Or. **Motto:** Semper proficimus. **Granted** 10 November 1950.

LEICESTERSHIRE

LETCHWORTH

LEWES

LICHFIELD

THE LEYS SCHOOL. Or, a cross gules, charged in the centre with a mullet of the field; on a chief ermine an open book argent embellished of the first between two roses of the second barbed and seeded proper. **Crest:** On a wreath of the colours, A wyvern proper resting the dexter claw on an antique lamp Or flaming gules. **Motto:** In fide fiducia. **Granted** 31 March 1914 to the Governing Body of the Leys School.

LICENSED VICTUALLERS' SCHOOL (SLOUGH, BUCKINGHAMSHIRE). Vert semée of ears of barley, a swan, wings elevated, ducally gorged, a bordure invected Or. **Crest:** Out of a coronet composed of hop fruit proper set upon a circlet Or, a cedar tree gold. **Granted** 20 October 1954, to the Society of Licensed Victuallers for the use of the school.

LICHFIELD, BISHOPRIC OF.* Per pale gules and argent, a cross potent quadrate in the centre per pale of the last and Or between four crosses patée, those to the dexter of the second and those to the sinister gold. Recorded in the College of Arms.

LICHFIELD, CITY OF (STAFFORDSHIRE).* Chequey of nine, Or a chevron gules, and ermine. **Supporters:** On the dexter side a representation of St. Chad vested in alb and amice proper, the orphreys vert embroidered Or, a dalmatic of the first embroidered of the second, and a chasuble of the second trimmed of the first embroidered of the second, gloves argent and shoes purpure, in the bend of his exterior arm a pastoral staff of the second and in his exterior hand a representation of Lichfield Cathedral proper; and on the sinister side a representation of a Guild Master of Lichfield in fifteenth century dress proper, carrying in his exterior hand a bunch of roses gules leaved and stalked proper. **Motto:** Salve magna parens. **Granted** 28 March 1950.

LICHFIELD RURAL DISTRICT COUNCIL (STAFFORDSHIRE). Vert, an eagle displayed, wings inverted, perched on a Stafford knot Or and charged on the breast with three arrows, barbs downwards, two in saltire and one in pale, proper banded gules; on a chief Or a pale ermine between two chevrons gules. **Crest:** Out of a coronet composed of four ears of wheat and as many acorns set alternately upon a rim Or. a demi stag sable charged on the shoulder with a sun in splendour gold. Mantled vert, doubled Or. **Motto:** Ora et labora. **Granted** 20 January 1964.

LINCOLN, BISHOPRIC OF. Gules, two lions passant guardant in pale Or; on a chief azure the Virgin ducally crowned sitting on a throne issuant from the chief, in her dexter arm the Infant Jesus and in her sinister hand a sceptre, all gold. Recorded in the College of Arms.

LINCOLN, CITY AND COUNTY BOROUGH OF.* Argent, on a cross gules a fleur-de-lis Or. **Motto:** Civitas Lincolnia; *or* Floreat Lindum.

LINCOLN COLLEGE (OXFORD UNIVERSITY).* Tierced in pale, the centre argent thereon an escutcheon of the Arms of the See of Lincoln ensigned with a mitre all proper, the dexter side barry of six argent and azure in chief three lozenges gules, the sinister side vert three stags trippant two and one argent attired Or. Recorded at the Visitation of 1574.

LINCOLN'S INN, THE HONOURABLE SOCIETY OF.* Azure semy of millrinds and on a canton Or a lion rampant purpure. Certified 10 May 1967.

LINCOLNSHIRE:—

PARTS OF HOLLAND COUNTY COUNCIL.* Or, three pink parrot tulips slipped proper; on a chief per pale sable and azure a ducal coronet and a mitre gold. **Crest:** Issuant from a coronet of six acorns slipped and leaved vert set upon a rim Or, a fleur-de-lys burgeonée azure. Mantled sable, doubled Or. **Supporters:** On either side a heron argent ducally gorged azure. **Motto:** Labore ipse merces. **Granted** 9 December 1954.

PARTS OF KESTEVEN COUNTY COUNCIL.* Vert, on a pale ermine an oak tree eradicated proper. **Crest:** On a wreath argent and vert, A heron, in the beak a pike proper. **Supporters:** On the dexter side a Roman legionary; and on the sinister side a Lincolnshire poacher of the early

LEWISHAM

LEYLAND

LICHFIELD BISHOPRIC

LINCOLN

LINCOLN COLLEGE

nineteenth century, both proper. **Motto:** Perseverantia vincit.

PARTS OF LINDSEY COUNTY COUNCIL.* Barry wavy of six argent and azure, a Viking ship Or, the sail set of the first; on a chief wavy of the second a bull's head caboshed proper between two garbs gold. **Crest:** On a wreath of the colours, Issuant from a wreath of laurel leaves, two arms embowed, the hand grasping a chain, all proper. **Motto:** Service links all. **Granted** 2 October 1935.

LINGUISTS, INSTITUTE OF. Ermine, a cross patonce Or fimbriated azure charged over all with a hurt, thereon a wolf's head erased argent; on a chief indented also azure a lion passant gold vulned in the dexter forepaw proper and langued azure. **Crest:** On a wreath argent, Or and azure, An inkhorn argent, garnished Or, perched thereon and raising the lid thereof with the dexter claw a dove, in the beak a sprig of laurel slipped proper. **Motto:** Universal understanding. **Granted** 1 March 1960.

LINNAEAN SOCIETY. Per fesse, the chief per pale gules and vert, the base sable, on a fesse argent a hurt charged with an egg erect proper. **Crest:** On a wreath of the colours, Behind a mount in which vegetates the linnaea-boreakis, the sun rising in splendour, all proper. **Supporters:** On the dexter side a lion Or gorged with a linnaea-borealis proper, therefrom a shield pendent per pale wavy argent and ermine charged with a rose slipped gules and a thistle fesseways proper; and on the sinister side an eagle rising proper, gorged as the dexter therefrom a shield pendent argent charged with a trefoil slipped vert. **Motto:** Naturae discere mores. **Granted** 1802.

LISBURN, BOROUGH OF (CO. ANTRIM). Azure, on a cross flory fitchy quadrate Or a mitte azure between in dexter chief a weaver's shuttle argent threaded Or, and in the sinister base an ostrich's head erased argent, in the beak a horseshoe Or. **Crest:** On a wreath of the colours, A mural crown gules, between two sprigs of flax flowered proper, perched on the battlements a gamecock sable, combed and wattled gules. **Supporters:** On either side a phoenix sable, beaked Or, enflamed proper, and murally crowned gules. **Motto:** Ex igne resurgam. **Granted** 15 November 1966.

LISKEARD RURAL DISTRICT COUNCIL (CORNWALL).* Or, two Cornish choughs respectant proper perched on the exterior lobes of a fleur-de-lys vert; on a chief sable, between two garbs, a lymphad gold, sail argent, flying flags and pennon of St. George. **Motto:** Dictis facta suppetant. **Granted** 1 November 1954.

LITTLEHAMPTON URBAN DISTRICT COUNCIL (WEST SUSSEX).* Per chevron engrailed azure and argent, in chief a martlet volant between two cross-crosslets fitchée of the second, and in base on water barry wavy proper a lymphad sable. **Motto:** Progress. **Granted** 29 July 1935.

LIVERPOOL, BISHOPRIC OF. Argent, an eagle rising sable, beaked and legged and a glory round the head Or, holding in the dexter claw an inkhorn proper; a chief per pale azure and gules charged on the dexter side with an open book Or inscribed in letters sable "Thy Word is Truth" and on the sinister side an ancient ship with three masts, sails furled, also Or. **Granted** 17 July 1882.

LIVERPOOL, CITY AND COUNTY BOROUGH OF (LANCASHIRE).* Argent, a cormorant, in the beak a branch of seaweed called laver, all proper. **Crest:** On a wreath of the colours, A cormorant, the wings elevated, in the beak a branch of laver, proper. **Supporters:** The dexter Neptune with his sea-green mantle flowing, the waist wreathed with laver, on his head an Eastern crown gold, in the right hand his trident sable, the left supporting a banner of the Arms of Liverpool; on the sinister a Triton wreathed as the dexter and blowing his shell, the right hand supporting a banner, thereon a ship under sail in perspective, all proper, the banner staves Or. **Motto:** Deus nobis haec otia fecit. Arms and Crest granted 22 March 1797; Supporters granted 23 March 1797.

LIVERPOOL, UNIVERSITY OF.* Azure, an open book argent inscribed "Fiat lux" in letters sable, bound and on the sinister side seven clasps Or, between three cormorants, otherwise called

PARTS OF HOLLAND

PARTS OF LINDSEY

LINCOLN'S INN

LISKEARD

PARTS OF KESTEVEN

livers, wings elevated, of the second, each holding in the beak a branch of seaweed, called laver, proper. **Motto:** Haec otia studia fovent. **Granted** 30 October 1903.

LIVERPOOL CATHEDRAL, DEAN AND CHAPTER OF. Argent, a cross patriarchal throughout gules. **Granted** 1 October 1931.

LIVERPOOL COLLEGIATE SCHOOL. Or, a cormorant, wings elevated and addorsed, sable, in the beak a rose gules barbed seeded slipped and leaved proper; on a chief azure an open book argent, edged and bound gold, between two roses silver. **Motto:** Ut olim ingenii necnon virtutis cultores. **Granted** 20 December 1962.

LLANDAFF, BISHOPRIC OF.* Sable, two pastoral staves endorsed in saltire, the dexter Or, the sinister argent; on a chief azure three mitres of the second. Recorded in the College of Arms.

LLANDUDNO URBAN DISTRICT COUNCIL (CAERNARVONSHIRE). Barry wavy of eight azure and argent, on a mount in base a representation of the Church of St. Tudno at Llandudno proper; on a chief per pale Or and gules two lions passant guardant counterchanged. **Crest:** On a wreath of the colours, Upon a mount vert charged with two pierced mullets argent, a dragon passant gules resting the dexter fore-claw on an escutcheon per bend sinister ermine and ermines a lion rampant Or. **Motto:** Hardd hafan hedd. **Granted** 14 July 1959.

LLANELLY, BOROUGH OF (CARMARTHENSHIRE).* Per chevron argent and gules, in chief two lymphads sable and in base a figure representing St. Elli of the first. **Crest:** Issuant from a mural crown proper, two dragons' wings gules each charged with a fess chequy Or and azure. **Motto:** Ymlaen Llanelli. **Badge:** In front of two miners' pick-axes in saltire and within a Stepney motor wheel, a wooden box containing a sheet of tin plate, all proper. Arms and Crest granted 21 October 1913; Badge granted 22 October 1913.

LLANELLY RURAL DISTRICT COUNCIL (CARMARTHENSHIRE).* Barry wavy of eight argent and azure, on a pile sable a cresset issuant Or, fired proper; ensigned with a coronet composed of four wheat-ears and as many acorns leaved, set alternately upon a rim gold. **Crest:** On a wreath Or and gules, Within a circlet of six daffodil flowers conjoined, a mount proper, thereon a dragon statant gules collared dancetty Or, flames issuant from the mouth proper. **Motto:** Diwidiant â harddwch. **Granted** 20 February 1962.

LLANTRISSANT AND LLANTWITFARDRE RURAL DISTRICT COUNCIL (GLAMORGANSHIRE).* Azure, two barrulets wavy argent between in chief three celestial crowns and in base as many mullets of six points Or. **Crest:** On a wreath of the colours, Out of the battlements of a tower argent a demi dragon gules supporting a staff proper, flying therefrom a banner tierced in fesse sable, silver and vert charged with a pair of scales Or. **Motto:** Llafur orfu bobpeth. **Granted** 2 December 1957.

LLOYDS, CORPORATION OF.* Per fesse argent and azure, in chief a cross with in the dexter canton a sword erect gules, and in base a fouled anchor in bend sinister Or. **Crest:** On a wreath of the colours, Upon waves of the sea a representation of H.M.S. La Lutine thirty-two gun frigate in full sail, all proper. **Supporters:** On either side a sea lion proper, the head and mane Or, supporting a trident erect also proper. **Motto:** Fidentia. **Granted** 10 December 1926.

LLOYDS BANK LIMITED. Azure, five bezants in chevron between two chevronels and three cocks argent, wattled, crested and armed Or. **Crest:** On a wreath of the colours, A griffin Or and a unicorn gules, armed unguled, crined and tufted argent, respectant and supporting between them a sword erect also gules, the blade enfiled by a mural crown gold. **Supporters:** On the dexter side a horse reguardant sable, knotted above the girths with a riband, the end flowing to the dexter argent; and on the sinister a goat reguardant argent, armed, unguled and gorged with an Eastern crown Or. **Motto:** Esto vigilans. **Badge:** A bezant charged with a horse forcene to the

LITTLEHAMPTON

LIVERPOOL CITY

LLANELLY BOROUGH

LIVERPOOL UNIVERSITY

LLANDAFF BISHOPRIC

sinister reguardant sable, knotted above the girths with a riband, the ends flowing to the dexter argent. **Granted** 17 February 1956.

LLOYD'S REGISTER OF SHIPPING.* Argent, a cross gules surmounted of an open book proper, edged Or bound also gules, thereon a lymphad, sail set, pennon and flags flying, of the last, the book ensigned with a mercantile crown azure. **Crest:** On a wreath of the colours, A woman proper, habited argent, crined and murally crowned Or, the dexter arm supporting a caduceus gold, the sinister hand resting on an anchor azure cabled sable. **Supporters:** On the dexter side a dolphin guardant Or charged with a cross paty sable, and on the sinister side a lion guardant gold charged with a sun in splendour gules. **Motto:** Sine praejudicio. **Badge:** On a cartouche gules environed of a torse of rope argent and Or a lymphad, sail set, pennon and flags flying, also argent, the whole ensigned with a mercantile crown azure. **Granted** 10 December 1957.

LOMBARD BANKING LIMITED. Or, six keys, three, two and one, wards upwards, gules; on a chief azure a Crown of Lombardy gold. **Crest:** On a wreath Or and azure, An eagle displayed sable, beaked and membered Or, each claw resting upon a bezant. **Supporters:** On either side a knight in full armour of the XVIth century sable, purfled, studded and spurred Or, holding in the exterior hand a sword erect gold. **Motto:** Nulli secundus (Originally Labor omnia vincit). Arms and Crest granted 21 February 1950; Supporters granted 10 October 1954.

LOMBARD MARCROFT LIMITED. Or, a dragon rampant gules charged on the underside of the wing with three bezants; on a chief ermine a representation of the Crown of Lombardy gold between two keys, wards upwards, azure. **Crest:** On a wreath of the colours, An eagle displayed sable, each claw resting upon a wheel Or. **Motto:** Semper fidelis. **Granted** 10 November 1954.

LONDON, BISHOPRIC OF.* Gules, two swords in saltire proper, hilts and pommels Or. Recorded in the College of Arms.

LONDON, CITY OF.* Argent, a cross gules, in the first quarter a sword in pale, point upwards, of the last. **Crest:** On a wreath of the colours. A dragon's sinister wing argent charged on the underside with a cross throughout gules. **Supporters:** On either side a dragon argent charged on the undersides of the wings with a cross throughout gules. **Motto:** Domine dirige nos. Arms "anciently recorded"; Crest (on a Peer's helmet) and Supporters confirmed and granted 30 April 1957.

LONDON, UNIVERSITY OF.* Argent, on a cross gules the Union rose irradiated and ensigned with the Imperial Crown proper; a chief azure thereon an open book also proper, the clasps gold. Granted by Royal Warrant exemplified 10 April 1838.

LONDON AND EDINBURGH GENERAL INSURANCE COMPANY LIMITED. Argent, a chevron, arched below embattled above, sable masoned Or, between in chief two swords, points upwards, gules and in base a tower with a conical roof sable, the port gules. **Crest:** On a wreath of the colours, A demi pegasus argent supporting an anchor sable. **Granted** 1 August 1969.

LONDON AND EDINBURGH LIFE ASSURANCE COMPANY LIMITED. Argent, issuant from waves in base the Tower Bridge, in chief two swords in saltire proper between two towers with conical roofs sable. **Crest:** On a wreath of the colours, A pegasus statant, in the mouth three stalks of wheat proper. **Granted** 1 August 1969.

LONDON AND LANCASHIRE INSURANCE COMPANY LIMITED. Gules, a pile between two piles reversed Or, the one in chief charged with a rose of the field barbed and seeded proper and the two in base with a sword erect also of the field. **Crest:** On a wreath of the colours, In front of and entwined with two swords in saltire a rose gules, barbed, seeded, stalked and leaved, proper. **Supporters:** On the dexter side a lion Or collared vair and on the sinister side a dragon argent

LLANELLY

LLOYD'S REGISTER OF SHIPPING

LLANTRISSANT

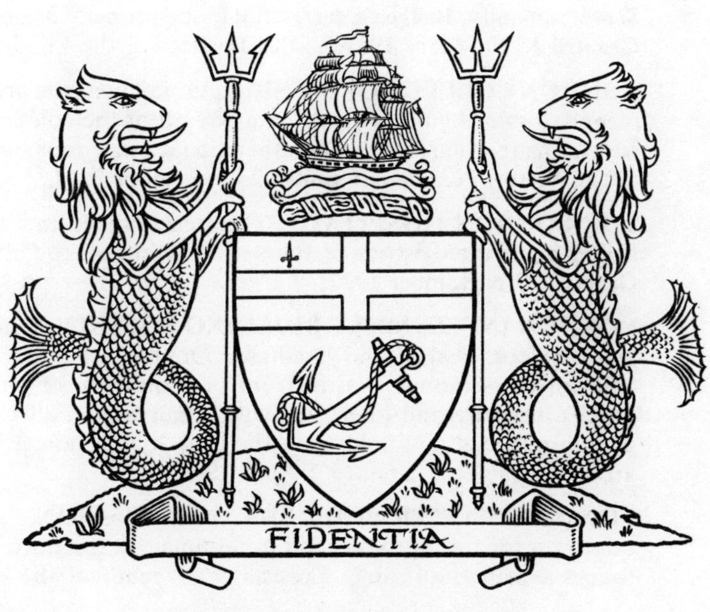

LLOYDS CORPORATION

charged on the wings with a cross gules; both langued of the last armed azure, and resting the interior hind leg on a rose also gules barbed and seeded proper. **Motto:** Security and Service. **Granted** 24 August 1949.

LONDON AND MANCHESTER ASSURANCE COMPANY LIMITED. Gules, on a cross argent a sword erect of the field; on a chief of the second upon waves of the sea a three-masted ship in full sail proper. **Crest:** On a wreath of the colours, A dragon's head argent gorged with a chain gules, pendent therefrom a bezant charged with a rose of the second barbed and seeded proper. **Supporters:** On either side a lion guardant Or crowned with a crown vallary and gorged with a collar gules. **Motto:** Be assured. **Granted** 26 March 1953.

LONDON ASSURANCE.* Argent, a cross cotised, in the first and fourth quarters a dagger erect gules; on a chief azure three anchors of the field. **Crest:** On a wreath of the colours, A female figure habited argent seated upon a terrestrial globe proper, resting the dexter hand upon a harp Or and supporting with the sinister hand a spear, point upwards, also proper, pendent therefrom by a riband gules an escutcheon of the Arms. **Supporters:** On the dexter side a figure representing Apollo and on the sinister side a figure representing Neptune, both proper. **Motto:** Mercatorum salus. **Granted** 30 September 1937.

LONDON CHAMBER OF COMMERCE. Argent, issuant from a mount in base vert a representation of the Great Beam of the City of London proper; on a chief per pale gules and azure a lymphad, sail set, Or and a caduceus of the field. **Supporters:** On either side a sea gull reguardant, the interior wing expanded and the exterior wing inverted, proper. **Motto:** Enterprise with prudence. **Granted** 11 January 1934.

THE LONDON CLINIC LIMITED. Argent, on a cross gules a rod of Aesculapius Or. **Crest:** On a wreath of the colours, In front of a demi-sun Or, a spray of three roses gules, barbed and seeded, slipped and leaved proper. **Supporters:** On the dexter side a dragon and on the sinister side a griffin Or, the dexter gorged with a collar gules, pendent therefrom by a ring of the last a rose also gules barbed and seeded proper, the sinister gorged with a coronet, pendent therefrom by a ring of the same a terrestrial globe also proper, surmounted over all of a rod of Aesculapius also gold. **Motto:** Serve humanity. **Badge:** A terrestrial globe proper, surmounted over all of a rod of Aesculapius Or. **Granted** 15 February 1961, to the Trustees of the London Clinic, Limited.

LONDON COLLEGE OF MUSIC. Azure, on a pale argent between two harps Or, stringed of the second, a sword gules. **Crest:** On a wreath of the colours, Five trumpets in pile Or enfiled with a riband azure. **Supporters:** On either side a swan rousant proper charged on the wing wth a harp azure. **Motto:** Persevere. **Granted** 23 December 1944.

THE LONDON HOSPITAL.* Quarterly argent and gules, a cross couped counterchanged; on a chief azure three ostrich feathers of the first quilled Or. **Motto:** Humani nihil a me alienum puto. **Granted** 25 November 1927.

LONDON INVESTMENT BUILDING SOCIETY. Barry wavy argent and azure, a male griffin gules, armed, beaked and irradiated Or; a chief gules masoned Or. **Crest:** On a wreath of the colours, On a mount vert, in front of a thorn bush proper a hammer erect and two shepherd's crooks in saltire and interlaced with a horseshoe, all Or. **Supporters:** On either side a hawk reguardant, belled and holding in the beak by the bow a key, the wards outward, Or. **Motto:** Integritas et vigilantia. **Granted** 5 April 1966.

LONDON MASTER BUILDERS' ASSOCIATION. Argent, a cross gules between in the first quarter a square, in the second a plummet, in the third a pair of compasses extended, and in the fourth a mallet, all sable. **Crest:** On a wreath of the colours, A quadrangular castle with four

LONDON BISHOPRIC

CITY OF LONDON

LONDON HOSPITAL

LONDON UNIVERSITY

LONDON ASSURANCE

towers proper. **Motto:** Fortiter et recte. **Granted** 6 March 1924.

LONDON RETAIL MEAT TRADERS' ASSOCIATION INCORPORATED.* Azure, two bull's heads and in base a ram's head all erased argent; on a chief of the last a boar's head erased gules. **Crest:** On a wreath Or and azure, In front of two sprigs of butcher's broom in saltire a bull's head caboshed. **Motto:** Qui unum tangit omnes tangit. **Granted** 1 February 1949.

LONDON SCHOOL OF ECONOMICS AND POLITICAL SCIENCE COLLEGE.* Sable, a beaver proper; on a chief Or two closed books purpure clasped of the third. **Granted** 12 September 1922.

LONDON UNDERWRITERS, INSTITUTE OF. Argent, a cross gules between in the first and fourth quarters a galley sable on water barry wavy proper and in the second and third quarters a lighthouse upon a rock all also proper. **Crest:** On a wreath of the colours, A sea lion proper supporting with the fins a fouled anchor sable. **Motto:** Aequitas actionum regula. **Granted** 12 April 1943.

LONDONDERRY, CITY AND COUNTY BOROUGH OF.* Sable, a human skeleton Or seated upon a mossy stone proper and in dexter chief a castle triple towered argent; on a chief of the last a cross and in the first quarter a sword erect gules (the Arms of the City of London). **Motto:** Vita Veritas Victoria. Confirmed by Daniel Molyneux, Ulster King of Arms, 1 June 1623; Certified by Garter and Norroy and Ulster Kings of Arms 28 April 1953.

LONDONDERRY, PORT AND HARBOUR COMMISSIONERS OF. Or, on a cross gules a tower proper; on a chief argent the representation of the entrance to the harbour and a ship with three masts sailing in, all also proper. **Crest:** On a wreath of the colours, A lighthouse standing on a rock proper. **Supporters:** Two dragons with wings expanded proper, each charged on the shoulder with a tower also proper. **Motto:** In Portu quies. **Granted** by Sir Bernard Burke, Ulster King of Arms, 9 February 1858.

LONDONDERRY COUNTY COUNCIL.* Per chevron gules and Or, in chief a flax flower proper between two garbs of the second, in base a dexter hand appaumée couped at the wrist of the first; the shield ensigned with a mural crown gold. **Supporters:** On either side a sea dragon argent, each charged on the wing with a cross gules and wreathed about the neck with a garland of oak stalked and leaved and fructed proper. **Motto:** Auxilium a Domino. **Granted** 1 February 1951.

LONDONDERRY HIGH SCHOOL. Argent, on a cross sable cotised gules a castle triple-towered of the first; on a chief azure an owl affrontee also argent between two open books of the same edged and bound Or. **Motto:** ΩΣ ΑΕΙ ΕΝΩΠΙΟΝ ΤΟΥ ΘΕΟΥ **Granted** 20 November 1957.

LONG EATON URBAN DISTRICT COUNCIL (DERBYSHIRE).* Barry wavy of six azure and argent, on a chevron Or two bars gemell sable, in base a Tudor rose barbed and seeded proper; a chief gold, thereon a representation of a piece of lace fessewise also sable. **Crest:** On a wreath of the colours, Issuant from the battlements of a tower azure charged with three fire-bombs in fesse proper, a demi lion Or holding a torch sable enfiled by a celestial crown gold and enflamed also proper. **Motto:** Progress by endeavour. **Granted** 8 April 1954.

LONGRIDGE URBAN DISTRICT COUNCIL (LANCASHIRE). Per chevron Or and vert, on a chevron sable between in chief two roses gules barbed and seeded proper and in base an eagle's leg erased of the first, three bars argent. **Crest:** On a wreath Or and purpure, Upon a rock proper a bull passant argent resting the dexter forehoof upon a shuttle erect Or. **Motto:** Sow for posterity. **Granted** 12 April 1954.

LORINERS OF THE CITY OF LONDON, WORSHIPFUL COMPANY OF. Azure, on a chevron argent between three manage bits Or as many bosses sable. These arms are of no authority.

LONDONDERRY C. C.

LONDON SCHOOL OF ECONOMICS

LONDONDERRY CITY

ONDON RETAIL MEAT TRADERS

LONG EATON

LOUGHBOROUGH, BOROUGH OF (LEICESTERSHIRE).* Or, on a bend sable between a maunch in chief and a bull's head erased in base of the last, a fret between two escallops of the first. **Crest:** Upon a wreath of the colours, A lion rampant Or holding in the dexter fore-paw a maunch and resting the dexter hind paw on a fret sable. **Motto:** In veritate victoria. **Granted** 10 April 1889.

LOUGHBOROUGH TECHNICAL COLLEGE. Sable, a cross engrailed argent surmounted of a like cross gules, in the first quarter a representation of Offa's cross, in the second a peacock in his pride, in the third an open book, and in the fourth a hammer, all Or. **Crest:** On a wreath of the colours, A sinister hand holding an open book proper, edged Or, the wrist entwined by a serpent also proper. **Motto:** Veritate, Scientia, Labore. **Granted** 9 November 1920.

LOUGHBOROUGH UNIVERSITY OF TECHNOLOGY. Sable, on a cross engrailed purpure fimbriated argent between in the first quarter a cross composed of the upper and lower limbs of a cross crosslet and the horizontal limbs of a cross formy, and in the fourth quarter a thunderbolt, an ancient lamp, all Or. **Crest:** On a wreath of the colours, A peacock proper supporting with the dexter claw a key purpure, the wards upward and irradiated Or. **Motto:** Veritate scientia habere. **Granted** 5 October 1966.

LOUTH, BOROUGH OF (LINCOLNSHIRE—PARTS OF LINDSEY).* Sable, a wolf rampant Or; on a chief of the last a plough turned towards the sinister azure between two garbs gules. **Motto:** Deo adjuvante non timendum. **Granted** 8 June 1954.

LOUTH RURAL DISTRICT COUNCIL (LINCOLNSHIRE—PARTS OF LINDSEY). Per fesse argent and barry wavy of the first and vert, on a fesse of the last between in chief two fleeces proper banded and ringed Or and in base a Lincoln Red Shorthorn bull's head caboshed and ringed also proper, three garbs gold. **Crest:** On a wreath of the colours, A demi greyhound sable charged on the shoulder with a Heneage knot argent, and supporting either paw a Danish double-headed axe, the head downwards, proper. **Motto:** Let us grow in service. **Granted** 5 December 1958.

LOWESTOFT, BOROUGH OF (EAST SUFFOLK).* Argent, on a chevron sable between in chief an antique crown between two roses gules, each rose charged with another rose argent all barbed and seeded proper, and in base a sun issuant Or, three Lowestoft china plates all proper. **Crest:** On a wreath of the colours, A demi figure representing St. Margaret holding in the hand a pearl, all proper. **Motto:** Point du jour. **Granted:** 14 February 1913.

LUDLOW, RURAL BOROUGH OF (SHROPSHIRE).* Azure, a lion couchant guardant between three roses argent. **Crest:** On a wreath of the colours, A porcupine quarterly Or and azure. Recorded at the Visitations of 1569, 1623 and 1663.

LURGAN, BOROUGH OF (CO. ARMAGH). Per pale Or and argent, eight martlets, three, two, three sable; a bordue charged with five escallops of the first and as many mullets of the second alternately. **Crest:** On a wreath of the colours, A greyhound statant Or semée of flax flowers stalked and leaved proper, and collared gules. **Supporters:** On either side a unicorn argent charged on the shoulder with a stalk of flax flowered and leaved proper. **Motto:** Be just and fear not. **Granted** 7 December 1951.

LUTON, COUNTY BOROUGH OF (BEDFORDSHIRE).* Quarterly gules and azure, on a cross argent between a garb in the first quarter, a beehive in the second, a rose slipped and leaved in the third, and a thistle also slipped and leaved in the fourth, all proper, a bee volant of the last. **Crest:** On a wreath of the colours, Upon a mount vert, a cubit arm in bend, vested azure cuff argent, the hand proper holding seven ears of wheat Or. **Motto:** Scientiae et labori detur. **Granted** 25 July 1876.

LUTON AND DUNSTABLE HOSPITAL.* Argent, on a cross gules between in the first and fourth quarters a fleur de lys azure and in the second and third quarters a hurt thereon two keys barwise in pale, wards to the dexter and downwards, surmounted on a sword erect, all of the first, a rod of Aesculapius erect proper. **Motto:** Deo operae scientiaeque fisi. **Granted** 16 June 1944.

LOUGHBOROUGH

LOWESTOFT

LUTON CO. BOROUGH

LOUTH BOROUGH

LUDLOW

LUTON RURAL DISTRICT COUNCIL (BEDFORDSHIRE).* Per chevron argent and vert, a pale counterchanged between three sickles proper on the argent. **Crest:** On a wreath argent, vert and Or, A bull's head Or, in the mouth an endless chain of nineteen links argent. Mantled vert, doubled argent and Or. **Granted** 20 September 1959.

LUTTERWORTH RURAL DISTRICT COUNCIL (LEICESTERSHIRE).* Or, on a chevron sable between in chief two bulls' heads caboshed gules and in base a torteau charged with a pierced cinquefoil ermine, an open book proper edged bound and clasped gold, between two lozenges of the first voided also gules. **Crest:** On a wreath of the colours, A demi Leicester ram proper supporting a torch sable enflamed also proper and winged Or. **Motto:** Lutter a ma puissance. **Granted** 12 April 1955.

LYDD, BOROUGH OF (KENT). . . . on water in base . . . to the dexter a representation of a church with tower and spire, thereon a forked pennon flying to the dexter near the centre of the field argent, and to the sinister side an ancient ship with one mast and sail furled passing behind the church, on the stern a man blowing a horn, all Or; on a canton also argent a cross between four lions rampant (?guardant) gules. Recorded (partially tricked) at the Visitation of 1574 and again (almost fully tricked) at that of 1619.

LYDNEY PARISH COUNCIL (GLOUCESTERSHIRE). Sable, a fess ermine: in chief two crosses formy Or; over all a representation of the Market Cross at Lydney issuant from the base proper. **Crest:** On a wreath argent and azure, Issuant from the hulk of an ancient ship and in front of a cresset sable, fired proper, between two stalks of wheat, each with three ears Or, a demi cog-wheel proper. **Motto:** Labores prosint ceteris. **Granted** 25 June 1969.

LYDNEY RURAL DISTRICT COUNCIL (GLOUCESTERSHIRE). Argent, on a pile wavy throughout vert a stag's head caboshed, between the attires a port between two towers Or; on a chief sable three crosses formy gold. **Crest:** Out of a coronet composed of four ears of wheat and as many acorns leaved alternately set upon a rim Or, a demi bull guardant gules ringed and a line therefrom reflexed over the back gold, holding between the legs a cogwheel gold. Mantled gules, doubled Or. **Motto:** 'Twixt Severn and Wye. **Granted** 20 May 1965.

LYMINGTON, BOROUGH OF (HAMPSHIRE).* Argent, on waves of the sea in base an ancient ship, sail furled, proper, pendent from the cross spar an escutcheon Or charged with three torteaux and a label of three points azure; on a bordure embattled gules three bezants between each three plates. **Crest:** On a wreath argent and gules, A demi winged sea lion azure, wings and fins argent, supporting a staff Or, flying therefrom a pennon gules charged with the Badge of the Borough of Lymington. Mantled azure, doubled argent. **Supporters:** On the dexter side a lion azure and on the sinister side a boar argent crined and unguled Or, **Motto:** By sea and forest enchanted. **Badge:** An ancient ship as in the Arms encircled by a chain, the links alternately argent and Or. **Granted** 2 November 1964.

THE LYMM GRAMMAR SCHOOL (LYMM, CHESHIRE). Argent, a chevron between three cormorants sable; on a chief azure a book open proper, edged and bound, between two garbs Or. **Crest:** On a wreath Or and azure, Between two ostrich feathers argent a cubit arm, vested gules, charged with a pale of lozenges and cuffed also argent, the hand proper grasping a torch erect gold, enflamed also proper. **Motto:** Olim meminisse juvabit. **Granted** 15 July 1960.

LYTHAM ST. ANNES, BOROUGH OF (LANCASHIRE).* Barry wavy of six argent and azure, a lymphad Or, the sail sable, thereon a bend of the first charged with three mullets gules; on a chief wavy of the second a cross flory between two lions rampant argent. **Motto:** Salus populi suprema lex. **Granted** 9 November 1922.

LYTHAM SCHOOLS FOUNDATION. Per pale azure, issuant from three bars wavy in base argent a cubit arm proper vested also argent, the hand grasping by the blade a representation of the sword Excalibur, point downwards, proper, and sable, a marigold slipped and leaved also proper and in base an escallop Or; the whole within a bordure ermine. **Crest:** On a wreath Or and azure, A cubit arm in armour proper, the gauntlet holding a riband Or suspended therefrom an escutcheon azure charged with three crosses of St. Cuthbert argent. **Granted** 3 April 1951.

LUTTERWORTH

LYMINGTON

LUTON R. D. C.

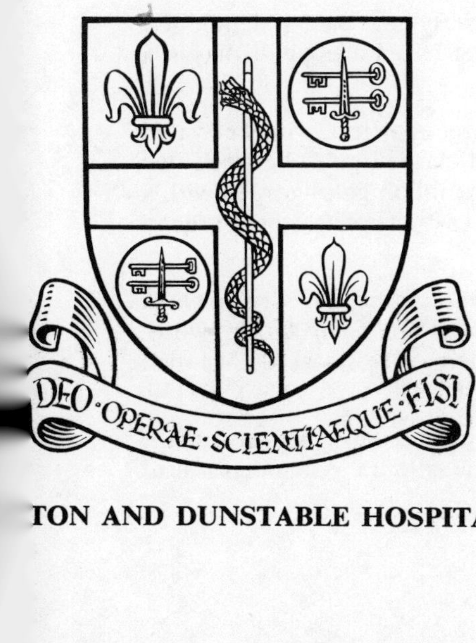

TON AND DUNSTABLE HOSPITAL

LYTHAM ST. ANNES

M

MABLETHORPE AND SUTTON URBAN DISTRICT COUNCIL (LINCOLNSHIRE—PARTS OF LINDSEY).* Per fesse embattled azure and Or, in chief two white lilies slipped and leaved proper, the stalks conjoined and entwined with the shank of an anchor interlaced with the bows of two keys fessewise, wards outwards and downwards, gold, and in base three dolphins naiant of the first. **Crest:** Out of a mural crown argent charged with three cross-crosslets sable, a demi lion gules gorged with a collar lozengy of the first and last. Mantled azure, doubled Or. **Motto:** Amoeniora litora nostra. **Granted** 10 February 1960.

MACCLESFIELD, BOROUGH OF (CHESHIRE).* Argent, a lion rampant azure holding between the forepaws a garb of wheat proper. **Crest:** On a wreath Or and azure, Out of a circlet composed of four towers conjoined with a castle wall gold, a unicorn's head argent, armed and crined of the first and gorged with a label of five points azure. **Supporters:** On each side a stag Or gorged with a wreath gold and azure, pendent therefrom by a guige proper an escutcheon, that on the dexter Gules a cross engrailed ermine, that on the sinister Argent a chevron between three bugle horns stringed sable. **Motto:** Nec virtus nec copia desunt. **Badge:** Upon a plate encircled by a torse Or and azure, a lion holding a garb as in the Arms. **Granted** 20 July 1960.

MACCLESFIELD RURAL DISTRICT COUNCIL (CHESHIRE).* Or, a stag rampant sable holding between the fore-legs a bugle-horn vert; on a chief of the last three garbs gold. **Crest:** On a wreath of the colours, A cross crosslet fitchy sable and two bugle-horns Or interlaced. Mantled vert, doubled Or. **Motto:** Memor ruris disciplinae custos. **Granted** 12 April 1955.

MAGDALEN COLLEGE (OXFORD UNIVERSITY).* Lozengy ermine and sable, on a chief of the last three lilies close couped argent. Recorded at the Visitation of 1574.

MAGDALENE COLLEGE (CAMBRIDGE UNIVERSITY). Quarterly per pale indented Or and azure, on a bend of the second between in sinister chief and dexter base an eagle displayed a fret between two martlets of the first. These are of no authority.

MAGEE UNIVERSITY COLLEGE (LONDONDERRY). Gules, three martlets, wings elevated and addorsed Or; on a chief sable an open book proper, bound and clasped gold, between two hawks' heads erased also gold. **Crest:** On a wreath of the colours, A demi lion gules gorged with a collar company azure and ermine and supporting between the paws a castle triple-towered argent. **Granted** 9 December 1954.

THE MAGISTRATES' ASSOCIATION.* Ermine, on a pale gules a mace Or. **Crest:** On a wreath ermine and gules, Issuant from clouds proper and in front of a sun rising Or, a sword, point upwards, proper, suspended from the reverse of the blade a pair of scales gold. Mantled gules, doubled argent. **Motto:** Ratione et consilio. **Granted** 30 May 1963.

MAIDENHEAD, BOROUGH OF (BERKSHIRE).* Azure, three pallets wavy argent issuant from a bridge of as many arches in chief Or. **Crest:** On a wreath of the colours, A maiden's head

MACCLESFIELD BOROUGH

MABLETHORPE

MAGISTRATES' ASSOCIATION

MACCLESFIELD R. D. C.

MAGDALEN COLLEGE

affrontée proper ensigned by a mullet azure and charged on the neck with a saltire couped gules. **Supporters:** On the dexter side a representation of St. Andrew proper, and on the sinister a representation of St. Mary Magdalene, both proper. **Motto:** Jewel of the Thames. **Granted** 21 May 1947.

MAIDSTONE, BOROUGH OF (KENT).* Or, a fesse wavy azure between three torteaux; on a chief gules a lion passant guardant Or. **Crest:** Issuant from a mural crown Or, a horse's head argent gorged with a chaplet of hops fructed proper. **Supporters:** On the dexter side an iguanodon proper collared gules, suspended therefrom by a chain Or a scroll of parchment also proper inscribed with the date One thousand five hundred and forty nine sable; and on the sinister side a lion Or collared gules, suspended therefrom by a like chain also Or, a scroll of parchment also proper inscribed with the date One thousand nine hundred and forty nine also sable. **Motto:** Agriculture and Commerce. Arms recorded (without tinctures) at the Visitation 17 August 1619; Arms confirmed and Crest and Supporters granted 30 June 1949.

MALMESBURY, BOROUGH OF (WILTSHIRE).* Per saltire argent and gules, a cross bottonnée between in chief a Saxon crown and in base an orb Or; on a chief sable a lion passant between a mitre and a crosier erect of the third. **Granted** 7 June 1950.

MALTBY URBAN DISTRICT COUNCIL (YORKSHIRE—WEST RIDING).* Argent, on a chevron gules between three parrots vert, collared of the second, a mitre of the field; on a chief also gules an open book proper, edged and bound gold, between two roses also argent, barbed and seeded proper. **Crest:** Out of a coronet composed of eight cog-wheels in mesh set upon a steel rim proper, a demi lion sable gorged with a collar gemel dancetty Or and holding between the paws a shuttle erect proper. **Motto:** Per laborem, scientiam, artem. **Granted** 2 June 1958.

MALTON URBAN DISTRICT COUNCIL (YORKSHIRE—NORTH RIDING).* Argent, three bars gules; an eagle displayed, wings inverted, Or, pendent from the neck by a guige an escutcheon also gules charged with a cross patonce of the field; on a chief azure three roses argent, barbed and seeded proper. **Crest:** Out of a mural crown Or, a demi griffin argent gorged with a collar azure, thereon three crescents Or, resting the sinister claw on the battlements of the crown and the dexter on an escutcheon lozengy also argent and gules. **Motto:** Vetera novaque tueri. **Granted** 30 October 1957.

MALVERN COLLEGE (WORCESTERSHIRE).* Or, five torteaux between two chevronels gules, all between three fountains. **Crest:** On a wreath Or and gules, A griffin sejant supporting a weather vane sable. **Motto:** Sapiens qui prospicit. **Granted** 16 August 1926.

MALVERN URBAN DISTRICT COUNCIL (WORCESTERSHIRE).* Argent, two lions passant queue fourchée gules; on a chief of the last a cross patonce Or between two fountains. **Crest:** On a wreath of the colours, In front of a pear tree fructed proper a stag lodged also proper. **Motto:** Levavi oculos meos in montes. **Granted** 2 October 1951.

MANAGEMENT CONSULTANTS, INSTITUTE OF, LIMITED. Gules, a barrulet argent charged with ten pellets, between in chief a cornucopia, the horn Or the fruit proper, and in base an open book proper, edged gold. **Crest:** On a wreath of the colours, A sun in splendour Or charged with a cogwheel sable. **Motto:** Knowledge & Progress. **Granted** 3 December 1964.

MANCHESTER, BISHOPRIC OF.* Or, on a pale engrailed gules three mitres of the field; a canton of the second, thereon three bendlets enhanced also of the field. **Granted** 5 January 1848.

MANCHESTER, CITY AND COUNTY BOROUGH OF (LANCASHIRE).* Gules, three bendlets enhanced Or; a chief argent, thereon on waves of the sea a ship under sail proper. **Crest:** On a wreath of the colours, A terrestrial globe semée of bees volant, all proper. **Supporters:** On the dexter side a heraldic antelope argent, attired, collared and chain reflexed over the back Or, and

MAIDENHEAD

MALTBY

MALMESBURY

MAIDSTONE

MALTON

on the sinister side a lion guardant Or, murally crowned gules; each charged on the shoulder with a rose of the last. **Motto:** Concilio et labore. **Badge:** An eagle displayed, wings inverted, Or, the tail feathers enfiled by a mural crown argent, the claws grasping the said crown, and charged upon the breast with a fesse dancetty of two point gules within an annulet of the same. Arms and Crest granted 1 March 1842; Supporters granted 2 March 1842; Badge granted 20 December 1957.

MANCHESTER, UNIVERSITY OF. Argent, a serpent nowed vert; on a chief nebulée azure a sun issuant Or. **Crest:** On a wreath of the colours [argent and azure], Between two branches of laurel, a palm tree proper, suspended in front thereof by a riband azure a shield argent thereon a lion rampant gules and a chief of the last charged with three bendlets Or. **Motto:** Arduus ad solem. Granted to Owens College, Manchester, 14 October 1871.

MANCHESTER AND SALFORD POLICE AUTHORITY. Per pale wavy gules and azure, a chief also per pale wavy argent and Or, six bees volant, two, two and two, proper. **Crest:** On a wreath Or, gules and azure, Issuant from a circlet gules charged with three bendlets Or, a demi lon rampant argent charged on the shoulder with two roses fessewise gules barbed and seeded proper. **Supporters:** On either side an heraldic antelope argent, armed and unguled, maned and tufted Or, about the neck a torse, the dexter Or and gules, the sinister Or and azure, conjoined by a chain reflexed over the backs and behind the shield Or, and each charged on the shoulder with a capstan proper. **Motto:** Labore et integritate. **Granted** 9 May 1969.

MANCHESTER CHAMBER OF COMMERCE. Gules, a balance within an orle of bees volant Or. **Supporters:** On the dexter a winged lion, and on the sinister a winged sea lion, the interior wing of each expanded and elevated, the other inverted, Or each supporting a staff flying a banner, that on the dexter Sable fretty wavy argent, and that on the sinister Sable three bendlets enhanced argent. **Motto:** Vigilans et utilis. **Granted** 14 September 1937.

MANCHESTER COLLEGE (OXFORD).* Gules, two torches inflamed in saltire proper; on a chief argent between two roses of the field, barbed and seeded, an open book also proper. **Crest:** Issuant from a celestial crown Or, a demi heraldic antelope argent, armed, collared and chained, the chain reflexed over the back gold, charged on the shoulder with a rose as in the Arms. **Motto:** Veritas, Libertas, Pietas. **Granted** 14 May 1934.

MANCHESTER COLLEGE OF SCIENCE AND TECHNOLOGY.* Gules, three bendlets enhanced Or; on a chief azure an open book proper, edged and bound, between two bees volant gold. **Crest:** Out of a coronet composed of four roses gules, barbed and seeded proper, set upon a rim Or, a demi lion guardant gold murally crowned of the first and supporting a torch erect sable fired proper. **Motto:** Scientia et labore. **Granted** 10 December 1956.

MANCHESTER LAW SOCIETY. Per pale gules and azure, in chief three bendlets enhanced Or and in base in front of a sword erect argent, hilt and pommel gold, a pair of scales also gold. **Crest:** On a wreath of the colours, A woman's head, blindfolded, couped at the shoulders, proper, habited per pale gules and azure three bendlets Or. **Granted** 9 May 1961.

MANCHESTER PORT HEALTH AUTHORITY. Party per pale Or and azure, a fesse indented and in base a beehive counterchanged, in the dexter chief three roses of Lancaster and in the sinister chief three bees volant Or. **Crest:** On a wreath of the colours, A terrestrial globe charged with a ship of the sixteenth century with three masts, in full sail, all proper flying three flags of St. George. **Motto:** Omnia pro bono. **Granted** 26 June 1940.

MANCHESTER STOCK EXCHANGE.* Per pale sable and gules, six bezants, three, two and one, that in centre chief charged with a rose gules, barbed and seeded proper, each of the others with a bee volant also proper. **Crest:** On a wreath Or and gules, A bear's head gules and a bull's head sable, armed Or, couped and addorsed, conjoined and gorged with a ducal coronet gold. **Motto:** Pacto fidelia. **Granted** 30 May 1960.

MALVERN COLLEGE

MANCHESTER COLLEGE (OXFORD)

MALVERN

NCHESTER COLLEGE OF SCIENCE

MANCHESTER BISHOPRIC

MANCHESTER STOCK EXCHANGE

MANDER COLLEGE (BEDFORD).* Azure, three bars wavy argent, in chief an open book proper, edged and clasped Or and bound gules, between on the dexter an estoile and on the sinister a cog-wheel and in base an escallop, all gold. **Crest:** On a wreath Or and azure, An eagle displayed and looking to the sinister Or, beaked and legged gules, on the breast a hurt charged with an estoile gold. **Motto:** Scientia sola non satis. **Granted** 28 February 1962.

MANOR HOUSE SCHOOL, ARMAGH, INCORPORATED (MILFORD, CO. ARMAGH). Gules fretty Or, issuant from the base a unicorn's head, the horn in pale, argent between in chief two lozenges of the last each charged with a trefoil slipped vert. **Granted** 1 February 1951.

MANSFIELD, BOROUGH OF (NOTTINGHAMSHIRE).* Quarterly sable and azure, a cross flory Or between in the first and fourth quarters a stag's head caboshed argent, attired of the third and in the second and third a cotton hank of the fourth. **Crest:** On a wreath of the colours In front of an oak tree proper two cross crosslets fitché saltirewise argent, and between as many mullets Or. **Motto:** Sicut quercus virescit industria. **Granted** 9 February 1892.

MANSFIELD COLLEGE (OXFORD UNIVERSITY).* Gules, an open book proper inscribed "Deus locutus est nobis in Filio" in letters sable, bound argent edged and clasped Or, between three cross crosslets gold. **Crest:** On a wreath of the colours, A unicorn sejant gules, armed, crined and unguled Or, gorged with a celestial crown gold and resting the dexter foreleg on a fountain. **Granted** 10 February 1956.

MARGATE, BOROUGH OF (KENT).* Per pale gules and azure, a chevron argent between in chief a demi lion passant guardant conjoined to the demi-hulk of a ship Or and in base a horse rampant of the third. **Crest:** On a wreath of the colours, A sea horse supporting the mast of a ship with yard and rigging, all proper. **Motto:** Porta maris portus salutis. **Granted** 12 January 1858.

MARIA ASSUMPTA TRAINING COLLEGE (KENSINGTON). Per fesse Or and argent, on a pale purpure a representation of Our Lady also argent, the numbus gold. **Motto:** Nil sine fide. **Granted** 6 December 1955.

MARIA GREY TRAINING COLLEGE. Or, on a pale engrailed azure between two torches sable, enflamed proper, a lion rampant Or. **Motto:** Servite in laetitia. **Granted** 15 April 1932.

MARINE AND GENERAL LIFE ASSURANCE SOCIETY.* Argent, a torch winged sable, enflamed proper; on a chief of the second a capstan also proper cabled Or between two escutcheons gold each charged with an escarbuncle Gules. **Crest:** On a wreath of the colours, Issuant from the battlements of a square tower sable, a demi figure representing St. Swithin, habited and mitred, proper supporting in the dexter hand a walking staff also sable ensigned with a cross paty convexed Or and holding with the sinister hand a book gules edged gold. **Supporters:** On the dexter side a sea horse (Hippocampus) azure and on the sinister side a Chinese Dragon azure tufted gules. **Motto:** Protect and provide. **Granted** 23 February 1955.

MARINE ENGINEERS, INSTITUTE OF. Argent, five barrulets wavy azure, a pile reversed and in chief a pair of calipers Or. **Crest:** On a wreath of the colours, A mercantile crown Or, therein on water barry wavy proper a sea lion Or, collared and lined gules, holding in the paws a cogwheel sable. **Supporters:** On either side a sea-lion (Otaria) proper, collared and lined gules, that on the dexter holding a torch sable, enflamed proper, and that on the sinister a caduceus sable, the serpents vert. **Motto:** Per mare scienter. **Granted** 20 January 1964.

MARITIME INSURANCE COMPANY LIMITED (LIVERPOOL). Azure, on a saltire argent between four fountains a cormorant's head erased holding in its beak a sprig of laver proper. **Crest:** On a wreath of the colours, A sea lion proper charged on the shoulder with a sprig of laver also proper. **Motto:** Per aequora et aethera securus. **Granted** 9 May 1949.

MANCHESTER, CITY

MANDER COLLEGE

MANSFIELD

MANSFIELD COLLEGE

MARGATE

MARKET BOSWORTH RURAL DISTRICT COUNCIL (LEICESTERSHIRE).* Per fesse dancetty of two points vert and sable, a fesse dancetty of two pieces argent; on a chief Or three torteaux, that in the centre charged with a pierced cinquefoil ermine, the two others each charged with a mascle gold. **Crest:** On a wreath of the colours, Out of a mural crown Or, a demi boar argent pierced in the breast with a sword fessewise also argent, hilt and pommel azure. **Motto:** Post proelia concordia. **Granted** 25 November 1954.

MARKET HARBOROUGH RURAL DISTRICT COUNCIL (LEICESTERSHIRE). Or, issuant from a base barry wavy of four argent and vert, a grassy mount, thereon a representation of the Gartre Bush formerly in the Hundred of Gartre proper; on a chief also vert a pierced cinquefoil ermine between two Leicester rams' heads caboshed also proper. **Crest:** On a wreath of the colours A sea horse argent ducally gorged and resting the dexter leg on an escutcheon Or charged with a fox's mask proper. Mantled vert, doubled Or. **Motto:** Ready all appear. **Granted** 23 December 1958.

MARKET HARBOROUGH URBAN DISTRICT COUNCIL (LEICESTERSHIRE).* Argent, on a chevron gules between three torteaux, those in chief each charged with a pierced cinquefoil ermine and that in base with a rose argent barbed and seeded proper, a cross flory between two leopards' faces Or. **Crest:** On a wreath of the colours, A demi ram argent, armed and unguled Or, gorged with a riband, pendent therefrom by a string of the last a bugle-horn gules, and holding between the fore legs an escutcheon azure charged with a fleur de lys gold. **Motto:** Nec temere nec timide. **Granted** 27 May 1953.

MARKETING AND SALES MANAGEMENT, INSTITUTE OF. Ermine, on a chevron vert between in chief two garbs and in base a pair of scales Or, five bezants; on a chief gules between a horseshoe and a pair of wings conjoined in base argent a lymphad with pennon and flags flying gold, the sail set also argent. **Crest:** On a wreath Or and vert, A dexter hand bendwise proper grasping a staff gules, headed Or, flying therefrom a banner vert fringed gold charged with two rods of Mercury in saltire of the last. **Supporters:** On either side a dragon argent, armed Or, winged vert, the underside of the wings bezanty, about the neck a chaplet of laurel fructed gold **Motto:** Bold in selling, honest in telling. **Granted** 20 March 1961.

MARK MASTER MASONS, GRAND LODGE OF. Per fesse gules and azure, in fesse an arch argent, masoned sable, the keystone charged with an equilateral triangle of the last. **Crest:** Issuant from a mural crown argent, masoned sable, a cubit arm proper, the hand grasping a keystone also argent charged with an equilateral triangle also sable. **Supporters:** On the dexter side a craftsman habited proper holding in the exterior hand a keystone argent and on the sinister side a warden habited and holding in the interior hand an axe proper. **Motto:** Lapis reprobatus caput anguli. **Granted** 17 August 1940.

MARKS AND SPENCER LIMITED.* Pily azure and gules, a pair of scales Or in an orle of roses argent barbed and seeded Or. **Crest:** On a wreath of the colours, In front of two cornucopiae in saltire a ladder erect proper. **Supporters:** On the dexter side a lion gules and on the sinister side an owl proper, each gorged with an Eastern crown Or. **Motto:** Strive, probe, apply. **Badge:** Issuant from clouds, a demi figure of St. Michael proper, wreathed about the temples, habited and winged argent, holding in the sinister hand a pair of scales Or and brandishing in the dexter a sword proper, guard and pommel Or. **Granted** 1 October 1968.

MARLBOROUGH, BOROUGH OF (WILTSHIRE).* Per saltire gules and azure, in chief a bull passant argent armed Or, in fesse two capons, and in base three greyhounds courant in pale of the third collared of the first; a chief also Or, thereon on a pale of the second between two roses gules a tower triple-towered argent. **Motto:** Ubi nunc sapientis ossa Merlini. Recorded at the Visitation of 1565 together with the ancient coat (identical with the pale in the above).

MARKET HARBOROUGH U. D. C.

MARKS AND SPENCER

MARINE AND GENERAL

MARKET BOSWORTH

MASONS OF THE CITY OF LONDON, WORSHIPFUL COMPANY OF.* Sable, on a chevron engrailed between three castles argent, garnished with doors and windows of the field, a pair of compasses extended also sable. **Crest:** On a wreath of the colours, A castle argent. **Motto used:** God is our guide. **Granted** 1472/3 by William Hawkeslowe, Clarenceux King of Arms (Crest painted but not blazoned); Confirmed 1520/1 by Thomas Benolt, Clarenceux King of Arms; entered at the Visitation of 1634.

MASTER MARINERS, HONOURABLE COMPANY OF. Argent, on waves of the sea a representation of the ship 'The Golden Hind' in full sail all proper; on a chief arched azure a terrestrial globe also proper between two mullets of the field. **Crest:** On a wreath of the colours, In front of a sun in splendour proper a quadrant Or. **Supporters:** On either side a sea horse proper gorged with a naval crown Or, that on the dexter supporting a staff proper headed Or, flying therefrom the Union Flag, and that on the sinister supporting a like staff, flying therefrom the Red Ensign also proper. **Motto:** Loyalty and Service. **Badge:** In front of an anchor Or, a fountain fimbriated of the first, thereon a seahorse proper gorged with a mural crown also of the first. Arms, Crest and Supporters granted 26 April 1927; Badge granted 8 November 1951.

MATHEMATICAL ASSOCIATION. Azure, a representation of a pentagon with diagonals Or; on a chief argent an open book proper inscribed with the Greek letters Pi and Epsilon sable and edged and clasped Or. **Crest:** On a wreath of the colours, A dexter hand couped at the wrist holding a crystal cylinder enclosing a like sphere, all proper. **Motto:** Tibi creditum debes. **Granted** 1 June 1965.

MATLOCK TRAINING COLLEGE FOR WOMEN.* Gules, a lion bicorporate rampant and counterrampant Or, in the fesse point on a plate fimbriated sable a Tudor rose barbed and seeded proper. **Granted** 18 December 1953 to the Derbyshire County Council for the use of the College.

MEASUREMENT AND CONTROL, INSTITUTE OF. Or, on a pile reversed sable a flambeau enfiling a cog-wheel Or, the flames proper; on a chief sable three pallets Or. **Crest:** On a wreath of the colours, From waves of the sea an albatross rising proper, in the beak a lightning flash. **Motto:** Divide et impera. **Badge:** An albatross rising Or within an annulet gobony Or and sable. **Granted** 20 September 1968.

MEAT, INSTITUTE OF.* Gules, two torches in saltire inflamed Or, in chief a sheep's head erased argent. **Crest:** On a wreath of the colours, In front of a bull statant gules a poleaxe erect proper. **Motto:** Per doctrinam ad dignitatem. **Granted** 21 November 1947.

MECHANICAL ENGINEERS, INSTITUTION OF. Sable, between the points of a pair of calipers inverted Or, a plate. **Crest:** On a wreath of the colours, Upon a terrestrial globe a grey horse forcene proper gorged with a coronet composed of four fleurs-de-lys with chain reflexed over the back Or. **Supporters:** On the dexter side a figure representing Archimedes holding in his exterior hand a pointer and on the sinister side a figure representing Vulcan resting his exterior hand upon a sledge hammer proper. **Motto:** Progress. **Granted** 17 October 1939.

MEDICAL HERBALISTS, NATIONAL INSTITUTE OF, LIMITED. Or, on a pale vert between two sprigs of rosemary flowered proper, a rod of Aesculapius gold; on a chief also vert three roses argent barbed and seeded also proper. **Supporters:** On the dexter side a representation of the goddess Isis holding in the palm of her dexter hand proper a bowl Or; and on the sinister side a representation of an Indian Medicine Man of North America proper, pendent from the outer hip a wampum pouch also proper, and holding in the sinister hand three stalks of wheat gold. **Motto:** Ex herbis remedia. **Granted** 20 September 1957.

MEDICAL LABORATORY TECHNOLOGY, INSTITUTE OF. Per pale argent and sable, in dexter chief an antique lamp enflamed proper, and in sinister a pile reversed of the first; over all

MARLBOROUGH

MATLOCK TRAINING COLLEGE

MASONS COMPANY

MELKSHAM

MEAT INSTITUTE

a cross gules charged with a staff of Aesculapius also proper. **Crest:** On a wreath argent, sable and gules, A cormorant proper, the wings elevated and displayed Or, charged on each wing with an open scroll also proper, and holding in the dexter claw a Norman sword erect likewise proper. **Motto:** Disce ut proficias. **Granted** 1 November 1960.

MEDICINE, ROYAL SOCIETY OF. Per pale vert and gules, the serpent of Moses Or entwined round a Tau cross Argent. **Crest:** On a wreath of the colours, Three sprigs of the herb "All Heal" proper. **Supporters:** On the dexter side a representation of St. Cosmas and on the sinister side a representation of St. Damian, both proper. **Motto:** Non est vivere sed valere vita. **Granted** 7 October 1927.

MELKSHAM URBAN DISTRICT COUNCIL (WILTSHIRE).* Per pale azure and vert, a fesse dancetté argent, in chief an ancient crown Or. **Crest:** On a wreath of the colours, In front of a cogwheel proper a stag's head affrontée gules attired argent. **Motto:** Unity and Progress. **Granted** 6 December 1948.

MEN OF KENT AND KENTISH MEN, ASSOCIATION OF.* Gules, a fesse wavy argent, thereon another azure, over all a horse forcene; a bordure argent charged with an orle wavy azure surmounted of four lymphads, sails set, pennons flying, Or. **Crest:** On a wreath of the colours, A Cubit arm grasping a sword bend sinisterwise proper, hilt and pommel Or, the arm encircled by two branches of oak fructed proper. **Motto:** Cantium nobis princeps. **Granted** 20 December 1963.

MERCERS OF THE CITY OF LONDON, WORSHIPFUL COMPANY OF.* Gules, issuant from a bank of clouds a figure of the Virgin couped at the shoulders proper, vested in a crimson robe adorned with gold, the neck encircled by a jewelled necklace, crined Or and wreathed about the temples with a chaplet of roses alternately argent and of the first, and crowned with a celestial crown; the whole within a bordure of clouds also proper. **Crest:** On a wreath of the colours, Issuant from a bank of clouds proper a figure of the Virgin as in the Arms. **Motto:** Honor Deo. Arms recorded at the Visitations of 1568, 1634 and 1687; Arms confirmed and Crest granted 22 April 1911.

MERCHANT ADVENTURERS OF THE CITY OF BRISTOL, COMPANY AND FELLOWSHIP OF THE. Barry wavy of eight argent and azure, on a bend Or a dragon passant with wings inverted and tail extended vert; on a chief gules a lion passant guardant of the third between two bezants. **Crest:** In a ducal coronet Or, a main-mast of the last with pennon flying argent charged with a cross gules, on the round top a man in armour proper, on his dexter arm a truncheon, his sinister hand supporting a carved shield of the second, from the round top six pikestaves, three on each side, issuing bendways of the first, the rigging from the round top to the coronet sable. **Supporters:** The dexter, a mermaid in the sea, all proper, crined Or, the midde fins at the joining of the borders of the last, holding in her sinister hand a mirror of the first, and supporting with her dexter hand an anchor of the second cabled proper; the sinister supporter, a winged satyr proper standing on a mount vert, winged and legged Or, holding in his sinister hand a scythe, the blade in base, all proper. **Motto:** Indocilis pauperiem pati. Recorded in the College of Arms.

MERCHANT ADVENTURERS OF THE CITY OF YORK, COMPANY OF. Barry wavy argent and azure, on a chief per pale gules and azure a lion passant Or between two roses argent barbed and seeded proper. **Crest:** On a wreath argent and gules, Leaping from water barry wavy argent and azure, a pegasus argent winged azure hooved Or. **Supporters:** On either side a pegasus argent, hooved Or, the wings azure, each charged with a rose argent barbed and seeded proper. **Motto:** Dieu nous donne bonne aventure. **Granted** 12 June 1969.

MERCHANT TAYLORS OF THE CITY OF LONDON, WORSHIPFUL COMPANY OF.*
Argent, a pavilion imperial purple [i.e. crimson] garnished Or [lined ermine] between two mantles

MEN OF KENT

MERCHANT TAYLORS COMPANY

MERIONETH

MERCERS COMPANY

also imperial purple [lined ermine]; on a chief azure a lion passant [guardant] gold. **Crest:** On a wreath argent and azure, On a mount vert a lamb argent in sunbeams Or. Mantled gules, doubled argent. **Supporters:** On either side a camel Or. **Motto:** Concordia parvae res crescunt. **Granted** 23 December 1586 by Robert Cooke, Clarenceux King of Arms, to replace an earlier grant of Arms and Crest (23 October 1481) by Sir Thomas Holme, Clarenceux King of Arms.

MERCHANT TAYLORS IN THE CITY OF YORK, COMPANY OF. Or, a pavilion purpure, lined ermine; on a chief azure a lion's head caboshed affrontée Or; over all two robes of estate lined purpure. **Crest:** Out of a coronet composed of four roses argent, barbed and seeded proper, and as many rose leaves Or set alternately on a circlet gold, a mount vert, thereon a Paschal Lamb proper. Mantled azure, doubled Or. **Supporters:** On either side a camel erminois gorged with a collar azure charged with a rose argent barbed and seeded proper. **Motto:** Concordia parvae res crescunt. **Granted** 5 March 1963.

MERIONETH COUNTY COUNCIL.* Azure, three goats salient argent, armed, crined and unguled Or; on a chief of the last issuant from barry wavy of four of the first and second a sun rising gules. **Crest:** Issuant from a coronet of six roses set upon a rim Or, a representation of Harlech Castle on a rock proper. **Supporters:** Upon a compartment of rock proper, on either side a dragon gules supporting an abbot's crozier and charged on the wing with five mullets Or. **Motto:** Tra Mor tra Meirion. **Granted** March 1952.

MERSEY AND RIVER WEAVER AUTHORITY. Per fess Or and azure, a fess wavy per fess wavy azure and argent, in chief three roses gules and in base a garb Or. **Crest:** On a wreath of the colours, On a rock in front of a fountain, a cormorant wings addorsed proper, beaked and legged gules, in the beak a branch of laver proper. **Supporters:** On the dexter side a figure representing Neptune mantled vert, and on the sinister side a lion guardant Or murally crowned and charged on the shoulder with a rose gules barbed and seeded proper. **Motto:** Vita ex aqua venit. **Granted** 1 March 1965.

MERSEY DOCKS AND HARBOUR BOARD. Argent, a bend wavy azure between in chief a cormorant, holding in the beak a branch of seaweed called laver, proper and in base an estoile of the second. **Crest:** On a wreath of the colours, On waves of the sea and in front of a lighthouse a dolphin naiant, all proper. **Supporters:** On the dexter side a representation of Neptune proper and on the sinister side a representation of Mercury proper. **Motto:** Business in Great Waters. **Granted** 30 January 1948.

MERSEY TUNNEL JOINT COMMITTEE.* Or masoned sable, a pellet; on a chief gules a cormorant between two estoiles of the field. **Crest:** On a wreath of the colours, Two lions salient respectant gules holding between their forepaws a wheel Or. **Supporters:** On the dexter side a representation of Apollo and on the sinister side a representation of Pluto, both proper. **Motto:** Ripae ulterioris amore. **Granted** 14 August 1952.

MERTHYR TYDFIL, COUNTY BOROUGH OF (GLAMORGAN).* Azure, a representation of St. Tydfil and in chief two crosses pattée fitchée all Or. **Motto:** Nid Cadern ond Brodyrdde. **Granted** 17 August 1906.

MERTON, LONDON BOROUGH OF.* Sable, a fret; on a chief Or two keys in saltire, wards upwards and outwards, surmounted by a sword, point downwards, between a double headed eagle displayed sable, armed and legged gules, and a lion passant sable, armed and langued gules. **Crest:** Issuant from a mural crown Or and in front of three sprigs of lavender proper a fret Or, thereon a Cornish chough proper. **Supporters:** On the dexter side a lion and on the sinister side an eagle, wings addorsed, sable, each gorged with a mural crown Or. **Motto:** Stand fast in honour and strength. **Badge:** On a fret Or two lions counterpassant sable. **Granted** 1 January 1965.

MERSEY TUNNEL

MERTHYR TYDFIL

MERTON COLLEGE

MERTON

MERTON COLLEGE (OXFORD UNIVERSITY).* Or, three chevronels per pale, the first and third azure and gules, the second of the same counterchanged. Recorded at the visitation of 1574. The College bears these impaled (to the sinister) with those of the See of Rochester.

METALS, INSTITUTE OF. Per pale Or and argent, an open book proper, thereon the alchemical signs for the non-ferrous metals sable. **Crest:** On a wreath Or and sable, Issuant from flames a crucible emitting oxide vapour proper. **Supporters:** On either side a male griffin sable, armed and tufted Or. **Motto:** De re metallica. **Granted** 23 December 1953.

METHODIST CHURCH PURPOSES, TRUSTEES FOR.* Argent, a cross between twelve escallops purpure, over all a castle of three [domed] towers proper. **Motto:** Nobis officium, allis usus, Deo gloria. **Badge:** In front of an escallop Or a cross purpure. **Granted** 7 June 1948 to the Trustees of the Methodist Church for Church Purposes.

METROPOLITAN LIFE ASSURANCE SOCIETY. Or, on a mount vert, a female figure proper vested argent, mantled azure, the right arm extended and entwined by a serpent, holding in the left hand a human skull, both also proper; a chief also azure, thereon a pallet ermine charged with a dagger erect gules, between two portcullis with chains Or. **Motto:** True faith, true policy. **Granted** 18 August 1885.

THE METROPOLITAN POLICE FORCE.* Azure, a portcullis chained within a double tressure flory counterflory argent. **Crest:** On a wreath of the colours, Three arrows, one in pale and two in saltire, barbs downward, proper, banded azure and ensigned by the Royal Crown proper. **Supporters:** On either side a lion guardant argent, gorged with a collar azure charged alternately with bezants and bees volant, grasping in the interior paw a column Or. **Badge:** A roundel azure, thereon the Royal Cypher of Her Majesty Queen Elizabeth the Second argent within a circlet azure fimbriated and inscribed with words 'Metropolitan Police' in letters argent, the whole upon a star of eight major and fifty-six lesser points argent, ensigned by the Royal Crown proper. **Granted** (pursuant to Royal Licence) 5 September 1967.

METROPOLITAN WATER BOARD.* Argent, on a pile vert a dexter hand Or issuing from a cloud in chief proper and scattering eight guttés d'eau, in base three bars wavy azure; on a chief nebuly of the first a Cross of St. George charged with a Lion of England. **Crest:** On a wreath of the colours, A hurt charged with a hand issuing from a cloud and scattering guttés as in the Arms. **Supporters:** On the dexter side a figure representing Hygeia vested argent mantled azure, and on the sinister side a figure representing Aquarius habited azure. **Motto:** Et plui super unam civitatem. Arms and Crest granted 10 February 1931; Supporters granted 11 February 1931.

MID ANGLIA POLICE AUTHORITY.* Per fess gules and argent, a fess enarched and embattled Or, masoned sable, between in chief two [open] crowns Or and in base three bars wavy [azure] and thereon two keys in saltire Or. **Granted** 20 December 1965.

THE MIDDLESEX HOSPITAL. Gules, three seaxes, points fessewise to the sinister, in pale proper, pommels and hilts Or; on a chief sable three rods of Aesculapius gold. **Motto:** Miseris succurrere disco. **Granted** 30 April 1926 to the President, Vice-Presidents, Treasurers and Governors of The Middlesex Hospital.

MID-ESSEX TECHNICAL COLLEGE AND SCHOOL OF ART. Or, a pegasus passant, in chief two greyhounds' heads erased sable. **Crest:** On a wreath of the colours, In front of an owl sable, two rays of lightning in chevron reversed Or. **Supporters:** On the dexter side a figure representing Urania holding in her exterior hand a terrestrial globe, and on the sinister side a figure representing a Vulcan resting his exterior hand on the haft of a hammer, all proper. **Motto:** Arte et scientia ditamur. **Granted** 26 July 1956.

MIDDLE TEMPLE, THE HONOURABLE SOCIETY OF THE.* Argent, on a cross gules a Paschal Lamb supporting a banner Or. Certified by the Kings of Arms 9 March 1949.

MID ANGLIA POLICE

MIDDLE TEMPLE

METROPOLITAN POLICE

METROPOLITAN WATER BOARD

METHODIST CHURCH PURPOSES

MIDDLETON, BOROUGH OF (LANCASHIRE).* Quarterly per pale nebuly gules and argent, on a fesse ermine between a cross patonce of the second in the first quarter, a mullet sable pierced of the field in the second, a silkworm moth volant in the third, and a rock in base thereon a stork in the fourth, three sprigs of the cotton tree slipped and fructed, all proper. **Crest:** On a wreath of the colours, Upon a mount vert, between two boars' heads erect and couped sable, a tower proper, suspended therefrom by a riband gules an escocheon Or charged with a lion passant also gules. **Motto:** Fortis in arduis. **Granted** 28 January 1887.

MIDLAND BANK LIMITED.* Quarterly, first and fourth azure a bend of lozenges conjoined Or, second and third per pale indented of the last and gules; over all a cross also gules, thereon in chief a sword erect proper, hilt and pomel of the second, and in fesse a mural crown between four ermine spots gold. **Crest:** On a wreath of the colours, Issuant from a mural crown proper, a dragon's wing gules bezantée. **Supporters:** On the dexter side a dragon and on the sinister side a griffin argent, each collared and with chain reflexed over the back Or. **Motto:** Vis unita fortior. **Badge:** Within a circlet of [twenty] bezants a griffin segreant Or. **Granted** 28 August 1952.

MIDLAND ASSURANCE LIMITED. Quarterly per pale indented azure and gules, a Roman shield Or. **Crest:** On a wreath of the colours, A demi lion holding the fasces proper, the faggots entwined with a snake vert. **Motto:** Commune bonum. **Granted** 4 September 1950 to The Midland Employers' Mutual Assurance Limited.

MIDWIVES, ROYAL COLLEGE OF. Azure, a sinister and dexter hand erect couped in fesse proper surmounted of a mullet of eight points the uppermost and lowest points extended palewise argent; a bordure quarterly of the last and sable. **Crest:** On a wreath of the colours, A pomegranate tree eradicated and fructed proper, the stem enfiled by an ancient crown Or. **Supporters:** On the dexter side a representation of Juno Lucina proper, vested vert, with veil argent, and diadem and sandals Or, holding on the interior arm a naked child and in the exterior hand a sheaf of white lilies, all also proper; and on the sinister side a representation of Hygeia likewise proper, vested also argent, with mantle purpure, and diadem and sandals gold, holding in the exterior hand a bowl of the last, the arm entwined by a serpent also vert. **Motto:** Vita donum Dei. **Granted** 15 December 1959.

MILFORD HAVEN CONSERVANCY BOARD. Barry wavy of ten argent and azure, two flaunches vert, each charged with a cross moline Or. **Crest:** On a wreath of the colours, A demi conical bouy, skirt chequy argent and sable, the lamp enflamed and radar reflector all proper. **Supporters:** On the dexter side an eagle [wings inverted] Or, and on the sinister side a sea dragon gules [the whole on a compartment per pale grass and water]. **Motto:** Nautis navibusque. **Granted** 1 June 1965.

MILK MARKETING BOARD. Vert, issuant from the sinister base three piles wavy bendwise conjoined at the dexter chief point argent. **Crest:** Within a crown palisado argent a mount vert, thereon a cow statant also argent. **Supporters:** On the dexter side a lion and on the sinister side a dragon argent. **Motto:** Together in enterprise. **Granted** 6 September 1954.

MILLFIELD SCHOOL LIMITED (SOMERSET).* Vert, the sails of a windmill saltirewise between four crosses bottonée argent. **Crest:** On a wreath argent and azure, On a mount vert a windmill gules between two branches of hawthorn proper. **Motto:** Molire molendo. **Granted** 9 September 1954.

MILL HILL SCHOOL.* Argent, on a cross quadrate gules an open book argent; on a chief azure three martlets Or. **Motto:** Et virtutem et Musas. **Granted** 25 September 1935.

MINING ELECTRICAL AND MECHANICAL ENGINEERS, ASSOCIATION OF. Quarterly argent and Or, three lozenges conjoined in fesse sable, the two in the flanks each charged

MIDLAND BANK

MIDDLETON

MILLFIELD SCHOOL

MILL HILL SCHOOL

MIRFIELD

with a thunderbolt also Or and that in the centre with a steel cogwheel proper. **Crest:** On a wreath argent, Or and sable, A mole proper ensigned with a mural crown sable masoned argent. **Motto:** Progress with safety. **Granted** 25 July 1960.

MIRFIELD URBAN DISTRICT COUNCIL (YORKSHIRE—WEST RIDING).* Azure, a chief gules; over all a ram's head caboshed between two ears of barley stalked and bladed in saltire Or. **Crest:** On a wreath of the colours, A demi knight affrontée in mail proper, with surcoat Argent two bars sable, supporting a representation of a church Or. **Motto:** Fruges ecce paludis. **Granted** 26 February 1935.

MONMOUTH, BISHOPRIC OF.* Per pale azure and sable, two croziers in saltire Or between in chief a bezant charged with a lion passant guardant gules, in fesse two fleurs de lys and in base one fleur-de-lys of the third. **Granted** 20 April 1922.

MONMOUTH, BOROUGH OF.* Azure, three chevronels Or, over all a fesse gules; the shield ensigned with a mural crown of the second. **Supporters:** On the dexter side a lion guardant murally crowned Or, and on the sinister side a heraldic antelope argent gorged with a mural crown Or. **Motto:** Monemus et munimus. **Granted** 8 August 1946.

MONMOUTHSHIRE COUNTY COUNCIL.* Per pale azure and sable, three fleurs-de-lys Or; on a chief of the last two towers triple-towered gules. **Crest:** On a wreath of the colours, A tower triple-towered gules charged with an escutcheon of the Arms of Somerset, that is to say Quarterly, first and fourth Azure three fleurs-de-lys Or, second and third Gules three lions passant guardant in pale Or, all within a bordure gobony argent and azure. **Supporters:** On the dexter side a lion guardant Or, grasping with the interior paw a rose gules barbed seeded stalked and leaved proper, and gorged with a coronet composed of four fleur-de-lys set upon a rim also gules; and on the sinister side a dragon of the last, grasping with the interior claw a leek also proper, and gorged with a like coronet gold. **Motto:** Utrique fidelis. **Granted** 28 January 1948.

MONTGOMERYSHIRE COUNTY COUNCIL.* Tierced in pairle reversed Or, argent and azure, three lions rampant gules, sable and gold; all within a bordure gobony sable and argent. **Crest:** Issuant from a mural crown gules, a swan rising, in the beak a sprig of oak slipped leaved and fructed proper. Mantled azure, doubled Or. **Supporters:** On either side a wyvern vert gorged with a riband, pendent therefrom by a ring a fleece Or. **Motto:** Powys Paradwys Cymru. **Granted** 23 January 1951.

MOORFIELDS EYE HOSPITAL. Per pale Or and sable, a sun counterchanged; on a chief azure a leopard's head argent, crowned with an eastern crown gold, between two fleurs-de-lis also gold. **Crest:** On a wreath of the colours, An elephant's head couped proper holding in the trunk a fleam Or. **Supporters:** On either side a peacock in its pride holding in the beak an ophthalmoscope proper, the dexter gorged with a chain, pendent therefrom a portcullis Or, the sinister also gorged with a chain, pendant therefrom an escallop argent, [the whole upon a compartment in the form of a stone plinth proper, thereon carved the] **Motto:** Fiat lux. **Granted:** 10 July 1958.

MORECAMBE AND HEYSHAM, BOROUGH OF (LANCASHIRE).* Per chevron Or and azure, in chief two roses gules, each charged with a rose argent, barbed, seeded, slipped and leaved proper, and in base a fishing-boat in full sail of the fourth. **Motto:** Beauty surrounds, health abounds. **Granted** 24 February 1926.

MORLEY, BOROUGH OF (YORKSHIRE—WEST RIDING).* Argent, on a fesse gules between a sprig of the cotton-tree slipped fructed and leaved proper between two pellets in chief and a pickaxe surmounted by a spade in saltire in base sable, a shuttle fessewise Or, thread pendant of the first. **Crest:** Upon a wreath of the colours, In front of a ram's head couped argent, a shuttle fessewise proper, thread pendant also argent. **Motto:** Industria omnia vincit. **Granted** 9 August 1887.

MONMOUTH

MORECAMBE AND HEYSHAM

MONMOUTH BISHOPRIC

MONMOUTHSHIRE C. C.

MORPETH, BOROUGH OF (NORTHUMBERLAND).* Barry of ten argent and gules, a tower triple-towered Or; a bordure azure charged with eight martlets gold. **Motto:** Inter silvas et flumina habitans. **Granted** 20 May 1552 by William Hervey, Norroy King of Arms.

MOTHERS' UNION, THE.* Per chevron, barry wavy argent and azure, and ermine, in base two chevronels gules; on a chief of the second a representation of the Holy Virgin and Child standing between two portcullis chained Or. **Motto:** For love of God and home. **Granted** 16 March 1927.

MOUNT ST. MARY'S COLLEGE (SPINKHILL, DERBYSHIRE). Or, a chevron between three crescents azure; on a canton of the last the Roman letters IHS between in chief a Passion Cross and in base three passion nails pilewise, all of the first. **Crest:** On a wreath of the colours, A lily flowered stalked and leaved proper between two wings displayed Or. **Motto:** Sine macula. **Granted** 23 June 1941.

MOTOR INDUSTRY, (INCORPORATED), INSTITUTE OF THE. Per fesse Or and gules, in chief a representation of Boadicea's chariot of the second, and in base six bees volant of the first. **Crest:** On a wreath of the colours, In front of a daw, wings extended and inverted, a open book proper, edged Or bound gules. **Supporters:** On either side a lion guardant, the dexter Or semée of bees volant gules, the sinister gules semée of bees volant Or. **Motto:** Integritas et scientia. **Granted** 1 November 1955.

MUNICIPAL AND COUNTY ENGINEERS, INSTITUTION OF.* Barry wavy of six argent and vert, a pale sable thereon in chief a torch Or fired and enfiled with a mural crown proper and in base a winged wheel gold. **Motto:** Amenity, Progress, Stability. **Granted** 7 May 1931.

MUNICIPAL AUTHORITIES OF NORTHERN IRELAND, ASSOCIATION OF.* Quarterly gules and Or, in the first quarter a mullet of six points argent charged with a dexter hand couped at the wrist of the first, and in the fourth a mural crown also argent. **Crest:** On a wreath of the colours, Upon a demi tower proper a mace fessewise Or. **Granted** 1 September 1954.

MUNICIPAL MUTUAL INSURANCE LIMITED. Or, two swords, points upwards, in saltire azure between in chief a rose gules barbed and seeded proper, and in fesse a thistle and a daffodil both stalked and leaved also proper. **Crest:** Upon a mural crown proper a portcullis chained Or, with a rose gules barbed and seeded also proper. **Motto:** Concordes ad serviendum. **Granted** 25 September 1950.

MUNICIPAL TREASURERS AND ACCOUNTANTS, INSTITUTE OF. Azure, in front of a balance Or two quill pens in saltire, points downward, surmounted of an open book with book marks proper; a chief embattled of the second, thereon three purses of the first. **Crest:** Out of a circlet of steel proper a demi talbot azure holding between the paws a fasces erect Or. **Supporters:** On either side a talbot Or gorged with a circlet of steel proper and charged on the shoulder with a key, wards downwards and inwards, gules. **Motto:** Fiscum serva fideliter. **Badge:** In front of a balance Or, two quill pens in saltire, points downward, surmounted of an open book with book-marks proper. **Granted** 20 June 1955.

THE MUSEUMS ASSOCIATION.* Azure, a lyre within an orle of nine estoiles Or. **Motto:** Musarum templa colamus. **Granted** 15 December 1960.

MUSICIANS OF THE CITY OF LONDON, WORSHIPFUL COMPANY OF.* Azure, a swan with wings expanded argent, within a double tressure flory counterflory Or; on a chief gules a pale between two lions passant guardant Or, thereon a rose gules barbed and seeded vert. **Crest:** On a wreath of the colours, A lyre Or. No motto is used at the present time but the following have been employed: A Deo et caelo symphonia; Harmony. **Granted** 15 October 1604 by William Camden, Clarenceux King of Arms.

MORLEY

MORPETH

MOTHERS' UNION

MONTGOMERYSHIRE

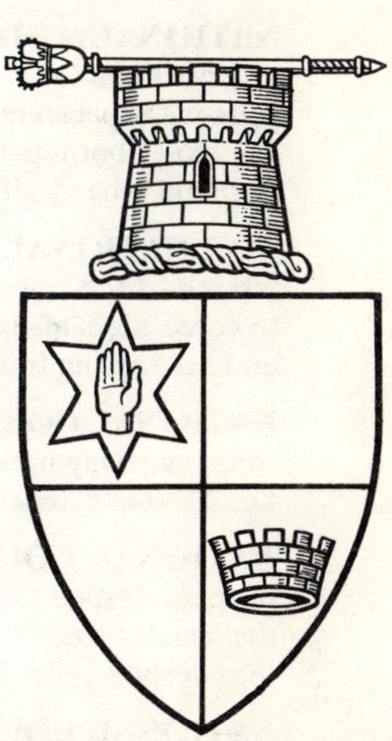

MUNICIPAL AUTHORITIES OF NORTHERN IRELAND

MUSICIANS COMPANY

MUNICIPAL AND COUNTY ENGINEERS

MUSEUMS ASSOCIATION

N

* *Denotes Illustration*

NATIONAL AND GRINDLAYS BANK LIMITED. Barry wavy of eight azure bezantée and argent. **Crest:** On a wreath of the colours, A demi lion gules supporting a cornucopia inverted proper. **Supporters:** On the dexter side an Indian elephant and on the sinister side an African elephant, both proper. **Motto:** Surgunt commercia gentes. **Badge:** A bezant charged with an elephant's head affrontée proper. **Granted** 4 August 1954 to the National Bank of India Limited.

THE NATIONAL BANK LIMITED.* Azure, a harp or within an orle of bezants. **Crest:** On a wreath of the colours, an Irish wolf hound couchant azure issuant from the port of a tower triple-towered or. **Supporters:** On either side an Irish wolf hound Or, gorged with a collar azure besanty and resting the interior hind paw on a bezant. **Granted** 5th February 1952.

NATIONAL COAL BOARD.* Per fesse argent and sable, three fusils conjoined in fesse counter-changed. **Supporters:** On either side a lion sable charged on the shoulder with a sun in splendour Or. **Motto:** E tenebris lux. **Granted** 26 April 1949.

NATIONAL COUNCIL FOR TECHNOLOGICAL AWARDS. Gules, in chief an open book proper, clasped Or, on the dexter page a representation of the atomic structure of crystal and on the sinister page a cogwheel, both sable, and in base a dexter hand couped at the wrist grasping a thunderbolt gold. **Motto:** With mind and hands. **Granted** 20 March 1958.

NATIONAL DOCK LABOUR BOARD. Per pale vert and water barry wavy proper, two Argosies with sails furled in pale Or, that in chief pointing to the dexter, the other turned about. **Crest:** On a wreath argent and vert, In front of three leaves of the dock plant a seagull rising proper. **Supporters:** On the dexter side a lion and on the sinister side a sea lion Or, both gorged with a collar of steel proper charged with a grappling-hook gold, attached to the lion's collar a steel chain containing a tension-screw, and to the sea lion's collar a rope, both reflexed over the back, also proper. **Motto:** Ne inviti otientur. **Granted** 7 July 1952.

NATIONAL EMPLOYERS' LIFE ASSURANCE COMPANY LIMITED. Azure, two battle-axes in saltire Or, surmounted in the centre with a bezant, between in pale as many pelicans' heads erased argent, beaked of the second, vulning themseves proper, and in fesse as many fleurs-de-lys also of the second. **Crest:** On a wreath argent and azure, A cubit arm vested azure and charged with a bezant, the hand proper supporting two battle-axes in saltire Or. **Supporters:** On either side a pelican argent, beaked and membered Or, vulning itself proper and charged on the wing with a hurt, thereon a bezant. **Motto:** Per mutua serviendo tutiores. **Granted** 1 December 1960.

NATIONAL FARMERS' UNION. Vert, a chevron ermine between in dexter chief a bull's head and in sinister chief a ram's head caboshed and in base three ears of wheat banded, all Or. **Crest:** On a wreath of the colours, A scythe and sceptre in saltire Or. **Motto:** Labore agricolae floreat civitas. **Granted** 9 September 1946.

NATIONAL BANK

NEATH R.D.C.

NATIONAL COAL BOARD

NATIONAL FEDERATION OF BUILDING TRADES

NATIONAL FEDERATION OF BUILDING TRADES EMPLOYERS.* Azure, an arch throughout proper, masoned Or. **Crest:** On a wreath of the colours, Issuant from a wreath of oak proper, fructed Or, a triple towered castle gold. **Granted** 25 January 1949.

NATIONAL GAS TURBINE ESTABLISHMENT. Gyronny of eight gules and argent, a chief embattled, thereon an astral crown, both counterchanged, between a rose also gules, barbed and seeded proper, and a pierced cinquefoil ermine. **Crest:** On a wreath of the colours, A phoenix proper gorged with an astral crown argent. **Motto:** Scientia vis augetur. **Granted** 15 August 1961.

NATIONAL HEART HOSPITAL. Argent, on a cross gules between four heartsease flowers proper, a heart Or. **Crest:** On a wreath of the colours, In front of a foxglove plant of three stalks erect flowered and leaved proper, a heart Or. **Granted** 16 May 1957.

NATIONAL LIBRARY OF WALES, THE. Sable, on a fesse between three open books argent embellished Or, a lion passant guardant gules. **Crest:** On a wreath of the colours, A dragon passant gules holding in the dexter claw a parchment roll proper tied with a riband azure. **Supporters:** On either side a dragon gules, each gorged with a collar and suspended therefrom by a chain Or a closed book argent embellished gold. **Granted** 12 November 1919.

NATIONAL PLAYING FIELDS ASSOCIATION. Per fesse azure and vert, in chief an eagle volant affrontée, head downwards and to the sinister, Or and in base a design consisting of a ring fessewise in perspective surmounted of two other rings palewise over-lapping argent. **Badge:** Set upon the wings of an eagle as in the Arms, a roundel vert, thereon within a ring a design as in the base of the Arms argent charged in the centre with a representation of a human eye also argent, the iris sable. **Granted** 20 December 1954.

NATIONAL SOCIETY. Per fesse argent and sable, in chief a cross cottised gules, thereon an open book proper garnished Or, and in base fishes naiant also proper within fretty Or. **Motto:** Piscatores hominum. **Granted** 5 April 1937.

NATIONAL WOOL TEXTILE EXPORT CORPORATION (BRADFORD). Barry wavy argent and azure, on a chevron gules between in chief two roses also gules, barbed and seeded proper, and in base a sheep passant Or, a daffodil flower gold between two thistles, slipped and leaved, also proper. **Crest:** On a wreath argent and gules, A winged lion sejant Or resting the dexter paw on a shuttle gules threaded gold. **Supporters:** On the dexter side a ram argent, armed and unguled Or, gorged with a collar, pendent therefrom an escutcheon gules charged with a rose of the first barbed and seeded proper, and on the sinister side a goat sable, armed and unguled Or gorged with a collar, pendent therefrom an escutcheon argent charged with a rose gules barbed and seeded proper. **Motto:** Vellera fiant aurea. **Granted** 25 April 1952.

NATIONWIDE BUILDING SOCIETY. Per chevron azure and Or, in chief on a rock proper a castle triple-towered gold, and in base a dragon couchant, wings lifted and addorsed, gules. **Crest:** On a wreath of the colours, Four keys, wards upwards and outwards, in saltire Or enfiled by a chaplet of daffodils proper, roses gules, and thistles and shamrocks also proper. **Supporters:** On either side a cockatrice argent, combed wattled and armed gules, each gorged with a collar Or, pendent therefrom an escutcheon barry wavy of ten also argent and azure. **Motto:** Step by step. **Badge:** A hurt charged with a representation of a pyramid Or standing upon the sands of the desert proper. **Granted** 27 September 1954 to the Co-operative Permanent Building Society.

NAVAL ARCHITECTS, INSTITUTION OF. Per fesse wavy azure and barry wavy of six argent and of the first, issuant from the fesse line a sun in splendour; over all a three-masted ship of the seventeenth century in full sail proper, pennon and flags flying also of the first. **Crest:** On a wreath of the colours, A lymphad proper, sail barry wavy of eight argent and azure charged with a sun in splendour Or, pennon and flags flying also azure. **Supporters:** On either side a dolphin Or, gorged with a naval crown with a rope pendent therefrom and reflexed over the back azure. **Motto:** Salum et carinae pignora vitae. **Badge:** A nautilus Or. **Granted** 10 February 1955.

NEATH, BOROUGH OF (GLAMORGAN). Per fesse Or and barry wavy azure and argent, on a mount vert in base point a tower double-towered gules between two lymphads issuant from the fesse line sable, flags and pennons per fesse of the third and vert, the sails also gules charged with a clarion gold. **Crest:** Out of a mural crown sable, a demi eagle displayed wings inverted Or, incensed proper and gorged with a collar of steel also proper, pendent therefrom an escutcheon argent charged with the astronomical sign for Mars also sable. **Supporters:** On either side a dragon gules gorged with an ancient crown Or, pendent therefrom an escutcheon, that on the dexter Or three chevronels gules, that on the sinister Quarterly argent and gules fretty Or a bendlet sable. **Motto:** Tu nidum servas. **Badge:** Upon an oval barry wavy of six argent and azure environed of a steel hawser proper and ensigned with an ancient crown Or, a tower as in the Arms. **Granted** 20 February 1961.

NEATH RURAL DISTRICT COUNCIL (GLAMORGAN).* Per pale Or and sable, a pale wavy paly wavy of four vert and argent between seven gouttés d'huile and as many gouttés d'Or; on a chief gules three clarions gold. **Crest:** Out of a circlet gules charged with three escallops Or, a mount vert, thereon a lamb passant proper unguled gold, gorged with a collar sable charged with three bezants, pendent therefrom a buglehorn stringed also sable, and supporting a staff Or, flying therefrom a banner also gules charged with three chevrons argent. **Motto:** Oni heuir ni fedir. **Granted** 1 June 1952.

NEEDLEMAKERS OF THE CITY OF LONDON, WORSHIPFUL COMPANY OF. Vert, three needles in fesse argent each ducally crowned Or. **Crest:** On a wreath of the colours, A Moor's head couped at the shoulders in profile proper, wreathed about the temples argent and gules, vested round the shoulder argent, in his ear a pearl also proper. **Supporters:** On the dexter side a man, and on the sinister side a woman, both proper, each wreathed round the waist with leaves of the last, in the woman's hand a needle argent. **Motto:** They sewed fig leaves together and made themselves aprons. These are of no authority.

NELSON, BOROUGH OF (LANCASHIRE).* Azure, on a chevron argent between two sprigs of the cotton tree slipped and fructed in chief and a fleece in base Or, two reed-hooks chevronwise proper. **Crest:** On a wreath of the colours, Upon a shuttle fessewise Or, a cock gules, holding in the beak a sprig of the cotton-tree slipped and fructed proper. **Motto:** By industry and integrity. **Granted** 5 May 1891.

NEW COLLEGE (OXFORD UNIVERSITY). Argent, two chevronels sable between three roses gules barbed and seeded proper. **Motto:** Manners makyth man. Recorded at the Visitation of 1574.

NEWARK-ON-TRENT, BOROUGH OF (NOTTINGHAMSHIRE). Barry wavy of six argent and azure, on a chief gules a peacock in his pride proper between a fleur-de-lis on the dexter and a lion passant guardant on the sinister Or. **Crest:** On a wreath argent and azure, A morsex argent beaked sable, holding in its beak an eel proper. Mantled gules, doubled argent. **Supporters:** On the dexter side an otter and on the sinister side a beaver, the latter langued gules. **Motto:** Deo fretus erumpe. **Granted** 8 December 1561. Although the tinctures of the supporters are not specified they are painted proper.

NEWBURY, BOROUGH OF (BERKSHIRE).* Gules, on a fesse argent between in chief a teazle flower between two garbs and in base as many swords in saltire, point upwards, Or, a bar wavy azure. **Crest:** On a wreath Or and azure, A castle of three towers domed gules, flying from the centre tower a forked pennant argent charged with a bar wavy azure, and from the exterior towers a flag also azure. **Motto:** Floruit, floreat. **Granted** 24 June 1948.

NEWCASTLE AND GATESHEAD BUILDING SOCIETY. Azure, a fesse wavy, in chief two crosses of St. Cuthbert and in base a triple-towered castle, all argent. **Crest:** On a wreath of the colours, On a mount vert an oak tree proper, pendent from the branches thereof a portcullis, the chain sable, all between two thrift flowers stalked and leaved proper. **Motto:** Service and security. **Granted** 20 December 1963.

NEWCASTLE REGIONAL HOSPITAL BOARD. Azure, a cross patonce Or between a dexter hand issuant downwards from clouds, a rod of Aesculapius erect argent, an antique lamp also argent enflamed proper, and a dove perched on a branch in the beak a sprig of olive likewise argent. **Crest:** On a wreath argent and azure, A castle triple-towered argent, issuant from the battlements thereof a demi lion guardant supporting with the paws a staff Or, flying therefrom a gonfannon azure charged with a winged bull statant also argent armed and unguled and the wings, and the cords and tassels of the gonfannon gold. **Motto:** Servare et sanare. **Granted** 20 March 1958.

NEWCASTLE-UNDER-LYME, BOROUGH OF (STAFFORDSHIRE).* Or, on a base barry wave of four argent and azure charged with three fishes naiant proper, a castle of three towers gules; on a chief also azure a lion passant guardant between two fleurs-de-lis of the first. **Crest:** On a wreath Or and gules, A demi lion queue fourchée argent charged on the shoulder with a Stafford knot gules and supporting a staff proper, flying therefrom a banner azure charged with three garbs Or. **Supporters:** On either side a lion guardant sable supporting a scythe proper. **Motto:** Prisca constantia. **Granted** 21 December 1951.

NEWCASTLE-UPON-TYNE, BISHOPRIC OF. Gules, a cross between four lions rampant Or; on a chief of the last three castles triple-towered of the first. **Granted** 29 September 1949.

NEWCASTLE-UPON-TYNE, CITY AND COUNTY BOROUGH OF (NORTHUMBERLAND).* Gules, three castles triple-towered argent. **Crest:** On a wreath of the colours, A castle as in the Arms, issuant therefrom a demi-lion guardant supporting a flagstaff Or, flying therefrom a forked pennon of the Arms of St. George. **Supporters:** On either side a sea horse proper, crined and finned Or. **Motto:** Fortiter defendit triumphans. Arms recorded and confirmed, Crest and Supporters granted 16 August 1575 by William Flower, Norroy King of Arms; Recorded at the Visitation of 1615; certified April 1954 by the Master of Sinclair, Bluemantle Pursuivant. Since in all these records there are variations in details we reproduce the official blazon of the latest certificate.

NEWCASTLE-UPON-TYNE, UNIVERSITY OF. Azure, a cross of St. Cuthbert argent; on a chief of the last a lion passant guardant gules. Granted to King's College, Newcastle-upon-Tyne, 28 January 1938; transferred by Royal Warrant 1 August 1963; exemplified 24 September 1963.

NEWCASTLE-UPON-TYNE INCORPORATED LAW SOCIETY. Per chevron sable and ermine, in chief two sea lions erect, the dexter contourné, Or supporting between them a sword, point upwards, argent; a bordure counterchanged. **Crest:** On a wreath ermine and sable, A dexter arm embowed vested sable, cuffed paly Or and gules, the hand proper grasping a scroll with two seals pendent therefrom also proper. Mantled sable, doubled argent. **Motto:** Justitiae fundamentum est fides. **Granted** 15 December 1960.

NEWCASTLE-UPON-TYNE ROYAL GRAMMAR SCHOOL. Gules, two horses' heads erased in chief and in base a tower triple-towered argent; on a chief of the second a torteau charged with a lion passant guardant Or between two hurts each charged with a fleur-de-lis gold. **Motto:** Discendo duces. **Granted** 11 November 1931.

NEWCASTLE URBAN DISTRICT COUNCIL (CO. DOWN). Vert, a pale wavy argent, thereon a pallet wavy azure surmounted of a castle triple-towered argent; on a chief dancetty Or between a trefoil and a harp vert a dexter hand appaumé couped at the wrist gules. **Crest:** On a

NEWCASTLE-UNDER-LYME

NELSON

NEWBURY

NEWCASTLE-UPON-TYNE

wreath of the colours, Between six bulrushes, three and three, leaved and fructed Or, a boar passant paly of six argent and azure, armed and unguled gules. **Granted** 1 September 1965.

NEW FOREST RURAL DISTRICT COUNCIL (HAMPSHIRE).* Ermine, a stag's head caboshed gules, between the antlers an arrow, point downwards, also gules surmounted by a stirrup sable; on a chief vert the head of an abbot's crosier between two crowns each consisting of four fleurs-de-lis affixed to a rim Or. **Crest:** On a wreath argent and gules, A lymphad Or flying flags and pennon of St. George, the sail sable charged with an acorn stalked, leaved and slipped gold and with a chief of the last thereon three gouttés d'huile. **Motto:** Old yet ever new. **Granted** 27 June 1955.

NEWHAM, LONDON BOROUGH OF.* Per fesse gules and Or, in chief a ship in full sail, flags flying, proper and two hammers in saltire Or, in base three chevronels gules; over all on a pale ermine a crozier Or. **Crest:** On a wreath of the colours, In front of a sword, point downwards, proper, hilt and pommel Or, and a crozier gold, in saltire, a sun rising proper. **Motto:** Progress with the people. **Granted** to the County Borough of West Ham 14 January 1887; transferred by Royal Warrant 1 January 1965; exemplified 20 May 1966.

NEW MALDON, BOROUGH OF (ESSEX). Per pale azure and argent, on the dexter side three lions passant reguardant in pale Or, and on the sinister on waves of the sea in base proper a ship of one mast sable, the mast ensigned by a fleur-de-lys gold and from the mast-head a pennon flying gules, the sail furled argent, at the stern a flagstaff erect ensigned by a like fleur-de-lys and flying therefrom a banner azure charged with three lions passant reguardant in pale Or. Confirmed 30 April 1562 by Sir Gilbert Dethick, Garter King of Arms; recorded at the Visitation of 1624.

NEWMARKET URBAN DISTRICT COUNCIL (WEST SUFFOLK). Vert, a horse courant argent; on a chief gules a lion rampant guardant between two Saxon crowns Or, therein as many arrows in saltire, points downwards, of the second. **Motto:** Respice finem. **Granted** 15 November 1951.

NEWNHAM COLLEGE (CAMBRIDGE UNIVERSITY).* Argent, on a chevron azure between in chief two crosses bottonée fitchée sable and in base a mullet sable, a griffin's head erased Or between two mascles of the field. **Granted** 27 February 1923.

NEWPORT, BOROUGH OF (ISLE OF WIGHT). Azure, on water barry wavy in base proper, an ancient ship Or, the sail argent, at the tip of the bowsprit and at right angles thereto a cross formy fitchy of the last. Recorded at the Visitation of 1622.

NEWPORT, COUNTY BOROUGH OF (MONMOUTHSHIRE). Or, a chevron reversed gules; the shield ensigned by a cherub proper. **Supporters:** On the dexter side a winged sea lion Or, and on the sinister side a sea dragon gules, the nether parts of both proper, finned gold. **Motto:** Terra marique. Arms granted 17 April 1929; Supporters granted 7 May 1958.

NEWPORT AND MONMOUTHSHIRE WATER BOARD. Argent gutty de larmes, a cherub proper, winged Or, and a chief nebuly azure. **Crest:** On a wreath argent and azure, A demi lion rampant Or with dragon's wings gules, holding between the paws a pitcher gold. **Motto:** Semper praebebimus. **Badge:** In front of an annulet Or, a cherub proper, the wings Or gutty de larmes. **Granted** 12 March 1962.

NEWPORT PAGNELL RURAL DISTRICT COUNCIL (BUCKINGHAMSHIRE).* Per fesse gules and sable, a bar wavy argent between in chief an oak tree, couped and fructed, and in base an eagle displayed, wings inverted, Or, in the flanks and over all two abbots' crosiers addorsed of the last. **Crest:** On a wreath of the colours, Out of a mural crown gules, a demi bull sable, armed, unguled and gorged with a torse of wheat Or, resting the sinister hoof on a Buckinghamshire lace-pillow proper. **Motto:** Fresh courage take. **Granted** 10 May 1957.

NEW FOREST

NEWHAM

NEWPORT PAGNELL R. D. C.

NEWPORT PAGNELL U. D. C.

NEWNHAM COLLEGE

NEWQUAY

NEWPORT PAGNELL URBAN DISTRICT COUNCIL (BUCKINGHAMSHIRE).* Or, two lions passant in pale, in base as many bars wavy azure; all within a bordure gyronny of eight gules and sable. **Crest:** On a wreath of the colours, Issuant from the battlements of a tower, a swan rising and supporting over the dexter shoulder a staff proper, flying therefrom a banner per pale gules and sable charged with a sword, point upwards, surmounted of two keys in saltire all gold. **Motto:** Praecepta non homines. **Granted** 17 May 1951.

NEWQUAY URBAN DISTRICT COUNCIL (CORNWALL).* Or, on a saltire azure four herrings respectant argent. **Crest:** On a wreath of the colours, Upon a block of granite ringed a bollard, perched thereon a Cornish chough, all proper. **Motto:** Ro an mor. **Granted** 4 June 1951.

NEW ROMNEY, BOROUGH OF (KENT). Azure, three lions passant guardant in pale Or. Recorded at the Visitation of 1619.

NEW TOWNS, COMMISSION FOR THE. Vert, a voided escutcheon argent, over all six towers Or in orle. **Crest:** Within a crown palisado Or a mount vert. **Supporters:** On the dexter side a beaver upon the stock of a tree, and on the sinister side a stag proper, attired and unguled Or. **Motto:** Semper aliquid novi. **Granted** 20 November 1963.

NEWTOWNABBEY URBAN DISTRICT COUNCIL (CO. ANTRIM). Or, on a bend wavy gules a Maltese cross between two towers argent. **Crest:** Out of a mural crown argent, a phoenix proper charged on the breast with a mullet of six points also argent. **Motto:** Septem in uno surgent. **Granted** 10 June 1958.

NEWTOWNARDS, BOROUGH OF (CO. DOWN). Per saltire argent and azure, in chief an eagle displayed gules, crowned Or, in fesse two fleurs-de-lys of the last, and in base a cross moline sable. **Crest:** On a wreath of the colours, Within and issuant from a crescent Or a dexter hand gules grasping a fleur-de-lys gold. **Supporters:** On the dexter side a unicorn and on the sinister side a lion Or, each supporting a pastoral staff sable. **Motto:** Fidelis etque fortis. **Granted** 29 August 1952.

NEW WINDSOR, ROYAL BOROUGH OF (BERKSHIRE). Per fesse argent and vert, a stag's head caboshed of the first, in chief between the attires sables an escutcheon of France Modern and England quarterly, in base a castle wall with three towers also argent, in the central tower a open port with portcullis raised Or. Arms entered (without tinctures) at the Visitation of 1532; Confirmed with tinctures at the Visitation of 1566; certified painting supplied by Richmond Herald in 1947.

NIDDERDALE RURAL DISTRICT COUNCIL (YORKSHIRE—WEST RIDING). Per chevron vert and Or, a chevronel wavy per chevron wavy argent and azure between in chief two garbs of the second and in base three arrows, one in pale and two in saltire, points downward, banded gules; on a chief of the last an apple slipped and leaved gold between two roses argent barbed and seeded proper. **Crest:** Out of a crown of rays of ancient Rome Or, a stag's head proper. Mantled vert, doubled Or. **Granted** 20 March 1959.

NORFOLK COUNTY COUNCIL.* Per pale Or and sable, a bend ermine; on a chief gules a lion passant guardant of the first between two ostrich plumes argent quilled each ensigned with a Prince's coronet of the first and transpiercing a label thereon the **Motto** 'Ich Dien' as borne on the banner of King Edward the Third. **Granted** by Royal Warrant 11 May 1904; exemplified 3 July 1904.

NORFOLK HERALD EXTRAORDINARY. See Arms, Officers of.

NORFOLK JOINT POLICE AUTHORITY. Gules, a castle proper, the portcullis raised Or and with three domes, flying from each a banner of St. George proper; on a chief bendy of six

NORFOLK

NORTHAMPTON CO. BOROUGH

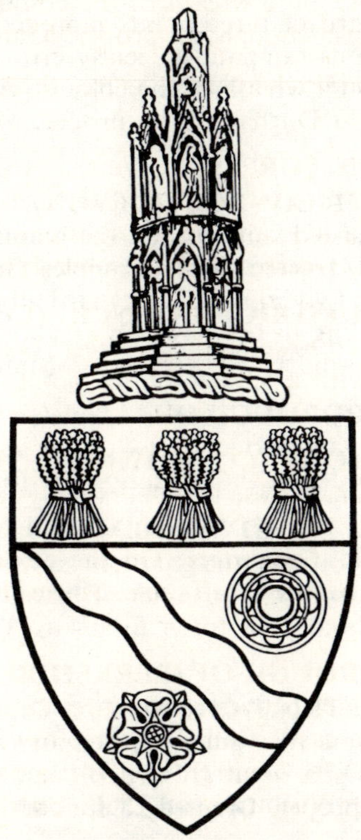

NORTHAMPTON R. D. C.

NORTHAM

NORTH COTSWOLD

Or, ermine and sable, a lion passant guardant Or dimidiated with a herring argent. **Motto:** E tribus unum. **Granted** 3 January 1968.

NORMANTON GRAMMAR SCHOOL. Paly of six Or and azure, a chief gules fimbriated gold. **Crest:** On a wreath of the colours, A demi Grey Friar affrontée proper charged on the breast with a trefoil slipped Or and clasping in the dexter hand a breviary also proper. **Motto:** Learn to be free. **Granted** 15 November 1960.

NORROY KING OF ARMS. See Arms, Officers of.

NORTHALLERTON URBAN DISTRICT COUNCIL (YORKSHIRE—NORTH RIDING). Per pale Or and azure, a standard of three points mounted on a car, the pole ensigned with a cross formy, all between two lions rampant anciently crowned, the dexter lion contournée, the whole counterchanged. **Crest:** On a wreath of the colours, A cushion gules, tasselled Or, charged with three roses argent, thereon a Durham mitre proper. **Motto:** For God and Crown. **Granted** 30 July 1957.

NORTHAM URBAN DISTRICT COUNCIL (DEVON).* Or, on a base of waves of the sea and pebbles, an ancient three-masted ship proper, the mainsail set argent charged with an apple tree couped above the root vert, fructed of seven apples Or, pennons flying silver each charged with a cross gules; on a chief vert two lions passant guardant gold. **Crest:** On a wreath Or and vert, A demi lion rampant gules holding in the paws an escallop argent, the lion between two wings addorsed ermine. **Motto:** Concordia vincit. **Granted** 5 March 1963.

NORTHAMPTON, COUNTY BOROUGH OF.* Gules, on a mount vert a tower triple-towered argent, the portcullis raised Or, supported by two lions rampant guardant of the last. **Motto:** Castello fortior concordia. Recorded at the Visitation of 1617.

NORTHAMPTON COLLEGE OF ADVANCED TECHNOLOGY (LONDON). Murrey, a chevron Or between in chief a lion passant guardant and in base a beacon fired, all Or. **Crest:** On a wreath of the colours, In front of a chaplet of laurel Or, a dexter hand couped below the wrist proper, habited murrey, holding a torch fired Or. **Motto:** Naturam ad usum tractamus. **Granted** 20 December 1962.

NORTHAMPTON RURAL DISTRICT COUNCIL.* Or, a bend wavy azure between in chief a roller-bearing proper and in base a rose gules, barbed and seeded also proper; on a chief of the second three garbs gold. **Crest:** On a wreath of the colours, A representation of the Northampton Queen Eleanor memorial cross proper. **Granted** 28 January 1952.

NORTHAMPTONSHIRE COUNTY COUNCIL. Argent, a rose gules, barbed and seeded proper; on a chief of the second a fetterlock Or between two roses of the first, barbed and seeded also proper. **Crest:** On a wreath of the colours, A falcon close argent gorged with a cord tied gules. **Supporters:** On the dexter side a hart argent gorged with an iron collar and chain reflexed over the back proper; on the sinister side a bull guardant sable gorged with a collar and line reflexed over the back Or. **Motto:** Rosa concordia signum. **Granted** 1 August 1939.

NORTH COTSWOLD RURAL DISTRICT COUNCIL (GLOUCESTERSHIRE).* Vert, a pallet argent, over all a fleece Or ringed and banded gules; on a chief enarched of the second two mitres also gules. **Crest:** Out of a coronet composed of four fleurs-de-lys set upon a rim Or, a swan rousant proper gorged with a ducal coronet, pendent therefrom an escutcheon gules charged with a sun gold. **Motto:** Montes excelsi refugio. **Granted** 9 September 1955.

NORTH EAST COAST INSTITUTION OF ENGINEERS AND SHIPBUILDERS. Azure, an ancient ship with sail set argent; on a chief of the second a tower triple-towered between two wheels of the first **Crest:** On a wreath of the colours, A sun in splendour Or encircled by a chain proper. **Motto:** By service, industry & honour. **Granted** 5 February 1934.

NORTHUMBERLAND

NORTH WALSHAM

NORTHWICH U. D. C.

NORWICH

NORTHWICH R. D. C.

NORTHERN ASSURANCE COMPANY LIMITED. Or, a lion rampant gules within a bordure sable charged with four roses of the second, barbed and seeded proper, and as many thistles slipped also proper alternately. **Crest:** Within a chaplet of eight roses gules, barbed and seeded proper, and as many thistles slipped also proper alternately linked gold, a lion rampant also gules. **Supporters:** On either side a unicorn argent, each collared Or, pendent therefrom an escutcheon, that on the dexter charged with the Arms of the City of London and that on the sinister with the Arms of the City of Aberdeen. **Granted** 5 September 1929.

NORTHERN BANK LIMITED (BELFAST). Vert, a gryphon statant, wings elevated, Or, in chief two bezants and in base a bell of the second. **Granted** 23 October 1947.

NORTHERN IRELAND FIRE AUTHORITY. Purpure, three tongues of flame issuing from the base; a chief of water barry wavy proper. **Crest:** On a wreath of the colours, A dexter arm embowed proper, the hand grasping a branchpipe Or. **Supporters:** On either side a hawk, wings addorsed and inverted Or, belled argent, charged on the breast with a dexter hand couped gules. **Motto:** Ardens in Ignis. **Granted** 15 May 1952.

NORTHERN ROCK BUILDING SOCIETY. Gules, issuant from water barry wavy proper a three-towered castle pierced at the base with two arches argent, all couped per chevron reversed in base; on a chief of the last a money balance between two pairs of compasses extended of the field. **Motto:** Aut maxima parati minimave. **Granted** 25 January 1951 to the Northern Counties' Building Society; transferred to the above by Royal Licence, exemplified 15 November 1965.

NORTH KESTEVEN RURAL DISTRICT COUNCIL (LINCOLNSHIRE—PARTS OF KESTEVEN). Vert, two bars wavy argent, over all an eagle displayed, wings inverted, Or; all within a bordure also argent charged with eight crosses couped gules. **Crest:** Out of a coronet composed of four ears of wheat and as many acorns leaved, set alternately upon a rim Or, clouds proper, thereon a lion statant guardant gules, between the forepaws a fleur-de-lys bendwise gules. **Motto:** Rectam viam sequi. **Granted** 25 November 1960.

NORTHLEACH RURAL DISTRICT COUNCIL (GLOUCESTERSHIRE). Azure, on a chevron between in chief two woolpacks and in base a garb Or, three mullets of six points gules. **Crest:** Out of a circlet vairy argent and gules, and in front of a demi double-headed eagle displayed sable charged on the breast with a long cross Or, in each beak an ostrich feather also gules, two spiked clubs in saltire gold. Mantled azure, doubled Or. **Motto:** Spirat in Deo. **Granted** 6 December 1960.

NORTH LONDON HOSPITAL. See University College Hospital.

NORTH RIDING OF YORKSHIRE COUNTY COUNCIL. See Yorkshire.

NORTH THAMES GAS BOARD. Or, issuing from a mount sable a burning bush proper; all within a bordure gules. **Supporters:** On either side a salamander gules, inflamed proper, charged on the shoulder with a pellet fimbriated Or, thereon a flame of fire also proper. **Motto:** Stet capitolium fulgens. **Badge:** A pellet fimbriated Or charged with a flame of fire proper. **Granted** 18 November 1949.

NORTHUMBERLAND COUNTY COUNCIL.* Paly of eight Or and gules, per fess embattled all counterchanged. **Crest:** On a wreath of the colours, In front of a castle proper thereon a lion passant tail extended azure, an escutcheon of the Arms. **Supporters:** On either side a lion Or, gorged with a collar paly gold and gules, supporting a staff proper, flying therefrom a banner of the Arms. On a scroll below the shield the word 'Northumberland'. **Granted** 4 December 1951.

NORTH WALSHAM URBAN DISTRICT COUNCIL (NORFOLK)*. Sable, a crosier between two ancient crowns Or; on a chief dancetty of the last a cross flory of the first between two garbs vert. **Crest:** On a wreath of the colours, In front of a sun in splendour Or a griffin sejant sable collared gules. **Motto:** Non nobis sed omnibus. **Granted** 19 December 1949.

NORTH WESTMORLAND RURAL DISTRICT COUNCIL. Per chevron, barry wavy vert and argent, and purpure, in base a castle of three towers of the second; on a chief Or between six annulets two and one, a pale sable, thereon an eagle displayed ermine. **Crest:** Out of a coronet composed of four wheat ears and as many acorns leaved, set alternately upon a rim Or, a stag's head gules. Mantled vert, doubled argent. **Motto:** Amoenitas et antiquitas. **Granted** 15 June 1959.

NORTHWICH RURAL DISTRICT COUNCIL (CHESHIRE).* Or, in front of an abbot's crozier erect issuant from the base azure, a stag's head caboshed gules; on a chief of the second three garbs gold. **Crest:** On a wreath of the colours, Upon a red sandstone rock proper, a wyvern sejant Or charged on the shoulder with a fountain and resting the dexter claw on a covered salt argent, garnished gold. **Motto:** Vale sape. **Granted** 11 December 1953.

NORTHWICH URBAN DISTRICT COUNCIL (CHESHIRE).* Azure, a pall wavy reversed argent between three garbs Or. **Crest:** On a wreath of the colours, An ancient three-masted ship, pennons flying Or, the mainsail azure charged with a wyvern sejant argent, the foresail gules charged with a mullet of six points gold and the mizzen sail also gules charged with a fountain. **Motto:** Sal est vita. **Badge:** An eagle displayed azure, ducally crowned gules, charged on the breast and wings with three garbs Or. **Granted** 10 September 1962.

NORTON URBAN DISTRICT COUNCIL (YORKSHIRE—EAST RIDING). Vert, an eagle displayed Or, beaked and membered gules, between in chief two roses argent, barbed and seeded proper, and in base a bezant; on a chief gold a ram's head caboshed between two boars' heads couped all sable, armed Or and langued gules. **Crest:** On a wreath of the colours, Upon a mount vert a horse courant sable, mounted thereon a jockey habited proper, the shirt green, the sash belt and cap ochre. Mantled vert, doubled Or. **Motto:** Providentia proficiemus. **Granted 20 September 1958.**

NORWICH, BISHOPRIC OF. Azure, three mitres, two and one, Or. Recorded in the College of Arms.

NORWICH, CITY AND COUNTY BOROUGH OF.* Gules, a castle triple-towered and domed argent; in base a lion passant guardant Or. Recorded and confirmed at the Visitation 2 July 1562.

NORWICH UNION FIRE INSURANCE SOCIETY LIMITED. Gules, a castle of three towers domed argent; on a chief barry wavy of six of the second and azure a pale also of the second charged with a sword erect of the field. **Crest:** On a wreath of the colours, A representation of Justice seated proper, habited azure, holding in her dexter hand a pair of scales Or and in her sinister hand a sword argent, pommel and hilt gold, the blade resting on her shoulder, and at her side a target also gold charged with two clasped hands issuant in bend proper cuffed also azure. **Supporters:** On the dexter side a lion azure and on the sinister side a salamander Or enflamed proper. **Motto:** Fide et fiducia. **Granted** 24 November 1947.

NORWICH UNION LIFE INSURANCE SOCIETY. Azure, two hands in union couped at the wrist proper within a serpent, the tail in the mouth, Or; on a chief embattled of the last an hour glass sable between two wings elevated of the field. **Crest:** On a wreath of the colours, On a serpent nowed, the head towards the sinister, a dove proper, from the mouth an escrol, thereon the words 'Prudens Simplicitas'. **Supporters:** On the dexter side a figure representing Atropos proper and on the sinister side a figure representing Time proper. **Motto:** Esto perpetua. Arms and Crest granted 9 February 1808 to the Amicable Society; regranted as above 14 April 1938.

NOTTINGHAM, CITY AND COUNTY BOROUGH OF.* Gules, issuant from the base, a ragged cross couped proper between two ducal coronets in chief Or, the lower limb of the cross enfiled with a like coronet. **Crest:** On a wreath of the colours, A castle walled triple-towered and capped proper, the dexter tower surmounted by a crescent argent and the sinister tower by an estoile Or. **Supporters:** On either side standing on a staff raguly erased, a royal stag guardant proper, ducally gorged Or. **Motto:** Vivit post funera virtus. **Badge:** A saltire raguly vert ensigned by a stag's head caboshed proper. **Standard:** Barry of six Or and argent, the bands gules edged gold inscribed sable; fringed gold and red. Arms recorded at the Visitation of 1614; Crest granted 10 June 1898; Supporters granted 3 November 1908 (to replace those granted 11 June 1898); Badge granted 7 November 1911.

NOTTINGHAM, UNIVERSITY OF.* Barry wavy of six argent and azure, a cross moline gules; on a chief of the last an open book proper clasped Or inscribed with the words 'Quaerenti Ostium' in Roman characters sable between two domed towers also proper, that to the dexter ensigned with an increscent of the first and that to the sinister with an estoile also Or. **Crest:** On a wreath of the colours, On a mount vert an oak tree proper, fructed Or, between two garbs resting against the trunk gold. **Motto:** Sapientia urbs conditur. **Granted** to the University College of Nottingham, 15 April 1948.

NOTTINGHAM AND DISTRICT TECHNICAL COLLEGE. Azure, a ragged cross of wood couped Or between in dexter chief a Tudor rose barbed and seeded proper [argent on gules] and in sinister base an acorn slipped gold. **Crest:** On a wreath of the colours, In front of a walled castle triple-towered, the towers surmounted with spires, proper, that on the dexter ensigned with an increscent argent, that on the sinister with an estoile Or, the castle charged with a Tudor rose, barbed and seeded also proper, a spade fessewise, blade to the dexter, likewise proper. **Supporters:** On the dexter side a stag guardant Or; on the sinister side a lion queue-fourchee sable. **Motto:** Dei auxilio faber est quisque fortunae suae. **Badge:** A torch enflamed proper surmounted of a shuttle fessewise also proper, the cotton azure. **Granted** 14 March 1956.

NOTTINGHAM HIGH SCHOOL. Ermine, a lozenge argent charged with three blackbirds rising proper; on a chief gules an open book also proper, garnished Or, between two ducal coronets of the last. **Crest:** On a wreath argent and gules, A squirrel sejant gules holding between the paws a ducal coronet Or. **Motto:** Lauda finem. **Granted** 22 March 1949.

NOTTINGHAMSHIRE COMBINED POLICE AUTHORITY. Quarterly vert and gules, issuant from the base a cross raguly couped quarterly counterchanged, fimbriated and in the first quarter an oak tree eradicated and in the second and third a ducal coronet Or. **Crest:** Out of a crown palisado azure, a garb Or between two towers with conical caps, the dexter surmounted of an increscent argent, the sinister of an estoile Or. Mantled azure, doubled argent. **Supporters:** On either side an Alsatian dog proper, each gorged with a torse argent and azure with line reflexed over the back azure. **Motto:** Salus populi nostra merces. **Granted** 2 December 1968.

NOTTINGHAMSHIRE COUNTY COUNCIL.* Vert, a fesse wavy per fesse wavy argent and azure, over all an oak tree fructed Or. **Crest:** Issuant from a mural crown, a garb Or charged with the blade of a miner's shovel sable. **Supporters:** On the dexter side a lion rampant queue fourchée sable gorged with a Saxon crown Or, and on the sinister side a greyhound argent gorged with a like crown with line reflexed over the back azure. **Motto:** Sapienter proficiens. **Granted** 19 July 1937.

NUFFIELD COLLEGE (OXFORD UNIVERSITY). Ermine, on a fesse Or between in chief two roses gules, barbed and seeded proper, and in base a balance of the second, three pears sable. **Crest:** On a wreath Or and gules, A demi bull gules, armed and unguled Or, resting the sinister hoof on a winged wheel gold. **Granted** by Royal Warrant 5 May 1958; exemplified 20 June 1958.

NUNEATON, BOROUGH OF (WARWICKSHIRE).* Per chevron argent and barry wavy of six azure and of the first, in chief two lozenges sable; on a chief gules a cinquefoil ermine between two fleurs-de-lys Or. **Crest:** On a wreath of the colours, Between two lozenges a bear's gamb erased sable enfiled by a mural crown Or and holding a cinquefoil slipped ermine. **Motto:** Prêt d'accomplir. **Granted** 21 April 1932.

NURSING, ROYAL COLLEGE OF. Azure, a sun in splendour and in chief three mullets Or. **Crest:** On a wreath of the colours, In front of an open book proper a Roman lamp Or nflamed also proper. **Granted** 18 September 1945.

NOTTINGHAMSHIRE C. C.

NOTTINGHAM UNIVERSITY

NUNEATON

NOTTINGHAM CITY

O

* *Denotes Illustration*

OADBY URBAN DISTRICT COUNCIL (LEICESTERSHIRE).* Gules, on a bend cotised flory counter-flory Or, a lion's gamb erased bendwise of the field, between two torteaux, that in chief charged with two keys in saltire, wards upwards and outwards, argent, and that in base with a pierced cinquefoil ermine. **Crest:** Out of a mural crown Or, a mount vert, thereon a lamb passant gorged with a collar of steel and resting the dexter forehoof upon a pelt, all proper. **Motto:** I pede fausto. **Granted** 6 December 1960.

OAKENGATES URBAN DISTRICT COUNCIL (SHROPSHIRE).* Or, an eagle displayed, wings inverted, azure grasping in the talons two abbots' crosiers sable; on a chief gules three acorns slipped and leaved gold. **Crest:** Out of a coronet composed of four laurel leaves set upon a rim Or, a demi wolf argent collared and lined gold and holding in the forepaws a tower sable, the battlements enflamed proper. **Motto:** Haec sunt nostra robora. **Granted** 15 September 1960.

OAKHAM RURAL DISTRICT COUNCIL (RUTLAND).* Vert semé of acorns and fretty Or; on a chief gules a pegasus courant argent between two horseshoes gold. **Crest:** On a wreath of the colours, Upon a rock Or a bull statant gules, armed and unguled gold. **Motto:** Parva componere magis. **Granted** 6 November 1958.

OBSTETRICIANS AND GYNAECOLOGISTS, ROYAL COLLEGE OF.* Per pale azure and sable, a mullet of eight points the lowest point extended towards the base argent. **Crest:** On a wreath of the colours, In front of a demi sun gules a crescent Or. **Supporters:** On the dexter side a woman, habited in a loose white robe with white sandals upon her feet, supporting in her exterior hand a staff vert ensigned with a crux ansata Or, and on the sister side a representation of Aesculapius proper, habited in a robe argent with white sandals upon his feet, holding in his interior hand a crescent argent and supporting with his exterior hand his staff Or. **Motto:** Super ardua. Arms and Crest granted 30 January 1931 to the British College of Obstetricians and Gynaecologists; Supportes granted 20 June 1950 to the Royal College of Obstetricians and Gynaecologists.

OFFICE MANAGEMENT, INSTITUTE OF. Or, on a pale sable between two flashes of lightning gules, three labels of three points Or; on a chief gules a pair of scales between a lymphad Or, sail set argent, pennon and flags flying Or, and an open book argent, edged and bound Or. **Crest:** On a wreath of the colours, Two cubit arms erect vested sable, cuffed argent, the hands proper holding a caduceus Or. **Supporters:** On the dexter side a stag lozengy Or and azure, attired Or, and on the sinister side a talbot, each supporting a quill pen argent. **Motto:** Non sibi sed toti. **Granted** 3 February 1966.

OLDHAM, COUNTY BOROUGH OF (LANCASHIRE).* Sable, a chevron invected plain cottised Or between three owls argent; on a chief engrailed of the second a rose gules, barbed and seeded proper, between two annulets also gules. **Crest:** On a wreath of the colours, In front of a rock thereon an owl argent, three roses fessewise gules, barbed and seeded proper. **Motto:** Sapere aude. **Granted** 7 November 1894.

OAKENGATES

OADBY

OAKHAM

OBSTETRICIANS AND GYNAECOLOGISTS

OPHTHALMOLOGICAL SOCIETY OF THE UNITED KINGDOM, THE. Sable, on an open book proper, edged and bound, an eagle rising Or; on a chief wavy gold a representation of the eye of Horus of the field. **Crest:** On a wreath Or and vert, in front of a demi archer habited vert, sleeved and belted gules, hooded sable, bow in full draught to the dexter proper, four escallops Or. **Supporters:** On the dexter side a figure representing Apollo proper holding in the exterior hand a lyre Or, and on the sinister side a representation of a Franciscan Friar holding in the exterior hand a magnifying glass also proper. **Motto:** Ad lucem. **Granted** 1 June 1965.

OPHTHALMOLOGISTS, FACULTY OF. Sable goutté-d'eau, a chief enarched nebuly gules, issuant from the base a pile Or. **Crest:** On a wreath Or, gules and sable, Issuing from a chaplet of thistle proper a demi figure representing St. Medana also proper, vested gules, mantled azure with garnishings Or, holding in the dexter hand a peg Or transfixing her two eyes proper, and resting the sinister hand on a fountain. **Supporters:** On either side a lynx guardant proper, crowned with a crown rayonée Or, each gorged with a chain, pendant from that of the dexter a staff of Aesculapius and from the sinister a fleam gold. **Granted** 20 September 1962.

ORAL SURGEONS, BRITISH ASSOCIATION OF. Sanguine, on a pale indented argent between an opinicus rampant contournée and an eagle, wings elevated and addorsed, Or, a rod of Aesculapius proper. **Crest:** On a wreath of the colours, Two fleams addorsed Or, interlaced in fesse of a serpent nowed vert. **Motto:** Scientia in unitate. **Granted** 30 June 1962.

ORIEL COLLEGE (OXFORD UNIVERSITY).* Gules, three lions passant guardant in pale Or; a bordure engrailed argent. Recorded at the Visitation of 1574.

ORIENTAL STUDIES, SCHOOL OF (LONDON UNIVERSITY). Argent, a cross gules, in the first quarter a sword in pale, point upwards, of the last; on a chief also gules an open book proper between a lotus bud on the dexter and a lotus slipped and leaved on the sinister, both Or. **Crest:** On a wreath of the colours, In front of a rising sun proper a lion passant guardant Or resting the dexter forepaw on a scroll also proper. **Supporters:** On the dexter side a camel, and on the sinister an elephant, both proper. **Motto:** Knowledge is Power. **Granted** by Royal Warrant 14 October 1917; exemplified 3 December 1918.

ORIENT STEAM NAVIGATION COMPANY LIMITED. Fusilly fesswise argent and azure; on a chief of the last a rising sun Or. **Crest:** Out of an Eastern crown Or, on waves of the sea a representation of the clipper ship 'Orient' proper. **Supporters:** On the dexter side a sea lion, and on the sinister side a kangaroo, both proper and gorged with an Eastern crown Or. **Motto:** Par non leonina societas. **Granted** 7 June 1957.

OSGOLDCROSS JOINT CREMATION BOARD. Quarterly, the first and fourth quarters barry wavy argent and azure, the second and third quarters sable, over all a cross Or, in the second quarter a rose argent, barbed and seeded proper, and in the third quarter a miner's lamp also proper; the whole within a bordure also argent. **Granted** 20 March 1959.

OSGOLDCROSS RURAL DISTRICT COUNCIL (YORKSHIRE—WEST RIDING).* Vert, a cross moline Or; a chief wavy argent, thereon on a pale sable between two lions' faces gules a ram's head couped also argent. **Crest:** On a wreath of the colours, In front of an oak tree proper, fructed Or, pendent from the branches an escutcheon Ermine charged with a saltire engrailed gules, three roses argent, barbed and seeded poper. **Motto:** Amor Angliae rusticae. **Granted** 30 March 1955.

OSWESTRY RURAL DISTRICT COUNCIL (SHROPSHIRE).* Per pale and per fesse indented argent and gules, two lions passant in pale counterchanged. **Crest:** On a wreath Or and azure, Out of the battlements of a tower gules a demi dragon Or gorged with a riband also gules, pendent therefrom a lozenge ermine charged with a saltire couped per pale argent and sable, and supporting a staff proper, flying therefrom a triangular pennon tierced in pale vert, argent and sable. Mantled

OLDHAM

OSGOLDCROSS

OSWESTRY

ORIEL COLLEGE

OTLEY

azure, doubled Or. **Motto:** Nec temere nec timide. **Granted** 1 August 1957.

OTLEY URBAN DISTRICT COUNCIL (YORKSHIRE—WEST RIDING).* Argent, on a pile azure, three towers, two and one, of the first; in the middle chief point two keys in saltire, wards upwards and inwards, Or. **Granted** 14 December 1951.

OXFORD, BISHOPRIC OF.* Sable, a fesse argent, in chief three demi ladies couped at the waist, heads affrontée, proper, [ducally] crowned Or, arrayed and veiled of the second; in base an ox also argent, horned and hoofed gold, passing a ford barry wavy of six argent and azure. Recorded in the College of Arms.

OXFORD, CITY AND COUNTY BOROUGH OF.* Argent, an ox gules, armed and unguled Or, passing over a ford of water in base barry wavy azure and argent; the shield encircled with a ribbon azure charged with a ribbon azure charged with four roses and four fleurs-de-lis alternately Or, the ribbon edged of the last. **Crest:** On a wreath of the colours, A demi lion rampant guardant Or, crowned with an Imperial Crown proper and semée of fleurs-de-lis azure, holding between the paws a rose gules charged with another argent. **Supporters:** On the dexter side an elephant ermines, eared argent, tusked Or, collared and lined Or; and on the sinister side a beaver vert, its tail barry wavy [= scaly] azure and argent, ducally gorged and lined Or. **Motto:** Fortis est veritas. Arms, Crest and Supporters recorded at the Visitation on 12 August 1634. The Crest differs from that granted with the Supporters in 1574.

OXFORD, DEAN AND CHAPTER OF THE CATHEDRAL CHURCH OF CHRIST. Quarterly azure and gules, on a cross argent between in the first and fourth quarters three fleurs-de-lis, two and one, and in the second and third quarters as many lions passant guardant in pale, all Or, an open book as in the Arms of the University of Oxford, the book ensigned of the Royal Crown proper. Recorded at the Visitation of 1574.

OXFORD, UNIVERSITY OF.* Azure, an open book proper, edged and garnished Or, leathered gules, pendent from the dexter side thereof seven seals gold, the pages inscribed 'In principio erat verbum et verbum erat apud Deum', the whole between three open crowns also gold. Recorded at the Visitation of 1574. The inscription of the book has varied from time to time; it currently reads 'Dominus illuminatio mea'.

OXFORDSHIRE COUNTY COUNCIL.* Azure, two bendlets wavy argent, between in chief a garb and in base an oak tree eradicated and fructed Or, in the fess point an ox's head caboshed gules. **Crest:** Issuing from a mural coronet gules, a mount vert, thereon a representation of St. George's Tower, Oxford Castle, proper. **Supporters:** On either side an Oxford Down ram proper gorged with a collar azure, thereon a bar wavy argent. **Motto:** Sapere aude. **Granted** 5 May 1949.

OXFORD CITY

OXFORD BISHOPRIC

OXFORD UNIVERSITY

OXFORDSHIRE C. C.

P

* *Denotes Illustration*

PACIFIC STEAM NAVIGATION COMPANY. Argent, on a cross azure between four anchors gules, a naval crown Or. **Crest:** On a wreath of the colours, A branch of coral gules. **Supporters:** On either side a dolphin azure gutty d'Or finned gold. **Motto:** Tranquillus et constans. **Badge:** Within a scroll ensigned with a naval crown Or and charged with the motto Tranquillus et constans in letters sable, a flag of the Arms flying from a staff gold. **Granted** 1957.

PAINTER-STAINERS OF THE CITY OF LONDON, WORSHIPFUL COMPANY OF.* Quarterly first and fourth azure, three escutcheons, two and one, argent; second and third, azure a chevron between three phoenix heads erased Or beaked gules. **Crest:** On a wreath Or and gules, a phoenix proper. Mantled azure, doubled ermine. **Supporters:** On either side a panther argent spotted with various colours, ducally crowned, collared and chained Or. **Motto:** Amor queat obedientiam. Recorded at the Visitation of 1634. The original Arms (which consisted of the second and third quarters above) and the Crest were granted 1486 by Sir Thomas Holme, Clarenceux King of Arms; recorded at the Visitation of 1568; confirmed 6 October 1530 by Thomas Benolt, Clarenceux King of Arms. (*Illustration on page* 305).

PARISH CLERKS OF THE CITY OF LONDON, WORSHIPFUL COMPANY OF.* Azure, a fleur-de-lys Or; on a chief gules a leopard's face Or between two prick-song books of the same, laced vert. **Crest:** On a wreath gules and azure, A cubit arm vested azure, cuffed ermine, holding an open prick song book, all proper. Mantled gules and azure, doubled ermine on the dexter and Or on the sinister. **Motto:** Unitas securitatis stabilitas. **Granted** 30 March 1582 by Robert Cooke, Clarenceux King of Arms, in place of an earlier coat granted 1469 or 1470 by Walter Bellinger, Ireland King of Arms, regranted 16 July 1482 by Thomas Holme, Clarenceux King of Arms, and confirmed 1530 by Thomas Benolt, Clarenceux King of Arms. (*Illustration on page* 305).

PARK ADMINISTRATION (INCORPORATED), INSTITUTE OF. Vert, on a cross argent cantoning two acorns in bend and as many roses in bend sinister Or, a fountain proper. **Crest:** On a wreath Or and vert, A dexter cubit arm proper grasping a winged torch Or enflamed also proper. **Motto:** Curamus quod populo servit. **Granted** 5 August 1958.

PATHOLOGISTS, COLLEGE OF. Sable, surmounting an open book a rod of Aesculapius proper, the serpent Or; on a chief argent a bar wavy gules between in chief two torteaux and in base a benzene ring sable. **Crest:** On a wreath of the colours, In front of a sprig of logwood leaved and fructed proper, an antique microscope proper. **Motto:** Sedes invenire et causas morborum. **Granted** 1 July 1964.

PATTENMAKERS OF THE CITY OF LONDON, WORSHIPFUL COMPANY OF. Gules, on a chevron argent between three pattens Or tied of the second, the ties lined azure, two cutting knives conjoined sable. **Crest:** On a wreath of the colours, A patten as in the Arms. **Motto:** Recipiunt foeminae sustentacula nobis. These are of no authority.

PEMBROKE BOROUGH

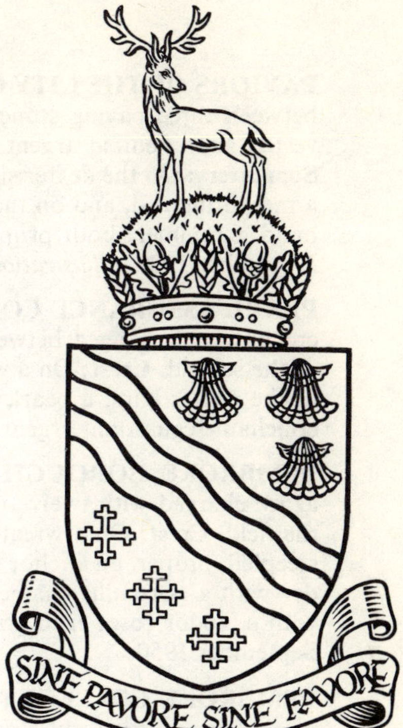

PENRITH R. D. C.

PEMBROKE COLLEGE
(CAMBRIDGE UNIVERSITY)

PEMBROKE COLLEGE
(OXFORD UNIVERSITY)

PEMBROKESHIRE

PAVIORS OF THE CITY OF LONDON, WORSHIPFUL COMPANY OF.* Argent, a chevron between three paving stones sable. **Crest:** On a wreath of the colours, A dexter arm embowed vested azure, cuffed argent, the hand grasping a pavior's pick, the handle fessewise, all proper. **Supporters:** On the dexter side a master pavior of the reign of Edward I resting the dexter hand on a measuring rod, and on the sinister side a pavior of the reign of Edward I holding in the sinister hand a rammer, both proper. **Motto:** God can raise to Abraham children of stone. **Granted** 4 November 1929. (*Illustration on page* 305).

PEARL ASSURANCE COMPANY LIMITED. Argent, a saltire gules surmounted by a sword erect counterchanged between a covered cup and a hind lodged pierced with an arrow in fesse of the second. **Crest:** On a wreath of the colours, A figure representing St. Margaret, vested gules, in the dexter hand a pearl, and in the sinister a palm branch, both proper, at her feet a dragon couchant reguardant argent. **Motto:** Damus plus quam pollicemur. **Granted** 30 November 1911.

PEMBROKE, BOROUGH OF.* Or, six chevronels gules within a bordure quarterly argent and azure charged with twelve martlets, those on the argent of the second and those on the azure of the field. **Crest:** On a wreath of the colours, In front of a castle with three towers, the outer two steepled, proper, an anchor sable. **Supporters:** On the dexter side a lion gules charged on the shoulder with a portcullis chained Or, and on the sinister side a lion argent charged on the shoulder with a Tudor rose; each gorged with a naval crown gold. **Motto:** Ung nous servons. **Granted** 12 September 1950.

PEMBROKE COLLEGE (CAMBRIDGE UNIVERSITY).* Barry of ten argent and azure, an orle of five martlets gules dimidiated with paly vair and gules, on a chief Or a label of five points throughout azure. Recorded at the Visitation of 1684.

PEMBROKE COLLEGE (OXFORD UNIVERSITY).* Per pale azure and gules, three lions rampant, two and one, argent; a chief per pale Or and argent, thereon on the dexter a rose of the second, barbed and seeded proper, and on the sinister a thistle also proper. **Granted** 1625 by St. George, Clarenceux King of Arms.

PEMBROKESHIRE COUNTY COUNCIL.* Quarterly, first and fourth per fesse gules and Or in chief a lion passant and in base two fleurs-de-lys counterchanged, second and third argent two bars gules; the whole surmounted by a cross sable and within a bordure argent charged with eight martlets and as many ermine spots sable alternately. **Crest:** Issuant from a mural crown Or, a rock proper, thereon an eagle, wings elevated and addorsed gold. **Supporters:** On the dexter side a lion Or gorged with a collar and charged on the shoulder with a fleur-de-lys gules, and on the sinister side a dragon gules gorged with a collar and charged on the shoulder with a fleur-de-lys Or. **Motto:** Ex unitate vires. **Granted** 11 October 1937.

PENINSULAR AND ORIENT STEAM NAVIGATION COMPANY. Per saltire argent, azure, gules and Or, in chief a lion statant gules, in fess a kangaroo erect proper and an elephant statant, on his back a castle Or, and in base a Chinese dragon azure. **Crest:** On a wreath argent and azure, Issuant from waves of the sea a sun in splendour Or. **Motto:** Quis nos separabit. **Granted** 16 June 1937.

THE PENNINE INSURANCE COMPANY LIMITED (HALIFAX). Per pale argent and gules, a chain palewise Or between two roses counterchanged, barbed and seeded proper. **Crest:** On a wreath of the colours, On a mount vert a Paschal Lamb proper in front of a beacon sable enflamed proper. **Supporters:** On each side a lion guardant Or resting the exterior forepaw on an anchor azure. **Motto:** Progressio et alacritas. **Granted** 30 June 1955.

PENRITH RURAL DISTRICT COUNCIL (CUMBERLAND).* Gules, on a bend wavy between three escallops shells and as many cross-crosslets fitchy argent, a bendlet wavy azure. **Crest:** Out of a coronet composed of four ears of wheat and as many acorns leaved set alternately upon a

PENRITH U. D. C.

PENYBONT

PERSHORE

ERFORMING RIGHT SOCIETY

PENZANCE

rim Or, a mount vert, thereon a stag reguardant gules, attired and unguled Or. Mantled azure, doubled argent. **Motto:** Sine pavore, sine favore. **Granted** 10 November 1961.

PENRITH URBAN DISTRICT COUNCIL (CUMBERLAND).* Per chevron azure and gules, issuant from the point of the chevron rays of the sun between two sheaves of corn Or, and in base a triple-towered castle gold. **Crest:** On a wreath of the colours, A saltire argent fimbriated azure enfiled by an ancient crown Or. **Motto:** Fide et fortitudine. **Granted** 28 February 1952.

PENYBONT RURAL DISTRICT COUNCIL (GLAMORGAN).* Gules, two abbots' croziers in saltire between in chief an anchor, in base a castle of three towers, and in fesse two clarions, the sinister contournée, all Or. **Crest:** On a wreath argent and vert, Issuant from a circlet of eight lozenges sable a limestone rock proper, thereon a dragon statant gules gorged with a collar of steel, attached thereto a chain of the same reflexed over the back also proper. **Motto:** Diwydiant ein cadernid. **Granted** 9 November 1960.

PENZANCE, BOROUGH OF (CORNWALL).* Argent, a Paschal Lamb proper, in base a Maltese cross azure; on a chief embattled of the last, between two keys in saltire, wards upwards, Or and a saltire couped argent, a plate charged with a dagger, point downwards, gules. **Crest:** Within a mural crown Or, an ancient ship with three masts in full sail, sinking by the stern and with guns firing, all proper. **Supporters:** On the dexter side a pirate holding in the exterior hand a cutlass, and on the sinister side a fisherman holding over his exterior arm a net, all proper. **Motto:** Quod improbum terret probo prodest. **Granted** 12 June 1934.

PERFORMING RIGHT SOCIETY LIMITED.* Per fesse embattled argent and azure, in chief five barrulets surmounted to the dexter by an Alto Clef sable; over all a dexter hand proper, the cuff erased Or, holding a baton erect also proper. **Crest:** On a wreath of the colours, Issuant from a wreath of laurel a swan rousant proper collared Or. **Granted** 14 July 1947.

PERSHORE RURAL DISTRICT COUNCIL (WORCESTERSHIRE).* Sable, on a chevron between in chief two plumes and in base a garb Or, three holly leaves vert; a base barry wavy argent and azure. **Crest:** Out of a coronet composed of four ears of wheat and as many acorns leaved set alternately upon a rim Or, a pear tree fructed proper. **Motto:** Progredi et conservare. **Granted** 20 June 1962.

PETERBOROUGH, BISHOPRIC OF.* Gules, two keys in saltire, the wards upwards, between four cross crosslets fitchée Or. Recorded in the College of Arms.

PETERBOROUGH, CITY OF (HUNTINGDONSHIRE).* Azure, two keys in saltire Or, enfiled by a mural crown argent; the shield ensigned with a mural crown of six towers gold. **Supporters:** On each side a lion ermine, winged argent, charged on the wing with three estoiles sable, the interior paw resting on a tree-trunk fessewise proper. **Motto:** Upon this rock. **Granted** 6 September 1960.

PETERHOUSE (CAMBRIDGE UNIVERSITY).* Or, four pallets gules; on a bordure of the last eight open crowns of the first. **Granted** 1575 by Robert Cooke, Clarenceux King of Arms.

PETERLEE DEVELOPMENT CORPORATION (CO. DURHAM).* Argent, a lion rampant azure; on a chief embattled gules three popinjays of the field. **Crest:** On a wreath argent and gules, Issuant from the battlements of a tower argent, masonry and coping sable, a staff ensigned with a cross formy quadrate Or, flying from the staff a banner azure, the socket gules, the banner charged with a cross patonce gold between four lions rampant argent. **Supporters:** On the dexter side the figure of a bishop habited in robes and mitre proper, holding in the exterior hand a pastoral staff Or, and on the sinister side the figure of a miner habited proper, holding in the exterior hand a miner's safety lamp and a pick resting on the sinister shoulder, all proper. **Motto:** Viam inveniam aut faciam. **Granted** 12 April 1955.

PETERLEE

PETERBOROUGH BISHOPRIC

ROYAL COLLEGE OF PHYSICIANS

PETERBOROUGH

PETERHOUSE

PETROLEUM, INSTITUTE OF. Or, an archaeopteryx displayed gules. **Granted** 4 July 1949.

PEWTERERS OF THE CITY OF LONDON, WORSHIPFUL COMPANY OF.* Azure, on a chevron Or between three strikes argent as many roses gules, stalked, budded and leaved vert. **Crest:** On a wreath of the colours, A mount vert, thereon two arms embowed vested argent, the hands proper grasping a pewter dish also argent. Mantled gules, doubled argent. **Supporters:** On either side a sea horse Or, tailed proper. Arms granted 26 May 1533 by Thomas Benolt, Clarenceux King of Arms to replace an earlier grant (13 August 1451) by Roger Leigh, Clarenceux; Crest and Supporters granted 1573 by Robert Cooke, Clarenceux King of Arms.

PHARMACEUTICAL SOCIETY OF GREAT BRITAIN. Or, on a cross gules between a dove holding in the mouth an olive branch in the first quarter, an aloe in the second, a staff erect entwined by a serpent in the third, and an alembic and receiver in the fourth, all proper, a pair of scales of the first; on a chief azure a stag lodged also of the first. **Crest:** On a wreath of the colours, A mortar, therein a pestle Or. **Supporters:** On the dexter side a figure intended to represent Avicenna, habited in a dark red robe with a white under vest, his shoes red, around his waist a shawl also red fringed gold, and upon his head a white turban, in his right hand a staff gold entwined with a serpent proper; and on the sinister side a figure intended to represent Galen, habited in a long white vest and loose robe, his sandals red, and holding in his right hand a steelyard Or. **Motto:** Habenda ratio valetudinis. Arms and Crest granted 14 March 1844; Supporters granted 27 March 1844.

PHARMACY, SCHOOL OF (LONDON UNIVERSITY). Argent, on a bend azure between two mortars, in each a pestle proper, a rod of Aesculapius Or; on a chief of the second a Tudor rose radiated between two open books also proper, edge and clasped gold. **Crest:** On a wreath of the colours, In front of a foxglove leaved and flowered, two poppy boles stalked and leaved in saltire, all proper. **Motto:** Salutifer Orbi. **Granted** 3 March 1950.

PHOENIX ASSURANCE COMPANY LIMITED. Azure, upon a billet fessewise Or inscribed 1782 in numerals sable, a phoenix proper. **Granted** 9 November 1936.

PHYSICIANS, ROYAL COLLEGE OF.* Sable, a hand proper, vested argent, issuing out of clouds in chief of the second rayonné Or, feeling the pulse of an arm proper issuing from the sinister side of the shield, vested argent, in base a pomegranate Or, between five demi fleurs-de-lis bordering the edge of the escutcheon of the last. Recorded in the College of Arms.

PICKERING URBAN DISTRICT COUNCIL (YORKSHIRE—NORTH RIDING).* Per fess wavy argent and barry wavy azure and argent; above a castle an ancient crown gules; on a chief of the last three roses argent barbed and seeded proper. **Crest:** On a wreath argent and gules, A pike fessewise argent, in the mouth an annulet Or. **Motto:** Ever loyal. **Granted** 15 September 1961.

PLANT ENGINEERS, THE INSTITUTION OF. Or, two barrulets between three wheels gules; a bordure per pale argent and vert, guttée counterchanged. **Crest:** On a wreath of the colours, In front of a demi sun Or dexter cubit arm, vested sable cuffed argent, the hand proper holding a pair of dividers extended and inverted gold. **Supporters:** On either side a Lynx proper gorged with a chain Or, pendant therefrom an escutcheon sable, that on the dexter charged with a pair of dividers extended gold and that on the sinister with an open book also proper edged and bound also gold. **Motto:** Instruendo, Praestando, Experiendo. **Granted** 20 July, 1959.

PLASTERERS OF THE CITY OF LONDON, WORSHIPFUL COMPANY OF.* Azure, on a chevron argent a rose gules budded Or, stalked and leaved vert, between two fleurs-de-lys azure, in chief a trowel fessewise between two plasterers' hammers palewise, all argent handled Or, and in base a plasterer's brush of four knots tied argent handled Or. **Crest:** On a wreath argent and azure, An arm vested bendy of four gules and Or, holding in the hand proper a plasterer's hammer as in the Arms. Mantled gules, doubled argent. **Supporters:** On either side an opinicus vert, winged, membered and eyed gules, the throat and belly purfled Or. **Motto:** Let brotherly love continue. **Granted** 20 January 1546; modern copy entered in the records at the instance of Charles George Young, York Herald. (*Illustration on page* 307).

PLYMOUTH

POCKLINGTON

PICKERING

PLYMOUTH COLLEGE

PONTEFRACT

PLASTIC SURGEONS, BRITISH ASSOCIATION OF. Gules, the branch of an apple tree, couped and leaved, proper, fructed Or, with a slip of apple tree leaved also proper grafted to the top, in dexter chief a dagger in bend, point upwards, gold, around the hilt and handle a thread loosely tied argent. **Crest:** On a wreath of the colours, Upon a rock a lizard proper. **Supporters:** On the dexter side a figure representing Podalirius habited in a robe argent, resting his exterior hand on a staff Or entwined by a serpent, and on the sinister side a figure representing Machaon habited as the dexter, holding in his exterior hand a dart broken, the point downwards, gold, around the neck of each figure a garland of flowers of the British Empire. **Motto:** Manu sciente. **Badge:** A dagger, point upwards, proper, hilt and pommel Or, around the hilt and handle a thread loosely tied sable. **Granted** 27 April 1950.

PLAYING CARD MAKERS OF THE CITY OF LONDON, WORSHIPFUL COMPANY OF. Gules, on a cross argent between four ace cards proper, videlicet those of hearts and diamonds in chief and those of clubs and spades in base, a lion passant guardant of the first. **Crest:** On a wreath of the colours, On arm in armour erect, holding in the hand an ace of hearts, all proper. **Supporters:** On either side a man in complete armour proper garnished Or, on each a sash gules. These are of no authority.

PLUMBERS OF THE CITY OF LONDON, WORSHIPFUL COMPANY OF.* Or, on a chevron sable between in chief a Jacob's staff of the second between two sounding leads proper, and in base a water level also sable, two soldering irons in saltire between on the dexter a cutting knife and on the sinister a shavehook argent. **Crest:** On a wreath Or and sable, a fountain argent, garnished and on the top thereof an archangel holding a sword and a balance Or. Mantled sable, doubled argent. **Motto** (Over the arms): Justicia et Pax; (below the arms) In God is all our hope. **Badge:** On a pellet a fountain argent garnished Or surmounted by a representation of the Archangel Michael holding in the dexter hand a sword and in the sinister hand a balance Or between two sounding leads proper. Arms and Crest granted 24 November 1588 by Robert Cooke, Clarenceux King of Arms; Badge granted 9 February 1925. (*Illustration on page* 307).

PLYMOUTH, CITY AND COUNTY BOROUGH OF (DEVON).* Argent, a saltire vert between four towers sable. **Crest:** Issuant from a naval crown azure, a lion's gamb erect Or grasping an anchor fessewise gules. **Supporters:** On either side a lion reguardant Or gorged with a naval crown azure, pendent therefrom by a riband gules a torteau charged with a boar's head couped argent. **Motto:** Turris fortissima est nomen Jehova. Arms recorded at the Visitation of 17 October 1620; Crest and Supporters granted 4 May 1931.

PLYMOUTH COLLEGE AND MANAMEAD SCHOOL.* Argent, a cross vert between four towers sable; a chief per pale, the dexter piece per pale gules and sable a castle of three towers argent, the sinister piece sable six bezants three two and one. **Motto:** Dat Deus incrementum. **Granted** 24 September 1956.

POCKLINGTON RURAL DISTRICT COUNCIL (YORKSHIRE—EAST RIDING).* Argent, on a cross vert an abbot's crosier in pale of the first between two mitres in fesse Or, over all two swords in saltire proper, embrued gules, hilts and pommels gold; on a chief sable a rose of the first, barbed and seeded proper, between two garbs also gold. **Crest:** On a wreath of the colours, A demi stag argent attired and unguled Or gorged with a collar company gold and azure and supporting with the sinister foreleg an escutcheon sable, thereon a griffin's head erased of the first. **Motto:** Sic nos non nobis laboramus. **Granted** 25 February 1958.

PONTEFRACT, BOROUGH OF (YORKSHIRE—WEST RIDING).* Per fesse wavy sable and barruly wavy argent and azure, a quadrangular castle in perspective only three of the four towers being visible, on the dome of each tower argent a flagstaff proper, flying therefrom to the sinister a banner gules. **Motto:** Post mortem patris pro filio. Recorded as a seal device (untinctured) at the Visitation of 1584.

THE PAINTERSTAINERS

THE CLARKS

THE PAVIORS

THE PEWTERERS

POOLE, BOROUGH OF (DORSET).* Barry wavy of eight sable and Or, a dolphin naiant embowed argent, langued gules; on a chief wavy of the third three escallops of the first. **Crest:** On a wreath of the colours, A mermaid proper supporting with her dexter hand an anchor cabled, without a beam, proper, and in her sinister hand a pellet. **Motto:** Ad morem villae de Poole. Arms recorded (without tinctures and with variations) at the Visitations of 1563 and 1623; Arms confirmed and Crest granted 19 June 1948.

PORTADOWN COLLEGE.* Argent, in chief between two lions rampant per fess gules and azure an ancient lamp of the last enflamed gules, and in base a like lion between two lozenges also gules. **Crest:** On a wreath of the colours, In front of a griffin's head argent, beaked gules, between two wings silver, three lozenges also gules. **Motto:** Fortiter et humaniter. **Granted** 12 March 1962.

PORTCULLIS PURSUIVANT. See Arms, Officers of.

PORTHCAWL URBAN DISTRICT COUNCIL (GLAMORGAN).* Per pale azure and gules, on a chevron wavy between in chief two eagles displayed and in base a lion rampant argent, a chevron wavy azure. **Crest:** On a wreath of the colours, Two dragons' legs embowed gules supporting an anchor erect Or fouled sable. **Motto:** Arf doeth yw pwyll. **Badge:** A fouled anchor azure enfiled with a circlet of ten escallops conjoined Or. **Granted** 1 March 1965.

PORTMAN BUILDING SOCIETY. Argent, on a pale sable between a thrift plant with two flowers and a sprig of oak slipped leaved and fructed proper, five bezants; on a chief azure a key wards to the dexter and downward, Or. **Crest:** On a wreath of the colours, A port between two towers, the portcullis raised, proper, astride the battlements an owl Or. **Supporters:** On either side a talbot argent, collared azure, charged on the shoulder with a fleur-de-lis and in the mouth a quill also Or. **Motto:** Securior quo paratior. **Granted** 5 February 1964.

PORT OF LONDON AUTHORITY. Azure, issuing from a castle argent a demi man vested, holding in the dexter hand a drawn sword and in the sinister a scroll Or, the one representing the Tower of London, the other the figure of St. Paul the patron saint of London. **Crest:** On a wreath of the colours, An ancient ship Or, the mainsail charged with the Arms of the City of London. **Supporters:** On either side a sea lion argent, crined, finned and tufted Or, issuing from waves of the sea proper, that to the dexter grasping the banner of King Edward the Second, that to the sinister the banner of King Edward the Seventh. **Motto:** Floreat Imperii Portus. **Badge:** A sea lion grasping a trident Or. **Standard:** Gules, the bands argent inscribed sable; fringed argent and azure. **Granted** by Royal Warrant 12 July 1909; Arms and Crest exemplified 23 August 1909; Supporters exemplified 26 August 1909; Badge granted 30 August 1909.

PORTORA ROYAL SCHOOL.* Or, on a fesse sable between in chief an open book proper, edged gules, bound and inscribed with the Roman numerals MDCVIII of the second, and in base a castle also proper, flying therefrom a banner of St. George, a harp between two fleurs-de-lys Or. **Crest:** On a wreath of the colours, A stag trippant proper, collared with a chain reflexed over the back Or, supporting with the dexter foreleg a staff of the last, flying therefrom a banner sable charged with a mural crown gold. **Granted** 2 February 1954.

PORTSMOUTH, BISHOPRIC OF.* Per fesse Or and gules, in chief upon waves of the sea proper a lymphad sable, and in base two keys conjoined, wards outwards, in bend, the uppermost Or, the other argent, a sword interposed between them in bend sinister argent, pommel and hilt Or. **Granted** 25 July 1927.

PORTSMOUTH, CITY AND COUNTY BOROUGH OF (HAMPSHIRE).* Azure, a crescent Or ensigned by an estoile of eight points of the last. **Motto:** Heaven's light our guide. Recorded at the Visitation of 1686.

THE POVLTERS

THE PLAISTERERS

THE PLVMMERS

PORTSMOUTH GRAMMAR SCHOOL. Per fesse gules and sable, in chief a lion couchant and in base two Cornish choughs and a crescent, therein between the horns an estoile of eight points, all Or. **Crest:** On a wreath of the colours, A horse's head per fesse gules and sable, charged in base with a sun in splendour Or. **Motto:** Praemia virtutis honores. **Granted** 20 March 1957.

PORT TALBOT, BOROUGH OF (GLAMORGAN).* Gules, three chevronels argent between as many clarion Or. **Crest:** On a wreath of the colours, Issuant from a clarion Or, a plume of ostrich feathers, gules, gold and vert. **Motto:** Duwiolldeb diwyrdwydd. **Granted** 11 June 1953.

POULTERS OF THE CITY OF LONDON, WORSHIPFUL COMPANY OF.* Argent, on a chevron azure between three (?cranes) proper as many swans of the first. **Crest:** On a mural crown gules a (?crane) rising proper. Mantled gules, doubled argent. **Supporters:** On either side a pelican, wings displayed and addorsed, Or vulning itself gules. **Motto:** Remember your oath. **Granted** 1634 by Sir Richard St. George, Clarenceux King of Arms. (*Illustration on page* 307).

POULTON-LE-FYLDE URBAN DISTRICT COUNCIL (LANCASHIRE).* Azure, on water barry wavy proper a lymphad, sail furled, Or, flags argent charged with a cross gules; on a chief of the second a rose of the fourth, barbed and seeded proper, between two crosses formy also of the fourth. **Crest:** On a wreath of the colours, A representation of Poulton-le-Fylde Market Cross and Stocks proper. **Motto:** Sub cruce floreamus. **Granted** 3 November 1950.

POULTRY ASSOCIATION OF GREAT BRITAIN (SPBA) LTD. Vert, on a cross engrailed argent between in the first and fourth quarters a chick and in the second and third quarters an egg Or, a cross throughout gules, thereon an ear of wheat, slipped and leaved, of the third. **Crest:** On a wreath of the colours, In front of seven game-cocks' feathers, three in bend, one erect and three in bend sinister, a cock's head couped, all proper. **Motto:** Ever vigilant. **Granted** 4 November 1948.

PREESALL URBAN DISTRICT COUNCIL (LANCASHIRE).* Azure, on a chevron between in chief two griffins' heads erased and in base a martlet Or, a rose gules, barbed and seeded proper, between two fountains. **Crest:** On a wreath of the colours, An ancient galley, sails furled, Or, with pennons of St. George, and pendent from the mast-head by a knot azure a cross-bow gules. **Motto:** Prae salutem notanda. **Granted** 2 June 1950.

PREPARATORY SCHOOLS, INCORPORATED ASSOCIATION OF. Quarterly azure and gules, over all a breastplate of the last, garnished Or, encircled by a girdle gold. **Crest:** On a wreath argent, gules and azure, A dexter hand couped at the wrist proper grasping a sword erect argent, hilt and pomel Or, the blade enfiled by a celestial crown resting on the quillons gold. **Supporters:** On either side a mounted knight in armour proper, crowned with a celestial crown Or and supporting a staff also proper, flying therefrom a pennon argent fringed gold and charged with a cross gules. **Motto:** Put on the whole armour of God. **Granted** 15 June 1959.

PRESCOT GRAMMAR SCHOOL (PRESCOT, LANCASHIRE). Or, an open book proper, edged gules; on a chief indented azure three plates. **Crest:** On a wreath of the colours, An eagle, wings elevated and addorsed, Or supporting with the dexter claw a torch erect gules fired proper. **Motto:** Futuram civitatem inquirimus. **Granted** 24 April 1933.

PRESTATYN URBAN DISTRICT COUNCIL (FLINTSHIRE).* Barry wavy of six azure and Or, on a mount in base vert a castle triple-towered; on a chief argent a rose gules, barbed and seeded, between two sprigs of oak fructed proper. **Crest:** Out of a circlet azure charged with three crescents Or, a demi dragon gules supporting a tree stock raguly in bend proper. **Motto:** Cynyddaf a llawenychaf. **Granted** 2 September 1964.

PRESTON, COUNTY BOROUGH OF (LANCASHIRE).* Azure, a Paschal Lamb couchant argent [nimbed Or] supporting a cross-staff Or flying a pennant of the second; in base the letters

POOLE

PORTSMOUTH

PORTHCAWL

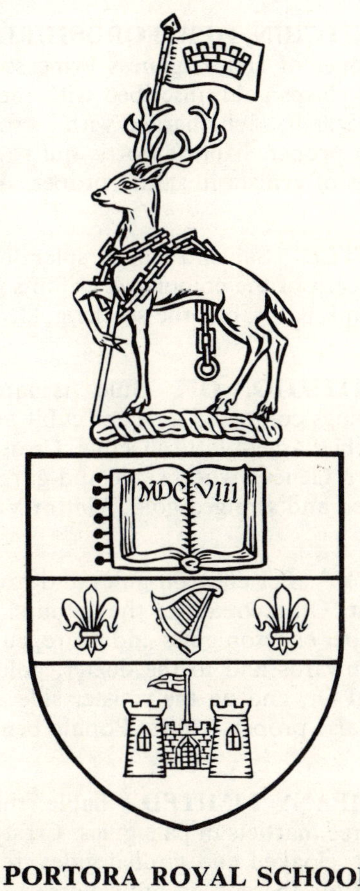

PORTORA ROYAL SCHOOL

PORTSMOUTH BISHOPRIC

PORTADOWN COLLEGE

PP of the third. Recorded without tinctures as a seal device at the Visitation of 1613; Confirmed by Kings' of Arms Certificate 6 March 1950.

PRESTON RURAL DISTRICT COUNCIL (LANCASHIRE).* Per saltire vert and Or, a fess wavy azure, charged with another wavy argent, between in chief an eagle displayed and in base a castle of three towers of the second. **Crest:** On a wreath of the colours, A dragon without wings passant, head erect and tail nowed, argent, gorged with a mural crown gules and grasping with the dexter forepaw a rose also gules, barbed, seeded, stalked and leaved proper. **Motto:** Unitate praestans. **Granted** 28 July 1948.

PRESTWICH, BOROUGH OF (LANCASHIRE).* Argent, on a pile between two roses gules, barbed and seeded proper, two swans' heads erased ermine in chief and a fleur-de-lys of the first in base. **Crest:** On a wreath of the colours, A lozenge azure charged with a fleur-de-lys argent, between two roses gules, barbed and seeded proper. **Supporters:** To the dexter a wyvern reguardant Or, and to the sinister a lion reguardant argent, each gorged with a riband and suspended therefrom a lozenge azure charged with a fleur-de-lys argent. **Motto:** Recte fac noli timere. Arms and Crest granted 20 September 1939 to the Prestwich UDC; Supporters granted to the Borough 10 November 1939.

PRINCESS HELENA COLLEGE (HITCHIN, HERTFORDSHIRE). Per fesse gules and azure, in chief a representation of the Coronet of Her Highness Princess Helena Victoria Or, and in base an open book argent, edges and clasps gold, inscribed with the words "fortis qui se vincit" sable; all between two flaunches also argent, each charged with a cross couped between two roses in pale also gules barbed and seeded proper. **Motto:** Fortis qui se vincit. **Badge:** A daisy erect slipped and leaved between two sprigs of genista in saltire proper. Arms granted 2 August 1928; Badge granted 20 September 1928.

PRINTING, INSTITUTE OF, LIMITED. Sable, a sun in splendour Or; on a chief embattled argent three torteaux. **Crest:** On a wreath of the colours, A griffin sejant sable, beaked and membered gules, holding in each claw an ink ball sable, the stocks gold. **Motto:** Imprimatur. **Granted** 1 March 1965.

PRODUCTION ENGINEERS, INSTITUTION OF. Gules, issuant from a segment of a clock face in base Or and in front of two wings conjoined a dexter cubit arm proper the hand grasping a torch gold enflamed also proper; a chief argent latticed sable. **Crest:** On a wreath of the colours, A demi bull holding between the legs a Geneva wheel sable and gorged with a collar Or, pendent therefrom a bugle horn gules garnished and stringed gold. **Motto:** Vires acquiunt eundo. **Granted** 28 February 1939.

PROVINCIAL BUILDING SOCIETY.* Per chevron gules and azure, in chief two bugle horns stringed and in base a fleece Or. **Crest:** On a wreath of the colours, Issuant from a port between two towers proper a cubit arm vested per chevron gules and azure, cuffed Or, the hand also proper grasping a key fessewise, wards downwards and to the dexter, gold. **Supporters:** On the dexter side a ram sable, horned and unguled Or, and on the sinister side an owl proper, both charged with a rose argent, barbed and seeded also proper. **Motto:** Populo bene servire. **Granted** 26 November 1945.

PRUDENTIAL ASSURANCE COMPANY LIMITED. Sable, three bars embattled Or; two flaunches argent each charged with three martlets in pale gules. **Crest:** On a wreath of the colours, A female figure proper, vested argent, cloaked and girdled gules, resting the sinister arm on the trunk of a tree eradicated and supporting thereon an hour-glass, and holding in the dexter hand a mirror which she is regarding and in the sinister an arrow entwined by a serpent, all proper. **Motto:** Fortis qui prudens. **Granted** 18 March 1904.

PRESTATYN

PREESALL

PRESTON CO. BOROUGH

POULTON-LE-FYLDE

PORT TALBOT

PUBLIC HEALTH INSPECTORS, ASSOCIATION OF.* Per fesse azure and gules, a pentagram Or. **Crest:** On a wreath of the colours, A phoenix proper, each wing charged with a mullet Or. **Motto:** Amicus humani generis. **Granted** 20 December 1957.

PUDSEY, BOROUGH OF (YORKSHIRE—WEST RIDING). Argent, on a chevron vert between two pairs of shuttles saltirewise in chief and a woolpack in base proper, three mullets pierced Or; all within a bordure engrailed gules charged with eight roses of the field. **Motto:** Be just and fear not. **Granted** 10 January 1901.

PURCHASING, INSTITUTE OF. Argent, a fesse per fesse indented throughout Or and gules between three purses azure, corded and tasselled gold. **Crest:** On a wreath of the colours, A cubit arm vested gules, slashed and embroidered Or, and ruffled at the wrist argent, the hand proper grasping a double-warded key fessewise, wards to the dexter, gold. **Supporters:** On either side a male griffin gules bezanty, armed, rayed and tufted Or, the forelegs of the same. **Motto:** Pactum serva. **Badge:** Two double-warded keys in saltire Or, surmounted of a purse azure, corded and tasselled gold, the cord enfiling the keys. **Granted** 20 January 1959 to The Purchasing Officers' Association.

PRESTON R. D. C.

PRESTWICH

PUBLIC HEALTH INSPECTORS

PROVINCIAL BUILDING SOCIETY

Q

** Denotes Illustration*

QUANTITY SURVEYORS, INSTITUTE OF.* Per pale Or and azure, a chevron between in chief two pyramids and in base a balance, all counterchanged. **Crest:** On a wreath of the colours, A Roman column Or supported on either side by kneeling figures representing Romulus and Remus proper, hair gold, vested gules. **Supporters:** On the dexter side a lion guardant gules, and on the sinister side a dragon azure, both billety Or. **Motto:** In veritate. **Granted** 20 November 1955.

QUARRYING, INSTITUTE OF.* Azure, an octagonal tower of Caernarvon Castle with two turrets proper; on a chief Or between two quarryers' jads sable a coronet composed of wattle-flowers and trefoils alternately set upon a rim vert. **Crest:** On a wreath argent and azure, On top of a quarry face proper, a lion sejant erect Or, the head and mane gules, supporting between the forelegs a key erect, wards outwards, argent. **Motto:** Terram autem filiis hominum. **Granted** 30 October 1958.

QUEEN ELIZABETH COLLEGE (LONDON UNIVERSITY). Argent a cross gules between four blazing hearths proper. **Granted** 21 June 1930 to King's College of Household and Social Science; transferred upon the change of name, 1953.

QUEEN ELIZABETH'S FREE GRAMMAR SCHOOL (GAINSBOROUGH, LINCOLNSHIRE).* Vert, a sun in splendour between a pair of scales in chief and an ancient crown in base, all within a chain in orle Or. **Crest:** On a wreath of the colours, A falcon, wings elevated and addorsed, argent, beaked, membered and belled Or, supporting with the dexter claw a link [= torch] gold enflamed proper. **Motto:** Fortiter prospicere gloriari praeteritis. **Granted** 3 March 1952.

QUEEN ELIZABETH'S FREE GRAMMAR SCHOOL (WAKEFIELD, YORKSHIRE).* Party per fesse, in chief per pale the dexter gules a lion statant guardant Or and sinister sable an owl argent, in base a book also argent, spine to the dexter, clasped, leaved and edged Or. **Crest:** On a wreath Or and sable, An owl argent crowned with an ancient crown Or and charged on the breast with a rose gules surmounted of another argent seeded and both barbed proper. **Motto:** Turpe nescire. **Badge:** On a woolpack Or an owl as in the Crest. **Granted** 5 March 1963.

QUEEN ELIZABETH'S HOSPITAL AT BRISTOL. Gules, on waves of the sea with dolphins' heads therein proper, the bow of a ship with cupola argent, garnished Or, issuant out of a port on the sinister silver, with mount vert impaling Gules, on a chevron argent three estoiles sable, in chief a martlet Or; over all on a chief azure a lion passant guardant between two fleurs-de-lis Or. **Crest:** On a wreath of the colours, On the stem of a tree couped and eradicated, entwined by a serpent proper, a bird, wings endorsed, argent. **Supporters:** On each side a sea horse proper, ducally gorged and crined Or. **Granted** 1591 by Robert Cooke, Clarenceux King of Arms.

QUEEN ELIZABETH TRAINING COLLEGE FOR THE DISABLED (LEATHERHEAD). Potent argent and azure, on a pale gules a chevron Or, thereon two bars gemel of the third, between in chief a garb and in base a martlet of the fourth; on a chief of the first a lion rampant of

QUANTITY SURVEYORS

QUARRYING INSTITUTE

QUEEN ELIZABETH'S FREE
MMAR SCHOOL (GAINSBOROUGH)

QUEEN'S COLLEGE
(OXFORD UNIVERSITY)

QUEEN ELIZABETH'S FREE
GRAMMAR SCHOOL (WAKEFIELD)

the second between two hurts both charged with a rose of the first barbed and seeded proper. **Crest:** On a wreath of the colours, A sun in splendour Or charged with a cross potent gules. **Supporters:** On either side a swan in front of a cedar tree proper; the whole resting on a bridge of fourteen arches over water also proper. **Motto:** Adversis major. **Granted** 8 August 1946.

QUEEN ETHELBURGA'S SCHOOL (HARROGATE). Azure, on a chevron ermine between in the dexter chief a sun in splendour Or, and in base an eagle, wings elevated, respecting the same, three ancient crowns gold. **Crest:** Out of a coronet composed of eight ostrich feathers set upon a rim argent, a mount vert, thereon a falcon also argent, armed, belled and jessed Or, wings elevated per chief dancetty Or and azure. **Motto:** Luce magistra. **Granted** 1 June 1962.

QUEEN MARGARET'S SCHOOL (ESCRICK, YORKSHIRE). Azure, on a cross formy between four crested tits Or, a rose argent, barbed and seeded proper; on a chief ermine an ancient crown gold. **Crest:** On a wreath Or, gules, azure, argent, gules and azure, Out of a chaplet of roses argent, barbed and seeded proper, a demi lion rampant gules, gorged with a collar gemel flory counterflory Or, supporting a key in bend gold. **Motto:** Filia regis. **Granted** 20 June 1962.

QUEEN MARY COLLEGE (LONDON UNIVERSITY). Azure, on three several clouds, sunbeams issuing from the base thereof proper, three triple imperial crowns Or; on a chief gules an open book proper, edged Or, inscribed 'Soli Deo Honor et Gloria' between two mullets gold. **Granted** 7 March 1921 to East London College, Stepney; re-certified on change in name.

QUEEN'S COLLEGE (BIRMINGHAM), THE. Purpure, an open book argent, edged and clasped Or, inscribed thereon in letters sable the words QUI UTUNTUR NON UTANTUR; in chief an ancient crown of four fleurs-de-lys of the third between two cocks of the second. **Granted** 17 April 1931.

QUEENS' COLLEGE (CAMBRIDGE UNIVERSITY). Quarterly of six, first barry of eight argent and gules (for Hungary); second azure semee-de-lis Or a label of three points gules (for Anjou-Sicily); third Agent a cross potent between four crosses couped Or (for Jerusalem); fourth azure semee-de-lis Or a bordure gules (for Anjou); fifth azure crusily two barbels haurient and addorsed Or (for Barr); sixth Or on a bend gules three allerions displayed argent (for Lorraine); the whole within a bordure vert. **Crest:** In a coronet of gold an eagle rousant sable winged gold. **Granted** 1575 by Robert Cooke, Clarenceux King of Arms.

QUEEN'S COLLEGE (OXFORD UNIVERSITY).* Argent, three eagles displayed, two and one, gules, [on the breast of that in dexter chief a pierced mullet of six points] and each beaked and legged Or. Recorded at the Visitation of 1574.

QUEEN'S SCHOOL (CHESTER). Or, a rose gules; on a chief azure a mitre and a garb of the first. **Crest:** On a wreath of the colours, An eagle Or, wings expanded azure, holding a banner Or charged with a rose gules. **Motto:** Honour wisdom. **Granted** 27 February 1936.

RADCLIFFE

RADNORSHIRE

RAMSGATE

RAWTENSTALL

R

** Denotes Illustration*

RADCLIFFE, BOROUGH OF (LANCASHIRE).* Argent, two bendlets engrailed sable between a cross potent voided of the field and a rose of the third, barbed vert, seeded Or. **Crest:** Upon a mural crown a lion passant guardant Or, the dexter forepaw resting on a pheon sable. **Supporters:** On the dexter side a bull argent, armed and unguled, gorged with a mural crown, attached thereto a chain reflexed over the back Or, and charged on the shoulder with a fleur-de-lys sable; and on the sinister side a lion sable, gorged and chained as the dexter and charged on the shoulder with a fleur-de-lys argent. **Motto:** Industria ditat. **Granted** 10 September 1935.

RADIO ENGINEERS, BRITISH INSTITUTION OF. Azure, on a pile Or a fess chequy of the first and argent between in chief a heart between two crescents gules and in base a boars' head erased sable. **Crest:** On a wreath of the colours, A representation of the head and shoulders of Mercury proper, the hair Or. **Supporters:** On the dexter side a buck proper, and on the sinister side a lion queue-fourchée barry of ten argent and gules. **Motto:** Scientia pro hominibus. **Granted** 10 February 1956.

RADIOGRAPHERS, SOCIETY OF. Azure, a sun in his splendour Or; on a chief sable a saltire argent surmounted by a rod of Aesculapius proper. **Crest:** On a rim Or a white owl proper holding with the dexter claw a rod of Aesculapius gold. Mantled azure, doubled Or. **Motto:** Ex umbris eruditio MDCCCCXX. **Granted** 3 May 1951.

RADIOLOGISTS, FACULTY OF. Barry wavy of ten argent and gules, on a pale azure an X-ray tube Or, irradiated at the centre also Or, and entwined of two serpents gold. **Crest:** On a wreath of the colours, Issuant from flames alternately gules and Or a skeletal cubit arm proper, the hand grasping a thunderbolt fessewise also proper. **Supporters:** On either side a griffin Or collared azure and charged on the shoulder with a rope also azure. **Motto:** Ex radiis salutas. **Granted** 15 May 1961.

RADIO MANUFACTURERS' ASSOCIATION. Azure, a bend dancetty Or cottised also dancetty argent between in chief a thunderbolt of the second and in base a terrestrial globe proper; a bordure ermines charged with eight mullets of six points argent. **Crest:** On a wreath of the colours, A bezant charged with a pair of wings and encircled with a wreath of laurel proper. **Motto:** Radio maximo arvo. **Granted** 14 October 1931.

RADLEY COLLEGE. See St. Peter's College, Radley.

RADNORSHIRE COUNTY COUNCIL.* Quarterly, first and fourth gules a lion rampant reguardant Or; second and third argent three boars' heads couped sable; all within a bordure compony of the second and azure; and the shield ensigned with a mural crown Or. **Motto:** Ewch yn uwch. **Granted** 21 November 1950.

RAMSGATE, BOROUGH OF (KENT).* Quarterly gules and azure, a cross parted and fretty argent between a horse rampant of the last in the first quarter, a demi lion passant guardant of the third conjoined to the hulk of a ship Or in the second, a dolphin naiant proper in the third,

RATING AND VALUATION OFFICERS

RAYLEIGH

READING

READING UNIVERSITY

and a lymphad also Or in the fourth. **Crest:** Issuant from a naval crown Or a pierhead, thereon a lighthouse, both proper. **Supporters:** On the dexter side a lifeboatman, and on the sinister side a coastguard holding in the exterior hand a telescope, all proper. **Motto:** Salus naufragis salus aegris. Arms and Crest granted 23 July 1884; Supporters granted 2 November 1935.

RATCLIFFE COLLEGE, LEICESTER. Azure, six mullets, three, two and one, argent; on a chief Or three pellets, the centre one charged with a lion rampant of the third, the dexter with a lily and the sinister with a swallow both of the second. **Crest:** On a wreath of the colours, A pelican in her piety affronte argent, vulning herself proper, the nest Or. **Motto:** Legis plenitudo charitas. **Granted** 23 September 1936.

RATING AND VALUATION OFFICERS, INCORPORATED ASSOCIATION OF.* Vert, a bend wavy argent charged with a bendlet wavy ermine; over all three mural crowns Or. **Crest:** On a wreath of the colours, Upon a rock proper semée of bezants and plates, a lion passant guardant Or supporting a staff gules, flying therefrom a pennon gold charged with two branches of laurel in saltire vert. **Supporters:** On either side a lion Or gorged with a collar, pendent therefrom by a chain an escutcheon gules charged with two branches of laurel in saltire gold. **Motto:** Diligenter et fideliter. **Granted** 25 October 1937.

RAWTENSTALL, BOROUGH OF (LANCASHIRE).* Or, on a fesse gules between two stags trippant at gaze in chief proper and a mound in base vert thereon two cows grazing and respecting each other sable, a wolf courant of the first between two bales of wool of the third; in the chief point a sinister hand couped at the wrist of the second. **Crest:** On a wreath of the colours, Upon a mount a squirrel sejant cracking a nut, between two sprigs of the cotton tree, slipped, leaved and fructed, all proper. **Motto:** Floret qui laborat. **Granted** 16 July 1871.

RAYLEIGH URBAN DISTRICT COUNCIL (ESSEX).* Argent, a wyvern vert, armed, langued and the jaws and underparts gules; on a chief gules a seax, point to the sinister, proper, hilt and pommel Or. **Crest:** On a wreath argent and gules, On a mount vert a roe doe statant proper, pendent from the neck by a chain Or an escutcheon argent charged with a Tudor rose also proper. **Motto:** In reliquiam laboramus. **Granted** 20 December 1962.

REA BROTHERS LIMITED. Gules, on a chevron between in chief a pair of scales and in base a lymphad, sails furled flags flying to the dexter, Or three mural crowns of the field. **Crest:** Out of a circlet Or a demi lion reguardant proper, armed gules and gorged with a riband gold, pendant therefrom an escutcheon argent charged with a cormorant's head erased, in the beak a sprig of seaweed called laver, proper, and holding in the paws a sword erect gules. **Motto:** Recte fac noli timere. **Granted** 10 March 1958.

READING, COUNTY BOROUGH OF (BERKSHIRE).* Azure, five maidens' heads in saltire couped at the shoulders and vested proper, each crined and wearing a necklace and pendant Or, the centre head imperially crowned gold, the cap gules, in fess the letters RE also gold. **Crest:** On a wreath argent and azure, Issuant from a circlet of four [inverted] escallops and as many lyres alternating Or, a mitre proper. **Supporters:** On either side a ram argent, armed and unguled Or, charged on the shoulder, the dexter with a portcullis chained azure, the sinister with a hurt thereon a plate charged with two bars wavy also azure. **Motto:** A Deo et Regina. Arms recorded at Visitations 6 October 1566, 1623 and 1665; certified 22 September 1893 by Henry Farnham Burke, Somerset Herald (there are considerable differences in details); Crest and Supporters granted 20 May 1953.

READING, UNIVERSITY OF.* Per fesse gules and sable, in chief three escallops fessewise Or, and in base on a cross engrailed argent a rose of the first barbed and seeded proper. **Granted** 7 August 1896 to the Reading University Extension College.

READING COLLEGE OF TECHNOLOGY. Or, on a saltire azure five maidens' heads affrontée couped at the shoulders, that in the centre crowned with a Saxon crown, all gold; on a chief

REDBRIDGE

RED HOUSE SCHOOL

REDDITCH

REFUGE ASSURANCE

gules an open book argent, edged and bound also gold, between two cogwheels of the same. **Crest:** On a wreath Or, azure and gules, On a mount vert and in front of an oak tree also vert fructed Or a lion passant guardant gold, at the base of the mount five escallops in fesse, the exterior and that in the centre reversed, also gold. Mantled azure and gules doubled Or. **Motto:** Ancora Imparo. **Granted** 6 September 1960 to the Reading Technical College.

REDBRIDGE, LONDON BOROUGH OF.* Ermine, an oak tree eradicated and fructed proper between four leopards' faces and three martlets alternating in orle Or, a base wavy barry wavy azure and argent. **Crest:** On a wreath argent and azure. Issuant from a chaplet of oak a demi buck proper supporting a cross flory argent. **Supporters:** On each side a figure, that to the dexter habited as a Benedictine abbess, holding in the exterior hand a book and supporting a crosier with sudarium, and that to the sinister as a forester, supporting with the exterior hand a bow, all proper. **Motto:** In unity progress. **Badge:** On a mount and in front of a hurst of trees, a stag trippant proper. **Granted** 3 December 1964.

REDDITCH URBAN DISTRICT COUNCIL (WORCESTERSHIRE).* Argent, on a cross engrailed vert a needle, point downwards, of the field, eyed and ensigned with an ancient crown Or; in the first quarter a salmon-fly in bend proper. **Crest:** On a wreath of the colours, In front of a demi-cogwheel, thereon a swift rising proper, an arrow fessewise Or. **Motto:** Reddite Deo. **Granted** 15 December 1943.

RED HOUSE SCHOOL LIMITED (STOCKTON-ON-TEES).* Ermine a chevron gules between three crosses cercelée sable; on a chief of the second as many mullets argent. **Crest:** On a wreath of the colours, A reindeer lodged proper gorged with a chain Or, pendant therefrom an escutcheon ermine charged with a cross cercelée sable. **Motto:** Veritas in Virtute. **Granted** 15 May 1950.

REFRACTORIES ASSOCIATION OF GREAT BRITAIN. Azure guttee d'eau, issuant from the base a sun in splendour Or; a chief enarched of firebricks proper. **Crest:** On a wreath Or and gules, Standing on a furnace fired argent a salamander passant in flames, all proper. **Motto:** Igne non frangor. **Granted** 25 April 1958.

REFUGE ASSURANCE COMPANY LIMITED.* Gules, a beehive Or; on a chief azure a pair of scales between a tower and a garb of the second. **Crest:** On a wreath of the colours, A representation of Noah's Ark proper. **Supporters:** On the dexter side the figure of a woman representing Justice proper, blindfolded and habited in a robe argent, in her dexter hand a pair of scales and in her other hand a sword erect Or. On the sinister side a lion guardant gules, murally crowned and charged on the shoulder with a rose gold. **Motto:** Refugium rebus adversis. **Granted** 19 September 1951.

REGENT'S PARK COLLEGE (OXFORD UNIVERSITY). Argent, on a cross gules an open Bible proper irradiated Or, the pages inscribed with the words 'Dominus Jesus' in letters sable; on a chief wavy azure a fish gold. **Crest:** On a wreath of the colours, A representation of the King John's Tower of the Baptist College formerly at Stepney. **Motto:** Omnia probate quod bonum tenete. **Granted** 3 March 1958.

REGIUS PROFESSORS (CAMBRIDGE UNIVERSITY). See Cambridge, Readers in the University of.

REIGATE, BOROUGH OF (SURREY).* Checky azure and Or; on a chief wavy sable, between two crosses potent quadrate gules fimbriated argent a mount, thereon in front of an oak tree of the last, the leaves charged with an escutcheon chequy azure and Or, a port with portcullis raised between two towers also argent. **Crest:** On a wreath of the colours A demi lion argent gorged with a mural crown and supporting with the paws a cross crosslet fitchée gules. **Supporters:** On either side a pilgrim with staff and scrip, and habited in traditional costume proper, the dexter having a cloak azure, the sinister a cloak vert, both buckled Or. **Motto:** Never wonne ne never shall. **Granted** 26 September 1951.

REIGATE

RHYLL

RICHMOND R.D.C.

RELIANCE MUTUAL

THE REINSURANCE CORPORATION, LIMITED. Gules, an anchor argent surmounted and interlaced by two torches in saltire Or, enflamed proper; over all a chevron rompu Or. **Crest:** On a wreath Or and gules, A tower of three stages gules, issuing from the battlements of the first stage a flagstaff proper, flying therefrom to the sinister and reflexed to the dexter a pennon per fesse argent and gules, the whole between two branches of oak fructed proper. **Supporters:** On either side a sea lion gules. **Motto:** Quae juncta firma. **Granted** 30 July 1964.

RELIANCE FIRE AND ACCIDENT INSURANCE CORPORATION LIMITED. Per chevron vert and argent, in chief a cannon barrel fessewise Or and in base an oak tree fructed and eradicated proper. **Crest:** On a wreath of the colours, Issuant from a criclet of eight bezants a talbot's head sable. **Supporters:** On either side a salamander enflamed proper charged on the shoulder with a portcullis chained Or in front of flames also proper. **Motto:** Fide et integritate. **Badge:** A portcullis chained Or in front of flames proper. **Granted** 6 March 1952.

RELIANCE MARINE INSURANCE COMPANY LIMITED. Per fesse wavy gules and barry wavy of ten argent and azure, on a pile of the second a cormorant rising proper holding in the beak an anchor of the first. **Crest:** On a wreath of the colours, A Lymphad sable, the sail set argent charged with a ship's steering wheel azure. **Motto:** Reliance. **Granted** 27 February 1947.

RELIANCE MUTUAL LIFE INSURANCE SOCIETY LIMITED.* Per chevron gules and argent, in chief a cannon barrel fessewise Or and in base a castle of three towers proper. **Crest:** On a wreath of the colours, Issuant from a chaplet of roses argent, barbed and seeded proper, a mitre gules, the two points ensigned with two crosses patée Or and the cap charged with a chevron also argent fimbriated gold thereon three escallops sable. **Supporters:** On either side a lion guardant Or charged on the shoulder with a portcullis chained sable, in front thereof a slip of thrift stalked leaved and flowered proper. **Motto:** Semper fidelis. **Badge:** In front of a portcullis chained sable, a slip of thrift stalked leaved and flowered proper. **Granted** 2 November 1951 to the Farringdon Reliance Mutual Life Insurance Society Limited.

RENDCOMB COLLEGE (GLOUCESTERSHIRE). Gules, a griffin passant, and issuant from the dexter chief a sun Or. **Crest:** On a wreath of the colours, In front of a sun in splendour Or a griffin's head erased gules. **Motto:** Quo lux ducit. **Granted** 10 June 1920.

RETAIL FRUIT TRADE FEDERATION LIMITED. Vert, a cornucopia erect Or, the contents proper, within an orle of [eight] crosses floretty gold. **Crest:** On a wreath of the colours, Between a pair of pheasant's wings a basket of divers vegetables, in the midst thereof an escallop, all proper. **Motto:** Vis unita fortior. **Badge:** In front of a sun in splendour a basket, all Or.

RHONDDA, BOROUGH OF (GLAMORGAN).* Vert, a pall wavy argent; on a chief dancetty of four points a balance between two acorns slipped and leaved Or. **Crest:** Out of a mural crown sable, masoned gules, a demi dragon also gules gorged with a riband, pendent therefrom an escutcheon Or charged with three chevronels of the second, and supporting a torch erect also sable enflamed proper. **Supporters:** On each side a sea dragon sable, fins and tail proper, gorged with a collar chequy argent and azure. **Motto:** Hwy clod na golud. **Granted** 12 May 1955

RHYLL URBAN DISTRICT COUNCIL (FLINTSHIRE).* Tenny, a pile barruly wavy argent and azure; over all a fish-weir sable, staked gules, in fess between a lymphad, sail set pennon and flags flying, gules and in base a salmon naiant proper. **Crest:** On a wreath of the colours, On a mount vert a dragon sejant gules supporting a staff proper, flying therefrom a banner of the Arms. **Motto:** Yr hafan dêg ar fin y dôn. **Granted** 1 August 1967.

RICHMOND, BOROUGH OF (YORKSHIRE—NORTH RIDING).* Gules, an orle argent; over all a bend ermine. **Crest:** Out of an ancient crown Or, a rose argent barbed and seeded proper. Arms recorded without tinctures 21 August 1665; confirmed with tinctures and Crest granted 4 August 1959.

RICHMOND HERALD. See Arms, Officers of.

RHONDDA

RICHMOND BOROUGH

RICHMOND-UPON-THAMES

RICKMANSWORTH

RICHMOND RURAL DISTRICT COUNCIL (YORKSHIRE—NORTH RIDING).* Gules, an eagle displayed, wings inverted, Or grasping in the claws two swords in saltire proper, hilted and pommelled gold; on a chief wavy of the last three abbots' crozier heads azure. **Crest:** On a wreath of the colours, Out of a mural crown azure charged with three roses argent, barbed and seeded proper, a stag's head holding in the mouth an ear of wheat stalked, leaved and slipped also proper, and gorged with a collar ermine. **Motto:** Vi Dei terraeque. **Granted** 22 September 1955.

RICHMOND-UPON-THAMES, LONDON BOROUGH OF.* Ermine, a portcullis chained Or; a bordure gules charged with eight fleur-de-lis Or. **Crest:** On a wreath argent and gules, Out of a mural crown gules, a swan rousant, in the beak a branch of climbing red roses leaved and entwined about the neck proper. **Supporters:** On either side a griffin gules, armed and beaked azure, each supporting an oar proper, the blade of the dexter dark blue and that of the sinister light blue. **Badge:** A rose Or, charged with a portcullis chained gules. **Granted** 7 March 1966.

RICKMANSWORTH URBAN DISTRICT COUNCIL (HERTFORDSHIRE).* Per fesse dancetty sable and Or semée of flowers gentil proper, in chief three plates above two estoiles of the second. **Crest:** On a wreath of the colours, Issuant from a wreath of watercress proper a garb Or charged with a lion's face azure. **Motto:** Nisi Dominus aedificaverit. **Granted** 30 November 1953.

RIDLEY HALL (CAMBRIDGE). Per pale gules and argent, on the dexter two swords in saltire, points upwards proper, hilt and pommel Or, and on the sinister a bull passant of the first and in base a rush plant flowered and eradicated also proper; the whole within a bordure ermine. **Crest:** On a wreath of the colours, A bishop's mitre between two slips of bulrush proper. **Motto:** Martyrii memores. **Granted** 29 September 1952.

RINGWOOD AND FORDINGBRIDGE RURAL DISTRICT COUNCIL (HAMPSHIRE).* Azure, issuant from the base point an oak tree, the trunk enfiled with a circlet Or, and fructed of sixteen acorns of the field; on a chief wavy gold a bridge of seven arches of the first. **Crest:** On a wreath of the colours, Out of a mural crown a New Forest pony's head between two sprigs of broom flowered, all proper. **Motto:** Ruris artes fovere. **Granted** 1 February 1961.

RIPLEY URBAN DISTRICT COUNCIL (DERBYSHIRE).* Vert, on a chevron Or between in chief two stags' heads caboshed and in base a fleur-de-lys argent, a chevronel sable surmounted by a Tudor rose barbed and seeded proper; all within a bordure also argent, thereon six horseshoes also sable. **Crest:** On a wreath of the colours, Out of a mural crown sable, flames proper, issuant therefrom a unicorn's head argent, armed and crined Or, charged with three spearheads erect, one and two, gules. **Motto:** Ingenium industria alitur. **Granted** 8 April 1954.

RIPON, BISHOPRIC OF.* Argent, on a saltire gules two keys in saltire, wards upwards, Or; on a chief of the second a Holy Lamb proper. **Granted** by Royal Warrant 3 November 1836; exemplified 21 November 1836.

RIPON, WAKEFIELD AND BRADFORD DIOCESAN TRAINING COLLEGE. Per pale gules and azure, two keys in saltire, wards upward and outward, in chief a bugle horn stringed Or; on a chief Or, a celestial crown between two fleurs-de-lis azure. **Crest:** On a wreath of the colours, Issuant from an antique crown [=ancient crown] Or, two sprigs of three roses, one in pale and two in saltire, barbed, seeded and leaved proper. **Motto:** Nisi Dominus frustra. **Granted** 20 December 1963.

ROAN SCHOOLS. Vert, three stags trippant within an orle of fourteen mullets Or. **Crest:** On a wreath of the colours, In front of a stag's head erased, in the mouth a sprig of oak, proper, an anchor fessewise, stock to the dexter, vert. **Motto:** Honore et labore. **Granted** 8 August 1927.

ROBERT JONES AND AGNES HUNT ORTHOPAEDIC HOSPITAL, THE (GOBOWEN, NEAR OSWESTRY). Per pale ermines and ermine, on the dexter side a dragon rampant Or and on the sinister side a saltire couped per pale argent and sable; a chief gules charged with a

RIPLEY

RIPON BISHOPRIC

ROCHFORD

ROCHESTER

RINGWOOD

ROSS-ON-WYE

ROCHDALE

leopard's face of the third between two sprigs of the plant Self-heal proper. **Crest:** On a wreath of the colours, A dexter cubit arm grasping in the hand a sprig of the plant Self-heal proper. **Motto:** Deo dante damus. **Granted** 2 December 1944.

ROCHDALE, COUNTY BOROUGH OF (LANCASHIRE).* Argent, a woolpack encircled by two branches of the cotton tree flowered and conjoined proper; a bordure sable charged with eight martlets of the field. **Crest:** Upon a wreath of the colours, A mill-rind sable, and above a fleece argent banded Or. **Motto:** Crede signo. **Granted** 20 February 1857.

ROCHDALE GRAMMAR SCHOOL FOR BOYS. Gules, a fleece Or; on a chief argent three keys, wards upward and to the dexter, gules. **Crest:** On a wreath Or, vert and sable, A dexter cubit arm vested per pale vert and sable, cuffed Or, the hand proper grasping a cross staff argent, the cross Or, between two sprigs each of two roses gules, barbed, seeded and leaved proper, all within four fleurs-de-lys argent. **Motto:** Aude et praevalebis. **Granted** 20 May 1966.

ROCHESTER, BISHOPRIC OF. Argent, on a saltire gules an escallop Or. Recorded in the College of Arms.

ROCHESTER, CITY OF (KENT).* Or, on a cross gules a letter R of the field; on a chief of the second a lion passant guardant gold. Recorded as a seal device (untinctured) at the Visitation 2 September 1574; Recorded with tinctures (as Arms) at the Visitation of 1619.

ROCHFORD RURAL DISTRICT COUNCIL (ESSEX).* Quarterly Or and gules, in the first quarter a bull's head caboshed sable. **Crest:** On a wreath Or and sable, Standing on a mount vert enfiled by an ancient crown Or a cock gules combed and wattled gold. **Motto:** Arate sulco recte. **Granted** 3 September 1954.

ROEDEAN SCHOOL LIMITED. Per fesse wavy azure and argent, on a mount vert in base over a book expanded proper a roe-deer also proper, collared and chained and charged on the shoulder with a gridiron Or. **Motto:** Honneur aulx dignes. **Granted** 7 December 1921.

ROMSEY, BOROUGH OF (HAMPSHIRE). Quarterly gules and sable, a pastoral staff in pale, head to the sinister, surmounted of a portcullis chained Or. **Crest:** Out of a mural crown gules, four ears of wheat and as many ears of barley alternately Or. **Supporters:** On the dexter side a lion queue fourchée, ducally crowned, Or supporting between the forelegs a staff proper, flying therefrom a banner argent charged with two pallets sable, and on the sinister side a hart royal proper, attired, unguled and gorged with an ancient crown Or, and supporting between the forelegs a like staff, flying therefrom a banner azure charged with two pallets wavy argent over all a mayfly proper. **Motto:** Quae recta tene. **Granted** 15 June 1959.

ROSSALL SCHOOL (FLEETWOOD, LANCASHIRE). Argent, on a pale gules between four roses of the last, a mitre Or between two open books proper. **Motto:** Mens agitat molem. **Granted** 1892.

ROSS-ON-WYE URBAN DISTRICT COUNCIL (HEREFORDSHIRE).* Per fesse gules and vert, on a fesse wavy argent between in chief two leopards' faces reversed jessant-de-lys and in base a fleur-de-lys Or, a bar wavy azure. **Crest:** Issuant from a coronet composed of four fleurs-de-lys set upon a rim gules, a demi eagle displayed, wings inverted, Or collared vert, the breast and each wing charged with a rose also gules, barbed and seeded proper. **Motto:** Porta Vagae. **Granted** 26 June 1953.

ROTHERHAM, COUNTY BOROUGH OF (YORKSHIRE—WEST RIDING).* Vert, above two bars wavy in base argent, a bridge of three arches throughout proper, in chief a mitre between two roses of the second. **Crest:** On a wreath of the colours, A hand proper grasping a caduceus Or. **Supporters:** On either side a stag Or gorged with a chain, pendent therefrom an escutcheon sable charged with a bee volant gold. **Motto:** Sic virescit industria **Granted** 22 October 1947.

ROTHERHAM CO. BOROUGH

ROYAL AIR FORCE COLLEGE

ROYAL ALEXANDRA
AND ALBERT SCHOOL

ROYAL AGRICULTURAL COLLEGE

ROTHERHAM R.D.C.

ROTHERHAM RURAL DISTRICT COUNCIL (YORKSHIRE—WEST RIDING).* Vert, a stag trippant Or; on a chief sable two swords in saltire proper, hilted and pomelled gold, between as many roses argent, barbed and seeded also proper. **Crest:** On a wreath of the colours, A demi griffin argent gorged with a collar lozengy argent and gules, pendent therefrom an escutcheon sable charged with a chevron between three leopards' faces Or, and holding between the claws a cross patonce also sable. **Motto:** Intento animo. **Granted** 20 June 1955.

N. M. ROTHSCHILD AND SONS. Azure, a lion passant guardant erminois grasping with the dexter forepaw five arrows, the pheons point downwards, all Or within a bordure gold. **Crest:** On a wreath Or and azure, Out of a crown vallery gules, the circlet charged with two bezants, a demi lion erminois holding between the paws five arrows as in the Arms, tied with a riband Or. **Supporters:** On the dexter side a lion Or, and on the sinister side a unicorn argent, pendent from each an escutcheon gules, the baldric gold buckled also gules. **Motto:** Concordia, integritas, industria. **Badge:** Within a chaplet of laurel proper, banded Or, a carved escutcheon gules charged with five arrows as in the Arms, tied with a riband gold. **Granted** 10 September 1962.

ROUGE CROIX PURSUIVANT. See Arms, Officers of.

ROUGE DRAGON PURSUIVANT. See Arms, Officers of.

ROYAL AGRICULTURAL COLLEGE (CIRENCESTER).* Per fesse indented azure and sable, over all a garb Or; in dexter chief an estoile argent. **Crest:** Out of a coronet composed of six garbs set upon a rim Or, a ram's head sable, armed gold. **Supporters:** On either side a Ram sable, armed and collared with a coronet composed of six garbs set upon a rim Or. **Motto:** Arvorum cultus pecorumque. **Granted** 20 September 1956.

ROYAL AIRCRAFT ESTABLISHMENT (FARNBOROUGH). Azure, a key in pale, wards downwards, Or; on a chief embattled of the last a mural crown between on the dexter a naval crown and on the sinister an astral crown of the first. **Crest:** Out of an astral crown Or, a pterodactyl displayed proper. **Motto:** Alis apta scientis. **Granted** 12 April 1954.

ROYAL AIR FORCE COLLEGE (CRANWELL).* Azure, on a chevron between three cranes volant argent, as many torteaux, each charged with a lion's face Or. **Crest:** On a wreath of the colours, A figure representing Daedalus proper. **Motto:** Superna petimus. **Granted** 19 December 1929.

ROYAL AIR FORCE STAFF COLLEGE. Argent, on a cross engrailed per pale sable and gules a spear in pale surmounted in the fess point by an annulet between two buck's heads caboshed Or; on a chief per pale argent and bleu celeste, to the dexter three pales sable and to the sinister a representation of the constellation Aquilla Or; all in a bordure per chief sable and bleu celeste. **Crest:** On a Royal Air Force Pilot's helmet proper, On a wreath argent and bleu celeste. Out of an astral crown Or the hawk of Horus proper. **Motto:** Visu et nisu. **Granted** 2 January 1970.

ROYAL ALEXANDRA AND ALBERT SCHOOL (REIGATE, SURREY).* Gules, a lion rampant Or; a chief of the last, thereon a fountain between two oak trees eradicated, fructed proper. **Motto:** Nisi Dominus frustra. **Granted** 11 June 1953.

ROYAL BELFAST ACADEMICAL INSTITUTION. Sable, between two Doric columns Or an open book proper, edged and bound of the second and inscribed in fesse with the Roman numerals MDCCCX of the first, in chief the Crown of Hanover gold. **Crest:** On a wreath of the colours, A seahorse erect Or supporting a torch of the last inflamed gold. **Motto:** Quaerere verum. **Granted** 3 August 1951.

THE ROYAL BERKSHIRE HOSPITAL (READING). Sable, on a cross gules between in the first and fourth quarters a hart trippant and in the second and third quarters an escallop Or, a cross gules charged with a sceptre in pale gold. **Motto:** Serviendo fidem tenemus. **Granted** 1 November 1937.

ROYAL CENTRAL ASIAN SOCIETY. Vert, a chevron engrailed cotised engrailed Or between three crescents argent; on a chief of the second the horns of the Ovis Poli proper. **Crest:** On a wreath of the colours. In front of the rising sun Or the horns of the Ovis Poli proper as in the Arms. **Motto:** Cornua levat super terras. **Granted** 26 September 1933.

ROYAL COLLEGE OF MIDWIVES. See Midwives

ROYAL DENTAL HOSPITAL OF LONDON, SCHOOL OF DENTAL SURGERY (LONDON UNIVERSITY). Quarterly purpure and vert, on a cross patonce quadrate in the centre argent between in the first and fourth quarters an antique crown and in the second and third quarters a rod of Aesculapius Or, an open book proper, bound gules edged Or. **Granted** 15 May 1950.

ROYAL EXCHANGE ASSURANCE COMPANY OF LONDON, THE GOVERNOR AND CORPORATION OF THE. Azure, on a hill the Royal Exchange, both proper, the last adorned with gold, in cheif two shipps under sail, the hull Or, masts sails and rigging proper, the sinister ship riding at anchor with the sails furl'd emblazoned as before. **Crest:** [On a wreath of the colours], A demy angell proper cloathed with a crimson garment girdled of the same wings displayed Or, in his right hand the sun, in his left a crescent and crowned with a ducal coronet, the North Starr issuing out of it Or. Supported on the dexter side by a Neptune proper crown'd with an Eastern crown gold, a mantle carelessly flung over his body purpure, in his right hand a trident erect Or staff purpure, on the sinister by a seaman proper, shirt chequered, vestment below blew lined, britches and stockings white, shoes black buckled silver, cap on his head blew turned up white, holding with his left hand an anchor gold cabled proper. **Motto:** Trade and Navigation. **Granted** 1721; certified 6 April 1905.

ROYAL FORESTRY SOCIETY OF ENGLAND, WALES AND NORTHERN IRELAND. Per fesse tenné and argent, a pale counterchanged, in chief between two fir trees proper a rose gules surmounted of a rose argent barbed and seeded, and in base a fir tree between a daffodil flower and a flax flower proper. **Crest:** On a wreath argent and vert, In front of an oak sapling leaved and fructed, a woodman's axe and a spade, handles upward, in saltire proper, all enfiled of an annulet Or. **Supporters:** On either side a lion guardant vert, gorged with an ancient coronet Or, supporting an oak sapling leaved and fructed proper. **Motto:** Serit arbores quae altem seculo prosunt. **Badge:** Within an annulet ensigned by an ancient coronet Or, an oak tree proper. **Granted** 20 November 1963.

ROYAL FREE HOSPITAL SCHOOL OF MEDICINE (LONDON UNIVERSITY). Quarterly per fesse indented and per pale sable and Or, in the first and fourth quarters a lion rampant gold and in the second and third a rod of Aesculapius also sable. **Crest:** On a wreath of the colours, Within the branches of a rose tree flowered gules, barbed and seeded, and leaved, an open book proper, bound and clasped Or. **Motto:** Virtute fideque. **Granted** 24 December 1954.

ROYAL GWENT HOSPITAL (NEWPORT, MONMOUTHSHIRE). Per pale azure and sable, three fleurs-de-lys Or; on a chief ermine a rod of Aesculapius between two ancient lamps or enflamed proper. **Crest:** On a wreath of the colours, An ancient lamp gules, enflamed proper, charged with a fleur-de-lys Or. **Motto:** Goreu olud iechyd. **Granted** 24 January 1919.

ROYAL HOLLOWAY COLLEGE. Ermine, on a cross gules another argent, over all in the fesse point an open book proper; on a chief of the second three crescents Or. **Granted** 1 May 1944.

THE ROYAL HORTICULTURAL SOCIETY. Vert, within a bordure an apple tree eradicated Or fructed gules. **Granted** 11 January 1928.

ROYAL INSTITUTION OF GREAT BRITAIN. Azure, the sun in splendour Or, in base the ocean proper; on a canton argent an escutcheon gules charged with a lion passant guardant of the second. **Crest:** Out of a mural crown Or an oak tree fructed proper. **Supporters:** (Dexter) a figure representing Minerva habited in a robe flowing to the feet argent, supervested with a tunic purpure, zoned Or, bearing on her breast a gorget charged with Medusa's head of the last, and on her head a helmet surmounted by an owl gold, the plume argent, in her dexter hand a spear erect proper; (Sinister) a figure representing Vesta habited in a flowing robe argent, banded from the right shoulder under the left breast, the band Or, her head encircled by a golden fillet, her vest thrown back, and her exterior hand holding a torch illumined proper. **Motto:** Illustrans commoda vitae. **Granted** 7 January 1800.

ROYAL LEAMINGTON SPA, BOROUGH OF (WARWICKSHIRE).* Per fesse argent and Or, a lion rampant double-queued vert, a chevron vair, in chief three mullets gules; all within a bordure azure charged with eight fleurs-de-lis of the second. **Crest:** On a wreath of the colours, In front of a staff raguly argent surmounted by a staff in bend sinister Or entwined with a serpent proper, two sprays of Forget-me-nots in saltire slipped, all proper. **Motto:** Sola bona quae honesta. **Granted** 16 November 1876.

ROYAL LONDON MUTUAL ASSURANCE SOCIETY.* Argent, a cross quarterly gules and vert between in the first and fourth quarters two swords in saltire of the second and in the second and third quarters an ancient crown of four fleurs-de-lys of the third. **Crest:** On a wreath of the colours, Upon a mount vert, in front of a representation of the White Tower of the Tower of London proper a lion couchant gules. **Supporters:** On either side a dragon argent charged on the shoulder with a fetterlock gules. **Motto:** Sustentet nos Deus. **Granted** 12 January 1934.

ROYAL MAIL LINES LIMITED.* Azure, upon waves of the sea proper a ship in full sail Or, the sails argent, flying from each mast a pennon also argent charged with a saltire gules; upon a chief also argent, a saltire also gules charged with a representation of the Imperial Crown proper. **Crest:** On a wreath argent and azure, Upon waves of the sea proper a ship in full sail, flying from each mast Or a pennon argent charged with a saltire gules and charged on each sail with a like saltire. **Supporters:** On either side a sea horse proper. **Motto:** Per Mare Ubique. **Badge:** Upon an ogress encircled by a rope Or, on waves of the sea a ship in full sail, flying from each mast a pennon, all gold, upon a scroll also gold the words 'Per Mare Ubique' in letters sable. **Granted** by Royal Warrant 14 February 1929; exemplified 17 April 1929 to the Royal Mail Steam Packet Company; transferred to the above, November 1932.

ROYAL MARSDEN HOSPITAL (LONDON). Per pale gules and azure, a dance argent surmounted by a rod of Aesculapius, ensigned by an ancient crown, between in base two coots Or. **Crest:** On a wreath of the colours, Between two rays of lightning Or a stag's head erased gules, thereon a bee volant gold. **Supporters:** On the dexter side an owl and on the sinister side an unicorn each resting the interior leg upon a crab Or. **Motto:** Labor omnia vincit. **Granted** 14 February 1963.

ROYAL MEDICO-PSYCHOLOGICAL ASSOCIATION. Or, a staff of Aesculapius gules; a bordure sable charged with four butterflies of the field. **Crest:** On a wreath of the colours, A looped cross Or between two wings sable. **Supporters:** On either side a serpent Or, langued gules. **Granted** 12 October 1926.

ROYAL MILITARY COLLEGE OF SCIENCE (SHRIVENHAM, WILTSHIRE). Azure, a cross Or surmounted by another gules, charged with an open book argent; in the first quarter three cannons in pale of the last. **Granted** 9 April 1948 to the Military College of Science.

ROYAL NATIONAL THROAT, NOSE AND EAR HOSPITAL (LONDON). Azure, on a pale Or between two candles, each grasped by a hand issuant from the dexter and sinister base, three sprigs of All-heal (Heradeum Panaces Linnaeus) stalked, leaved and flowered also proper. **Crest:** On a wreath of the colours, Issuant from a chaplet of twelve roses gules, barbed and seeded, an open book proper, thereon a lion's head and a unicorn's head, both erased and respectant of the first. **Supporters:** On the dexter a representation of Aesculapius proper vested gules doubled argent, holding in the exterior hand a retort, and on the sinister a representation of Hygeia proper, robed

ROYAL LEAMINGTON SPA

ROYAL LONDON MUTUAL ASSURANCE

ROYAL MAIL LINES

ROYAL TUNBRIDGE WELLS

argent and azure, a serpent coiled about her neck, and holding in the exterior hand an ancient lamp Or enflamed also proper. **Motto:** Audient surdi multique loquentur. **Granted** 28 September 1951.

ROYAL OVERSEAS LEAGUE. In a shield a representation of a seascape, thereon an ancient ship in full sail, flying a pennon and flags of St. George, all within a bordure of clouds proper **Crest:** On a wreath argent, gules and azure, Two hands, that to the dexter sable, and that to the sinister carnation, supporting a terrestrial globe, the sea Or, the land gules. **Supporters:** On the dexter side a winged sea-unicorn argent, armed, crined, finned and the wings Or, and on the sinister side a winged sea-lion also argent, maned, finned and the wings gold. **Motto:** Ubique navigamus. **Badge:** The letter S within the letter O, the whole ensigned with an ancient ship in full sail Or, the sails argent, flying a pennon and flags of St. George, and on waves of the sea proper. **Granted** 7 January 1960.

ROYAL RADAR ESTABLISHMENT. Per fesse vert and barry wavy of six argent and azure, a pale Or surmounted of another also azure charged with a representation of amplitude signals of successively increasing amplitude, equally paced on a vertical time base of the second. **Crest:** Out of an astral crown a lion rampant Or. Mantled vert, doubled argent. **Motto:** Ubique video. **Granted** 20 August 1959.

ROYAL SANITARY INSTITUTE.* See Health, Royal Society of.

ROYAL SCHOOL FOR DAUGHTERS OF OFFICERS OF THE ARMY (BATH). Per pale gules and azure, a fesse embattled argent between in chief a lion passant guardant Or and in base three bees also argent. **Motto:** Dominus sapientiam dat. **Granted** 10 March 1952.

ROYAL SCHOOL OF CHURCH MUSIC. Argent, five barrulets azure, over all a lyre between six nightingales, three and three, respectant in pale Or; on a chief of the second an open book proper between two stars of eight points of the third. **Crest:** On a wreath of the colours, A demi figure of St. Nicholas vested in pontificals proper, mitred, and holding in his dexter hand a pastoral staff and in his sinister hand three purses Or. **Motto:** Psallam spiritu et mente. **Granted** 12 October 1950.

ROYAL SEAMEN'S PENSION FUND.* Argent, eight ship's bells, four, three and one, sable; on a chief per pale gules and vert, between two anchors an ostrich feather of the first enfiled with a naval crown Or. **Crest:** On a wreath of the colours, Two compass needles in saltire, each per fesse azure and argent, the pivot cap Or. **Granted** 10 September 1932.

ROYAL SOCIETY.* Argent, on a quarter gules three lions passant guardant in pale Or. **Crest:** On a ducal coronet Or, an eagle with wings endorsed proper supporting with his dexter foot an escutcheon gules charged with three lions passant guardant in pale Or. **Supporters:** Two talbots proper ducally gorged Or. **Motto:** Nullius in verba. **Granted** by Sir Edward Walker, Garter King of Arms.

ROYAL TUNBRIDGE WELLS, BOROUGH OF (KENT).* Gules guttée d'eau, on a pile Or between two fountains in base, a lion rampant gules. **Crest:** On a wreath of the colours, A well proper, issuant therefrom a demi lion gules holding between the paws a fountain. **Motto:** Do well, doubt not. **Granted** 19 July 1889.

ROYAL WOLVERHAMPTON SCHOOL.* Azure, on a chevron argent between three bezants, a cross patée gules; all within a bordure Or charged with three Stafford knots gules. **Crest:** Issuant from a crown palisado Or, between two keys in saltire, wards upwards and outwards, a torch erect sable, fired proper. Mantled gules, doubled Or. **Motto:** Nisi Dominus frustra. **Granted** 8 May 1946.

ROYSTON URBAN DISTRICT COUNCIL (HERTFORDSHIRE).* Argent, a fesse gules, thereon another chequy of the first and sable, in chief two Tudor roses barbed and seeded, and in

ROYAL SOCIETY

ROYAL WOLVERHAMPTON SCHOOL

ROYSTON (HERTFORDSHIRE)

ROYSTON (YORKSHIRE)

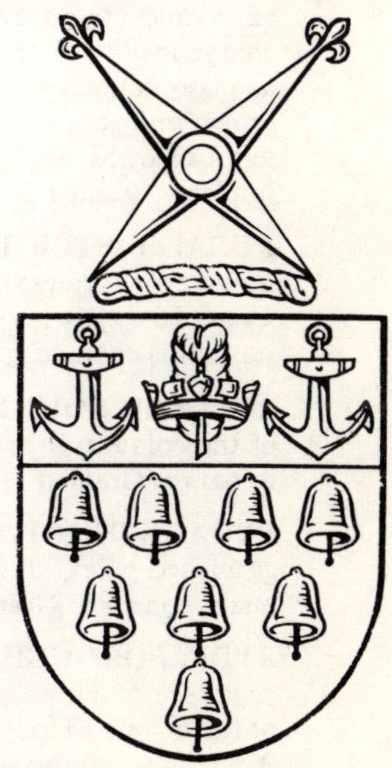

ROYAL SEAMEN'S PENSION FUND

base a stag trippant, the whole surmounting an archiepiscopal staff, all proper. **Crest:** On a wreath of the colours, Perched upon a representation of the Royse Stone a hooded crow proper. **Motto:** A bonis ad meliora. **Granted** 19 May 1952.

ROYSTON URBAN DISTRICT COUNCIL (YORKSHIRE—WEST RIDING).* Ermine, on a saltire gules between in chief and in base a bee volant and in either flank nine ears of wheat banded Or, a fountain; on a chief sable a Paschal Lamb proper between two covered cups argent. **Crest:** On a wreath argent and gules, Out of a wreath of oak fructed proper, a demi lion sable holding in the sinister paw a miner's pick, head to the dexter, and gorged with a chain, pendent therefrom a rose argent, barbed and seeded proper. **Motto:** Fide et industria. **Granted** 3 December 1964.

RUGBY, BOROUGH OF (WARWICKSHIRE).* Per chevron engrailed azure and Or, in chief a bezant charged with a rose gules, barbed and seeded proper, between two griffins' heads erased of the second, and in base a bear erect sable, collared and supporting a ragged staff of the third. **Crest:** On a wreath of the colours, A thunderbolt Or, the flames proper, between two lions' gambs erased gold, each holding a date branch fructed also proper. **Motto:** Floreat Rugbeia. **Granted** 27 September 1932.

RUGBY FOOTBALL UNION. Per chevron engrailed azure and argent, in chief two griffins' heads erased Or and in base a triple rose gules, barbed and seeded, stalked, and with five leaves proper; a bordure Or. **Crest:** On a wreath of the colours, A demi lion guardant Or charged on each leg with two roses gules, barbed and seeded, and resting the sinister paw on a Rugby football fesswise proper. **Motto:** Rugbeia floreat ubique. **Granted** 10 June 1970.

RUGBY SCHOOL.* Azure, on a fesse engrailed between three griffins' heads erased Or, a fleur-de-lys of the first between two roses gules, barbed and seeded proper; a bordure of the second. **Crest:** On a wreath of the colours, A lion's gamb erased Or charged with two roses in pale as in the Arms and holding a branch of dates, the fruit gold in pods argent, the stalks and leaves vert. **Motto:** Orando laborando. **Granted** 9 March 1932.

RUNCORN URBAN DISTRICT COUNCIL (CHESHIRE).* Or, on a base barry wavy of four azure and argent a lymphad proper, flying flags and pennon of St. George, the sail also azure charged with a garb gold; on a chief gules two flaying knives in saltire proper, handles Or, between as many fountains. **Crest:** Out of a mural crown gules, a demi lion sable crowned with an ancient crown and supporting an abbot's crosier Or, pendent therefrom by the guige an escutcheon also gules charged with four fusils conjoined in pale each fessewise gold. **Motto:** Navem mercibus implere. **Granted** 30 October 1956.

RURAL DISTRICT COUNCILS ASSOCIATION. Vert, three garbs Or, each enfiled with a mural crown gules; on a chief per pale of the last and gold a lion passant guardant counterchanged. **Crest:** In a crown vallary Or, a mount, thereon an oak tree fructed proper, and in front thereof a portcullis chained gold. **Motto:** Rura diligere, consilio adjuvare. **Granted** 8 June 1954.

RUTLAND COUNTY COUNCIL.* Vert, semée of acorns, a horseshoe Or. **Crest:** On a wreath of the colours, In front of a horseshoe an acorn Or, leaved and slipped proper. **Motto:** Multum in parvo. **Granted** 1 May 1950.

RYDAL SCHOOL. Ermine, two dolphins naiant in pale Or; on a chief azure an open book proper garnished gules, clasped Or, between two lions sejant respectant of the second. **Motto:** Prodesse quam conspice. **Granted** 9 January 1933.

RYDE, BOROUGH OF (ISLE OF WIGHT).* Argent, in base on waves of the sea a schooner yacht under sail proper, within a bordure azure charged with eight estoiles Or. **Crest:** On a wreath of the colours, Upon a rock a sea-horse proper, charged on the body with two estoiles Or. **Motto:** Amoenitas, salubritas, urbanitas. **Granted** 18 February 1869.

RUGBY

RUGBY SCHOOL

RUNCORN

RUTLAND

RYDE

S

* *Denotes Illustration*

SADDLERS, OF THE CITY OF LONDON, WORSHIPFUL COMPANY OF.* Azure, a chevron between three saddles furnished Or. **Crest:** On a wreath of the colours, A horse passant argent, bridled, saddled, and trapping Or, on its head a plume of three feathers carnation. Mantled gules, doubled argent. **Supporters:** On either side a horse argent, hoofed and bridled Or, on its head a plume of three feathers carnation. **Mottoes:** Hold fast, sit secure; Our trust is in God. Arms confirmed and Crest and Supporters granted 20 October 1585 by Robert Cooke, Clarenceux King of Arms. (*Illustration on page* 351).

SAFFRON WALDEN, BOROUGH OF (ESSEX).* Vert, within a representation of town walls having a gateway between two towers argent, three saffron flowers issuant from the battlements of a gateway blown and showing the stamens proper. **Crest:** On a wreath of the colours, Upon a chapeau gules turned up ermine, a lion rampant azure grasping in the dexter paw a representation of the ancient mace of the Borough of Saffron Walden proper. **Granted** 20 November 1961.

ST. AIDAN'S SOCIETY (DURHAM UNIVERSITY). Per chevron argent and sable, in chief two ancient Northumbrian crosses gules, in base two keys in saltire, wards upwards, of the first. **Crest:** Out of an ancient crown Or, two lions' gambs argent, armed gules, the paws grasping an estoile Or. **Motto:** Super fundamentis certis. **Granted** 31 May 1957.

ST. ALBANS, BISHOPRIC OF.* Azure, a saltire Or, over all a sword erect in pale proper, pomel and hilt of the second, in chief a celestial crown gold. **Granted** 8 June 1877.

ST. ALBANS, CITY OF (HERTFORDSHIRE).* Azure, a saltire Or. Recorded without tinctures at the Visitation of 1634; certified by King's of Arms Certificate 23 October 1951.

ST. ALBANS RURAL DISTRICT COUNCIL (HERTFORDSHIRE).* Or, an eagle displayed, wings inverted, gules charged on the breast with a mural crown of the first; all within a bordure azure charged with eight saltires couped also of the first. **Crest:** On a wreath of the colours, A stag's head proper, attired Or, charged on the neck with a pellet, thereon an escallop argent, and in the mouth three ears of wheat, the stalks bound with a riband, gold. **Motto:** Exemplo sint virtutis. **Granted** 10 August 1954.

ST. ANDREW'S SCHOOL (EASTBOURNE) LIMITED. Azure, a saltire argent surmounted in pale by a torch enflamed proper. **Crest:** On a wreath of the colours, Two fish, their heads downwards and outwards, their tails interlaced and entwined with as many swords in saltire points downwards proper, pommels and hilts Or. **Motto:** ΑΝΔΡΕΙΑ. **Granted** 4 September 1950.

ST. ANNE'S COLLEGE (OXFORD UNIVERSITY). Gules, on a chevron between in chief two lions' heads erased argent and in base a sword of the second, pommelled and hilted Or and enfiled with a wreath of laurel proper, three ravens also proper. These are of no authority.

ST. ANTHONY'S COLLEGE, THE WARDENS AND FELLOWS OF (OXFORD UNIVERSITY).* Or, on a chevron between three Tau crosses gules, as many pierced mullets of the field. **Granted** 30 November 1953.

SAFFRON WALDEN

ST. ALBANS CITY

ST. ALBANS BISHOPRIC

ST. ANTHONY'S COLLEGE

BARTHOLOMEW'S HOSPITAL

ST. ALBANS R.D.C.

ST. ASAPH, BISHOPRIC OF. Sable, two keys in saltire, wards upwards, argent. Recorded in the College of Arms. Sable, a key in bend dexter surmounted of a pastoral staff in bend sinister argent. Recorded in the Parliament Roll of 1512.

ST. BARTHOLOMEW'S HOSPITAL (LONDON).* Per pale argent and sable, a chevron counterchanged. Recorded in the College of Arms.

ST. CATHERINE'S COLLEGE, THE MASTER AND FELLOWS OF (CAMBRIDGE UNIVERSITY).* Gules, a Catherine wheel Or. Recorded at the Visitation of 1684.

ST. CATHERINE'S COLLEGE (OXFORD UNIVERSITY).* Sable, a saltire ermine between four Catherine wheels Or. **Motto:** Nova et vetera. **Granted** 10 June 1963.

ST. CHAD'S COLLEGE (DURHAM UNIVERSITY). Vert, a cross potent Or, in chief a Durham mitre of the last between two lions rampant argent. **Crest:** On a wreath of the colours, Two hands proper grasping a plate, thereon a cross pattée quadrate gules. **Motto:** Non vestra sed vos. **Granted** 17 December 1951.

ST. CLEMENT DANES GRAMMAR SCHOOL. Azure, an anchor Or, the stock banded vert; on a bordure engrailed gold eight hearts gules. **Badge:** An anchor as in the Arms within an annulet Or, thereon a chain gules. **Granted** 10 September 1963.

ST. CUTHBERT'S SOCIETY (DURHAM UNIVERSITY). Vert, a representation of St. Cuthbert's cross proper; a bordure argent. **Crest:** Out of an ancient crown Or an eider duck rising proper. Mantled vert, doubled argent. **Motto:** Gratia gratiam capit. **Granted** 31 May 1957.

ST. DAVIDS, BISHOPRIC OF.* Sable, on a cross Or five pierced cinquefoils of the field. Recorded in the College of Arms.

ST. DAVIDS COLLEGE OF (LAMPETER). Sable, between four cinquefoils in cross Or a figure representing St. David standing in his archiepiscopal robes in a niche under a canopy, holding in his dexter hand a crosier and in his sinister a book, all gold. **Motto:** Gair Duw Gorew Dysg. **Granted** 1830.

ST. EDMUND HALL (OXFORD UNIVERSITY). Or, a cross patonce between four sea-pies sable, winged argent. These are of no authority.

ST. EDMUNDSBURY AND IPSWICH, BISHOPRIC OF. Per pale and azure, between three ducal coronets a demi lion passant guardant conjoined to a demi hull of an ancient ship [all Or]. **Granted** 12 August 1949.

ST. ENDELLION, PREBENDAL FOUNDATION OF. Per chevron wavy azure and vert, in chief a crown vallary between two heifers' heads caboshed and in base a cow couchant guardant Or. **Granted** 27 November 1950.

ST. FAITH'S AND AYLSHAM RURAL DISTRICT COUNCIL (NORFOLK).* Azure, on a pile Or between two ostrich feathers ermine, the quill of each piercing a scroll argent, a dexter arm issuant from the sinister vested with a maunch gules, the hand proper grasping a rose gules, barbed slipped and seeded proper. **Crest:** On a wreath of the colours, Out of a mural crown argent charged with a cinquefoil sable between two fleurs-de-lys azure, a bull's head also sable wreathed about the neck with a torse of the first and vert. **Motto:** Studio fide animis. **Granted** 20 August 1957.

ST. FELIX SCHOOL LIMITED (SOUTHWOLD). Vert, a chevron between in chief to the dexter a Catherine wheel and to the sinister a lymphad, and in base a mitre, all Or. **Crest:** Issuant out of a coronet composed of six roses set upon a rim Or, a griffin's head holding in the beak a taper inflamed proper. **Motto:** Felix quia fortis. **Granted** 10 October 1933.

ST. CATHERINE'S COLLEGE
(OXFORD UNIVERSITY)

ST. CATHERINE'S COLLEGE
(CAMBRIDGE UNIVERSITY)

ST. DAVIDS BISHOPRIC

ST. FAITH'S AND AYLSHAM

ST. HILDA'S COLLEGE

ST. HELENS

ST. GEORGE'S HOSPITAL (LONDON). Or, the staff of Aesculapius in pale proper surmounted by a celestial crown azure. **Crest:** On a wreath of the colours, A lion rampant Or resting the forepaws on an antique shield charged with the figure of St. George slaying the dragon proper. **Supporters:** On the dexter side a figure representing Aesculapius proper habited in a robe purpure, supporting with the left hand his staff also proper, and on the sinister side a figure representing Hygeia, vested argent, holding in the exterior hand the patera and serpent proper. **Motto:** Deus incubat angui. **Granted** 28 February 1835.

ST. HELENS, COUNTY BOROUGH OF (LANCASHIRE).* Argent, two bars azure, over all a cross sable; in the first quarter a saltire gules and in the second and third a griffin sergeant of the third. **Crest:** On a wreath of the colours, A lion passant guardant proper charged on the body with two fleurs-de-lis gules, resting the dexter fore paw on an ingot of silver. **Motto:** Ex terra lucem. **Granted** 17 January 1876.

ST. HILDA'S COLLEGE (DURHAM UNIVERSITY). Purpure, three ammonites in bend between two cotices, in chief a lion rampant supporting a bourdon and in base a cross formy quadrate argent. **Crest:** On a wreath of the colours, A crozier head Or. **Motto:** Supra montem posita. **Granted** 10 June 1962.

ST. HILDA'S COLLEGE (OXFORD UNIVERSITY).* Azure, on a fesse Or between in chief two unicorns' heads couped and in base a coiled serpent argent, three estoiles gules. **Granted** 20 May 1960.

ST. HUGH'S COLLEGE (OXFORD UNIVERSITY). Azure, a saltire ermine between four fleurs-de-lys Or. These are of no authority.

ST. IGNATIUS COLLEGE (TOTTENHAM). Per fesse argent and Or, in chief a caldron suspended by a chain sable, supported by two wolves rampant gules, and in base three bendlets vert. **Crest:** On a wreath argent and vert, A torch sable, enflamed proper, between four ostrich feathers, the inner Or, the outer gules. **Motto:** Ad majorem Dei gloriam. **Granted** 18 December 1953.

ST. JOHN'S COLLEGE (CAMBRIDGE UNIVERSITY).* Quarterly France Modern and England; a bordure company argent and azure. Recorded in the College of Arms.

ST. JOHN'S COLLEGE (DURHAM UNIVERSITY). Quarterly argent and azure, in the first and fourth a cross formy quadrate gules, in the second an eagle wings elevated and inverted Or, in the third a lion rampant crowned with an ancient crown of the last; all within a bordure quarterly of the second and gold. **Crest:** Out of an ancient crown Or, two lions' gambs argent, armed gules, the paws grasping a pair of wings conjoined in base gold. Mantled azure, doubled Or. **Motto:** Fides nostra victoria. **Granted** 31 May 1957.

ST. JOHN'S COLLEGE (OXFORD UNIVERSITY). Gules, on a bordure sable eight estoiles Or, on a canton ermine a lion rampant of the second; in chief an annulet gold (for difference). These are of no authority.

ST. JOHN'S COLLEGE (YORK).* Per chevron vert and Or, in chief two pairs of keys in saltire, wards upwards and outwards, of the last and in base an eagle displayed sable. **Crest:** On a wreath of the colours, An eagle displayed sable charged on the dexter wing with a torch inflamed and on the sinister wing with a key erect, the ward upwards and to the sinister, Or. **Granted** 29 September 1952.

ST. JOHN OF JERUSALEM, THE GRAND PRIORY IN THE BRITISH REALM OF THE VENERABLE ORDER OF THE HOSPITAL OF. Gules, a cross argent, in the first quarter a representation of the Royal Crest of England. **Granted** by Royal Warrant 1 February 1926; exemplified 15 March 1926.

SALE

ST. JOHN'S COLLEGE (YORK)

ST. JOHN'S COLLEGE (CAMBRIDGE UNIVERSITY)

ST. MARGARET'S SCHOOL

ST. PETER'S HALL

ST. PETER'S SCHOOL

ST. JOHN'S SCHOOL (HURSTPIERPOINT). Per pale argent and ermine, dexter on a bend cottised sable a cross couped between two martlets of the first, on a chief gules an eagle, round the head a crown of glory, Or, sinister two wolves passant counterpassant also gules; all within a bordure engrailed azure. **Motto:** Beati mundo corde. **Granted** 1 June 1931.

ST. LAWRENCE COLLEGE (RAMSGATE) ALIAS SOUTH EASTERN COLLEGE. Gules, an open book argent edged and surmounted by a celestial crown Or; on a chief of the second an annulet between two crosses patée of the first. **Crest:** On a wreath of the colours, In front of two amphibanes entwined Or, an escallop argent. **Motto:** In bono vince. **Granted** 15 April 1929.

ST. LOYES COLLEGE FOR THE TRAINING AND REHABILITATION OF THE DISABLED. Or, a chevron potent between two leopards' faces and in base an eagle displayed sable; on a chief argent between two crosses gules a Tudor rose barbed and seeded proper. **Crest:** On a wreath of the colours, In front of a torch azure fired Or two keys in saltire of the last. **Supporters:** On either side a shoveller close in front of an apple tree proper fructed Or; the whole resting upon a compartment gules between water also proper. **Granted** 12 January 1950.

ST. MARGARET'S SCHOOL (BUSHEY, HERTFORDSHIRE).* Or, on a cross gules a Saxon crown gold; on a chief vert an open book proper, bound also gules, edged of the first. **Motto:** Sursum corda, habemus ad Dominum. **Granted** 26 September 1957, to The Governors of the Society for Clothing, Maintaining and Educating Poor Orphans of Clergymen of the Established Church in that Part of the United Kingdom called England until of age to be put apprentice, for the use of the School.

ST. MARK AND ST. JOHN, COLLEGE OF (CHELSEA). Argent, two swords in saltire, points upwards, between four fusils gules; on a chief per pale azure and of the second, to the dexter a winged lion sejant guardant Or resting the dexter fore paw on an open book proper, and to the sinister a Paschal Lamb also proper. **Motto:** Abeunt studia in mores. **Badge:** Upon a closed book proper, clasped Or, a lamb argent, winged Or, supporting with the dexter fore leg a staff proper, flowing therefrom a banner azure charged with a winged lion sejant Or resting the dexter fore paw on an open book proper. **Granted** 18 September 1925.

ST. MARTIN'S COLLEGE OF EDUCATION (LANCASTER). Azure, a sword in bend argent, hilt and pomel Or, cotised between a mitre and a mantle bisected in pale argent. **Crest:** On a wreath of the colours, In front of a mantle as in the Arms, a sword proper, hilt and pomel to the dexter Or, perched on the blade a martin azure, in the beak a rose gules barbed, seeded, stalked and leaved proper. **Motto:** Scio cui credidi. **Granted** 1 August 1966.

ST. MARY'S SOCIETY (DURHAM UNIVERSITY). Argent, a cross formy quadrate gules; a chief azure, thereon a Durham mitre Or between two lilies proper. **Crest:** Out of an ancient crown Or two lions' gambs argent, armed gules, the paws grasping a rose also argent. Mantled gules, doubled argent. **Motto:** Ancilla Domini. **Granted** 31 May 1957.

ST. MICHAEL'S COLLEGE (LEEDS). Azure, a sword erect enflamed proper, pomel and hilt Or; a bordure argent gutty de sang. **Motto:** Quis ut Deus. **Granted** 10 April 1967.

ST. PETER'S COLLEGE, RADLEY. Argent, an open book [proper] garnished gules, clasps and buckles Or, thereon inscribed the words 'Sicut serpentes sicut columbae' between three crosses patée of the second; on a chief of the last a key in bend sinister of the first surmounted by a like key in bend dexter gold between to the dexter a serpent nowed and erect and to the sinister a dove, both proper. **Motto:** Sicut serpentes sicut columbae. **Granted** 14 May 1908.

ST. PETER'S HALL (OXFORD UNIVERSITY).* Per pale vert and argent, dexter two keys in saltire Or surmounted by a triple towered castle of the second masoned sable, sinister a cross gules surmounted by a mitre of the third between four martlets sable; the whole within a bordure gold. **Granted** 19 December 1929.

ST. PETER'S SCHOOL (YORK).* Azure, a key in bend, ward upwards, Or surmounting a like key in bend sinister argent, between in chief an ancient crown of the second and three double roses, two in fesse, and one in base, also argent, barbed and seeded proper. **Crest:** On a wreath of the colours, An ancient tiara, the cap argent, the crown and mound gold. **Motto:** Super antiquas vias. **Granted** 23 July 1953.

ST. SWITHIN'S SCHOOL (WINCHESTER). Azure, on a pale between two keys, wards upwards and outwards, Or, a representation of St. Swithin of the first. **Crest:** On a wreath of the colours, A lion rampant Or supporting with the forepaws a key, ward upwards, azure and resting the dexter hind leg on a hurt. **Motto:** Caritas, Humilitas, Sinceritas. **Granted** 9 June 1936.

ST. THOMAS' HOSPITAL (LONDON). Argent, on a cross between in the first quarter a sword erect gules and in the second quarter a chough proper, a roach haurient of the first; on a chief azure a rose of the field, barbed and seeded proper, between two fleurs-de-lys Or. **Crest:** On a wreath of the colours, Between four spears, points upwards, sable, embrued gules, three Madonna lilies argent, stalked and leaved vert. **Supporters:** On the dexter side a chough, and on the sinister side a nightingale, both proper. **Granted** 14 February 1950.

ST. THOMAS' HOSPITAL MEDICAL SCHOOL. Argent, on a cross between in the first quarter a sword erect and in the fourth quarter a rod of Aesculapius gules, a torch Or inflamed proper; a chief azure, thereon a rose of the first, barbed and seeded proper, between two fleurs-de-lys also of the first. **Granted** 28 January 1949.

ST. THOMAS OF CANTERBURY ROMAN CATHOLIC SECONDARY SCHOOL (BLACKPOOL, LANCASHIRE). Argent, on a bend azure between two Cornish choughs proper, in the beak of each a rose gules, barbed, seeded, stalked and leaved proper, an open book argent, edged, bound, and between two celestial crowns Or. **Crest:** On a wreath of the colours, Perched upon the battlements of a tower Or charged with three roses gules, barbed and seeded, a Cornish chough proper crowned with a celestial crown Or. **Motto:** Pro Deo prodeo. **Granted** 10 October 1967.

SALE, BOROUGH OF (CHESHIRE).* Azure, on a pile argent between two garbs Or, three lozenges sable. **Crest:** On a wreath of the colours, Upon the battlements of a tower argent, a moorcock sable, combed and wattled gules, beaked and legged Or. **Supporters:** On the dexter side a unicorn argent, armed and unguled Or, maned and tufted azure, and on the sinister side a badger proper, each gorged with a wreath of sallow twigs also proper. **Motto:** Salus et felicitas. Arms and Crest granted to the Sale UDC 23 September 1920; **Supporters** granted to the Borough 15 August 1945.

SALESIAN COLLEGE (CHERTSEY). Per pale Or and argent, two keys addorsed in bend sinister, the bows interlaced in base, gules and azure, within an orle of six sprigs of oak fructed proper; on a chief per pale azure and gules a lily flower and a chalice gold with the Host also argent. **Granted** 5 August 1964.

SALFORD, CITY AND COUNTY BOROUGH OF (LANCASHIRE).* Azure, semée of bees volant, a shuttle between three garbs Or; on a chief of the last a bale corded proper between two mill-rinds sable. **Crest:** On a wreath of the colours, A demi lion argent supporting a lance proper, therefrom flowing to the sinister a flag azure charged with a shuttle Or. **Supporters:** On the dexter side a wolf Or, around the neck a chain and pendent therefrom an escocheon gules charged with a mill-rind also Or; on the sinister side an heraldic antelope argent, armed crined and unguled Or, around the neck a chain and pendent therefrom an escocheon gules charged with a rose also argent. **Motto:** Integrity and Industry. **Badge:** Within a collar argent fimbriated Or, set thereon four roses gules, barbed and seeded proper, and as many letters S also gules alternately, a hurt, thereon issuant from a wreath of sallow a demi lion also argent. Arms and Crest granted 5 November 1844; Supporters granted 6 November 1844. Badge granted 15 September 1959.

SALFORD, UNIVERSITY OF. Azure, a sun of sixteen rays within and conjoining the links of a circular chain Or; on a chief gold a lion passant guardant proper between two roses gules barbed and seeded proper. **Crest:** On a wreath of the colours, A demi lion argent, collared vair, supporting a lance proper, flying therefrom a forked pennon per fesse of the first and azure charged in the hoist with a rose as in the Arms. **Motto:** Altiora petamus. **Granted** 15 December 1959 to the Royal Technical College, Salford; transferred to the above 19 March 1968.

SALFORD HOSPITAL MANAGEMENT COMMITTEE. Azure, a chief Or, and over all a pale counterchanged, in chief an ancient lamp Or, inflamed proper, between two roses gules, barbed and seeded, and on the pale a rod of Aesculapius proper. **Crest:** On a wreath of the colours, A demi heraldic antelope argent, armed and unguled, maned and tufted, Or, about the neck a chain gules, supporting between the legs a crux ansata Or. **Motto:** Salus populi curanda. **Granted** 12 March 1968.

SALISBURY, BISHOPRIC OF.* Azure, Our Lady crowned, holding in her dexter arm the Infant Jesus, in her sinister hand a sceptre Or, round both heads circles of glory of the last. Recorded in the College of Arms.

SALISBURY, CITY OF (WILTSHIRE).* Azure, four bars Or. **Supporters:** On either side an eagle displayed with two heads Or, ducally gorged azure. Recorded at the Visitation of 1565 and with variations at that of 1623.

SALISBURY AND WILTON RURAL DISTRICT COUNCIL (WILTSHIRE). Barry or and vert, three lions rampant argent; on a chief of the second a coronet composed of four ears of wheat and as many acorns leaved alternately set upon a rim gold. **Crest:** On a wreath of the colours, A demi double-headed eagle, wings displayed, sable, gorged with a naval crown Or and holding in each beak a branch of palm proper. **Motto:** Unity is strength. **Granted** 20 November 1959.

SALTBURN AND MARSKE-BY-THE-SEA URBAN DISTRICT COUNCIL (YORKSHIRE—NORTH RIDING).* Azure, rising from waves a seagull affrontée proper; on a chief Or three tridents' heads gules. **Crest:** On a wreath argent and azure, On water barry wavy a Roman ship proper with three pennons flying to the dexter gules, the sail also proper charged with two wings conjoined in lure azure. **Motto:** Surgimus. **Granted** 19 June 1935.

SALTERS OF THE CITY OF LONDON, WORSHIPFUL COMPANY OF.* Per chevron azure and gules, three covered salts argent garnished Or, the salt shedding on both sides of the salt argent. **Crest:** On a wreath argent and gules, Issuing from water proper an arm embowed carnation holding in the hand a salt as in the Arms. **Supporters:** On either side an ounce sable bezanty ducally gorged and chained Or. **Motto:** Sal sapit omnia. Arms granted 17 November 1530 by Thomas Benolt, Clarenceux King of Arms; Crest and Supporters granted 25 September 1591 by Robert Cooke, Clarenceux King of Arms; the whole recorded at the Visitations of 1634 and 1687.

THE SALVAGE ASSOCIATION. See Association for the Protection of Commercial Interests as respects Wrecked and Damaged Property.

SANDBACH URBAN DISTRICT COUNCIL (CHESHIRE).* Azure, on a fesse argent between in chief two garbs and in base a representation of the Saxon crosses of Sandbach Or, a fesse gules. **Crest:** On a wreath Or and azure, In front of a garb Or banded with silk ribbons alternately azure and gules, a demi wheel of the last. **Motto:** Principia non homines. **Granted** 20 June 1956.

SANDWICH, BOROUGH OF (KENT).* Per pale gules and azure, three demi lions passant guardant Or conjoined to the hulks of as many ships argent. Recorded at the Visitation of 1574.

SAVE AND PROSPER GROUP LIMITED. Or, semée of hexagons gules voided of the field, over all three keys fessewise in pale, wards to the dexter, sable. **Crest:** On a wreath Or and Sable, A rising Sun Or charged with three keys erect in fesse, wards to the sinister, sable. **Supporters:**

SALFORD

SALISBURY BISHOPRIC

SALISBURY

SALTBURN AND MARSKE

On either side a lion triple-queued and grasping in the exterior paw a key erect, wards inwards, sable. **Motto:** Save and Prosper. **Granted** 15 June 1960 to the Bank Insurance Trust Corporation Limited; regranted to the above 10 December 1962.

SAVINGS AND LOAN SOCIETY LIMITED. Argent, a saltire gules, over all a balance counterchanged between in chief and in base a purse of the second. **Crest:** Out of an Eastern crown Or, a demi lion guardant gules gorged with a chain, pendent therefrom a key, wards to the dexter, gold. **Motto:** Memores polliciti nostri. **Granted** 28 September 1956.

SAVOY HOTEL LIMITED. Gules, on a cross argent an ostrich feather ermine between in pale two millrinds gules and in fess two fleurs-de-lys azure; on a chief argent a Paschal Lamb couchant proper between two roses gules, barbed and seeded proper. **Crest:** On a wreath of the colours, In front of a wheel Or an eagle displayed sable. **Motto:** For excellence we strive. **Badge:** On a mount vert, in front of a triple-towered castle a falcon rising proper. **Granted** 5 May 1966.

SAWBRIDGEWORTH URBAN DISTRICT COUNCIL (HERTFORDSHIRE).* Gules, a garb Or between two barge rudders addorsed argent furnished gold, the dexter tiller superimposing the sinister; a chief enarched per fess indented throughout azure and argent. **Crest:** On a wreath argent and gules, On a mount vert, between two oast houses each garlanded with apple blossom, a hart lodged, all proper. **Motto:** Concordia, amicitia, conjuncta. **Granted** 20 July 1962.

SCARBOROUGH, BOROUGH OF (YORKSHIRE—NORTH RIDING).* Per fesse wavy gules and barry wavy of six argent and azure, issuant in chief to the dexter a lymphad and to the sinister a square tower, in the chief point an estoile, all of the second. **Crest:** On a wreath of the colours, In front of a lymphad sable and sail gules charged with an estoile Or, three roses argent, barbed and seeded proper. **Supporters:** On either side a stag reguardant gules, that to the dexter gorged with a chain Or, pendent therefrom a rose argent barbed and seeded proper, that to the sinister gorged with a like chain, pendent therefrom a bugle horn gold. **Motto:** Per pericula ad decus ire juvat. **Granted** 3 December 1935.

SCARBOROUGH COLLEGE. Per chevron enarched azure and sable, in chief a sun issuant Or and in base a dolphin haurient argent. **Crest:** On a wreath argent and vert, Perched on a mural crown gules, an owl proper between two sprigs of laurel vert. Mantled vert, doubled Or. **Motto:** Pensez fort. **Granted** 20 December 1963.

SCHRODERS LIMITED. Argent, a fesse gules, in chief three roses also gules, barbed, seeded, stalked and leaved proper, their stalks intertwined in saltire, in base three mullets of six points, two and one, azure; all within a bordure of the last charged with eight bezants. **Crest:** Out of an ancient coronet Or, a rose as in the Arms, the stalk erect, between two buffalo horns argent, each banded gules, the band charged with a bezant. **Supporters:** On the dexter side a lion argent charged on the body with three bezants palewise, and on the sinister side a unicorn also argent, armed, unguled, crined and tufted gold, and charged likewise with three bezants. **Granted** 9 December 1959.

SCIENCE AND TECHNOLOGY, THE UNIVERSITY OF WALES INSTITUTE OF (ARTHROFA GWYDDENIAETH A THECHNOLOG PRIFYSGOL CYMRU). Azure, four annulets, two and two, that in dexter chief enclosing a cross throughout, that in sinister chief a bezant, and that in sinister base a barrulet throughout, all Or; a bordure argent. **Crest:** On a wreath of the colours, A dragon passant gules charged on the wing and holding in the dexter claw an annulet embattled Or. **Motto:** Dawn dysg deall. **Badge:** On a bezant embattled Or a hurt charged with four annulets, two and two, that in dexter chief enclosing a cross throughout, that in sinister chief a bezant, and that in sinister base a barrulet throughout, all Or. **Granted** 19 December 1969.

SCIENTIFIC INSTRUMENT MAKERS, COMPANY OF. Tierce in pairle azure, Or and argent, ten cubes conjoined in perspective, four, three, two and one, the tops also Or, the dexter

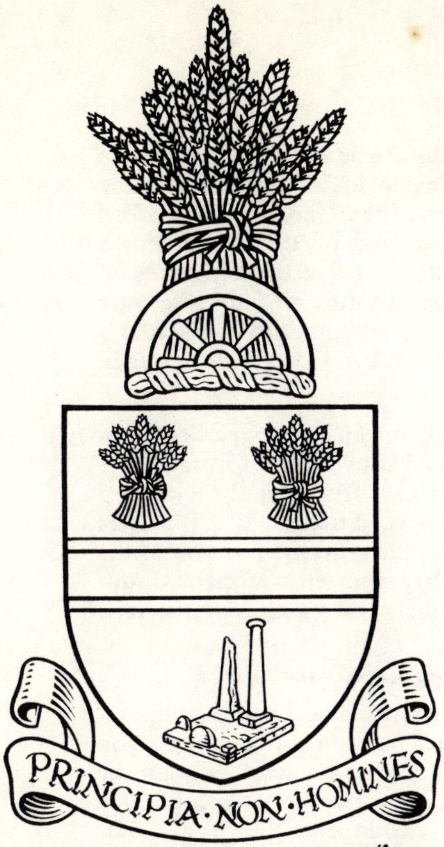

SANDBACH

SANDWICH

SAWBRIDGEWORTH

SCARBOROUGH

SCUNTHORPE

[and sinister] sides sable and azure respectively. **Crest:** On a wreath of the colours, An antique bronze bust of Minerva proper, the eyes argent. **Supporters:** On the dexter side a figure representing Michael Faraday habited in a festal gown of a Doctor of Civil Law of the University of Oxford and holding in the exterior hand a representation of his coil proper, and on the sinister side a figure representing Sir Isaac Newton habited in a gown of a Master of Arts of the University of Cambridge and holding in the exterior hand his telescope also proper. **Motto:** Sine nobis scientia languet. **Badge:** On a roundle azure a quartz crystal proper within a representation of Faraday's Ring argent, the coil Or. Arms, Crest and Supporters granted 10 December 1956; Badge granted 15 December 1960.

THE SCOUT ASSOCIATION. Per fess Or and argent, a lion rampant guardant gules between two tilting spears palewise proper between four fleurs-de-lys azure and four crosses formy in orle gules. **Crest:** Issuant out of a crown vallary Or, two oak branches proper, fructed and enclosing a fleur-de-lys Or charged on each lobe with a mullet vert. Mantled vert, doubled Or. **Supporters** On either side a Scout, the dexter in the uniform of the present, the sinister in the uniform of the past, upon a compartment representing Brownsea Island with a bay and jetty proper. **Motto:** Be prepared. **Badge:** A fleur-de-lys Or charged on the dexter and sinister lobe with a mullet vert. **Granted** 10 March 1969.

SCRIVENERS OF THE CITY OF LONDON, WORSHIPFUL COMPANY OF.* Azure, an eagle volant Or, holding in its beak a penner and inkhorn sable stringed gules, standing upon a book gules garnished Or. **Crest:** On a wreath Or and azure, A dexter hand proper holding a pen argent, the sleeve Or turned up argent, issuing from a cloud proper, over all a scroll bearing the motto 'Scribite scientes'. Mantled gules, doubled argent. **Supporters:** On either side a councillor proper standing upon a scroll beneath the Arms also bearing the motto as over the Crest. Additional motto (replacing the latter): Littera scripta manet. Arms confirmed and Crest and Supporters granted 11 November 1634 by Sir Richard St. George, Clarenceux King of Arms. (*Illn. page* 351).

SCUNTHORPE, BOROUGH OF (LINCOLNSHIRE—PARTS OF LINDSEY).* Vert, a chain of five links in fesse between in chief two shells (Gryphoea incurva) and in base a garb Or. **Crest:** On a wreath of the colours, The top of a blast furnace, issuant therefrom flames, all proper. **Motto:** Refulget labores nostros coelum. **Granted** 25 September 1936.

SEAFARERS' EDUCATION SERVICE. Barry wavy of eight argent and azure, an ancient ship Or, the sail gules, flying from the main mast a pennant argent charged with a cross also gules, in chief a merchantile crown Or between two open books proper, edged and bound also Or. **Crest:** On a wreath of the colours, A sea dog sejant azure, finned gold, supporting with the dexter fore paw a torch also gold, enflamed proper. **Motto:** Salo extendere scientiam. **Granted** 25 February 1958.

SEAFORD URBAN DISTRICT COUNCIL (EAST SUSSEX).* Argent, on water barry wavy a lymphad sailing to the sinister proper, pennons flying gules; a chief per pale of the last and Or, thereon to the dexter two demi lions passant guardant gold conjoined with as many sterns of ships of the field in pale, and to the sinister an eagle displayed sable. **Motto:** E ventis vires. **Granted** 18 April 1953.

SEAHAM URBAN DISTRICT COUNCIL (CO. DURHAM).* Tierced in pairle reversed vert, sable and azure, in chief a garb and a miner's lamp Or and in base on water barry wavy a cargo steamer affrontée proper. **Crest:** On a wreath Or and azure, A pick and spade in saltire sable, hafts downward, and tied with a ribbon Or. **Motto:** By courage and Faith, **Granted** 28 September 1951.

SEA INSURANCE COMPANY LIMITED. Per fesse, barry wavy azure and argent, and sable, in chief two lymphads of the last, sails also argent, pennons and flags flying gules, and in base a

THE SADLERS

THE SALTERS

THE SCRIVENERS

THE SHIPWRIGHTS

phoenix proper. **Crest:** On a wreath argent and sable, A cormorant proper supporting with the beak an anchor Or. **Granted** 20 March 1957.

SEATON URBAN DISTRICT COUNCIL (DEVON).* Azure, a lymphad, sail furled, Or, flying flags and pennon of St. George, between in chief two dolphins haurient respectant Or; on a chief wavy argent a demi eagle issuant, wings displayed, purpure. **Crest:** On a wreath of the colours, Out of a Saxon crown Or a demi lion gules charged on the shoulder with two crozier-heads conjoined in the form of a letter S Or, and holding in the paws a unicorn's head erased argent. **Motto:** Seek, strive, attain. **Granted** 15 August 1967.

SECRETARIES, CHARTERED INSTITUTE OF. Ermine, on a pale engrailed azure between two keys, wards downwards and outwards, a pen Or; on a chief gules a lion passant guardant erminois. **Crest:** On a wreath argent and azure, Upon a key fessewise, wards downwards to the sinister, Or a Secretary bird proper. **Supporters:** On either side a lion guardant Or charged on the shoulder with an escutcheon gules, thereon a rose gold barbed and seeded proper. **Motto:** Semper vigilans rege adjuvante. Arms (without chief and with quill pen argent) and Crest granted 2 May 1903; Arms changed, Crest confirmed and Supporters granted 9 January 1928.

SECRETARIES, CORPORATION OF.* Or, a terrestrial globe proper; on a bordure gules eight bees of the field. **Crest:** On a wreath of the colours, In front of a Secretary bird holding in the dexter claw a quill pen point downwards, an open book, all proper. **Supporters:** On either side a lion Or, gorged with a collar gules charged with three bees gold, pendent from the collar an escutcheon azure, the dexter charged with a balance and the sinister with a torch enflamed also gold. **Motto:** Virtute officii. **Granted** 25 June 1954.

SECRETARIES' ASSOCIATION, THE. Azure, an open book proper, leaves edged Or and binding gules; a chief of the second, thereon between two pens of the first a hurt charged with the head of Mercury couped at the shoulders proper. **Motto:** Prorsum semper honeste. **Granted** 10 June 1925.

SECURITY LIFE ASSURANCES LIMITED.* Azure fretty argent, an anchor Or; on a chief gules a mullet between a fleece and a garb Or. **Crest:** On a wreath of the colours, On a mount vert, in front of a sun rising proper a cup argent. **Granted** 30 May 1963.

SEDGEFIELD RURAL DISTRICT COUNCIL (CO. DURHAM).* Sable, a pick and shovel in saltire Or; on a chief of the last a cross couped between two garbs Or. **Crest:** Issuant from a coronet composed of oak leaves and acorns proper set alternately upon a rim, a horseshoe Or. **Motto:** Ex terra vigemus. **Granted** 27 September 1954.

SEISDON RURAL DISTRICT COUNCIL (STAFFORDSHIRE).* Argent fretty gules cloué Or, a bordure vert charged with twelve Stafford knots gold. **Crest:** On a wreath of the colours, Issuant from flames proper a demi unicorn argent, armed, crined, tufted and unguled Or, supporting a Roman sword, point downwards, also proper, hilt and pomel gold. **Motto:** Honeste progrediemur conando. **Granted** 5 September 1952.

SELWYN COLLEGE, THE MASTER, FELLOWS AND SCHOLARS OF (CAMBRIDGE UNIVERSITY).* Per pale gules and argent, a cross potent quadrate [per pale] argent and Or between four crosses paty, those to the dexter argent, those to the sinister Or, for the See of Lichfield, impaling Argent, on a bend cotised sable three annulets Or, for Selwyn; all within a bordure sable. **Crest:** On a wreath Or and purpure, In front of a book erect, bound gules, edged, clasped and garnished Or, a representation of the pastoral staff of Bishop Selwyn. **Motto:** ΑΝΔΡΙΣΕΣΘΕ. **Badge:** A mitre Or within an annulet purpure. **Granted** 3 December 1964.

THE SERVICES KINEMA CORPORATION. Gules, four swords saltirewise, points inwards, argent, hilts and pomels and the blades interlaced with a wreath of oakleaves Or enfiling on the

SEAHAM

SEAFORD

SEATON

SECURITY LIFE ASSURANCES

SECRETARIES CORPORATION

dexter side a naval crown and on the sinister side an astral crown argent. **Crest:** On a wreath Or, gules and azure, On a demi terrestrial globe Or, a cat-a-mountain statant guardant proper ducally crowned and supporting with the dexter forepaw a trident erect Or. Mantled gules and azure, doubled Or and argent. **Motto:** Lux ib tenebris. **Badge:** Surmounting two swords saltirewise argent, hilts and pomels and within a wreath of oak leaves bound in base by the riband to a foul anchor Or, over all in fesse two wings argent and a cat-a-mountain rampant guardant proper, crowned Or. **Granted** 30 September 1969.

SETTLE RURAL DISTRICT COUNCIL (YORKSHIRE—WEST RIDING). Per pale Or and gules, on a mount in base a representation of the Market Cross of Giggleswick proper supported by a lion azure and a lion argent. **Crest:** On a wreath argent and vert, In front of a representation of the summit of Ingleborough, thereon a Craven heifer statant guardant proper, a rose argent, barbed, seeded, slipped and leaved proper. Mantled vert, doubled argent. **Motto:** Cavendo tutus adversa sperno. **Granted** 20 November 1964.

SEVENOAKS URBAN DISTRICT COUNCIL (KENT).* Gules, on a pall azure fimbriated argent seven acorns Or. **Crest:** Out of a circlet argent charged with eight lozenges throughout gules, a demi horse supporting a lance erect argent tipped Or entwined about with a branch of vine fructed proper. Mantled gules, doubled Or. **Motto:** Floreant septem quercus. **Granted** 3 December 1964.

SHEFFIELD, BISHOPRIC OF. Azure, a crozier in pale, ensigned by a fleur-de-lis, between in fess a key surmounted by a sword in saltire to the dexter and to the sinister eight arrows interlaced and banded saltirewise, all Or. **Granted** 21 April 1914.

SHEFFIELD, CATHEDRAL CHAPTER OF THE CATHEDRAL CHURCH OF ST. PETER AND ST. PAUL. Per fess gules and sable, a sword in bend sinister, point upwards, argent, hilt and pomel Or, surmounted of a key in bend, ward upward and outward, of the last, in chief eight arrows fretted in saltire, points downward, banded of the third. **Granted** 9 February 1951.

SHEFFIELD, CITY AND COUNTY BOROUGH OF (YORKSHIRE—WEST RIDING).* Per fesse azure and vert, in chief eight arrows interlaced saltirewise banded argent and in base three garbs fessewise Or. **Crest:** On a wreath of the colours, A lion rampant argent, gorged with a collar and holding between the paws an antique shield azure charged with eight arrows as in the Arms. **Supporters:** On the dexter side a figure habited as Thor resting his exterior hand on a hammer all proper, and on the sinister side a figure habited as Vulcan standing in front of an anvil and in the dexter hand a pair of pincers all also proper. **Motto:** Deo adjuvante labor proficit. Arms and Crest granted 26 July 1875; Supporters granted 31 August 1893.

SHEFFIELD, UNIVERSITY OF. Azure, an open book proper, edged gold, inscribed with the words 'Disce Doce', between in fess two sheaves of eight arrows interlaced saltireways and banded argent, in chief an open crown Or, and in base a rose also argent, barbed and seeded proper. **Motto:** Rerum cognoscere causas. **Badge** (for the use of Earnshaw Hall): An eagle's leg erased sable, armed gules, charged on the thigh with a pomegranate Or, seeded proper, the talons upward and grasping an arrow pointing to the dexter argent transfixing two wooden wedges proper. **Badge** (for the use of Stephenson Hall): A falcon's head erased gules, beaked Or, gorged with a collar vair, pendent therefrom an escutcheon vert charged with two arrows in saltire, barbs downward, Or, in the beak an arrow in bend, barb downward, azure. Arms granted 28 June 1905; first Badge granted 20 May 1966; second Badge granted 5 October 1966.

SHEFFIELD AND ROTHERHAM POLICE AUTHORITY. Vert, in base two barrulets wavy argent, issuing therefrom a bridge of three arches proper and in chief three garbs Or. **Crest:** On a wreath of the colours, A stag rampant argent, resting the dexter hind foot on a dragon's head erased proper, and holding between the forefeet eight arrows in saltire Or, banded argent. **Supporters:** On the dexter side a lion, and on the sinister side a stag Or, each gorged with a collar

SEDGEFIELD

SEISDON

SELWYN COLLEGE

SEVENOAKS

SHEFFIELD

azure, pendant therefrom a rose argent barbed and seeded proper, lined gules. **Motto:** Sic virescit lux. **Badge:** In front of an arch of a bridge proper, a saltire azure, over all a garb Or. **Granted** 4 March 1968.

SHERBORNE SCHOOL FOR GIRLS. Argent, on a cross gules a fleur de lys of the first, over all on the dexter a bishop's crook erect Or; on a chief azure a plate charged with a candlestick and a candle vert, enflamed proper, between two pairs of wings conjoined in lure of the third. **Granted** 7 July 1949.

SHERINGHAM URBAN DISTRICT COUNCIL (NORFOLK).* Per chevron vert and argent, in chief two pine cones Or and in base on water barry wavy a three-masted fishing vessel of the sixteenth century in full sail proper. **Crest:** On a wreath of the colours, A hurt fimbriated and charged with a lobster Or. **Motto:** Mare ditat pinusque decorat. **Granted** 26 March 1953.

SHIPLAKE COURT LIMITED.* Azure, a chevron gules fimbriated argent, between in chief two Viking ships, pennons flying, Or, sails set silver, and in base a pair of scales gold. **Crest:** On a wreath tenné, azure and gules, in front of the battlements of a tower sable, an owl proper. **Granted** 20 September 1962.

SHIPPING FEDERATION LIMITED. Gules, a ship's steering wheel with twelve spokes Or, on a chief azure two mercantile crowns gold. **Crest:** On a wreath Or and azure, Between two towers sable, masoned argent, on each a lighted cresset proper, on waves of the sea also proper, a lymphad Or sailing to the dexter, the sail azure charged with three purses gold, pennons flying per fesse gules and argent. **Supporters:** On either side standing on a rock proper a sea dog azure, the spines and fins Or. **Granted** 20 December 1956.

SHIPWRIGHTS OF THE CITY OF LONDON, WORSHIPFUL COMPANY OF.* Azure, in a sea proper the hull of a ship Or and for difference in the dexter chief point a sword erect, point upward, of the last; on a chief argent a cross gules charged with a lion passant guardant Or. **Crest:** On a wreath of the colours, On an ark sable resting upon a mount vert, a dove bearing an olive branch proper, and for difference in the prow of the ark a sword as in the Arms. Mantled gules, doubled argent. **Motto:** Within the Ark safe for ever. **Granted** by Royal Warrant 2 March 1920; exemplified 24 June 1920. (*Illustration on page* 351).

SHREWSBURY, BOROUGH OF (SHROPSHIRE).* Azure, three lions' faces Or. **Motto:** Floreat Salopia. Recorded at the Visitation of 1623.

SHROPSHIRE COUNTY COUNCIL.* Erminois, three piles azure, two issuant from the chief and one in base, each charged with a leopard's face Or. **Motto:** Floreat Salopia. **Granted** 18 June 1896.

SIDMOUTH URBAN DISTRICT COUNCIL (DEVON). Gules, on water in base barry wavy proper an ancient galley in full sail, oars in action, Or; on a chief argent a cross couped of the first between two fleurs-de-lys azure. **Crest:** On a wreath of the colours, Issuant from water barry wavy proper a demi lion gules holding between the paws a sun in splendour Or. **Granted** 24 October 1949.

SIDNEY SUSSEX COLLEGE (CAMBRIDGE UNIVERSITY).* Argent, a bend engrailed sable, impaling Or, a pheon azure. **Granted** by Sir Edward Walker, Garter King of Arms, 1675.

SILCOATES SCHOOL (WAKEFIELD). Or, on a chevron between in chief two roses and in base a phoenix gules, an open book between two roses argent; on a chief wavy azure a three-masted sailing ship in full sail of the fourth. **Motto:** Clarior ex ignibus. **Granted** 1 December 1924.

SILSDEN URBAN DISTRICT COUNCIL (YORKSHIRE—WEST RIDING).* Or, on a chevron sable between in chief a patriarchal cross vert, on either side thereof three sparrow-bills, two in

SHERINGHAM

SHROPSHIRE

SHIPLAKE COURT

SHREWSBURY

SILSDEN

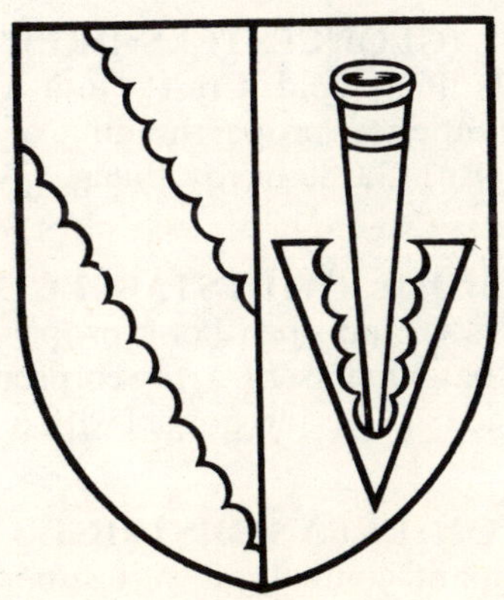

SIDNEY SUSSEX COLLEGE

SIR THOMAS RICH'S SCHOOL

saltire and one in pale, points downwards, of the second, and in base a ram's head caboshed proper, a rose argent barbed and seeded also proper between two demi suns gold. **Crest:** On a wreath of the colours, A wyvern gules grasping in the dexter claw a sprig of flax slipped, leaved and flowered proper. **Motto:** Unity and Service. **Granted** 6 October 1954.

SINO-BRITISH FELLOWSHIP TRUST. Per chevron azure and argent, in chief a pair of hands issuant from clouds and in base an open book with clasps, the dexter page inscribed 'Different in Race but United in Mind' and on the sinister side the same in Chinese characters, all proper. **Crest:** On a wreath of the colours, On a mount vert a Chinese phoenix holding in the beak a wild rose proper. **Supporters:** On the dexter side a lion guardant and on the sinister side a Chinese dragon, all proper. **Motto:** Gentes diversi Mente concordes. **Granted** 23 February 1955 to the British United Aid to China.

SIR ANTHONY BROWNE'S SCHOOL COMMONLY CALLED BRENTWOOD SCHOOL. Gules, a chevron between two lions' gambs erased and a bordure argent, in the honour point a fleur-de-lys Or, on a chief also argent an eagle displayed looking to the sinister sable, beaked and legged and anciently crowned gold, for Browne, impaling Quarterly, first and fourth argent, a chevron gules between three lions' faces sable, for Farington, second gules three pierced cinquefoils argent, for Farington, third argent a cross engrailed sable between four torteaux, for Clayton; the whole within a bordure gules. **Motto:** Virtue, learning, manners. **Badge:** A lion's gamb erased argent enfiled with an ancient crown and grasping an eagle's wing sable. **Granted** 19 July 1957.

SIR JOHN CASS'S FOUNDATION AND RED COAT CHURCH OF ENGLAND SECONDARY SCHOOL, THE GOVERNING BODY OF. Argent, on a chevron sable cottised and between in chief two ship's helms and in base a passion cross gules, three fountains. **Crest:** On a wreath argent and gules, A dexter cubit arm proper, vested gules purfled argent, cuffed ermine, the hand holding a quill pen in bend sinister gules. **Badge:** A ship's helm Or surmounted by a plate charged with three bars wavy azure. **Granted** 7 March 1966.

SIR ROBERT MCALPINE AND SONS LIMITED. Per chevron vert and Or, two chevronells argent and azure, a bordure embattled gules. **Crest:** On a wreath of the colours, Issuant from the battlements of a tower a dexter cubit arm grasping a chaplet of pine fructed, all proper. **Supporters:** On either side a labourer (or navvy) habited in working clothes of the late nineteenth century, the dexter resting the exterior hand upon a shovel and the sinister upon a pick, the whole upon a compartment of a podium of brick topped with coping stones, all proper. **Motto:** Build sure. **Badge:** A dexter cubit arm erased grasping a wreath of pine fructed and interlaced by a pick and shovel in saltire, the handles upward, all proper. **Granted** 1 September 1965.

SIR THOMAS RICH'S SCHOOL (GLOUCESTERSHIRE).* Or, on a saltire raguly per saltire gules and azure, five cross crosslets fitchy gold. **Crest:** On a wreath Or and azure, A dexter arm embowed in armour, the hand gautletted proper holding a cross formy fitchy Or, the elbow enfiled of a mural crown gold. **Motto:** Garde ta foy. **Badge:** A saltire raguly per saltire gules and azure. **Granted** 23 October 1962.

SIR WILLIAM NOTTIDGE SCHOOL (WHITSTABLE). Azure, on a chevron between in chief two garbs and in base a fleece Or, an open book proper, bound gules. **Crest:** On a wreath of the colours, Issuant from the battlements of a tower proper, a boar's head and neck erect gules, bristled and armed Or, langued azure, and gorged with a collar erminois. **Granted** 16 February 1953.

SITTINGBOURNE AND MILTON URBAN DISTRICT COUNCIL (KENT).* Or, a lion rampant gules and a dragon rampant combattant vert supporting a scroll of parchment erect proper; on a chief azure a Saxon crown between two escallops of the field. **Crest:** On a wreath of the colours, On a mount a cherry tree fructed proper. **Motto:** Known by their fruits. **Granted** 28 July 1949.

THE SKINNERS

THE SOAPMAKERS

THE STARCHMAKERS

THE STATIONERS

The arms of the Soapmakers Company and the Starchmakers Company are now obsolete and the blazon is not given therefore in the text.

SKINNERS OF THE CITY OF LONDON, WORSHIPFUL COMPANY OF.* Ermine, on a chief gules three caps of the first tasselled and enfiled with coronets Or. **Crest:** On a wreath Or and gules, A lynx statant proper, about the neck a wreath leaved vert purfled Or. Mantled azure, doubled argent. **Supporters:** On the dexter side a lynx proper and on the sinister side a marten sable, about the neck of each a wreath leaved vert. **Mottoes:** (above the Crest) In Christo fratres; (below the Arms) To God only be all glory. Arms confirmed and Crest and Supporters granted 1 October 1550 by Thomas Hawley, Clarenceux King of Arms; certified by Henry Farnham Burke, Somerset Herald, in 1908. (*Illustration on page* 359).

SKIPTON BUILDING SOCIETY. Gules, a sheep statant Or; on a chief chequy Or and azure a castle triple-towered argent, masoned sable. **Crest:** On a wreath of the colours, A bezant masoned sable with a chaplet of [four] roses argent, barbed and seeded [and leaved] proper. **Motto:** Industria et spe. **Granted** 20 May 1965.

SKIPTON URBAN DISTRICT COUNCIL (YORKSHIRE—WEST RIDING).* Vert, a fleece Or between in chief two roses argent, barbed and seeded proper; a chief chequy Or and azure. **Crest:** On a wreath of the colours, A wyvern sejant gules supporting a staff proper, flying therefrom a banner barry of eight Or and gules, thereon a port between two towers argent. **Motto:** Industria et spe. **Granted** 12 October 1951.

SLEAFORD URBAN DISTRICT COUNCIL (LINCOLNSHIRE—PARTS OF KESTEVEN).* Gules, on a chevron Or, three estoiles sable; on a chief argent as many trefoils slipped vert. **Crest:** On a wreath of the colours, An eagle, wings extended and head downwards and to the sinister, proper holding in the beak an ear of wheat, stalked and leaved, Or. **Granted** 26 October 1950.

SLOUGH, BOROUGH OF (BUCKINGHAMSHIRE).* Per chevron argent and gules, in chief two roses of the last, barbed and seeded proper, and in base a swan holding in the beak a white pink slipped and leaved also proper; on a chief azure the astronomical symbol of Uranus irradiated between two brick-axes Or. **Supporters:** On the dexter side a figure of Mercury proper, vested argent, mantled azure, and on the sinister side a figure of Vulcan proper, vested argent, holding in the dexter hand a pair of pincers also argent. **Motto:** Fiducia et Vi. **Granted** 3 September 1938.

SODBURY RURAL DISTRICT COUNCIL (GLOUCESTERSHIRE). Argent, on a fess dancetty sable between two lions passant guardant gules, three clarions Or. **Crest:** On a wreath argent and gules, In front of a portcullis sable, chained argent, a tower Or. **Motto:** Civibus sodalibusque. **Granted** 5 October 1966.

SOCIETIES. See under the operative term, e.g., for Society of Dyers and Colourists see Dyers and Colourists, Society of.

SOLICITORS OF THE CITY OF LONDON, WORSHIPFUL COMPANY OF. Quarterly argent and gules, in sinister chief a deed with seals pendent proper, in dexter base a Roman lamp of the first: over all a sword, point upwards, in bend of the second. **Crest:** On a wreath of the colours. Upon a fasces fessewise, rods gules, axe and binding Or, an owl argent. **Motto:** Lex Libertatis Origo. **Granted** 25 August 1926.

SOLIHULL, COUNTY BOROUGH OF (WARWICKSHIRE).* Argent, within two barrulets between in chief as many pierced mullets and in base a Saxon crown gules, a greyhound courant sable. **Crest:** On a wreath of the colours, Issuant from the battlements of a tower, an mount, thereon an oak tree eradicated proper, fructed Or, in front thereof also issuant two sickles, the hafts in saltire and blades outwards, also proper. **Motto:** Urbs in rure. **Granted** 10 September 1948.

SOMERSET COUNTY COUNCIL.* Or, a dragon rampant gules holding in its claws a mace erect azure. **Motto:** Sumorsaete ealle. **Granted** 29 December 1911.

SITTINGBOURNE AND MILTON

SLEAFORD

SKIPTON

SOMERSET

SLOUGH

SOLIHULL

SOMERSET HERALD. See Arms, Officers of.

SOMERVILLE COLLEGE (OXFORD UNIVERSITY). Argent, three mullets in chevron reversed gules between six crosses crosslet fitched sable. These are of no authority.

SONS OF THE CLERGY, CORPORATION OF THE. Lozengy argent and sable; on a chief purpure a cross patée Or between two books of the first, garnished and clasped of the fourth. **Crest:** On a wreath of the colours, A female figure, the emblem of Charity, vested in a loose garment sable, head, breast, hands and feet proper, hair dishevelled Or, accompanied with three naked boys, one on the dexter side, and one in each arm, of the second, crined of the third. **Motto:** Quod eorum minimis mihi. **Granted** 29 November 1685 by Dugdale, Garter, and St. George, Clarenceux, to The Society for the Relief of Clergymen's Widows and Orphans.

SOUTHAM RURAL DISTRICT COUNCIL (WARWICKSHIRE).* Gules, a chevron between in chief two escallops and in base a cross cercelé argent; on a bordure also argent eight cross crosslets of the field. **Crest:** On a wreath of the colours, Out of a mural crown gules, masoned argent, therein a circle of wheat ears Or, a mount vert, thereon a lion passant guardant gold holding erect in the dexter forepaw a sword embrued proper. **Motto:** Sincerity. **Granted** 15 July 1959.

SOUTHAMPTON, CITY AND COUNTY BOROUGH OF (HAMPSHIRE).* Per fess argent and gules, three roses counterchanged. **Crest:** On a wreath silver and gules, On a mount vert a castle gold, out of the castle a Queen in her imperial majesty holding in her right hand the sword of justice, in the left hand the balance of equity. Mantled gules, doubled silver. **Supporters:** Out of two ships proper upon the sea, standing in the forepart of the ships two lions rampant gold. Arms and Crest confirmed and Supporters granted 4 August 1575.

SOUTHAMPTON, UNIVERSITY OF.* Argent, a hart trippant gules; on a chief azure an open book proper, edged and bound Or. **Crest:** On a wreath of the colours, A dragon rampant Or supporting a staff proper, flying therefrom to the sinister a flag per fesse argent and gules charged with three roses counterchanged [two and one] barbed and seeded also proper. **Motto:** Strenuis ardua cedunt. **Granted** 1 March 1948 to the Hartley University College, Southampton; certified to the above on change in name and status.

SOUTHAMPTON HARBOUR BOARD. Gules, a branch of mayflower, flowered and leaved, proper; on a chief argent two roses gules, barbed and seeded also proper. **Supporters:** On the dexter side a Triton, and on the sinister side a seahorse, both proper. **Motto:** Janua maris. **Granted** 15 April 1954.

SOUTHBOROUGH URBAN DISTRICT COUNCIL (KENT).* Per chevron gules and Or, in chief two sprigs of broom stalked, leaved and flowered of the last, and in base an oak tree fructed and eradicated proper; on a chief gold a torteau between two billets fessewise of the first. **Crest:** On a wreath of the colours, Issuant from a chaplet of oak leaves Or, a ram's head sable. **Motto:** Propria tuemur. **Granted** 14 December 1953.

SOUTH EAST DERBYSHIRE RURAL DISTRICT COUNCIL.* Vert, on a chevron Or between in chief two garbs of the last and in base a fountain, four annulets sable. **Crest:** On a wreath of the colours, Issuant from a circlet of eight bezants a tower azure. **Motto:** Quanti est sapere. **Granted** 17 March 1952 to Shardlow RDC.

SOUTH EASTERN ELECTRICITY BOARD.* Quarterly gules and azure, a cross triparted and fretted Or between in the first quarter a horse rampant argent, in the second quarter a representation of the crown of King Edgar of the third, and in the third and fourth quarters a martlet also of the third. **Crest:** On a wreath of the colours, A Catherine Wheel rayonné Or. **Supporters:** On either side a lion Or collared sable, each conjoined with a line also sable and supporting a flag-

SOUTHAMPTON

SOUTH EAST DERBYSHIRE

SOUTHAM

SOUTHBOROUGH

SOUTHAMPTON UNIVERSITY

staff proper, flying therefrom a pennon sable of four points gules charged with a thunderbolt Or. **Motto:** Jubeo et ardet. **Granted** 1 June 1948.

SOUTH EASTERN GAS BOARD. Or, a bar wavy azure; on a chief embattled sable three lions' faces of the field, langued of the third. **Crest:** On a wreath Or and sable, A demi lion passant guardant Or, armed and langued sable, conjoined to a demi hulk of an ancient ship gold. **Supporters:** On either side an Anglo-Saxon habited proper. **Motto:** In rupe aedificabimus. **Granted** 20 January 1950.

SOUTHEND-ON-SEA, COUNTY BOROUGH OF (ESSEX).* Azure, on a pile argent between on the dexter an anchor erect, on the sinister a grid-iron, and in base a trefoil slipped Or, a flower vase, issuing therefrom a spray of lilies proper. **Crest:** Issuant out of a mural crown gules, the mast of a ship proper, flowing therefrom a flag argent charged with a cross throughout gules. **Supporters:** On the dexter side a mediaeval fisherman holding a net with his exterior hand all proper, and on the sinister side a Cluniac monk proper holding in the dexter hand a book gules and in the exterior hand a staff also proper. **Motto:** Per mare per ecclesiam. Arms and Crest granted 1 January 1915; Supporters granted 2 January 1915.

SOUTHEND-ON-SEA HIGH SCHOOL FOR BOYS. Gules, two keys in pile, bows interlaced, wards upwards and inwards, Or surmounted by a sword erect argent, pommel and hilt of the second; on a chief sable a cross engrailed of the third charged with an ermine spot of the fourth. **Crest:** On a wreath Or and vert, Issuant from the battlements of a tower gules two keys and a sword as in the Arms. **Motto:** Forti nihil difficile. **Granted** 15 February 1934.

SOUTHEND-ON-SEA HIGH SCHOOL FOR GIRLS. Gules, three lilies argent issuant from a stalk enfiled in base by the bows of two keys interlaced in pile, the wards inwards, Or; on a chief sable a cross engrailed of the second charged with an ermine spot of the fourth. **Crest:** On a wreath Or and vert, Issuant from the battlements of a tower gules, masoned argent, three lilies and two keys as in the Arms. **Motto:** Ad Dei gloriam. **Granted** 10 May 1938.

SOUTHERN GAS BOARD. Per pale Or and gules, three flames counterchanged; on a chief wavy per pale gules and Or a lion passant also counterchanged. **Crest:** On a wreath of the colours, Upon a mount sable a bush vert inflamed proper. **Supporters:** On either side a salamander azure inflamed Or. **Motto:** Flamma fumo est proxima. **Granted** 20 December 1956.

SOUTH KESTEVEN RURAL DISTRICT COUNCIL (LINCOLNSHIRE—PARTS OF KESTEVEN).* Argent, on waves of the sea in base barry wavy azure and of the first, a Norse ship sable, sail, shields and oars Or, the sail charged with a raven proper, flag flying to the dexter gules; on a chief vert a mitre between two garbs of the fourth. **Crest:** On a wreath argent and vert, Issuant from the battlements of a tower, a demi savage, girdled and wreathed about the temples with oak leaves proper, grasping with the dexter a flagstaff, the flag Or fretty azure. **Motto:** Ora et ara. **Granted** 26 October 1948.

SOUTHLANDS COLLEGE OF EDUCATION (LONDON). Azure, on a chevron cotised between in chief two fleurs-de-lys and in base a lamp Or inflamed proper, three escallops gules. **Crest:** On a wreath of the colours, In front of a demi sun Or a pelican in her piety proper. **Motto:** Light, love, life. **Granted** 12 February 1968.

SOUTH LONDON HOSPITAL FOR WOMEN AND CHILDREN (INCORPORATED). Azure, a cross potent and quadrate between in chief a sun in splendour and in base an ancient lamp Or fired proper and two flaunches of the second. **Motto:** Et dato gaudetis. **Granted** 16 October 1947.

SOUTHPORT, COUNTY BOROUGH OF (LANCASHIRE).* Argent, a fesse dancettée between in chief three cross crosslets fitchée sable and in base upon waves of the sea a lymphad proper, flags flying gules. **Crest:** Issuant from a mural crown Or a cross crosslet fitchée as in the Arms entwined by a serpent gold. **Motto:** Salus populi. **Granted** 28 April 1923.

SOUTHEND-ON-SEA

SOUTH KESTEVEN

SOUTHPORT

SOUTH EASTERN ELECTRICITY BOARD

SOUTH STAFFORDSHIRE BUILDING SOCIETY. Gules masoned argent, a cross formy Or; on a chief gold a Stafford knot sable. **Crest:** On a wreath Or and gules, A sprig of thrift of three flowers proper entwined with two keys in saltire, the wards in the form of a letter S, upward and outward Or. Mantled gules doubled Or. **Motto:** Security and Service. **Granted** 20 September 1962.

SOUTH STAFFORDSHIRE WATERWORKS COMPANY. Sable, on a pile barry wavy argent and azure, fimbriated vert, a Stafford knot Or, all between three fountains. **Crest:** On a wreath argent and vert, Issuant from water a mound of sand, thereon a knot (Calidris canutus) in winter plumage, all proper. **Motto:** Nil sine aqua. **Badge:** A fountain charged with a Stafford knot Or. **Granted** 20 November 1964.

SOUTH WALES AND MONMOUTHSHIRE, UNIVERSITY COLLEGE OF (CARDIFF). Gules, three chevronels Or within a bordure engrailed of the last charged with seven mullets of the field. **Crest:** Issuant from a coronet composed of eight mullets set upon a rim Or an angel affrontée, wings expanded, proper, vested azure, with girdle and halo gold, holding in her hands an open book also proper. **Motto:** Nerth gwlad ei gwybodau. **Granted** 16 November 1943.

SOUTH WALES AND MONMOUTHSHIRE SCHOOL OF MINES. Azure, in front of a spur wheel, pendent therefrom a miner's safety lamp, two geological hammers in saltire, all Or. **Crest:** On a wreath of the colours, A dragon passant gules resting the dexter claw on an antique lamp Or. **Motto:** Luce scientiae vinces. **Granted** 15 June 1915.

SOUTH WALES ELECTRICITY BOARD. Per chevron vert and sable, in chief a thunderbolt Or. **Crest:** On a wreath of the colours, A sun in splendour rising Or charged with a fess wavy azure. **Supporters:** On the dexter side a dragon gules gorged with two bars dancetty Or. On the sinister side a lion Or gorged with two bars dancetty gules. **Motto:** Experiendo. **Granted** 2 June 1949.

SOUTHWARK, BISHOPRIC OF. Argent, eleven fusils conjoined, seven in pale fessewise, four in fesse palewise, and in the dexter chief a mitre, all gules. **Granted** 19 June 1905.

SOUTHWARK, LONDON BOROUGH OF.* Gules, on a cross argent a well-head between four cinquefoils gules; on a chief chequy Or and vert a lymphad, sail furled, sable, and a rose gules, barbed and seeded proper. **Crest:** On a wreath Or and azure, An oak tree proper, fructed and dimidiating a garb Or, both banded wavy per fess wavy argent and azure. **Supporters:** On the dexter side an Elizabethan player habited as for the role of Hamlet, holding a skull in the exterior hand, and on the sinister side a youth habited in early fifteenth century dress, all proper. **Motto:** United to serve. **Granted** 15 August 1966.

SOUTHWELL, BISHOPRIC OF. Sable, three fountains proper; a chief Or, thereon a pale azure charged with a representation of the Virgin Mary seated bearing the Infant Christ Or, between on the dexter side a stag lodged proper and on the sinister two staves raguly crossed vert. **Granted** 27 June 1884.

SOUTH WEST ESSEX TECHNICAL COLLEGE AND SCHOOL OF ART. Gyronny argent and gules, an open book proper, bound sable, edged and clasped Or, charged with two cog-wheels in fesse also sable. **Crest:** On a wreath of the colours, A demi stag [Or] attired and unguled sable, charged on the shoulder with a cogwheel also sable, and supporting between the forelegs a seax, blade upwards argent, pommel and hilt gold. **Motto:** Ductus per scientiam. **Granted** 17 September 1959.

SOUTH WESTMORLAND RURAL DISTRICT COUNCIL.* Argent, two barrulets gules, in chief a water bouget between two escallops, in fesse two water bougets, and in base an escallop sable. **Crest:** On a wreath of the colours, Issuant from the battlements of a representation of a pele tower argent, masoned sable, a damson tree fructed proper. **Granted** 20 December 1955.

SOUTHWARK

SOUTHWOLD

SOUTH WESTMORLAND

SPALDING R.D.C.

SPENBOROUGH

SPALDING U. D. C.

SOUTHWOLD, BOROUGH OF (EAST SUFFOLK).* . . . two arrows in saltire, points downward, enfiled with a ducal coronet . . . **Motto:** They ryght defend. Recorded (without tinctures) at the Visitation of 1561.

SPALDING RURAL DISTRICT COUNCIL (LINCOLNSHIRE—PARTS OF HOLLAND).* Or, a cross pall reversed barry wavy argent and azure between in chief two cornucopiae addorsed gules and in base a heron's head erased proper; all within a bordure of the third charged with ten cross-crosslets of the field. **Crest:** On a wreath of the colours, Issuant from the battlements of a tower gules, a demi lion reguardant argent gorged with a collar sable, pendent therefrom by a chain Or a hurt charged with a mullet of seven points gold, the collar charged with a bezant. **Motto:** Progress through endeavour. **Granted** 15 April 1954.

SPALDING URBAN DISTRICT COUNCIL (LINCOLNSHIRE—PARTS OF HOLLAND).* Azure, an estoile between three garbs, two and one, Or; on a chief of the last an open book proper, bound gules, edged of the second, between two tulips of the third, stalked and leaved vert. **Crest:** On a wreath of the colours, A lymphad Or with pennons of St. George flying to the dexter, the sail azure charged with a lily stalked and leaved proper. **Motto:** Vicinas urbes alit. **Granted** 28 June 1950.

SPECTACLE MAKERS OF THE CITY OF LONDON, WORSHIPFUL COMPANY OF. Vert, a chevron Or between three pairs of nose-spectacles proper, framed of the second. **Crest:** On a wreath Or and vert, Two arms embowed vested vert cuffed Or, the hands proper holding a sun in splendour within an annulet gold. **Supporters:** On either side a falcon proper belled Or charged with a sword erect gules. **Granted** 18 September 1950.

SPENBOROUGH, BOROUGH OF (YORKSHIRE—WEST RIDING).* Gules a lamb passant proper supporting a staff Or, flying therefrom a pennon argent charged with a cross of the first; in chief three roses of the third, barbed and seeded also proper. **Crest:** On a wreath argent and gules, A lion rampant purpure resting the sinister paw on an escutcheon argent charged with a saltire gules and a label of five points azure. **Motto:** Industry enriches. **Granted** 5 September 1949.

SPENNYMOOR URBAN DISTRICT COUNCIL (CO. DURHAM).* Quarterly gules and sable, a cross Or charged with ten gouttes de sang; in the first and fourth quarters a lion rampant argent, and in the second and third quarters a fleur-de-lis gold. **Crest:** Standing upon the battlements of a mural crown, a salamander sable enflamed proper grasping with the dexter claw a sword erect also proper, hilt and pomel Or. **Motto:** Spe nemo ruet. **Granted** 25 March 1952.

STAFFORD, BOROUGH OF.* Gules, a quadrangular castle in perspective, the four towers domed argent and each surmounted by a pennon Or, between in chief two Stafford knots and in base a lion passant guardant of the last. **Badge:** A domed tower argent ensigned with a staff flying a pennon Or within a circlet composed of Stafford knots conjoined Or. Arms recorded at the Visitation of 1614; certified by J. A. Frere, Bluemantle Pursuivant, c.1953; Badge granted 20 June 1962.

STAFFORDSHIRE COUNTY COUNCIL.* Or, on a chevron gules a Stafford knot of the first; on a chief azure a lion passant guardant of the field. **Crest:** Issuant out of a mural crown proper a Stafford knot Or. **Supporters:** On the dexter side a lion reguardant gules crowned with a ducal coronet Or, and on the sinister side a gryphon reguardant Or. **Motto:** The knot unites. **Granted** 31 January 1931.

STAINES URBAN DISTRICT COUNCIL (SURREY).* Gules, on a fesse barry wavy of four argent and azure between in chief two swans respectant proper and in base a representation of London Stone Or between two seaxes, blades upwards and outwards, of the second, hilted and pommelled, a representation of the Staines Bridge gold. **Crest:** On a wreath of the colours, Upon the

STAFFORDSHIRE C. C.

SPENNYMOOR

STAFFORD

STAINES

STANDARD BANK

battlements of a tower Or a greyhound sejant gules. **Motto:** Ad pontes prospicimus. **Granted** 4 June 1951.

STALYBRIDGE, BOROUGH OF (CHESHIRE).* Argent, a chevron engrailed gules between two crosses pointed voided in chief sable and a mullet in base also sable and pierced of the field, with two flanches azure each charged with a cinquefoil of the field. **Crest:** On a wreath of the colours, A garb Or, in front thereof a wolf statant argent. **Motto:** Absque labore nihil. **Granted** 18 June 1857.

STAMFORD, BOROUGH OF (LINCOLNSHIRE—PARTS OF KESTEVEN). Per pale, dexter side Gules three lions passant guardant in pale Or, and the sinister side Chequy Or and azure. Recorded at the Visitation of 1634.

STAMFORD MUTUAL INSURANCE COMPANY LIMITED. Or, an escarbuncle; on a chief azure three bezants. **Crest:** On a wreath of the colours, Two arms embowed in armour, the hands gauntletted, grasping an escarbuncle Or. **Supporters:** On the dexter side a lion Or, and on the sinister side a seahorse proper. **Motto:** Strength. **Granted** 10 December 1965.

STANDARD BANK LIMITED.* Azure, flying from a staff proper in bend sinister a standard [= banner] with cords and tassels Or. **Crest:** On a wreath of the colours, A three-masted sailing ship of the nineteenth century in full sail proper, the sails azure, the foresail, mainsail and mizzen sail each charged with a bezant, flags flying to the dexter gules. **Supporters:** On either side an antelope proper, collared Or, resting the interior hind leg upon a bezant. **Motto:** Prodeant vexilla. **Badge:** An antelope trippant proper, supporting with the dexter foreleg over the shoulder in bend sinister a staff proper, flying therefrom a standard [= banner] with cords and tassells as is in the Arms. **Granted** 30 March 1955 to the Standard Bank of South Africa Limited; transferred to the above on change of name 20 July 1962.

STANLEY URBAN DISTRICT COUNCIL (CO. DURHAM).* Per fess argent and vert, a representation of the Causey Arch at Stanley in fess throughout proper between in chief three popinjays vert collared gules and in base a cross of St. Cuthbert Or the inner angles enflamed proper. **Crest:** On a wreath of the colours, Out of a circlet vert a demi bull argent, armed and unguled Or, pendent from the neck by a chain argent a Roman shield sable charged with a thunderbolt and on a bordure Or ten pellets. **Motto:** On, Stanley, on! **Granted** 25 April 1968.

STATIONERS' COMPANY ALIAS THE MASTERS AND KEEPERS OR WARDENS AND COMMONALTY OF THE MYSTERY OR ART OF A STATIONER AND NEWSPAPER-MAKER OF THE CITY OF LONDON,* Azure, on a chevron between three books with clasps, all Or an eagle volant gules with a nimbus Or, between two roses gules leaved vert, in chief issuing out of a cloud proper radiated Or a Holy Spirit, wings displayed, argent with a nimbus Or. **Crest:** On a wreath of the colours, An eagle, wings expanded, with a diadem above its head, perched on a book fessewise, all Or. **Supporters:** On either side an angel proper, vested argent, mantled azure, winged and blowing a trumpet Or. **Motto:** Verbum Dei manet in aeternum. Arms granted 6 September 1557 by Sir Gilbert Dethick, Garter King of Arms; Crest and Supporters granted 30 July 1951. (*Illustration on page* 359).

STERLING OFFICES LIMITED. Azure, two martlets and a cap of Mercury argent; on a chief Or a bridge of one arch proper. **Crest:** On a wreath of the colours, In front of a rising sun an ingot fessewise Or. **Motto:** Concordant nomini facta. **Granted** 30 January 1931.

STEVENAGE DEVELOPMENT CORPORATION (HERTFORDSHIRE).* Or, a four-barred gate sable; a chief indented azure. **Crest:** On a wreath of the colours, An oak tree fructed and eradicated proper enfiled at the base with a mural crown gules. **Supporters:** On either side a stag

STANLEY

STEVENAGE DEVELOPMENT CORPORATION

THE STOCK EXCHANGE

STEVENAGE U. D. C.

proper gorged with a chain, pendent therefrom an escutcheon Or charged with an acorn slipped also proper. **Motto:** Consider thy purpose. **Granted** 26 October 1950.

STEVENAGE URBAN DISTRICT COUNCIL (HERTFORDSHIRE).* Argent, on a mount in base point vert an oak tree eradicated proper, fructed Or, transfixed with a sword in bend sinister, point downward, also proper, hilt and pommel also Or, and over all a fesse gules charged with six mullets of six points gold. **Crest:** Out of a crown palisado Or, a demi hart proper, its sinister foreleg resting upon a cogwheel gold. **Motto:** The heart of a town lies in its people. **Granted** 10 March 1958.

THE STOCK EXCHANGE, THE TRUSTEES AND MANAGER OF (LONDON).* Argent, a cross and in the first quarter a sword erect gules; on a chief of the second a balance Or. **Crest:** On a wreath of the colours, In front of a tower proper a lion passant guardant Or. **Supporters:** On either side a griffin sable, [wings inverted] gorged with a mural crown Or. **Motto:** Dictum meum pactum. **Granted** 10 September 1923.

STOCKPORT, COUNTY BOROUGH OF (CHESHIRE).* Azure, semée of cross crosslets, three lozenges Or; a bordure of the last charged with three garbs and as many double headed eagles displayed [wings inverted] alternately of the first. **Crest:** Issuant from a mural crown Or, a mount vert, thereon a castle with two towers proper. Mantled azure, doubled Or. **Supporters:** On either side a lion argent, that to the dexter gorged with a collar vairy Or and gules, pendent therefrom by a chain gold a plate charged with a rose gules, barbed and seeded proper, that to the sinister likewise collared and pendent from the collar by a like chain a hurt charged with a garb also gold. **Motto:** Animo et fide. Arms and Crest granted 5 December 1932; Supporters granted 1 December 1959.

STOCKPORT GRAMMAR SCHOOL. Sable, a chevron between three fusils erminois, a bordure Or. **Crest:** On a wreath Or and sable, An unicorn rampant Or, crined and unguled argent, resting the dexter hind leg on a book erect sable garnished gold. **Motto:** Vincit qui patitur. **Granted** 10 December 1962.

STOCKTON RURAL DISTRICT COUNCIL (CO. DURHAM). Or, on a chevron sable between three fountains, as many cressets gold enflamed proper; on a chief azure two pallets between as many mullets argent. **Crest:** On a wreath of the colours, Upon a garb fesswise Or a dragon statant gold gorged with a collar counter-compony argent and azure. **Motto:** Tempori parendum. **Granted** 10 February 1958.

STOKE-ON-TRENT, CITY AND COUNTY BOROUGH OF (STAFFORDSHIRE).* Argent, a cross gules fretty Or between in the first quarter a representation of the Portland Vase, in the second a camel kneeling charged on the body with an escutcheon argent, thereon a cross gules, in the third an eagle displayed sable, and in the fourth a scythe also proper; on a chief of the second a boar's head erased between two Stafford knots of the third. **Crest:** On a wreath of the colours, A potter of ancient Egypt at his wheel argent. **Motto:** Vis unita fortior. **Granted** 20 March 1912.

STONYHURST COLLEGE (LANCASHIRE). Quarterly argent and vert, in the first and fourth quarters a lion rampant guardant, and in the second and third quarters an eagle displayed, wings inverted, counterchanged; all within a bordure engrailed gules charged with eight patriarchal crosses of the first. **Crest:** On a wreath of the colours, A unicorn's head erased argent, armed and crined Or, gorged with a collar engrailed azure charged with three crescents ermine. **Motto:** Quant je puis. **Granted** 28 December 1953.

STOURBRIDGE, BOROUGH OF (WORCESTERSHIRE). Azure, the span of a bridge argent, masoned sable, suspended therefrom by a chain of the last a fleece, and in chief two pears slipped and leaved, all Or. **Motto:** One heart, one way. **Granted** 6 November 1917.

STOURPORT-ON-SEVERN URBAN DISTRICT COUNCIL (WORCESTERSHIRE).* Barry wavy of six argent and azure, a representation of a Severn trow Or; on a chief sable a cross moline

STALYBRIDGE

STOCKPORT

STOWE SCHOOL

STOURPORT

STROOD

STOKE-ON-TRENT

between two bees volant Or. **Crest:** On a wreath of the colours, A cockatrice sejant argent, beaked, combed and wattled Or, the underwing charged with three cross-crosslets fitchy gules, gorged with a collar, attached thereto a chain of steel reflexed over the back, and holding in the dexter claw a torch sable enflamed proper. **Motto:** Dum defluat amnis. **Granted** 20 June 1962.

STOWE SCHOOL.* Quarterly indented argent and Or, first a lion rampant azure, second a pile gules, third a pile vert thereon a cross of the second bearing five torteaux, fourth three martlets of the third. **Motto:** Persto et praesto. **Granted** 1923.

STRANMILLIS TRAINING COLLEGE (BELFAST). Azure, a lion rampant guardant Or, in chief on a mullet of six points argent between two keys, wards upward and inward, of the second, a dexter hand couped at the wrist gules. **Motto:** Docendo discimus. **Granted** 20 June 1961.

STRATFORD-UPON-AVON, BOROUGH OF (WARWICKSHIRE). Or, a chevron azure between three leopards' faces gules. Recorded (without tinctures) as a seal of the Arms at the Visitations of 1619 and 1682. Certified by Kings' of Arms Certificate 4 June 1958.

STRETFORD, BOROUGH OF (LANCASHIRE). Argent, on a fesse gules between in chief a flail and a scythe in saltire proper between two roses of the second, barbed and seeded, and in base upon waves of the sea a lymphad, sail furled, oars in action, proper, a lion passant Or. **Crest:** Issuant from a coronet composed of eight roses as in the Arms set upon a rim Or, a cubit arm, the hand proper grasping a thunderbolt gold. Mantled gules, doubled Or. **Motto:** Service and Efficiency. **Granted** 20 February 1933, to the Stretford UDC.

STROOD RURAL DISTRICT COUNCIL (KENT).* Vert, two quill pens in saltire, points downwards, Or between in chief a port between two towers argent and in base a cornucopia gold, the fruit proper; two flaunches barry wavy of six also argent and azure. **Crest:** On a wreath of the colours, Issuant from a Saxon crown Or a ship's mast proper, the sail gules charged with a horse rampant argent, pennon flying also gules. **Motto:** Spes patriae rus. **Granted** 26 June 1953.

STROUD URBAN DISTRICT COUNCIL (GLOUCESTERSHIRE).* Vert, a bendlet wavy argent between six billets gules, each fimbriated Or. **Crest:** On a wreath alternately argent and vert and argent and gules, A demi man habited in the Arms Gules a fesse chequy Or and azure in dexter chief an annulet gold. Mantled vert and gules, doubled argent. **Motto:** Persevera. **Granted** 1 July 1960.

STRUCTURAL ENGINEERS, INSTITUTION OF. Per fesse azure and barry wavy of the first and argent, a fesse embattled of the second masoned sable, issuant therefrom three piles Or, in chief a lion passant guardant of the last and issuant from the base rocks proper. **Crest:** On a wreath of the colours, Issuant from the battlements of a tower argent masoned sable, a demi lion guardant supporting a slide rule in bend sinister Or. **Motto:** Fundamento semper stabili. **Granted** 23 April 1935.

STURMINSTER RURAL DISTRICT COUNCIL (DORSET).* Vert, a saltire wavy argent between in pale two crosses moline and in fesse two garbs Or. **Crest:** Out of a coronet composed of four ears of wheat and four sprigs of oak fructed set upon a rim Or, a mount sable, thereon an heraldic panther statant guardant proper. Mantled vert, doubled argent. **Motto:** Quis metuit. **Badge:** Within an annulet rayonée Or, a bull's head caboshed gold. **Granted** 1 December 1961.

SUDBURY, BOROUGH OF (WEST SUFFOLK).* Sable, a talbot sejant argent; on a chief gules a lion passant guardant between two fleurs-de-lis Or. **Crest:** On a wreath of the colours, A talbot's head erased Or between two ostrich feathers erect argent. **Granted** 20 September 1576.

SUFFOLK AND IPSWICH FIRE AUTHORITY. Party per pale sable and azure, a cross engrailed between in the first and fourth quarters a leopard's face and in the second and third quarters a martlet Or, and on the sinister three demi-hulks of ships conjoined to the impalement line

STROUD

STURMINSTER

SUFFOLK, EAST

SUNBURY

SUGAR BOARD

SUDBURY

of the last. **Crest:** On a wreath of the colours, A lion rampant gules holding between the forepaws a bezant charged with a phoenix displayed also gules. **Motto:** Swift to serve. **Granted** 4 August 1950.

SUFFOLK, EAST, COUNTY COUNCIL.* Sable, a cross engrailed Or; on a chief ermine, between two leopard's faces of the second a pale azure, thereon upon waves of the sea proper an ancient galley to the sinister, sail set, and issuant from the sinister chief the sun in splendour also of the second. **Crest:** On a wreath of the colours, Upon a rock proper a falcon, belled, wings expanded, Or, the inside of the wings azure, supporting with the dexter claw a staff erect also proper, flying therefrom a banner also azure charged with a garb gold. **Motto:** Opus nostrum dirige. **Granted** 14 December 1935.

SUFFOLK, WEST, COUNTY COUNCIL. Azure, a cross fleury between five martlets Or; on a chief sable between two mitres argent two arrows in saltire also argent enfiled with an ancient crown gold. **Crest:** On a wreath of the colours, In front of two arrows in saltire proper, a castle with two domed towers, flags flying thereon, Or. **Motto:** For King, Law and People. **Granted** 9 June 1959.

SUGAR BOARD.* Azure, a ship's mast with derricks and the sail furled proper, the pennon flying to the dexter gules, surmounted below the sail of a pair of scales Or, in the dexter pan three piles of coin proper, and in the sinister pan as many bales of sugar also proper. **Crest:** On a wreath Or and azure, A lion sejant guardant gules between two sugar canes proper, resting the dexter fore-paw upon a sugar beet also proper. **Granted** 12 September 1958.

SUMMER FIELDS SCHOOL TRUST LIMITED (OXFORD). Gules, two bars argent between in chief two bezants and in base three lily flowers proper. **Crest:** On a wreath of the colours, Upon a mount vert, in front of a port between two towers Or an ox passant gules. **Motto:** Mens sana in corpore sano. **Granted** 1 July 1963.

SUNBURY-ON-THAMES URBAN DISTRICT COUNCIL (SURREY).* Per fesse Or and argent, on a fesse vert between in chief two shepherds' crooks in saltire and in base as many bars wavy azure, a mitre between two Saxon crowns of the first. **Crest:** On a wreath argent and vert, In front of a sun rising Or, a seax fessewise, point to the dexter, azure, hilted gules. **Motto:** Sol et pastor Deus. **Granted** 9 November 1948.

SUNDERLAND, COUNTY BOROUGH OF (CO. DURHAM).* Argent, a sextant sable; on a chief azure two keys, wards upwards and outwards, in saltire argent between as many mitres of the last both enfiled with a ducal coronet Or. **Crest:** On a wreath argent and azure, A lymphad sable, the sail azure charged with the cross of St. Cuthbert, flags flying argent charged with a cross gules. **Supporters:** On either side a lion argent, the dexter supporting an anchor and the sinister a pickaxe Or. **Motto:** Nil desperandum auspice Deo. **Granted** 10 August 1949.

SUNDERLAND BUILDING SOCIETY. Argent, a lymphad sable, flying flags and pennon of St. George, the sail azure charged with a representation of the cross of St. Cuthbert argent; on a chief embattled gules a sprig of three Thrift flowers between two keys erect, wards upwards and outwards, Or. **Crest:** Out of a mural crown sable a cubit arm proper, the hand grasping a sextant also sable. Mantled sable and gules, doubled argent. **Supporters:** On either side a lion argent, crowned Or, gorged with a chain, pendent therefrom a lozenge sable charged with an anchor gold. **Motto:** Nil timendun auspicibus nos. **Granted** 5 March 1963.

SUNNY HILL GIRLS' SCHOOL (BRUTON).* Per chevron azure and argent, in chief a sun in splendour issuant Or and in base a cross botony vert. **Crest:** On a wreath Or and azure, A laurel wreath proper enclosing an estoile irradiated Or. **Motto:** Follow the gleam. **Granted** 6 September 1960.

ROYAL COLLEGE OF SURGEONS

SUNNY HILL GIRLS' SCHOOL

SURREY C. C.

SUNDERLAND

SURREY UNIVERSITY

SURGEONS OF ENGLAND, ROYAL COLLEGE OF.* Quarterly Or and argent, a cross gules (being that of St. George) thereon the Imperial Crown proper between two anchors erect in pale and two portcullises in fess of the first, in the first and fourth quarters a serpent nowed and in the second and third a lion couchant guardant proper; on a chief of the third a lion passant guardant of the first being part of the Royal Arms of England. **Crest:** On a wreath of the colours, An eagle reguardant imperially crowned proper, the dexter claw supporting a mace erect gold. **Supporters:** On the dexter side a figure representing Machaon habited in a robe, holding in the exterior hand a dart broken, the point downwards, and on the sinister a figure representing Podalirius, habited as the dexter, holding in his exterior hand a staff entwined by a serpent, all proper. **Motto:** Quae prosunt omnibus artes. **Granted** by Royal Warrant 16 December 1821; exemplified 17 October 1822.

SURREY, UNIVERSITY OF.* Or, three swords palewise, points downwards, gules; on a chief sable a pale checky azure and Or between two woolpacks argent. **Crest:** On a wreath Or and azure, A stag trippant proper, resting the dexter forehoof on a key Or. **Granted** 5 October 1966.

SURREY COUNTY COUNCIL.* Per pale azure and sable, a fess per pale ermine and Or, in chief a representation of the crown of King Edgar proper and a sprig of oak fructed argent. **Badge:** On a roundel per pale azure and sable, a sprig of oak fructed argent, the stem enfiled with a representation of the crown of King Edgar proper. Arms granted 8 August 1934; Badge granted 20 January 1958.

SUSSEX, UNIVERSITY OF.* Argent, on a chevron per pale azure and gules six martlets Or, between in chief two Saxon crowns and in base a dolphin naiant sable. **Crest:** On a wreath argent and gules, Two dolphins embowed, heads downwards, enfiled by a Saxon crown Or. **Supporters:** On either side a pelican in her piety proper [= vulning itself] standing upon a book gules, edged Or, each supporting a staff also proper, that on the dexter flying a banner of the second charged with a lion passant guardant gold dimidiating the hull of an ancient ship argent, and that on the sinister flying a banner of the second charged with a stag's head caboshed silver. **Motto:** Be still and know. **Granted** 15 March 1962.

SUSSEX, EAST, COUNTY COUNCIL.* Gules, six martlets three, two and one, and in chief Saxon crown Or. **Granted** 10 September 1937.

SUSSEX, WEST, COUNTY COUNCIL.* Azure, six martlets, three, two and one, and a chief Or. **Granted** 18 May 1889.

SUSSEX POLICE AUTHORITY. Azure, a tower between five martlets Or. **Granted** 30 May 1969.

SUTTON, LONDON BOROUGH OF.* Per chevron azure and argent, on a chevron gules between in chief a bezant and a plate each charged with a key, wards upward and outward, the dexter azure, the sinister gules, and in base an inescutcheon of the first charged in chief with a representation of an Hannibal aircraft volant argent and in base a sun rising Or, a fountain between two sprigs of oak leaved and fructed argent. **Crest:** On a wreath of the colours, Perched on a mural crown Or charged with a rose gules thereon another argent, barbed and seeded, a popinjay proper, gorged gules, holding in the dexter claw a cross formy fitchy sable. **Supporters:** On the dexter side a lion queue fourché gules, and on the sinister side a greyhound sable, each gorged with a mural crown Or charged with a rose gules thereon another argent barbed and seeded proper. **Motto:** Per ardua in fide servite Deo. **Granted** 5 April 1966.

SUTTON COLDFIELD, BOROUGH OF THE ROYAL TOWN OF (WARWICKSHIRE).* Argent, on a cross sable, a stag's head couped between four doves of the field, in the first quarter a mitre proper; on a chief vert two stags courant Or. **Crest:** Issuant from a mural crown Or, a demi stag proper supporting between the legs two keys, wards upwards and outwards, in saltire

SUSSEX UNIVERSITY

SUSSEX, EAST

SUSSEX, WEST

SUTTON

SWADLINCOTE

gold and a sword erect proper, banded with a riband gules. [Mantled gules, doubled Or]. **Supporters:** On the dexter side a greyhound Or gorged with a mural crown gules, and on the sinister side a dragon gules gorged with a like crown Or, pendent from each crown by a chain gold an escutcheon argent, thereon a rose gules charged with another argent, barbed and seeded proper. **Granted** 15 May 1935.

SWADLINCOTE URBAN DISTRICT COUNCIL (DERBYSHIRE).* Quarterly ermine and gules, a cross quarterly counterchanged between in the first and fourth quarters a Tudor rose barbed and seeded proper, and in the second and third quarters a fleur-de-lys argent; the whole within a bordure vairy of the first and second. **Crest:** On a wreath argent and gules, Upon a mount sable inflamed a cubit arm holding in the hand proper a billet fessewise Or. **Motto:** E terra divitiae. **Granted** 14 May 1947.

SWANSEA, CITY AND COUNTY BOROUGH OF (GLAMORGAN).* Per fess wavy azure and barry wavy of six argent and of the first, a double-towered castle Or, in chief on an inescutcheon of the third a lion passant guardant gules. **Crest:** On a wreath of the colours, An osprey rising, holding in the beak a fish proper. **Supporters:** On the dexter side a lion gules gorged with a mural crown Or, and on the sinister side a dragon gules gorged with a mural crown Or. **Motto:** Floreat Swansea. **Granted** 27 October 1922.

SWANSEA AND BRECON, BISHOPRIC OF. Per fesse azure and Or, in chief surmounting a Catherine Wheel issuant an eagle rising reguardant of the second, and in base a fleur-de-lys of the first. **Granted** 4 February 1924.

SWANSEA, UNIVERSITY COLLEGE OF. Vert, an anchor in bend dexter, a pickaxe in bend sinister and a hammer in pale, surmounted by an open book all proper; on a chief argent a dragon passant gules. **Motto:** Gweddw crefft heb ei dawn. **Granted** 6 May 1921.

SWINDON, BOROUGH OF (WILTSHIRE).* Quarterly per fesse nebuly azure and gules, a pile argent thereon three crescents of the second in the first quarter, three castles one and two of the third in the second, a mitre Or in the third, and a winged wheel of the last in the fourth; a chief also of the third, thereon a locomotive engine proper. **Crest:** On a wreath of the colours, A dexter arm embowed proper grasping two hammers in saltire Or. **Motto:** Salubritas et industria. **Granted** 23 September 1901.

SWINTON AND PENDLEBURY, BOROUGH OF (LANCASHIRE).* Gules, a cockatrice Or; on a chief per pale of the second and argent a lion passant guardant between two roses of the first, barbed and seeded proper. **Crest:** On a coronet composed of six roses gules, barbed and seeded proper, set upon a rim Or, a boar's head erased argent, armed azure. **Supporters:** On either side a lion rampant Or holding in the interior paw a pickaxe gules. **Motto:** Salus populi suprema lex. **Granted** 1 October 1934.

SWANSEA

SUTTON COLDFIELD

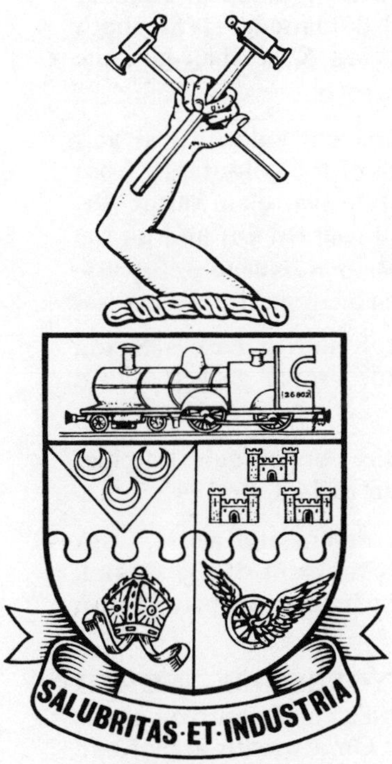

SWINDON

SWINTON AND PENDLEBURY

T

** Denotes Illustration*

TADCASTER RURAL DISTRICT COUNCIL (YORKSHIRE—WEST RIDING).* Per fesse vert and sable, on a fesse wavy argent between in chief a garb between two stalks of barley and as many swords in saltire, and in base a representation of the head of a Roman centurion's standard with the letters SPQR, thunderbolt, laurel wreath and eagle displayed of gold, a bar wavy azure; over all on the fesse a mitre gold. **Crest:** On a wreath of the colours, In front of a unicorn's head erased gules, armed and crined Or, a rose argent, barbed and seeded proper. **Motto:** By service let us govern. **Granted** 15 April 1954.

TALLOW CHANDLERS OF THE CITY OF LONDON, WORSHIPFUL COMPANY OF. Per fesse azure and argent, a fesse counterchanged and three doves of the second, membered gules, each holding in its beak an olive branch Or. **Crests:** (On the dexter, the helmet contournée) On a wreath of the colours, an angel issuant from clouds proper, holding a platter Or, thereon the head of St. John the Baptist also proper. [Mantled gules, doubled ermine] (On the sinister) On a wreath of the colours, On a charger proper rayonée Or the head of St. John the Baptist also proper. [Mantled gules, doubled ermine.] **Supporters:** On either side on a mount vert an angel vested winged and crowned with stars [= celestial crown] Or. **Motto:** Ecce Agnus Dei qui tollit peccata mundi. **Badge:** A dove, wings expanded and inverted, argent, beaked and membered gules, in the beak a branch of olive Or. Arms and first Crest granted 24 September 1456 by John Smert, Garter King of Arms; Arms confirmed, second Crest and Supporters granted 29 January 1603, by William Camden, Clarenceux King of Arms; Badge granted 20 January 1962; both crests confirmed 9 September 1961. The original motto was 'Delite in God & he shall give the thy desyre'. In 1603 it was 'Quae arguuntur a lumine manifestantur'.

TAMWORTH, BOROUGH OF (STAFFORDSHIRE).* Per fess azure and gules, a fess vair between in chief a saltire and in base a fleur-de-lis Or. **Crest:** On a wreath of the colours, In front of a mount vert, thereon a representation of Tamworth Castle proper, two swords in saltire Or. **Supporters:** On the dexter side a bear argent, muzzled gules, collared and chained Or, and on the sinister side a lion gules crowned Or. **Badge:** A saltire Or surmounted by a fleur-de-lys azure. **Granted** 1 May 1965.

TAUNTON, BOROUGH OF (SOMERSET).* Azure, in chief a cherub and in base a Saxon crown Or. **Crest:** Issuant from a mural crown Or a peacock in his pride proper gorged with a Saxon crown Or. **Motto:** Defendamus. **Granted** 23 October 1934.

TAXATION, INSTITUTE OF.* Azure, a garb Or charged with a saltire couped gules; a chief chequy of the last and second. **Motto:** In Regem Civemque Justicia. **Granted** 14 June 1945.

TEES CONSERVANCY COMMISSIONERS. Barry wavy of twelve argent and azure, on a chief ermine an anchor surmounted by a castle sable between two lions rampant of the second. **Crest:** On a wreath of the colours, A lymphad, on the prow a burning brazier proper. **Motto:** Meliora sperans. **Granted** 11 November 1914.

TEESSIDE, COUNTY BOROUGH OF (CO. DURHAM AND YORKSHIRE—NORTH RIDING).* Argent, an ancient ship, sails furled, pennons flying, sable; on a chief azure, on a pale sable fimbriated and between two crucibles argent, a basilisk Or. **Crest:** On a wreath argent and

TADCASTER

TAMWORTH

TEESSIDE

TAUNTON

azure, On a grassy mount proper, an anchor Or between two cogwheels sable. **Supporters:** On the dexter side a lion Or resting the interior hind paw on three ingots of steel proper, and on the sinister side a seahorse argent, scales, dorsal fin and tail Or, each collared azure thereon a barrulet wavy argent; the whole upon a compartment per pale of a grassy mount and waves of the sea proper. **Motto:** Progress in unity. **Badge:** A tau cross azure, enfiling a mural crown Or. **Granted** 26 March 1968.

TEES VALLEY WATER BOARD. Sable, a cross argent surmounted by another invected gules, in the first and second quarters a lion passant guardant of the second; on a chief Or a water-bouget azure between two fountains proper. **Motto:** Collectos spargere fontes. **Granted** 3 February 1900.

TEMPERANCE PERMANENT BUILDING SOCIETY. Azure, a pile reversed Or surmounted in fesse of a wall gold, masoned sable, pierced with an archway of the first, the keystone charged with a fountain, in the archway a key in pale, wards downwards to the dexter, also gold. **Crest:** On a wreath of the colours, A demi lion ermine crowned with Saxon crown Or, gorged with a collar sable charged with three fountains, and grasping by the blade a sword erect gules. **Supporters:** On either side a greyhound reguardant ermine, gorged with a collar sable charged with three fountains. **Motto:** Janua securitas. **Granted** 3 December 1954.

TENBY, BOROUGH OF (PEMBROKESHIRE).* Or, three cinquefoils sable; on a chief barry of four argent and azure three martlets, two and one, gules. **Crest:** On a wreath argent and azure, A lymphad Or, the sail gules charged in base with a mount vert thereon a port between two towers Or, pennon and flags flying azure, each charged with a fleur-de-lys argent. **Supporters:** On either side a dolphin Or charged with a roundel gyronny of sixteen argent and sable, thereon a mural crown Or, supporting between the fins a staff proper, flying therefrom a forked pennon, that on the dexter per fess argent and azure, that on the sinister per fess argent and vert. The compartment a mount issuant from waves of the sea proper. **Motto:** ΘΑΛΑΣΣΑ ΚΛΥΖΕΙ ΠΑΝΤΑ ΤΑΝΘΡΩΠΩΝ ΚΑΚΑ. **Granted:** 1 August 1963.

TENTERDEN, BOROUGH OF (KENT).* Gules, in base waves of the sea proper and thereon a ship of three masts Or, the sail on the foremast furled, the mainsail per pale gules and azure thereon three demi lions passant guardant Or conjoined to as many hulks of ships also argent, the mizzen charged with the Arms Argent on a bend sable between four lions' heads erased gules three mullets of six points Or. Recorded without tinctures at the Visitation of 1574; Recorded with tinctures at the Visitation of 1619.

TEWKESBURY, BOROUGH OF (GLOUCESTERSHIRE).* Gules, a cross engrailed Or; on a chief per pale argent and gules a castle proper, flying from each flanking turret a flag counterchanged, between two roses counterchanged barbed and seeded proper. **Crest:** On a wreath argent and gules, Out of a Saxon crown Or a demi lion double-queued vert holding in the paws a pear sable. **Supporters:** On the dexter side a panther guardant argent, semy of torteaux, hurts and pomeis alternately, issuant from the mouth and ears flames proper, collared, with a chain reflexed over the back, Or; and on the sinister side an eagle, wings expanded and inverted, argent, beaked and legged Or; upon a compartment vert a pall wavy argent charged with another azure. **Motto:** In consilio sapientia. **Granted** 10 April 1964.

THE TEXTILE INSTITUTE. Gules, a fesse argent fretty sable between in chief three shuttles erect and in base two distaffs in saltire Or. **Crest:** On a wreath of the colours, Issuant from clouds, a terrestrial globe proper. **Supporters:** On either side a weaver bird holding in the beak two strands of grass proper. **Motto:** Omnia sunt hominum pendentia filio. **Granted** 2 November 1951.

THINGOE RURAL DISTRICT COUNCIL (WEST SUFFOLK).* Ermine, on a chevron vert between in chief two garbs of barley and in base the sails of a windmill saltirewise Or, a mitre argent between two ancient crowns each enfiling as many arrows, points downward, in saltire gold. **Crest:** On a wreath argent and vert, A demi ounce sable bezantée, gorged with a collar counter-compony argent and azure. **Motto:** Attingo rura. **Granted** 20 February 1958.

TENBY

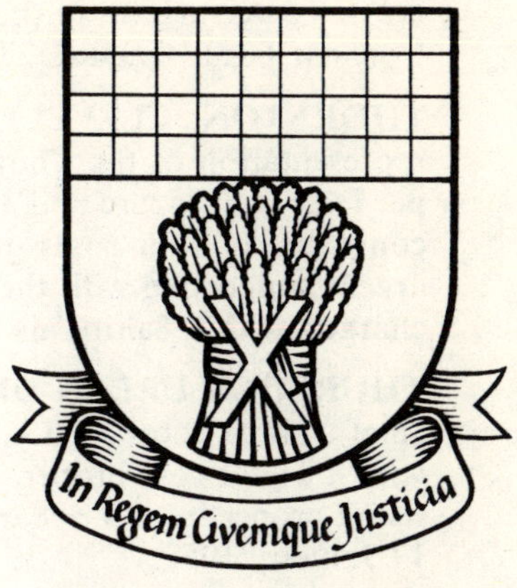

TAXATION INSTITUTE

TENTERDEN

TEWKESBURY

THINGOE

THORNBURY RURAL DISTRICT COUNCIL (GLOUCESTERSHIRE). Per chevron Or and barry wavy of eight argent and azure, on a chevron between in chief two bulls' heads caboshed gules and in base as many wings conjoined fessewise Or, a cross-crosslet fitchée between two crosses patée argent, in the centre chief point an apple pendent slipped and leaved proper. **Motto:** Coronat fides. **Granted** 27 March 1953.

THORNTON CLEVELEYS URBAN DISTRICT COUNCIL (LANCASHIRE).* Vert, a representation of the Thornton Marsh Mill proper; on a chief Or, issuant from a barrulet wavy per fesse wavy azure and argent a sun rising gules. **Crest:** On a mount vert issuant from a coronet composed of four roses gules barbed and seeded proper set upon a rim Or, a wolf reguardant argent supporting with the dexter forepaw a flagstaff also proper, flying therefrom a banner azure charged with a saltire also argent. **Motto:** Terra marique. **Granted** 24 October 1950.

THURROCK URBAN DISTRICT COUNCIL (ESSEX).* Argent, on a fesse wavy between in chief a ship's screw and a wheel azure and in base a Celtic cross also azure charged in the centre with a Tudor rose proper, three lymphads argent. **Crest:** On a wreath of the colours, An albatross rising proper from a bollard sable roped Or. **Motto:** Secundum Tamesim quovis gentium. **Granted** 17 January 1957.

THE TIMES PUBLISHING COMPANY. Argent, eight barrulets sable, over all a caduceus in pale Or. **Supporters:** On either side a pegasus sable, winged, crined and unguled Or, holding in the mouth a sprig of oak fructed gold. **Motto:** Tempus fuit est et erit. **Badge:** Issuant from a mural crown Or, a dexter arm embowed proper grasping in the hand a thunderbolt gold. **Granted** 23 December 1929.

TINPLATE WORKERS OF THE CITY OF LONDON, WORSHIPFUL COMPANY OF. Sable, a chevron Or between three lamps, two in chief with one burner each, the burners inwards, and one in base with two burners, argent garnished Or. **Crest:** On a wreath of the colours, A spherical ship's lantern Or ensigned with a royal crown of the seventeenth century all proper. **Supporters:** On either side a tinplate worker of the eighteenth century vested proper. **Motto:** Amore siti uniti. **Granted** by Royal Warrant 26 January 1956; exemplified 6 September 1957.

TOBACCO PIPE MAKERS AND TOBACCO BLENDERS, COMPANY OF. Argent, on a mount vert in base a tobacco plant proper; a bordure murrey. **Crest:** On a wreath Or and murrey, A hand couped at the wrist holding a root briar pipe, all proper. **Supporters:** On the dexter side a North American Negro and on the sinister side a South Rhodesian native, both proper. **Motto:** Producat terra. **Granted** 8 November 1956.

TODMORDEN, BOROUGH OF (YORKSHIRE—WEST RIDING).* Or, on a fesse wavy azure between a rose gules in chief and a rose argent in base, both barbed and seeded, slipped and leaved proper, a shuttle in bend sinister and a spindle in bend of the fourth. **Crest:** On a wreath of the colours, Upon a mount vert an obelisk proper. **Motto:** By industry we prosper. **Granted** 31 December 1896.

TONBRIDGE SCHOOL.* Quarterly gules and azure, a cross fillet Or between in the first and fourth quarters a fesse raguly between three boars' heads couped argent, armed and langued azure, and in the second and third quarters three lions rampant gold. **Crest:** On a wreath of the colours, A boar's head erased per pale gules and sable, armed and langued azure, gorged with a coronet composed of fleurs-de-lis Or. **Motto:** Deus dat incrementum. **Granted** 16 March 1923, to The Free Grammar School of Sir Andrew Judd.

TONBRIDGE URBAN DISTRICT COUNCIL (KENT).* Argent, five pallets wavy azure, a chief Or; over all a bridge of five arches masoned proper and in base an ancient ship with oars sable, sail set and colours flying gules. **Crest:** On a wreath of the colours, A port between two towers masoned proper, their conical roofs azure, on the dexter tower a torteau charged with a lion passant guardant Or and on the sinister tower a bezant charged with three chevronels gules. **Motto:** Salus populi suprema lex. **Granted** 30 September 1935.

THORNTON CLEVELEYS

THURROCK

TODMORDEN

TONBRIDGE SCHOOL

TORBAY

TORBAY, COUNTY BOROUGH OF (DEVON).* Azure, a lymphad Or flying flags and streamer of St. George, sail argent, pendent from the masthead by a cable Or the beams and stocks of four anchors conjoined in cross gules; on a chief enarched Or a mural crown gules. **Crest:** On a wreath of the colours, A crosier erect Or between two dolphins, heads downward and outward, azure, finned Or, all enfiled through a horseshoe argent. **Supporters:** On either side a sea lion proper, head and mane gules, and pendent from a cable about the neck proper a Tau cross Or. **Motto:** Salus et felicitas. **Badge:** On a fountain four Tau crosses conjoined in cross, the whole encircled by a cable proper and murally crowned gules. **Granted** 12 March 1963.

TOTNES, BOROUGH OF (DEVON).* Sable, on water in base proper a triple-towered castle, the portcullis raised, and upon each outer tower a banner, between two keys, wards upwards and outwards, all argent. Recorded in this form at the Visitation of 1572 and with variations in 1564, 1620, and 1644; Certified painting of 1572 version obtained from Bluemantle Pursuivant in 1958.

TOWER HAMLETS, LONDON BOROUGH OF.* Argent, out of a base wavy azure thereon two bars argent a lymphad, sail furled, sable, pennon and flags flying gules; on a chief azure, between a pair of fire-tongs and a weaver's shuttle, a pale argent charged with a sprig of mulberry fructed proper. **Crest:** On a wreath of the colours, In front of a representation of the White Tower of the Tower of London proper, two anchors in saltire Or. **Supporters:** On the dexter side a sea horse and on the sinister side a talbot proper. **Motto:** From great things to greater. **Granted** 1 September 1965.

TOWN CLERKS, SOCIETY OF. Azure, a sword argent, the hilt in base Or, between five martlets gold. **Crest:** Out of a mural crown argent, within a wreath of oak fructed proper, a beaver Or supporting with the dexter forepaw an open book proper, edged gold, bound gules. **Supporters:** On either side a beaver, the dexter Or and the sinister gules. **Motto:** Leges civitatemque servamus. **Granted** 30 August 1962.

TRENT RIVER AUTHORITY.* Barry wavy of eight azure and argent, a saltire couped gules, and in chief an ancient crown Or. **Crest:** On a wreath of the colours, Standing on a fish wheel Or a heron proper collared Or. **Supporters:** On the dexter side a lion sable supporting between the forelegs a ditching spade proper, and on the sinister side a stag likewise supporting a pipette proper. **Motto:** Pax fiat per fluminis aquas. **Badge:** A bar wavy azure surmounted by a sceptre [with fleur-de-lys atop] gules. **Granted** 1 August 1967.

TREVELYAN COLLEGE (DURHAM UNIVERSITY). Gules, issuant from water in base barry wavy of four argent and azure a demi horse rampant Or, in chief three crosses of St. Cuthbert argent. **Crest:** Out of a coronet composed of sixteen fleurs-de-lys set upon a rim, alternately large and small, a lyre Or. **Motto:** Vera fictis libentius. **Badge:** Within a torse argent and gules a lyre Or. **Granted** 9 September 1966.

TRINITY COLLEGE (CAMBRIDGE UNIVERSITY).* Argent, a chevron between three roses gules, barbed and seeded proper; on a chief of the second a lion passant guardant between two closed books, all Or. Recorded at the Visitation of 1575.

TRINITY COLLEGE (CARMARTHEN).* Azure, a penner and ink-horn argent, garnished and tied with a cord Or; on a chief of the last three cinquefoils sable. **Crest:** On a wreath Or and Azure, Issuant from a celestial crown Or a demi dragon gules holding two keys addorsed, wards upwards, gold surmounted by a plate charged with a cross cottised also gules thereon an open book proper. **Granted** 1 May 1963.

TRINITY COLLEGE (OXFORD UNIVERSITY).* Per pale Or and azure, on a chevron between three griffins' heads erased, four fleurs-de-lys, all counterchanged. These are of no authority.

TRINITY COLLEGE OF MUSIC. Azure, a lyre Or; on a chief of the last three cherubs' heads winged of the first. **Motto:** Gloria in Excelsis Deo. **Granted** 13 March 1913 to replace an earlier grant (23 May 1912).

TONBRIDGE

TOWER HAMLETS

TOTNES

TRINITY COLLEGE (CAMBRIDGE)

TRENT RIVER AUTHORITY

TRINITY COLLEGE (CARMARTHEN)

TRINITY HALL (CAMBRIDGE UNIVERSITY).* Sable, a crescent within a bordure ermine. Granted 1575 by Robert Cooke, Clarenceux King of Arms.

TRINITY HOUSE GUILD OF FRATERNITY. Argent, a cross gules between four ships of three masts, each under full sail all proper, on each pennant and ensign a cross gules, and each quarter representing a sea-piece. **Crest:** On a wreath of the colours, A demi lion rampant guardant and regally crowned Or holding in the dexter paw a sword erect argent, hilted and pommelled of the first. **Motto:** Trinitas in unitate. **Granted** 1573 by Sir Gilbert Dethick, Garter King of Arms to The Master, Wardens and Bretheren of the Navy Royall.

TROWBRIDGE URBAN DISTRICT COUNCIL (WILTSHIRE).* Or, a fleece sable and band gules fimbriated argent; on a chief also gules a mural crown between two garbs gold. **Crest:** On a wreath of the colours, Out of a circlet composed of six arches of a bridge Or, a demi-lion gules tufted and queued gold. **Motto:** Respice prospice. **Granted** 5 December 1951.

TRURO, BISHOPRIC OF. Argent, on a saltire gules a key, ward upwards, surmounted by a sword, point downwards, saltirewise Or, in base a fleur-de-lis sable; a bordure of the last charged with fifteen bezants. **Granted** 28 April 1877.

TRURO, CITY OF (CORNWALL).* Gules, a representation of an ancient ship of three masts under sail Or in the sea proper, and in base two fish naiant in pale also proper. **Supporters:** On the dexter side a miner habited and holding in the exterior hand a pick, its handle downwards, all proper; and on the sinister side a fisherman habited and holding in the exterior hand a coil of rope, all proper. **Motto:** Exaltum cornu in Deo. Arms recorded at Visitations of 1573 and 1620; Supporters granted 3 November 1877.

TUNBRIDGE WELLS. See Royal Tunbridge Wells.

TURNERS OF THE CITY OF LONDON, WORSHIPFUL COMPANY OF. Azure, a Catherine Wheel between two columns Or, in chief an imperial crown Or and in base a hatchet fessewise to the sinister, head downwards, argent, handled Or. **Crest:** On a wreath Or and azure, The figure of St. Catherine crowned Or, wearing a mantle azure furred ermine, holding in the dexter hand a Catherine Wheel Or and in the sinister a sword argent, hilted Or, the point downwards, [dressed in a pink gown beneath her azure mantle, with a gold girdle about the waist and a nimbus around her crowned head]. Mantled gules, doubled argent. **Motto:** By faith I obteigne. **Granted** 17 December 1634 by Sir Richard St. George, Clarenceux King of Arms.

TYLERS AND BRICKLAYERS OF THE CITY OF LONDON, WORSHIPFUL COMPANY OF. Azure, a chevron Or, in chief a fleur-de-lys argent between two brick-axes palewise Or, in base a brush also Or. **Crest:** On a wreath Or and azure, A dexter arm embowed vested party per pale Or and gules cuffed argent, holding in the hand proper a brick-axe Or. Mantled gules, doubled argent. **Motto:** In God is all our trust, let us never be confounded. **Granted** by Sir Gilbert Dethick, Garter King of Arms, Robert Cooke, Clarenceux King of Arms, and William Flower, Norroy King of Arms,3 February 1569.

TYNEMOUTH SCHOOL. Gules, two keys in saltire between in chief a representation of St. Cuthbert's pectoral cross Or, in base an ancient crown, and in fesse two like crowns Or. **Crest:** On a wreath of the colours, A representation of H.M.S. Royal Sovereign of early nineteenth century date Or, the lower mainsail gules charged with a lion's head affrontée crowned with a naval crown gold. **Motto:** Moribus civilis. **Granted** 30 October 1961.

TYRONE COUNTY COUNCIL.* Per fesse indented sable and argent, in chief a mullet of eight points of the second charged with a fleur-de-lys of the first, in base a dexter hand appaumé gules. **Crest:** On a wreath argent and gules, On a mount and in front of a castle of two towers, a hurst, issuant from the battlements of the castle a dexter arm embowed in armour, the hand grasping a sword in bend sinister, all proper. **Supporters:** On either side a lion rampant, that to the dexter Or gorged with a ribbon, pendent therefrom an escutcheon argent charged with a cross gules, and that to the sinister gules gorged with a ribbon argent, pendent therefrom an escutcheon azure charged with a saltire also argent. **Motto:** Consilio et Prudentia. **Granted** 24 May 1951.

TRINITY COLLEGE (OXFORD)

TRINITY HALL

TRURO

TROWBRIDGE

TYRONE

U

** Denotes Illustration*

UCKFIELD RURAL DISTRICT COUNCIL (EAST SUSSEX).* Argent, on a field in base vert an oak tree fructed and leaved proper between two martlets respectant in fesse azure; all within a bordure gobony of the first and last. **Crest:** On a wreath of the colours, Upon a mount vert a boar rampant sable, armed and unguled Or, supporting a cresset fired proper. **Motto:** Like as the oak. **Granted** 30 January 1948.

ULLATHORNE GRAMMAR SCHOOL (COVENTRY). Quarterly Or and argent, a chevron azure between three crosses potent gules. **Crest:** On a wreath Or and gules, A bear sejant sable supporting with the dexter paw a patriarchal cross staff Or. **Motto:** Soli Deo. **Granted** 23 April 1934, to the Ullathorne Roman Catholic Secondary School.

ULSTER BANK LIMITED (BELFAST).* Gules, on a cross argent cottised Or a dexter hand of the field couped at the wrist. **Crest:** Out of an ancient Irish crown Or a spear [=a tilting spear] erect Argent [the inside of the hand guard] garnished gold, a bell fastened thereto by a chain also gold. **Supporters:** On either side an Irish Wolfhound proper, collared chequy [of two rows only] argent and gules, chained Or, the chain passing through the mouth and reflexed behind the head gold. **Granted** 20 November 1957.

ULSTER KING OF ARMS. See Arms, Officers of.

ULSTER TRANSPORT AUTHORITY. Vert, a bend argent between six earls' coronets Or. **Crest:** On a wreath Or and vert, A winged horse rampant Or charged on the shoulder with a dexter hand appaumée couped at the wrist gules. **Supporters:** On the dexter side a lion gules, and on the sinister side an Irish Elk proper, both gorged with a mural crown Or. **Motto:** Transportatio cultum significat. **Granted** 9 December 1959.

ULVERSTON URBAN DISTRICT COUNCIL (LANCASHIRE).* Argent, two bars gules, a pale sable fretty of the first between two abbots' crosiers addorsed also sable; on a chief azure an anchor between two fleurs-de-lys Or. **Crest:** Out of a coronet composed of four roses gules, barbed and seeded proper, set upon a rim Or, a demi wolf sable breathing flames and gorged with a leather collar proper, buckled and pendent therefrom by a chain an escutcheon gold charge with a ray of lightning throughout in bend also gules surmounted of an Ankh Vert, and supporting a garb also gold. Mantled sable, doubled argent. **Motto:** Optimum sufficit. **Granted** 1 December 1955.

UNIGATE LIMITED. Vert, a Guernsey cow grazing proper; on a chief argent three slips of white clover flowered and leaved also proper. **Crest:** Issuant from a chapeau vert, turned up argent, three slips of white clover joined at the base, flowered and leaved proper. Mantled azure, doubled argent. **Supporters:** On the dexter side a unicorn argent, and on the sinister side a white dairy cow reguardant proper, both armed, unguled and tufted Or, and collared gules. **Motto:** In unitate cum Natura. **Granted** 15 February 1962.

UCKFIELD

UNITED KINGDOM ATOMIC ENERGY AUTHORITY

ULSTER BANK

ULVERSTON

UNION CASTLE MAIL STEAMSHIP COMPANY LIMITED. Gules, a chief sable, over all a lymphad, flags and pennant flying Or, the sail charged with a castle triple-towered per fesse also sable and of the field. **Crest:** On a wreath of the colours, A demi lion contournée and a demi springbok supporting between them a trident erect sable, the haft gules. **Motto:** Vigilans et audax. **Granted** 7 December 1956.

UNION DISCOUNT COMPANY OF LONDON LIMITED. Argent, on a chevron sable between in chief two swords erect and in base a sheet bend knot of rope gules, five bezants. **Crest:** On a wreath of the colours, Issuant from flames proper a demi lion guardant gules gorged with a collar counter-compony argent and sable, holding between the paws a bezant charged with a cock's head erased also sable combed and wattled also gules. **Granted** 20 May 1954.

UNITED BIRMINGHAM HOSPITALS [BOARD]. Or, a bend of five lozenges between seven crosses couped, four in chief and three in base, gules. **Crest:** On a wreath of the colours, A demi double headed lion azure holding between the paws a torch Or enflamed proper. **Motto:** Heal, teach, learn. **Badge:** On a cross couped gules fimbriated argent, an antique lamp enflamed proper. **Granted** 16 December 1953.

UNITED KINGDOM ATOMIC ENERGY AUTHORITY.* Sable semée of plates, a pile barry dancetty Or and gules. **Crest:** On a wreath argent and sable, A sun in splendour of thirty-two points Or charged with a voided escutcheon gules, therein a martlet sable. **Supporters:** On either side a pantheon gules, unguled Or, semée of mullets, thirteen of six points, two of seven, and gorged with a crown palisado, affixed thereto and reflexed over the back a chain gold. **Motto:** E minimis maxima. **Badge:** A lion passant guardant gules supporting with the dexter forepaw a pile sable. **Granted** 12 April 1955.

UNITED KINGDOM TEMPERANCE AND GENERAL PROVIDENT INSTITUTION. Argent, on a pale wavy azure a lion rampant Or and a unicorn rampant of the field. **Crest:** On a wreath of the colours, In front of a sundial proper a fountain. **Supporters:** On either side a lion rampant reguardant Or collared azure, the dexter resting the interior hind leg on a spinning wheel proper and the sinister resting the interior hind leg on a globe also proper. **Motto:** Quoniam sumus in vicem membra. **Granted** 4 September 1940.

UNITED REINSURERS LIMITED.* Argent, a rose gules, barbed and seeded proper; on a chief barry of four azure and of the field, a pale also argent charged with a cross throughout between in the first and fourth quarters a sword in bend, point upwards, also gules. **Crest:** On a wreath of the colours, In front of a torch azure, enflamed proper, two keys in saltire, wards upwards and outwards, gold. **Supporters:** On either side a talbot Or gorged with a cord gules, suspended therefrom by a like cord an escutcheon argent thereon within a bordure also gules a rose of the last barbed and seeded proper. **Motto:** Let the Losse Lighte Easillie. **Badge:** In front of an escutcheon enhanced to the dexter chief gules, another argent charged with a rose of the first barbed and seeded proper. **Granted** 3 October 1956.

UNIVERSITIES. See Aston in Birmingham; Bath; Birmingham; Bradford; Bristol; Brunel; Cambridge; City; Durham; East Anglia; Essex; Exeter; Hull; Keele; Lancaster; Leeds; Leicester; Liverpool; London; Kent at Canterbury; Manchester; Newcastle-upon-Tyne; Nottingham; Oxford; Reading; Salford; Sheffield; Southampton; Surrey; Sussex; Wales; York.

UNIVERSITY COLLEGES. See Aberystwyth; Cardiff; Hartley; Hull; Magee; North Staffordshire; South Wales and Monmouthshire; South West of England; Swansea.

UNIVERSITY COLLEGE (OXFORD UNIVERSITY).* Azure, a cross patonce between four martlets Or. Recorded at the Visitation of 1574. In practice five martlets are shown.

UNIVERSITY COLLEGE HOSPITAL OR NORTH LONDON HOSPITAL.* Per fesse Or and azure, an ancient galley proper, the sail argent charged with a serpent nowed vert, the pennon

UNITED REINSURERS

URMSTON

UNIVERSITY COLLEGE (OXFORD)

UPTON-UPON-SEVERN

UNIVERSITY COLLEGE HOSPITAL

gules, and in chief two maple leaves slipped also proper. **Crest:** On a wreath of the colours, A pelican in her piety proper charged on the breast with a plate, thereon a cross gules. **Motto:** Ratione dirige cursum. **Granted** 7 June 1907.

UPHOLDERS OF THE CITY OF LONDON, WORSHIPFUL COMPANY OF. Sable, three spervers ermine, trimmed azure and gules, in base upon a pillow Or a lamb couchant argent beneath a cross formy fitched gules. **Crest:** On a wreath of the colours, A King Eider drake proper standing on a cushion Or. **Supporters:** On either side a lamb argent unguled and gorged with a plain collar Or, pendent therefrom a cross formy fitchy gules. **Motto:** Sustine bona. Arms granted 11 December 1465 by William Hawkeslowe, Clarenceux King of Arms; certified by Kings' of Arms Certificate 1 April 1963; Crest and Supporters granted 10 June 1963.

UPTON-UPON-SEVERN RURAL DISTRICT COUNCIL (WORCESTERSHIRE).* Per fesse gules and sable, on a fesse barry wavy of six argent and azure between in chief two cross crosslets and in base a crescent Or, two pallets that to the dexter embattled counter-embattled of the last **Crest:** On a wreath argent and azure, On a mount vert, in front of a pear tree proper fructed sable, a pelican Or vulning herself gules. Upon a scroll beneath the shield the words 'Upton super Sabrinam'. **Granted** 18 November 1948.

URMSTON URBAN DISTRICT COUNCIL (LANCASHIRE).* Per chevron azure and barry wavy argent and of the first, on a chevron ermine between in chief a griffin segreant and an oak tree eradicated Or and in base a bezant charged with an anvil sable, a rose gules, barbed and seeded proper between two martlets also Or. **Crest:** On a wreath of the colours, A squirrel sejant proper, holding with the forepaws a balance Or. **Motto:** Salus populi suprema est lex. **Granted** 10 June 1942.

URSULINE CONVENT HIGH SCHOOL, THE (BRENTWOOD, ESSEX). Azure, two lilies argent, seeded Or, slipped vert, in base an antique lamp Or, enflamed argent; on a chief gules a dove volant affronty gold. **Crest:** On a wreath of the colours, In front of three arrows, one in pale and two in saltire azure, barbs downward and argent, a cross formy Or charged with a rose gules barbed and seeded proper. Mantled azure, doubled Or. **Motto:** Duty. **Badge:** A cross formy Or, thereon a torteau charged with an antique lamp gold enflamed argent. **Granted** 2 September 1964.

URWICK, ORR AND PARTNERS LIMITED. Argent, on a bend engrailed sable, plain cottised gules, a plate between two lozenges, each palewise argent and charged with a saltire also gules. **Crest:** On a wreath of the colours, A terrestrial globe proper, ensigned with a pair of dividers chevronwise Or, and at the base, a slide rule fessewise gold. **Motto:** Verum nobilissimum est. **Granted** 20 March 1957.

* *Denotes Illustration*

V

VALUERS AND AUCTIONEERS, INCORPORATED SOCIETY OF, LIMITED. Per pairle reversed argent, Or and azure, in the first a gavel sable, in the second a Tee-square interlaced with an open foot-rule proper, and in the third a pair of scales Or. **Crest:** On a wreath of the colours, Issuant from a crown palisado Or, a mount vert, thereon a dexter hand, holding a flambeau erect, fired proper, between two stalks of wheat bladed, each with three ears Or. **Supporters:** On the dexter side a Roman citizen holding in the exterior hand a scroll, and on the sinister side an Ancient Briton holding in the exterior hand a club resting on the shoulder all proper. **Motto:** Value with integrity. **Badge:** A tower and a garb Or, looped about with a cord knotted between them azure. **Granted** 20 June 1968.

VINTNERS COMPANY

VAYNOR AND PENDERYN

VICTORY INSURANCE

VETERINARY SURGEONS

VALUERS' INSTITUTE. Per chevron azure and Or, in chief two gavels of the second and in base an Iron gateway sable. **Crest:** Issuant from a crown palisado Or a mount vert, thereon a lion passant guardant between two stalks of wheat bladed, each with three ears gold. **Motto:** Omnino adjuvando. **Granted** 17 August 1938 to the National Association of Auctioneers, House Agents, Rating Surveyors and Valuers, Limited; transferred by endorsement to the above 1949.

VAN MILDERT COLLEGE (DURHAM UNIVERSITY). Gules, two scythe blades in saltire, in chief the cross of St. Cuthbert argent. **Crest:** On a wreath of the colours, In front of a castle of three towers sable, a silver pennannular brooch proper, the ends charged with gilded crosses of St. Cuthbert. **Motto:** Sic vos non vobis. **Badge:** A silver brooch proper, the ends charged with gilded crosses of St. Cuthbert. **Granted** 3 February 1966.

VAYNOR AND PENDERYN RURAL DISTRICT COUNCIL (BRECKNOCKSHIRE).* Argent, between two piles issuant from the base vert a fire beacon enflamed proper, the basket Or; on a chief azure two bars wavy of the field surmounted by three church steeples gold. **Crest:** Issuant from a coronet composed of four pairs of wings erect set upon a rim Or, a demi horned sheep argent. **Motto:** Gwella braint heb golli bro. **Granted** 20 December 1955.

VETERINARY SURGEONS, ROYAL COLLEGE OF.* Argent, a cross engrailed gules between a horse's head erased in the first quarter, an arrow in bend entwined by and piercing a serpent in the second, a horse-shoe in the third, all proper, and a bull's head erased sable in the fourth. **Crest:** On a wreath of the colours, A centaur proper holding a shield argent charged with an aloe also proper. **Motto:** Vis unita fortior. **Granted** 1 July 1844.

VICKERS LIMITED. Azure, a chevron reversed between a lion's head caboshed affrontée in chief and two mullets in base Or. **Crest:** On a wreath of the colours, Three mullets Or in front of two ostrich feathers forming the Roman letter V azure. **Supporters:** On either side a sea griffin azure, beaked, winged and finned Or, armed and langued gules, each gorged with an ancient crown, attached thereto a chain reflexed over the back gold. **Motto:** Service in peace and war. **Badge:** Out of an ancient crown Or two ostrich feathers forming the Roman letter V azure. **Granted** 5 March 1963.

VICTORIA COLLEGE (BELFAST). Per pale sanguine and sable, on the dexter a harp Or and on the sinister an open book proper, edged and bound gold; a chief vair, thereon a pale azure charged with a bee argent. **Motto:** Honor fidelitas praemium. **Granted** 27 April 1951.

VICTORY (EX-SERVICES) ASSOCIATION LIMITED. Ermine, a torse of dark blue, gules and pale blue silk proper, in the form of the letter V, enfiled in chief with a naval crown and a mural crown and in base by an astral crown Or. **Crest:** On a wreath Or, azure and gules, An eagle, wings addorsed and inverted, azure between an anchor and a sword Or, the dexter claw grasping the anchor. **Motto:** We served. **Granted** 20 January 1958.

VICTORY INSURANCE COMPANY LIMITED.* Barry wavy of six argent and azure, a chevronel reversed gules. **Crest:** On a wreath of the colours, Issuant from flames a dexter hand apaumée proper. **Motto:** Uberrima fides. **Granted** 23 October 1944.

VIGILANT ASSURANCE COMPANY LIMITED. Tierce in pairle reversed sable, vert and argent semée of flames gules, in chief an edelweiss flower proper between a fountain and a broken wheel Or. **Motto:** Vigilans non cadit. **Granted** 10 November 1959.

VINTNERS OF THE CITY OF LONDON, WORSHIPFUL COMPANY OF.* Sable, a chevron between three wine tuns argent. **Crest:** On a wreath of the colours, A caravel Or laden with tuns proper, the sails gules, the mainsail charged with a cartwheel Or, and from the masthead a pennon argent. **Supporters:** On either side a swan, the dexter a cob, the sinister a pen, both nicked in the beak with the mark of the Company, all proper, about the neck of each a riband azure, pendant therefrom a bunch of grapes also proper. **Motto:** Vinum exhilarat animum. Arms granted 17 September 1447 by Roger Leigh, Clarenceux King of Arms; confirmed at the Visitations of 1590 and 1634; Crest and Supporters granted 20 June 1957.

THE WATERMEN

THE WAXCHANDLERS'

THE WEAVERS

THE WOOLPACKERS

W

** Denotes Illustration*

WADHAM COLLEGE (OXFORD UNIVERSITY). Gules, a chevron between three roses argent barbed and seeded proper, impaling Gules, a bend Or between two escallops argent. These are of no authority.

WAKEFIELD, BISHOPRIC OF. Or, a fleur-de-lis azure; on a chief of the last three celestial crowns of the field. **Granted** 17 June 1905.

WAKEFIELD, CITY AND COUNTY BOROUGH OF (YORKSHIRE—WEST RIDING).* Azure, a fleur-de-lys Or fimbriated ermine. **Granted** 3 March 1932.

WAKEFIELD GIRLS' HIGH SCHOOL. Per chevron sable and azure, in chief two leopards' faces and in base a fleur-de-lys Or; a bordure ermine. **Crest:** On a wreath Or, azure, argent and sable, An owl argent, crowned with an ancient crown Or, standing within a chaplet of leaves proper and roses silver, barbed and seeded proper, and between two pens azure, the quills gold. **Motto:** Each for all—all for God. **Badge:** An owl argent standing on a woolpack and crowned with an ancient crown Or. **Granted** 10 January 1963.

WALES, REPRESENTATIVE BODY OF THE CHURCH IN. See Church in Wales.

WALES, UNIVERSITY COLLEGE OF (ABERYSTWYTH). Per chevron Or and vert, in chief two dragons combatant gules, armed and langued azure, and in base an open book proper. **Crest:** On a wreath of the colours, A castle battlement in flames, arising therefrom an eagle, all proper. **Motto:** Nid byd byd wybodaeth. **Granted** 7 May 1928.

WALES, UNIVERSITY OF.* Argent, on a fess murrey three mediaeval lamps Or; all within a bordure of the second charged with eight mullets of the third. **Crest:** On a wreath of the colours, A dragon statant gules, resting the dexter claw on an open book proper inscribed with the words 'Gorev awen gwirioned'. **Motto:** Scientiam ingenium artes. **Granted** 2 May 1910.

WALES, UNIVERSITY OF. See also Science and Technology.

WALLASEY, COUNTY BOROUGH OF (CHESHIRE).* Or, on waves of the sea a three-masted ship in full sail proper; on a chief azure, to the dexter three garbs, two and one, of the first, and to the sinister a bugle horn proper stringed and garnished gold. **Crest:** On a wreath of the colours, A dolphin, head downwards, proper entwining a trident erect Or. **Motto:** Audemus dum cavemus. **Granted** 8 September 1910.

WALLINGFORD, BOROUGH OF (BERKSHIRE).* Gules, a portcullis Or, studded sable chained argent, ensigned with an ancient crown of the second; all within an orle of bezants. **Crest:** On a wreath of the colours, Issuant from water barry wavy a castle [of two towers] proper. **Supporters:** On either side a knight in armour proper, wearing a surcoat of the Arms, mounted on a horse argent caparisoned likewise of the Arms, holding in his dexter gauntlet a tilting spear also proper, his helm bearing the Crest. **Granted** 23 August 1955.

WALES UNIVERSITY

WALLSEND

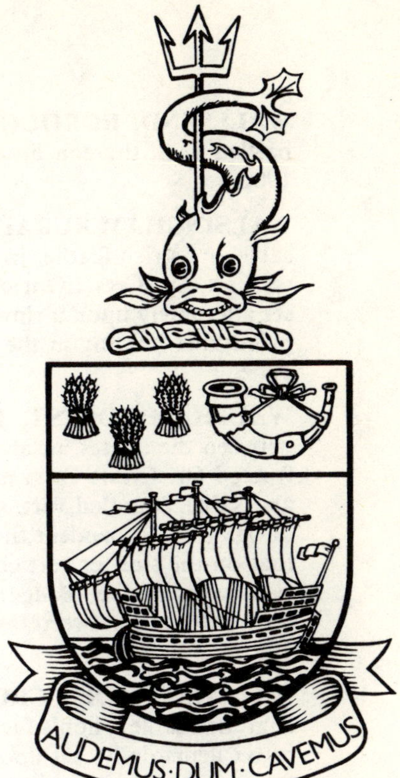

WALLASEY

WAKEFIELD

WALLINGFORD

WALLSEND, BOROUGH OF (NORTHUMBERLAND).* Sable gutté-d'Or, in base an embattled wall, thereon an eagle displayed Or. **Motto:** Situ exoritur Segeduni. **Granted** 8 October 1902.

WALSINGHAM RURAL DISTRICT COUNCIL (NORFOLK). Checky Or and vert, on a cross sable an ostrich feather in pale ermine, the quill transfixing a scroll argent, between two lymphads, sails set, Or. **Crest:** Out of a coronet composed of four ears of wheat and as many acorns leaved set alternately upon a rim Or, in front of five ostrich feathers argent a demi stag sable, attired, unguled, and holding in the mouth a horseshoe gold. **Motto:** Fide et Labor. **Granted** 20 December 1962.

WALTHAM FOREST, LONDON BOROUGH OF.* Vert, a stag's head caboshed proper, between the attires an ancient crown Or; on a chief wavy argent three oak trees couped proper fructed Or. **Crest:** On a mural crown and in front of a cross staff Or, a lion passant per pale Or and sable. Mantled vert, doubled argent. **Supporters:** On either side a stag gorged with a wreath of oak proper, pendent therefrom a billet, that on the dexter gules charged with an anchor argent, that on the sinister vert charged with a sword, point upwards, argent, hilt and pomel Or. **Motto:** Fellowship is life. **Badge:** A stag's head caboshed proper charged on the forehead with a cross formy Or, and between the attires three oak trees, two and one, as in the Arms. **Granted** 1 January 1965.

WALTHAM HOLY CROSS URBAN DISTRICT COUNCIL (ESSEX).* Argent, on a cross engrailed sable a lion's face between four crosses bottonnée Or. **Crest:** Out of a coronet composed of six fleurs-de-lys set upon a rim Or, a demi stag at gaze proper charged on the shoulder with a fountain and holding in the mouth a seax, the blade argent, the hilt and pommel gold. Mantled gules, doubled argent. **Motto:** Sanctae nomine crucis. **Granted** 9 November 1956.

WALTON AND WEYBRIDGE URBAN DISTRICT COUNCIL (SURREY).* Or, on a fesse wavy azure between in chief two Tudor roses, barbed and seeded proper, and in base an eagle displayed gules, two barrulets wavy argent, surmounted by as many palets of the field. **Crest:** On a wreath of the colours, A swan's head erased proper gorged with a Saxon crown Or and holding in the beak a sprig of oak, leaved and fructed, also proper. **Motto:** Dum defluat amnis. **Granted** 29 March 1946.

WALTON-LE-DALE URBAN DISTRICT COUNCIL (LANCASHIRE).* Per chevron argent and gules, a chevron per chevron counterchanged, in chief two crosses patonce sable and in base a demi pelican issuant, wings expanded and inverted, argent vulning herself gules. **Crest:** Out of a circlet Or charged with three gouttés de sang, a demi lion purpure supporting a staff proper, flying therefrom a banner sable charged with three bars argent. **Motto:** De bon cuer. **Granted** 4 April 1952.

WANDSWORTH, LONDON BOROUGH OF.* Per pale indented argent and azure, a fesse chequey azure and Or, each of the last charged with a goutté azure. **Crest:** On a wreath of the colours, An ancient ship, at the prow a dragon's head, sable, four oars in action and as many shields Or resting against the bulwarks, pennon flying to the dexter gules, the sail charged with the Arms of the London Borough of Wandsworth. **Supporters:** On the dexter side a dove, wings elevated and addorsed, azure, the underside of the wings charged with four mullets Or, in the beak a sprig of lavender proper, and on the sinister side a dragon sable, wings elevated and addorsed argent, the underside of the wings charged with four crosses couped gules. **Motto:** We serve. **Badge:** A fountain charged with a crown palisado Or. **Granted** 1 March 1965.

WARE URBAN DISTRICT COUNCIL (HERTFORDSHIRE).* Azure, two posthorns in saltire Or between in pale two barge rudders paly of six argent and gules, furnished gold, and in fesse as many garbs of barley of the last, banded gules. **Motto:** Cave. **Granted** 26 March 1956

WALTHAM FOREST

WALTHAM HOLY CROSS

WALTON AND WEYBRIDGE

WANDSWORTH

WARLEY, COUNTY BOROUGH OF (WORCESTERSHIRE).* Per saltire vert and Or, two lions rampant in pale Or, in fess of either flank a club in bend sinister surmounted by a caduceus in bend proper; on a chief Or a lion passant vert. **Crest:** Issuant from a Saxon crown Or, a demi lion rampant double queued vert holding with the dexter paw an arrow, barb downwards, proper. **Supporters:** On the dexter side a lion gules, in the mouth an arrow proper; on the sinister side a dragon gules, in the mouth an anchor Or. **Motto:** Unity and Progress. **Granted** 30 June 1966.

WARMINSTER URBAN DISTRICT COUNCIL (WILTSHIRE). Or, a mounted figure [riding] to the sinister in armour, brandishing a sword in bend sinister proper, his surcoat and shield azure lined gules, the horse sable with bardings of the third lined with the second. **Granted** 29 November 1948.

WARRINGTON, COUNTY BOROUGH OF (LANCASHIRE).* Ermine, six lioncels rampant, three, two and one, gules, within a bordure azure charged with eight covered cups Or. **Crest:** On a wreath of the colours, Upon a rock proper a unicorn rampant argent, armed, maned and unguled, supporting a flagstaff Or, thereon hoisted a flag flying to the sinister per pale argent and azure charged with a rose gules, barbed and seeded of the first, and a garb of the second. **Motto:** Deus dat incrementum. **Granted** 18 May 1897.

WARWICK, BOROUGH OF.* Sable, a walled town with three towers argent, issuing from each of the flanking towers a demi figure representing a nightwatchman respectant winding a horn argent, habited and capped gules, the central tower charged with an escutcheon gules, thereon a ragged staff bendwise, between in chief a mullet of six points and an increscent silver. **Crest:** On a wreath of the colours, A demi bear supporting a ragged staff sable. **Motto:** Antiquum obtinens. **Granted** 10 April 1964.

WARWICK, UNIVERSITY OF.* Quarterly gules and sable, in the first quarter an elephant statant, on the back a castle triple towered, Or, in the second and third quarters representations of the two isotopes of lithium, that in the second quarter having six and that in the third seven protons and neutrons in its nucleus, with electrons in orbit, argent, in the fourth quarter a bear and ragged staff argent, muzzled gules, collared and chained Or; on a chief argent a representation of a DNA double helix, spirals azure lined gules, with connecting lines gold. **Crest:** On a wreath of the colours, An open book bound and clasped argent, the pages Or, inscribed thereon in Roman capitals sable MENS AGITAT MOLEM, and resting on a book fesswise argent, the foredge to the front Or. On an escrol beneath the shield the words UNIVERSITAS WARWICENSIS. **Granted** 5 October 1966.

WARWICK SCHOOL. See King's School, Warwick.

WARWICKSHIRE COUNTY COUNCIL.* Gules, a bear erect argent, muzzled of the first, collared and chained Or, supporting a ragged staff of the second, the chain reflexed over the back and encircling the staff, on a chief of the third three cross crosslets of the first; the shield ensigned with a mural crown gold. **Motto:** Non sanz droict. **Granted** 7 July 1931.

WASHINGTON DEVELOPMENT CORPORATION (CO. DURHAM).* Per chevron argent and azure, in base a cross Or, over all two bars and in chief three mullets gules. **Crest:** On a wreath of the colours, In front of an eagle, wings addorsed, sable, three mullets gules. **Motto:** Eodem signo Coniuncti. **Granted** 10 May 1965.

WATER POLLUTION CONTROL, INSTITUTE OF. Barry wavy of six argent and azure, on a pile reversed sable semy of plates, a sword in pale proper, hilt and pommel Or. **Crest:** On a wreath of the colours, In front of three fountains a kingfisher proper, in the beak a sword proper, hilt and pommel Or. **Granted** 10 April 1967.

WATER SUPPLY INDUSTRY TRAINING BOARD. Azure, two bars wavy and a chief wavy argent; over all a torch Or, inflamed proper. **Crest:** On a wreath of the colours, In front of water

WALTON-LE-DALE

WARLEY

WARWICK

WARE

WARRINGTON

barry wavy of four argent and azure, a torch Or, inflamed proper, supported by two demi lions azure gutty d'eau and issuant from the water. **Motto:** Amicitia progredimur. **Granted** 1 August 1967.

WATERMEN AND LIGHTERMEN OF THE CITY OF LONDON, WORSHIPFUL COMPANY OF. Argent, in base barry wavy of six azure and argent, a boat proper; on a chief azure two oars in saltire Or between two cushions argent fretted gules trimmed argent tasselled Or. **Crest:** On a wreath argent and gules, A dexter arm embowed vested argent, holding in the hand proper an oar erect Or. **Supporters:** On either side a dolphin haurient argent, finned, eyed and tusked Or. **Motto:** At commaundement of owre superiors. **Granted** 18 September 1585 by Robert Cooke, Clarenceux King of Arms. (*Illustration on page* 399).

WATFORD, BOROUGH OF (HERTFORDSHIRE).* Gules, on a pale wavy argent between two escallops Or, a pallet wavy azure charged with a fasces erect of the second; on a chief of the third a hurt, charged with a saltire also of the third, between two harts statant of the first. **Motto:** Audentior. **Granted** 16 October 1922.

WAX-CHANDLERS OF THE CITY OF LONDON, WORSHIPFUL COMPANY OF. Azure, on a chevron argent between three mortiers royal Or, as many roses gules seeded Or. **Crest:** On a wreath Or and gules, A maiden vested of cloth of gold furred with ermine, kneeling amongst divers flowers proper and making thereof a garland. **Supporters:** On either side a unicorn argent, gorged with a garland of various flowers proper, the horn wreathed Or and gules. **Motto:** Truth is the light. Arms and Crest (mantling azure, doubled ermine) granted 3 February 1485 by Sir Thomas Holme, Clarenceux King of Arms; Supporters granted 11 October 1530 by Thomas Benolt, Clarenceux King of Arms; the whole confirmed 12 October 1536 (mantling gules, doubled argent) by Thomas Hawley, Clarenceux King of Arms; The whole entered as above (the supporters being originally different) at the Visitation of 1634. (*Illustration on page* 399).

WEAVERS OF THE CITY OF LONDON, WORSHIPFUL COMPANY OF. Azure, on a chevron argent between three leopards' faces, each holding in the mouth a shuttle Or, as many roses gules. **Crest:** On a wreath argent and gules, A leopard's head affrontée crowned and holding in the mouth a shuttle Or. Mantled azure, doubled ermine. **Supporters:** On either side a wyvern ermine, langued and membered gules, on the wings displayed and garnished Or a rose gules. **Motto:** Weave trust with trust. Arms and Crest granted 4 August 1490 by Sir Thomas Holme, Clarenceux King of Arms; confirmed in 1530 by Benolt and in 1590 by Cooke; Supporters granted 10 August 1616 by Sir William Segar, Garter King of Arms. (*Illustration on page* 399).

WEIR, ANDREW, INSURANCE COMPANY LIMITED. See Andrew Weir Insurance Company Limited.

THE WELDING INSTITUTE. Sable, a pile reversed throughout Or, guttée gules in base; over all a broken fess per pile argent and of the third. **Motto:** E duobus unum. **Granted** 20 December 1968.

WELFARE INSURANCE COMPANY LIMITED. Azure, an annulet and an armillary sphere interlaced Or. **Crest:** Out of a coronet composed of roses gules, barbed and seeded proper, set upon a rim Or, a compass card argent, marked and lettered azure. **Supporters:** On either side a lion Or gorged with a cord gules, pendent therefrom an escutcheon azure, that on the dexter charged with two keys in saltire gold, and that on the sinister with two clasped hands issuant in fesse also gold. **Motto:** Welfare. **Badge:** An annulet and an armillary sphere interlaced as in the Arms. **Granted** 9 March 1956.

WELLINGBOROUGH RURAL DISTRICT COUNCIL (NORTHAMPTONSHIRE). Gules, a chevron vair between in chief two garbs and in base a bulls' head caboshed Or, three roses gules,

WARWICKSHIRE C. C.

WATFORD

WARWICK UNIVERSITY

WASHINGTON

barbed and seeded proper. **Crest:** Out of a Saxon crown Or a mount vert, thereon a representation of the Saxon tower of the Church at Earls Barton proper. **Motto:** Tam cras quam hodie. **Granted** 4 August 1954.

WELLINGBOROUGH SCHOOL. Quarterly gules and vert, a pile Or surmounted of a fesse wavy argent, in chief a rose of the first, barbed and seeded proper, and in base an open book of the last. **Motto:** Altiora peto. **Granted** 11 November 1924.

WELLINGBOROUGH URBAN DISTRICT COUNCIL (NORTHAMPTONSHIRE).* Sable, on a chevron between in chief two leopards' faces and in base a garb Or, five fountains. **Crest:** On a wreath of the colours, Issuant from flames proper a demi bull sable, armed, unguled and supporting a crosier Or, suspended from his neck by a riband gold an escutcheon argent charged with a Tudor rose proper. **Motto:** Aspice, respice. **Granted** 23 August 1949.

WELLINGTON SCHOOL (SOMERSET). Sable, an open book proper, edged and clasped Or and inscribed with the words 'Nisi Dominus frustra'; on a chief Or, between two dragons rampant combatant, a pale gules charged with a cross argent, in each canton five plates in saltire. **Granted** 2 November 1926.

WELLINGTON URBAN DISTRICT COUNCIL (SHROPSHIRE).* Argent fretty gules, a lion rampant sable; on a chief of the last a castle of the first between two fleurs-de-lys Or. **Crest:** On a wreath of the colours, In front of a portcullis chained sable, a bugle horn stringed Or. **Motto:** Deo adjuvante. **Granted** 14 March 1951.

WELLS, CITY OF (SOMERSET).* Argent, in base a mount vert, thereon an ash tree proper between three wells gules; the shield ensigned by a mural crown Or. **Motto:** Hoc fonte derivata copia. **Granted** 23 August 1951.

WELTON RURAL DISTRICT COUNCIL (LINCOLNSHIRE—PARTS OF LINDSEY).* Gules, a cross patonce Or between five fountains; on a chief azure a pallet ermine betwen two lions passant guardant gold. **Crest:** Out of a circlet vert charged with three ears of wheat Or, two ostrich feathers argent, between the same a demi lion gold, gorged with a collar gules, holding in the forepaws a battle-axe, the haft sable, the head proper. **Motto:** Prests pour nostre pays. **Granted** 20 June 1955.

WELWYN GARDEN CITY URBAN DISTRICT COUNCIL (HERTFORDSHIRE).* Vert, two pairs of dividers in fesse, inverted and extended, the interior points contiguous, argent, between three ears of wheat, stalked, leaved and slipped, Or; on a chief of the last as many bees volant proper. **Crest:** On a wreath of the colours, In front of a willow tree, a hart lodged proper murally gorged Or. **Motto:** By wisdom and design. **Granted** 15 December 1958.

WESLEY HOUSE (CAMBRIDGE). Gules, a cross between four escallops Or; on a chief sable a book argent edged and clasped Or. **Motto:** Lux vita caritas. **Granted** 24 March 1926.

WEST BROMWICH, COUNTY BOROUGH OF (STAFFORDSHIRE).* Azure, a stag's head caboshed argent between three fers-de-moline Or; a bordure of the second charged with four mullets and as many fleurs-de-lis alternately of the first. **Crest:** On a wreath of the colours, In front of four feathers erect azure, a stag lodged argent, supporting with the dexter foot a fer-de-moline sable. **Granted** 16 October 1882.

WEST BROMWICH BUILDING SOCIETY. Azure, a stag's head caboshed argent, between the antlers a Stafford knot Or; on a chief embattled sable a sprig of thrift gold between two keys, wards upwards and outwards, also gold. **Crest:** Issuant from a celestial crown Or, a demi dragon sable grasping a lance erect gold, tipped argent, flying therefrom a pennon of the Arms of St. George. Mantled azure, doubled argent. **Motto:** Sapientia aedificatur domus. **Granted** 22 July 1955.

WELLINGBOROUGH U. D. C.

WELLINGTON

WELLS

WELWYN GARDEN CITY

WELTON

WESTFIELD COLLEGE (LONDON UNIVERSITY).* Sable, a cross quadrate Or; on a chief of the last an open book proper bound gules between two mascles that on the dexter enclosing a sinister hand couped appaumée, that on the sinister a lion's paw erased, all of the first. **Granted** 15 February 1934.

WEST MERCIA POLICE AUTHORITY.* Per fesse gules and azure, on a fesse between in chief a lion passant guardant argent and in base a leopard's face Or, three pears sable. **Granted** 10 October 1967.

WEST MIDLANDS GAS BOARD. Per fess azure and sable, on a fess wavy argent a bar wavy azure, in chief a Stafford knot Or between two flames proper, and in base a blacksmith's hammer erect Or. **Crest:** On a wreath of the colours, In front of flames proper, two cog-wheels engaged sable, voided argent, upon each an ermine spot. **Supporters:** On the dexter side a Hereford Bull proper, and on the sinister side a male figure in Tudor dress, a sheaf of arrows at his back and holding in the exterior hand a longbow stringed proper, the whole upon a grassy mount and thereon two pears proper. **Motto:** E terra marique vis. **Granted** 30 May 1967.

WEST MIDLANDS POLICE AUTHORITY. Or, a cross formy gules between four lions rampant [queue fourchée] vert; on a chief azure a stag's head caboshed between two bears sejant respectant argent, muzzled gules, each supporting a ragged staff argent and collared and chained Or. **Crest:** On a wreath of the colours, In front of a pear tree, fructed, a representation of the Keep of Dudley Castle on a grassy mount proper charged with a Stafford knot Or. **Motto:** Quinque in uno. **Granted** 1 August 1967.

WESTMINSTER, CITY OF.* Azure, between two wolves' heads erased argent and on a base wavy argent and azure, a female figure affrontée vested and mantled and on her sinister arm a child also vested, around the head of each a halo, all Or; on a chief of the last a pallet azure, thereon a cross flory between five martlets Or, being the Arms of King Edward the Confessor, between two united roses argent upon gules. **Crest:** On a wreath Or and azure, A portcullis sable studded and chained Or, between on the dexter side a united rose, the flower argent upon gules, and on the sinister side a lily, both stalked, leaved and erect proper. **Supporters:** On either side a lion ermine, the dexter gorged of a mural crown azure charged with three lily flowers argent, the sinister gorged of a like crown Or charged with two swords in saltire gules. **Motto:** Custodi civitatem Domine. **Badge:** A portcullis chained and ensigned of a mural crown between on the dexter side a united rose and on the sinister side a lily, both stalked and leaved, all Or. Arms, Crest and Supporters granted 2 September 1964; Badge granted 1 March 1965.

WESTMINSTER, COLLEGIATE CHURCH OF ST. PETER. DEAN AND CHAPTER. Azure, a cross patonce between five martlets Or; and on a chief Or a pale quarterly of France Modern and England between two roses gules [barbed and seeded proper]. Confirmed and exemplified 5 October 1966. **DEPUTY HIGH STEWARD. Badge:** A cross patonce Or surmounted by a portcullis sable studded Or. **Granted** 3 February 1967.

WESTMINSTER CHAMBER OF COMMERCE. Or, a portcullis chained sable; a bordure azure charged with five bezants alternately with as many martlets gold. **Crest:** On a wreath Or and azure, An ancient ship in full sail Or, flying from each masthead a pennon argent charged with a cross gules, the mainsail [azure] charged with a bezant thereon a portcullis chained sable. **Supporters:** On either side a red squirrel proper, pendent from a chain about the neck a key, wards downwards and outwards, Or. **Motto:** Fortuna meliores sequitur. **Granted** 10 March 1958.

WESTMINSTER COLLEGE, THE GOVERNORS OF (OXFORD). Or, on a chevron azure three escallops argent, between in chief two lions rampant guardant, the dexter contourné gules, supporting with their forepaws a portcullis chained sable, studded of the fourth, and in base a lion rampant guardant also gules. **Crest:** On a wreath of the colours, The battlements of a tower triple-towered argent, standing upon the centre tower a peacock proper, ducally gorged Or. **Motto:** Virtute et fide. **Granted** 6 September 1956.

WESTFIELD COLLEGE

WEST BROMWICH

WEST MERCIA POLICE

WESTMORLAND

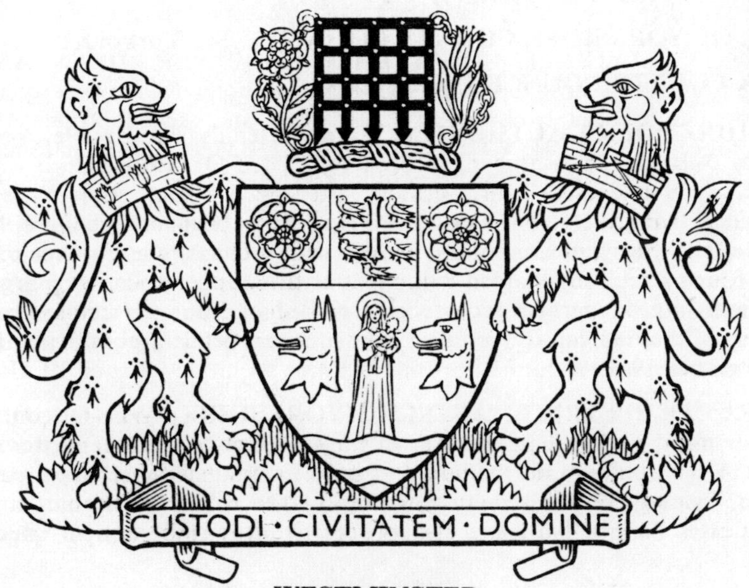

WESTMINSTER

WESTMINSTER HOSPITAL. Azure, a cross patonce between three martlets Or; a chief of the last, thereon on a pale of the first between two roses gules, each surmounted by another argent, barbed and seeded proper, a portcullis chained of the second ensigned with the Imperial Crown also proper. **Granted** 1 February 1940 to the President, Vice Presidents, Treasurers and Governors of the Westminster Hospital pursuant to Royal Warrant 12 December 1939.

WESTMORLAND COUNTY COUNCIL.* Argent, two bars gules; over all an apple tree with seven branches fructed and eradicated Or. **Crest:** On a wreath of the colours, A Herdwick ram's head proper charged on the forehead with a shearman's hook Or. **Granted** 2 June 1926.

WESTONBIRT SCHOOL (GLOUCESTERSHIRE). Per chevron gules and argent, in chief a slip of White Amaryllis flowers leaved proper, and a Catherine Wheel also argent, and in base a cedar tree eradicated also proper; on a chief of the second between two greyhounds' heads erased sable, an open book likewise proper, bound gules, edged and clasped Or, thereon the words 'Te Deum Laudamus' in letters also sable. **Motto:** Bono malum superate. **Granted** 20 August 1960.

WESTON-SUPER-MARE, BOROUGH OF (SOMERSET).* Per fesse Or and argent, in chief to the sinister a setting sun issuant gules, and in base a lymphad also gules; on a quarter sable a castle of three towers silver. **Crest:** On a wreath argent and sable, In front of a lighthouse set upon a rock, a seagull volant proper. **Supporters:** On the dexter side a lion guardant azure, collared Or, pendent therefrom by a chain also Or an escutcheon gules charged with a chevron argent between three clarions gold, and on the sinister side a wolf argent collared gules, pendent therefrom by a chain Or an escutcheon sable charged with a fesse ermine. **Motto:** Ever forward. **Granted** 15 January 1960.

WEST PENWITH RURAL DISTRICT COUNCIL (CORNWALL).* Azure, on a chevron between in chief two lymphads in sail, and in base a roundel Or charged with a cross pommy gules, a chevron engrailed sable charged with five bezants. **Crest:** On a wreath of the colours, Out of a mural crown argent a mount vert, thereon in front of four ears of wheat, stalked and leaved, a Cornish chough proper supporting in the dexter claw a torch erect sable, enflamed also proper. **Motto:** Aspice finem. **Granted** 10 December 1953.

WEST RIDING OF YORKSHIRE COUNTY COUNCIL. See Yorkshire.

WEST SUSSEX COUNTY COUNCIL. See Sussex.

WEST YORKSHIRE POLICE AUTHORITY. Or, a portcullis chained gules; on a chief dancetty azure three roses of seven petals argent, barbed and seeded Or. **Crest:** On a wreath argent and azure, A falcon, wings addorsed, azure, beaked and legged argent, supporting with the dexter talon a staff argent, flying therefrom a banner of the Arms. **Supporters:** On either side a griffin reguardant azure, beaked, membered and collared, with a chain reflexed over the back, pendant from the collar four portcullises chained conjoined at their upper ends in cross surmounted by a rose of seven petals argent, barbed and seeded Or. **Badge:** Four portcullises conjoined at their upper ends in cross, chained gules; over all a rose of seven petals argent, barbed and seeded Or. **Granted** 10 September 1969.

WETHERBY RURAL DISTRICT COUNCIL (YORKSHIRE—WEST RIDING).* Argent, two bars wavy azure; on a chief gules a wether passant between two ears of wheat slipped and leaved Or. **Crest:** On a wreath of the colours, In front of a castle with two towers each surmounted by a staff proper, flying therefrom a banner argent charged with a cross gules, a Knight Templar holding in his dexter hand a battleaxe also proper. **Motto:** Imperium in imperio. **Granted:** 7 January 1938.

WESTON-SUPER-MARE

WEST PENWITH

WHISTON

WEYMOUTH

WETHERBY

WEYMOUTH AND MELCOMBE REGIS, BOROUGH OF (DORSET).* Azure, on waves of the sea in base proper, a ship of three masts tackled and rigged all Or, on the fore and mizzen masts two square banners, that on the first per pale gules and vert three lions passant guardant in pale Or, that on the latter quarterly, 1 and 4 argent a lion rampant purpure, 2 and 3 gules a tower triple-towered Or; on the hulk of the ship an escutcheon Per fesse Or and gules, in chief three chevronels also gules, in base three lions passant guardant in pale also Or. **Seal:** Azure, a bridge double-embattled argent standing in the sea proper, in the chief an escutcheon Per fess Or and gules, in the first three chevrons gules and in the second three lions passant guardant in pale gold. **Granted** 1 May 1592.

WHEELWRIGHTS OF THE CITY OF LONDON, WORSHIPFUL COMPANY OF. Gules, a chevron between three wheels Or; on a chief argent a broad axe, blade to the sinister, proper. **Crest:** On a wreath argent and gules, A dexter arm embowed, vested azure, cuffed argent, the hand proper holding a mullet Or. **Supporters:** On either side a horse argent, each gorged with a circlet, pendent therefrom over the foreleg a chain terminated by a ring Or. **Motto:** God grant unity. **Granted** 20 November 1964.

WHISTON RURAL DISTRICT COUNCIL (LANCASHIRE).* Argent, a griffin segreant sable, the beak and forelegs Or, charged on the shoulder with an escallop of the field, in chief three crescents gules; all within a bordure of the second charged with eleven ermine spots also of the field. **Crest:** On a wreath argent and gules, Within a circlet composed of four fleurs-de-lys argent and as many mullets sable alternately, a mount vert, thereon an eagle rising, neck embowed, Or, in the beak a rose gules, barbed, seeded, stalked, leaved and slipped, proper. **Motto:** Labora si vis tondere. **Granted** 22 January 1957.

WHITBY RURAL DISTRICT COUNCIL (YORKSHIRE—NORTH RIDING).* Per fesse wavy vert and purpure, a barrulet wavy argent between three coiled serpents Or; on a chief also argent three lymphads, sails furled, sable. **Crest:** On a wreath of the colours, Issuant from a circlet composed of eight fusils conjoined Or, a demi unicorn ermine, armed and unguled also Or, gorged with a wreath of rose leaves vert charged with three roses argent, and supporting a staff gold, flying therefrom a forked pennon per fesse argent and azure charged in the hoist with a cross formy also gold. **Motto:** Amoenitate quies. **Granted** 10 February 1958.

WHITBY URBAN DISTRICT COUNCIL (YORKSHIRE—NORTH RIDING).* Barry wavy of ten argent and azure, three serpents coiled proper. **Crest:** On a wreath of the colours, In front of an anchor sable, three roses, two and one, argent, barbed and seeded proper. **Motto:** Fuimus et sumus. **Granted:** 3 July 1935.

WHITCHURCH PARISH COUNCIL (SHROPSHIRE).* Azure, a chevron erminois between in chief two garbs Or, the dexter charged with a cross engrailed floretty sable, and in base a leopards face gold. **Crest:** On a wreath of the colours, In front of the sun rising Or, a representation of the old Parish Church of Whitchurch proper. Mantled azure, doubled Or. **Motto:** Floreant concilia Salopiae. **Granted** 20 March 1962 to the Whitchurch UDC.

WHITLEY BAY, BOROUGH OF (NORTHUMBERLAND). Per fesse gules and barry wavy azure and argent, a fesse embattled Or; in chief three ducal coronets of the last and in base over all a lymphad, sail furled, sable with pennon and flags flying of the Arms of St. George. **Crest:** Out of a coronet of four lily flowers set upon a rim argent, a mount vert, thereon a representation of the lighthouse of St. Mary's Island proper. Mantled azure, doubled Or. **Supporters:** On either side a sea lion proper, head and mane Or, each gorged with a collar company gold and gules, pendent therefrom by a link vert an escutcheon, that on the dexter Azure five lozenges conjoined in fess Or, that on the sinister Ermine two bars vert. **Motto:** Non sibi sed omnibus. **Granted** 23 April 1954.

WIGAN

WHITBY U.D.C.

WHITCHURCH

WHITBY R.D.C.

WIDNES, BOROUGH OF (LANCASHIRE). Quarterly argent and azure, a cross per cross quarterly counterchanged, in the first and fourth quarters a rose gules barbed and seeded proper, and in the second and third a beehive between four bees volant saltirewise Or. **Crest:** Upon a wreath of the colours, A furnace, thereon an alembic, all Or. **Motto:** Industria ditat. **Granted** 5 June 1893.

WIGAN, COUNTY BOROUGH OF (LANCASHIRE).* Gules, a castle with three towers argent surmounted [=ensigned] by a crown composed of fleurs-de-lis Or. **Crest:** On a wreath of the colours, In front of a king's head affrontée, couped below the shoulder, proper, vested gules, crowned and crined Or, a lion couchant guardant gold. **Supporters:** On either side a lion Or holding in the exterior paw a branch of mountain ash proper. **Motto:** Ancient and Loyal. **Granted** 28 April 1922.

WIGAN AND DISTRICT MINING AND TECHNICAL COLLEGE.* Sable, a sunburst proper, and in chief an open book Or. **Motto:** Lux ex tenebris. **Granted** 18 March 1948.

P. WIGHAM-RICHARDSON AND COMPANY LIMITED. Barry Or and azure, on a pale argent a leopard's face azure between two acorns slipped and leaved proper. **Crest:** On a wreath of the colours, Out of a mercantile crown Or, the sails argent, a dexter cubit arm in armour proper, holding a scroll argent. **Supporters:** On the dexter side a griffin Or, winged azure, charged on the wing with a tower Or, and on the sinister side a sea griffin likewise Or, winged azure, charged on the wing with an anchor Or. **Motto:** Peragimus quod coepit conditor. **Granted** 2 September 1964.

WIGSTON URBAN DISTRICT COUNCIL (LEICESTERSHIRE).* Vert, between two piles issuant from the base argent a plate fimbriated Or charged with Tudor rose, barbed, seeded, stalked and leaved, proper, in chief the driving wheel of a railway engine gold. **Crest:** On a wreath of the colours, A tiger passant guardant holding in the dexter paw a shuttle proper. **Motto:** Finis coronat opus. **Granted** 25 November 1953.

WILMSLOW URBAN DISTRICT COUNCIL (CHESHIRE).* Argent, on a bend between two bendlets wavy azure, three garbs Or. **Crest:** On a wreath of the colours, Issuant from an antique crown Or enfiled round the base with a wreath of cotton proper, a bear's head sable, muzzled gules, charged on the neck with an estoile argent. **Motto:** Nobis habitatio felix. **Granted** 21 June 1951.

WILTSHIRE COUNTY COUNCIL.* Barry of eight argent and vert, on a canton of the last a dragon rampant gules. **Crest:** On a wreath of the colours, A Bustard, wings elevated and addorsed, proper. **Badge:** On a roundel barry of eight argent and vert a Bustard, wings addorsed, proper. Arms and Crest granted 5 April 1937; Badge granted 30 June 1967.

WIMBLEDON AND PUTNEY COMMON CONSERVATORS. Vert, a dove volant argent within a chain in orle Or. **Crest:** On a wreath of the colours, Set upon a brick wall gules, a representation of the old windmill on Wimbledon Common proper charged with three escallops in bend argent. **Motto:** Custodes ruris in urbe. **Badge:** A representation of the old windmill on Wimbledon Common environed by an oval band Or. **Granted** 21 June 1945.

WIMBORNE AND CRANBORNE RURAL DISTRICT COUNCIL (DORSET).* Azure, a stag's head caboshed, between the attires a cross flory, Or; on a chief argent a fleur-de-lys between two Saxon crowns gules. **Crest:** Out of a coronet composed of two fleurs-de-lys Or and as many roses gules, barbed and seeded proper, set alternately upon a rim gold, a demi lion ermine, ducally gorged also gold and holding between the paws a chapeau gules turned up ermine. **Motto:** Serio servire. **Granted** 29 May 1959.

WINCHESTER, BISHOPRIC OF. Gules, two keys, endorsed and conjoined at the bows, in bend, wards in chief, the uppermost Or, the lower argent, a sword, the point in chief, interposed between them in bend sinister of the third, pomel and hilt gold. Recorded in the College of Arms.

WIGSTON

WIMBORNE AND CRANBORNE

WILMSLOW

WILTSHIRE

WIGAN TECHNICAL COLLEGE

WINCHESTER, THE DEAN AND CHAPTER OF THE CATHEDRAL CHURCH OF. A mynster or churche sylver masoned sable, in the yate of the churche the holye image of the blessed Trynyte golde and silver crowned imperiall with a dyademe golde of the most high and mighty prince the Kinge their founder, a canton party par palle gueules and silver a rose with the sonne beames celestiall counterchanged of the fylde the sede pomeley golde with these words of Poisie scz. Benedicta sit Scã Trinitas. **Granted** by Sir Christopher Barker, Garter King of Arms, 1 June 1541.

WINCHESTER, CITY OF (HAMPSHIRE).* Gules, five castles triple-towered in saltire argent, and on either side of the centre castle a lion passant guardant, that to the dexter contourné Or. Recorded at the Visitation of 1686.

WINCHESTER RURAL DISTRICT COUNCIL (HAMPSHIRE).* Azure, two garbs and in base a naval crown Or, on a chief of the last a rose gules, barbed and seeded proper, between two lymphads of the first; all within a bordure argent charged with six trout naiant pursuant from the dexter sable alternating with as many slips of watercress also proper. **Crest:** Issuant from a Saxon crown Or, a demi lion guardant gules holding in the paws a mullet gold. **Motto:** Ardua vince merendo. **Granted** 20 April 1953.

WINDSOR, BOROUGH OF. See New Windsor.

WINDSOR HERALD. See Arms, Officers of.

WINDSOR RURAL DISTRICT COUNCIL (BERKSHIRE).* Vert, on a fess wavy argent between in chief two acorns slipped and leaved and in base a horseshoe (racing plate) Or, two barrulets wavy azure. **Crest:** On a wreath of the colours, Out of a circlet of park palings argent, a demi hart royal proper, unguled and attired Or, between two sprigs of azalea stalked and leaved vert and flowered gold. **Motto:** In counsel is stability. **Granted** 1 December 1962.

WISBECH, BOROUGH OF (CAMBRIDGESHIRE).* Azure, representations of St. Peter and St. Paul standing within a double canopy Or. **Crest:** On a wreath of the colours, A sixteenth century ship with three masts Or, on each mast a square sail azure, the center one charged with two keys in saltire, wards upwards, and the other two charged with a castle gold. **Granted** 11 November 1929.

WISBECH RURAL DISTRICT COUNCIL (CAMBRIDGESHIRE).* Barry wavy of eight argent and vert, a cornucopia erect Or, the fruit proper; all within a bordure gules charged with eight ducal coronets gold. **Crest:** Out of a circlet argent charged with three mullets sable, a demi lion also argent gorged with a ducal coronet Or and supporting a staff of the first, flying therefrom a banner azure charged with a lily flower also argent. Mantled vert, doubled argent. **Motto:** Thesauros in agro. **Granted** 11 October 1954.

WITNEY GRAMMAR SCHOOL (OXFORDSHIRE). Azure, a fess argent surmounted of another invected gules charged with a lion passant guardant Or, in chief an open book proper, bound, edged and clasped gold, between two griffins' heads erased of the last, and in base a like griffin's head also gold. **Crest:** On a wreath Or and azure, A demi griffin per fesse gules and Or, armed gold, the under wing azure, between a crescent and a star also gold. **Motto:** Studio floremus. **Granted** 20 March 1959.

WITNEY URBAN DISTRICT COUNCIL (OXFORDSHIRE).* Vert, on a fess wavy argent between in chief a sinister glove of the last between two leopards' faces each holding in the mouth a shuttle Or, and in base a representation of the Butter Cross at Witney gold, a barrulet wavy azure. **Crest:** On a wreath of the colours, Upon a mount vert, between a crescent and a star Or, a Paschal Lamb proper. **Motto:** Ingenio floremus. **Granted** 9 September 1955.

WINCHESTER R. D. C.

WINCHESTER CITY

WINDSOR

WISBECH BOROUGH

WISBECH R. D. C.

WITNEY

WOKING URBAN DISTRICT COUNCIL (SURREY).* Quarterly Or and gules, a cross flory between in the first and fourth quarters a fleur-de-lis and in the second and third quarters a fret, all counterchanged. **Motto:** Fide et diligentia. **Granted** 18 June 1930.

WOKINGHAM, BOROUGH OF (BERKSHIRE).* Or, semée of acorns vert, a chevron ermine, thereon a Tudor rose, barbed and seeded, proper. **Crest:** On a wreath of the colours, Issuant from a Saxon crown Or a demi stag at gaze proper supporting a crosier Or. **Motto:** E glande quercus. **Granted** 29 September 1953.

WOKINGHAM RURAL DISTRICT COUNCIL (BERKSHIRE).* Argent, two bars wavy vert, over all a stag's head caboshed proper; on a chief gules, in front of two pastoral staves in saltire Or, a mitre, the infulae entwined with the staves, argent. **Crest:** Out of a coronet composed of four ears of wheat and as many acorns leaved, set alternately upon a rim Or, a mount vert, thereon a lion passant guardant gold supporting with the dexter forepaw an oar erect proper. **Motto:** Unum e pluribus. **Granted** 12 March 1962.

WOLVERHAMPTON, COUNTY BOROUGH OF (STAFFORDSHIRE).* Gules, a cross formée Or between a pillar in the first quarter, a woolpack in the second, an open book in the third, all argent, and in the fourth a padlock of the second. **Crest:** On a wreath of the colours, In front of a beacon sable, fired proper, two keys in saltire, wards upwards, Or. **Motto:** Out of darkness cometh light. **Granted** 31 December 1898.

WOLVERHAMPTON AND DISTRICT BUILDING SOCIETY. Or, in front of a beacon sable, fired proper, two keys in saltire, wards upwards and outwards, also sable; on a chief azure a Stafford knot between two sprigs of thrift, each of three flowers, gold. **Crest:** On a wreath of the colours, Issuant from the battlements of a tower Or a demi wolf sable charged on the shoulder with a Stafford knot and holding between the forepaws a key in pale, wards outwards, gold. **Motto:** Progress with security. **Granted** 20 December 1963 to Wolverhampton and District Permanent Building Society.

WOLVERHAMPTON GIRLS' HIGH SCHOOL. Gules, a cross formy throughout, interlaced by a Stafford knot Or, all between four towers argent each charged with an ermine spot sable. **Crest:** On a wreath of the colours, Between two wings, a triangle, point downward, Or. **Motto:** Ludus supra praemium. **Badge:** On a cross formy interlaced by a Stafford knot Or, four ermine spots inward sable. **Granted** 15 August 1962.

WOLVERHAMPTON HOSPITAL MANAGEMENT COMMITTEE. *Argent, a cross gules quarter pierced; on a chief sable three wolves' heads erased Or. **Granted** 24 June 1949 to the Wolverhampton Local Management Committee.

WOLVERHAMPTON ROYAL HOSPITAL. Argent, a cross gules; on a chief sable three wolves' heads erased Or. **Granted** 30 July 1930 to The Royal Hospital Wolverhampton.

WOODSTOCK, BOROUGH OF (OXFORDSHIRE).* Gules, the stump of a tree couped and eradicated argent and in chief three stags' heads caboshed of the same; all within a bordure of the last charged with eight oak leaves vert. **Crest:** Out of a ducal coronet Or, an oak tree proper leaved vert. **Supporters:** On either side a savage proper, wreathed about the head and loins with oak leaves vert, holding over his exterior shoulder a club proper. **Motto:** Ramosa cornua cervi. Recorded at the Visitation of 1634; Certified painting obtained in 1949.

WOOLMEN OR WOOLPACKERS OF THE CITY OF LONDON, WORSHIPFUL COMPANY OF. Gules, a woolpack argent. **Crest:** On a wreath of the colours, In front of two distaffs in saltire gules, flaxed Or, the wheel of a spinning wheel Or. **Motto:** Lana spes nostra. **Granted** 19 November 1954. (*Illustration on page* 399).

WOKINGHAM BOROUGH

WOKING

WOKINGHAM R. D. C.

WOLVERHAMPTON H. M. C.

WOLVERHAMPTON CO. BOROUGH

WOODSTOCK

WOOLWICH POLYTECHNIC. Barry wavy of six argent and azure, a pale sable, thereon a gun barrel erect surmounted on the breech by a lion's face argent; on a chief also sable a cogwheel between two open books Or. **Crest:** On a wreath of the colours, Issuant from a wreath of oak fructed Or, a boar's head erased sable. **Granted** 25 November 1953.

WORCESTER, BISHOPRIC OF.* Argent, ten torteaux, four, three, two and one. Recorded in the College of Arms.

WORCESTER, CITY AND COUNTY BOROUGH OF.* Quarterly sable and gules, a castle triple-towered argent. **Motto:** Civitas in bello et pace fidelis. Recorded at the Visitations of 1569 and 1634. Argent, a fesse between three pears sable. Recorded at the Visitation of 1634.

WORCESTER COLLEGE (OXFORD UNIVERSITY). Argent, two chevronels between six martlets, three, two and one, gules. These are of no authority.

WORCESTER ROYAL GRAMMAR SCHOOL. Gules, an ancient crown Or, on a chief argent three pears sable. **Crest:** On a wreath of the colours, In front of the battlements of a castle triple-towered argent, masoned sable, a Roman lamp Or, inflamed gules. **Motto:** Respice et prospice. **Granted** 24 July 1961 to The Royal Free Grammar School of Queen Elizabeth alias Worcester Royal Grammar School.

WORCESTERSHIRE COUNTY COUNCIL.* Argent, issuant from a mount on water in base, a pear tree proper fructed sable; the shield ensigned with a mural crown Or. **Granted** 21 May 1947.

WORKINGTON, BOROUGH OF (CUMBERLAND).* Sable, between two piles Or billettée azure, a garb of the second. **Crest:** On a wreath of the colours, Issuant from a mural crown Or, a unicorn's head argent holding in the mouth an anchor in bend sable. **Supporters:** On the dexter a representation of Vulcan, and on the sinister a representation of Themis, both proper. **Motto:** Levavi oculos meos in montes. [Motto on patent—Floreat oppidum laborans]. **Granted** 15 November 1950.

WORKS MANAGERS, INSTITUTE OF. Or, a pair of scales surmounted of a pair of keys addorsed, bows interlaced in base, between three pierced mullets sable; on a chief vert three crosses patonce argent. **Crest:** On a wreath of the colours, A demi man in mail, the coif and mittens loose, proper, with a surcoat argent, thereon framed within a mascle sable, a sun in splendour throughout Or, holding in the dexter hand a pyramid argent, masoned sable, and the sinister supporting by the scabbard a sheathed sword also sable, garnished, hilt, pommel and quillons gold, the pommel resting on his hip. Mantled gules and sable, doubled Or. **Supporters:** On the dexter side a lion guardant sable, and on the sinister side a bull guardant also sable, unguled gules, and supporting a cresset, the basketwork fretty also sable, studded Or, enflamed proper, the pole gules, ferruled also sable [on a compartment consisting of a steel girder, draped around which is the] **Motto:** Ducit qui conducit. **Granted** 10 May 1962.

WORKSOP, BOROUGH OF (NOTTINGHAMSHIRE).* Argent, on a cross azure between in the first quarter a lion rampant per fesse sable and gules, in the second quarter a martlet of the last, in the third quarter a miner's shovel and pick in saltire proper, and in the fourth quarter an oak tree eradicated also proper, five ducal coronets Or. **Crest:** On a mural crown Or two squirrels sejant addorsed proper. **Supporters:** On the dexter side a knight in armour proper supporting with the exterior hand a shield azure, thereon a cross flory Or, and on the sinister side a man habited as a forester supporting with the exterior hand a longbow proper. **Motto:** Sans Dieu rien. **Granted** 10 June 1932.

WORKSOP RURAL DISTRICT COUNCIL (NOTTINGHAMSHIRE). Per saltire vert and sable, on a saltire argent between two garbs palewise Or and two stags' heads caboshed fessewise

WORCESTERSHIRE C. C.

WORKINGTON

WORCESTER BISHOPRIC

WORCESTER CITY

WORKSOP

also argent, two tilting spears in saltire gules, their points uppermost. **Crest:** On a wreath argent and sable, in front of two sprigs of oak entwined, leaved and fructed proper, a lozenge sable; over all a stag's head caboshed argent, attired and langued gules. **Motto:** Work supports all. **Granted** 31 July 1952.

WORK STUDY, INSTITUTE OF.* Tierce in pairle gules, azure and argent, in chief an open book proper, bound and garnished Or, and in base two cranes respectant, each grasping in the dexter claw a rock, all counterchanged. **Crest:** On a wreath argent and gules, An owl proper grasping in the dexter claw a torch Or enflamed also proper. **Motto:** Veritatem petimus. **Granted** 1 November 1960.

WORSLEY URBAN DISTRICT COUNCIL (LANCASHIRE).* Argent, a lion rampant gules; on a chief of the last a fountain between two lozenges of the field, on each a pheon sable. **Crest:** Out of a coronet composed of eight roses gules, barbed and seeded proper, set upon a rim Or, a demi lion sable gorged with a wreath of oak also proper and holding between the paws a cross patonce argent. **Motto:** Non nobis solum. **Granted** 14 February 1956.

WORTHING, BOROUGH OF (WEST SUSSEX).* Barry wavy of six azure and argent, three fishes naiant in pale proper; on a chief wavy Or, a cornucopia also proper. **Crest:** On a wreath of the colours, A female figure proper habited argent and azure, grasping in both hands a snake also proper. **Motto:** Ex terra copiam e mari salutem. **Granted** 30 October 1919.

WREKIN COLLEGE, WELLINGTON, LIMITED (SHROPSHIRE).* Azure, a lion rampant Or; on a canton of the last a sprig of bay slipped proper. **Crest:** On a wreath of the colours, Within a chaplet of bay proper a lion rampant Or. **Motto:** Aut vincere aut mori. **Granted** 26 February 1951.

WREXHAM, BOROUGH OF (DENBIGHSHIRE). Ermine, two croziers in saltire Or; on a chief dancettée per pale gules and Or two lions passant guardant counterchanged. **Crest:** On a wreath of the colours, Upon a mount vert a dragon gules resting the dexter claw upon a shield Or charged with the character of Mars sable. **Motto:** Fear God, Honour the King. **Granted** 6 November 1857.

WREXHAM RURAL DISTRICT COUNCIL (DENBIGHSHIRE).* Vert, two croziers in saltire Or between in pale two bull's heads caboshed proper and in fesse as many lozenges of the second both charged with a lozenge sable. **Crest:** On a wreath of the colours, In front of an oak tree proper, fructed Or, a dragon passant resting the dexter claw on an escutcheon gules, masoned argent. **Motto:** Suum cuique tribuere. **Granted** 1 December 1948.

WYCLIFFE COLLEGE (STONEHOUSE, GLOUCESTER). Quarterly sable and gules, a griffin passant between two crescents [in pale] Or. **Crest:** On a wreath of the colours, Within a circlet of eight crescents sable, a griffin passant Or. **Motto:** Bold and loyal. **Granted** 30 September 1931 to the Protestant Episcopal Divinity School Corporation for the use of Wycliffe College.

WORK STUDY INSTITUTE

WORSLEY

WORTHING

WREKIN COLLEGE

WREXHAM R. D. C.

Y

** Denotes Illustration*

YARMOUTH. See Great Yarmouth.

YEOVIL, BOROUGH OF (SOMERSET).* Azure, a representation of St. John the Baptist standing within a doorway Or, in his sinister hand a torteau charged with a Paschal Lamb proper, all between two croziers turned outwards and each ensigned with an ancient crown gold. **Crest:** Out of a Saxon crown gold, issuant from flames proper a demi bull sable, armed and unguled Or, supporting between the hoofs an escutcheon azure charged with a dexter glove appaumé Or. **Supporters:** On the dexter side a lion Or gorged with a collar azure charged with two spear heads gold, pendent from the collar by a rope proper an escutcheon Per fesse sable and vert over all fretty Or; and on the sinister side a horse Or gorged with a like collar, pendent therefrom by a rope proper an escutcheon Argent with a chevron between three roses gules, barbed and seeded proper, thereon. **Motto:** Industria virtute et labore. **Granted** 23 June 1954.

YEOVIL RURAL DISTRICT COUNCIL (SOMERSET).* Or, on a pall purpure a pall wavy argent; a chief vert, thereon a rural crown Or between a sinister and a dexter glove appaumy argent. **Crest:** On a wreath of the colours, In front of a demi-eagle Or, wings inverted, charged on the breast with a crescent enclosing an estoile of twelve rays sable and on each wing six bezants, four roses gules, barbed and seeded proper. **Motto:** Pro rure et focis. **Granted** 20 May 1953.

YORK, ARCHBISHOPRIC OF.* Azure, an archiepiscopal staff in pale argent ensigned by a cross patée Or, surmounted of a pallium of the second fringed of the third and charged with five crosses patée fitchée sable. Gules, two keys in saltire argent, in chief a regal crown Or. Both coats recorded in the College of Arms. The second is here illustrated.

YORK, CITY, COUNTY OF THE CITY, AND COUNTY BOROUGH OF.* . . . on a cross . . . five lions passant guardant . . . Recorded without tinctures at the Visitation of 1584.

YORK, UNIVERSITY OF, TRUST FUND.* Azure, on a chevron ermine three books fessewise, each with two clasps downwards, Or. **Crest:** On a wreath Or and azure, Out of a mural crown argent, masoned sable, two keys in saltire Or and silver, wards upward and outward, surmounted by a rose also argent, barbed and seeded proper. **Motto:** In limine sapientiae. **Badge:** Out of a mural crown argent, masoned sable, two keys in saltire Or and silver, wards upward and outward, surmounted by a rose also argent, barbed and seeded proper. **Granted** 20 June 1962.

YORK HERALD. See Arms, Officers of.

YORK AND NORTH EAST YORKSHIRE POLICE AUTHORITY. Argent, within a cross voided gules, an eagle displayed azure between four lions passant guardant gules; on a chief per pale azure and sable, three roses argent, barbed and seeded proper. **Crest:** On a wreath argent, gules and azure, Out of a mural crown argent, a mount vert, thereon a sea lion sejant azure, the head and mane Or, grasping in the dexter claw three roses argent barbed and seeded and the stalks conjoined in pale, proper. **Badge:** Three roses argent, barbed and seeded and the stalks conjoined in pale, proper. **Granted** 20 May 1969.

YEOVIL BOROUGH

YORK ARCHBISHOPRIC

YEOVIL R. D. C.

YORK CITY

YORK UNIVERSITY

YORKSHIRE BANK LIMITED.* Argent, a cross gules surmounted by another engrailed Or; on a chief per pale azure and of the second three roses of the first, barbed and seeded proper. **Granted** 1 May 1934 to the Yorkshire Penny Bank, Limited.

YORKSHIRE, EAST RIDING OF, COUNTY COUNCIL.* Per chevron argent and Or, in chief two garbs proper and in base an eagle displayed azure; on a chief sable three roses of the first, barbed and seeded proper. **Crest:** On a wreath of the colours, On a garb fessewise Or an eagle displayed azure. **Motto:** Solis ortum conspicere. **Granted** 28 February 1945.

YORKSHIRE, NORTH RIDING OF, COUNTY COUNCIL.* Argent, a cross gules; on a chief azure three roses argent, barbed and seeded proper. **Granted** 1 March 1928.

YORKSHIRE, WEST RIDING OF, COUNTY COUNCIL.* Ermine, a rose argent, barbed and seeded proper and en soleil Or; on a chief gules three roses of the second, barbed vert, seeded gold; the whole ensigned by a mural crown Or. **Motto:** Audi consilium. **Badge:** A rose argent, barbed and seeded proper, ensigned by a mural crown Or. **Standard:** Gules, the bands argent, inscribed sable, fringed argent and gules. **Granted** 2 February 1927.

YORKSHIRE RESIDENTIAL SCHOOL FOR THE DEAF (DONCASTER). Gules, a port between two towers with flags flying argent, the portcullis raised sable, in chief three roses in fesse of the second, barbed and seeded proper. **Motto:** Video vincam. **Granted** 26 September 1952.

YSTRADGYNLAIS RURAL DISTRICT COUNCIL (PEMBROKESHIRE). Per fess Or and azure, in chief a Davy lamp sable, the glass proper, between two horological balance wheels also sable, and issuant from the base a mount vert, thereon a port between two towers argent, perched on the battlements of the port a nightingale also proper. **Crest:** On a wreath of the colours, A dragon segreant gules, supporting with the sinister foreclaw and dexter hindclaw a pick, head downwards, proper. **Motto:** Amser yw'n golud. **Granted** 9 November 1951.

Z

ZOOLOGICAL SOCIETY OF LONDON. Gules, a lion passant guardant Or, armed and langued azure, holding in the dexter paw a torch gold, enflamed proper, the flame irradiated also gold. **Crest:** On a wreath Or and sable, An osprey, wings extended, perched upon and grasping in talons a fish fessewise proper. **Supporters:** On either side a zebra proper, collared Or. **Motto:** Curae genus omne animantium. **Badge:** A lion passant guardant Or, armed and langued gules, holding in the dexter paw a torch gold enflamed proper, the flame irradiated also gold. **Granted** 10 February 1959.

YORKSHIRE, EAST RIDING

YORKSHIRE, WEST RIDING

YORKSHIRE, NORTH RIDING

YORKSHIRE BANK

SUPPLEMENTARY LIST OF THE CIVIC AUTHORITIES WHOSE ARMS HAVE BECOME OBSOLETE

A

Acton, Borough of (Middlesex). Arms and Crest granted 15 November 1921.

Aston Manor, Borough of (Warwickshire). Arms and Crest granted 22 March 1904.

B

Barking, Borough of (Essex). Arms, Crest and Supporters granted 16 October 1931.

Barnes, Borough of (Surrey). Arms and Supporters granted 5 October 1932.

Battersea, Metropolitan Borough of. Arms and Crest granted 30 September 1955.

Beckenham, Borough of (Kent). Arms and Crest granted (to UDC) 17 December 1931; Supporters granted 9 September 1935.

Beddington and Wallington, Borough of (Surrey). Arms and Crest granted 3 July 1937.

Bermondsey, Metropolitan Borough of. Arms and Crest granted 25 March 1901.

Bexley, Borough of (Kent). Arms and Crest granted (to UDC) 16 October 1937.

Billingham Urban District Council (Co. Durham). Arms and Crest granted 1 May 1951.

Bilston, Borough of (Staffordshire). Arms, Crest and Supporters granted 15 September 1933.

Bocking Parish Council (Essex). Arms and crest granted 23 November 1927.

Brentford and Chiswick, Borough of (Middlesex). Arms, Crest and Supporters granted 1 September 1932.

Brierley Hill Urban District Council (Staffordshire). Arms and Crest granted 19 June 1942.

Bromley, Borough of (Kent). Arms and Crest granted 19 April 1904.

Burslem, Borough of (Staffordshire). Arms and Crest granted 26 April 1928.

C

Camberwell, Metropolitan Borough of. Arms and Crest granted 7 May 1901; Badge granted 10 February 1927.

Cambridgeshire County Council. Arms and Crest granted 17 June 1914; Supporters granted 18 June 1914.

Carshalton Urban District Council (Surrey). Arms and Crest granted 14 May 1952.

Chelsea, Metropolitan Borough of. Arms granted 28 February 1903.

Chingford, Borough of (Essex). Arms and Crest granted 26 September 1938.

Coseley Urban District Council (Staffordshire). Arms and Crest granted 2 May 1951.

Coulsdon and Purley Urban District Council (Surrey). Arms and Crest granted 24 March 1953.

Crayford Urban District Council (Kent). Arms granted 22 January 1945.

Croydon, County Borough of (Surrey). Arms and Crest granted 10 August 1886.

D

Dagenham, Borough of (Essex). Arms and Crest granted (to UDC) 8 July 1936.

Devonport, County Borough of (Devon). Arms and Crest granted 6 November 1876.

E

Ealing, Borough of (Middlesex). Arms granted 22 February 1902.

East Barnet Urban District Council (Hertfordshire). Arms and Crest granted 9 September 1955.

Edmonton, Borough of (Middlesex). Arms, Crest and Supporters granted 2 October 1937.

Enfield, Borough of (Middlesex). Arms and Crest granted (to UDC) 20 September 1946; Supporters granted 26 October 1955.

Erith, Borough of (Kent). Arms and Crest granted (to UDC) 27 February 1906.

Eston Urban District Council (Yorkshire—North Riding): Arms and Crest granted 5 December 1955.

F

Feltham Urban District Council (Middlesex). Arms and Crest granted 19 June 1945.

Finchley, Borough of (Middlesex). Arms, Crest and Supporters granted 10 July 1933.

Finsbury, Metropolitan Borough of. Arms, Crest and Supporters granted 7 May 1931.

Friern Barnet Urban District Council (Middlesex). Arms and Crest granted 10 August 1938.

Fulham, Metropolitan Borough of. Arms and Crest granted 12 October 1927.

G

Gloucester, City of. Arms granted 18 October 1538.

Gravesend, Borough of (Kent). Arms recorded at Visitation of 1619.

Great Berkhamsted, Borough of (Hertfordshire). Arms recorded at Visitation of 1634.

Greenwich, Metropolitan Borough of. Arms and Crest granted 15 July 1903.

H

Hackney, Metropolitan Borough of. Arms and Crest granted 31 May 1924.

Hadleigh, Borough of (Suffolk). Arms and Crest granted 18 February 1618.

Hammersmith, Metropolitan Borough of. Arms and Crest granted 23 December 1897.

Harrow, Borough of (Middlesex). Arms and Crest granted (to UDC) 3 May 1938; Supporters granted 10 September 1954.

Hayes and Harlington Urban District Council (Middlesex). Arms and Crest granted 12 October 1950.

Hendon, Borough of (Middlesex). Arms, Crest and Supporters granted 24 September 1932.

Heston and Isleworth, Borough of (Middlesex). Arms granted 16 April 1932.

Holborn, Metropolitan Borough of. Arms and Crest granted 3 May 1906; Supporters granted 25 May 1906.

Hornchurch Urban District Council (Essex). Arms and Crest granted 14 September 1948.

Hornsey, Borough of (Middlesex). Arms granted 17 March 1904.

Huntingdonshire County Council. Arms and Crest granted 9 April 1937.

I

Ilford, Borough of (Essex). Arms, Crest and Supporters granted 17 October 1926.

Isle of Ely County Council. Arms and Crest granted 1 May 1931.

Islington, Metropolitan Borough of. Arms and Crest granted 2 May 1901.

K

Kensington, Royal Borough of. Arms granted 23 May 1901.

Kingston-upon-Thames, Royal Borough of (Surrey). Arms recorded at Visitations of 1572 and 1623.

L

Lambeth, Metropolitan Borough of. Arms and Crest granted 22 April 1922.

Lewisham, Metropolitan Borough of. Arms, Crest and Supporters granted 27 November 1950.

Leyton, Borough of (Essex). Arms and Crest granted 27 October 1926.

London County Council. Arms granted by Royal Warrant 29 July 1914; Badge granted 12 March 1956.

M

Malden and Coombe, Borough of (Surrey). Arms and Crest granted 14 August 1936.

Merton and Morden Urban District Council (Surrey). Arms granted 12 July 1943.

Middlesbrough, County Borough of (Yorkshire—North Riding). Arms and Crest granted 8 November 1911.

Middlesex County Council. Arms granted 7 November 1910.

Mitcham, Borough of (Surrey). Arms and Crest granted 14 September 1934.

N

Nottingham, City and County Borough of. Supporters granted 11 June 1898.

O

Oldbury, Borough of (Worcestershire). Arms and Crest granted (to UDC) 15 April 1926.

Orford, Borough of (Suffolk). Arms recorded in the College of Arms.

Orpington Urban District Council (Kent). Arms and Crest granted 30 July 1956.

P

Paddington, Metropolitan Borough of. Arms granted 5 April 1902.

Paignton, Urban District Council (Devon). Arms and Crest granted 2 April 1947.

R

Redcar, Borough of (Yorkshire—North Riding). Arms and Crest granted 10 October 1922.

Richmond, Borough of (Surrey). Arms and Crest granted 19 June 1891.

Romford, Borough of (Essex). Arms and Crest granted 24 May 1938.

Rowley Regis, Borough of (Staffordshire). Arms, Crest and Supporters granted 20 September 1933.

Ruislip-Northwood Urban District Council (Middlesex). Arms and Crest granted 22 June 1937.

S

St. Marylebone, Metropolitan Borough of. Arms and Crest granted 17 August 1901.

St. Pancras, Metropolitan Borough of. Arms and Crest granted 7 December 1936.

Smethwick, County Borough of (Staffordshire). Arms and Crest granted 15 November 1907.

Soke of Peterborough County Council. Arms and Crest granted 10 November 1950.

Southall, Borough of (Middlesex). Arms, Crest and Supporters granted 23 September 1936.

Southgate, Borough of (Middlesex). Arms, Crest and Supporters granted 15 September 1933.

Southwark, Metropolitan Borough of. Arms granted 14 June 1902.

Stepney, Metropolitan Borough of. Arms and Crest granted 8 August 1931.

Stockton-on-Tees, Borough of (Co. Durham). Arms, Crest and Supporters granted 19 March 1951.

Stoke Newington, Metropolitan Borough of. Arms and Crest granted 12 June 1934.

Surbiton, Borough of (Surrey). Arms, Crest and Supporters granted 17 July 1936.

Sunderland Rural District Council (Co. Durham). Arms and Crest granted 5 February 1952.

Sutton and Cheam, Borough of (Surrey). Arms and Crest granted 16 October 1934.

T

Tettenhall Urban District Council (Staffordshire). Arms and Crest granted 29 September 1938.

Thaxted, Borough of (Essex). Arms recorded in the College of Arms.

Thornaby-on-Tees, Borough of (Yorkshire—North Riding). Arms and Crest granted 23 January 1893.

Tipton, Borough of (Staffordshire). Arms, Crest and Supporters granted 8 November 1938.

Torquay, Borough of (Devon). Arms and Crest granted 29 May 1893.

Tottenham, Borough of (Middlesex). Arms and Crest granted (to UDC) 4 September 1924; Arms, Crest and Supporters granted 13 September 1934.

Twickenham, Borough of (Middlesex). Arms and Crest granted (to UDC) 30 October 1913.

U

Uxbridge, Borough of (Middlesex). Arms and Crest granted (to UDC) 18 May 1948; Supporters granted 26 November 1955.

W

Walthamstow, Borough of (Essex). Arms, Crest and Supporters granted 6 December 1929.

Wandstead and Woodford, Borough of (Essex). Arms, Crest and Supporters granted 6 October 1937.

Wandsworth, Metropolitan Borough of. Arms and Crest granted 6 July 1901.

Wednesbury, Borough of (Staffordshire). Arms and Crest granted 1904.

Wednesfield Urban District Council (Staffordshire). Arms and Crest granted 20 May 1965.

Wembley, Borough of (Middlesex). Arms, Crest and Supporters granted 25 January 1938.

West Ham, County Borough of (Essex). Arms and Crest granted 14 January 1887.

Westminster, City of. Arms granted 1 October 1601; regranted by Royal Warrant 6 November 1901; exemplified 6 February 1902; Crest granted 24 October 1902; Supporters granted 27 October 1902.

Weston-super-Mare, Borough of (Somerset). Arms and Crest granted (to UDC) 9 August 1928; Supporters granted 6 October 1937.

Willenhall Urban District Council (Staffordshire). Arms and Crest granted 10 April 1935.

Willesden, Borough of (Middlesex). Arms, Crest and Supporters granted 1933.

Wimbledon, Borough of (Surrey). Arms and Crest granted 15 October 1906.

Wood Green, Borough of (Middlesex). Arms and Supporters granted 1 August 1933.

Woolwich, Metropolitan Borough of. Arms granted 9 August 1934.

Y

Yiewsley and West Drayton Urban District Council (Middlesex). Arms and Crest granted 20 May 1953.